Principles of Tort Law

Presenting the law of tort as a body of principles, this authoritative textbook leads students to an incisive and clear understanding of the subject. Each tort is carefully structured and examined within a consistent analytical framework that guides students through its preconditions, elements, defences and remedies. Clear summaries and comparisons accompany the detailed exposition ~~and further support is provided by numerous~~ diagrams and tables, which clarify complex ~~aspects of the law. Crucial discussion of legal judgments~~ students to develop s~~~~ and leading cases from ~~~~ ~~~~s in tort law. A rich co~~~~ ore advanced areas of t~~~~ts, the text is also ideal ~~~~ omprehensive and accur~~~~

Rachael M~~~~ ~~~~ty of London, where sh~~~~ ~~~~cern tort law and class~~~~ ~~~~has frequently assisted ~~~~irms, on tort-related a~~~~akes extensive law refo~~~~ ~~~~f England and Wales. F~~~~ ~~~~dations to the Governm~~~~ ~~~~(or 'damages-based ag~~~~ as a litigation solicitor ~~~~tor), and then predomi~~~~

Birmingham | Bristol | Chester | Guildford | London | Manchester | York

Principles of Tort Law

Rachael Mulheron

Professor of Law, Queen Mary University of London

CAMBRIDGE
UNIVERSITY PRESS

CAMBRIDGE
UNIVERSITY PRESS

University Printing House, Cambridge CB2 8BS, United Kingdom

Cambridge University Press is part of the University of Cambridge.

It furthers the University's mission by disseminating knowledge in the pursuit of
education, learning and research at the highest international levels of excellence.

www.cambridge.org
Information on this title: www.cambridge.org/9781107151369

© Rachael Mulheron 2016

First published 2016
Printed in the United Kingdom by Clays, St Ives plc

A catalogue record for this publication is available from the British Library

ISBN 978-1-107-15136-9 Hardback
ISBN 978-1-316-60566-0 Paperback

Additional resources for this publication at www.cambridge.org/mulheron

Summary contents

Pages preceded by ◑ indicate that the relevant content is locatable in the materials available at the Online Torts Hub (available at www.Cambridge.org/Mulheron).

Detailed contents

Barristers (when conducting matters in court) ❧   1

Foreword

There are few areas of the law which are as rewarding to study and have as practical an impact on our daily lives as, to borrow from Professor Mulheron, the 'motley bunch of causes of action which fall within English Tort Law!' Not only does detailed study provide an in-depth insight into the development of the common law and of the incremental, precedent-based, common law method in action, it also raises challenging questions of principle. Questions concerning the role that tort law plays in our legal system and wider society, the extent to which the law should impose liability for harm on individuals and the circumstances when it should do so, whether it is underpinned by an overarching principle or by a variety of principles, remain matters of interest and debate. And from a practical perspective, the boundaries of tort law help shape the contours of everyday life. Whether we consider the steps manufacturers must take to ensure that their products are safe for sale or – as in *Donoghue v Stevenson* – consumption, the steps that professionals, such as doctors or lawyers, must take to treat their patients or advise their clients appropriately, or that employers must take to secure the safety of their workers, the law of tort provides the framework.

In this new book, *Principles of Tort Law*, Professor Mulheron, drawing on her extensive experience of the field both in practice in Australia and teaching tort law at Queen Mary University of London, provides a clear, detailed and challenging account of the law of tort. By utilising the method taken by the American Law Institute in its famous Restatements of the Law of Tort – statement of principle followed by detailed exegesis drawing on relevant case law, statutory provision and, where relevant, comparative jurisprudence – she presents a meticulous analysis in a thoroughly accessible manner. This work is a most welcome contribution to the field, one that will be of great benefit to students, practitioners, academics and judges and to anyone interested in gaining a proper understanding of the fundamental nature of this central part of the law. I cannot commend it highly enough.

The Right Honourable Lord Dyson,
Master of the Rolls

Preface

This book aims to do what it 'says on the tin' – to state the corpus of Tort law as a body of principles. Tort lawyers commonly talk of 'the principles of Tort', and yet, when examining case after case, that ethos can easily become lost, in amongst factual distinctions, common law complexities, statutory interventions and appellate cases which frequently contain multiple judgments of differing ratio.

My interest in writing a book which addresses this area of law as a set of principles, with an in-depth underlying analysis, was motivated by four influences:

i. Teaching undergraduate Torts students has enriched my understanding of just how important it is to delve into, and isolate, the principles which we, as academics, seek to convey to those students who are encountering the subject for the first time. Questions such as, 'When should we use *Bolam* and when should we use *Bolitho*?'; 'Is *Donoghue v Stevenson's* ratio still relevant?'; 'Is the test of foreseeability the same for duty of care, breach, and remoteness?', and literally hundreds of similar-type queries and discussion points, have been an important genesis for this book.

It is intended that this text will, primarily, have utility to the student who is studying Tort law. Students may take on board some of the principles per chapter, and omit others, in accordance with the depth and direction of study being undertaken. The book has been written in a style that incorporates presentational tools to assist the student in his or her studies, by employing frameworks for analysis per chapter, tables of legal analysis, diagrammatic depictions of the parties' relationships in leading cases, boxes illustrating comparative judicial reasoning, and the like.

ii. Whilst in legal practice, I was frequently engaged in Tort litigation, and came to realise that exposition of principle in concise, but in-depth, treatment, is the nadir of what this area of the law should seek to achieve. After all, Tort law is there to serve society in all of its guises, to enable claimants to seek (usually compensatory) redress for their grievances, and to provide defendants with a logical set of defences to such actions. Its complexity and (occasional) opaqueness should not obscure the fact that the law should be capable of being understood by 'the reasonable person on the London underground' (an identity of such importance in Tort law!).

iii. The subject-matter of Tort law is undeniably interesting, and very relevant to everyday life, and hence, a work that seeks to espouse the principles of Tort will be of interest to a wider readership than the student body to which it is principally directed. Notably, it is envisaged that this book will also have utility for those audiences (e.g., judiciary, legal practitioners, legislators and academics) who are already familiar with Tort law, but who are grappling with particular issues and points of complexity associated with distinct principles.

iv. Lastly, one of the key features of Tort law is the extent to which legal and public policy influences, and informs, the development of jurisprudence in this area. Whilst it is called a set of 'principles', much discussion surrounding Tort law is directed to what the Law *should* be – and an explicit acknowledgement and elucidation of that fact is one of the driving interests which motivated the writing of this book. For this reason, key law reform commission opinion is canvassed in those areas in which, for policy reasons, those commissions suggested that the law should perhaps change. Occasionally, comparative vignettes are also referenced in chapters, to show how similar problems in Tort law can yield differing solutions, depending upon differing judicial (or legislative) attitudes in other jurisdictions.

It is an ancillary aim of the book to promote and activate a debate, among policy-makers, reformers, judiciary and academics, about the utility of a *Restatement*-type project of English Tort law. I do not envisage that Tort law should be codified, in the sense that a 'blank sheet of paper' should be the starting point of Tort law for this jurisdiction. Rather, the depth and nuances of the common law of Tort (with occasional statutory enactments), and the jurisprudence generated over its long and distinguished history, are worth preserving in all of its grand complexity. However, as the analysis in this book demonstrates, there are pockets of uncertainty, of unsettled law, of appellate judgments which differ and where 'the circle cannot be squared', and of law reform proposals which remain unenacted. The text of principles and analysis undertaken herein could serve as a useful reference point for a future *Restatement* project, should that be considered desirable.

Grateful thanks are due to many people, whose guidance, input, interest, and insights throughout this long journey have been extremely valuable and much appreciated. The support and encouragement provided by my publishers, particularly by Ms Valerie Appleby and Ms Kim Hughes; by my parents whose constant belief in the value of the project were both vital and sustaining in the long years that this project has taken; and by my family and friends whose patience with, and interest in, the book were always much appreciated, are all (inadequately, but with heartfelt gratitude) acknowledged herein. Grateful thanks are also due to my colleagues at the Department of Law at Queen Mary University of London, Mr Ian Yeats and Ms Margaret Cunningham, both of whom, in combination, kindly provided very helpful feedback on numerous draft chapters; to several colleagues in practice who provided useful insights and/or materials along the way, especially: Mr David Body, former partner of Irwin Mitchell solicitors; Ms Beverley Barton, Ms Martha Castaneda-Wilcox and Ms Susan Scott, all of Practical Law; Mr John Brown, litigation partner of McCarthy Tetrault LLP, Toronto, Canada; Dr Duncan Fairgrieve, Director of Projects at the British Institute of International and Comparative Law; Mr Peter Farr, Chief Executive of the Civil Justice Council of England and Wales; Mr Robert Gapes, partner of Simpson Grier Solicitors, Auckland; His Honour Judge David Grant, of the Technology and Construction Court; Mr Gregory Jones QC; Prof Vince Morabito of Monash University, Australia; Mr John Spencer, foundation partner of Spencer Solicitors; and Ms Anne Ware, partner of Kennedys Lawyers (whose feedback on the chapter entitled 'Defective Products' was highly insightful and helpful). I also wish to record my deep gratitude to Mr Justice Ross Cranston FBA, whose support and encouragement for the worth of the project was unwavering during the years that it has taken to complete. I am also grateful to the various anonymous reviewers who provided feedback on various chapters during the publishing process, and whose insights were very helpful. Finally, the careful production of the case table was primarily due to the unstinting efforts of Ms Holly Abbott, to whom I am deeply indebted. It goes without saying that any errors in either the manuscript, or in the preliminary tables, are solely my own.

Finally, I would like to convey my thanks to all the copyediting and typesetting team at Cambridge University Press and associated entities (especially Rachel Cox, Deborah Hey, and Preeti Saani) for providing valuable editorial and other assistance in order to bring this book to fruition.

The ongoing development of Tort law, particularly in case law, is inevitable and under constant review. To the best of my knowledge, the law is stated as at 31 July 2015, although some reference to later 2015 cases has been possible during the final preparation of the manuscript.

Rachael Mulheron

How to use this book

Print and online chapters

Principles of Tort Law is comprised of 28 chapters in total, 18 of which are print chapters and a further 10 of which are available as online chapters at the accompanying Online Torts Hub (available at www.Cambridge.org/Mulheron).

The print chapters focus upon those particular areas which tend to arise commonly in Torts curricula in England and Wales. In addition to a detailed consideration of the tort of Negligence, the print chapters also cover particular manifestations of negligence (*viz*, the Occupiers' Liability Act regimes, and the law associated with Public Authority liability) and some separate torts altogether (*viz*, Defamation, Private Nuisance, the Rule in *Rylands v Fletcher* and the torts encompassed by Trespass to the Person). Vicarious liability, a strict liability doctrine which forms an important part of the modern Torts curriculum, is also included as a print chapter.

The online chapters, on the other hand, deal with torts, or issues arising from Tort Law, which do not feature as commonly in Torts curricula, but which nevertheless may arise for student consideration from time to time. Of course, some Torts curricula do incorporate the study of particular manifestations of negligence, such as the statutory regimes enacted for defective products and for damage caused by animals, and also consider wider torts such as Public Nuisance, Privacy or the statutory tort of Harassment. The online chapters fully cater for that type of Torts curriculum. Additionally, the often tricky concepts associated with multiple defendants in Tort, and the issues to do with when a tortious cause of action 'accrues', limitation periods, and when a defendant's liability in tort ends, are also dealt with in the online chapters. The online content may also assist students who are studying aspects of Tort as part of other law modules (such as Media Law, Public Authorities and the Law, or Medical Negligence Law), or who are studying such issues for the purposes of mooting, writing research essays, legal advice clinic work and the like.

Occasionally, a section of a print chapter is excised from that chapter and is available online. For example, some of the categories of defendants for whom a duty of care has been a legal issue (e.g., barristers, parental liability for their children's negligence, parental liability to their children and regulators/inspectors/certifiers) are contained in Chapter 2 as online content only.

The system of principle numbering

The numbering of the print chapters follows sequentially throughout the book, from Chapter 1, 'The Role of Modern Tort Law', to Chapter 18, 'Vicarious Liability'. The online chapters appear in the Table of Contents – and for the convenience of readers, their content is also included in the Tables of Cases and Legislation.

The principles in the print chapters adopt the numbering of the particular chapter, so that each principle has a unique identifier. For example, for Chapter 8, 'Causation of Damage', the principles commence at §8.1, and follow sequentially throughout the chapter, until the final principle of that chapter, §8.34.

The principles in the online chapters adopt their numbering from an acronym of the particular chapter, so that, again, each principle has a unique identifier. For example, principle 12 in each of the online chapters is designated as follows: §DP.12, for the 'Defective Products' chapter; §AN.12, for the 'Liability for Animals' chapter; §EM.12, for the 'Employers' Liability' chapter; §SD.12, for the 'Breach of Statutory Duty' chapter; §HA.12, for the 'Statutory Tort of Harassment' chapter; §WD.12, for 'The Rule in *Wilkinson v Downton*' chapter; §PR.12, for the 'Privacy' chapter; §PU.12, for the 'Public Nuisance' chapter; §MD.12, for the 'Multiple Defendants' chapter; and §BE.12, for the 'Beginning and End of Liability' chapter.

Where, within a print chapter, a small section of the chapter is available online, the principles in that online-only section uses a separate referencing system, whereby the principle adopts the chapter number, but uses an alphabetical identifier. For example, as noted above, Chapter 2 is a print chapter, but contains some small sections of online content. For the first online section in that chapter concerning 'Barristers', the principle in that section is numbered as §2.A. The next online section in that chapter concerns 'Parental liability for their children's negligence', in which the relevant principles are numbered as §2.B and §2.C. The next online principle in Chapter 2 is under the section, 'Parental liability to their children', and is numbered as §2.D.

Hence, each principle in the book, whether contained in the print chapters or the online chapters, has a unique identifier which directs the reader to its precise location.

The system of page numbering

As mentioned above, the online chapters appear in the Table of Contents – and for the convenience of readers, their content is also included in the Tables of Cases and Legislation. The online content of the book is paginated sequentially from 1 to 476, as evident from the materials available at the accompanying Online Torts Hub.

Hence, in the Table of Contents, Table of Cases, Table of Legislation, and Index, an entry appearing at, say, p 20 of the print book will be designated merely as '20'; whereas an entry appearing at p 20 of the online part of the book will be designated as ◐ 20, to signify that it is to p 20 of the online content that a reader must refer.

Table of cases

The full citation of each case is locatable at the corresponding page reference which appears in the table below. Pages preceded by ⬤ indicate that the relevant case is locatable in the materials available at the Online Torts Hub (available at www.Cambridge.org/Mulheron).

Table of legislation

Pages preceded by ◐ indicate that the relevant statutory provision is locatable in the materials available at the Online Torts Hub (available at www.Cambridge.org/Mulheron).

Abbreviations

General

[10]	paragraph 10
10	page 10
AG	Attorney General
AHA	Area Health Authority
aka	also known as
Art, Arts	Article, Articles
Ass	Assurance
Assn	Association
Aus or Aust	Australian
BBC	British Broadcasting Corp
BC	Borough Council, or British Columbia (depending upon the context)
Bros	Brothers
CC	County Council, City Council, or Chief Constable (depending upon the context)
Civ	Civil
CN	Contributory negligence
Co	Company
Comm	Commission
Commr	Commissioner
Co-op	Co-operative
Corp	Corporation
CPS	Crown Prosecution Service
CP	Consultation Paper
dB	decibel/s
Dept	Department
DP	Discussion Paper
edn	Edition
Govt	Government
HA	Health Authority
HHJ	His/Her Honour Judge
HMP	Her Majesty's Prison
HMRC	Her Majesty's Revenue and Customs
Hosp	Hospital
Ins	Insurance
Intl	International
J	Justice
LBC	London Borough Council

Litig	Litigation
LJ	Law Journal or Lord Justice (depending upon the context)
LRC	Law Reform Commission
L Rev	Law Review
MBC	Metropolitan Borough Council
MC	Municipal Council
MOD	Ministry of Defence
MR	Master of the Rolls
NLJ	New Law Journal
NHS	National Health Service
P	President
PCC	Press Complaints Commission
PD	Practice Direction
pp	pinpoint
PSLA	damages for pain, suffering and loss of amenity
PTSD	post-traumatic stress disorder
r, rr	rule, rules
reg	regulation
RSC	Rules of the Supreme Court
Rwy	Railway
Sec	Secretary
Soc	Society
s, ss	section, sections
TC	Town Council
US	United States
WHO	World Health Organisation

Legislation

CPA	Consumer Protection Act 1987
CPR	Civil Procedure Rules 1998
ECHR	European Convention on Human Rights
FAA	Fatal Accidents Act 1976
HRA	Human Rights Act 1998
LR(MP) Act	Law Reform (Miscellaneous Provisions) Act 1934
OLA 1957	Occupiers' Liability Act 1957

OLA 1984   Occupiers' Liability Act 1984
UCTA   Unfair Contract Terms Act 1977

Courts

ABCA   Alberta Court of Appeal
ABQB, or Alta QB   Alberta Court of Queen's Bench
ACTSC   Australian Capital Territory Supreme Court
Alta SC App Div   Alberta Supreme Court Appeal Division
Alta TD   Alberta Trial Division
BCCA   British Columbia Court of Appeal
BCSC   British Columbia Supreme Court
CA   Court of Appeal
Ch   Chancery Court
Cal Sup Ct   California Supreme Court
CSIH   Scottish Court of Session (Inner House)
CSOH   Scottish Court of Session (Outer House)
Div Ct   High Court of Justice Divisional Court
ECJ   European Court of Justice
ECtHR   European Court of Human Rights
EWCA Civ   England and Wales Court of Appeal (Civil Division)
EWHC   England and Wales High Court
EW Misc   England and Wales Courts – Miscellaneous (via Bailii)
Exch Ct   Exchequer Court
FCA   Federal Court of Australia
FCAFC   Federal Court of Australia, Full Court
FJHC   Fiji High Court
HCA   High Court of Australia
HKCFA   Hong Kong Court of Final Appeal
HKCFI   Hong Kong Court of First Instance
HKDC   Hong Kong District Court
HL   House of Lords
IEHC   High Court of Ireland
IESC   Supreme Court of Ireland
INSC   India Supreme Court
KB   England and Wales High Court (King's Bench Division)
LRKB   Law Reports, King's Bench
Man CA   Manitoba Court of Appeal
MLJU   Malaysia Federal Court of Appeal
MLJU(HC)   High Court of Malaysia
NICA   Northern Ireland Court of Appeal
NICh   High Court of Justice, Northern Ireland, Chancery Division

NIQB   High Court of Justice, Northern Ireland, Queen's Bench Division
NSWSC   New South Wales Supreme Court
NSWCA   New South Wales Court of Appeal
NTSC   Northern Territory Supreme Court
NZCA   New Zealand Court of Appeal
NZSC   New Zealand Supreme Court
Ont SCJ   Ontario Superior Court of Justice
PC   Privy Council
QB   England and Wales High Court (Queen's Bench Division)
QB (TCC)   High Court of Justice, Queen's Bench Division, Technology and Construction Court
QCA   Queensland Court of Appeal
QSC   Queensland Supreme Court
SASC   South Australian Supreme Court
SC   Supreme Court (United Kingdom)
SCC   Supreme Court of Canada
Scot CS   Scottish Court of Sessions Decisions
SGHC   Singapore High Court
SGCA   Singapore Court of Appeal
Tas SC   Tasmanian Supreme Court
UKEAT   United Kingdom Employment Appeals Tribunal
UKFTT   United Kingdom First Tier Tribunal (Tax Chamber)
UKHL   United Kingdom House of Lords
UKPC   United Kingdom Privy Council
UKSC   United Kingdom Supreme Court
Ves Sen   Vesey Senior's Chancery Reports
Vic SC   Victorian Supreme Court
Vic CA   Victorian Court of Appeal
WADC   Western Australian District Court
WASC   Western Australia Supreme Court
WASCA   Western Australia Supreme Court, Court of Appeal
ZASCA   South African Supreme Court, Court of Appeal

Law Reports

A 2d   Atlantic Reporter, Second Series (United States)
AC   Law Reports, Appeal Cases (Third Series)
ACD   Administrative Court Digest
ACWS (3d)   All Canada Weekly Summaries, Third Series

AER	All England Law Reports	Cr App R	Criminal Appeal Reports
All ER	All England Law Reports	Dears	Dearsley's Crown Cases Reserved
All ER(D)	All England Direct Law Reports (Digests)	Dears & B	Dearsley and Bell's Crown Cases Reserved
All ER Rep Ext	All England Law Reports Reprint Australian Extension Volumes	De G & Sm	De Gex and Smale's Chancery Reports
ALJR	Australian Law Journal Reports	Dick	Dickens Chancery Reports
ALR	Australian Law Reports	DLR	Dominion Law Reports
App Cas	Law Reports, Appeal Cases (Second Series)	E & B	Ellis and Blackburn's Queen's Bench Reports
AR	Alberta Reports	Ed CR	Education Case Reports
ATR	Australian Tax Reports	EGLR	Estates Gazette Law Reports
B & Ad	Barnewall and Adolphus' King's Bench Reports	EHRR	European Human Rights Reports
B & C	Barnewall and Cresswell's King's Bench Reports	ELR	Education Law Reports
		EMLR	Entertainment and Media Law Reports
BCC	British Company Law Cases	Env LR	Environmental Law Reports
BCLC	Butterworths Company Law Cases	ER	English Reports
Bing	Bingham's Common Pleas Reports	Ex, or Ct Exch	Law Reports, Exchequer Division
Bing NC	Bingham's New Cases, English Common Pleas	F 2d	Federal Reporter, Second Series
		F & F	Foster and Finlayson's Nisi Prius Reports
BLR	Building Law Reports	Fam	Law Reports, Family Division
BMLR	Butterworths Medico-Legal Reports	FCR	Butterworths Family Court Reports
B & S	Best and Smith's Queen's Bench Reports	FLR	Family Law Reports (England and Wales)
Burr	Burrows King's Bench Reports (tempore Mansfield)	FSR	Fleet Street Reports
C & L	Connor and Lawson's Irish Chancery Reports	Hare	Hare's Chancery Reports
		HLC (Clark's)	Clark and Finnelly's House of Lords Reports, New Series
Cal 3d	Californian Reports (Third Series)	HLR	Housing Law Reports
Cal Rptr	Californian Reporter	H & C	Hurlstone & Coltman's Exchequer Reports
Camp	Campbell's Nisi Prius Cases		
Car and P, or C & P	Carrington and Payne's Nisi Prius Reports	Hurl & N, or H&N	Hurlstone & Norman's Exchequer Reports
CB (NS)	Common Bench Reports, New Series	H & Tw	Hall and Twell's Chancery Reports
CCL Rep	Community Care Law Reports	ICR	Industrial Court Reports
CCLT	Canadian Cases on the Law of Torts	IR, or Ir R	Irish Reports
Ch	Law Reports, Chancery Division (3rd Series)	Ir Jur Rep	Irish Jurist Reports
		IRLR	Industrial Relations Law Reports
CL	Current Law Monthly Digest (UK)	JP	Justice of the Peace Reports
CLC	CCH Commercial Law Cases	KB	Law Reports, King's Bench
CLR	Commonwealth Law Reports	KIR	Knight's Industrial Reports
CLY	Current Law Yearbook	LD Raym	Lord Raymond's King's Bench and Common Pleas Reports
CMLR	Common Market Law Reports		
CM & R	Crompton, Messon and Roscoe's Exchequer Reports	LGR	Local Government Reports
		LJCP	Law Journal Reports, Common Pleas New Series
Co Rep	Coke's King's Bench Reports		
Con LR	Construction Law Reports	LJQB	Law Journal Reports, Queen's Bench New Series
Cr & M	Crompton and Meeson's Exchequer Reports		

Lloyd's Rep	Lloyd's Law Reports	P 2d	Pacific Reporter, Second Series
Lloyd's Rep Med	Lloyd's Law Reports (Medical)	PIQR	Personal Injuries and Quantum Reports
Lloyd's Rep PN	Lloyd's Law Reports (Professional Negligence)	PNLR	Professional Negligence and Liability Reports
Lofft	Lofft's King's Bench Reports	PTSR	The Public and Third Sector Reports
LR	Law Reports (First Series)	QB	Law Reports, Queen's Bench (3rd Series)
LRCP	Law Reports, Common Pleas		
LR Eq	Law Reports, Equity Cases	Qd R	Queensland Reports
LR Ex	Law Reports, Exchequer Cases	RPC	Reports of Patent, Design and Trade Mark Cases
LRKB	Law Reports King's Bench		
LT Rep	Law Times Reports (England and Wales)	RTR	Road Traffic Reports
		SA	South African Law Reports
L & TR	Landlord and Tenant Reports	SASR	South Australian State Reports
M & S	Maule and Selwyn's King's Bench Reports	SC	Session Cases (Scotland)
M & W	Meeson and Welsby's Exchequer Reports (England and Wales)	SC(HL)	Session Cases, House of Lords (Scotland)
Med LR	Medical Law Reports	SCLR	Scottish Civil Law Reports
Mod	Modern Reports (England and Wales)	Scot CS	Scottish Court of Session Decisions
NBR	New Brunswick Reports	SCR	Supreme Court Reports (Canada)
NE	North Eastern Reporter	SJLB	Solicitors' Journal Law Brief (UK)
NI	Northern Ireland Law Reports	SLT	Scots Law Times
NJ Super	New Jersey Supreme Court Reports	SR(NSW)	New South Wales State Reports
NPC	New Property Cases	Taunt	Taunton's Common Pleas Reports
NY	New York Reports	TCLR	Technology and Construction Law Reports
NYS	New York Supplement		
NZAR	New Zealand Administrative Reports	TLR	Times Law Reports
NZLR	New Zealand Law Reports	VLR	Victorian Law Reports
OAC	Ontario Appeal Cases	VR	Victorian Reports
OR	Ontario Reports	Wils KB	Wilson's King's Bench and Common Pleas Reports
P 2d	Pacific Reporter (Second Series) (United States)		
P	Law Reports, Probate	WLR	Weekly Law Reports
PD	Law Reports, Probate, Divorce and Admiralty Division	WN	Weekly Notes of Cases
		WTLR	Wills and Trusts Law Reports
		WWR	Western Weekly Reports

Notes on mode of citation

1. In each case citation, the court is referred to in parentheses in all instances where it is not obvious from the report series or mode of citation which court made the decision. Neutral citations have been used wherever available.
2. The expression 'English law' should be understood to include the law of Wales (unless indicated otherwise).
3. Throughout this book, 'C' denotes 'claimant'; and 'D' denotes 'defendant'; and the plural of each is denoted by 'Cs' and 'Ds', respectively.
4. Throughout this book, the masculine personal pronoun is used, for the sake of convenience and, as and where appropriate, should be taken to denote the feminine pronoun.
5. The scholarship and opinion of many entities (including law reform commissions) and persons are referenced throughout this book. All reasonable efforts have been made to reference and to pinpoint as accurately and fulsomely as possible. It should be noted that wherever quotations appear, and in the interests of brevity, footnotes within those quotations have not been reproduced, and the conventional usage of 'footnotes omitted' should be assumed throughout.
6. Wherever available, paragraph numbers are used as pinpoints in preference to page numbers.

1

The role of modern Tort law

WHAT IS A TORT?

§1.1   A tort is a wrongful act or omission, for which compensation or other remedy can be awarded to C (the claimant, or the person aggrieved) against D (the defendant, or tortfeasor). The corpus of Tort law, in general, excludes wrongs which are remediable as a breach of contract (albeit that some claims may give rise to concurrent liability in contract and in tort), a crime (albeit that occasionally a tort may also be a crime), an equitable cause of action, or a restitutionary cause of action.

The word 'tort' is derived from the Old French, *tortus*, meaning 'twisted' or 'crooked', and from the medieval Latin, *tortum*, meaning 'wrong' or 'injustice'.[1] Hence, the definition above aptly conveys that a great many causes of action fit under the Tort law 'umbrella'.

The corollary is that any shared or common characteristics among the torts – apart from the fact that all are claims for which damages are obtainable in a civil court – are nigh to impossible to identify. Indeed, it is a motley bunch of causes of action which fall within English Tort law!

The range of modern torts in English law

§1.2   There are at least 33 different torts which are recognised in English law.

The following Table provides an alphabetical list of those torts which, so far as the author's searches can ascertain, represent currently-recognised torts in the English jurisdiction. Each tort is either defined (with reference to a relatively recent authority in which the tort is discussed) or is referenced to detailed analysis elsewhere in this book:

---

[1] *Oxford Dictionary of English* (2nd edn, revised, 2006) 1862. See too *Oxford Dictionary of Law* (6th edn, 2006) 537; and J Penner, *The Law Student's Dictionary* (Oxford University Press, 2008) 292.

	The tort	Nutshell definition (or chapter treatment)
1	Abuse of judicial process	Originating in *Grainger v Hill* (1838), the tort requires that: D brings legal process principally for an improper, collateral, or ulterior purpose; and where the improper use to which the process was applied causes C damage (see, e.g., *Land Securities plc v Fladgate Fielder (a firm)*[a] and *Crawford Adjusters v Sagicor General Insurance (Cayman) Ltd*[b])
2	Assault	See Chapter 14, and the definition at §14.3 and §14.9
3	Battery	See Chapter 14, and the definition at §14.3 and §14.4
4	Breach of statutory duty	See 'Breach of statutory duty' (an online chapter), and the definition at §SD.1
5	Causing loss by unlawful means	The tort requires that: D interferes with the liberty of others; D's interference was intentional; D's interference was via unlawful means; and the interference with others (e.g., customers) causes C damage (see, e.g., *OBG Ltd v Allan; Douglas v Hello! Ltd*[c]). The unlawful means does not require any actual threat on D's part, thereby distinguishing the tort from that of Intimidation; and there is no need for a contract between C and the other party, thereby distinguishing the tort from Inducing Breach of Contract, and Interference with Contractual Relations
6	Champerty	The tort (now abolished as a tort in England, although it can still render a contract void as being contrary to public policy) requires that: D supports C's legal action in which D has no legitimate concern, without just cause or excuse; and contracts for a share of the proceeds of C's action or for some other pecuniary benefit if the action succeeds (see, e.g., *R (Factortame Ltd) v Sec of State for Transport, Local Govt and the Regions (No 8)*[d])
7	Conspiracy to injure	The tort requires: an agreement between two or more persons (Ds, the conspirators) to commit an act or omission with the intent of causing damage to C's trade or reputation; D's act or omission is *either* unlawful in nature (known as 'unlawful means conspiracy') *or* lawful in nature but where D had the sole or predominant purpose of injuring C (known as 'lawful means conspiracy'); and C suffers damage as a result of the conspirators' act or omission. The tort does not enable recovery for injury to C's reputation or injury to feelings, but is primarily directed to the recovery of financial loss (see, e.g., *Total Network SL v HMRC*[e] and *Aerostar Maintenance v Wilson*[f]). Conspirators can join the agreement at different times (per *QBE Management Services (UK) Ltd v Dymoke*[g])

[a] [2009] EWCA Civ 1402, [2010] 1 Ch 467. Although there was much debate as to whether such a tort existed in England ('the last reported successful action in this jurisdiction for the tort abuse of process was either about 140 or 170 years ago': at [41]), all CA members affirmed that it existed in limited form.

[b] [2013] UKPC 17, [2014] 1 AC 366.

[c] [2007] UKHL 21, [2008] 1 AC 1, [6]–[8], [45]–[64] (Lord Hoffmann).

[d] [2002] EWCA Civ 932, [2003] QB 381, [32] (Lord Phillips MR). See too: s 14(1), (2) of the Criminal Law Act 1967 (discussed in: Mulheron and Cashman, 'Third Party Funding of Litigation: A Changing Landscape' (2008) 27 *Civil Justice Quarterly* 312, 318–19; and *Code of Conduct for Litigation Funders* (Jan 2014).

[e] [2008] UKHL 19, [2008] 1 AC 1174.

[f] [2010] EWHC 2032 (Ch).

[g] [2012] EWHC 80 (QB) [198].

	The tort	Nutshell definition (or chapter treatment)
8	Conversion (aka trover, its ancient description[h])	The tort requires that: D's dealings with goods (e.g., depriving C of their possession) were inconsistent with C's rights, where C owned, possessed, or was entitled to immediate possession of the goods; D's conduct was intentional and not accidental; and D's conduct was sufficient to exclude C from being able to use and/or possess the goods (see, e.g., *Kuwait Airways Corp v Iraqi Airways Co (Nos 4 and 5)*[i] and *Glenbrook Capital LP v Hamilton*[j])
9	Defamation	See Chapter 15, and the definition at §15.1 and §15.2
10	Deceit (aka fraudulent misrepresentation)	The tort requires: a false (fraudulent) representation by D, which D either knows to be untrue or is recklessly indifferent as to whether it is true; D intended that C should act in reliance on the false representation; C, in fact, relied on the representation; and C suffered loss (see, e.g., *VTB Capital plc v Nutritek Intl Corp*[k] and *Derry v Peek*[l])
11	False imprisonment	See Chapter 14, and the definition at §14.13
12	Harassment	A statutory tort, created by the Protection from Harassment Act 1997. See 'The Statutory Tort of Harassment' (online), and the definition at §HA.1
13	Inducing (or procuring) breach of contract (aka the tort in *Lumley v Gye*[m])	The tort requires that: X commits an actionable breach of his contract with the other contracting party, C; D's conduct procured X to commit that breach of contract; D intended to induce X to breach his contract with C, or was recklessly indifferent (i.e., 'turned a blind eye') as to whether it was breached; D knew or foresaw that the conduct which was being induced would result in a breach of X and C's contract; and C suffered loss (see, e.g., *OBG Ltd v Allan; Douglas v Hello! Ltd*[n])
14	Interference with another's contractual relations	The tort requires that: D prevented or hindered X's performance of his contract with the other contracting party, C; D procured X to prevent/hinder the performance of his contract with C; D intended to induce X to hinder/prevent his contract with C, or was recklessly indifferent as to whether or not it was so; and C suffered loss (see, e.g., *OBG Ltd v Allan; Douglas v Hello! Ltd*[o]). D can be liable, even without the contracting party, X, actually committing an actionable breach of contract (distinguishing the tort from Inducing breach of contract)

[h] Also encompassed, statutorily, in the Torts (Interference with Goods) Act 1977, s 1(a).
[i] [2002] UKHL 19, [2002] 2 AC 883, especially [37]–[44] (Lord Nicholls).
[j] [2014] EWHC 2297 (Comm).
[k] [2012] EWCA Civ 808.
[l] (1889) LR 14 App Cas 337 (HL).
[m] (1853) 2 E&B 216.
[n] [2007] UKHL 21, [2008] 1 AC 1, [3]–[5], [39]–[44] (Lord Hoffmann).
[o] [2005] EWCA Civ 106, [2005] QB 762, and not discussed in detail on appeal, *ibid*.

	The tort	Nutshell definition (or chapter treatment)
15	Intentional infliction of mental distress or physical harm (aka the rule in *Wilkinson v Downton*)	See 'The Rule in *Wilkinson v Downton*' (online), and the definition at §WD.1
16	Intimidation	The tort requires: a threat made by D to do something unlawful or 'illegitimate'; which can take the form of *either* a threat to C that, unless C acts in a certain way, D will act impermissibly against C *or* a threat to X that, unless X acts in a certain way towards C, D will act impermissibly towards X; D's threat was intended to coerce C to take, or refrain from taking, some course of action; the threat did coerce C to take that action; and C suffered loss (see, e.g., *Berezovsky v Abramovich*[p])
17	Libel	See Chapter 15 (Defamation), and the definition at §15.2
18	Maintenance	The tort (now abolished as a tort in England, although it can still render a contract void as being contrary to public policy) requires that: D 'supports litigation, in which he has no legitimate concern, without just cause or excuse' (see, e.g., *R (Factortame Ltd) v Sec of State for Transport, Local Govt and the Regions (No 8)*,[q] and involves the notion of 'improperly stirring up litigation and strife by giving aid to one party to bring or defend a claim' (see, e.g., *Trepca Mines Ltd (No 2)*[r])
19	Malicious falsehood (aka injurious falsehood)	The tort requires that: D published false allegations about C; *either* knowing them to be false *or* being indifferent as to their truth or falsity; D published the information with malice; and C suffered loss (per *Friend v Civil Aviation Authy*,[s] and *Cornwall Gardens Ltd v RO Garrard & Co Ltd*[t]). It is not necessary that C suffers any loss of reputation; the tort is focused primarily upon C's economic or commercial interests (e.g., where D dishonestly tells C's customers that C has ceased trading (per *Gregory v Portsmouth CC*[u])). The tort may sometimes duplicate the tort of Defamation (per *Reachlocal UK Ltd v Bennett*[v])

[p] [2011] EWCA Civ 153, [2011] 1 WLR 2290, [5]; and earlier: [2010] EWHC 647 (Comm) [128].

[q] [2002] EWCA Civ 932, [2003] QB 381, [32] (Lord Phillips MR). See too: s 14(1), (2) of the Criminal Law Act 1967 (discussed in: Mulheron and Cashman, 'Third Party Funding of Litigation: A Changing Landscape' (2008) 27 *Civil Justice Quarterly* 312, 318–19.

[r] [1963] Ch 199 (CA) 219.

[s] [2005] EWHC 201 (QB) [235] (Eady J).

[t] [2001] EWCA Civ 699, [2002] 1 WLR 713.

[u] [2000] UKHL 3, [2000] AC 419.

[v] [2014] EWHC 3405 (QB) [65].

	The tort	Nutshell definition (or chapter treatment)
20	Malicious procurement of a search warrant	The tort requires: a successful application for a search warrant by D; a lack of reasonable and probable cause to make the application; *either* D knew that he had no power to apply for the warrant and that it would probably injure C, *or* D was recklessly indifferent as to whether that act would injure C; and C suffered loss or damage as a consequence of the issue or execution of the warrant (see, e.g., *Keegan v CC of Merseyside*[w] and *Crawford v Jenkins*[x]). The tort also extends to the malicious presentation of a bankruptcy petition or a winding-up petition
21	Malicious prosecution (aka injurious prosecution)	The tort requires: *either* a criminal *or* a civil claim was brought by D against C maliciously and in the absence of reasonable and probable cause; the proceedings ended in C's favour; D acted with malice in instituting the claim; C suffered loss or damage (e.g., damage to his reputation, if the matter is scandalous; damage to his person, if he is imprisoned; or damage to his property, if he is put to charges and expenses) (see, e.g., *Crawford Adjusters (Cayman) Ltd v Sagicor General Ins (Cayman) Ltd,*[y] and *Land Securities plc v Fladgate Fielder (a firm)*[z]). The prosecution is usually for a criminal charge, but the tort of maliciously bringing civil proceedings is also recognised
22	Misfeasance in public office	The tort requires that: D, a public officer, purported to exercise some power or authority; *either* D knew that his disregard of his duty would injure C *or* was recklessly indifferent to the consequences for C; D's exercise of power or authority was done with malice or dishonestly or 'in bad faith'; and C suffered loss (see, e.g., *Three Rivers DC v Governor of Bank of England*[aa] and *N v Sec of State for the Home Dept*[bb])
23	Misuse of private information (Privacy)	See 'Privacy' (online), and the definition at §PR.1
24	Negligence	See Chapter 2, and the nutshell analysis above at §2.1
25	Negligent misstatement	See Chapter 4, and the definition at §4.3

[w] [2003] EWCA Civ 936, [2003] 1 WLR 2187, [13], citing: *Gibbs v Rea* [1998] AC 786 (HL). Subsequently applied in: *Fitzpatrick v Commr of Police* [2012] EWHC 12.

[x] [2014] EWCA Civ 1035, [48].

[y] [2013] UKPC 17, [2014] AC 366.

[z] [2009] EWCA Civ 1402, [2010] 1 Ch 467, [67], [100], [110]. See earlier: *Gregory v Portsmouth CC* [2000] UKHL 3, [2000] AC 419 (especially Lord Steyn, 'The extension of the tort to civil proceedings').

[aa] [2000] UKHL 33, [2000] 2 WLR 1220.

[bb] [2014] EWHC 3304 (QB).

	The tort	Nutshell definition (or chapter treatment)
26	Passing-off	The tort requires that: D conducts his business on the basis that it misleads the public to believe that D's goods and/or services are those of C's business; at the time of the acts complained of, C had a significant reputation or goodwill; and D's acts gave rise to a false message which would be understood, by a not insignificant section of his market, that his goods have been endorsed, recommended or approved by C (see, e.g., *Irvine v Talksport Ltd*,[cc] and *Cranford Community College v Cranford College Ltd*[dd]). It is not necessary to prove that D intended to deceive; innocent passing-off is actionable as a tort
27	Private nuisance	See Chapter 16, and the definition at §16.1
28	Public nuisance	See 'Public Nuisance' (online), and the definition at §PU.1
29	*Rylands v Fletcher*, the rule in	See Chapter 17, and the definition at §17.1
30	*Scienter*, action for	This tort is now replaced as described in 'Liability for animals' (online), and the text under §AN.1
31	Slander	See Chapter 15 and the definition at §15.2
32	Trespass to chattels	The tort requires: a direct and immediate interference by D with goods; where those goods were in the possession of C at the time of the interference; and where the act of interference can constitute touching, handling, damaging or removing those goods; without C's permission or licence (see, e.g., *White v Withers LLP*[ee])
33	Trespass to land	The tort requires: D entered land without permission, or remained on that land which was entered into with permission following the withdrawal of that permission, and a reasonable opportunity to leave the land has passed; the land was owned by, or in the exclusive possession of, C; and D's entry, or remaining there, was intentional, negligent or innocent (see, e.g., *Monsanto plc v Tilly*[ff])

[cc] [2002] EWCA Civ 423.
[dd] [2014] EWHC 2999 (IPEC).
[ee] [2009] EWCA Civ 1122, [2009] 3 FCR 435, [44]–[50].
[ff] [1999] EWCA Civ 3044, [2000] Env LR 313.

There are some causes of action, ostensibly tortious,[2] which do **not** appear in the abovementioned Table, and the reasons for their exclusion are noted below:

---

[2] Not 'tortuous', even though the claims may feel to be just that by the litigants and their lawyers! This inaccuracy occasionally turns up even in law reports, e.g., *Watkins v Home Office* [2006] UKHL 17, [32].

	The 'non-tort'	Why it is excluded
a.	Breach of confidence	Although sometimes called a tort (e.g., in *Venables v NGN Ltd*[a]), this cause of action was developed by the Courts of Chancery during the 18th and 19th centuries, and modern appellate decisions have referred to it (correctly) as an *equitable* cause of action (see, e.g., *Tchenguiz v Imerman (Rev 4)*,[b] and *Wainwright v Home Office*[c])
b.	Detinue	This tort was abolished by the Torts (Interference with Goods) Act 1977. Detinue was proven where there was a wrongful detention of goods by the possessor of those goods, D, after C, their rightful owner, lawfully requested their return. The 1977 Act now governs that right of recovery[d]
c.	Wrongful interference with a body	English law does not currently recognise the tort of wrongful interference with a body (where D removes and retains organs from a child's body without knowledge or consent of the parent) (per *AB v Leeds Teaching Hosp NHS Trust*[e])
d.	Conversion of contractual rights	English law does not recognise a tort of conversion of contractual rights (e.g., where a receiver is invalidly appointed and wrongfully takes control of a company's, C's, contractual rights and business) – because there can be no conversion of intangible choses in action (per *OBG Ltd v Allan*[f])

[a] [2001] EWHC QB 32, [2001] 2 WLR 1038, [7] (President Elizabeth Butler-Sloss). Also, e.g.: *Campbell v MGN Ltd* [2002] EWCA Civ 1373, [2003] QB 633, [69] (Lord Phillips MR).

[b] [2010] EWCA Civ 908, [2011] 2 WLR 592, [74] ('A claim based on confidentiality is an equitable claim. Accordingly, the normal equitable rules apply': Lord Neuberger MR, writing for the court).

[c] [2003] UKHL 53, [2004] 2 AC 406, [18] (an 'equitable action for breach of confidence': per Lord Bingham).

[d] See s 2(1), subject to the following saving provision in s 2(2): 'An action lies in conversion for loss or destruction of goods which a bailee has allowed to happen in breach of his duty to his bailor (that is to say it lies in a case which is not otherwise conversion, but would have been detinue before detinue was abolished)'.

[e] [2004] EWHC 644 (QB), [2005] 2 WLR 358, [161] (Gage J).

[f] [2005] EWCA Civ 106, [2005] QB 762, [49]–[58].

Finally, as a matter of terminology, some so-called torts are merely generic, or compendious, terms for a 'bunch' of individual torts. To clarify:

This is not a tort *per se* ...	... but a generic term by which to describe other torts ...
Trespass to the person	... a series of common law torts whose purpose is to protect against violations of C's person, *viz*: assault; battery; and false imprisonment. See Chapter 14.
Wrongful interference with goods	... certain common law torts (*viz*, conversion, and trespass to chattels), and statutory torts (to the extent that the Torts (Interference with Goods) Act 1977 preserves a cause of action which would have operated in detinue).

Disparities among the torts

§1.3   There are numerous disparities across the torts, such that a common or shared characteristic among them is virtually impossible to identify.

This section highlights **ten (10)** disparities across the torts arising in English law:

i. Actionable *per se* versus proof of damage. For those torts which have, as their principal aim, the protection or vindication of C's rights, they are actionable without proof of damage. Trespasses to the person (assault, battery and false imprisonment), and wrongful interferences with goods (trespass to chattels, and conversion), fall into that category. However, for torts where compensation is the primary purpose, the tort will not be actionable unless there is some proof of compensable damage – negligence, the tort in *Wilkinson v Downton*, private nuisance, and the rule in *Rylands v Fletcher*, are examples of the latter category.

ii. Strict liability versus fault. For some torts, it is irrelevant if D was 'at fault', or whether D exercised reasonable (or even the utmost) care to avoid the harm to C. D will be strictly liable in tort, regardless. These torts include: the rule in *Rylands v Fletcher*, liability for defective products under the Consumer Protection Act 1987; defamation; and in some cases of breach of statutory duty. For the majority of torts, however (e.g., negligence; trespasses to the person such as assault, battery and false imprisonment; and private nuisance), some proof of fault or wrongdoing will be required.

iii. Intentional versus non-intentional conduct. Some torts require proof of intentional conduct, which may include a reckless indifference on D's part (e.g., the rule in *Wilkinson v Downton*, and trespasses to the persons, generally fall within this category, although, exceptionally, negligent conduct may be sufficient for battery). For other torts, intentional conduct is not required. For example, in negligence, and public or private nuisance, then careless, or even careful, conduct, respectively – which is not intended to harm C at all – is sufficient to make out the causes of action.

iv. The type of interests protected. The main purpose of the tort of negligence is to protect against damage to the person, property, or economic interests, of C. However, some causes of action protect different interests entirely. For example: defamation serves to protect the reputation of individuals or entities; trespasses to the person (assault, battery and false imprisonment), and the rule in *Wilkinson v Downton*, aim to protect personal bodily integrity; the torts such as passing-off, conspiracy to injure, intimidation; the rule in *Rylands v Fletcher*, and private nuisance primarily serve to protect C's economic or commercial, interests; and the protection of C's interest in personal property is addressed by torts such as conversion, and trespass to chattels.

v. C's personal culpability as a defence differs. For some torts, the careless or wrongful conduct of C constitutes a (partial) defence to the tort (e.g., the defence of contributory negligence is available in a claim for negligence as a matter of statutory law, via the Law Reform (Contributory Negligence) Act 1945). For other torts, however, any culpability on C's part is not a defence, or, at least, it is very doubtful, on current authority, whether a defence can be made out (as, e.g., for assault and battery).

vi. Availability of remedies differs. Remedies across the torts are not uniform either. For most torts, the appropriate remedy is that of damages (whether compensatory, aggravated, exemplary, or restitutionary – although the availability of these types of damages has not been confirmed across all torts). For limited torts, however (e.g., private nuisance, or trespass to land), self-help remedies are also available (i.e., abatement of the nuisance, or ejection of the trespasser, respectively), permitting C to protect his rights without recourse to judicial determination.

vii. **Some torts are crimes, but most are not.** Trespass to land is a tort, but is not usually a crime (unless exceptional circumstances apply, such as trespassing on diplomatic or consular premises), and hence, any sign, '*Trespassers will be prosecuted*', is commonly misleading, if no criminal prosecution is possible.[3] Some torts, however, are commonly crimes too (e.g., assault, battery, public nuisance and dangerous driving arising from negligent conduct), which can give rise to prosecution of D by the State.

viii. **Standing to sue.** Some torts restrict standing, by reference to C's proprietary or possessory rights. For example, for private nuisance, and the rule in *Rylands v Fletcher*, the claim is only capable of being brought if C has proprietary rights or exclusive occupation of the land upon which the interference occurred. For other torts, however (e.g., negligence, trespass to the person, the rule in *Wilkinson v Downton*), proprietary rights are irrelevant in establishing standing to sue.

ix. **Source of the law.** Some torts are vested in, or defined by, statute, and hence, are properly considered to be statutory torts. For example, the tort of harassment arises from the Protection from Harassment Act 1997; and the law of occupiers' liability, regarding liability towards lawful entrants or towards trespassers, is governed by the Occupiers' Liability Act 1957 and the Occupiers' Liability Act 1984, respectively. For most torts, however, they are sourced to judicial decision-making in case law.

x. **Limitation periods.** The period in which C may maintain an action in tort varies considerably. The general rule is that, by virtue of s 2 of the Limitation Act 1980, an action founded on a tort may not be brought after the expiration of six years from the date on which the cause of action accrued. However, that general rule is overridden by numerous other provisions, which impose different limitation periods for specific torts. Limitation periods are discussed in 'The beginning and end of liability' (an online chapter). For example, the variation can be briefly illustrated as follows: for an action for negligence, nuisance, or breach of statutory duty, which consists of, or includes, damages for personal injuries to C or to any person, the limitation period is three years; for defamation (whether libel or slander), the limitation period is only one year; and an action under the Protection from Harassment Act 1997 is permitted six years. Many law reform commissions have criticised the lack of uniformity of limitation periods in Tort law. The Alberta Law Reform Institute, for example, remarked that 'there is neither a sound theoretical nor practical foundation for the practice of assigning different fixed limitation periods to different categories of claim'.[4] Nevertheless, differing limitation periods remain the reality for the English landscape.

THE PURPOSES OF TORT LAW

§1.4   The are *seven* judicially-identified purposes of Tort law, the principal one of which is to provide compensation to C as a victim of the civil wrong committed by D against C, for the harm or damage suffered as a consequence of that civil wrong.

---

[3] Noted, e.g., in: *Oxford Dictionary of Law* (6th edn, Oxford University Press, 2006) 546.

[4] *Limitations* (DP 4, 1986) [2.63], and also cited in Irish LRC, *Limitation of Actions* (Rep 104, 2011) [2.02].

The purposes outlined below may be singly, or (sometimes) concurrently, evident in any one piece of Tort litigation. In other cases, the purposes may clash, and pull in different directions. However, in combination, they provide the basic reasoning as to why the subject has occupied an extremely important part of common law legal systems around the world.

i. Compensatory function. The compensatory function of Tort law has frequently been judicially acknowledged. For example, in *Devenish Nutrition Ltd v Sanofi-Aventis SA (France) (Rev 1)*, Arden LJ remarked, '[t]he aim of the law of tort is to compensate for loss suffered';[5] whilst in *Gregg v Scott*, Baroness Hale observed that, '[t]ort law is not criminal law. The criminal law is there to punish and deter those who do not behave as they should. Tort law is there to compensate those who have been wronged, [although] some wrongs are actionable whether or not the claimant has been damaged'.[6]

However, that cannot be its only function. Indeed, in *Smith New Court v Citibank*,[7] Lord Steyn observed that any view that the 'the sole purpose of the law of tort generally … should be to compensate the victims of civil wrongs' was 'far too narrow'. In that particular case (which concerned the tort of deceit), the deterrent function also had an important role to play (as discussed below).

The 'compensatory' function of Tort law must be qualified in two respects. First, it is usually (but not always) met by an award of compensatory damages – assessed so as to put the victim, C, in the position in which he was placed before the tort was committed by the tortfeasor, D (insofar as money can do so). However, other awards of damages, where appropriate for the tort in issue, will also satisfy the 'compensatory' function. These include: *restitutionary* damages (where the purpose of the award is to strip D of his profit or to cause the reversal of a benefit conferred by C); *user* damages (where the purpose of the award is to assess the fair value of a right of which D's tortious conduct has wrongly deprived C, even if C would not have sought to use that right and so incurred no loss); *aggravated* damages (where the purpose of the award is to compensate C where the tortious conduct of D, or the circumstances surrounding the commission of the tort, subjected C to humiliation, distress or embarrassment); and even *nominal* damages (where C has not suffered any damage from the wrong committed by D, but nevertheless the award denotes that a legal right has been infringed).

Secondly, the victim of a tort is, invariably, **not** compensated for the entirety of his grievances. Some heads of damage are simply unavailable (e.g., damages for mere distress are not awardable in some Torts); some have been abolished altogether (e.g., damages for loss of consortium – the right of one spouse to the company, assistance and affection of the other – were abolished by the Administration of Justice Act 1982); and for some heads of general damage, the quantum may be either stipulated by pre-set awards or capped by statute (as discussed in Chapter 11). Hence, full compensation is not necessarily the aim of Tort law.

ii. Deterrent function. The fact that Tort law accommodates an award of exemplary damages – albeit in limited circumstances, and only where D's conduct deserves to be punished because it is egregious and worthy of condemnation – confirms that this strand of civil liability endorses a deterrent function.

---

[5] [2008] EWCA Civ 1086, [2009] Ch 390, [2].   [6] [2005] UKHL 2, [2005] 2 AC 176, [217].
[7] [1997] AC 254 (HL) 279–80.

That an award of compensatory damages may also fulfil a deterrent function accords with senior English judicial views, thereby acknowledging that deterrence is not exclusively the province of the criminal law. For example, in *Cassell & Co Ltd v Broome (No 1)*,[8] Lord Kilbrandon noted that compensatory damages, especially 'very large compensatory damages', carry an adequate deterrent function of themselves. Further, according to *Rookes v Barnard*, 'if, and only if, the amount [of compensatory damages] is inadequate to punish [D] for his outrageous conduct, to mark the disapproval of such conduct and to deter [D] from repeating it' can exemplary damages be awarded – thereby acknowledging that compensatory awards may have, themselves, some capacity to punish.[9]

Subsequently, in *Gleaner Co Ltd v Abrahams (Jamaica)*, the Privy Council approved of the 'orthodox view of the dual function of compensatory damages', so that 'compensatory damages may also have a punitive, deterrent or exemplary function', but that '[w]hat distinguishes exemplary damages ... is that they do not have a compensatory function'.[10]

iii. Striking a balance between competing rights. Another principal purpose of Tort law is to allocate responsibility for the obligations which one person owes to another; and to protect the rights that one person is permitted to assert against another – a disarmingly bland statement which belies the difficulties/conflicts which arise in practice and which is the role of Tort law to resolve. The problem was no better explained than by Lord Scott in *Ashley v CC of Sussex Police*:

> the civil law, in particular the law of tort, must strike a balance between conflicting rights. Thus, for instance, the right of freedom of expression may conflict with the right of others not to be defamed. The rules and principles of the tort of **defamation** must strike the balance. The right not to be physically harmed by the actions of another may conflict with the rights of other people to engage in activities involving the possibility of accidentally causing harm. The balance between these conflicting rights must be struck by the rules and principles of the tort of **negligence**. As to **assault and battery** and self-defence, every person has the right in principle not to be subjected to physical harm by the intentional actions of another person. But every person has the right also to protect himself by using reasonable force to repel an attack or to prevent an imminent attack.[11]

iv. Public vindication. Public enquiries or investigations of what happened to C, at the hands of D, are typically undertaken via one of three means: criminal trials, coronial inquests and a formal public enquiry. Can a tortious cause of action fulfil that role too? Is that a legitimate purpose of Tort law?

In *Ashley v CC of Sussex Police*,[12] the House of Lords (by majority) held that it could. C was entitled to proceed with the claim for battery and assault, in that case, for 'vindicatory purposes', even if no damages could be awarded, due to a prior concession on damages by the police. Lord Scott commented that, '[a]lthough the principal aim of an award of compensatory damages is to compensate [C] for loss suffered, there is no reason in principle why an award of compensatory damages should not also fulfil a vindicatory purpose ... They want a finding of liability on their assault and battery claim in order to obtain a public vindication of the deceased's right not to have been subjected to a deadly assault ... They have pleaded a case that, if reasonably arguable on the facts, cannot be struck out as being unarguable in law. Why, therefore, should

---

[8] [1972] AC 1027 (HL) 1134.   [9] [1964] AC 1129 (HL) 1228 (Lord Devlin).
[10] [2003] UKPC 55, [2004] AC 628, [41].   [11] [2008] UKHL 25, [2008] 1 AC 962, [18].
[12] *ibid*, with quotes at [22]–[23], [60].

they be denied the chance to establish liability at a trial?' The following statement in *Chester v Afshar* was also cited, in *Ashley*: '[t]he function of the law [of Tort] is to enable rights to be vindicated and to provide remedies when duties have been breached' – because unless an infringed right obtained an adequate remedy, the tortious obligation would become 'a hollow one, stripped of all practical force and devoid of all content'.[13]

In practice, the vindicatory purpose also manifests where the only damages awarded to C are nominal in nature. The very award proves that C's right was infringed by D's conduct.

v.   A 'gap-filler' in the general common law. The law of tort also has the function of 'perform[ing] a gap-filling role to provide a needed remedy which otherwise would not be available' (as the Scottish Outer House commented in *Realstone Ltd v J&E Shepherd*[14]). That court noted that this function has been evident in negligently-inflicted pure economic loss (as discussed in Chapter 4). For example, in *White v Jones*,[15] Lord Goff explicitly noted that creating a tortious duty of care may be justified because of 'the simple filling of an unacceptable gap' in the common law (that gap was indeed 'filled' in *White v Jones*), while, in *Williams v Natural Life Health Foods Ltd*, Lord Steyn expressly acknowledged that 'the law of tort, as the general law, has to fulfil an essential gap-filling role'.[16]

vi. A vehicle for the apportionment of risk. In Contract law, the apportionment of risk between the contracting parties is a matter of negotiation and/or consent, and the loss falls where it is agreed (affirmed, e.g., in *Caledonia North Sea Ltd v British Telecommunications plc (Scotland)*[17]).

In Tort law, by contrast, the obligations falling upon C and D are imposed by law. In determining where the loss should fall, Tort pays particular regard to two factors (both of which were described, e.g., in *Re Deep Vein Thrombosis and Air Travel Group Litig*[18]):

- which, of C or D, is better equipped to insure against the risks associated with D's acts or omissions? If D is in a better position to distribute the loss (i.e., the liability to pay tortious damages) among its customers or clients, of what would otherwise be 'a crushing burden upon those few unfortunate enough to become accident victims', then doctrine may be construed accordingly; and
- which, of C or D, is better positioned to minimise or prevent C's injury or loss? When the event which caused the injury or loss is solely within D's capacity to control or to influence, then the risk apportionment theory of liability suggests that liability for that risk manifesting should be D's to bear.

Depending upon the outcome of this query, the compensatory purpose may be subjugated to the conclusion that C, the 'injured party', was better-placed to insure against the loss which he suffered (a verdict arrived at, e.g., in *West Bromwich Albion Football Club Ltd v El-Safty*,[19] a leading pure economic loss case discussed in Chapter 4).

vii. An alternative to statutory compensation. C may be entitled to statutory compensation when injured by D, and for which compensation derived in a tortious action can serve as a 'top-up'. There have also been various *proposed* statutory schemes for tortiously-caused injuries

[13] [2005] 1 AC 134, [87] (Lord Hope).   [14] [2008] CSOH 31, [19] (Lord Hodge).
[15] [1995] UKHL 5, [1995] 2 AC 207, 268.
[16] [1998] UKHL 17, [1998] 1 WLR 830, 837, and cited with approval in: *Riyad Bank v Ahli Bank (UK) plc* [2006] EWCA Civ 780, [40]–[41].
[17] [2002] UKHL 4, [2002] 1 Lloyd's Rep 553, [13].   [18] [2002] EWHC 2825 (QB) [47], [106]–[108].
[19] [2007] PIQR P7 (CA) [63] (Rix LJ), [84] (Mummery LJ).

in England (e.g., as discussed in Chapter 17, brief consideration will be given to the suggested statutory scheme for damage caused by the escape of dangerous things in place of the tortious action under *Rylands v Fletcher*, which scheme has never been enacted). A snapshot of the principal and currently-available statutory compensation schemes is contained in the following Table:

Snapshot of some English statutory compensation schemes

- **the Criminal Injuries Compensation Scheme 2012**, 'a government funded scheme to compensate blameless victims of violent crime. Payment can never fully compensate for the injuries suffered, but it is a recognition of public sympathy';[a]
- **the compensation regime for road traffic accidents**, operated by the Motor Insurers' Bureau (MIB), per the Road Traffic Act 1988 (RTA). The MIB 'functions under two separate Agreements between Government and the motor insurance industry', and has responsibility for administering three separate regimes: (1) the Uninsured Drivers' Scheme, which requires the MIB to meet unsatisfied Civil Court Judgments against identified motorists who may not have been insured, as required by the RTA[b]; (2) the Untraced Drivers' Scheme, which requires the MIB to consider applications for compensation from victims of 'hit and run' motorists; and (3) the Green Card Scheme, which requires the MIB to act as the deemed insurer of visiting motorists, for the purpose of paying claims.[c] All insurers who offer compulsory motor insurance are required to belong to the MIB and to contribute to its funding;
- **the workers' compensation scheme**, governed by the Social Security Contributions and Benefits Act 1992. For example, under s 94(1) of that Act, 'industrial injuries benefit shall be payable where an employed earner suffers personal injury ... by accident arising out of and in the course of his employment'. Additionally, several diseases are stipulated by the Social Security (Industrial Injuries) (Prescribed Diseases) Regs 1985, as falling within the scheme, and include, say, diffuse mesothelioma, occupational asthma, and anthrax;[d]
- **compensation for designated diseases**, purportedly caused by the pertussis vaccination of either child or pregnant mother, under the Vaccine Damages Payments Act 1979 (providing for a fixed payment in circumstances of 80% disability, later amended to lower the level of minimum disability to 60% and raise the statutory sum to £100,000, per the Vaccine Damages Payments Act 1979 Statutory Sum Order 2000).[e]

[a] See: Criminal Injuries Compensation Authy, *A Guide to the Criminal Injuries Compensation Scheme 2012* (5 Mar 2013), Section 1, [1].
[b] Pursuant to s 143(1)(a).
[c] See: Motor Insurers' Bureau, 'Frequently Asked Questions', available at: http://www.mib.org.uk/making-a-claim/what-we-do/.
[d] See Regs 2, 43, and Sch 1 and 4.
[e] SI 2000/1983. Also: Regulatory Reform (Vaccine Damages Payments Act 1979) Order 2002, SI 2002/1592.

Occasionally, senior judicial figures have acknowledged that Tort law plays a crucial role in delivering compensation to **some** aggrieved parties, even if it fails to deliver to others – in circumstance where Parliament has not acted to facilitate statutory compensation, whether for political, economic, cultural or societal reasons. Compensation schemes require a political will which may be entirely lacking. As Lord Hoffmann observed in *Matthews v MOD*, whether a tort-based system of compensation should be supplanted or supplemented is 'a matter of national policy', and that whether a tort-based system 'is the most sensible way of providing compensation for accident victims is controversial ... the existing [Tort law] system is expensive and, in many respects, unfair'.[20]

Of course, sometimes Tort law may not provide **any** alternative to C at all, in the circumstances. Where C is injured by D's driving, then frequently that driving will have been negligent, giving rise to the right to court-ordered compensation, or the statutory and administrative arrangements governing road traffic accidents (as noted in the Table above) may enable C to recover compensation for his injuries. Nevertheless, there may still be those few who suffer from injuries arising from the driving of a vehicle by another, and who cannot recover anything at all, where negligence cannot be proven – e.g., where D, the driver, suffered from a hitherto-unknown hypoglacaemic state, as in the English case of *Mansfield v Weetabix Ltd*,[21] or a latent sick sinus condition, as in the Irish case of *Counihan v Bus Atha Cliath-Dublin Bus*,[22] which caused the respective drivers to black out whilst at the wheel, and cause serious injury and damage to C. Such cases inevitably attract judicial sympathy, as evident in *Snelling v Whitehead*,[23] where Lord Wilberforce noted:

> This case is one which is severely distressing ... [and] should attract automatic compensation, regardless of any question of fault. But no such system has yet been introduced in this country, and the courts, including this House, have no power to depart from the law as it stands. This requires that compensation may only be obtained in an action for damages and ... as a condition of the award of damages against the [driver], a finding of fault, or negligence, on his part.

Nevertheless, for all of the drawbacks, disadvantages, and vagaries which Tort jurisprudence may demonstrate, it must be reiterated that statutory compensation schemes can be afflicted with several difficulties too, both with their design and their application/outcomes. The following Table illustrates some of the conundrums, with reference to well-known statutory compensation schemes:

Statutory compensation schemes: a snapshot

Some examples:

New Zealand: originally, the Accident Compensation Act 1972, and subsequently replaced by: Injury Prevention, Rehabilitation and Compensation Act 2001[a]

Florida: the Birth-Related Neurological Injury Compensation Act (1988)[b]

Design features:

- **what range it covers** – comprehensive (NZ statute); or situation-specific (Florida statute)
- **what residual rights to pursue common law proceedings remain:** whether the regime entirely precludes a common law action; *or* precludes a common law action for personal injury only; *or* precludes a common law action for compensatory damages but permits an action for exemplary

[a] In force, 1 Apr 2002, and amended by: Injury Prevention, Rehabilitation and Compensation Amendment Act (No 2) 2005, mainly in force 1 Jul 2005.
[b] See subsequently: s 7666.302 of the Florida Statute.

---

[20] [2003] UKHL 4, [2003] 1 AC 1163, [2].   [21] [1998] 1 WLR 1263 (CA).
[22] [2005] IEHC 51, [2005] 2 IR 436.   [23] The Times (31 Jul 1975), [1998] RTR 385 (HL) 386.

damages; *or* precludes a common law action for statutorily-specified injuries, but allows a common law action for everything else; *or* precludes a common law action until C fails to establish that it is covered by the regime, whereupon a common law action is available; *or* precludes a common law action below a certain threshold of injury, but permits a common law action above that threshold; *or* puts C to an election, *viz*, either a common law action or a statutory action;

- **defining the triggers for compensatory awards** – e.g., note the triggers in the Florida statute: 'injury to the brain or spinal cord of a live infant [in excess of a minimum birth weight] caused by oxygen deprivation or mechanical injury occurring in the course of labor, delivery or resuscitation in the immediate post-delivery period in a hospital, which renders the infant permanently and substantially mentally and physically impaired. This definition shall apply to live births only, and shall not include disability or death caused by genetic or congenital abnormality'. Contrast the triggers in the NZ legislation: 'a personal injury suffered in New Zealand and [which] is caused by an accident, a medical misadventure, or a gradual process, disease or infection that is work-related, or [by] a medical misadventure, or as a result of a personal injury or its treatment';
- **what (if any) injury or disability thresholds apply** for eligibility for payment to arise;
- **whether any rights of appeal are available** (and if so, whether to court or to some other forum);
- **whether the regime is compulsory; opt-in; or opt-out,** in relation to either victim C, or the paying party D (and, if non-compulsory, what notice and consent requirements must be met, to ensure valid involvement);
- **what, and how, damages or expenses are compensated** (e.g., capped, indexed, or scaled); and **how those payments should be made** (whether lump-sum, periodical or other);
- **practically speaking,** how the claims should be processed, and how the claims facility should be funded.

Hence, there are considerable legal and policy conundrums vested in the exercise of drafting a statutory compensation scheme – as the somewhat problematical, and oft-litigated, regimes in Florida and New Zealand aptly demonstrate. (An analysis of that jurisprudence falls outside the scope of this book.)

TORTS IN CONTEXT

Obtaining monetary compensation

§1.5 More than one cause of action may be pleaded by C, in respect of the same grievance, from different legal avenues. However, C will recover the monetary redress to which he is entitled only once, regardless of how many causes of action are successfully instituted against D.

Tort law protects rights *in personam*, which amount to an injury to C's person or property, or economic well-being, or his reputation). Three other avenues of redress may protect the same type of rights:

Avenues, apart from Tort law

Contract law The cause of action for breach of contract requires three matters to be proven:
- formation of a contract;
- breach of that contract; and
- the absence of any factor that would vitiate the contract's formation.[a]

Equity This avenue includes numerous causes of action, e.g.:
- breach of confidential information;
- breach of fiduciary relationship;
- undue influence.[b]

Restitution This avenue includes, e.g.:
- an action for *quantum meruit*, for a reasonable value of goods or services obtained, following rescission (or, more rarely) termination of a contract
- disgorgement of benefits conferred on D as a result of C's mistake of fact or of law.[c]

[a] See, e.g.: N Andrews, *Contract Law* (2nd edn, Cambridge University Press, 2015); M Chen-Wishart, *Contract Law* (4th edn, Oxford University Press, 2012).
[b] See, e.g.: A Hudson, *Equity and Trusts* (8th edn, Routledge, 2014); G Virgo, *The Principles of Equity and Trusts* (Oxford University Press, 2012).
[c] See, e.g.: A Burrows, E McKendrick and J Edelman, *Cases and Materials on the Law of Restitution* (2nd edn, Oxford University Press, 2007); R Goff and G Jones, *The Law of Restitution* (7th edn, Sweet & Maxwell, 2007).

Concurrently-prosecuted tortious wrongs are perfectly permissible, and indeed, are very common, albeit that pleading numerous causes of action does not guarantee success in any one of them:

> In *Keegan v CC of Merseyside*,[24] police officers, D, considered that there were reasonable grounds to arrest X on suspicion of involvement in armed robberies. However, the premises mistakenly targeted in the raid were those of the Keegan family, C, who pursued D for three causes of action: malicious procurement of a search warrant; trespass to land; and false imprisonment. **Held:** all three causes of action failed. D had a proper motive in deciding to seek a warrant and there was no malice involved; D's entry to the premises was lawful and not a trespass to land; and there was no false imprisonment.

Even where C may prove **all** concurrently-pleaded causes of action, C is only entitled to recover his damages **once**, if all claims are in respect of the same injury to C. In that respect, the causes of action are the doorways through which C must try to enter the room; and once in that room, C is entitled to monetary award, to redress the injury or damage which he has suffered. As Lord Rodger explained in *Ashley v CC of Sussex Police*,[25] double-recovery is **not** possible: 'as a general rule, the damages recoverable under both causes of action will be the same. Since the damages are intended to provide compensation for the injuries suffered by [C], he is entitled to the same damages, whether he succeeds on one cause of action or on both. The only material advantage to [C] in succeeding on both causes of action is that he will be entitled to retain his damages, even if an appeal court later holds that he should not have succeeded on one of them'.

[24] [2003] EWCA Civ 936, [2003] 1 WLR 2187.   [25] [2008] UKHL 25, [2008] 1 AC 962, [58].

Indeed, the interaction between pleas for breach of contract and for negligence, arising out of the same grievance, have given rise to some controversy, and is discussed in the following section.

Concurrent liability in Contract and in Tort

In their contract, the parties, C and D, can freely allocate the risks and responsibilities between themselves as they see fit during negotiations (or lay off some of the risk to other parties involved in the project). Any risks and responsibilities in Tort, however, are imposed by law – the parties have no say in that allocation. Hence, in analysing the obligations and responsibilities which arise in Contract, the court is scrutinising the express terms (whether written or oral), and the implied terms (if any). In negligence, however, the obligations are determined by asking what duty of care arose between C and D, under one of the relevant tests governing duty (as discussed in Chapter 2).

Why it matters

The significance of plucking, and pleading, different causes of action from different avenues usually comes down to specific matters – and it is no different when choosing between Contract and Tort actions:

The measure of damages. There is a prospect of the measure of damages differing, depending upon which cause of action/s succeeds for C. The function of an award of damages in Contract is quite different from that of Tort. As Lord Scott stated, in *Rees v Darlington Memorial Hosp NHS Trust,*[26] for claims for breach of contract, C 'is entitled to the benefit of the contract and entitled, therefore, to be placed in the position, so far as money can do so, in which he would have been if the contractual obligation had been properly performed. But where the claim is in Tort, there being no contract to the benefit of which [C] is entitled, [C] is entitled to be placed in the position in which he would have been if the tortious act, the wrong, had not been committed'. Additionally, in Contract, the damages may be capped or circumscribed (e.g., liquidated) by the contract itself.

In addition, the rules of remoteness of damage differ between the actions. In Contract, the rule in *Hadley v Baxendale*[27] restricts the scope of damages recoverable to those for which a party assumed contractual responsibility as having been in the contemplation of the parties, or which arise normally in the course of things (per *Transfield Shipping Inc v Mercator Shipping Inc (The Achilleas*[28])). By contrast, in Tort, the remoteness rules are wider: provided that the type or kind of damage was reasonably foreseeable, and falls within the scope of the duty, then the damage is recoverable (per *Jolley v Sutton LBC*[29]).

The fact of damage. Proving damage **may** be necessary for the Tort action (e.g., in respect of negligence, '[i]t is trite law that damage is the gist of the action', per *Chester v Afshar*[30]), whereas it is **not** an element of the action, say, for breach of contract. Nominal damages can be awarded for a breach of contract, whereas substantive damage must be proven for an action in negligence. Hence, in the absence of any compensable damage, C will prefer a remedy in Contract, because it is the very defect, whether it be in the provision of a building, a chattel, or a service, which is actionable (see, e.g., the discussion by Stanley Burnton LJ in *Robinson v PE Jones (Contractors) Ltd*[31]).

[26] [2003] UKHL 52, [2004] 1 AC 309, [130].   [27] (1854) 9 Ex 341 (QB).   [28] [2009] 1 AC 61 (HL).
[29] [2000] UKHL 31, [2000] WLR 1082.   [30] [2004] UKHL 41, [2005] 1 AC 134, [9] (Lord Bingham).
[31] [2011] EWCA Civ 9, [2012] QB 44, [94].

Limitation periods. The limitation period for contract is generally more onerous, i.e., shorter, than for Tort, given that the limitation period starts running, in Contract, from the moment of the alleged breach; whereas the limitation period starts running, in Tort, from the moment that damage is allegedly incurred (a point which may occur much later than the breach itself, as discussed in 'The beginning and end of liability' (an online chapter). In *Henderson v Merrett Syndicates Ltd*, it was argued that the differences which may exist between the limitation periods in Contract and Tort should mean that no concurrent liability in Contract and in Tort should exist – for 'the temptation of elegance'.[32] However, this argument did not prevail (see below).

The standard of care. The standard of care expected of D may be quite different in Contract and in Tort – a point which is often seen in construction or in manufacturing contracts. In contract, D may undertake not to create a defective piece of workmanship, product or article. Any defect will thereby amount to a breach of contract on D's part (unless D has limited, excluded or off-loaded its liability for such defect by some other contractual clause). On the other hand, in the tort of negligence, D is under a duty to use reasonable care and skill to avoid causing damage to C as a result of any defective workmanship, but does not guarantee to produce something which is free of defects – otherwise, negligence would impose an obligation of perfection, or a warranty of a perfect outcome, which the law will not do. Hence, the duty in contract may be more onerous than, and not co-extensive with, the duty in tort – so that it is in C's interests to rely upon the contractual duty if possible (per *Payne v John Setchell Ltd*[33]).

The general principle

§1.6   As a general principle, the mere fact that C and D are in a contractual relationship does not preclude D from owing a tortious duty of care to C too, provided that D assumed a responsibility towards C to exercise reasonable care to avoid causing C loss or damage. C may, therefore, have concurrent remedies in contract and in tort against D, permitting C, if successful in both, to choose the most advantageous remedy.

The permissibility, in English law, of seeking concurrent remedies in contract and in tort was confirmed by Lord Goff in *Henderson v Merrett Syndicates Ltd*:[34]

an assumption of responsibility, coupled with the concomitant reliance, may give rise to a tortious duty of care, irrespective of whether there is a contractual relationship between the parties, and in consequence, unless his contract precludes him from doing so, [C], who has available to him concurrent remedies in contract and tort, may choose that remedy which appears to him to be the most advantageous.

In *Henderson v Merrett Syndicates Ltd*, C were underwriting members at Lloyds (aka Names) who entered into underwriting agency agreements with Merrett, managing agents of the syndicate, D. In at least one group of actions (Gooda Walker), the Names alleged that D were contractually liable for their failure to exercise reasonable care and skill in relation to such underwriting. C's claims for pure economic loss were framed both in contract and tort. **Held:** C were entitled to pursue their remedies in contract and tort.

---

[32] [1995] 2 AC 145 (HL) 186.   [33] [2001] EWHC 457 (TCC) [23].
[34] [1995] 2 AC 145 (HL) 194 (Lords Keith, Mustill, Nolan and Browne-Wilkinson agreeing).

Lord Goff considered the two options open to the House: that a contractual relationship should preclude any tortious action from arising (as applies in the French legal system); or that a tortious action could lie alongside a contractual action concurrently (as in the German legal system). Albeit recognising that the arguments favouring, or disfavouring, concurrent remedies, were finely-balanced, ultimately, *Henderson* permits C to choose, as between concurrent causes of action and concurrent remedies, that which best suits C's interests (indeed, this principle has been applied more widely – when C has a choice as between recovery under a statutory regime, and in restitution[35] – albeit that such discussion is beyond the scope of this book). Although *Henderson* itself concerned a claim by C to recover damages for pure economic loss, the principle applies where C is claiming for personal injury or physical damage to property too (per *Biffa Waste Services Ltd v Maschinenfabrik Ernst Hese GmbH*[36]).

Precondition for concurrent duties. A necessary condition for the imposition of a concurrent liability in contract and in negligence is that D must have *assumed a responsibility* to avoid the particular damage of which C complains (be it personal injury, property damage or, most controversially, economic damage sustained). Professional Ds, in particular, tend to give rise to the requisite assumption of responsibility, which will entail, for that D, that he owes a contractual duty to C, and a parallel (concurrent) duty in tort. Indeed, concurrent duties in contract and in tort have applied to the following:

- architects (per *Bellefield Computer Services v E Turner & Sons Ltd*[37]);
- builders who exercise design functions as well as workmanship (suggested obiter in an earlier decision in *Bellefield Computer Services Ltd v E Turner & Sons Ltd*[38]);
- insurance brokers (per *Punjab National Bank v DeBoinville*[39]);
- bankers to their customers to whom they provide, e.g., investment advisory services (per *Riyad Bank v AHLI United Bank (UK) plc*[40]), or creditworthiness references (as in *Hedley Byrne and Co Ltd v Heller and Partners Ltd*[41]);
- solicitors (per *Midland Bank Trust Co Ltd v Hett, Stubbs & Kemp*[42]);
- underwriting/managing agents (per *Henderson v Merrett Syndicates Ltd* itself);
- valuers and surveyors (per *Smith v Eric S Bush*[43]);
- accountants (per *Caparo Industries plc v Dickman*[44]); and
- engineers (per *Mirant-Asia Pacific Ltd v Oapil*[45]).

That will not always be the case – D may **not** have assumed responsibility to C, in tort, to avoid causing C damage, as Jackson LJ pointed out in *Robinson v PE Jones (Contractors) Ltd*:

> the conceptual basis, upon which the concurrent liability of professional persons in tort to their clients now rests, is assumption of responsibility ... [However], [w]hen one moves beyond the realm of professional retainers, it by no means follows that every contracting party assumes responsibilities ... to the other parties co-extensive with the contractual obligations. Such an analysis would be nonsensical. Contractual and tortious duties have different origins and different functions.

---

[35] *Deutsche Morgan Grenfell Group plc v Inland Revenue* [2006] UKHL 49, [2007] AC 558, [50]–[51], [136].
[36] [2008] EWHC 6 (TCC) [169(3)] (Akenhead J).   [37] [2002] EWCA Civ 1823, [73] (May LJ).
[38] [2000] EWHC Admin 284 (Schiemann LJ).   [39] [1992] 1 Lloyd's Rep 7 (CA).
[40] [2006] EWCA Civ 780, [36]–[47].   [41] [1964] AC 465 (HL).
[42] [1979] Ch 384. Approved in *Henderson v Merrett Syndicates Ltd* [1995] 2 AC 145 (HL) 184–94 (Lord Goff).
[43] [1990] 1 AC 831, and approved by Lord Goff in *Henderson, ibid.*
[44] [1990] 2 AC 605 (HL).   [45] [2004] EWHC 1750 (TCC) [357], [395]–[396].

Contractual obligations spring from the consent of the parties and the common law principle that contracts should be enforced. Tortious duties are imposed by law, as a matter of policy, in *specific situations*. Sometimes a particular set of facts may give rise to identical contractual and tortious duties, but self-evidently that is not always the case.[46]

For example, the current view is that builders do not owe concurrent duties of care in contract and in tort to protect their employers (developers) against any economic loss brought about by their defective workmanship (per Stanley Burnton LJ in *Robinson v PE Jones Ltd*, who stated that, to the extent that first-instance decisions had recognised concurrent obligations in contract and in tort, those decisions were wrongly decided[47]).

Disapproval of previous authority. A decade before *Henderson* was handed down, the Privy Council had taken quite the opposite view, in *Tai Hing Cotton Mill Ltd v Liu Chong Hing Bank Ltd*,[48] holding that a duty of care in tort should not co-exist with obligations arising under a contract. Lord Scarman (writing for the court) held, in dicta, that, in commercial relationships, 'it is correct in principle, and necessary for the avoidance of confusion in the law, to adhere to the contractual analysis: on principle, because it is a relationship in which the parties have, subject to a few exceptions, the right to determine their obligations to each other; and for the avoidance of confusion, because different consequences do follow according to whether liability arises from contract or tort, e.g. in the limitation of action'.

As it turned out, the approach of *Tai Hing* has been substantially 'reconsidered' in the light of *Henderson* (per *Biffa Waste Services Ltd v Maschinenfabrik Ernst Hese GmbH*[49]).

Query for the future. Recently, there has been some query, judicially, as to whether concurrent duties should apply, given the significant differences between contract and tort. In *Wellesley Partners LLP v Withers LLP*, Nugee J said this:[50]

> it has been established at the highest level that a professional retained by a client has (usually) a concurrent liability in tort as well as contract ... the well-known consequence of the client being able to sue in either contract or tort is to enable him to take advantage of the longer limitation period available in tort. Given that the test for remoteness of damage is different in tort from that which it is in contract, I do not think it is open to me to say ... that a client who chooses to sue in tort cannot equally take advantage of the more generous rules for remoteness of damage available in tort. If that step is to be taken, I think it must be by a higher court.

Whether that step is taken, and the Privy Council's views in *Tai Hing* reinstated, remains to be seen.

Exceptions

§1.7 The principle of concurrent liability will not apply in exceptional circumstances, where: (1) any tortious duty is so inconsistent with the contract so as to be excluded; and (2) a group of contracts governs the relevant obligations.

---

[46] [2011] EWCA Civ 9, [2012] QB 44, [74] (emphasis added), a theme to which Jackson LJ returned in a recent extra-curial lecture to the Technology and Construction Bar Assn and the Socy of Construction Law, 'Concurrent Liability: Where Have Things Gone Wrong?' (30 Oct 2014) [copy on file with the author].

[47] [2011] EWCA Civ 9, [2012] QB 44, [95].   [48] [1986] AC 80 (HL) 107.

[49] [2008] EWHC 6 (TCC) [74].   [50] [2014] EWHC 556 (Ch) [214].

Concurrent duties in contract and in tort may not be recognised, for the following reasons:

i. **The contract precludes concurrent duties between C and D.** As Lord Goff's classic statement in *Henderson* confirms, the contract between C and D may expressly preclude any tortious action from arising. There would be no room for concurrent liability in contract and tort (said Lord Goff) where the tortious duty was so inconsistent with the applicable contract that such tortious liability had to be taken as being excluded.[51] Of course, it all depends upon how the contract is worded.

As Akenhead J reiterated in *Biffa Waste Services Ltd v Maschinenfabrik Ernst Hese GmbH*, 'a duty of care should not be permitted to circumvent or escape a contractual exclusion or limitation of liability for the act or omission that would constitute the tort'.[52]

> In *Robinson v PE Jones (Contractors) Ltd*,[53] James Robinson, C, bought his house from PE Jones, D, the builder, in April 1992, when the building work was completed. Then, in Oct 2004, C arranged to have the gas fires in the house serviced by British Gas, and the fires were declared unsafe, because of alleged defects in their construction and with the flues connected to them. The fires had to be uninstalled and rectified at great expense. C sued D in contract, and in tort, for those costs. **Held:** C's claim in contract was statute-barred. The claim in tort also failed, because it was precluded by cl 10 of the contract:
>
>> The Vendor shall not be liable to the Purchaser ... under the Agreement or any document incorporated therein in respect of any defect, error or omission in the execution or the completion of the work, save to the extent, and for the period, that it is liable under the provisions of the NHBC Agreement on which alone his rights and remedies are founded.

That clause was reasonable under the Unfair Contract Terms Act 1977, and also excluded concurrent liability in tort: '[t]he parties expressly agreed that [D's] only liability to [C] should be that arising from the NHBC agreement ... the only sensible interpretation of cl 10 is that the parties are agreeing to exclude any liability in negligence'.

ii. **A group's contractual arrangements.** Where a *group of contracting parties* have entered into an arrangement, whereby they have each chosen the party/parties with whom to contract, but where one member of the group, C, then seeks to pursue a claim in tort against a party with whom that party has no contract (D), then C is using tort to circumvent the contractual arrangements formed among the group members. In such cases, the question (according to *Pacific Associates v Baxter*[54]) is whether, to permit C to pursue D in tort, would 'cut across and be inconsistent with the structure of relationships created by the contracts' (per Ralph Gibson LJ) – or, '[g]iven the contractual structure between the contractor and the employer, can it be fairly said that it was ever within the contemplation of the contractor [C] that, outside the contract, it could pursue a remedy against the engineer [D]' (per Russell LJ).

Actually, this is not strictly a *Henderson v Merrett Syndicates* scenario, because the court is not considering whether D owes C a parallel duty of care in negligence as well as an obligation in contract. Nevertheless, in such cases, the same principles have been broadly applied.

---

[51] [1995] 2 AC 146 (HL) 193–94.   [52] [2008] EWHC 6 (TCC) [169(4)].
[53] [2011] EWCA Civ 9, [2012] QB 44, quote at [84]–[85] (Jackson LJ).   [54] [1990] 1 QB 993 (CA) 1032, 1037.

In *BSkyB Ltd v HP Enterprise Services UK Ltd (Rev 1)*,[55] British Sky Broadcasting Ltd (BSkyB) and Sky Subscribers Services Ltd (SSSL), C, provided satellite broadcasting services. They had a dispute with those providing IT services to them, EDSC, D. The 'prime contract' was between SSSL and D, to which BskyB was not a contracting party. BSkyB sued D in tort, for alleged losses resulting from the unsuccessful IT systems (approx. £709m). **Held:** D did not owe a duty of care to BSkyB. Otherwise, if it did, that would circumvent the contractual arrangements which the parties had put in place. The parties had not included any provision within the prime contract which expressly referred to any liability of D towards BSkyB, when they could have done so. Hence, the contractual structure negated any possibility that such a duty of care should arise in these circumstances.

TORT LITIGATION

Sources of Tort law

§1.8 There are three principal sources of English Tort law: (1) domestic case law; (2) domestic legislation; and (3) the jurisprudence under the Human Rights Act 1998.

Dealing briefly with each in turn:

i. Domestic case law. As a 'black letter' common law subject, the vast majority of the law discussed in this book is derived from English judicial decisions. Courts from highest appellate level (whether Supreme Court or, previously, the House of Lords) to County Courts and Employment Tribunals, have pronounced on important points of Tort law which have been sufficiently noteworthy to include herein.

    Of course, in accordance the doctrine of authoritative precedent, great care must be taken, in the law of Tort, to distinguish, in a case, the *ratio decidendi* (Latin for 'the reason for deciding') from the *obiter dictum* (Latin for 'a remark in passing'). Only the ratio of a case – the reasoning of the court in reaching its decision on the facts of the case before it – is binding upon lower courts; dicta does not form part of the ratio of the case and creates no binding precedent, but is merely persuasive authority, no matter which court utters it.[56]

    Where appropriate, comparative vignettes of judicial viewpoint, sourced from other common law jurisdictions, have been cited throughout the book, if they provide a different perspective or varying case scenarios which shed light on the point of Tort law under consideration. These are, of course, of persuasive precedent only.

ii. Domestic legislation. As will be evident throughout the book (and from a cursory examination of the Legislation Table in the preliminaries), legislation has had a considerable impact upon substantive Tort law – e.g., from how tortious remedies can be sought in the event that the tortfeasor brings about the death of a victim (see below), to the allocation of damages between culpable Ds, all of whom have wrongfully exposed C to asbestos and where C suffers from mesothelioma as a result (see 'Multiple defendants', an online chapter).

There have been notable occasions, however, where the Law Commission of England and Wales has strongly recommended that an area of Tort law be clarified by the enactment of

---

[55] [2010] EWHC 86 (TCC) [538]–[543].

[56] See, e.g., the order of precedential authority in: *Oxford Dictionary of Law* (6th edn, Oxford University Press, 2006) 393, 404, 439.

legislation, but where Parliament has steadfastly refused to follow that recommendation (the area of negligently-inflicted psychiatric damage, examined in Chapter 5, readily springs to mind).

iii. **The Human Rights Act 1998.** The Human Rights Act 1998 (HRA), and the Convention rights to which it gives further effect,[57] has had a considerable impact upon the development of some areas of English Tort law. This has come about for two reasons.

First, the definition of a 'public authority' in the HRA includes a court or tribunal (per s 6(3)). Hence, courts must ensure that English Tort law is compatible with the Convention, when deciding disputes between purely private parties (the so-called 'horizontal effect' of the HRA). In that regard, it has been evident that, at times, domestic Tort law has been rendered incompatible with Convention rights and 'cannot survive the Human Rights Act' (as recognised by the Court of Appeal in *JD v East Berkshire Community Health NHS Trust*,[58] speaking of the decision in *X (Minors) v Bedfordshire CC*, as discussed in Chapter 13). On other occasions, however, it has not been necessary to develop (i.e., amend, reverse or supplement) English Tort law in order to ensure its compatibility with the Convention – the no-duty-to-rescue principle in 'Bad Samaritan' negligence law (see Chapter 2), and the lack of any *general* tort of privacy (see 'Privacy', an online chapter) being two notable examples where English courts have refused to re-write established doctrine.

The second impact of the HRA on English Tort law – of a more indirect nature – is that C may allege concurrent suits against D, one pleaded as a cause of action in Tort, and the other framed as a claim under the HRA against D, as a public authority which has allegedly acted in a way that was incompatible with C's Convention rights. For example, as discussed in Chapter 13, claims by the vulnerable and disadvantaged against public authorities which have obligations to provide social, housing or educational services are frequently brought in both negligence and under the HRA (as occurred, e.g., in the horrific abuse case of *X & Y v Hounslow LBC*[59]).

Costs rules in tort litigation

A general appreciation of how costs rules operate in English Tort law may be of value, in order to highlight the significant financial risks that both sides of the litigation run, and to canvass some recent and important changes to the costs rules that govern civil (including Tort) litigation.

§1.9   In English civil litigation, the general rule of costs-shifting applies. However, in respect of some areas of Tort litigation, exceptional scenarios have been legislatively-created, since the Jackson Costs Review.

The general rule of costs-shifting

The ramifications of C's losing his Torts suit against D may be very expensive, because of the general rule that 'costs follow the event' (also called the 'two-way' costs rule, the 'costs-shifting'

---

[57] Per the European Convention for the Protection of Human Rights and Fundamental Freedoms 1950 (in Sch 1 to the Human Rights Act 1998), in force Oct 2000.

[58] [2003] EWCA Civ 1151, [2004] QB 558, [83] (Lord Phillips MR, who delivered the judgment of the court).

[59] [2008] EWHC 1168 (QB) [84].

rule, the 'English rule', and the 'loser pays winner' rule – the terms are synonymous). Essentially, it means that the 'winner' of the litigation recovers the reasonable costs incurred in bringing, or defending, the litigation. English law follows the costs-shifting principle for contentious litigation[60] (which embraces all of the Tort litigation referenced in this book), although the court does retain a wide discretion to vary that order[61] (including a discretion not to award the winning party any costs at all).

Limits on recoverability. Costs-shifting does **not**, however, enable the recovery of all of the costs to which the successful party may be put. Broadly speaking, regardless of whether it is C or D who wins the litigation, there is likely to be a substantial discrepancy between the amount of the winner's actual costs in pursuing or defending the Tort action (termed the solicitor and client costs), and the amount that he will be entitled to recover from the unsuccessful opponent (termed the party and party costs).

The costs-shifting rule has been perceived to pose considerable barriers to bringing, or defending, civil litigation, given that each party faces two potential burdens: he must pay his own lawyers' fees and disbursements (of which he will receive only *a portion* of those total costs back, if successful), plus he faces the added burden of being liable for the opponent's party and party costs, if he loses the litigation. However, costs-shifting has the oft-cited benefit of deterring speculative, weak or blackmail claims – given that the party bringing the action has a 'skin in the game'.

The alternative costs rules. There are two other primary costs rules.

Under the **'no-way' costs rule** (also called the 'American rule', in recognition of the fact that a no-way costs rule frequently, but not always, operates in that jurisdiction[62]), the court does not award costs to the successful party. Rather, each party bears his own costs of the litigation, regardless of success or failure. The rule is perceived to give rise to the risk of abuse, for C may be more inclined to bring frivolous/blackmail actions, knowing that, if he loses, he will not have to pay D's costs.

The **one-way costs rule** entails that an award of costs can be made against a losing D, but not against a losing C. This means that D will generally be ordered to pay the costs of a winning C but, subject to certain exceptions, will not recover his own costs if he successfully defends the claim. It is perceived to be a means of removing the risk that C may become liable to pay D's costs in any litigation which C may wish to bring.

A changing costs landscape in Tort litigation

As a result of the ground-breaking costs review conducted by Sir Rupert Jackson, commencing in 2008,[63] progressing to a detailed preliminary report in 2009,[64] and culminating with a final report in 2010,[65] the application of the costs-shifting rule has undergone some significant changes in recent times, which directly impinge upon Tort litigation.

---

[60] Per: CPR 44.3(2)(a).   [61] CPR 44.3(2)(b).

[62] A principle from an 1853 statute, subsequently codified as: 28 USC ¶1920, 1923(a), and see too: *Alyeska Pipeline Service Co v Wilderness Soc*, 421 US 240, 247 (1975) (as a general rule, 'the prevailing litigant is ordinarily not entitled to collect a reasonable attorney's fee from the loser'). See further: Mulheron, *The Class Action in Common Law Legal Systems: A Comparative Perspective* (Hart Publishing, 2004), ch 12.

[63] See: 'Lord Justice Jackson to Head Civil Costs Review' (2008) *Solicitors' Journal* (4 Nov 2008).

[64] *Review of Civil Litigation Costs: Preliminary Report* (May 2009).

[65] *Review of Civil Litigation Costs: Final Report* (Jan 2010).

The potential for radical changes to English law's traditional costs rule were flagged up quite early in the review, and the ultimate recommendations reflected that train of thought.

> **The law reform corner: Costs rules**
>
> **Sir Rupert Jackson's Costs Review (2010) recommended that:**[66]
> - a regime of qualified one-way costs shifting (QOCS) be introduced for personal injury cases (qualified, in that costs-shifting could resume, depending upon the financial resources of C, and the conduct of C in bringing and conducting the suit);
> - QOCS could be introduced for private nuisance claims in the future, if other changes in costs and funding showed that they were an obstacle to access to justice for those types of claims; and
> - QOCS could be introduced for defamation and breach of privacy claims.

On 1 April 2013, QOCS was introduced for personal injury cases,[67] but at the time of writing, the recommendations for QOCS to be introduced in the other areas noted above has not occurred. These costs reforms are likely to have a large impact upon the commencement and conduct of a considerable amount of Tort-related litigation, and represent an important adjustment in the landscape (additional to the other innovative aspect of the Jackson reforms, *viz*, the introduction of percentage contingency fees, or 'damages-based agreements', for 'contentious' legal business for the first time in English law[68]).

In any event, a brief familiarity with the costs rules governing Torts litigation provides a sense of what is *at stake* (albeit that the rules do not impact whatsoever upon *substantive* Tort law).

Strike-out applications in Tort litigation

§1.10   Some of the most important Torts cases in English legal history have been determined as strike-out applications. However, these decisions should arguably not be regarded as being of any lesser precedential value, merely for that reason.

A court has the power to strike out C's claim, where it appears to the court that the claim discloses no reasonable grounds for bringing the claim.[69] A decision on a preliminary point of law[70] serves the same purpose; indeed, the two avenues are 'indistinguishable' for practical purposes (said the Court of Appeal in *Kent v Griffiths*[71]). Notably, although the hearing proceeds on a statement of agreed facts, a decision in a strike-out application is a decision on the merits.[72]

---

[66] *Review of Civil Litigation Costs: Final Report* (2010), chh 19, 31, 32. Earlier: 'Review of Civil Litigation Costs: Information that Would be Helpful for the Costs Review' (27 Nov 2008), published in: *Costs, Collective Redress, Contingency Fees ... The Way Forward?* (Practical Law, London, 26 Feb 2009), s 2.

[67] Per CPR 44.13–44.17.

[68] See the Damages-Based Agreements Regulations 2013, reviewed by an MOJ Working Group chaired by the author in: *The Damages-Based Agreements Reform Project: Drafting and Policy Issues* (Aug 2015).

[69] CPR 3.4(2)(a).   [70] CPR 3.1(2)(i).   [71] [2000] EWCA Civ 3017, [2001] QB 36, [38].

[72] See: A Zuckerman, *Zuckerman on Civil Procedure* (2nd edn, Thomson Sweet & Maxwell, 2006) 279–82.

The strike-out procedure has its limitations in English law too. In *Barrett v Enfield LBC*,[73] Lord Browne-Wilkinson pointed out that a court must not be too eager to strike out a tortious claim, especially where a novel area of law is taking shape. His Lordship referred to his previous judgment in *X (Minors) v Bedfordshire CC*,[74] that, 'in an area of the law which was uncertain and developing (such as the circumstances in which a person can be held liable in negligence for the exercise of a statutory duty or power), it is not normally appropriate to strike out ... it is of great importance that such development should be on the basis of actual facts found at trial, not on hypothetical facts assumed (possibly wrongly) to be true for the purpose of the strike out'. Lord Browne-Wilkinson summed up the position thus: there must be 'a clear and obvious case calling for striking out' – and several evolving areas of Tort law simply do not fall into that category. These judicial sentiments have been useful to various claimants in English Tort law, where the law has been unsettled and developing, enabling them to survive a strike-out application and resolutely carry on (either to settlement or trial).

As a corollary, the strike-out application has assumed an historical importance in Tort law. In *Vicario v Commr of Police for the Metropolis*,[75] Jacobs LJ noted that numerous important authorities governing whether D owed C a duty of care in negligence have been decided 'in strike-out or preliminary point circumstances'. By way of example:

Some notable strike-out cases in English negligence law

- *Donoghue v Stevenson* (1932)
- *Hedley Byrne & Co v Heller & Partners Ltd* (1964)
- *Dorset Yacht Co v Home Office* (1970)
- *Anns v Merton LBC* (1978)
- *Hill v CC of West Yorkshire Police* (1989)
- *Calveley v CC of Mersey* (1989)
- *Caparo Industries plc v Dickman* (1990)
- *X (Minors) v Bedfordshire CC* (1995)
- *Marc Rich & Co v Bishop Rock Marine Co* (1995)

- *Arthur JS Hall & Co v Simons* (2002)
- *JD v East Berkshire Community NHS Trust* (2005)
- *Brooks v Commr of Police of the Metropolis* (2005)

In addition (and not referred to in *Vicario*):
- *Sion v Hampstead HA* (1994)
- *W v Essex CC* (2001)
- *Michael v South Wales Police* (2014)
- *Kent v Griffiths* (1999)

Jacobs LJ added that, '[o]ne cannot imagine what our current law of negligence would look like without these cases, all decided without a trial. Standing above all is *Donoghue v Stevenson*. Not only was it decided on the Scottish equivalent of what the English used to call a demurrer [a strike-out], but no one knows whether there ever was a snail in the bottle'.[76] The view that strike-out applications have played an important role in English Tort law has drawn support in subsequent novel cases (e.g., in *Mitchell v Glasgow CC*[77]), in the evolving and difficult areas of Tort with which courts have had to grapple.

By contrast, some judicial suggestions that strike-out applications are of lesser weight, given their context, do occur from time to time – e.g., in *Taylor v A Novo (UK) Ltd*,[78] Lord

---

[73] [2001] 2 AC 550 (HL) 557.   [74] [1995] 2 AC 633 (HL) 740–41.
[75] [2007] EWCA Civ 1361, with examples at [44].
[76] *ibid*, [45].   [77] 2008 SC 351, 2008 SLT 368 (IH) [134].   [78] [2013] EWCA Civ 194, [34].

Dyson MR remarked that a key case concerning negligently-inflicted psychiatric injury, *W v Essex CC*, was 'a strike-out case. All that the House of Lords decided was that the claim should not have been struck out because it raised an arguable case. For that reason alone, it is of limited value'.

However, and notwithstanding such sentiments, the strike-out applications which have guided, determined, and in some cases, revamped, English Tort law, are given the prominence in this book which, in the author's opinion, they so richly deserve. Some of their doctrines and influence have endured for decades, and 'good English law' would not be the same without them!

TORTS AND DEATH

§1.11   When a person dies as a result of D's tort, two potential actions are available: an action by the person's estate, under the Law Reform (Miscellaneous Provisions) Act 1934; and an action by the person's dependants, under the Fatal Accidents Act 1976.

Although it may seem somewhat odd to confront the subject of torts giving rise to death so early in this book, it will quickly become apparent from subsequent chapters that, unfortunately, whether through D's negligence, battery, breach of statutory duty, or some other tort, a person (the Deceased) may die as a result of D's acts or omissions. It is important to appreciate, from the outset, how claims may legally be brought in that event. In fact, **two** distinct claims are potentially available:

- a 'survival action', whereby the Deceased's estate (the Estate) may bring an action on behalf of the Deceased *for the Deceased's own losses*, pursuant to the Law Reform (Miscellaneous Provisions) Act 1934 ('the 1934 Act');[79] or
- a 'wrongful death action', whereby the Deceased's dependants (the Dependants) may sue, *on their own behalf*, for *their* loss of dependency, pursuant to the Fatal Accidents Act 1976 ('the FAA').[80] This is also called 'an FAA action', a 'dependency claim', or a 'Lord Campbell's Act action'.

The action against D is brought by either the Estate or by the Dependant (either of whom is C for these purposes, depending upon the Act being relied upon). Dealing with each in turn:

An action by/against the Estate

§1.12   Pursuant to s 1(1) of the 1934 Act, when the Deceased dies, all causes of action vested in him (or subsisting against him) survive for the benefit (or burden) of his Estate – subject to two exceptions: (1) claims for defamation, and (2) bereavement damages. When pursuing an action against wrongdoer D, the Deceased's Estate must prove that the Deceased had a 'cause of action', which was 'vested' in him at his death.

The key provision: Section 1(1) of the 1934 Act provides that, 'all causes of action subsisting against or vested in him shall survive against, or, as the case may be, for the benefit of, his

---

[79] In force 25 Jul 1934.
[80] In force 1 Sep 1976. It did not apply to any cause of action arising on a death before then (s 7(2)).

estate. Provided that this subsection shall not apply to causes of action for defamation'. This means that a tortious right of action by (or against) the Deceased may legally commence, following the Deceased's death. The action can be brought by, or against, the personal representatives of the Deceased's Estate.

On the one hand, where the Deceased's Estate makes a claim under the 1934 Act, then it is for the loss and damage *which the Deceased suffered* as a result of D's tort. On the other hand, where an action is brought *against the Deceased's Estate*, then any damages ordered to be paid by the estate (for the Deceased's wrong) becomes a liability which the Deceased's Estate must meet, because that liability is passed to the Deceased's Estate by virtue of the 1934 Act.

Where the Deceased's Estate is sued by C, the timing of events is important. In the usual case where D commits a tort (say, his negligent driving caused C's injury), and then D dies, C can continue his action against D's Estate, that death notwithstanding. However, under s 1(4), where the Deceased 'dies before, or at the same time as, the damage was suffered', then a cause of action is 'deemed' to have subsisted against that Deceased before his death. This covers circumstances where D dies instantaneously in the same car accident which injured C; or where C does not suffer his injury until some time after that car accident in which D died.

The previous common law: The 1934 Act reversed the harsh position which had prevailed at common law – in which, where a victim died as the result of D's tort, no cause of action either arose or could be continued. C's right of action in tort died with him, in that death extinguished the right to bring any action in tort. Similarly, at common law, where the wrongdoer D died as a result of the tort which he committed against C, then C (or, if C also died in the accident, his Dependant under the Fatal Accidents Act 1846, considered below) could not continue his action against D's Estate. This rule was known by the maxim, '*actio personalis moritur cum persona*' (a personal right of action dies with the person).

Exceptions: There are rare instances, however, where an action in tort does **not** survive the death of either C or of D. Where C complains that he was defamed by D, and then either C or D dies, that action is excluded by the 1934 Act, and does not survive the Deceased's death (per s 1(1)). Moreover, where C (whilst alive) had a claim against D for bereavement damages under the FAA, for the negligently-caused death of a spouse or child, but then either C or D dies, that claim for bereavement damages does not survive for the benefit of the Deceased's Estate either (per s 1(1A)[81]).

Two legal issues are particularly necessary to check, when the Deceased's estate is seeking to sue a tortious wrongdoer, D, under the 1934 Act:

Nutshell analysis: An action pursuant to the 1934 Act

Elements of the action:

1 A 'cause of action' had arisen, which the Deceased could either pursue or to which he was subject
2 That cause of action was 'vested' in or against the Deceased, at the time of death

---

Element #1: Cause of action. There is no statutory definition of what amounts to a 'cause of action' in the 1934 Act. Hence, the expression bears its ordinary meaning (per *Harris v*

[81] Inserted by the Administration of Justice Act 1982, s 4(1).

Lewisham and Guy's Mental Health Trust[82]), and was defined in *Letang v Cooper* to mean 'a factual situation, the existence of which entitles one person to obtain from the court a remedy against another person'.[83]

The effect of the 1934 Act is that it is **not** necessary to ask whether a Deceased's claim against D was a 'personal action' which could be assignable by operation of law. In *Ronex Properties Ltd v John Laing Construction Ltd*,[84] it was said that s 1(1) of the 1934 Act made 'comprehensive provision' for the survival of causes of action 'over the whole field'. Provided that the Deceased had a 'cause of action', then the benefit of it passed to his estate under the 1934 Act – whether it was a 'personal action' or not. However, not all benefits conferred by, or recoverable under, all statutes survive the victim's death. For example, in *D'Este v D'Este*,[85] an application for financial provision under the matrimonial causes legislation was not a cause of action.

Element #2: Vested in the Deceased. For a cause of action to be 'vested' in the Deceased at the time of his death, its elements must be complete. This means that if the tort is one which requires proof of damage, and if the Deceased had not suffered any relevant damage prior to his death, then there can be no cause of action 'vested' in the Deceased at his death. All the Deceased had was a potential cause of action, in the event that loss was to be suffered. In that case, s 1(1) has no effect, because there is nothing to 'survive' for the benefit of the Estate (per Carnwath LJ in *Daniels v Thompson*[86]).

As noted previously, s 1(4) is wider, in that it extends the survival of the action in tort *against* a Deceased's Estate, where the Deceased died *before* damage was incurred; but there is no similar extension for an Estate which is claiming on behalf of the Deceased.

Damages. As originally enacted, the 1934 Act permitted the recovery by the Estate of a wide array of damages on the Deceased's behalf. However, since s 1 of the Administration of Justice Act 1982 took effect on 1 January 1983, the damages recoverable in a survival action are limited to only certain types – loss of earnings, special damages, physical injury, pain and suffering and loss of amenity (PSLA), funeral expenses, and care and assistance for the Deceased. Conversely, certain heads of damage are not recoverable by the Estate in a survival action: damages for loss of expectation of life, or for fear of impending death; and bereavement damages. These issues are considered further in Chapter 11.

Contributory negligence. Some fault in causing the Deceased's death may rest with either the Deceased himself, or with someone in the Deceased's Estate (e.g., if the Deceased's wife's killed the Deceased due to her negligent driving). The effect of that contributory negligence is considered in Chapter 10.

The dependants' action

§1.13   Whereas, under the 1934 Act, the Estate seeks to recover damages accruing to the Deceased, a 'wrongful death' action under the FAA permits designated 'dependants' of the Deceased to recover specific damages for the deprivation of financial income or financially-measurable support caused to those dependants by the Deceased's death.

---

[82] [2000] EWCA Civ 87, [30] (also known as *Andrews v Lewisham and Guy's Mental Health Trust*).
[83] [1965] 1 QB 232 (CA) 242–43 (Diplock LJ).   [84] [1983] QB 398 (CA) 405.
[85] [1973] Fam 55, 59, and cited in *Harris* [2000] EWCA Civ 87, [30(6)].
[86] [2004] EWCA Civ 307, [59]–[60].

Although both a survival action and an FAA action arise out of the Deceased's death, the types of damages, and for whom they are awarded, are entirely different. Note that any damages awarded under the 1934 Act do **not** fall to be deducted from damages awarded under the FAA.

The purpose of the FAA: The FAA confers a right upon the dependants of the Deceased, who died as a result of D's tort, to enable those dependants to recover the loss of financial support arising from the Deceased's wrongful death – provided that the Deceased would have been able to recover damages from D, but for his death. It was first introduced as the Fatal Accidents Act 1846 (known as Lord Campbell's Act). It has been judicially described as an action 'to recover the loss caused to those dependants by the death of the breadwinner' (per *Pickett v British Rail Engineering Ltd*[87]).

The Dependant's claim is both derivative from, and independent of, the Deceased's claim. It is derivative, because it will depend upon the validity of any claim which would have been open to the Deceased (i.e., if the claim was barred to the Deceased, it will be barred to the Dependant). However, the claim is independent, because the Dependant's claim is for damages in his own right, i.e. for damages sustained by him personally (per *Dick v Falkirk Burgh*[88]). As Denning LJ described in *Gray v Barr*, the Dependants 'stand in [the Deceased's] shoes in regard to *liability*, but not as to *damages*'.[89]

The previous common law: Until 1846, the common law applied, per *Baker v Bolton*,[90] whereby the death of another human being could not be complained of as an injury. Hence, where the Deceased died due to D's tort, then anyone who suffered financial loss as the result of that breadwinner's wrongful death was unable to recover damages for that loss (unless C had an independent cause of action arising from the Deceased's death, such as loss of consortium). This harsh result caused much disquiet among lawmakers. Indeed, the Law Commission has noted that the FAA 'was a response to fatalities on the railways',[91] whereby a lot of husbands/fathers were killed in railway accidents, due to faulty tracks and signalling equipment (if any), demolition works which went awry, and poor weather conditions.

The elements of an FAA action are as follows:

Nutshell analysis: The FAA action

Elements of the action:

1 The Deceased would have had a claim against D
2 The Dependant is an appropriate claimant under the Act
3 The Dependant has suffered loss of dependency
4 The action is not barred or excluded

Element #1: The Deceased would have had a claim against D. Under s 1(1) of the FAA, the death of the Deceased must have been 'caused by any wrongful act, neglect or default [of D]', and would have 'entitled the [Deceased] to maintain an action and recover damages in respect

---

[87] [1978] UKHL 4, [1980] AC 136, 146.   [88] 1976 SC (HL) 1, 18–21 (Lord Wilberforce).

[89] [1971] 2 QB 554 (CA) 569 (original emphasis), quoted in EWLC, *Claims for Wrongful Death* (Rep 263, 1999) [2.2], fn 61.

[90] (1808) 170 ER 1033 (KB) (C was a publican, and his wife, who died in a stage coach accident because of D's negligence, had been useful in the business; C recovered £100 for his wife's loss of consortium).

[91] EWLC, *Claims for Wrongful Death* (1999) [2.1], fn 59, citing: *Hansard*, 21 Aug 1846, vol 88, col 926.

thereof'. Hence, it must be shown that, at the time of his death, the Deceased would have had a claim against D.

For example, insofar as a negligence action is concerned, the Deceased must have been able to prove that D's act or omission caused his injury and damage (i.e., death) – whether on the usual principle of 'but-for' causation or under one of the exceptional causal theorems (discussed in Chapter 8). In *Barker v Corus UK Ltd*,[92] which is authority for one of those exceptional theorems, the House of Lords noted that '[t]he approach to damages payable on a Fatal Accidents Act 1976 claim would be no different', whether it was C, or a Dependant under the FAA, bringing the claim. Similarly, where D's negligence caused some physical injury to the Deceased and the Deceased thereafter commits suicide, then for the Deceased's Dependant to claim damages under the FAA, the suicide must not be treated as an intervening act which breaks the chain of causation, and nor must it be too remote at law to be compensable (per *Corr v IBC Vehicles*,[93] where the Deceased's suicidal jump from a multi-storey carpark, after suffering horrendous facial injuries due to D's negligence, was neither an intervening act nor too remote, and hence, Mrs Corr and her two sons could recover under the FAA).

Element #2: The Dependant is an appropriate claimant. Any person who claims a loss of dependency resulting from the Deceased's death must be able to bring himself within the statutorily-prescribed categories of a Dependant. While s 1(2) provides that every such action shall be for the benefit of such Dependants of the Deceased, the term, 'dependant', is defined in s 1(3), to cover **only** the following:

(a) the spouse of the Deceased, including any former spouse who was financially supported by the Deceased (including one whose marriage to the Deceased was dissolved, annulled or declared void);

(b) a co-habitant of the Deceased – provided that the Dependant and the Deceased had been living in the same household as man and wife (or as same-sex partners)[94] for at least two years immediately before the Deceased's death. According to *Kotke v Saffarini*,[95] parties will be 'in the same household' if they are tied by their relationship – that tie being manifest, not by merely living under the same roof, but by 'the public and private acknowledgement of their mutual society, and the mutual protection and support which binds them together'.

> In *Kotke v Saffarini*, Trevor Snowdon and his partner, Ms Kotke, C, were hit by D's car while walking across a bridge in Bath. Hurled over the parapet wall into the River Avon below, Mr Snowdon was killed, and C was severely injured but survived. C sued D under the FAA. **Held:** her claim failed. She was not a suitable Dependant, not being Mr Snowdon's spouse, nor having lived with him in the same household for at least two years before his death. Their relationship 'did not cross the statutory threshold into the final stage'. Mr Snowdon kept a separate home in Doncaster with his wardrobe and possessions, and lived out of an overnight bag when staying with C in Bath. The splitting of shopping expenses 'was evidence of a sharing relationship, but one which fell short of the establishment of a joint household'.

(c) any parent or other ascendant (e.g., grandparent) of the Deceased;

(d) any person who was treated by the Deceased as his parent;

---

[92] [2006] UKHL 20, [2006] 2 AC 572, [63].   [93] [2008] UKHL 13, [2008] 1 AC 884.
[94] Pursuant to the Civil Partnership Act 2004, s 83.
[95] [2005] EWCA Civ 221, [23], with quote in case description at [59].

(e) any child or other descendant of the Deceased (including step-children, adopted and illegitimate children, and any unborn child conceived by the Deceased and born after the Deceased's death);

(f) any child (not the Deceased's own child) of any marriage to which the Deceased was a party and whom Deceased treated as a child of the family in relation to that marriage; and

(g) any person who is, or is the issue of, a brother, sister, uncle or aunt of the Deceased.

Element #3: The Dependant can prove loss of dependency. According to the 'reasonable expectation' test, each Dependant must separately prove that he reasonably expected to receive a pecuniary benefit arising from his relationship with the Deceased; and that he would have received it, but for the Deceased's death. That follows from s 3(1), which provides that damages under the FAA 'may be awarded as are proportioned to the injury resulting from the death to the dependants respectively'. Hence, individual amounts will generally be awarded to **each** Dependant named in the suit.

The 'reasonable expectation test' seems to have originated in 1858 in *Franklin v South Eastern Railway Co*,[96] where the correct question put to the jury was whether the Dependant, an old and infirm father, 'had any such reasonable expectation of benefit from the continuance of his son's life', where his son, 21, was negligently killed in a railway collision. More recently, in *Drake v Starkey*, it was said that '[t]his reasonable expectation test is a judicial interpretation of the archaic and somewhat diffuse wording of the [FAA Act]'.[97]

> In *Drake v Starkey*, James Wilson died of mesothelioma which he contracted as a result of his exposure to asbestos when working for D as a boiler erector at Dartford power station. His two daughters, his grandson, his six other grandchildren, and four great-grandchildren, could each separately prove that they reasonably expected to receive a pecuniary benefit arising from the family relationship (e.g., birthday gifts, weekly shopping contributions, one-off purchases of white-goods), and that they would have received those benefits, but for Mr Wilson's death.

The date for assessing whether the claimant was a Dependant is assessed when the Deceased died. The dependancy cannot, say, reduce after the Deceased's death, because the Dependant happened to take over the Deceased's business, earning a good income in the process. As remarked by Smith LJ in *Welsh Ambulance Services v Williams*,[98] 'dependency is fixed at the moment of death; it is what the Dependants would probably have received as benefit from the Deceased, had the Deceased not died. What decisions people make afterwards is irrelevant'.

> In *Welsh Ambulance v Williams*, Mr Williams was killed when negligently hit by D's ambulance. **Held**: Mr Williams' wife and children were his Dependants when he died. 'The fact that each of them was as well off after the death as before – because David and Sarah took over responsibility for managing the business, and did so successfully – is nothing to the point'.

Of course, where the claimants cannot prove dependancy upon the Deceased who died as a result of D's tort, then no FAA claim is possible (as, e.g., in *Hicks v CC of South Yorkshire*,[99] where the parental claimants were not dependent upon their two daughters killed in the Hillsborough disaster).

---

[96] (1858) 157 ER 448 (Exch Ct) 448.   [97] [2010] EWHC 2004 (QB) [44].
[98] [2008] EWCA Civ 81, [49]-[50].   [99] [1991] UKHL 9.

Element #4: The FAA action is not barred or excluded. A number of factors may bar the Dependant from bringing an FAA action against D. These 'preclusive factors' – itemised both by the English Law Commission,[100] and in *Dick v Falkirk Burgh*[101] – consist of the following:

- where the Deceased had already obtained judgment against D in respect of the cause of action. Since the enactment of s 3 of the Damages Act 1996, an award of provisional damages to the Deceased (awarded where the victim of D's tort faces the prospect of a serious deterioration of his condition in the future, and where preferred to a lump sum damages award) does not bar an FAA claim, although it will be taken into account when assessing damages payable to the Dependant;
- where the Deceased had settled his claim prior to his death 'in full and final settlement of this claim' against D, thus precluding any further action by a Dependant (discussed in '**Multiple defendants**', an online chapter);
- where defences such as *volenti*, or illegality, were available against the Deceased; or
- where a contract, or an expired limitation period which could not be extended by the exercise of judicial discretion, excludes a claim by the Deceased against D.

Damages. Although FAA damages are *principally* awarded for the Dependant's financial or pecuniary loss, certain non-pecuniary heads of damage are also recoverable, as discussed further in Chapter 11.

Contributory negligence. As under the 1934 Act, some fault in bringing about the Deceased's death may rest with either the Deceased himself, or with a Dependant of the Deceased who is claiming under the FAA. The effect of that contributory negligence is considered in Chapter 10.

---

[100] *Claims for Wrongful Death* (1999) [2.3]–[2.5].   [101] 1976 SC (HL) 1.

Part 1

Negligence

2

Duty I – General principles governing duty of care

INTRODUCTION

The framework for negligence

In order to prove the cause of action in negligence, C must establish **four** requirements, *viz*:

Nutshell analysis: **The tort of negligence**

1 D owed C a duty of care to avoid causing C the type of injury of which he complains
2 D breached the duty of care, by falling below the standard of reasonable care which the law demands
3a D's breach caused the damage complained of by C
3b the damage complained of by C was not too remote (unforeseeable) at law to be recoverable

---

This, and the following three chapters, deal solely with the first element – the establishment of a duty of care – in a variety of scenarios. English courts have long drawn a distinction between the existence of a duty of care in the context of loss caused by *physical injury or property damage*, on the one hand (the subject of analysis in this chapter); and where *economic loss* or *psychiatric injury* is caused, on the other. In the latter scenarios, special rules apply for the establishment of a duty of care, which are the subject of consideration in Chapters 4 and 5, respectively.

In *JD v East Berkshire Community Health NHS Trust*,[1] Lord Rodger somewhat pessimistically remarked that, 'the world is full of harm for which the law furnishes no remedy'. That lack of remedy may be entirely attributable to the lack of any duty of care (as it was in *JD* itself). In that regard, this element is a **very** important control mechanism in restricting D's liability for the tort of negligence – and its use in restricting the ambit of liability has become a more

---

[1] [2005] UKHL 23, [2005] 2 AC 373, [100].

modern trend. A lack of duty can preclude D's liability in negligence, even where *every other element* of negligence is satisfied by C.

§2.1 A duty of care is a legal duty imposed on D, by law, to exercise reasonable care and/or skill to avoid the risk of injury to C. Whether a duty of care is owed by D, on a set of given facts, is a question of law.

This proposition (per Lord Thankerton in *Bourhill v Young*[2]) contains several points of significance:

- a duty is *imposed* upon D – it is not a legal obligation which D agrees to (or can contract out of);
- the duty is to exercise *reasonable* care, not to achieve perfection or a guaranteed perfect outcome;
- a duty of care is owed by D to either C, or a class of persons of whom C was one. It is not usually imposed upon D towards the *world-at-large*, in respect of any one act or omission of negligence (although there are exceptions, e.g., manufacturers to consumers of defective products).

Whether a duty of care arises on the facts is determined by one or more of **three** potential approaches. Before considering these, however, a brief canvass of the development of the duty of care concept is apposite.

A brief historical overview

The ease with which C has been able to establish a duty of care in English negligence law has waxed and waned over time. In fact, Lord Walker's description of negligence (in *Customs and Excise Commrs v Barclays Bank plc*[3]) as being, 'not one of steady advance along a broad front, [but] ... a much more confused series of engagements with salients and beachheads, and retreats as well as advances', is as appropriate to the element of duty of care as it is to the tort as a whole.

Recognition of the tort of negligence actually **preceded** the seminal case of *Donoghue v Stevenson* (1932),[4] but the treatment of the duty concept, before and after it, has frequently been in a state of evolution – noted in the Table below:

The duty of care over the years

Early 19th century — There were a few 'recognised cases' in which a duty of care was acknowledged to exist (outside of a contractual relationship) – per Lord Buckmaster's dissenting judgment in *Donoghue v Stevenson*.[a] These consisted of: road-users who injured others ('cases of collision and carriage'); manufacturers towards consumers where the product was dangerous (e.g., a gun, as in *Langridge v Levy*,[b] although that was probably a case of fraudulent misstatement, not of negligence); and occupiers who invited visitors onto their premises, where there was 'some hidden danger' on those premises.

However, there was **no** general principle of law, as to when a duty of care would be owed by D to C.

---

[a] [1932] AC 562 (HL) 573 (Lord Buckmaster, citing Brett MR in *Heaven v Pender* (1883) 11 QBD 503, 509).
[b] (1837) 2 M&W 519, 150 ER 863.

[2] [1943] AC 92 (HL) 98 (Lord Thankerton), 104 (Lord Macmillan). [3] [2006] UKHL 28, [2007] 1 AC 181, [69].
[4] [1932] AC 562 (HL).

1842   In *Winterbottom v Wright*:[c]

a faulty mail carriage was hired by manufacturer, D, to the Postmaster-General (the other contracting party), and it collapsed, injuring the driver, C. As between manufacturer and a third party, there was no recognised category of a duty of care. **Held:** C could not recover against manufacturer D, as there was no cause of action by which to bring his claim (there was no contract between C and D, and to uphold a duty would undermine privity of contract).

Per Alderson B: 'The only safe rule is to confine the right to recover to those who enter into the contract. If we go one step beyond that, there is no reason why we should not go fifty'. Hence, the Postmaster-General could have sued in negligence, but not driver C. Liability in negligence was aligned with contractual, or quasi-contractual, relationships only.

1883   In *Heaven v Pender (t/as West India Graving Dock Co)*:[d]

a dockowner, D, supplied and put up scaffolding for a ship, under a contract with the shipowner. A painting firm contracted with the shipowner to paint the ship, and an employed painter, C, was injured when the scaffolding partly collapsed. **Held:** D was liable in damages to C, on the basis of an *implied invitation* by D to those painting the ship to use the scaffolding provided by him (i.e., there was a quasi-contractual, rather than any direct, relationship existing between C and D).

However, Brett MR (later to become Lord Esher) (dissenting) attempted to fashion a **general** principle upon which, apart from contract, the relationship between C and D could create a duty to take ordinary care: 'whenever one person [D] is, by circumstances, placed in such a position with regard to another [C] that everyone of ordinary sense ... would at once recognise that, if he did not use ordinary care and skill in his own conduct with regard to those circumstances, he would cause danger of injury to the person or property of [C], a duty arises to use ordinary care and skill to avoid such danger'. Hence, the suggestion was floated that a duty of care should be recognised in wider circumstances, independent of contractual relationships.

However, the majority members of the CA (Cotton and Bowen LJJ) declined to support that 'larger principle' put forward by Brett MR.

1893   In *Le Lievre v Gould*:[e]

a surveyor, D, provided completion certificates to lenders, C, who, on the faith of those certificates, advanced monies progressively to a builder. The certificates contained negligent statements. Surveyor D had not been appointed by lenders C, and hence, there was no contractual relationship between them. **Held:** D owed no duty to C to exercise care in giving his certificates.

Importantly, Lord Esher appeared to resile from his earlier statement in *Heaven v Pender*: 'But can [C] rely upon negligence, in the absence of fraud? ... What duty is there, when there is no relation between the parties by contract? A man is entitled to be as negligent as he pleases towards the whole world, if he owes no duty to them'.

---

[c] (1842) 10 M&W 109 (Ct Exch) 115, 152 ER 402.
[d] (1883) 11 QBD 503 (CA) 509–10.
[e] [1893] 1 QB 491 (CA) 497.

1906   In *Cavalier v Pope*:[f]

a landlord, D, let a house with a dangerous floor to a tenant, and he contracted to repair it. Before he did so, part of the floor gave way, and the tenant's wife, C, was injured. **Held:** D owed no duty of care to C to remedy the defect.

Lord James endorsed the requirement for privity of contract to substantiate a duty of care: 'there was but one contract, and that was made with the husband. The wife cannot sue upon it ... I regret this result, because [C] has been injured entirely through the failure of D's agent to fulfil the contract he made. But moral responsibility ... is not identical with legal liablity'.

1929   In *Mullen v AG Barr*:[g]

Mr Mullen bought a bottle of brewed ginger beer (manufactured by D) from a shop retailer, and poured the drink for his two children, C. After they had drunk some of it, Mr Mullen poured out the rest, and a decomposed mouse came out. The suggestion that the bottle was tampered with deliberately after it left D's factory as a practical joke or to damage its business was rejected. C sued manufacturer D in negligence (albeit that Lord Hunter noted that, 'the injury sustained was so slight that [C] might have been well advised to leave litigation alone'). **Held (3:1):** D owed no duty to C, with whom D had no contract.

Lord Anderson (for the majority): 'where the goods of [D] are widely distributed throughout Scotland, it would seem little short of outrageous to make the manufacturer responsible to members of the public for the condition of the contents of every bottle which issues from their works ... [D] might be called on to meet claims of damages which they could not possibly investigate or answer'.[h]

Lord Hunter (dissenting): 'To open the bottles would be prejudicial to the beer, and the tabs on the corks are intended to give the consumer confidence that the bottles have not been tampered with after they have left [D's] premises. The bottles are so dark in colour as to prevent the retail dealer or the consumer from detecting the presence of foreign or deleterious matter by any ordinarily careful examination of the bottle ... In these circumstances, ... there is such a relationship between the manufacturer and consumer as to impose a duty upon the former to exercise care that the latter does not suffer injury'.[i] It was this dissenting view which came to reflect the law, three years later.

1932   In *Donoghue (or M'Alister) v Stevenson*:[j]

Miss Donoghue's friend purchased a bottle of ginger beer in a café in Paisley, near Glasgow. The ginger beer was manufactured by Stevenson, D, manufacturer of 'aerated waters'. Some contents were poured into the glasses of C and her friend, and they drank some. The remainder was then poured into their glasses, and the bottle turned out to contain the decomposed remains of a snail. Being an opaque bottle, the snail could not be detected until the greater part of the contents had been drunk. C alleged that she suffered from shock and severe gastro-enteritis, and sued manufacturer D in negligence. **Held (3:2):** C could, as a preliminary point of law, recover damages in negligence. The case was remitted back to trial for proof (and, on that point, the allegation that a snail was in the bottle was never proved[k]).

---

[f] [1906] AC 428 (HL) 430.

[g] [1929] Sess Cas 461, 1929 SLT 341 (SCIH). This was joined with a similar case: *McGowan v Barr & Co*, also concerning a decomposed mouse in a bottle of ginger beer.

[h] *ibid*, 479.

[i] *ibid*, 477.

[j] [1932] AC 562 (HL) 580–81 (Lord Atkin, for the majority, with Lords Tomlin and Buckmaster dissenting).

[k] A point made in, e.g.: *Vicario v Commr of Police* [2007] EWCA Civ 1361, [45].

Per the majority, Lords Atkin, Macmillan, and Thankerton:

(1) a duty of care no longer depended on a contractual (or quasi-contractual, per *Heaven v Pender*) relationship between C and D. A duty could be imposed by law between C and D, nevertheless;

(2) a *new* category of duty of care was created (i.e., manufacturer–consumer, where no contractual relationship existed between them, and where there was no possibility of intermediate examination of the product in question, because of its presentation); and

(3) the 'neighbour principle' was proposed by Lord Atkin in these terms: a duty of care is owed by D to 'persons who are so closely and directly affected by my act that I ought reasonably to have them in contemplation as being so affected, when I am directing my mind to the acts or omissions called into question'; and where there is proximity, 'not confined to mere physical proximity; but be used ... to extend to such close and direct relations that the act complained of directly affects [C]'.

1964 In *Hedley Byrne & Co Ltd v Heller & Partners Ltd:*[l]

a bank, D, was asked about the creditworthiness and financial stability of one of the bank's customers, where it was made clear that the party on whose behalf the enquiry was being made, C, wished to know whether it could prudently lend a substantial sum of money to that customer. Bank D gave a favourable reference, but with a disclaimer of responsibility. C did extend credit to the customer, in reliance on the reference, but ultimately lost the money. **Held:** D was not liable, due to the disclaimer; but were it not for the disclaimer, a duty of care could arise in relation to negligent statements.

The basis of a duty of care could be predicated upon the so-called 'voluntary assumption of responsibility/reliance' test of duty of care (per Lord Morris). The case was notable, as the first occasion upon which negligence was (but for the disclaimer) available for economic loss resulting from C's reliance on a negligent misstatement (as discussed in Chapter 4).

1970 In *Home Office v Dorset Yacht Co:*[m]

Lord Reid described the difference between the 'categorisation approach' to a duty of care (i.e., that, when a new or novel scenario arises, it is necessary to ask whether it is covered by existing authority) and the 'principled approach' (i.e., that a single general principle, as espoused in *Donoghue v Stevenson*, should be applied in all new circumstances to determine the existence of a duty of care). Lord Reid favoured the latter approach: 'when a new point emerges, one should ask, not whether it is covered by authority, but whether recognised principles apply to it ... I think that the time has come when we should say that [the principled approach] ought to apply, unless there is some justification or valid explanation for its exclusion'. This view had the potential to expand the scope of a duty of care considerably.

1978 In *Anns v Merton LBC:*[n]

the question was whether a local authority, D, could be liable in negligence to long-term lessees, C, occupying maisonettes which were built on inadequate foundations, where the building had not complied with relevant statutory building regulations, and where D had not discovered by inspection the inadequacy of the foundations before they were covered over. **Held:** C had a cause of action against local authority D in negligence, for the cost of repairing cracks in the structure and of underpinning the foundations (i.e., physical damage).

[l] [1964] AC 465 (HL) 497, 502–3, 514.
[m] [1970] AC 1004 (HL) 1026–27.
[n] [1978] AC 728 (HL) 751–52.

2013	In *Woodland v Essex CC*,[v] the incremental approach to the development of the law, as espoused in *Caparo*, was again endorsed: '[t]he common law is a dynamic instrument. It develops and adapts to meet new situations as they arise. Therein lies its strength. But therein also lies a danger, the danger of unbridled and unprincipled growth to match what the court perceives to be the merits of the particular case. So it must proceed with caution, incrementally by analogy with existing categories, and consistently with some underlying principle' (Lady Hale). Further, even though the assumption of responsibility test in *Hedley Byrne* arose in the context of economic loss, it may incrementally apply, whether the potential loss is economic or physical (Lord Sumption).

[v] [2013] UKSC 66, [2014] 1 All ER 482, [28], [11].

This rather tortuous development of the concept of a duty of care aptly demonstrates the dynamic and evolving nature of the common law's development. Thankfully, the tests which govern the existence of a duty of care in English jurisprudence are far more settled now, and we now turn to those.

THE MODERN DUTY OF CARE TESTS

The three approaches: general

§2.2   As an overarching framework for analysis, three broad approaches have been adopted in English law, to assess whether a duty of care is owed by D to C: (1) the *Caparo* tri-partite test; (2) the *Hedley Byrne* 'voluntary assumption of responsibility/reliance' test; and (3) the incremental test.

In *Customs and Excise Commrs v Barclays Bank plc*,[5] the House of Lords outlined the 'conceptual basis' for deciding whether a duty of care exists in particular circumstances:

The three duty of care tests

The test	The definition	The source
The *Caparo* test	whether the '*Caparo* ingredients' are met: • harm to C was actually foreseen, or reasonably foreseeable, by D; • the requisite proximity (or 'neighbourhood') existed between C and D; and • it is fair, just and reasonable to impose a duty of care (or that no legal or public policy reasons preclude the imposition of a duty of care)	*Caparo Industries plc v Dickman* (per Lord Bridge)[a]

[a] [1990] 2 AC 605 (HL) 617–18 (Lord Bridge) ('*Caparo*').

[5] [2006] UKHL 28, [4] (Lord Bingham), [82] (Lord Mance).

The voluntary assumption of responsibility/ reliance test	applies where D, possessed of special skill, undertook to apply that skill for the assistance of C, who relied upon that skill. It requires: • an assumption of responsibility by D towards C to conduct himself with due care and/or skill; and • a reciprocal reliance by C upon D in so conducting himself	*Hedley Byrne & Co Ltd v Heller & Partners Ltd* (per Lord Morris)[b]
The incremental test	any new or novel duty of care scenarios should develop incrementally, by close analogy with established categories, 'rather than by a massive extension of a *prima facie* duty of care restrained only by indefinable considerations which ought to negative, or to reduce or limit the scope of the duty or the class of person to whom it is owed'. In other words, courts should 'hug the coastline' of established duties of care	*Caparo* (per Lord Bridge)[c]

[b] [1964] AC 465 (HL) 502–3.
[c] [1990] 2 AC 605 (HL) 618 (Lord Bridge).

In reality, these provide convenient reference points, or 'high-level' principles, of what a court will search for, in order to fix D with a duty of care – but to call them 'tests' is rather artificial. In truth, without teasing out the detailed factors which point in favour of, or away from, say, 'proximity', an 'assumption of responsibility', or public policy, the tests all verge upon meaningless phraseology. Several judgments make this point. The concepts are said to 'operate at a high level of abstraction', and that '[w]hat matters is how, and by reference to what lower-level factors, they are interpreted in practice' (per Lord Mance in *Customs & Excise Commrs v Barclays Bank plc*[6]). As Lord Hoffmann also said in *Customs and Excise*, '[t]here is a tendency ... for phrases like "proximate", "fair, just and reasonable", and "assumption of responsibility", to be used as slogans, rather than practical guides to whether a duty should exist or not. These phrases are often illuminating, but discrimination is needed to identify the factual situations in which they provide useful guidance'.[7] In *Caparo*,[8] Lord Bridge earlier held that the requirements of 'proximity', 'reasonable foreseeability' and 'policy', were labels only; were not definitive, or even capable of precise definition; but were all relevant in an appropriate case. Hence, when discussing these tests, close attention will inevitably have to be paid to the 'lower-level factors' which have been particularly important in assessing whether D owed C a duty of care.

[6] [2007] 1 AC 181, [83], citing: *Caparo* [1990] 2 AC 605 (HL) 617–18 (Lord Bridge), 633 (Lord Oliver).
[7] *ibid*, [35].   [8] [1990] 2 AC 605 (HL) 617–18.

The close interplay among the three elements of the *Caparo* test has been oft-cited. Indeed, it was said by Lord Oliver that they are 'merely facets of the same thing',[9] while Dyson LJ noted, in *Carty v Croydon LBC*, that 'these issues overlap, and it is not always possible to draw hard and fast lines between them'.[10]

§2.3   The *Caparo* tri-partite test is considered to be the <u>primary</u> test for novel negligence scenarios involving personal injury or property damage. However, the test of 'voluntary assumption of responsibility/reliance' may be used instead of, or in conjunction with, the *Caparo* test. The 'incremental test' serves primarily as a cross-check.

Inevitably, the fact that the House of Lords approved **all three** tests in *Customs and Excise*[11] gives rise to some degree of uncertainty and 'slipperiness' in the law of negligence.

That said, the *Caparo* test has been indicated, at the highest appellate level, to have the most prominent role of the three tests – whether in the area of pure economic loss out of which it arose (covered in Chapter 4) or in personal injury or property damage. In *Van Colle v CC of Hertfordshire Police*, Lord Bingham noted that *Caparo* was 'currently ... the most-favoured test' for imposing a duty of care in novel negligence scenarios,[12] an observation approved in *Mitchell v Glasgow CC*[13] – both of which were personal injury cases. That preference is partly because the *Caparo* test provides a structure which 'makes the analysis more easily intelligible' (per *Neil Martin Ltd v HMRC*[14]). Judges have certainly perceived the *Caparo* approach to be a distinct improvement on the liberalism that went before it, when the so-called 'generalist' approach was in vogue. In *Everett v Comojo (UK) Ltd (t/as the Metropolitan)*, Lady Justice Smith remarked, in 2011, that *Caparo* is 'the correct starting point' for the existence of a duty of care, and that it, 'provides some guide to the touchstone which eluded [previous courts]. If not a touchstone, the threefold test provides a process by which judges can determine whether a duty should exist and, if so, to determine its scope'.[15]

In any event, there are instances where the assumption of responsibility test really does not work well. The concept of whether D assumed any responsibility towards C is objectively-determined. Hence, 'the further this test is removed from the actions and intentions of the actual [D], and the more notional the assumption of responsibility becomes, the less difference there is between this test and the threefold [*Caparo*] test' (per Lord Bingham in *Customs and Excise*[16]). It follows that, where D did not **know** of the existence, let alone the identity, of C, at the time of the allegedly negligent act or omission, then to hold that D objectively assumed responsibility towards that unknown party, or that D knew, or should have known, that C was relying upon his skill, knowledge or expertise, tends to be a highly artificial analysis. The problem exists in reverse too. To say that C relied upon D, when he was never aware of D's existence or of his role in the arrangements for C's welfare, is very strained. That issue arose in *Marc Rich & Co v Bishop Rock Ltd*, where Lord Steyn refuted any application of the assumption of responsibility test: '[g]iven that the cargo owners [C] were not even aware of NKK's [D's] examination of the ship, and that the cargo owners simply relied on the undertakings

---

[9] [1990] 2 AC 605 (HL) 633 (Lord Oliver).
[10] [2005] 1 WLR 2312 (CA) 2318, citing: *A v Essex CC* [2004] 1 WLR 1881 (CA) (Hale LJ).
[11] [2006] UKHL 28, [2007] 1 AC 181, [4] (Lord Bingham).   [12] [2008] UKHL 50, [2009] 1 AC 225, [42].
[13] [2009] UKHL 11, [2009] 1 AC 874, [21] (Lord Hope).   [14] [2006] EWHC 2425 (Ch) [86].
[15] [2011] EWCA Civ 13, [2012] 1 WLR 150, [26]–[27], [29].   [16] [2006] UKHL 28, [5].

of the shipowners, it is ... impossible to force the present set of facts into even the most expansive view of the doctrine of voluntary assumption of responsibility'.[17] In those sorts of circumstances, the *Caparo* test will be the go-to test for the duty of care analysis.

To complicate matters, however, the tests have sometimes been used in conjunction together. The full 'battery' has been employed in some cases of serious personal injury (e.g., as in *Watson v British Boxing Board of Control*,[18] *Kent v Griffiths*,[19] and *Geary v JD Wetherspoon plc*[20]). The *Caparo* test is by no means the exclusive test for physical injury or property damage cases. In any event, in *Merrett v Babb*, May LJ stated that 'it is reaching for the moon – and not required by authority', to expect that one 'single short abstract formulation' of when a duty of care arises could be framed.[21] Some courts have noted that the various tests are 'mutually supportive, and likely to lead to the same conclusion' (per *Niru Battery Manufacturing Co v Milestone Trading Ltd*[22]). However, that conclusion has not always followed. One recent example of where a duty of care was proven under the *Caparo* test, but where it could not be proven under the assumption of responsibility/reliance test, occurred in *Biddick v Morcom*[23] (discussed later in this chapter).

Some decisions have also tended to conflate the proximity requirement of *Caparo* with the assumption of responsibility/reliance test – e.g., in *Geary v JD Wetherspoon plc*, that '[D] assumed no such responsibility towards [C], and there was no such reliance. In those circumstances, I do not consider that the necessary proximity has been demonstrated';[24] and *Watson v British Boxing Board of Control Ltd*, that, where there was no reliance or assumption of responsibility (re emergency services such as the police), then 'there is no close proximity between the services and the general public'.[25]

Hence, whilst three different approaches may provide desirable flexibility, it does create what appears, at times, to be a fluid and pragmatic (some would say, haphazard!) answer to the legal question: does D owe C a duty of care?

Assuming the existence of a duty of care

General rule

§2.4   Where C sustains personal injury or property damage, then if C can align his relationship with D with one of the recognised categories in which a duty of care has, traditionally, arisen as a matter of law, there is no need for C to prove the individual ingredients of the duty of care tests.

In some scenarios, a duty of care will be presumed, where C can align his scenario with one of the 'distinct and recognisable situations' in which a duty of care has been said to arise as a matter of law (per Lord Bridge in *Caparo*[26]). In 'real life' litigation, D will frequently *concede* a duty in such cases.

If, however, the scenario giving rise to C's grievance against D falls outside one of the traditional categories – or falls within an existing category, but arises out of a hitherto unconsidered or rarely-considered fact scenario – then a legal analysis of whether a duty of care should attach to D is always called for. It is in these scenarios that the three tests of duty of care essentially come into play.

The following Table outlines, by reference to a sample authority, the recognised categories of duty of care which arise in English law, where C suffers personal injury:

---

[17] [1996] AC 211 (HL) 242.   [18] [2001] QB 1134 (CA) [35]-[45].   [19] [2001] QB 36 (CA) [37]-[52].
[20] [2011] EWHC 1506 (QB).   [21] [2001] EWCA Civ 214, [2001] QB 1174, [41] (May LJ).
[22] [2003] EWCA Civ 1446, [2004] QB 985, [38].   [23] [2014] EWCA Civ 182.   [24] [2011] EWHC 1506 (QB) [68].
[25] [2001] QB 1134 (CA) [77] (Lord Phillips).   [26] [1990] 2 AC 605 (HL) 617–18 (Lord Phillips).

Relationships traditionally giving rise to a duty of care

School and teacher, D, to pupil, C, for his physical welfare and educational needs (except where TP does the harm to C – a duty is not 'assumed' there)	*Carmarthenshire CC v Lewis*[a] (a nursery school 'certainly owes a duty to the child to protect him from injury'); *X (Minors) v Bedfordshire CC*[b] (re older school pupils); except where third parties do the harm to the pupils, in which case the duty of care is a novel, not a recognised, scenario: *Webster v Ridgeway Foundation School*[c]
Road-user, D, towards other road-users (whether they be pedestrians, or bystanders nearby to the road, or passengers or drivers of other vehicles on or near the road)	*Mitchell v Glasgow CC* (per Lord Hope):[d] 'where a person is injured in the course of his employment, or in a road traffic accident … then it can be taken for granted that the employer owes a duty of care to the person who is in his employment, or that a duty is owed to other road users by the driver of a vehicle which causes an accident. If commonplace situations of that kind had to be analysed, … the duty is owed not simply because loss, injury or damage is reasonably foreseeable … there is a relationship of proximity between the employer and his employees, and the driver and other road users. This is sufficient in law to give rise to a duty of care … this is so obvious that there is no need to ask whether it is fair, or whether it is just and reasonable, that [C] should recover damages'. An illustrative authority, *Nettleship v Weston,*[e] held that a duty of care owed by one road-user to another was 'clear'
Employers, D, who cause physical injury to their employees, C	See Lord Hope's discussion in *Mitchell v Glasgow CC* above; and the discussion and authorities in 'Employers' liability', an online chapter
Transport operator (bus company, ferry operator, train operator, etc), D, towards passenger C	*Silverlink Trains Ltd v Collins-Williamson*[f] (a duty owed by the train company was uncontentious); *Fernquest v City of Swansea*[g] (bus companies owe a duty to their passengers, but not once they have alighted at their stop)
Healthcare practitioner (doctor, nurse, physiotherapist, midwife, etc), D, towards patient C	*Sidaway v Bethlem Royal Hosp Governors*[h] (a doctor owes a duty to his patients, which is 'a single comprehensive duty covering all the ways in which a doctor is called on to exercise his skill and judgment in the improvement of the physical or mental condition of the patient'); nurses (per *Barnett v Chelsea and Kensington HMC*[i]), and other health professionals

[a] [1955] AC 549 (HL) 563.
[b] [1995] 2 AC 633 (HL) 766.
[c] [2010] EWHC 157 (QB).
[d] [2009] UKHL 11, [2009] 1 AC 874, [16].
[e] [1971] 2 QB 691 (CA) 700.
[f] [2009] EWCA Civ 850.
[g] [2011] EWCA Civ 1712.
[h] [1985] 1 AC 871 (HL) 893 (Lord Diplock).
[i] [1969] 1 QB 428.

Jailers/custodian, D, towards prisoners C	*Ellis v Home Office*[j] ('[t]he duty on those responsible for one of Her Majesty's prisons is to take reasonable care for the safety of those within, and that includes those who are within against their wish'); *Home Office v Dorset Yacht Co Ltd*[k] ('a duty of care for their safety and welfare was owed by the Home Office to prisoners in a prison' (although D was not prepared to concede that such an automatic duty was owed to prison visitors)
Occupier of premises, D, who invites visitors, C, and C is injured from the state of the premises	This recognised duty of care relationship is now governed by statute, as discussed in Chapter 12

[j] [1953] 2 All ER 149 (CA) 154 (Singleton LJ).
[k] [1970] AC 1004 (HL) 1047 (Viscount Dilhorne).

Caveat

However, even in cases involving a relationship that traditionally gives rise to a duty of care, the common law may carve out, from that general duty, certain scenarios in which no duty is owed, or it may nominate certain classes of Cs to whom no duty is owed – regardless of the fact that C and D are in a recognised category of relationship that traditionally does give rise to a duty of care. For example:

- the doctor–patient relationship is one of the 'recognised categories' of a duty of care – yet not all scenarios in which a doctor carelessly causes physical injury to patient C give rise to a duty in C's favour. For example, case law has limited/precluded a doctor's duty to warn in some scenarios (as discussed in Chapter 3), and insofar as sterilisation operations are concerned, a doctor's duty is **not** to avoid or minimise **all** adverse consequences flowing from a failed sterilisation (as discussed later in this chapter);
- the employer–employee relationship is another 'recognised category', which applies to physical injury suffered by an employee, C. However, *psychiatric* injury incurred by an employee in the workplace does not automatically give rise to a duty on the employer D's part; rather, that is subject to special rules governing the existence of a duty of care (as discussed in Chapter 5).

The rest of this chapter considers the constituent elements of the relevant duty of care tests. As a result of the overlap of the *Caparo* elements noted previously, some of the factors identified in this chapter may be listed herein as going to proximity, whereas others may prefer the view that they are, more suitably, matters of legal and public policy. Regardless, it is worth noting Ouseley LJ's comment, in *Islington LBC v University College London Hosp NHS Trust*, that 'it may matter little under which particular heading the particular factors are posted. There is after all only one question: is there a duty of care?'[27] However, for the purposes of clarity of principle, the three elements of *Caparo*, and the two elements of the *Hedley Byrne* test, will be analysed separately.

[27] [2005] EWCA Civ 596, [49].

REASONABLE FORESEEABILITY OF HARM (*CAPARO* #1)

General principles

Different tests of foreseeability

D cannot be liable in negligence for the unforeseen or the unforeseeable. No reasonable D would take any precautionary steps or modify his conduct to avoid a risk that he does not know, or foresee, could occur, and the law does not expect that of him either.

Tests of foreseeability actually arise at recurrent stages of the negligence analysis – in the duty of care, breach of duty and remoteness of damage stages. The reality is that these may closely duplicate each other. Separate Courts of Appeal have made the point that the tests 'inevitably overlap' (per *Gabriel v Kirklees MC*[28]), that the different stages of negligence 'run continually into one another' (per *Roe v Minister of Health*[29]) and that '[t]his overlap between duty and remoteness of damage, and what constitutes negligent conduct in the circumstances of the case, means that [the analysis of foreseeability] can be telescoped into one issue of fact' in some cases (per *Billington v Maguire*[30]).

Clearly, how straightforward the test of foreseeability is to satisfy is a direct consequence of the specificity with which the question is framed in the first place. At duty stage, it is at its widest. The reality is that, where C suffers from physical injury or property damage, as a result of D's acts or omissions, then *some* injury of that nature is likely to have been a reasonably foreseeable occurrence. Many English cases show that a more specific, and factually focused, test of foreseeability is appropriately posed at the *breach-of-duty* stage, and then again at the *remoteness-of-damage* stage. This trend is particularly evident where C and D are already within a recognised or distinct category of relationship, discussed in the previous section, which traditionally points towards a duty of care; and where it is entirely foreseeable that C may suffer some harm from D's acts or omissions, but where subsequent enquiries of foreseeability cannot be met by C. Hence, the analysis adopted in several cases, and in this book, follows an inverted pyramid:

The differing tests of foreseeability in negligence

Duty of care stage – at its widest, 'was some type of harm reasonably foreseeable?'

Breach stage – somewhat narrower, 'was the type of accident or incident which befell C reasonably foreseeable, against which D should have taken some precautionary steps?' If a reasonable D should not have reasonably foreseen the type of accident which occurred, then D would not have taken precautionary steps or alternative actions to prevent or guard against that accident happening.

Remoteness stage – at its narrowest, 'was the kind or type of harm suffered by C reasonably foreseeable?'

[28] [2004] EWCA Civ 345, [27] (Moses LJ). [29] [1954] 2 QB 66 (CA) 73.
[30] [2001] EWCA Civ 273, [21] (Sir Anthony Evans).

A few cases illustrate the distinction, and illustrate how easy the test is to satisfy at duty-of-care stage:

How the test of foreseeability becomes more focused, from duty of care to the latter stages

Road user to another road user: one road user owes a duty of care to another road user. The circumstances of the road accident may be so unusual or unpredictable so as to render the injury to C unforeseeable, but that is a question of breach. In *Billington v Maguire*,[a] D parked his van and trailer by the road and blocked the cycle lane; and cyclist C ran into the van and trailer, not having seen it ahead of her – 'it affronts common sense to say that [D] owed [C] no duty'. The trial judge held that the circumstances were so unusual that the risk of injury to C, by D's parking his van where he did, was not foreseeable, but that was overruled on appeal; a breach was proven (with 70% CN against C).

Hospitals/doctors and patients: where patient C attends hospital for surgical treatment by doctor/surgeon/ anaesthetist D, it is reasonably foreseeable that *some* physical injury may result, if reasonable skill is not exercised by D. The doctor–patient relationship is a recognised category of duty. However, if the accident suffered by C was so unusual, and hitherto unknown, so as to have been unforeseeable, then no precautionary steps should have been taken by D (e.g., as in *Roe v Minister of Health*[b] – where a duty was owed, but no 'act of negligence' was proven).

Employer and employees: employer D will owe a duty of care to its employee C in avoiding the risk of physical injury which the workplace (or work systems) pose to C. However, how the harm befalls C may be so unusual that it could not have been foreseeable, and no reasonable employer would have acted differently to prevent it (e.g., as in *Williams v Univ of Birmingham*,[c] where a duty of care was admitted by D, but breach towards C failed).

An accident victim and his rescuer: where D is negligent, and imperils himself or his property (or someone else), then it is reasonably foreseeable that people might attempt to rescue D (or that someone else), and that some accident may befall the rescuer, C, during the rescue. A duty will be owed (where C suffers physical injury); but if C's injury happens in a very unusual and unpredictable way, then that injury will be adjudged to be too remote, as in *Crossley v Rawlinson*,[d] where C saw D's lorry on fire beside the road, picked up a fire extinguisher and raced down a trodden path towards the lorry, stepped into a hidden rabbit-hole, and suffered a leg injury.

[a] [2001] EWCA Civ 273, [23] (Sir Anthony Evans).
[b] [1954] 2 QB 66 (CA) 83–85 (Denning LJ).
[c] [2011] EWCA Civ 1242.
[d] [1982] 1 WLR 369 (CA) 374–75. Cf: *Videan v British Transport Comm* [1963] 2 QB 650 (CA) 669 (rescuer stationmaster, killed whilst saving his son; negligence proven).

Foreseeability at duty of care stage

§2.5   D must have either actually foreseen (i.e., actually appreciated), or reasonably foreseenx (i.e., a reasonable person in D's position would have anticipated) the risk that his failure to exercise reasonable care and/or skill might cause harm of some type to C individually, or to a class of persons of whom C was one. A risk is reasonably foreseeable if it is a 'real risk', i.e., more than a mere possibility.

This principle brings two separate concepts into play.

Some general type of harm. Several leading House of Lords decisions have confirmed that the enquiry as to reasonable foreseeability is a very high-level one, at this early stage of the negligence action. In *Caparo v Dickman plc*,[31] Lord Bridge referred to a foreseeability test in the most general of terms – *viz*, 'the foreseeability of damage' – as 'an ingredient' of a duty of care. In this aspect of his judgment, he endorsed the very same wide test of foreseeability which was favoured at duty-of-care stage by Lord Wilberforce in *Anns v Merton LBC*.[32] Subsequently, in *Van Colle v CC of Hertfordshire Police*, Lord Bingham described the first limb of *Caparo* in the same very wide terms: 'it must be shown that harm to [C] was a reasonably foreseeable consequence of what [D] did or failed to do'.[33] The width with which this test of foreseeability has been enunciated explains why the 'unforeseeable claimant' is a rarely-sighted creature indeed!

Reasonable foreseeability is a rather ill-defined concept. Buxton LJ remarked, in *Islington LBC v UCL London Hosp NHS Trust*, that it was a matter of 'fluidity or flexibility', and that '[t]he level of certainty required for an outcome to be deemed, after the event, to have been foreseeable is, to a large extent, a matter of impression'.[34] However, its difficulty should not be overstated, because the threshold for establishing a reasonably foreseeable risk of injury to C has proven to be a very low one indeed. It must be a 'real risk, and not a mere possibility' – i.e., one which a reasonable person 'would not brush aside as far-fetched' (per *Overseas Tankship (UK) Ltd v Miller Steamship Co Pty*[35]). In *AG v Hartwell (British Virgin Islands)*,[36] Lord Nicholls said that it must not be 'fanciful'. It follows that merely possible (i.e., very small or far-fetched) risks may be foreseeable – after all, a person with a sufficiently vivid imagination or an obsessively worried disposition can probably foresee anything – but those risks are not *reasonably* foreseeable.

Certainly, the test of reasonable foreseeability does **not** require a balance of probabilities, or 'likelihood', that the risk of injury would happen. On several early occasions, the House of Lords did, unhelpfully, say that a reasonably foreseeable risk must be 'probable' or 'likely' to occur – e.g., in *Glasgow Corp v Muir* (D 'should have reasonably anticipated as a natural *and probable* consequence of neglect'[37]); and in *Dorset Yacht Co Ltd v Home Office* (one that was 'very likely' to occur[38]). However, later House of Lords' decisions have distanced the law from that view. As stated in *Smith v Littlewoods Organisation Ltd*, whenever the word, 'probable', is used in the context of reasonable foreseeability, it decidedly does not entail any proof on the balance of probabilities: '[i]t is not used in the sense that the consequence must be more probable than not to happen, before it can be reasonably foreseeable'.[39] In *Mitchell v Glasgow CC* too, it was said that, '[t]he concept of reasonable foreseeability embraced a wide range of degrees of possibility, from the highly probable to the possible but highly improbable'.[40] Hence, when asking whether a risk of injury was reasonably foreseeable, the use of terms such as 'probable' or 'likely' do not bear the same meaning as in an assessment of causation (as will be discussed in Chapter 8). The Scottish Outer House recently pointed out that, in the context of reasonable foreseeability, the 'balance of probabilities' meaning is completely inappropriate; rather, 'probable' is 'used in the sense of reasonably likely to occur'.[41]

---

[31] [1990] 2 AC 605 (HL) 618.   [32] [1978] AC 728 (HL) 751–52.   [33] [2009] 1 AC 225 (HL) [42].

[34] [2005] EWCA Civ 596, [14].   [35] [1967] 1 AC 617 (PC, on appeal from NSWSC) 642–43 (Lord Reid).

[36] [2004] UKPC 12, [2004] WLR 1273, [38].   [37] [1943] AC 448 (HL) 454 (Lord Thankerton) (emphasis added).

[38] [1970] AC 1004 (HL) 1018 (Lord Wilberforce).   [39] [1987] AC 241 (HL) 269 (Lord Griffiths).

[40] [2009] UKHL 11, [2009] 2 WLR 481, [18] (Lord Hope), citing: *A-G (British Virgin Islands) v Hartwell* [2004] UKPC 12, [2004] 1 WLR 1273, [21] (Lord Nicholls).

[41] *French v Strathclyde Fire Board* [2013] Scot CS 3 (CSOH) [38].

All of this sets a very undemanding test – especially when combined with the fact that all that C has to prove, at the duty of care stage, is that *some physical injury or property damage* was reasonably foreseeable as a result of D's acts or omissions. As such, the first limb of *Caparo's* test has **not** acted as a stringent control mechanism in English negligence jurisprudence. The limb is, perhaps, slightly more likely to feature in cases involving pure omissions by D (see later below) and in failure-to-supervise-third-party cases (discussed in Chapter 3), although even there, reasonable foreseeability of physical injury or harm may be the **only** *Caparo* limb that C managed to prove (as, e.g., in *Hill v CC of West Yorkshire Police*[42] and *Palmer v Tees HA*,[43] where each C suffered the most extreme personal injury of all – murder – and yet reasonable foreseeability was the only *Caparo* limb which was met). Away from those contexts, it is difficult to identify **any** case since *Caparo* was handed down, in which the first limb of the *Caparo* test has failed. A couple of examples may demonstrate how unlikely is the 'unforeseeable claimant'.[44]

> In the Manitoba case of *Urbanski v Patel*[45] (referenced by the author elsewhere[46]), where a doctor, D, operated on a patient, and mistook an out-of-place kidney for an ovarian cyst and removed it (with that turning out to be that patient's only kidney, due to a congenital accident never suspected), and where the patient's father, C, donated one of his kidneys, thereby suffering physical injury, could it be reasonably foreseeable, at the time that the doctor operated, that C (a person related to the patient) could suffer some physical injury? The answer in *Urbanski* was 'yes', but it is questionable whether an English court would follow suit. In the New York case of *Palsgraf v Long Island Rwy Co*,[47] C was standing on a train platform, when a man running for a train and carrying the package was pulled into the train by a train guard, D. The man dropped the package onto the railway line (unknown to D, it contained fireworks), and it exploded, whereupon scales at the other end of the platform got knocked over, hitting C. C was held to be an unforeseeable C. Under the *Caparo* test, however, C's injury was surely foreseeable, in that some physical injury to persons within a zone of danger from the explosion of fireworks would be a 'real possibility'. Twisting those facts as *a hypothetical example*, suppose that a person shopping at a supermarket drops his shopping bag, breaking some eggs. One of the eggs was rotten, and a passerby, C, suffered an allergic reaction from the sulphur dioxide emanating from the egg, when no physical injury resulting from that dropped shopping bag could be envisaged to anyone else. C's injury may plausibly be unforeseeable under the *Caparo* test.

C individually, or as one of a class. It is not necessary to prove that D ought to have reasonably foreseen harm *to C specifically* as a result of D's acts or omissions. Of course, where C is known to D personally, then C may be an actually *foreseen* victim – as a passenger will be to a negligent driver in whose car that passenger is travelling (per *Nettleship v Weston*[48]). However, where C and D never had any prior relationship before the allegedly negligent event happened and where C is unknown to D, then it is sufficient if C was foreseeable as one of a class of persons whose person or property might be harmed by D's activities (say, a class defined by its geographic location).

---

[42] [1989] AC 53 (HL).   [43] [1999] EWCA Civ 1533, (1998) 39 BMLR 35.

[44] The author is grateful to her colleague, Mr Ian Yeats, for helpful discussions on this interesting point.

[45] (1978), 84 DLR (3d) 650 (Man QB).

[46] Mulheron, *Medical Negligence: Non-Patient and Third Party Claims* (Ashgate Publishing, 2010) 69–71.

[47] 248 NY 339 (NY Ct App, 1928).   [48] [1971] 2 QB 691 (CA).

In *Bolton v Stone*,[49] Miss Stone, C, was one of a class of residents living nearby to Cheetham Cricket Club's cricket ground and whose property or persons could be hit by errant cricket balls hit out of D's cricket ground. A duty of care was owed to C; but there was no breach. The risk of C's being hit by an errant cricket ball was 'infinitesimal', so small that a reasonable cricket club in D's position was justified in disregarding it (considered in Chapter 7).

Exceptionally, in some contexts, even if the class of persons which is foreseeably at risk from D's act or omission *is the entire world* (of whom, of course, C is one), that does not necessarily preclude the test of foreseeability from being met. For example, where D drives negligently, then harm to any member of the public who is on or near the road is entirely foreseeable, but a duty of care is owed to the particular road user or pedestrian who is in fact injured. Where a manufacturer distributes defective products for widespread public consumption, then any member of the public may foreseeably be harmed by using/consuming the product, but a duty of care crystallises when a particular claimant suffers injury (discussed in 'Defective products', an online chapter).

Hence, because of the requirements of a 'limited class of whom C was one', and 'a duty attaches when the damage crystallises', there is no prospect of D being liable to the whole world, even where there is a foreseeable risk of injury to the general public as a result of D's negligence. Additionally, the other limbs of *Caparo* (considered below) provide better 'brakes' on liability. Hence, although, in *Jones v Wright*,[50] Stocker LJ noted that '[s]ome limitations must be put upon what is reasonably foreseeable, if a duty of care is not to be owed to the whole world at large', the reality is that the restraints imposed by the test of foreseeability are fairly non-existent at duty of care stage.

§2.6   Although reasonable foreseeability is an objective test, it is the *particular D* whose breach caused the injury to C to whom that test must be applied.

The test of foreseeability, whilst an objective test, is **not** to be applied to a completely-hypothetical D. Rather, it is a reasonable person *in that particular D's shoes* whose mindset is in issue. Should *that D* have reasonably foreseen that a lack of reasonable care and/or skill on his part might give rise to C's injury? The answer is that, if the particular D 'possesses a significant degree of knowledge' as to how some injury may manifest to C as a result of D's act or omission, then the test of reasonable foreseeability will, inevitably, be easier to satisfy.

In *Islington LBC v UCL Hosp NHS Trust*,[51] a cardiac surgeon's secretary informed patient C, Mrs J, that her operation was cancelled and that she should not recommence her Warfarin medication. C suffered a stroke, during the period when she was not taking Warfarin. With her lack of medical knowledge, the secretary could not have foreseen the ramifications of the care which C would require, should she suffer a stroke. Hence, it would not have been possible to sue the secretary in negligence, and to sue the NHS Trust, D, vicariously for that negligence. Rather, it was necessary to sue D directly for systemic (direct) negligence. **Held:** C's injury was reasonably foreseeable to D (and a duty was owed to her).

---

[49] [1951] AC 850 (HL), on appeal from: [1950] 1 KB 201 (CA).   [50] [1991] 3 All ER 88 (CA) 114.
[51] [2005] EWCA Civ 596, quotes in text and case description at [15]–[16].

'The failure in this case was not that, or simply that, of the secretary. The failure was an institutional one, in that University College Hospital [operated by D] did not make proper arrangements for advising persons whose drug regime had been varied in anticipation of an operation and whose operation was then cancelled. The question is therefore what was foreseeable by the Trust ... the institutional body whose notional foresight has to be judged possesses a significant degree of medical knowledge.'

This case illustrates how important it is to select the relevant D carefully, when the test of foreseeability under *Caparo's* first limb is being considered.

§2.7 Reasonable foreseeability of injury to C is a necessary, but not sufficient, condition to prove a duty of care. *All* ingredients of the *Caparo* test must be met.

Given the liberal nature of the reasonable foreseeability test, the restraints on a duty of care are effectively set by a careful application of the proximity and policy tests. These are the *Caparo* limbs which **most effectively** act as factors which limit D's liability in negligence.

Occasionally, it has been judicially suggested that, where C suffers physical or personal injury, then 'reasonable foreseeability of harm is usually enough, in accordance with the principle in *Donoghue v Stevenson*, to generate a duty of care' (per Lord Hoffmann in *Customs & Excise Commrs v Barclays Bank plc*[52]). In *Perrett v Collins* too, the fact that C's claim was for a foreseeable physical injury was said to be, of itself, a 'potent factor' pointing to the existence of a duty.[53] However, such statements must be accorded real caution. Even in cases of foreseeable physical injury, proximity may be lacking, and public policy may preclude a duty of care. This has been particularly evident where C suffers personal injury or property damage in the failure-to-control-third-parties cases (per *Hill v CC of West Yorkshire Police*, where the House of Lords reiterated that, 'foreseeability of likely harm is not, in itself, a sufficient test of liability in negligence. Some further ingredient is invariably needed to establish the requisite proximity of relationship between [C] and [D] ... The nature of the ingredient will be found to vary in a number of different categories of decided cases'[54]). The paradigm example of the adage that reasonable foreseeability is never enough, on its own, to point to a duty is that of the blind man walking towards the cliff's edge – it is clearly foreseeable to bystander D, who says and does nothing, that the blind man will walk to severe injury or death, and yet, D owes no duty of care to him ('trite law', as Coulson J said in *Geary v JD Wetherspoon plc*[55]). The policy reasons which preclude a duty of care in that scenario are discussed below (under *Caparo* element #3).

Hence, any pre-*Caparo* cases which suggest that reasonable foreseeability was sufficient to prove a duty of care, in the context of C's suffering personal injury, must now be held to have been wrongly reasoned. Such cases resemble too closely the now-discredited *Anns* test (per *MacDonald v Aberdeenshire CC*[56]).

For some particular claimants – those susceptible to injury, and those unborn at the time of the alleged negligence – foreseeability of their injury is worth expansion.

Claimants susceptible to injury

§2.8 Where, unknown to D, C was particularly susceptible or vulnerable to the risk of the physical injury which befell him, as a result of D's acts or omissions (when no harm to an able-bodied

---

[52] [2006] UKHL 28, [2007] 1 AC 181, [31].   [53] [1998] PNLR 77, 114, 2 Lloyd's Rep 255 (CA).
[54] [1989] AC 53 (HL) 60.   [55] [2011] EWHC 1506 (QB) [61].   [56] [2012] ScotCS 101 (OH) [47].

person would have been foreseeable whatsoever), that harm to C *may* nevertheless be reasonably foreseeable, C being within a class of persons to whom a duty is owed by D.

This principle applies, even where: (1) a duty would **not** have been owed to a person of ordinary physical robustness, because it could not have been foreseeable that an able-bodied person would have suffered any harm; (2) the harm to the physically-vulnerable C was, statistically speaking, very small; and (3) D was not personally aware of C's physical vulnerability, i.e., where C was one of a potential class of physically-vulnerable Cs. If any further evidence were needed, this aptly emphasises the wholly undemanding nature of the test of reasonable foreseeability at duty stage.

> In *Haley v London Electricity Board*,[57] Mr Haley, C, had been blinded in an accident. He lived in Woolwich, London, and worked as a telephone operator for the London CC. Each day, he walked to the bus stop, and had learned to avoid ordinary obstacles with the aid of his white stick. However, unknown to C, the London Electricity Board, D, had been digging a trench, and put a long punner-hammer around it to warn pedestrians of the spot. C tripped over the punner-hammer, struck his head hard on the pavement, and was rendered deaf. **Held:** D, as electricity providers, owed a duty of care to blind persons affected by their servicing work. Some physical harm to C was reasonably foreseeable, even though the hammer would have warned a sighted person. Statistically, 1 in 500 people in London was blind, and many of them 'must walk pavements unaccompanied'. Hence, they were a foreseeable class to whom a duty was owed.

Note, however, that this is **not** an illustration of the so-called 'egg-shell skull' principle – the latter is a principle of remoteness of damage, and is considered in Chapter 9.

The unborn claimant

§2.9   Where C is born with a disease, deformity or abnormality which was due to the alleged negligence of D, whether caused whilst C was *in utero*, or pre-conception via parental treatment, the child, C, has the capacity to sue D for that ante-natal injury – provided that C was born alive.

The capacity for C to sue for injuries sustained as a result of acts or omissions committed whilst C was *in utero*, or because of treatment given to C's parent/s pre-conception, is statutorily-guaranteed, by virtue of s 1(1) of the Congenital Disabilities (Civil Liability) Act 1976 ('the 1976 Act'). The Act confers a right of action upon **a child** – born alive but disabled – because of 'an occurrence' which affected either parent's ability to have a normal, healthy child, or which affected the mother during pregnancy or affected her or the child during the child's birth, so that child C is born disabled (per s 1(2)(a) and (b), respectively). This is **not** a parental claim. The Act recognises a duty of care in favour of *the child*.

It follows that any of the following could fall within the scope of the Act, as an 'occurrence':

- something occurring pre-conception (e.g., where D negligently caused an injury to the mother's reproductive system before conception, condemning any child conceived thereafter, C, to disability);
- something which 'affected' C's mother during the mother's pregnancy (i.e., an act or omission which damaged C whilst *in utero*). The English Law Commission gave a number of examples in its 1973–74 study *Injuries to Unborn Children*.[58] (Notably, some of the scenarios postulated did

---

[57] [1965] AC 778 (HL) 791.   [58] (CP 47, 1973) [6]–[14].

not involve the mother herself being 'injured', thus suggesting that the Act covers a wider array of circumstances than that, where C may suffer an ante-natal injury because of some act or omission by D which involved the mother but which did not injure her.) Just to mention a few examples of how C's claim could arise: where a trauma is inflicted upon C's mother by some car or train accident caused by D; or where harmful drugs were taken by the mother during pregnancy that cause injury to C *in utero* (the Commission's final report noted[59] the extraordinary statistic that '[t]here are known to be about 1,500 drugs having teratogenica effects (i.e., capable of causing damage to the foetus) with varying (usually slight) degrees of risk'); or where the mother's womb was irradiated whilst the foetus was *in utero* (e.g., where a pregnancy was actually misdiagnosed as a uterine tumour, leading to an X-ray that proved to be detrimental to C *in utero*); or where some diagnostic investigations or medical procedure performed on the mother damaged C *in utero*; or

- an event which affected C's mother during C's birth (e.g., where C's oxygen supply was cut off during birth, or shoulder dystocia affected C's delivery, either of which caused C hypoxia).

Additionally, disabled child, C, has an actionable claim where C's disability was caused by damage to the selection or handling of gametes (i.e., unfertilised human sperm and eggs) or embryo outside the mother's body during infertility treatment. This action was inserted in 1990, as s 1A(1)(b) of the 1976 Act.[60] There has not, to date, been any judicial decision turning on this provision – although in the Scottish case of *Holdich v Lothian Health Board*,[61] the court was somewhat quizzical of s 1A, noting that some of its wording was 'more immediately intelligible' in s 1 (the general provision providing C with a cause of action) than in s 1A. In particular, it is unclear whether s 1A actually sanctions a 'wrongful life' action (see Chapter 3).

Triggers for the Act to apply

The Act applies to any birth in England that occurred **after** 22 July 1976 (per s 4(5)), and displaces the common law. Given the time which has elapsed since the Act was passed; the 3-year limitation period that applies to personal injury cases; and the maximum suspension of limitation periods in English law, any litigation involving this type of C will be now covered by the Act, and not by the common law.

§2.10 Under the Act, there are several criteria for a duty of care to be owed to the unborn claimant, C. These do not replicate the common law requirements set by the *Caparo* (or any other) test, but are defined uniquely by the Congenital Disabilities (Civil Liability) Act 1976.

The Act sets **four** criteria for a duty of care, where a child is born disabled, allegedly due to D's negligence:

i. C is born alive. From a combined reading of s 1(1) and s 4(2), a cause of action is only vested in C, for ante-natal injury suffered, if C is born alive and viable. Section 4(2)(a) specifically provides that being 'born' means 'born alive (the moment of a child's birth being when it first has a life separate from its mother'), however brief that separation might be. Hence, if C dies

---

[59] EWLC, *Report on Injuries to Unborn Children* (Rep 60, 1974) [21].

[60] By virtue of the Human Fertilisation and Embryology Act 1990, s 44(1), and in force 1 Aug 1991.

[61] [2013] CSOH 197, [27]. The 1976 Act does not apply to Scotland; and this case concerned a parental claimant in any event. Hence, there was no requirement to consider s 1A.

prior to delivery/birth because of D's negligence and is still-born, C's estate has no capacity to sue under the Act. (Other suits may be possible, however – whether by the mother of that child, per *Grieve v Salford HA*,[62] or by one who may claim damages for psychiatric injury as a secondary victim, as discussed in Chapter 5.[63])

ii. C is born 'disabled', with disabilities which would not have been present, but for D's acts or omissions. 'Disability' is defined in s 4(1), and includes being born with 'any deformity, disease or abnormality'. The Act gives no cause of action for C with naturally-occurring or congenital disabilities, because the disability itself must result from the 'wrongful act' of D (per s 1(1)). Further, if C is born with some particular characteristic (e.g., skin colour) to which C objects, that will not constitute a 'disability' for the purposes of the Act.

> In *A (a minor) v A Health and Social Services Trust*,[64] twins C were born as a result of IVF treatment provided by D's IVF facility. C's parents were white; and they were anxious that their child would have the same skin colour. D inseminated C's mother's eggs with sperm labelled, 'Caucasian (Cape coloured)'. The Cape coloured community in South Africa was derived from races of different skin colouring, including white, black and Malay, giving rise to C's being darker-skinned than their parents. **Held:** the 1976 Act could not apply, because C had suffered no 'disability' that would trigger its operation: 'these are healthy and normal children. In a modern civilised society the colour of their skin – no more than the colour of their eyes or their hair, or their intelligence, or their height – cannot and should not count as connoting some damage to them. To hold otherwise would not only be adverse to the self-esteem of the children themselves, but anathema to the contemporary views of right thinking people'.

iii. The disability was caused by an 'occurrence' attributable to D, which occurred before C's birth. The definition of an 'occurrence' has been noted above. Some aspects of an 'occurrence' necessary to trigger the 1976 Act have not been entirely clarified. For one thing, it is not entirely clear whether the event could be a drawn-out circumstance (e.g., the gradual accumulation of a drug in the mother's system), affecting the mother's ability to have a healthy child; or whether it must be something more singular and 'one-off'. In *Multiple Claimants v Sanifo-Synthelabo Ltd (the FAC Group Litigation)*,[65] Andrew Smith J noted that, in the insurance context, 'occurrence' signifies 'a degree of unity in relation of cause, locality, time, and, if initiated by human action, the circumstances and purposes of the persons responsible'. For another, defining the precise 'occurrence', when D's pharmaceutical product is in issue, can be very unclear.

> In *The FAC Group Litigation*, a group of children, C, were born to mothers, each of whom suffered from epilepsy, and who took an anti-epileptic anti-convulsant drug, Epilim, manufactured by D, during their pregnancies. C argued that Epilim was a known teratogen, which crossed the placenta and which caused various deformities for foetuses exposed to it. It was likely that the risk to the foetus also depended upon the mother's genetic makeup. C argued that the 'occurrence' was 'the trans-placental spread' of the product to the embryo/foetus, which then affected embryonic and foetal development; whereas D argued that the only 'occurrence' that affected the mothers' ability

---

[62] [1991] 2 Med LR 295 (QB).   [63] See pp 239–40.

[64] [2010] NIQB 108, with quotes at [10] and [18], and aff'd: [2011] NICA 28, [9].

[65] [2007] EWHC 1860 (QB) [55]–[57], citing: the award of Mr Michael Kerr QC in the Dawson's Airfield Arbitration dated 29 Mar 1972, re the meaning of 'occurrence' in the context of insurance policies.

to have a healthy baby was their epilepsy that required anti-epilepsy drugs, and that any trans-placental spread of the drug could not constitute an 'occurrence'. This point could not be decided as a preliminary issue, but would require evidence at trial, as to whether the spread was caused by genetic make-up or the mothers' consumption of Epilim.

iv. C's claim is derivative upon a claim against C's parent/s. C's claim against D can only be maintained under the 1976 Act if D was under an actual or potential tort liability to either parent of C, for the act or omission which led to C's disability – except that it does not matter (per s 1(3)) if the parent has suffered no *actual injury*. Hence, if, say, C's mother takes a pharmaceutical drug during her pregnancy, and suffers no injury herself, but C does suffer injury whilst *in utero*, then C can still bring an action against the manufacturer of that drug, D. In that regard, C's claim under the 1976 Act is unusual for an action in tort, in that C's action is *derivative* upon D's tortious duty to the parent/s – but it is unnecessary to show that the parent suffered any actionable injury.

It also follows, from the derivative liability imposed by the 1976 Act and from the terminology of s 1(7), that any 'shared' negligence which may be pleaded by D as against the child's parent/s, will reduce the child's, C's, damages too. This is not contributory negligence as such (as it is not C's negligence which is at issue, but his parents' conduct). Furthermore, s 1(4) is worth noting: as a defence under the Act, D is not responsible to the child, if the child's parent/s knew, pre-conception, of the risk of C's disability.

What the Act does not do. The Act does **not** assist at all to prove whether D committed any breach of duty towards C, whether that breach (if any) caused C's harm, or whether C's harm was too remote at law to be compensable. These other aspects of the negligence action remain for determination solely according to common law principles – and indeed, they may be very difficult for C to prove.

> In *McCoy v East Midlands Strategic HA*,[66] Brodie McCoy, C, was born severely brain-damaged, on 22 March, at 39 weeks. C sued her mother's treating doctors, D, for failing to carry out a cardiotocograph scan at 37 weeks. C argued that an earlier CTG trace had been 'suspicious'; a further scan would have shown a similarly-worrying fetal heart pattern indicating that the mother's placenta was failing; steps would have been taken to deliver C early by induced labour or by caesarean section; and if C had been delivered earlier, the brain injury would have been avoided. **Held:** C could bring a claim under the 1976 Act, but no negligence proven. Although D committed a breach in regarding the earlier CTG trace as satisfactory, that breach did not cause C's injury because, on the balance of probabilities, a further scan would not have led to an intervention to deliver C earlier than 22 March.

The other options

The 1976 Act was prompted by the recommendations of the EWLC (in *Injuries to Unborn Children*[67]), which endorsed the view that statutory standing be conferred on an unborn C, for injuries negligently-inflicted prior to that child's birth. At the time, English law was uncertain on this point, and the EWLC noted that, 'where a doubt exists as to what the law is on an important topic such as this, there is a strong case for resolving that doubt by legislation'.[68]

---

[66] [2011] EWHC 38 (QB). [67] See EWLC, *Injuries to Unborn Children* (CP 47, 1973), and (Rep 60, 1974).

[68] *ibid*, [4(c)], and see [4]–[15], for discussion and quotes in the Table.

The point of the Act is that, '[f]or there to be any cause of action there must be a live birth. The cause of action can be said to crystallise at birth',[69] because the damage was actually incurred at the point of a live birth. However, the EWLC had two other options to consider, on this point of standing.

The law reform corner: Standing to sue for the unborn claimant: three options

Option #1 (approved by the EWLC): according to the English Court of Appeal in *Burton v Islington HA*,[70] a child injured *in utero*, born alive, was owed a duty of care, because that risk of damage was reasonably foreseeable. Tina Burton, C, alleged negligence by medical staff when they carried out a dilation and curettage (D&C) procedure at a time when C's mother was about five weeks pregnant with C. D failed to carry out a pregnancy test before the procedure, where circumstances should have put experienced medical staff on enquiry. The common law applied (C was born on 26 April 1967, so being pre-22 Jul 1976, the Act did not apply). Earlier English authority supported that too. In *[an unnamed case cited by the EWLC]*,[71] a ladder fell upon a pregnant woman, caused by D's negligence. The child was born the next day and lived just one day. D paid $100 into court when the parents brought a claim for damages for loss of expectation of life, in settlement of the claim. The *Burton/* EWLC view was also endorsed in other jurisdictions. In *Watt v Rama*,[72] C suffered injury *in utero*, allegedly caused when D collided negligently with C's mother's vehicle. C's mother was rendered a paraplegic from the accident, and C, her son, was born with brain damage and epilepsy. In *Montreal Tramways Co v Léveillé*,[73] due to the negligence of the tram's motor man, C's mother fell from the tramcar and was injured. Two months later, she gave birth to C, who was born with club feet. Each C could pursue a negligence claim against D, provided that they were born alive and viable, in respect of their disabilities, even though the disabilities were caused *in utero*.

Option #2: was to recognise C, a damaged foetus, as a legal entity, separate from the mother, even if the foetus did not survive birth (permitted in some US jurisdictions in cases of still-birth[74]). That would enable C to recover heads of damage such as funeral expenses, and loss of expectation of life (albeit that damages for PSLA would be irrelevant). In *Burton*, Dillon LJ noted that earlier English authority[75] did not endorse the view that a foetus enjoyed an independent legal personality – 'a foetus cannot, while a foetus, sue and cannot be made a ward of court'. The EWLC[76] did not favour the proposition either, describing it as a 'fiction', and 'practically difficult'.

Option #3: was to deny any duty of care owed to C who was negligently injured *in utero*, even if the child was born alive. That view applied in the 1891 Irish decision in *Walker v Great Northern Rwy Co of Ireland*,[77] where C's mother, whilst pregnant with C, fell from D's

[69] See EWLC, *Report*, [32].   [70] [1992] EWCA Civ 2, [1993] QB 204.
[71] *Injuries to Unborn Children* (CP 47, 1973) fn 1, citing (1939) 83 Sol J 185 (Liverpool Assizes). The author's efforts to locate the name of this case have proven unsuccessful.
[72] [1972] VR 353 (CA) (Gillard J) 356.
[73] [1933] SCR 456 (SCC) 464 (a majority decision, re a Quebec statute: at 462–63).
[74] EWLC, *Injuries to Unborn Children* (CP 47, 1973) fn 3, citing: *White v Yup*, 458 P 2d 617 (1969).
[75] [1993] QB 204 (CA) 226, citing: *Paton v BPAS* [1979] QB 276; *Re F* [1988] Fam 122 (CA).
[76] (CP 47, 1973) [36].   [77] (1891) 28 LR (Ire) QB & Ex 69.

train because of D's alleged negligence. C was born crippled and deformed. C's statement of claim disclosed no cause of action. In *Burton*, the Court of Appeal considered *Walker* 'profoundly unsatisfactory'.[78] One of the reasons was that the *Walker* majority had 'attached weight to the fact that the Railway Company as a common carrier had sold the pregnant mother one ticket and not two – a conclusion which, if valid today, would carry the consequence that a child under three who can travel without a ticket on British Railways would have no remedy against British Railways if injured by the negligence of the British Rail employees'. The *Burton* court simply regarded *Walker* to be of 'no assistance today'.

PROXIMITY (*CAPARO #2*)

§2.11   The concept of proximity describes the degree of closeness or neighbourhood between C and D which must be proven to justify imposing a duty of care on D. It is traditionally proven via a combination of: geographical proximity; temporal proximity; relational proximity; and causal proximity. However, no particular proximity factor has a 'clinching' status.

The proximity enquiry requires the factual matrix to be examined, so as to show that C was a person 'so closely and directly affected by [D's] act that [D] ought reasonably to have [C] in contemplation as being so affected' (to revisit the words of Lord Atkin in *Donoghue v Stevenson*[79]). It was frankly acknowledged, in *Caparo Industries plc v Dickman*,[80] that 'proximity' is merely a label, and that, in novel cases, ascertaining whether the parties were sufficiently proximate could be viewed as the ultimate exercise in judicial pragmatism.

Four types were outlined by the High Court of Australia in *Sutherland SC v Heyman*,[81] and for the purposes of English law, were approved in *Stovin v Wise* as a 'valuable exposition' of proximity.[82]

The types of proximity – what they mean	
geographical proximity	the physical closeness between C, when the damage was suffered, and D, when the breach occurred
temporal proximity	the closeness in time between when C suffered the damage, and when the breach by D occurred
relational proximity	an enquiry into several matters, e.g.: • was C in a vulnerable position vis-à-vis D? • was D exercising control over the circumstances in which C was harmed or injured? • did C and D have a pre-existing relationship, in which C obviously relied upon D to exercise reasonable care, or where D assumed responsibility to exercise care towards C?

[78] [1993] QB 204 (CA) 231 (Dillon LJ).   [79] [1932] AC 562 (HL) 580 (Lord Atkin).
[80] [1990] 2 AC 606 (HL) 618 (Lord Bridge), 633 (Lord Oliver).
[81] (1985) 50 ALR 1 (HCA) 55.   [82] [1996] AC 923 (HL) 932 (Lord Nicholls).

	• was C at 'special risk' as a result of D's breach, over and above the risk faced by the general public? If the same measure of risk was faced by all, or a large cross-section of the public, then the requisite proximity between D and C is unlikely
causal proximity	whether D precluded a step which, had it occurred, would have almost certainly protected C from the harm that eventuated – the availability of that intervening step (so that not taking it exacerbated C's vulnerability) can enhance a finding of proximity between D and C

Different weightings may be given to these various types of proximity, in different fact scenarios, and none of them is an absolute pre-requisite or unifying characteristic, for legal proximity between C and D to be found. It all depends upon a close scrutiny and analysis of the facts and circumstances of the case at hand. However, they have all proven to be of *some* relevance, under the *Caparo* test.

Although it has been judicially said that proximity has 'an uncertain status' (per *Islington LBC v University College London Hosp NHS Trust*[83]), and is a 'slippery word' (per *Stovin v Wise*[84]), it has certainly proven effective in circumscribing the number of Cs who have scrambled through the duty of care door in English jurisprudence. Of course, for the recognised categories of duty of care, proximity is a 'given'; but in novel cases, 'the nexus is not given, but has to be found' (per *K v Sec of State for the Home Dept*[85]). The application of proximity, as a control mechanism, has been particularly noticeable in failure-to-control-third-party cases (as discussed in Chapter 3).

Where D has physically injured C, or caused C property damage, by reason of his acts or omissions, then proximity is, generally speaking, a non-contentious matter. As Lord Hoffmann remarked in *Customs and Excise*, there will usually be geographical and temporal proximity wherever D has physically injured C's person or property. However, in some cases, relational proximity (especially control over C's safety) may be entirely absent, in which case proximity will fail, the physical proximity notwithstanding.

In *Harrison v Technical Sign Co Ltd*,[86] Cluttons, D, the landlord's agent of a shop in Putney, was asked by the lessee, Maison Blanc, to inspect a defective awning over the shop, to ascertain whether the landlord might pay for repairs. Following the inspection, the fascia of the shop became detached from the building and fell onto the pavement, causing serious injuries to passerby, Gillian Harrison, C. **Held:** D did not owe C a duty of care. D's inspection had nothing to do with ensuring the safety of passers-by, but only to see whether the shop fixtures had sustained damage for which the landlord might be liable. If D had been asked by Maison Blanc to inspect the awning to ensure that it did not pose a danger to passers-by, the requisite proximity would probably have existed between C and D, because the very purpose of D's inspection would have been to ensure the public's safety. (Alternatively, by accepting such instructions, D would assume responsibility for the safety of passers-by, because then D would become involved in an activity which gave him a measure of control over, and responsibility for, their safety – per the assumption of responsibility/reliance test discussed later in the chapter.) But that was not the case here

[83] [2005] EWCA Civ 596, [20] (Buxton LJ).   [84] [1996] AC 923 (HL) 932 (Lord Nicholls).
[85] [2002] EWCA Civ 775, [26].   [86] [2013] EWCA Civ 1569, [14].

and, hence, there was insufficient proximity between D and any passer-by injured by the awning. In *Stagecoach South Western Trains Ltd v Hind*,[87] Kathleen Hind owned Rose Cottage, situated adjacent to the railway in Staines. She arranged for an arborist, D, to cut out the dead wood in an ash tree. Subsequently, one of C's trains collided with a branch of the ash tree which had fallen onto the railway line. C sued D in negligence for the cost of repairing the damage to its train. **Held:** D did not owe a duty of care to C. D was engaged for the specific purpose of clearing dead wood, which had nothing to do with the safety of those using the railway. It was analogous to *Harrison*, above. D was not involved in an activity which gave him a measure of control over, and responsibility for, the safety of C's trains.

A school and its pupils provide a useful example of proximity in action. In this context, a school encompasses the school as an entity (in devising its systems), and the principal and teachers for their individual acts or omissions (for which the school may be vicariously liable). A school which accepts a pupil for tuition assumes responsibility for his physical well-being, as well as for his educational needs (per *X (Minors) v Bedfordshire CC*[88] and *Webster v Ridgeway Foundation School*[89]). There is also relational proximity, in that the principal and teachers bear the standard of a 'careful parent' (per *Gower v Bromley LBC*[90]). Temporally, a duty to exercise reasonable care towards pupils applies during school hours, and extends 'for a reasonable period after the end of the school day while [the pupil] was still on the school's premises' (per *Webster*[91]), as well as for a reasonable period before school actually begins (*Kearn-Price v Kent CC*,[92] where a duty applied to an incident at 8.40am). Geographically, the duty may also extend beyond the physical boundaries of the school grounds, if a student is being bullied frequently on the journey to and from school (per *Bradford-Smart v West Sussex CC*[93]). More controversially, the requisite proximity between school and pupil may also apply, where the pupil is attacked by outsiders (per *Webster*, where the attack took place after the end of the school day, on school premises, and where the requisite proximity was found) – an illustration of the difficult scenario where, by his omissions, D facilitates the opportunity for a third party to do harm to C, and where proximity is always at issue.

Even where C and D were geographically and relationally proximate, however, proximity may not be proven. It all depends upon the circumstances. In *Geary v JD Wetherspoon plc*,[94] C and D were entrant and occupier, yet no proximity was made out (there was nothing defective about the state of D's premises, and hence, the Occupiers' Liability Acts discussed in Chapter 12 did not apply, and the case had to proceed as a common law negligence claim).

In *Geary v JD Wetherspoon plc*, Ruth Geary, C, visited D's pub, which was situated at the Union Rooms in Newcastle, with some work colleagues. The premises (previously a gentlemen's club) retained the original feature of a grand open staircase in the centre of the building, with sweeping banisters on both sides. When leaving at the end of the night, C hoisted herself onto one of the banisters to slide down it 'like Mary Poppins', but she fell backwards, landed on her back on the marble floor four metres below, and broke her back, suffering tetraplegia. **Held:** D owed C no duty of care, as proximity was lacking. The mere relationship of occupier–entrant could not, of itself, give rise to sufficient proximity. Further, there was no third party involved, so no proximity could arise where the allegation was that D's duty was to protect C from her own foolish actions, as opposed to protecting her from the actions of third parties.

---

[87] [2014] EWHC 1891 (TCC) [95]–[96].   [88] [1995] 2 AC 633 (HL) 766.   [89] [2010] EWHC 157 (QB).
[90] [2000] 2 LGLR 237 (CA) 240 (Auld LJ).   [91] [2010] EWHC 157 (QB) [121].   [92] [2002] EWCA Civ 1539.
[93] [2002] EWCA Civ 7.   [94] [2011] EWHC 1506 (QB) [58], [67]–[72].

§2.12 The gravity of harm to C, resulting from D's breach, has no impact upon the question of proximity.

Say that C dies as a result of D's negligence. Grievous injury to C, of itself, does **not** supply a nexus, or proximity of relationship, between C and D, sufficient to create a duty of care. This point was explicitly made in *K v Sec of State for the Home Dept*[95] (re an escapee awaiting deportation who raped C, a member of the public, while at large), and illustrated in *Geary* (where C suffered tetraplegia) and in *Palmer v Tees HA*[96] (where C was raped, murdered and mutilated). To hold otherwise would be to render D 'the world's insurer against grave danger' (per *K*[97]).

POLICY FACTORS (*CAPARO* #3)

General principles

§2.13 Both legal and public policy factors inform an assessment as to whether it is fair, just and reasonable to impose a duty of care on D. That judicial assessment of policy may change over time. The assessment of policy factors is a balancing exercise in novel fact scenarios, whereby some factors will support a duty of care, and others will disfavour it.

It is fair to say that there are distinctly contrasting perceptions of the role which policy plays in setting the existence of a duty of care under *Caparo*. At its most positive, an assessment of policy infuses a considerable degree of fluidity, which enables the court to come to the 'correct decision' on whether or not D **should** be liable in negligence. Lord Clyde put it this way, in *Phelps v Hillingdon LBC*:

> [policy considerations] have the advantage of flexibility, enabling the court to define the boundaries of claims for negligence, in the light of new situations and the recognition that incremental growth may require to be controlled, albeit at the risk of some uncertainty, at least in the prediction of the directions in which the law may develop.[98]

On the other hand, that very flexibility makes predicting the outcome of a duty of care in novel fact scenarios very uncertain. This was admitted a long time ago – back in 1824 – when Burrough J pithily stated, in *Richardson v Mellish*, that public policy was 'a very unruly horse, and when once you get astride of it, you never know where it will carry you'.[99]

In modern English law, it is hard to avoid the impression that the third limb of *Caparo* enables the court to dip into a 'bucket' of policy factors; extract from the bucket those which most suit the outcome which the court is seeking to achieve; return to the bucket those which do not 'suit' the desired outcome – and then 'dress the outcome' up as pragmatic judicial decision-making. At least Lord Pearson was honest in his assessment, in *Home Office v Dorset Yacht Co Ltd*,[100] that whether or not a duty of care was owed in that case 'must be a matter of impression and instinctive judgment as to what is fair and just'. In *Watson v British Boxing Board of*

---

[95] [2002] EWCA Civ 775, [24]–[30]. [96] (1998) 45 BMLR 88 (QB) 101 (Gage J). [97] [2002] EWCA Civ 775, [35].
[98] [2001] 2 AC 619 (HL) 671–72. [99] (1824) 2 Bing 229, 252. [100] [1970] AC 1004 (HL) 1054.

Control Ltd[101] too, Lord Phillips MR noted that, 'it is difficult, or perhaps impossible, to avoid a degree of subjectivity when considering what is fair, just and reasonable'.

This impression is surely enhanced by Buxton LJ's elliptical comment, in *Islington LBC v University College London Hosp NHS Trust*, that '"fair just and reasonable" is not to be read literally, nor is it to be read solely in the context of the relationship between the instant [C] and [D]. It still assumes ... that wider issues of policy may have to intervene'[102] (and, having duly 'intervened' in that case, a duty of care was 'a leap too far'). This passage emphasises a further important point – that while it may appear fair, just and reasonable for *that particular C* to recover for his injury or loss, his entitlement may be forsaken, because of other types of aggrieved Cs who could seek to press through the doorway over time.

To add to the uncertainty, policy has a tendency to change over time too. For example, no duty may be owed for public policy reasons by the police in 1989,[103] whereas in 2008, the House of Lords can admit that (although no duty remains the law) those reasons 'do not all stand up to critical examination today'.[104] That 'unruly horse' can change direction, responding to stimuli from its surroundings.

Lastly, an unfortunate terminological confusion has been introduced to this area, especially since 1999, by judicial references to 'public policy' and 'legal policy' factors under the third limb of *Caparo*. In *McFarlane v Tayside Health Board*,[105] Lord Millett remarked that '[l]egal policy, in this sense, is not the same as public policy, even though moral considerations may play a part in both. The court is engaged in a search for justice, and this demands that the dispute be resolved in a way which is fair and reasonable, and accords with ordinary notions of what is fit and proper'. Three years later, in *Rees v Darlington Memorial Hosp NHS Trust*,[106] Lord Steyn again distinguished the two types: '[t]he House did not rest its decision [in *McFarlane*] on public policy in a conventional sense ... Instead the Law Lords relied on legal policy'. However, neither of these judges explained precisely what was the difference between the types. Furthermore, other courts, before and since *McFarlane*, have used 'public policy' in precisely the sense in which Lord Millett described 'legal policy'. For example, in *Mitchell v Glasgow CC*,[107] Lord Hope used the terms interchangeably. As a result, it is not clear what the difference between legal and public policy factors actually is! Hence, the generic term, 'policy factors', will be used throughout this section, in the context of *Caparo's* third limb.

Under the now-overruled *Anns* two-stage test proposed by Lord Wilberforce, public policy was used to counter, or limit, the scenarios in which a duty of care could be owed. Under the *Caparo* line of authority, however, policy factors are used in a true balancing, or competing, exercise, whereby some factors will positively support a duty of care being owed.

A non-exhaustive sample of the most common policy arguments in novel fact scenarios involving personal injury or property damage to C, are summarised in the Table below:

---

[101] [2000] EWCA Civ 2116, [2001] QB 1134, [86].

[102] [2005] EWCA Civ 596, [34]; and also [53] (Ouseley LJ).

[103] *Hill v CC of West Yorkshire* [1989] AC 53 (HL) 63–64 (Lord Keith).

[104] *Smith v CC of Sussex Police; Van Colle v CC of Hertfordshire Police* [2008] UKHL 50, [2009] 1 AC 225, [73] (Lord Hope), referring to suits against the police for failing to prevent crime.

[105] [2000] 2 AC 59 (HL) 108.

[106] [2003] UKHL 52, [2004] AC 309, [29] (Lord Bingham drawing the same distinction at [6]).

[107] [2009] UKHL 11, [2009] 1 AC 874, [25]–[26].

Public policy factors: a deep 'bucket'

'corrective justice'	this rule of policy provides that, 'the first claim on the loyalty of the law [is] that wrongs should be remedied', or that 'every wrong should have a remedy' (per *X (Minors) v Bedfordshire CC*[a]). It has been described as 'the primary requirement of public policy' (per *Arthur JS Hall & Co v Simons*[b]) and 'the ideal of a system' (per *McFarlane v Tayside Health Board*[c]). Hence, if D has harmed C by his conduct without justification, then the balance between them should be restored by holding that a duty of care was owed
'distributive justice'	who would the 'commuters on the London Underground' consider should justly bear the burden of the loss suffered as a result of D's activities: C or D? (per *McFarlane v Tayside Health Board*[d]). This factor takes account of whether losses are being allocated in a way that gives the public confidence in the legal system (per *Arthur JS Hall & Co v Simons*) – albeit that '[j]udges do not have, and do not claim to have, any special insight into what contemporary society regards as fair and reasonable' (per *Rees v Darlington Memorial Hosp NHS Trust*[e]). Distributive justice 'is not a principle of English law recently adopted so as to allow free rein to ignore basic principles long established' (per *Tameside and Glossop NHS Trust v Thompstone*[f])
'floodgates concerns'	if to hold that D owed a duty of care would expose similarly-situated Ds to potential liability from many persons in C's position, and would likely increase the volume of litigation against similarly-situated Ds in the future, then that may preclude a duty of care (per *Hill v CC of West Yorkshire Police*[g])
'defensive practices'	if to impose a duty on D would promote overly cautious practices / assessments / treatments/etc, which could put third parties at risk, because D was not game to act for the protection of the public, for fear of ensuing litigation, then that may militate against a duty of care (per *Hill*[h])
'diversion of resources'	if to find a duty of care would divert D's manpower, money and staff resources away from frontline services into reviews of old cases or to defending litigation, that may preclude a duty (per *Hill*[i])

[a] [1995] 2 AC 633 (HL) 663 (Sir Thomas Bingham MR), and also 749 (Lord Browne-Wilkinson).
[b] [2002] 1 AC 615 (HL) 727 (Lord Hutton), citing: *Arenson v Arenson* [1977] AC 405 (HL) 419 (Lord Simon).
[c] [2000] 2 AC 59 (HL) 82 (Lord Steyn).
[d] [1999] UKHL 50, [2000] 2 AC 59, 82 (Lord Steyn).
[e] [2003] UKHL 52, [2004] AC 309, [14] (Lord Nicholls).
[f] [2008] EWCA Civ 5, [2008] 1 WLR 2207, [47] (Waller LJ).
[g] [1989] AC 53 (HL) 65 (Lord Templeman).
[h] *ibid*, 64 (Lord Keith).
[i] *ibid*.

'the no-need' policy reason	a duty of care may not be warranted, if it is unnecessary to afford C a remedy via negligence (i.e., if C has other forms of redress available, or there are other ways for making D accountable, e.g., public law remedies in respect of exercise of statutory powers; health departments subject to ministerial oversight; health workers subject to departmental disciplinary regimes; a criminal injuries compensation scheme; or complaints to an Ombudsman). Obversely, if D has other protections available to him, even where he is potentially liable in negligence, then that may favour a duty of care being imposed (per *Harris v Evans*[j])
'the insurability factor'	which of C or D could, and should, have insured himself against the loss suffered? Is the loss one against which C ought to have insured himself? If so, then the loss does (or should) fall upon the C's insurer, and not on D (*Marc Rich & Co AG v Bishop Rock Marine Co Ltd*[k]). The availability of insurance, both to C against the risk of injury, or to D against the risk of legal liability, is a divisive issue, as to whether or not it is potentially relevant (see text below)
'conflict of duties'	would D's duty to C require him to put C's interests above those of another party to whom he owes a duty of care? Any conflict of duties (actual or potential) will preclude a duty to C. On the other hand, if what is required of D to discharge any duty to C would *also* discharge his duty to the other party, then the duties are coincident, no conflict arises, and a duty may be upheld (*Capital and Counties plc v Hampshire CC*[l])
'the indeterminate liability problem'	if the losses sustained by C were very large, and if the time period over which losses were sustained was lengthy, and if the numbers of Cs could be very large, then the prospect of exposing D to indeterminate liability may preclude a duty of care (per *Ultramares Corp v Touche*,[m] who described the 'three indeterminates' as: 'a liability in an indeterminate amount for an indeterminate time to an indeterminate class', and was cited with approval in *Caparo Industries plc v Dickman*[n]). This tends to arise more frequently in cases of pure economic and pure psychiatric loss than in cases of personal injury or property damage. However, the mere prospect of indeterminate liability does not, of itself, preclude a duty of care from arising (as, e.g., in the context of consumers of a product, per *Wattleworth v Goodwood Road Racing Co Ltd*[o])

[j] [1998] EWCA Civ 709, [1998] 1 WLR 1285.
[k] [1996] 1 AC 211 (HL).
[l] [1997] QB 1004 (CA) 1036.
[m] 255 NY 170, 179 (1941) (Cardozo J).
[n] [1990] 2 AC 605 (HL) 621–22.
[o] [2004] EWHC 140 (QB) [122] (Davis J).

'the law's preference for personal injury'	if C is claiming only for economic loss, and not for personal injury, any duty to avoid such economic loss is more likely to be precluded by policy, personal injury being considered more worthy of compensation. Conversely, the law will more readily recognise a duty of care where physical harm has been inflicted upon C (per *Caparo*; and *Vowles v Evans*[p])
'a matter for the ballot box, or for Parliament'	if D's liability is better decided by elected parliamentarians, then the court should not usurp that democratic function (per *Hill*,[q] and *Home Office v Dorset Yacht Co Ltd*[r])
the 'what would it achieve?' factor	if to impose a duty of care on D would neither enhance the standard of care expected of D nor provide the general public with any greater confidence in D's activities, that may count against a duty (per *Hill*[s] – '[t]he court would have to decide whether an inspector is to be condemned for failing to display the acumen of Sherlock Holmes and whether a constable is to be condemned for being as obtuse as Dr Watson ... But that finding will not help anybody or punish anybody')
'the incalculables problem'	why should D be the subject of a duty of care, when C obtained benefits, resulting from D's breach, which are incalculable/unquantifiable/immeasurable? Those incalculables may count against a duty being imposed on D (per *McFarlane*[t])
'treating Ds alike'	if imposing a duty of care upon D would 'bring D into line' with other professions/similarly-situated Ds, that is a factor in favour of a duty (per *Arthur JS Hall & Co v Simons*[u])
'the-protection-of-the-public' argument	the purpose of negligence law is, in part, to set standards of D's behaviour for the public's benefit. Hence, if to impose a duty of care would 'weed out the bad eggs' amongst the profession/trade of which D is a member; or would otherwise fill a gap in redress for C, that may count in favour of a duty (per *Arthur JS Hall v Simons*[v])
'compromise of D's liberty/altruistic motives'	if to impose a duty of care on D would compromise D's individual liberty to act without positively hurting others; would seek to elevate an altruistic/moral motive to a legal duty; and/or would expose D to liability for acting/not acting, when others in the 'same boat' may not be sued in negligence, then that may militate against a duty (per *Stovin v Wise*[w])

[p] [2003] EWCA Civ 318.
[q] [1989] AC 53 (HL).
[r] [1970] AC 1004 (HL) 1026–27.
[s] [1989] AC 53 (HL) 64 (Lord Templeman).
[t] [2000] 2 AC 59 (HL) 111.
[u] [2002] 1 AC 615 (HL) 672.
[v] *ibid*, 729.
[w] [1996] AC 923 (HL).

'battle conditions'	where D must make difficult decisions with little or no time for considered thought, which decisions can expose C to physical injury, then it may be inappropriate to impose a duty of care, given that the fear of a negligence suit may compromise D's ability to make those critical decisions (per *Mulcahy v MOD*[x])
'subordination of the individual to the wider public good'	where C's ability to sue for compensation must be subordinated to a wider public or collective good, where D has acted as the executive arm of government (per *Bici v MOD*[y]) or in a quasi-state role (per *Marc Rich v Bishop Marine*[z]), that may count against a duty
'a lacuna in remedy'	if there is no lacuna in the law (i.e., no gap in compensation) that requires filling by imposing liability on D towards C, the courts will not fill it. But if there is a lacuna, in that C lacks a remedy against anyone other than D, then finding a duty in C's favour may be fair and just (per *Perrett v Collins*[aa])
'the disproportionate problem'	no duty will be imposed if it would have a punitive element, i.e., that to impose a duty 'might result in a burden of liability on [D] to so many people which was disproportionate to their tortious conduct' (per *McFarlane v Tayside Health Board*[bb])

[x] [1996] EWCA Civ 1323, [1996] QB 732.
[y] [2004] EWHC 786 (QB).
[z] [1996] AC 211 (HL).
[aa] [1999] PNLR 77 (CA) 90–91.
[bb] [2000] 2 AC 59 (HL) 96.

These various policy factors are considered, as and where appropriate, in the discussion which follows. Other 'one-off' policy factors have also arisen in specific scenarios, also discussed below.

Obviously, the **huge** array of factors gives an indication as to why the 'unruly horse' of policy has been hard to tether. It is 'an important but amorphous concept which the courts must keep within its proper limits' (per *Proactive Sports Management Ltd v Rooney*[108]). Certainly, English courts have had **ample** grounds upon which to say that any duty towards C would **not** be 'fair, just and reasonable'.

§2.14 Wherever policy reasons consistently dictate against a duty of care being imposed – with respect to a particular type of D, or a particular type of scenario – that effectively creates an immunity for D in negligence. That immunity must be justifiable, in light of C's right of access to the court, which is preserved both at common law and under Art 6(1) of the ECHR.

Immunities which D enjoys from suit in negligence have long caused concern at common law, because of the compromise of the access to justice which any such immunity entails.

Since the implementation of the Human Rights Act 1998, C's right of access to the court is enshrined in Art 6(1) of the ECHR. In *Golder v UK*, the European Court of Human Rights reiterated

[108] [2011] EWCA Civ 1444, [53].

that, '[t]he principle whereby a civil claim must be capable of being submitted to a judge ranks as one of the universally "recognised" fundamental principles of law; the same is true of the principle of international law which forbids the denial of justice. Article 6(1) must be read in the light of these principles'.[109] The Art 6 right is not absolute, but 'may be subject to limitations', brought about by either the state legislature or by the court (per *Fayed v UK*[110]). Any limitation, though, will only be justifiable if it is designed to pursue a legitimate aim, and is proportionate. If the restriction which the immunity imposes on C's right to access to justice is disproportionate to the public policy aims sought to be achieved by the immunity, then it will be incompatible with Art 6(1). Some categories of Ds, and scenarios, considered in this section, have inevitably entailed some very close judicial scrutiny, as to whether the policy reasons can withstand an Art 6 challenge.

Furthermore, as a matter of conceptual clarity – in some scenarios below, courts have consistently described D as having 'an immunity', whilst others have (more correctly) discussed the absence of liability as being attributable to no duty of care being owed by D. In *Jones v Kaney*[111] (which concerned the duty of care of an expert to the client who retained him), the Supreme Court internally divided. Lord Dyson suggested that reference to 'immunities' was outmoded, because the principle of immunity arose prior to the formation of the modern law of negligence – whilst Lord Collins remarked that it may not matter which terminology is used, '[b]ut it would be preferable to treat it as an immunity, to emphasise the strong element of policy involved'. In modern jurisprudence, however, an 'absence of a duty of care' is surely preferable. Any so-called 'immunity' conferred upon a particular type of D is only based on *policy grounds* which preclude a duty from arising, under *Caparo's* third limb. Furthermore, since the ECHR's implementation, appellate courts dislike speaking of 'blanket immunities', as they can tend to create an erroneous impression to the Strasbourg courts. Typical of this is Lord Steyn's comment, in *Brooks v MPC*,[112] that 'it would be best' for police duties of care to be 'reformulated in terms of the absence of a duty of care, rather than a blanket immunity'.

§2.15 English law is unsettled as to whether the (non)availability of insurance either to C (against the risk of injury) or to D (against the risk of legal liability) is a relevant policy factor governing a duty of care.

Pragmatically speaking, the law of negligence is about allocating losses among various parties – and if C suffers some injury as a result of D's negligence, then if a court considers that insurance for such liabilities 'naturally lie' with C rather than with D, that may be a policy reason for holding that it would not be fair, just and reasonable to impose a duty of care on D.

Some appellate authorities certainly take the view that, regardless of where the risk should lie, insofar as insurance availability or actual cover is concerned, that is **not** legally relevant. According to *Watson v British Boxing Board of Control Ltd*,[113] the argument that no duty of care should be imposed on a non-profit-making organisation (i.e., the British Boxing Board) because it did not carry insurance could not succeed, because '[c]onsiderations of insurance are not relevant [to the duty of care issue]'. Lord Phillips MR followed Buxton LJ's earlier view in *Perrett v Collins*[114] in that regard.

---

[109] (1975) 1 EHRR 524, 535–36, [35].   [110] (1994) 18 EHRR 393, 429–30, [65].
[111] [2011] UKSC 13, [2011] 2 AC 398, with quotes in text at, respectively, [111] and [73].
[112] [2005] UKHL 24, [2005] 1 WLR 1495, [27].   [113] [2001] QB 1134 (CA) [89].   [114] [1999] PNLR 77 (CA).

On the other hand, a differently-constituted Court of Appeal, in *Vowles v Evans*,[115] stated that the availability of insurance 'could bear on the policy question of whether it is fair, just and reasonable to impose a duty of care on referees'. It was also a key factor in *West Bromwich Albion Football Club Ltd v El-Safty*, so that where the medical mistreatment of employees (such as football player Michael Appleton in that case) caused the employer (the football club, WBA) financial loss, the Court of Appeal considered that insurance against that financial loss 'naturally lies with their employers'.[116] It was not reasonable to expect a surgeon to insure against additional loss of an economic kind, suffered by someone *other than his patient*, which was a factor against any duty of care being owed by the surgeon. Most crucially of all, however, the House of Lords has endorsed the relevance of insurance in a duty of care analysis in *Marc Rich & Co v Bishop Rock Ltd*.[117] A classification society owed no duty of care to a cargo owner (whose goods sank with an unseaworthy ship), partly because of the nature and function of a classification society such as NKK, and in the context of the complex arrangements for sharing, limiting and insuring the risks inherent in carriage of goods by sea.

The particular conundrum of whether an occupier should be liable for the acts or omissions of an independent contractor engaged by that occupier, where that contractor did not carry any public liability insurance, and whether the occupier's ignorance of that fact demonstrated that he had not taken sufficient care in selecting that contractor, is a separate issue which is discussed in Chapter 12.

The particular facts and reasoning of these disparate cases will be considered, as and where relevant, under the particular scenarios below (categories are arranged in roughly alphabetical order).

Children (young)

§2.16 Very young children do not owe a duty of care to those injured or killed by their acts or omissions.

So far as the author's searches can ascertain, there are no English authorities which expressly deal with whether a very young child, D, owes a duty of care to C to whom he causes injury or death, or at what precise age a duty of care does arise on the child's part. However, what case law there is, suggests that no duty of care is owed by very young children.

In *Carmarthenshire CC v Lewis*,[118] in which a very young child's actions caused C's death, Lord Reid said that 'the child was not old enough to be responsible' (albeit that the precise reason for that was not explained). None of the other members of the House explicitly addressed any discussion on the question of when a child would be an appropriate D, but all accepted that this child was not.

In *Carmarthenshire CC v Lewis*, 3-year-old David Morgan wandered out of his classroom at D1's nursery school, whilst the kindergarten teacher, D2, was attending to another child's cut knee. David was dressed up in coat and scarf and was waiting to go for a walk with the teacher and another nursery mate as a treat. Unexpectedly, he left the room, walked through a gate (that should have been locked), and out onto the adjacent main road, and into the path of Mr Lewis, C, who was driving his lorry. C swerved to avoid David, hit a lamppost, and was killed. His widow sued D1 (directly for

---

[115] [2003] EWCA Civ 318, [2003] WLR 1607, [12].   [116] [2007] PIQR P7 (CA) [63] (Rix LJ), [84] (Mummery LJ).
[117] [1996] AC 211 (HL) 239–41 (Lord Steyn, writing for the majority).   [118] [1955] AC 549 (HL) 563 (Lord Reid).

negligence, and vicariously for D2's lack of supervision of David). **Held:** D2 was not negligent; but D1 was liable in systemic negligence for allowing David to 'escape' the confines of the kindergarten.

Moreover, since the 'rise' of the concept of distributive justice (in *McFarlane v Tayside Health Board*[119]), it is surely the case that to consider that a young child owes a duty of care in his conduct is inimical to what the commuter on the London underground would think fair and just. The child lacks judgment, maturity, voluntariness and, of course, insurance.

However, those same commuters would surely consider that, at some (hitherto judicially-unspecified) age, a child should be responsible for the harm inflicted by his acts or omissions. This is reflected in the findings of contributory negligence which have been held against children as young as 12 (e.g., in *Young v Kent CC*[120]). Of course, even if a duty were owed by a very young child, regardless of the points noted above, the standard of care expected of him would likely be suppressed to the point of negligibility (as discussed in Chapter 6).

The law reform corner: Child defendants

Irish LRC: As explained in *Liability in Tort of Minors and the Liability of Parents for Damage Caused by Minors*,[121] the allocation of responsibility in Tort depends upon the concept of voluntariness of D's conduct, which 'involves the direction and control over conduct by a conscious mind'. Canadian authority[122] has held that the actions of a 3-year-old child (in pulling an infant out of a pram and dragging her several metres) were not voluntary. Hence, it is against public policy to impose a duty of care upon a very young child who cannot act voluntarily; but older children, who can understand the consequences of their actions, can owe a duty of care.

Doctors: 'wrongful conception' claims

§2.17   'Wrongful conception' cases arise where a parent, C, seeks compensation for the consequences of a child which was born as a result of a negligently-caused conception. The negligence may occur because C's surgeon, D, failed to take reasonable care when performing a sterilisation operation, failed to advise C to use other contraceptive methods for a period thereafter, or failed to advise C on the risks of pregnancy.

When they arise. This area has been described, in *DN v Greenwich LBC*, as an 'exceptionally difficult area of the law of professional negligence'.[123] The leading authority is a House of Lords' Scottish case.

In *McFarlane v Tayside Health Board*,[124] Mr McFarlane underwent a vasectomy, as he and Mrs McFarlane (both Cs) wished to limit their family to four children. After negligent advice from his consultant surgeon, D, some six months later, that Mr McFarlane was now infertile and his sperm counts were negative, C ceased using other contraceptive measures. Mrs McFarlane then fell pregnant, giving birth to a healthy baby girl, Catherine. C sued jointly for the loss and damage incurred as a consequence of the birth of Catherine. **Held:** negligence proven, with certain damages recoverable.

---

[119] [1999] UKHL 50, [2000] 2 AC 59, 82 (Lord Steyn).   [120] [2005] EWHC 1342 (QB).
[121] (Rep 17, 1985) 2–3.   [122] *Tillander v Gosselin* [1967] 1 OR 203 (HC, Grant J), cited *ibid*, 3.
[123] [2004] EWCA Civ 1659, [77].   [124] [2000] 2 AC 59 (HL), on appeal from CSIH.

It is notable, however, that 'wrongful conception' actions have been extended to encompass **any** situation where, had the parents been carefully advised not to conceive a child (because, say, the mother suffered from a particular condition), they would then have taken steps not to conceive.

> In *Less v Hussain*,[125] Ms Less, C, had a complicated past medical and obstetric history, and together with her partner, sought advice before deciding whether or not to try to conceive and sustain a pregnancy. C consulted gynaecologist, D, who advised that there was 'no reason not to conceive, and that they could go ahead'. C's pregnancy was difficult, and the child (son Luis) was ultimately stillborn. To add to the tragedy, when Luis was taken away and photographs were taken of him at the hospital, he was wearing a dress, because that clothing was all that could be found. **Held:** C was owed a duty of care by D. However, negligence failed, because a causal link between D's breach (the advice) and C's damage (the conception of Luis) was not proven.

In wrongful conception cases, it is the actual conception, and not the birth, which is the injury or legal wrong suffered by C (per *Less v Hussain*[126]). Whatever happens after the point of conception merely goes to the question of damages. There are **three** possible outcomes for the parents, following a wrongful sterilisation (assuming that the mother, C, remains alive): the baby may be lost during pregnancy (i.e., stillborn, as in *Less*); the child may be born healthy; or the child may be born disabled.

Although healthcare practitioner D owes the parental C a duty of care to treat/sterilise/advise that parent carefully – wrongful conception is always a *parental* claim – the extent, or scope, of D's duty is limited, in that not **all** damages suffered by the parent/s will be recoverable. Although this question is perhaps more relevant to the 'scope of the duty', and hence, to the question of remoteness-of-damage (that was certainly Lord Hope's view in *McFarlane*), the majority in *McFarlane* held that it was not 'fair, just and reasonable' to impose a duty on D to avoid all the damages which the parental C may suffer in these circumstances. Hence, policy was invoked to limit the ambit of the undoubted duty of care which D owes to C in such a distinct and recognisable category as doctor–patient.

§2.18   D owes a duty of care to both his patient, C, who was negligently sterilised or who relied upon his negligent advice, and (according to dicta) to the *existing* sexual partner of C. However, C cannot recover damages for the costs of raising a child who was conceived and born subsequent to the failed sterilisation – except where the child is disabled, whereupon the costs associated specifically with the child's disability can be recovered.

A healthy child. In *McFarlane*, Lord Slynn framed the physical damage as 'the physical effects of the pregnancy and birth', and that the costs of raising and maintaining a healthy child were 'consequential [economic] responsibilities' resulting from that physical damage.[127] All members of the House of Lords unanimously held that the parental C is **unable** to recover those costs of raising and maintaining a healthy child, conceived and born following a failed sterilisation – as it is not fair, just or reasonable to impose liability for them on the negligent healthcare practitioner, D. Interestingly, prior to *McFarlane*, there was authority each way: in *Udale v*

---

[125] [2012] EWHC 3513 (QB).   [126] [2012] EWHC 3513 (QB) [168]–[169].

[127] [2000] 2 AC 59 (HL) 67 (noting that, at first instance, the Lord Ordinary had held that C's pregnancy 'could not be equiparated with a physical injury').

were attributed to that parent; or perhaps because the father had deliberately withdrawn from any involvement in the child's upbringing.

In other cases in which one or other of the parents has undergone a failed, negligently-performed, sterilisation, both parents have brought the action and recovered damages in a joint claim (e.g., *Thake v Maurice*[155] and *McFarlane*[156]). In *McFarlane*, none of the House discussed whether, and why, the surgeon owed Mrs McFarlane (the non-patient) a duty of care – this appears to have been assumed. Clearly the damages for the pain, suffering and inconvenience of pregnancy and childbirth were Mrs McFarlane's alone (and even as a non-patient, the majority held that she was entitled to recover these). Subsequently, the New South Wales Supreme Court remarked, in *McDonald v Sydney South West Area Health Service*, that the *McFarlane* decision 'does not assist on the issue of whether the duty of care of the doctor extends to the partner of his patient'.[157]

However, there is some English dicta support for the proposition that the biological parent of the child born of a failed sterilisation – but who was not the sterilised parent – can claim damages for economic injury from D who performed the operation. For example, in *Islington LBC v UCL London Hosp NHS Trust*, the Court of Appeal remarked, just because the surgeon's advisory letter was addressed to Mr McFarlane alone, did not mean that there was no duty to Mrs McFarlane.[158] Also, in *Parkinson*, where Mrs Parkinson was the patient, there was no claim for damages by Mr Parkinson against the surgeon, and the issue of his legal status did not arise on the facts, but Hale LJ commented that the proximity between D as surgeon, and his patient's sexual partner, was 'quite close', and that where any claim was made by a father 'who not only has, but meets, his parental responsibility to care for the child', then her 'tentative view' was that the father should have a potential claim against D too.[159] Interestingly, however, the Irish High Court was not prepared to award the father (who was the non-patient) any damages in *Ahern v Moore*, noting that Hale LJ's comment was 'obiter and conditional', and that there was 'no legal rule that would permit [the court] to award him damages'.[160]

In that light, the legal status of the biological parent of a child born of a wrongful conception to sue for damages against D, who performed the sterilisation operation on his or her partner, is not entirely settled.

§2.19   By contrast, no English authority supports a duty of care on D's part, to avoid *any* of the losses sustained by a future sexual partner of the patient in a wrongful conception action.

Where D negligently performs a sterilisation operation on a patient, and years later, that patient conceives a child with a partner, C, who, at the time of the operation, was not known to the patient, much less to D, then D will **not** be in a sufficiently proximate relationship with that future sexual partner, C. It follows that C will be unable to recover **any** costs associated with the birth (and the child-rearing costs would not be recoverable in any event, since *McFarlane*).

In *Goodwill v British Pregnancy Advisory Service*,[161] Mr MacKinlay, M, underwent a vasectomy operation, and was thereafter advised by the BPAS, D (a charity which arranged and provided for sterilisation operations, and counselling services) of 'permanent sterility'. The operation spontaneously

---

[155] [1986] QB 644 (CA).   [156] [2000] 2 AC 59 (HL).   [157] [2005] NSWSC 924, [64].
[158] [2004] EWHC 1754 (QB) [37].   [159] [2001] EWCA Civ 530, [2002] QB 266, [93].
[160] [2013] IEHC 72, final para.   [161] (1996) 31 BMLR 83 (CA), quote at 91.

reversed, without warning of this being given to M by D. Ms Goodwill, C, subsequently entered into a relationship with M, and relying on what M told her about his prior vasectomy, C stopped using other contraceptive measures. C conceived a child, 3 years after M's operation. C and M then separated, and given her lack of financial means, C sued D for the expenses associated with her daughter's birth, including the costs of raising her. **Held:** D owed no duty of care to C. It was 'manifestly unsustainable'.

Evidently, this verdict was the result of both policy factors under *Caparo's* third limb, and the lack of temporal and relational proximity between C and D which *Caparo's* second limb entails.

Doctors: 'wrongful birth' claims

§2.20 'Wrongful birth' claims arise where a healthcare practitioner, D, failed to exercise reasonable care to diagnose or to detect a condition which, had it been pointed out to the mother, C, would have resulted in C's electing to abort her child which was afflicted with that condition (and which ultimately caused, in her child, physical or mental disabilities, or both). The central tenet of the claim is that, because of the misdiagnosis, D permitted the pregnancy to continue, so that C was deprived of the opportunity to terminate lawfully her pregnancy.

When they arise. A parental C may seek to sue for wrongful birth, where the substance of the suit is that the healthcare practitioner, D, failed to detect an already-existing condition in their child *in utero*. These conditions could comprise, say: Down's Syndrome (as in *Rand v East Dorset HA*[162] and *McLelland v Greater Glasgow Health Board*[163]); spina bifida (as in *Lee v Taunton and Somerset NHS Trust*[164]); the congenital abnormality of Smith Magenis Syndrome which affects chromosome 17 (as in *Conway v Cardiff and Vale NHS Trust*[165]); foetal disabilities arising from the mother's contraction of rubella during pregnancy (as in *Hardman v Amin*[166]); and muscular dystrophy, which genetic testing of the X-linked recessive gene would have revealed (as in *Anderson v Forth Valley Health Board*[167]). C's claim is that, had these conditions been identified, they would have led to the mother's undertaking a lawful abortion of the foetus. This (hereafter, 'Type 1' wrongful birth) is the most common type of wrongful birth suit.

> In *Rand v East Dorset HA*,[168] Mrs and Mr Rand, C, were the parents of K, a child born with Down's Syndrome. While Mrs Rand was pregnant with K, her treating doctors, D, failed to inform her of the results of a routine scan which indicated that C was likely to give birth to a child suffering from Down's Syndrome. Had C been informed of that, she would have elected to abort K. D conceded negligence, but disputed the heads of damages to which C was entitled. **Held:** C recovered £118,746 for the claim. Mr Rand recovered general damages of £5,000 separately, to reflect 'the true nature of the wrong done to the Rands, who have been deeply affected in their private lives by having to devote more time to the care and upbringing of K than the care and upbringing of a healthy child would have involved'. In *Lee v Taunton & Somerset NHS Trust*,[169] both Mr and Mrs Lee, C, suffered from epilepsy, for which they each had to take anti-convulsant medication, including

---

[162] [2000] Lloyd's Rep Med 181 (QB)   [163] 2001 SLT 446 (SCIH).
[164] [2001] Fam Law 103, [2001] 1 FLR 419.   [165] [2004] EWHC 1841.
[166] [2000] Lloyd's Rep Med 498 (QB). Also: *Salih v Enfield HA* [1991] 3 All ER 400 (CA) (congenital rubella).
[167] 1998 SLT 588 (CSOH).   [168] (2000) 56 BMLR 39 (QB), quote at 69 (Newman J).
[169] [2001] 1 FLR 419 (QB).

As in *McFarlane's* wrongful conception suit, the ordinary costs of raising the child cannot be recovered in a wrongful birth suit. This was made plain in *Groom v Selby*, where the Court of Appeal was clearly discussing *wrongful birth* when it analogised *Parkinson*, and said: 'as in *Parkinson*, an award of compensation which is limited to the special upbringing associated with rearing a child with a serious disability would be fair, just and reasonable'.[181] In that light, the views of Toulson J in *Lee v Taunton and Somerset NHS Trust* – although coming to the same 'bottom line' – were quite different, and must now be considered to have been overruled. Toulson J suggested that the **whole** costs of raising the disabled child should be recoverable ('I cannot see a barrier to Mrs Lee recovering the full costs of [George's] maintenance'), but subject to an off-setting exercise ('she was wanting to bear a healthy child. If, following a termination of her pregnancy with George, she had continued with her attempts and had been successful, she would have incurred the costs of bringing up a healthy child in any event'). *Lee* was referred to in *Groom v Selby*, but this reasoning was not referred to. In any event, *Groom* stands for the proposition that only the **extra** costs associated with the raising of the disabled child are recoverable in a wrongful birth suit.

- general damages – including for: pain and suffering relating to the pregnancy and birth – these would not have occurred, had an abortion been undertaken (per *Rand v East Dorset HA*[182]); for shock and distress upon discovering the birth of a disabled child (although *Hardman v Amin* indicated that the award of damages under this head 'would be modest'[183]); and for loss of amenity, *viz*, the additional strain resulting from the care of a disabled child, as compared with a healthy child (per *Rand*);

- special damages, of the type recoverable in wrongful conception (per *McFarlane*).

  In *FP v Taunton and Somerset NHS Trust*,[184] FP, C, brought a wrongful birth claim, for the birth of her very disabled son, RP. C sought an interim payment, plus a stay of a trial of the action whilst RP's prognosis (especially life expectancy) remained uncertain. **Held:** an interim payment of £1.2m was made. Damages were awardable to C for a period up to RP's life expectancy of 20–30 years, plus special damages including: therapies; education; mobility aids and equipment; specially-adapted seating and furniture, beds and accessories, bathing aids; adapted accommodation requirements; computers and electronic equipment; and extra burdens associated with travel, holidays, and leisure pursuits.

§2.21   English law is presently unsettled as to whether a father may bring a wrongful birth suit against D who did not detect the congenital disability or incompatibility, separately from the suit commenced by the mother.

Which parent/s may claim? Given that wrongful birth scenarios are associated with a misdiagnosis of the disabled foetus, the mother is the obvious claimant. It will be the mother who ought to have been advised of any disability *in utero* that would have prompted her election to abort.

At times, the mother has been the sole claimant (e.g., in *Hardman v Amin*, where the mother, C, was exposed to rubella during her pregnancy and which went undiagnosed, her husband

---

[181] [2001] EWCA Civ 1522, [24] (Brooke LJ).   [182] (2000) 56 BMLR 39 (QB) 43, 58, 68.
[183] [2000] Lloyd's Rep Med 498 (QB) [10].   [184] [2011] EWHC 3380 (QB).

was closely involved in the care of their disabled son, but not a party to the litigation). In such cases, it may be that the damages incurred by the father have been recovered by the mother, who then held the sum recovered on trust for the father (a suggested explanation of such cases in *Schumann v Wasbrough*[185]).

Occasionally in wrongful birth claims, the father has brought a **joint** claim with the mother, in respect of the negligent failure to provide advice that would have resulted in the termination of the pregnancy, but with no judicial discussion as to the status of the father in the law suit (as in, e.g., *Salih v Enfield HA*,[186] and in the Scottish case of *Anderson v Forth Valley Health Board*,[187] where both parents were joint claimants). According to Laws LJ in *Whitehead v Searle*, '[i]n some of the wrongful birth cases, it seems to have been assumed, without argument, that the father as well as the mother may claim. The possibility is certainly not ruled out in the learning. It is clear ... that the law on the topic is still developing'.[188] In the Scottish case of *McLelland v Greater Glasgow Health Board*[189] too, the father recovered some damages in his own right in a wrongful birth suit – but without any detailed discussion of why D owed the father a duty of care.

Quite what status the father has, to bring a wrongful birth claim, is presently uncertain in English law – but the question of whether or not an independent claim for wrongful birth can be brought by the biological father of the disabled child may become very important where, *viz*, the financial burdens become the father's alone to bear. This may arise where the mother commits suicide and the father takes over the care of the disabled child (as in *Whitehead v Searle* itself); where the mother dies in childbirth and the father takes on the burden of raising the child (a hypothetical example given in *Whitehead*[190]); or where the father provided gratuitous care to the disabled child which would give rise to a claim for damages on the father's part (as in *Schumann v Wasbrough*). In *Whitehead*, Rix LJ said that there was a 'potentially difficult but realistically arguable claim by [the father] in his own right, once he had shouldered parental responsibility, for the extra costs of [the child's] care, over and above those costs which would have been involved in a normal birth'.[191] Unfortunately, the other two members of the Court of Appeal did not comment on the issue. Subsequently, in *Schumann v Wasbrough*, Dingemans J reiterated that whether the father had any personal action against a healthcare practitioner for the wrongful birth is 'not settled in English law'.[192]

Emergency services: fire brigade and coastal rescue services

§2.22   The emergency services of fire brigade and coastguard owe no duty of care to members of the general public to turn up to an emergency when summoned to do so. Exceptionally, a duty of care is owed where the rescue/protective services, through their own negligence, create the danger which caused C's injury or harm by some positive act of misfeasance (i.e., made the situation worse).

The distinction drawn in the principle above is entirely attributable to the different functions which the various emergency services perform. (For discussion about the legal principles applicable to the duty of care, if any, owed by the *police*, readers are referred to the separate section, 'Police', below.)

---

[185] [2013] EWHC 3730 (QB) [61].   [186] [1991] 3 All ER 400 (CA).   [187] 1998 SLT 588 (CSOH).
[188] [2008] EWCA Civ 285, [50] (also known as *Whitehead v Hibbert Pownall & Newton (a firm)*).
[189] 2001 SLT 446 (SCIH).   [190] [2008] EWCA Civ 285, [63].
[191] *ibid*, [67].   [192] [2013] EWHC 3730 (QB) [61].

Further discussion of the 'making it worse' principle, giving rise to a duty of care, is contained in Chapter 13.

Emergency services: the ambulance service

§2.23   By contrast to the fire brigade and coastal rescue services, the ambulance service generally owes a duty of care to any specific individual who summons the ambulance, and where the ambulance accepts that request to attend.

The ambulance is in a different legal position from rescue services and fire brigade (and the police, discussed below). The ambulance's duty is to assist **specific individuals** who are in need of medical attention (per *Kent v Griffiths*[198]). Where the ambulance is called upon to render emergency services to C and agrees to assist, that agreement induces reliance on C's part, invoking a duty of care. With the ambulance, it is not a matter of 'general reliance' (as there is on the part of property owners and the fire brigade), but rather, of 'specific reliance' – the ambulance is 'dealing with a named individual upon whom the duty becomes focused'.[199]

> In *Kent v Griffiths*, Mrs Griffiths, C, was pregnant, when she suffered a serious asthma attack at home. Her GP was summoned, and assessed that C urgently required hospital treatment. A 999 call was placed by her GP at 4.25 pm, and accepted by the ambulance, D, via its service operator. When no ambulance turned up, there were two follow-up calls made (at 4.38 pm and 4.54 pm), in which the operator again assured that an emergency ambulance was 'on its way'. The ambulance arrived at 5.05 pm, and C arrived at hospital at 5.17 pm. C suffered a respiratory arrest during the journey, and suffered a miscarriage and brain damage as a result of the delay in reaching hospital. The trial judge found that the record prepared by a member of the ambulance crew was deliberately falsified to indicate that the time of arrival at C's home was not 5.05 pm, but 4.47 pm. No satisfactory explanation for the ambulance taking 34 minutes to travel 6.5 miles from its base to C's home was ever given. **Held:** D owed C a duty of care, and negligence proven. No policy reasons precluded a duty of care on D's part here. As no explanation for the delay was given, conflicting resourcing issues was not a relevant consideration.

This case, and its reasoning, is also dealt with in Chapter 13 and later in this chapter, under the 'Assumption of responsibility/reliance' test, given that that is where the focus of the court's reasoning really lay. With respect to policy, however, *Kent v Griffiths* did suggest that, in a different set of circumstances, a duty **may** be precluded for policy reasons (but not in this case).

Policy reasons relevant to ambulance emergency services

- *conflicts of interest/resources:* Where the ambulance service, D, has undertaken to respond to a specific request by C to attend, there *could* feasibly be some conflict between the interests of one caller and the public-at-large (say, where the ambulance had to attend a large-scale incident which injured

---

[198] [2001] QB 36 (CA), with quotes in box locatable at [14], [27], [45]–[49], [51]–[52] (Lord Woolf MR).

[199] *ibid*, [9]. See too: *Aitken v Scottish Ambulance Service* [2011] CSOH 49 (duty of care arguable on ambulance's part where 999 call made).

numerous people), placing conflicting demands on D's resources. Any such conflicts of interest among different individuals would **either** render a duty of care infeasible, or a duty could still be owed when D gave the undertaking to assist, but no *breach* of duty would be found because D's conduct would be reasonable in the circumstances – either way, C's claim would fail. But in the absence of such facts, no policy reasons precluded a duty of care from arising on D's part;

- *corrective justice:* expectations of 'common humanity' and 'a well-informed member of the public' would consider it to be the *right* outcome for a duty of care to be owed by the ambulance in a case like *Kent v Griffiths*;

- *'Bad Samaritan' rule inapplicable:* the policy reasons precluding D from having to assist someone in need did not apply to the ambulance service, as they were not 'volunteers', but rather, paid from the public purse.

Police

§2.24   Unless 'special and exceptional' circumstances apply, a police service, D, in the course of carrying out its functions of investigating, detecting and combatting crime, owes no duty of care to any individual member of the public, C, who suffers physical injury or property damage via the activities of criminals. Even where C is pre-identified to D, as a person in a vulnerable position with respect to actual or criminal activity, no duty of care is owed by D to C.

Known as the '*Hill* core principle', the source of this still-controversial proposition is to be found in the tragic case of Jacqueline Hill, who was the 13th and final murder victim of the 'Yorkshire Ripper'.

> In *Hill v CC of West Yorkshire*,[200] Jacqueline Hill, C, a 20-year-old law student at Leeds University, and the last victim of Peter Sutcliffe (PS), the 'Yorkshire Ripper', was murdered in Leeds in Nov 1980. PS was arrested in Sheffield in Jan 1981, confessed under interrogation, and was eventually convicted of 13 murders and 8 attempted murders from 1969–80, all bearing the same *modus operandi*. C's estate sued the West Yorkshire police service, D, claiming that D had been negligent in investigating the crimes committed by PS, and that if they had exercised reasonable care and followed reasonable lines of enquiry, D would have captured PS much earlier, thus preventing C's murder. (Ms Hill proposed to donate any damages awarded to a charity, but sought to establish that a police force owed a duty to members of the public, re the investigation of crime.) **Held (trial, CA, and HL):** C's claim was struck out. No duty of care was owed by D to C, as the victim of a crime. There was reasonable foreseeability of likely harm to persons such as Ms Hill, if PS were not identified and apprehended promptly – but the requisite proximity between D and C was lacking; plus several policy reasons precluded a duty of care.

The *Hill* principle was affirmed by two more 'milestone' House of Lords' decisions (to adopt the terminology in *An Informer v CC*[201]) – albeit that these further decisions do not lay down any wider principle of immunity from negligence suits than was suggested in *Hill* itself (per *Desmond v CC of Nottinghamshire Police*[202]). In both cases, C's claim was struck out as disclosing no cause of action:

---

[200] [1989] 1 AC 53 (HL).   [201] [2012] EWCA Civ 197, [2013] 2 WLR 694, [87].   [202] [2009] EWHC 2362 (QB) [39].

The *Hill* core principle has manifested in a variety of scenarios, for the police's benefit. In each of the following,[209] the claim was struck out as disclosing no cause of action, as no duty of care was owed:

In *Michael v South Wales Police*,[210] Joanna Michael, C, made a 999 mobile phone call from her home east of Cardiff in the early hours of the morning. An operator with Gwent Police, D1, took the call. C said that her former partner, Cyron Williams (CW), had just found her with another man, had assaulted her, and had taken the man away in his car to drive him home, saying he would return to 'kill' or to 'hit' her (that bit of the 999 call was described as being inaudible). D1's call operator told C that her call would be passed on to South Wales Police, D2, who would want to call her back, and to keep the phone free; and she graded C's call as requiring 'immediate response' (response time: 5 mins). D1's operator passed the details to D2's emergency control room, but did not refer to CW's threat to kill C. The information was relayed to D2's police officers on mobile patrol, but the call was accidentally downgraded in priority (response time: 60 mins). C made a further 999 call 15 mins later, screaming, but that stopped suddenly during the call. D2's officers immediately attended C's premises, and found her stabbed to death. CW was convicted of C's murder. C's estate sued both D1 and D2 in negligence, but lost. Given that a 999 call had been logged, there was an 'investigation into criminal activity' already on foot, thus placing the case squarely within the *Hill* core principle. In *Alexandrou v Oxford*,[211] Socrates Alexandrou, C, occupied retail clothing store, Ziggys, in Birkenhead, in which he had installed a burglar alarm system. When activated, this raised an alarm at the local police station, with a recorded message re the alarm's location. One Sunday night, burglars entered C's store, stole a large quantity of clothing, and trashed the premises. The alarm sounded at 19.23. The police, D, attended, but because of their failure to properly inspect the rear of the shop when the alarm stopped at 21.26 (the burglars destroyed it), the burglary continued undetected. C sued D in negligence for failing to respond adequately to the alarm, but lost. If the police did owe a duty to an occupier of a property protected by a burglar alarm, then D would owe a similar duty to any person who informed them, whether by a 999 call or in some other way, that an actual or suspected crime was being committed against them/their property. This was unrealistic. It was 'unthinkable that the police should be exposed to potential actions for negligence at the suit of every disappointed or dissatisfied maker of a 999 call'. The *Hill* core principle also applied to emergency calls either not answered or answered ineffectually. In *Robinson v West Yorkshire Police*,[212] Mrs Robinson, C, was walking along a busy road in Huddersfield. Mr Williams was dealing in 'Class A' drugs on the opposite footpath. Plainsclothes police officers, D, arrested Mr Williams in the street, and in the ensuing struggle and melee, their momentum caused them to crash into C, who was injured. C sued D for arresting Mr Williams negligently, but lost. The act of arresting criminals was part of the 'core functions' of D and fell within the *Hill* core principle. It also had an 'obvious public interest', so that the risk of injury to passers-by like C was trumped by the risk to public as a whole if drug dealers were permitted to operate on the street. In *Osman v Ferguson*,[213] schoolteacher Paul Paget-Lewis (PL) formed an unhealthy attachment to a male pupil, Ahmet Osman, C, 15. PL made unfounded accusations of a sexual nature against C (accusing C of having a sexual relationship with a school friend). PL changed his name by deed poll to Osman; damaged and defaced the family's property and car, slashing tyres, spreading excrement over the Osman property, removing light bulbs and supergluing their locks, etc. PL also followed the

---

[209] See too: *CLG v CC of Merseyside Police* [2015] EWCA Civ 836, [22] (serving a witness summons, etc, part of the core functions of the police).

[210] [2015] UKSC 2, [2015] 2 WLR 343 (a 5:2 majority decision), affirming: [2012] EWCA Civ 981.

[211] [1993] 4 All ER 328 (CA) 334 (Slade LJ).

[212] [2014] EWCA Civ 15, [47].   [213] [1993] 4 All ER 344 (CA).

family when they were going about their daily business, causing serious traffic incidents. The police, D, were well aware of the harassment and interviewed PL, who said that the loss of his job was distressing, and he was concerned about doing something criminally insane. Almost a year after the campaign of harassment began, PL followed C and his family to their flat, shot and severely injured C, and killed C's father, Ali Osman. C's action against D for negligence was struck out.

Where C is a pre-identified victim. This scenario clearly did not arise in *Hill*, as Jacqueline Hill was not a pre-identified victim (or nor even a member of a small ascertainable class). However, in *Van Colle/Smith*, *Michael* and *Osman*, the dangerous predicament in which those Cs found themselves was clearly well known to the police – and yet, still no duty of care arose, for the reasons of policy articulated in *Hill*. Hence, even where C is a particular member of the public whose vulnerability or exposure to risk is well known to the police, the *Hill* principle will apply.

In *Osman*, there was an 'arguable case' (said the Court of Appeal[214]) that 'a very close degree of proximity amounting to a special relationship' between the Osman family and the police, D, was established, given the regular and long-standing dealings between the family and D. Yet, it was against policy to impose a duty of care because *Hill* applied, even in the case of these pre-identified victims.

However, whether the *Hill* principle **should** apply, in the case of a pre-identified victim who is at risk from criminal activity, has proven to be very controversial. In *Smith*, Lord Bingham CJ dissented,[215] and considered that a duty of care should be owed by the police to C in that case, pursuant to the so-called 'liability principle', defined as follows: 'where C, a member of the public, provides police officer D with credible evidence that a third party (whose identity and whereabouts are known) presents a specific and imminent threat to his life or physical safety, then D owes C a duty to take reasonable steps to assess such threat and, if appropriate, to take reasonable steps to prevent the threat from being carried out'. However, the *Smith* majority disagreed that any such principle should apply in English law.[216] More recently, the Supreme Court (by majority) again rejected Lord Bingham's liability principle, in *Michael v South Wales Police*,[217] in large part drawing upon the majority's reasoning in *Smith* (whereas Lord Kerr, dissenting in *Michael*,[218] endorsed a modified 'liability principle' which closely resembled Lord Bingham CJ's in *Smith*). Their contrasting views are set out in the Table below:

For and against: The 'liability principle'	
Against (per the majorities in *Smith* and in *Michael*)	**For (per the dissenters in *Smith* and in *Michael*)**
• the liability principle may fit well with the facts of *Smith*, but in other cases it could be difficult to apply. The threat may not be so credible or as obvious, or the information may come to the police D via someone other than C (*Smith*);	• in *Smith*, C fulfilled the principle because his relationship with D was one of close proximity, based on direct, face-to-face meetings;

---

[214] *ibid*, 350 (by majority, Beldam LJ reserving the question).
[215] [2009] AC 225 (HL) [44], with quote in Table at [60].
[216] *ibid*, [77] (Lord Hope), [100] (Lord Phillips), [109] (Lord Carswell), [129] (Lord Brown).
[217] [2015] UKSC 2, [117]–[130] (Lord Toulson, with whom Lords Neuberger, Mance, Reed and Hodge, agreed).
[218] *ibid*, [162]–[172], quote at [168]. Lady Hale agreed (at [197]–[198]).

- it is for D to judge whether the threat is credible and imminent. This would be difficult for a judge to decide, with all of the attendant difficulties and uncertainties of tracking back through an investigation which *Hill* articulated (*Smith*);
- the liability principle did not deal with several *Hill* policy reasons which apply, even if C was a pre-identified victim, e.g., defensive policing, the diversion of resources (*Smith*);
- why should the liability principle be limited to threats to life or to physical safety? Why not threats to property too? Where should its limits properly be set? (*Smith*);
- the court could not assume, 'on the basis of intuition', that the liability principle would either reduce domestic violence or improve police investigations (*Michael*);
- if there should be compensation of pre-identified victims of crime where D failed to prevent violence to C, then the criminal injuries compensation fund, and redress under Arts 2, 3 or 8 of the ECHR, may be available. Beyond that, it was for Parliament to legislate for such a scheme, and not for the common law to plug the gap (*Michael*).

- in *Smith*, D assumed responsibility to C by visiting him, assuring him that investigations were progressing, and inviting C to call 999 if concerned;
- C approached 'a professional force having a special skill in the assessment of criminal risk and the investigation of crime, [and] whose main public function is to maintain the Queen's peace, prevent crime and apprehend criminals' (*Smith*);
- public policy favoured a duty of care being owed by D to take reasonable steps to assess the threat to C and, if appropriate, take reasonable steps to prevent the harm from arising;
- the requisite proximity should not only arise where there was an assumption of responsibility (for that could depend upon the form of words used in the communications between C and the police, sometimes in a highly-stressful scenario). Rather, it should be determined by D's knowledge of 'an imminent threat to a particular individual, and that they have the means of preventing that threat and protecting the individual concerned' (Lord Kerr).

In various decisions since, victims of crime have attempted to distinguish *Hill*, but largely without success. In any circumstance where the police are investigating or combatting alleged criminal activity, and for any police activity which has, as its aim, the protection of the public, the case will fall within the *Hill* principle. Additionally, any attempt to invoke the 'liability principle' – as prevailing over the *Hill* principle – seems firmly closed to a victim of crime now, in light of *Michael* and *Smith*.

No blanket immunity. It is important to reiterate that the police do **not** enjoy a 'blanket immunity' from suits, whether in tort generally or in negligence specifically. In fact, in *Hill* itself, **none** of the Law Lords stated that they were proposing a blanket immunity for the police from suits in negligence.

Nevertheless, the decision in *Osman v Ferguson*[219] became the trigger for a marked dispute between the domestic courts and the European Court of Human Rights, on this very point. The Osman family – having failed in their suit against the police in the English Court of Appeal – took their case to the European Court of Human Rights, in *Osman v UK*,[220] alleging violations by the State of its obligations under Arts 2, 6, 8 and 13 of the ECHR. The European

---

[219] [1993] 4 All ER 344 (CA).   [220] [1998] ECHR 101, (2000) 29 EHRR 245, [149]–[151].

Court disapproved of what it termed an 'exclusionary rule' which the House of Lords had laid down in *Hill*, and considered that the principle gave the police a 'blanket immunity' in respect of their policy and operational decisions. This type of reasoning – 'without further enquiry into the existence of competing public-interest considerations' – amounted to an 'unjustifiable restriction' on the Osmans' claims to have the merits of their claim against the police determined, as a 'deserving case'. Hence, to the extent that *Hill* represented an immunity upon any prosecution of the police in negligence, the European Court held that it could not withstand Art 6 of the ECHR.

However, that critique adopted by the European Court was later toned down in *Z v UK*[221] (which concerned the liability of local authorities for alleged failures in the performance of their functions regarding children in care, discussed in Chapter 13). In *Z*, the European Court admitted that it had misunderstood the precise ambit and source of the *Hill* immunity. Specifically, its reasoning in *Osman* 'was based on an understanding of the [English] law of negligence which has to be reviewed, in light of the clarifications subsequently made by the domestic courts, and notably the House of Lords ... the law of negligence, as developed in the domestic courts since the case of *Caparo* ... include fair, just and reasonable criterion as an intrinsic element of the duty of care, and that the ruling of law concerning that element in this case does not disclose the operation of an immunity'. Domestically, this somewhat embarrassing retreat by the European Court not only entrenched the *Hill* principle in English jurisprudence, but also led to statements of the type of Lord Steyn's in *Brooks*, that it 'would be best for the principle in *Hill* to be reformulated in terms of the absence of a duty of care, rather than a blanket immunity'.[222]

There was some indication, after *Z v UK*, that English courts might become more reluctant to strike out claims by C against the police, arising out investigations of alleged criminal activity (as, e.g., in *Commr of Police v Reilly*[223]). However, that reluctance has not manifested since. Appellate courts have not hesitated to strike out claims against the police (as in, e.g., *Smith*, *Michael*, and *Vicario v Commr of Police*[224]), if the *Hill* principle applied.

Exceptional circumstances where a duty will be owed. The House of Lords, in both *Brooks* and *Van Colle/Smith*, acknowledged that 'exceptional cases on the margins of the *Hill* principle' will entail a duty of care being owed by the police to C. But what are these exceptional categories, which fall outside the *Hill* core principle? Several judgments in *Brooks* and *Smith/Van Colle* unhelpfully make 'broad unspecified references to potential exceptions' (as the Northern Ireland Queen's Bench put it in *Rush v Police Service of Northern Ireland*[225]), without defining what they may be.[226]

However, a more explicit attempt to articulate the exceptional categories was usefully made by Arden LJ in *An Informer v CC*[227] and by Lord Brown in *Smith/Van Colle*.[228] Referring to these (and adding a couple of others which also emerge from an analysis of the case law):

i. Where the police themselves created dangerous situations for C. Rarely will the police proactively put members of the public in danger – but where that occurs, the activity will lie outside the *Hill* principle. In each of the following, a duty of care was owed, and negligence was proven

---

[221] (2002) 34 EHRR 3, [100]. [222] [2005] UKHL 24, [2005] 1 WLR 1495, [27]. [223] [2008] EWHC 2217 (QB). [224] [2007] EWCA Civ 1361. [225] [2011] NIQB 28, [24].

[226] See, e.g. *Smith/Van Colle*: 'there might be exceptional cases where liability must be imposed. ... [but] I should prefer to leave the ambit of such exceptions undefined at present': [2008] UKHL 50, [109] (Lord Carswell).

[227] [2012] EWCA Civ 197, [2013] 2 WLR 694, [94]–[96] (Lady Justice Arden). [228] [2009] 1 AC 225 (HL) [135].

(although contrast *Robinson v West Yorkshire*,[229] considered previously, where a member of the public could not prove this exception):

> In *Rigby v CC of Northamptonshire*,[230] C's gun shop was at risk from a lunatic, and the police, D, came to deal with the situation. D fired a canister of capsicum spray gas into the shop to flush out the suspect, knowing that it could cause a high risk of fire, but without ensuring that the fire engine which had previously been available was there to put out any fire that resulted. In *Gibson v Orr*,[231] the police left the scene of an unsafe bridge which had collapsed as a result of flooding, without leaving any cones or barriers or warning signs. C's car went onto the bridge and fell into the river, causing the death of two occupants and severely injuring the third.

ii. **Assuming a specific responsibility.** The police owe a duty of care to C where they have assumed specific responsibility for C's safety, and have knowledge of C's identity and vulnerability, and where there is a reciprocal reliance by C. This will occur rarely, but as the Supreme Court affirmed in *Michael v South Wales Police*,[232] such cases lie outside the ambit of the *Hill* principle altogether.

> Examples include: where the police, D, assume a responsibility for the *physical* safety and well-being of police informants, particularly from threats by those being informed upon (per *Swinney v CC of Northumbria Police Force*,[233] and *An Informer v CC*,[234] although in the latter case, D owed C no duty to protect his *economic* interests); where C agreed with the CPS lawyer that his previous offences would be taken into account and that he would not have to appear on charges of theft, but that agreement was not honoured due to a negligent oversight by the CPS lawyer, and C was arrested when he did not appear on the theft charges (per *Welsh v CC of Merseyside Police*[235]); where D explicitly told a threatened person to do away with bodyguard protection because they would ensure his safety (an example by Lord Brown in *Smith/Van Colle*); and where D set up a sting to catch a criminal in a blackmail or abduction case, putting a participant in the sting at risk of physical injury (an example in *Commr of Police v Reilly*[236]).

Indeed, as the Northern Ireland Queen's Bench pointed out in *Rush*,[237] this exceptional category frequently carries with it public policy reasons in favour of a duty of care being imposed, which must be taken to outweigh the policy reasons in *Hill*. For example, in *Swinney*, the public interest in ensuring the protection of informants, thereby encouraging the solving of crimes, was to be regarded as outweighing the public interest in protecting the police from liability in negligence.

An assumption of responsibility towards those who are particularly vulnerable has also arisen by the police, D, to a prisoner, or to one who has suffered harm from another prisoner's actions.

> In *Kirkham v CC of the Greater Manchester Police*,[238] D knew that prisoner C had self-harmed and had suicidal tendencies, but failed to pass on that information to prison authorities. C then hanged himself whilst on remand in custody. **Held:** a duty was owed to C, and it was breached. In *Orange v CC of West Yorkshire*,[239] D did not know that C presented a suicide risk, merely because he had been

---

[229] [2014] EWCA Civ 15.   [230] [1985] 1 WLR 1242 (CA).
[231] 1999 SC 420 (CSOH), and approved in *Smith/Van Colle*, [53] (Lord Bingham CJ), [79] (Lord Hope).
[232] [2015] UKSC 2, [69]ff.   [233] [1997] QB 464 (CA).   [234] [2012] EWCA Civ 197, [2013] QB 579.
[235] [1993] 1 All ER 692 (CA).   [236] [2008] EWHC 2217 (QB) [16].   [237] [2011] NIQB 28, [19].
[238] [1990] 2 QB 283 (CA).   [239] [2001] EWCA Civ 611, [2002] QB 347, [47].

heavily drinking. C killed himself by hanging himself by his belt, and it was alleged that the belt should have been removed before he was placed into a cell. **Held:** no duty was owed: 'the special and unusual duty is one which is only owed where the [police] authorities know, or ought to know, of a suicide risk in an individual prisoner's case'.

However, in the latest word upon the subject by the Supreme Court majority in *Michael v South Wales Police*,[240] a pre-identified victim of crime is not able to assert that, where the police knew of an imminent threat to C's safety, an assumption of responsibility was undertaken towards him by the police. The decision also places the circumstances of a 999 call, and precisely what phrases were used by C and by a call operator in a highly-stressful and charged atmosphere, 'front and centre', as to whether an assumption of responsibility can be cast by that call (a proposition which Lord Kerr, dissenting, rightly called 'surely unacceptable'[241]).

> In *Michael v South Wales Police*, the fact that the 999 operator of Gwent Police, D1, told C that South Wales Police, D2, would want to call C back, and to keep the line free, did not constitute any exceptional scenario in which the police assumed responsibility for C's safety. This was an 'expectation', and not an 'assurance'. By assuring C that the call would be passed onto D2, D1's call operator did not promise how quickly D2 would respond. The case was distinguished from *Kent v Griffiths*, because in the latter, the 999 operator assured the GP that an ambulance would be there 'shortly'. In *Vicario v Commr of Police*, the police, D, investigated allegations of indecent assault and cruelty made by C against her step-father. The step-father was arrested and interviewed, but D decided not to take further action. In conducting those investigations, D did not assume responsibility to C in deciding whether or not to proceed with a prosecution. Nor was there any specific reliance on D by C (in adjusting C's position on the strength of that reliance – that would be 'unpleadable').

iii. Some other police function. The police owe a duty of care where the activities under scrutiny are **not** done in the course of investigating or suppressing crime, but as part of some other police function.

> In *Desmond v CC of Nottingshire Police*,[242] collating information for the Criminal Records Bureau, and for on-forwarding to C's employer, was arguably not an activity that fell within the *Hill* core principle.

iv. System of work. The police service, as an employer, owes a duty of care to a police employee, C, where the system of work established for police operations (whether for the investigation and suppression of crime, or for other operations) requires that the police assume substantial or total control of, and responsibility for, C's safety and well-being.

> Examples include: *Costello v CC of Northumbria Police*,[243] in respect of a female police constable's, C's, injuries inflicted by a female prisoner, whilst another senior police officer was standing by and did not come to C's aid; and *Donachie v CC of the Greater Manchester Police*,[244] where an employed officer was put at grave risk during a tagging operation because of defective batteries in the device.

v. Public safety at risk from known danger. The police may owe a duty of care where the police knew that public safety was in extreme jeopardy because of a known danger, and yet the police stood by and did nothing to prevent it or to assist C.

---

[240] [2015] UKSC 2, [138], and earlier: [2012] EWCA Civ 981, [22] (Longmore LJ).   [241] *ibid*, [167].
[242] [2009] EWHC 2362 (QB) [49].   [243] [1999] 1 All ER 550 (CA).   [244] [2004] EWCA Civ 404.

In *Rush v Police Service of Northern Ireland*, the court refused to strike out a claim by the estate of Libby Rush, who was murdered by a bomb placed by the Real IRA in a car at Main Street, Omagh in 1998. The police, D, knew that a bomb had been placed in the street with date and time nominated, and despite the exactitude of information, arguably stood by and did not prevent the bomb from exploding.

Significantly, some 'outrageous negligence' on the police's part will **not** constitute an exception to the *Hill* core principle. In *Brooks*, Lord Steyn contemplated (in dicta) this as an exceptional category, but in *Smith/Van Colle*, the majority cast rejected that proposition. Indeed, Lord Phillips noted that, on the assumed facts of *Smith*, it came close to 'outrageous negligence' towards Mr Smith, but that was not sufficient to put the case outside the *Hill* core principle.[245]

Extension of the *Hill* principle. Although the *Hill* principle precludes a claim by a member of the general public who has been the victim of crime, it may also apply where C is a police employee, 'by analogy'. It applied in both of the following cases, involving aggrieved police employees:

In *Hughes v National Union of Mineworkers*,[246] PC Hughes, C, was injured during disturbances at a colliery in North Yorkshire in 1984 during the national miners' strike. C sued the Union, and also his police employer, D, for failing to provide him with adequate protection, and for inadequately coordinating the police forces available. Foreseeability and proximity were conceded. As a matter of public policy, no duty was owed. In *Calveley v CC of Merseyside Police*,[247] various police officers, C, sued their employer, D, in negligence, on the basis that disciplinary proceedings against them had been negligently conducted. C were eventually reinstated after the proceedings, and sued for loss of overtime payments which they would have received, had they not been suspended. D owed no duty of care to C.

Policy reasons precluding a duty of care

- *defensive practices*: if senior police officers were liable to individual officers under their command, where those employees were injured by attacks from rioters, that would be detrimental to the control of public order (*Hughes*);
- *battle conditions*: in arranging riot control, when employed officers could be in danger of physical injury, police must make critical decisions urgently, and to expose them to negligence claims would be likely to affect the decisions of those police, 'to the prejudice of the very tasks which the decisions are intended to advance' (*Hughes*);
- *treating like cases alike:* 'if no duty of care is owed by a police officer investigating a suspected crime to a civilian suspect, it is difficult to see any conceivable reason why a police officer who is subject to investigation under the Regulations of 1977 should be in any better position' (*Calveley*).

The ECHR tack. Given the *Hill* core principle, it may prove more fruitful for C to sue for infringement of the ECHR, alleging that the police failed to investigate properly. Whilst some cases have failed in that attempt (e.g., *Osman v UK*;[248] *Van Colle*[249]), some recent case law has demonstrated more success. For example, in *DSD v Commr of Police*,[250] the victims of the convicted London 'black cab rapist', successfully sued the police under Art 3, for their failure to

---

[245] [2008] UKHL 50, [2009] 1 AC 225, [101]. [246] [1991] ICR 669 (QB) 680. [247] [1989] AC 1228 (HL) 1238.
[248] (1998) 29 EHRR 245 (ECtHR). [249] [2009] AC 225 (HL).
[250] [2015] EWCA Civ 646, affirming: [2014] EWHC 436 (QB). No claim in negligence was instituted.

conduct an effective investigation into the allegations of serious sexual assault. In *Michael*,[251] the Supreme Court permitted Miss Michael's estate to proceed with an Art 2 claim that D failed to protect C's right to life, and that they should have appreciated that there was 'a real and immediate risk to the life of an identified individual/s from the criminal acts of a third party' (per the test laid down in *Osman*[252]).

The 'Bad Samaritan'

§2.25 Under English common law, there is no duty of care imposed upon D, a bystander, to intervene and to offer assistance to a stranger, C, who is endangered, imperilled or injured.

The general proposition. The 'Bad Samaritan' is one who does not help others in danger or distress. With reference to the 'Good Samaritan' parable,[253] and per *Home Office v Dorset Yacht Co Ltd*:[254]

> The very parable of the good Samaritan ... illustrates, in the conduct of the priest and of the Levite who passed by on the other side, an omission which was likely to have, as its reasonable and probable consequence, damage to the health of the victim of the thieves, but for which the priest and Levite would have incurred no civil liability in English law.

The proposition applies to lay persons **and** doctors, so that 'a doctor who happened to witness a road accident will very likely go to the assistance of anyone injured, but he is not under any legal obligation to do so, save in certain limited [statutorily-set] circumstances which are not relevant' (per *Capital and Counties plc v Hampshire CC*[255]).

Whilst, in *Kent v Griffiths*,[256] the Court of Appeal accepted as 'good sense' the general no-duty-to-assist rule in English common law, some judicial examples of lawful 'Bad Samaritan'-type activity may sound rather dreadful to a layman's ears. **None** of the following scenarios could give rise to liability in negligence, because a duty to exercise reasonable care to intervene/assist/rescue is not owed:

The unhelpful strangers

- failing to stop a blind stranger stepping out in front of busy traffic (cf. the positive act of carelessly propelling him into the traffic which may give rise to actionable negligence) (per *Gibson (AP) v Orr, Strathclyde Police*[a]);
- watching a person who is pre-occupied about to walk over a cliff (per *Yuen Kun-Yeu v A-G of Hong Kong*[b]);

[a] [1999] Scot CS 61, Scot SC 420 (OH) 435.
[b] [1988] AC 175 (PC) 192 (Lord Keith); and: *Mitchell v Glasgow CC* [2009] UKHL 11, [15] (Lord Hope).

[251] [2015] UKSC 2, [139] (but trial would need to establish how D1's operator should have understood C's call).
[252] (1998) 29 EHRR 245 (ECtHR) [116].
[253] Gospel of Luke 10:25–37. See also: Mulheron, *Medical Negligence: Non-Patient and Third Party Claims* (Ashgate, 2010) ch 5 ('"Bad Samaritan" Liability'), from which some analysis herein is drawn.
[254] [1970] AC 1004 (HL) 1060 (Lord Diplock), and approved in, e.g.: *Mitchell v Glasgow CC* [2009] UKHL 11, [39], and *Smith (or Maloco) v Littlewoods Org Ltd* [1987] AC 241 (HL) 261, 271.
[255] [1997] QB 1004 (CA) 1035 (Stuart-Smith LJ).   [256] [2001] QB 36 (CA), [18]–[19].

- eating lunch on a beach while watching another beach-goer drown in the sea (per *Horsley v Ma-cLaren*[c]);
- watching a neighbour's goods destroyed by rain or fire, when minimal effort would have salvaged them (per *Home Office v Dorset Yacht Co Ltd*[d]);
- watching a child drown in shallow water, although he could have been easily saved (per *R v Evans*[e]);
- failing to stop a naval serviceman, with a known drink problem, from drinking himself to death on a remote military base in Norway (per dicta in *Barrett v MOD*[f]).

[c] (1970), 11 DLR (3d) 277 (CA) [34] (Jessup J), aff'd: [1972] SCR 441 (SCC), and cited in: EWLC, *Administrative Redress: Public Bodies and the Citizen* (CP 187, 2008) [3.161].
[d] [1970] AC 1004 (HL) 1060 (Lord Diplock).
[e] [2009] EWCA Crim 650, [17] (Lord Judge CJ).
[f] [1995] 1 WLR 1217 (CA) (dicta, because the deceased's colleagues eventually intervened to assist).

Notably, the ease with which D could have saved C; the resources or ability on D's part to provide assistance; and the degree of danger faced by C, have no apparent impact upon the principle under consideration. In *Smith v Littlewoods Organisation Ltd*,[257] Lord Goff spoke, no doubt for many reasonable thinkers, when he stated that, 'this proposition may be repugnant to modern thinking. It may therefore require one day to be reconsidered'. (However, to date, that has not occurred, except for certain exceptional circumstances, discussed shortly.) Two overall factors contribute to this rather sobering legal position in English law.

i. Various policy reasons. First, a number of policy reasons preclude a duty of care from arising (derived, principally, from *Stovin v Wise*[258] and *Mitchell v Glasgow CC*[259]), as shown in the Table below.

Policy reasons: no duty to rescue

- *individual liberty*: to compel D to rescue would sit uncomfortably with the individual liberty of doing as one chooses – provided that D does not *do harm* to other people: '[i]n political terms, it is less of an invasion of an individual's freedom for the law to require him to consider the safety of others in his actions than to impose upon him a duty to rescue or protect' (*Stovin v Wise*). Besides, D would have to be constantly on the look-out to prevent all foreseeable harm, placing him under an 'intolerable burden' (*Mitchell v Glasgow CC*);
- *indeterminate liability*: if D failed to intervene to help C, then many others may have 'looked the other way' too, meaning that any duty to rescue 'may apply to a large and indeterminate class of people who happen to be able to do something' (*Stovin*);
- *the 'why pick on me?' argument*: obversely, if C only sues D, out of a large group of bystanders who did nothing to help (whether D is chosen at random, or has the 'deepest pocket', or is on unfriendly terms with C), then this gives rise to a 'moral' dilemma (*Stovin*);
- *altruistic motive*: imposing a duty of care on D would elevate an altruistic/moral motive to a legal duty (*Stovin*);
- *imposing expenditure or danger on D not justifiable*: the common law cannot justify a principle that requires bystander D, who is not involved with C's activities *and* who has not created the

[257] [1987] AC 241 (HL) 271.   [258] [1996] AC 923 (HL), with quotes in Table locatable at 943–46 (Lord Hoffmann).
[259] [2009] UKHL 11, [2009] 1 AC 874, with quotes in Table locatable at [89] and [55].

danger himself, to spend money on behalf of, or put himself at risk during, C's rescue (*Stovin*). As the tragic facts of *Baker v TE Hopkins & Son Ltd*[a] showed, rescues can involve extreme danger to the rescuer (Dr Baker lost his life in that rescue attempt). Casting any burdens of this type on D deters recognising any duty to rescue at all;

- *potential causation problems*: where an omission to act is at issue, causation problems arise, because D has, at best, created the opportunity for harm to occur. By failing to stop a blind man from walking over a cliff, has the bystander D's omission to shout out a warning caused the blind man's injury or death? Other, more immediate, causes of the tragedy are: (1) the blind man's own disability, and (2) the natural features of the land. In *Mitchell v Glasgow CC*, Lord Rodger noted that such a bystander 'plays no part in the events'. Also, if D's omission enables a third party's criminal act to harm C, that criminal act may be a *novus actus interveniens* (per *Smith v Littlewoods Organisation Ltd*[b]). While these issues are, strictly speaking, causally-related, Lord Goff noted that they 'throw back to the duty of care', and whether one should be owed at all.

[a] [1959] 1 WLR 966 (CA).
[b] [1987] AC 241 (HL) 271 (Lord Goff).

In response to this draconian position, some law reform commentary has queried whether, if no general duty to rescue exists, a duty of 'easy rescue' should be imposed. However, that notion has never gained any significant judicial support in England.

The law reform corner: 'Easy rescues'

Irish LRC:[260] the Commission defined an 'easy rescue' as one which did not impose expense, danger, or undue inconvenience upon the bystander. However, it recommended against any duty to perform an easy rescue, principally because of its 'uncertain nature'. What was 'easy' would be subjective, and dependent upon the particular onlooker concerned; requiring some 'least effort' standard may benefit the victim very little, if at all; and identifying the borderline between an 'easy' and a 'difficult' rescue 'would pose a virtually impossible task'.

ii. A pure omission. A second reason for the law's reluctance to impose a duty to assist on the Bad Samaritan – indeed, the 'fundamental reason', according to Lord Goff in *Smith v Littlewoods Org Ltd*[261] – is that his failure to intervene, rescue, etc, rings of an **omission** to do something. The common law does not, generally speaking, impose liability for what are considered to be 'pure omissions' or 'mere omissions' (a controversial topic discussed in Chapter 3[262]). Indeed, in *Bishara v Sheffield Teaching Hosp NHS Trust*,[263] arising from an alleged failure to intervene, Sedley LJ noted that, 'whether the case is one of simple omission, and therefore excluded as a matter of policy from the arena of tort liability, has to be decided in the light of the facts'.

[260] *Civil Liability of Good Samaritans and Volunteers* (CP 47, 2007) [2.47]–[2.49], [2.88]–[2.89], citing: E Weinrib, 'The Case for a Duty to Rescue' (1980) 90 Yale LJ 247, 248.
[261] [1987] AC 241 (HL) 271–72. [262] See pp 146–52.
[263] [2007] EWCA Civ 353, [11], citing: *Stovin v Wise* [1996] AC 923 (HL).

The recent enactment of the Social Action, Responsibility and Heroism Act 2015[264] (the 'SA-RAH Act') does not appear to change the law in that respect, limited as it is to circumstances in which D 'was acting for the benefit of society',[265] or was 'carrying out an activity',[266] or when a person was 'acting heroically'.[267] Although the application of this controversial statute is yet to be tested in the courts, its wording seems, on its face, to preclude any application to the 'Bad Samaritan' scenario.[268]

Exceptions. However, there are some scenarios in which D will owe a duty of care to C to intervene, rescue, or assist, in an emergency scenario:

i. Doctors and hospitals in A&E departments: For hospital doctors, a duty of care at common law arises, whenever a person in need of medical assistance is 'accepted for treatment' (per *Cassidy v Ministry of Health*[269]), and hence applies, 'once a patient has been received or admitted into a NHS hospital, [so] the duty to provide (and thereafter to go on providing) treatment arises, whether the patient is competent or incompetent, conscious or unconscious' (per *R (on the application of Burke) v GMC*[270]). The point of 'acceptance' may occur (and a duty of care may arise) without a hospital doctor in A&E/casualty actually laying eyes, let alone hands, on the victim:

> In *Barnett v Chelsea and Kensington Hosp Management Committee*,[271] three night-watchmen attended D's casualty department, complaining to the nurse on duty that they had been vomiting for three hours after drinking tea at the Technical College where they worked. Mr Barnett, C, was so poorly that he lay down on the chairs. The on-duty A&E doctor was himself sick upstairs on the 2nd floor, and the nurse rang through to him, reporting the men's complaints. In a reference to the fact that it was New Year's Eve, the A&E doctor replied, 'Well, I am vomiting myself and I have not been drinking. Tell them to go home and go to bed and call in their own doctors' if the symptoms persisted. The men left the hospital (never having seen a doctor), and some five hours later, C died. An inquest held that arsenic had been introduced into the tea by person/s unknown, from which C died. An issue was whether the A&E officer owed any duty of care to C, when he had not actually sighted C. **Held:** D owed a duty of care to C (but C's estate ultimately failed because of the absence of a causal link, as discussed in Chapter 8).

The duty to assist/intervene was owed, because of a combination of factors: the casualty department was open and receiving patients; C presented himself complaining of illness or injury for the very purpose for which the A&E department offered its services; the symptoms of long-term vomiting warranted an examination of the watchmen by the A&E officer, rather than leaving any observation to the nurse on duty; and (in modern duty of care parlance), the advice which the A&E officer gave – to see their own GP's if their symptoms persisted (no matter how rudimentary) – demonstrated an assumption of responsibility for their care and treatment. In these circumstances, Nield J was satisfied that there was 'such a close and direct relationship between the hospital and the watchmen that there was imposed upon the hospital a duty of care which they owed to the watchmen'.[272]

---

[264] In force 13 April 2015, pursuant to the SARAH Act (Commencement and Transitional Provision) Regulations 2015, reg 2.

[265] SARAH Act 2015, s 2.   [266] *ibid*, s 3.   [267] *ibid*, s 4.

[268] The *Explanatory Notes* to the Act shed no light on the scope of the Act. See, generally, Mulheron, R, 'Legislating Dangerously: Bad Samaritans, Good Society, and the Heroism Act 2015' (2016) *Modern Law Review* [forthcoming].

[269] [1951] 2 KB 343 (CA) 360 (Denning LJ).   [270] [2004] EWHC 1879 (Admin) [85].

[271] [1969] 1 QB 428.   [272] *ibid*, 436.

There is no 'blanket duty' of care imposed on doctors who work in an A&E department, however. For example, in *Barnett*, Nield J noted that if a casualty department of a hospital closes its doors and says no patients can be received; or if a receptionist at A&E discovers that the person presenting there is already seeing his GP about a medical problem and only wants a second opinion; or if the victim has a small cut which an A&E nurse can easily treat without calling on the services of the A&E doctor on duty, then there would be no duty of care owed by an A&E doctor to the person attending, to either see or to examine him. 'Casualty departments are misused from time to time.'

ii. **An emergency request, an affirmative undertaking and reliance:** Wherever C *requests* medical or other assistance from D; and there is a reciprocal and affirmative *undertaking* given by D to provide that assistance; and C then *relies* on D, a duty of care will arise on D's part. This exception – whereby D cannot ignore the peril or difficulties in which C finds himself – arises by virtue of an application of the test of assumption of responsibility/reliance, discussed elsewhere in the chapter.[273] The scenario itself is best illustrated by *Kent v Griffiths*[274] (described above, under 'Emergency services').

Notably, *Kent v Griffiths* concerned a scenario where D undertook to assist C who was in medical need. However, where C requests assistance from D, and there is **no** undertaking by D to assist – indeed, quite the reverse, the request is refused – then there is no English authority to date which imposes a duty on D. Rather, the general rule would apply: that D is under **no** duty to go to C's rescue. There is certainly no decision that matches the pivotal Australian case of *Lowns v Woods*,[275] where the New South Wales Court of Appeal held (by majority) that a doctor who declined to attend an emergency did owe a duty of care to the patient in peril, and on whose behalf the request was made.

The comparative corner: **An Australian perspective**

In *Lowns v Woods*, Patrick Woods, C, 11, suffered an epileptic fit one morning in a flat where his family was holidaying, whilst his mother was out for a walk. Upon return, C's mother urgently sent her 18-year-old son to fetch an ambulance, and her 14-year-old daughter Joanna was dispatched to 'get a doctor'. Joanna ran to D's GP surgery about 300 metres away, and told him that her brother was 'having a bad fit', and requested him to come. D asked for C to be brought to his surgery. Joanna said, 'he's having a bad fit, we can't bring him down', to which D replied that an ambulance should be called for. Joanna said, 'we need a doctor. We have already got an ambulance', but D declined to attend. (D's case was that this conversation never occurred, but on that point, the evidence of Joanna was preferred by the trial judge.) C was treated by ambulance officers at the flat, but the fitting could not easily be brought under control, and C suffered serious and irreversible brain damage. Had D attended to C at the point of request, he would have used rectal Valium, which would have commenced 17–20 minutes earlier than it did, and C would not have suffered brain damage. **Held (CA, 2:1):** D owed a duty to attend/assist C in this emergency, and was negligent not to do so (C was awarded damages of approx A\$3.2m).

---

[273] See pp 113–22.   [274] [2001] QB 36 (CA). Lord Woolf MR delivered the judgment of the CA.
[275] [1996] Aust Torts R ¶81-376 (NSWCA, Kirby P and Cole JA, with Mahoney JA dissenting.

As the author has argued elsewhere,[276] it is very doubtful that *Lowns v Woods* would be followed in English law, were a similar fact scenario to come before this jurisdiction's courts. For one thing, England does not have any equivalent to the statutory provision that proved to be so important in *Lowns v Woods*, whereby the definition of 'misconduct' by D expressly covered non-attendance at an emergency without reasonable cause. For another, *Kent v Griffiths* is clearly distinguishable from *Lowns v Woods* on its facts, because an express undertaking to assist occurred in *Kent*, but not in *Lowns*. Indeed, in *Capital and Counties* (which was decided a year after *Lowns*), the Court of Appeal decided that there could be no assumption of responsibility, or duty of care, on the fire brigade's part towards any *one* property owner merely by taking control of the fire-fighting operations. Reliance there may have been, but an undertaking was not, and that was crucial to no duty of care being found.

Those who need rescuing

§2.26   Where D puts himself (or others) in a position of danger and peril, and rescuer C assists D (or others) and suffers physical injury in the course of the rescue, D owes C a duty of care, as a matter of policy. However, no duty will be owed by D, where rescuer C suffers from pure psychiatric injury as a result of carrying out the rescue.

In an oft-cited statement by American judge Cardozo J in *Wagner v Intl Rwy*:[277] '[d]anger invites rescue. The cry of distress is the summons to relief'. Closer to home, Morris LJ stated, in *Baker v TE Hopkins & Sons Ltd*,[278] that, '[t]here is, happily, in all men of goodwill, an urge to save those who are in peril'. However, those rescuers (i.e., Good Samaritans) may be seriously injured during the course of rescue. Does the rescued owe a duty of care to those brave souls who answer the cry?

In *Wagner*, Cardozo J remarked that, if D created the danger from which he then had to be rescued by C, then 'the wrongdoer may not have foreseen the coming of the deliverer [rescuer, C]. He is accountable as if he had'. However, the position in English law is that an attempt at rescue is *entirely* foreseeable. As canvassed earlier, where D imperils himself (or others), or someone else, then it is reasonably foreseeable that someone might attempt to rescue D or that someone else, and that some accident may befall rescuer C during the rescue (per *Crossley v Rawlinson*[279] and *Videan v British Transport Comm*,[280] respectively).

The rescuer C has not always been viewed so positively by English law, with some early cases holding that the rescuer voluntarily assumed the risk of his own injury by getting involved, where a dangerous situation was brought about by D's negligence, and that no liability towards C could arise (per *Dann v Hamilton*[281]).

However, some significant cases since undermined that view, and treated the 'Good Samaritan' rescuer far more kindly. As case examples: a policeman who intervened to stop bolting horses from trampling women and children in their path in Rotherhithe (*Haynes v Harwood*[282]); a bystander who pulled the dead and injured from the wrecked train carriages in the Lewisham train disaster (*Chadwick v British Rwys Board*[283]); and a doctor who went to the help of two men stuck down a well filled with carbon monoxide fumes and who died in the process of the

---

[276] Mulheron, *Medical Negligence: Non-Patient and Third Party Claims* (Ashgate, 2010) 173–82.

[277] 232 NY 176, 180–81 (1921), and cited in, e.g.: *Baker v TE Hopkins & Son Ltd* [1959] 1 WLR 966 (CA) 980 (Willmer LJ); *Frost (White) v CC of South Yorkshire Police* [1992] 1 AC 310 (HL) 408 (Lord Oliver).

[278] [1959] 1 WLR 966 (CA) 975.   [279] [1982] 1 WLR 369 (CA) 374–75.   [280] [1963] 2 QB 650 (CA) 669.

[281] [1939] 1 KB 509, 517.   [282] [1935] 1 KB 146.   [283] [1967] 1 WLR 912 (QB).

rescue (in *Baker v TE Hopkins & Son Ltd*[284]), all recovered in negligence for their injuries from those who put them in the situation of danger in the first place. The most recent authority on the issue – *Tolley v Carr* – reiterates that modern English law supports the imposition of a duty of care on D who imperils himself, and where C responds to the 'cry of distress' and suffers physical injury in the process.

In *Baker v TE Hopkins & Son Ltd*, TE Hopkins, D, a building company, was engaged to clear a deep well of water on a farm in Derby, by means of a petrol-driven pump. The operation of the pump created a haze of fumes, including carbon monoxide gas, in the well. Two workmen descended into the well, despite instructions from Mr Hopkins to wait for assistance to clear the well of dangerous fumes. The workmen were overcome by the poisonous gas, and fell unconscious. Dr Baker, C, was summoned, and was lowered into the well, with a rope tied to his body, to see whether he could rescue the workmen (even though C himself was also warned not to enter the well). Efforts to then pull C to the surface failed, because the rope which was tied to him became caught in a downpipe. By the time it was disentangled by the fire brigade (using suitable breathing apparatus), C and the two workmen had all died. **Held:** D owed a duty of care to rescuer C, and was liable in negligence for his death. It was foreseeable that, as a result of D's negligence towards its two workmen, they could be put in peril, that someone would attempt to rescue them, and that the rescue could have potentially dire consequences. In *Tolley v Carr*,[285] Claire Carr, D1, lost control of her vehicle on a high-speed motorway, and David Tolley, C, saw her predicament, stopped his car, and went to assist. Her car was partly in the outside fast lane, and C tried to move it further off the road, onto the central reservation. Whilst he was 'half in and half out' of the car, turning its hazard lights on, he was hit by two vehicles driven by D2 and D3. He suffered a broken spine, and almost total paralysis. **Held:** all Ds (including Ms Carr, D1) owed C a duty of care as rescuer, and negligence was proven, with 'very substantial damages' likely.

Policy reasons favouring a duty of care

- *corrective justice*: the law should encourage altruistic and moral behaviour, where mishaps occur: '[i]t would indeed be regrettable if the message delivered by the law of Tort, to a member of the public faced with a cry for help, is that if they intervene, they do so at their own risk; and that it would be wiser to pass by on the other side ... neither the law nor morality has ever sought to encourage imitation of the Levite' (per *O'Neill v Dunnes Stores*[a]);
- *distributive justice*: if D places C, his rescuer, in peril, then it is 'indeed ungracious' of D to suggest that C took on the risk of injury voluntarily. 'If C, actuated by an impulsive desire to save a life, acts bravely, and subjugates any timorous over-concern for his own well-being or comfort, I cannot think that it would be either rational or seemly to say that he freely and voluntarily agreed to incur the risks of the situation which had been created by D's negligence' (per *Baker v Hopkins*[b]). A duty of care owed to rescuers is a way for the common law 'to acknowledge the actions of such men, which often involve bravery as well as bare humanity' (per *Tolley v Carr*[c]).

[a] [2010] IESC 53, [2011] 1 IR 325, [51] (O'Donnell J).
[b] [1959] 1 WLR 966 (CA) 976.
[c] [2010] EWHC 2191 (QB) [21].

---

[284] [1959] 1 WLR 966 (CA).   [285] [2010] EWHC 2191 (QB) (Chester District Registry).

unwelcome detour, via Strasbourg, because of the argument that any such immunity violated C's Art 6 right to a consideration of the merits of his claim. As discussed previously, this episode eventually culminated in the conclusion, in Strasbourg[298] and reiterated in the House of Lords,[299] that the *Hill* principle was best **not** expressed as a 'blanket immunity', but in any event, there was no violation of Art 6. Given this history alone, it is surprising that the *Smith* majority preferred the recognition of an immunity, separate from *Caparo's* third limb. In any event, the terms, 'combat doctrine' and 'combat immunity' will be employed interchangeably in this section.

Sometimes, the doctrine has been couched in terms of a defence – e.g., in *Bici v MOD*, Elias J noted that combat immunity is '[e]xceptionally a defence to the government, and indeed individuals, who take action in the course of actual or imminent armed conflict, and cause damage to property and injury (including possibly death) to fellow soldiers or civilians'.[300] However, the statement is **not** to be taken literally, for as with all scenarios which invoke the third limb of *Caparo*, it **cannot** operate as a defence which places the burden on D. The burden remains on C to prove that a duty is owed to him.

The effect of the doctrine is powerful, as Elias J also pointed out in *Bici* (where it did **not** apply): 'the court is being deprived of its historic and jealously-guarded role of determining a dispute where a citizen claims that his rights have been unlawfully infringed by an act of the executive'.[301] As a result, it is not to be widely-construed (a notion affirmed as correct in *Smith v MOD*[302]).

The role of policy. Although the doctrine was described in *Smith v MOD*[303] as being 'well-recognised', it is not one of long standing, at least in English law.

The decision of *Mulcahy v MOD*[304] (1996) was the **first** occasion upon which an English court decided that no duty of care in Tort could be owed by one soldier to another, when engaging the enemy in battle conditions. Until 1987, s 10 of the Crown Proceedings Act 1947 had precluded proceedings being brought in respect of the death of, or personal injury to, a member of the armed forces caused by the negligence of another member of the armed forces and attributable to service. However, s 2 of the Crown Proceedings (Armed Forces) Act 1987 removed the blanket protection of s 10, thereby raising for judicial consideration (in *Mulcahy*, *Smith*, etc) the existence and ambit of the duty of care owed to a combatant who is injured or killed whilst on active service, and the policy reasons that preclude a duty.

In fact, several policy reasons have militated against any duty of care being owed in circumstances of combat:

The policy reasons in play

- *battle conditions:* acts or omissions during wartime operations should not be subject to judicial control or interference which constitute 'battle conditions' (*Mulcahy*);
- *subordination of the individual's interests to the wider public:* the interests of armed service colleagues must necessarily be subordinated to attaining the objectives set out in military operations. A duty is not owed where C (whether employees or civilians) 'are the "innocent" victims of action which is taken out of pressing necessity in the wider public interest arising out of combat' (*Bici*);

---

[298] (2002) 34 EHRR 3 (ECtHR).   [299] *Brooks v Commr of Police* [2005] UKHL 24, [2005] 1 WLR 1495.
[300] [2004] EWHC 786 (QB) [90] (Leeds District Registry).   [301] *ibid*, [84], and for quote in the box, see [101].
[302] [2013] UKSC 41, [90].   [303] [2012] EWCA Civ 1365, [2013] 2 WLR 27, [55].
[304] [1996] EWCA Civ 1323, [1996] QB 772, quote in Box at [47]; leave to appeal: [1997] 1 WLR 294 (HL).

- *the interplay with statute:* although the immunity of the armed services from actions in tort was removed by s 2 of the Crown Proceedings (Armed Forces) Act 1987, the fact that there was no statutory protection available to D did not mean that all protection for D at common law should be removed (*Mulcahy*);
- *the role of Parliament:* the allocation of resources to the armed services, and as between the different branches of the services, and as to what equipment should be procured, is a political decision more appropriate for Parliament than by a court ('[i]t does not follow from the fact that decisions about procurement are taken remote from the battlefield that they will always be appropriate for review by the courts': *Smith*[a]).

[a] [2013] UKSC 41, [65].

What is 'combat', for the purposes of the immunity? It has become important for courts to carefully articulate and delimit the scope of D's 'combat immunity'.

Its availability does **not** depend solely upon C's being killed or injured in combat. Rather, D's act or omission must have occurred in the 'heat of battle', or during the terms of 'actual engagement', or in the 'course of hostilities', or as part of 'the full width of active operations'. What falls within this ambit, to which the doctrine attaches, is a question of fact (and depends upon 'the factual matrix for each case', per *Durrheim v MOD*[305]). Decisions as to training/ equipment for future combats are not taken during 'active operations', and hence, cannot fall within the immunity (for, otherwise, 'it is difficult to see how anything done by the Ministry of Defence falls beyond it', according to Moses LJ in *Smith v MOD*,[306] a view affirmed by the majority of the Supreme Court in the same case[307]). However, the difficulties in assessing what falls within 'active operations' has troubled the judiciary. In *Shaw Savill and Albion Co Ltd v Cth*[308] (1940), and in a passage approved in *Mulcahy v MOD*,[309] Dixon J, of the High Court of Australia, remarked that:

> a real distinction does exist between actual operations against the enemy and other activities of the combatant services in time of war. For instance, a warship proceeding to her anchorage, or manoeuvring among other ships in a harbour, or acting as a patrol, or even as a convoy, must be navigated with due regard to the safety of other shipping, and no reason is apparent for treating her officers as under no civil duty of care ... It may not be easy under conditions of modern warfare to say, in a given case, upon which side of the line it falls. But, when ... the matters complained of formed part of, or an incident in, active naval or military operations against the enemy, then ... the action must fail on the ground that, while in the course of actually operating against the enemy, the forces of the Crown are under no duty of care to avoid causing loss or damage to private individuals.

For English purposes, in *Smith v MOD*,[310] Lord Hope accepted that the 'combat', necessary to trigger the immunity, could cover active operations against the enemy in which service personnel are exposed to attack/threat of attack when under actual or imminent armed conflict. However, the majority of the Supreme Court disagreed with the suggestion, in *Mulcahy v MOD*,[311] that the planning of, and preparation for, operations in which service personnel may come

---

[305] [2014] EWHC 1960 (QB) [63], [66].   [306] [2012] EWCA Civ 1365, [62].   [307] [2013] UKSC 41, [90].
[308] (1940) 66 CLR 75 (HCA) 361.   [309] [1996] EWCA Civ 1323, [29].   [310] [2013] UKSC 41, [90].
[311] [2003] EWHC 1134 QB (Admin, Owen J) [2.C.20, 3b].

under attack or meet armed resistance and suffer injury, was also within the province of the doctrine. Such preparation could encompass activities 'taken far away in place and time from those operations themselves', which would extend the 'immunity' far too widely.

Notwithstanding this guidance, there is no doubt that, when considering this description of 'combat', English cases have, to date, shown how very finely-balanced that line is, in practice. On the one hand, the combat doctrine did **not** apply in the following cases:

In *Smith v MOD*,[312] Private Hewett, C1 (and son of Susan Smith) was killed whilst travelling in a Snatch Land Rover when passing over an IED (improvised explosive device). His estate alleged that the vehicle was not fitted with electronic counter measures (ECMs) and other technology and equipment that would have prevented the incident. Corporal Allbutt, C2, was killed by 'friendly fire' during the offensive on Basra, whilst travelling in a Challenger II tank. His estate alleged that the MOD failed to provide available technology to protect against the risk of 'friendly fire' and adequate vehicle recognition training. Many of these acts or omissions being challenged as negligent (i.e., the choice and fitting out of the vehicles with technology and equipment, the recognition training given to soldiers) happened well before the active operations in which the soldiers were killed. Hence, the claims could not be struck out. In *Hopps v Mott Macdonald Ltd*,[313] Graham Hopps, C, was an electrical engineer, employed by MOD, working around Basra on projects designed to restore Iraq's shattered infrastructure. In Oct 2003, he was travelling in a vehicle, which was being escorted by a Land Rover following behind. C's vehicle drove over an explosive device, and C was badly injured, whilst soldiers also travelling in the vehicle were killed. The invasion of Iraq took place in March 2003, and by 30 April, the war phase was over, so no immunity applied in these circumstances. In *Bici v MOD*,[314] British soldiers, D, who were involved in a UN peacekeeping operation in Kosovo in 1999, shot at two Kosovar Albanians whilst they were passengers in a car travelling in Kosovo around midnight. Mohamet Bici, C1, was shot in the face but not killed, whilst his cousin, Skender Bici, C2, was not actually shot but suffered psychiatric injury. The shots were aimed at a third party on the roof of the car, Mr Fahri Bici, who was killed, but there was no intent on D's part to shoot either C1 or C2. The combat immunity did not apply, because D had not shot at the men in the car because of 'wider concerns which necessitated such draconian measures in the public interest, nor even that any such interest arose in the course of combat, however widely that concept is construed'. There was no concern that the men in the car were part of a wider group intending to attack buildings, civilians, or the soldiers, given that, 'the car was being driven away at increasing speed from that building'.

Combat immunity, which precluded a duty of care, **did** (or **could**) apply in the following cases, however, enabling the actions to be struck out as disclosing no cause of action:

In *Smith v MOD*,[315] in a conjoined case, Private Ellis, C3, was killed by an IED detonated beside his vehicle, a Snatch Land Rover, whilst on duty in Iraq. His estate alleged that the MOD failed to provide suitable equipment, by re-introducing Snatch Land Rovers, having earlier withdrawn them from use following the deaths of soldiers. Some of the allegations in the Ellis claim (that D should have limited C's patrol to medium or heavily-armoured vehicles) did occur in a phase in which there was a constant threat of enemy action, in which case it was arguable that the combat doctrine applied; that part of the case was to be left to trial. In *Mulcahy v MOD*,[316] Richard Mulcahy, C, was part of the allied forces during the Gulf War in 1991. His battalion was in Saudi Arabia (firing into

---

[312] [2013] UKSC 41 (4:3), affirming: [2012] EWCA Civ 1365. [313] [2009] EWHC 1881 (QB).
[314] [2004] EWHC 786 (QB) [101]. [315] [2013] UKSC 41, [96]. [316] [1996] EWCA Civ 1323, [1996] QB 732, 737.

Iraqi territory). C was employed specifically to man a M110 8 inch Howitzer gun, and to swab out the breech of the gun after each firing. Only a colleague sergeant was allowed to fire the gun as gun commander. C was to the front of the gun when the gun commander negligently caused the gun to fire. The discharge knocked C off his feet, and caused hearing problems thereafter. When the incident happened, C was engaged as part of a gun crew, firing shells on enemy targets, although there was no return fire, nor had there been for several days before it. However, this constituted 'battle conditions' sufficient for combat immunity to apply. In *Multiple Claimants (Bell) v MOD*,[317] several former members of the armed forces, C, sued in negligence for psychiatric injury allegedly as a consequence of exposure to the stress and trauma of combat. Some Cs had been engaged in anti-terrorist policing and peacekeeping operations (e.g., as in Northern Ireland, Bosnia and Kosovo). Again, combat immunity applied to such operations, because those were operations 'in which service personnel come under attack or threat of attack'.

The type of C. The immunity applies to protect D, regardless of whether C is a member of the armed forces engaged in the heat of battle, or a civilian caught up in cross-fire. Either way, a duty of care is ruled out for policy reasons (per *Smith v MOD*[318]). Earlier, Sir Iain Glidewell had opined, in *Mulcahy v MOD*, that '[i]f, during the course of hostilities, no duty of care is owed by a member of the armed forces to civilians or their property, it must be even more apparent that no such duty is owed to another member of the armed forces.'[319]

The type of D. The immunity applies, whether D: is an armed services colleague of C, whose acts or omissions allegedly caused C's injury or death; is an employer (i.e., the MOD) who is being sued for a direct claim in systemic negligence; or is an employer being sued vicariously for the alleged breaches of an employed member of the armed forces. Whatever capacity D is being sued in, where injuries or death are sustained by C in active operations, the immunity applies (per *Mulcahy v MOD*[320]).

The type of damage. The immunity applies, whether C is claiming for death, personal injury (including psychiatric injury), or property destruction or damage.

In *Burmah Oil Co (Burma Trading) Ltd v Lord Advocate*,[321] Burma Oil Co's, C's, installations near Rangoon were destroyed by the British army, D, to prevent their falling into the hands of the Japanese army when Japan invaded Burma. They were destroyed the day before Japanese forces took control of Rangoon. The case was governed by English law. **Held (3:2):** compensation was payable to C, where D was exercising a prerogative power. However, all members of the House agreed that the destruction 'did not arise out of the military operations', so no question of combat immunity arose. Moreover, although the damage inflicted by D here was deliberate, the immunity could apply (said the court in dicta) in cases of accidental damage to C's property, where, say, a house 'had the misfortune to be in the centre of a battlefield', and was accidentally demolished during warfare; its owner 'can have no claim'.

Further, the territorial limits of combat immunity, for the purposes of negligence claims, were not necessary to explore in *Mulcahy*,[322] although it is clear, from the facts of that case (and affirmed in *Smith v MOD*), that the immunity applies to war zones well away from British shores.

---

[317] [2003] EWHC 1134.   [318] [2012] EWCA Civ 1365, [57] (Moses LJ) and aff'd on appeal: [2013] UKSC 41, [90].
[319] [1996] EWCA Civ 1323, [1996] QB 732, [62].   [320] *ibid*, [65] (Sir Iain Glidewell).
[321] [1965] AC 75 (HL) 111.   [322] [1996] EWCA Civ 1323, [1996] QB 732, [47].

Sporting contests: referees, participants and others

§2.29   Amateur referees owe a duty of care to participants of sporting contests, as a matter of policy.

Unfortunately, in sporting contests, matters can go very seriously wrong for participants, and the referees of those matches in which the participants are hurt can thereafter be sued in negligence. In many cases, the referee will be of amateur, and not professional, status.

The *Caparo* tripartite test[323] is again the relevant test in such cases (per *Vowles v Evans*[324]). The Court of Appeal adopted that test as the rightful premise, and held, further, that its first and second limbs would be met, as between participant C and referee D (i.e., it was reasonably foreseeable that, if D failed to exercise reasonable care in refereeing the match, injury to C might result; and the relationship between them was sufficiently proximate). The whole duty of care question revolved around whether it was 'fair, just and reasonable' to impose on an amateur referee a duty of care towards the players in the match.

> In *Vowles v Evans*, Richard Vowles, C, was playing hooker for the Llanharan Rugby Football Club 2nd XV in a 'local Derby' in an amateur game. David Evans, D, was refereeing in an amateur capacity. During the game, C's team lost their loose-head prop when he dislocated his shoulder, and had no trained front row forward on the bench to replace him, nor anyone who had recent or significant experience of playing in the front row. D was aware that C's team did not have a suitable replacement on the bench, so he told their captain that they could provide a replacement from within the scrum, or opt for non-contestable scrummages. C's team mate, Christopher Jones, playing as a flanker, said that he would 'give it a go' as front row forward. D agreed to this without enquiring of Mr Jones, the captain, or anyone else, about Mr Jones's previous experience. During injury time, the opposing team aimed for a 'push-over' try from a scrum which, if converted, would enable them to snatch a victory. During that scrum, the scrum collapsed, and C was seriously injured, suffering tetraplegia. **Held:** D owed C a duty of care, and was liable in negligence.
> In *Smoldon v Whitworth & Nolan*,[325] Mr Smoldon, C, 17, was playing hooker in an <19 colts game, and had his neck broken when a scrum collapsed. C claimed that the referee, D, owed him a duty of care to enforce the Laws of the Game and to 'effect control of the match so as to ensure that the players were not exposed to unnecessary risk of injury'. **Held:** a duty of care was conceded by D (and breach was proven, and *volenti* rejected).

The policy reasons in favour of a duty of care were multifarious, as described in *Vowles v Evans*:[326]

The policy reasons in play

• *the availability of insurance:* even if it was 'public knowledge' that the Welsh Rugby Union (the referee's employer) was heavily in debt (and insurance was expensive), and that public liability insurers were considering excluding cover for participants' sporting injuries, judicial notice could not be taken of the WRU's finances or the intentions of public liability insurers. It was possible for referees, or the WRU, to obtain insurance cover against legal liability, which helped to favour a duty of care;

---

[323] [1990] 2 AC 605 (HL).   [324] [2003] EWCA Civ 318, [2003] WLR 1607.   [325] [1997] PIQR P133 (CA) P137.
[326] [2003] EWCA Civ 318, with relevant discussion in the box at [11]–[25], quote at [24] (Lord Phillips MR).

- *defensive practices:* re arguments that the supply of amateur referees would 'be in danger of drying up' if they were liable in negligence, and that it was in the public interest that amateur referees should be available for amateur sports and offering their services for free without the risk of legal liability, that risk was covered by the availability of insurance and/or vicarious liability. Further, the very small risk of a player sustaining a serious injury and suing for it would not mean that it would 'discourage those who take their pleasure in the game by acting as referees';
- *treating D's alike:* policy considerations did not alter, whatever the age of C and whatever the type of game that D was refereeing: 'we do not consider that the distinction between a colts game and an adults game can affect the answer to the question of whether a referee owes any duty of care to the players';
- *preference for personal injury:* in a rugby match, which is an inherently-dangerous sport, some of the laws of the game are specifically designed to minimise the inherent dangers, and players are dependent for their safety on the enforcement of the rules by the referee. It is very unusual for the law to preclude a duty of care by D, whose acts or omissions are capable of causing physical harm to others in a structured relationship. There were no good reasons for treating rugby football as an exceptional case;
- *no indeterminate liability:* that there may be many participants in a sport, to whom a duty of care could be potentially owed, does not amount to indeterminate liability. A large but finite number of potential Cs is not the same as indeterminate liability.

Of course, as *Smoldon* demonstrated, whether a breach is proven – in circumstances where the game is fast-moving, and intentionally physical among the participants – is an entirely separate question.

THE VOLUNTARY ASSUMPTION OF RESPONSIBILITY TEST

§2.30   The second test by which to establish a duty of care in novel scenarios is to prove that D assumed responsibility to C in respect of his conduct towards C, and in turn, C relied on D to exercise due skill and care in that conduct.

The genesis of the test was the banking case of *Hedley Byrne & Co Ltd v Heller & Partners Ltd*,[327] where Lord Morris stated that 'if someone possessed of a special skill undertakes, quite irrespective of contract, to apply that skill for the assistance of another person who relies upon that skill, a duty of care will arise'. *Hedley Byrne* (discussed in detail in Chapter 4) was, of course, a world away from the personal injury and property damage suits being considered in this chapter – but the test has come to have a considerable application to these contexts too (albeit that economic loss cases are where it is *still* most significant). Its application to a wider ambit of scenarios than merely to *Hedley Byrne's* giving of information/advice was reiterated by the Supreme Court in *Michael v South Wales Police*.[328]

The analysis below draws out the key principles underpinning the two components of the test, in the context of both personal injury and property damage scenarios.

---

[327] [1964] AC 465 (HL) 502–3.   [328] [2015] UKSC 2, [67].

Proving an assumption of responsibility

§2.31   An assumption of responsibility on D's part is, specifically, an undertaking to exercise reason-able care, judgment, expertise and skill in the provision of goods or services, and to apply any relevant special skills in a careful and reasonable manner.

D's undertaking is **not** to bring about a positive result or a perfect outcome for C, nor to prom-ise a particular result for C. That sort of assumption of responsibility does not (indeed, cannot) arise in negligence – it can only result from a *contract*, in which D guarantees the outcome, but such a guarantee will only be upheld if it was given in clear and unequivocal terms.[329] The exercise of reasonable care by D may result in a terrible outcome for C, but that cannot give rise to negligence.

> In *Wattleworth v Goodwood Road Racing Co Ltd*,[330] facts previously, **held:** no breach by the Motor Sports Assn (MSA), D, proven. It could not (and did not) give a guarantee as to track safety or safety barriers which would ensure the safety of drivers at the circuit, even though, 'on occasion at trial, [C's] case came close to saying that there must have been negligence on the part of someone, just because Mr Wattleworth was killed'.

When it arises

§2.32   The 'paradigm situation' in which D assumes legal responsibility to C is where their relation-ship is something akin to a contractual relationship – albeit that an assumption can legally arise even where such a relationship does not exist. Responsibility is not truly 'assumed' by D, however, but is imposed by operation of law. Any assumption of responsibility on D's part is to be determined objectively, from all the surrounding circumstances, and not by reference to what D thought or intended.

An assumption of responsibility is most likely, where the parties are in some relationship 'hav-ing all the indicia of contract, save consideration', according to Lord Bingham in *Customs and Excise Commrs v Barclays Bank plc*.[331] Some personal injury scenarios have involved situa-tions which are contractual or 'close to contract', enhancing an assumption of responsibility, as noted below.

However, as Lord Slynn pointed out in *Phelps v Hillingdon LBC*, the phrase, 'assumed re-sponsibility', can be misleading: 'it can suggest that the professional person [or other D] must knowingly and deliberately accept responsibility ... [but] the phrase means simply that the law recognises that there is a duty of care. It is not so much that responsibility is assumed, as that it is recognised or imposed by law'.[332] This seems counter-intuitive, because the test seems to imply that, subjectively speaking, D voluntarily *chose* to exercise some responsibility for the task undertaken for C. That, however, is not the legal position. Hence, D may be taken to have assumed responsibility for the performance of a task or service that affects C, even where he does not consciously *intend* to do so.

---

[329] *Thake v Maurice* [1986] QB 644 (CA) 688. See also: *Dow v Tayside Uni Hosp NHS Trust* 2006 SCLR 865 (Sheriff Ct). In neither case was a guaranteed successful outcome upheld.

[330] [2004] EWHC 140, [124].   [331] [2006] UKHL 28, [2007] 1 AC 18, [4].

[332] [2001] 2 AC 619 (HL) 654. See also: *Merrett v Babb* [2001] EWCA Civ 214, [2001] QB 1174, [41].

From an analysis of English case law, a number of factors have emerged, whether alone or in combination, to point to an assumption of responsibility on D's part. Many of these exhibit some degree of control or power by D or some vulnerability on C's part. Those circumstances in which the police may, exceptionally, assume a responsibility to victims, prisoners, etc, have been discussed earlier in this chapter.[333] Drawing upon other contexts (with illustrative authorities), this section highlights the key factors which will point to some legally-enforceable undertaking having been given:

i. Teaching or instruction: Where D instructed or taught C in something that he was unfamiliar with, where D made C aware of the dangers or risks of a certain activity – but where the instruction was not sufficient to prevent the harm that eventually befell C – an assumption of responsibility may arise:

> In *Fowles v Bedfordshire CC*,[334] Mr Fowles, C, visited a gym owned/operated by D, and received some instruction on how to use the gym mats when doing a forward somersault, but he was not made aware of the dangers of practising these without supervision, or of how to use the crash mat properly. On his 2nd visit, when using the mats without supervision, C suffered serious injury. **Held:** D owed a duty of care to C, because, '[h]aving assumed the task of teaching [C] how to perform the forward somersault, [D] voluntarily assumed a responsibility to teach him properly and to make him aware of the dangers. They failed to do either.'

Such cases may occur (as with *Fowles* itself) where C is an entrant to D's premises, of which D is an occupier, but where it is not an 'Occupiers' Liability' case, because there was nothing wrong with the state of the premises, and hence, C's action must be brought in negligence.

Also, where D's relationship with C was one of superior rank, and where that relationship meant that D's teaching/instruction/authorisation were unquestioningly followed because of that rank, then D can be taken to have assumed responsibility to prevent C, a subordinate, from taking undue risks (of which he should have been aware), when knowing that C was very likely to follow the instructions or permissions. In such cases, assumption of responsibility is enhanced where C is not likely to question D's judgment. The military employment relationship, where 'authority derives from rank' (whether on- or off-duty), where 'following those more senior is fundamental', and where 'although the officers and men were relaxing off-duty [when the accident happened], rank and military discipline remained relevant', is a classic instance of this.

> In *MOD v Radclyffe*,[335] officers and soldiers in an army unit in Germany were taking a break in between Adventure Training exercises. Captain Jones, D, was the officer-in-charge. Some army members wanted to jump from a bridge into a reservoir (about 20 metres below), and asked D for permission. He told them to check the bridge and the water depth, and authorised the guardsmen to do the jump. D and Mr Radclyffe, C, a junior army officer who had newly joined the unit, watched. D suggested that it would be 'bad form' if officers did not do the same. C did the jump without mishap. The next day, other guardsmen wished to jump from the same bridge, and C decided that he should demonstrate how to do it. He entered the water badly, and was severely injured. **Held:** D owed C a duty of care, based upon an assumption of responsibility.

---

[333] See pp 95–99.   [334] [1995] PIQR P380 (CA) P390 (Millett LJ).
[335] [2009] EWCA Civ 635, quotes in text at [20]–[22].

no control over, or responsibility for, providing safe drinking water to the citizens of Bangladesh: D 'had no connection with the drinking water project, and no-one asked them to test the water for potability. They owed no duty to the government or people of Bangladesh to test the water for anything'. In *Yates v National Trust*,[344] Jamie Yates, C, was a member of a team of tree-fellers, independent contractors who were engaged by the National Trust, D, to take down a horse chestnut tree in Morden Hall Park, a property owned by D. C was working on the tree, about 50 feet up, when he fell to the ground, suffering permanent paraplegia. **Held:** D did not owe a duty of care to C. D was not his employer, and as hirer of the independent contractor, D did not owe any duty of care to that contractor's employees either. D did not exercise control over the tree-felling team so as to assume responsibility for C's welfare. The case was distinguishable from *Perrett* and *Watson*, and was analogous to *Sutradhar*. Further, the principle that an occupier owed a duty of care to C, for acts or omissions on the part of an independent contractor, if he did not take reasonable steps to satisfy himself that the contractor was competent and the work was properly done, applied only to ultra-hazardous activities – and whilst tree-felling was hazardous, it was not hazardous enough to fall within that principle (as discussed in Chapter 12).

A most unusual application of the assumption of responsibility principle – which falls broadly under this scenario of 'rules and regulations' – occurred in a religious context, where a caterer provided food for the bridal party and guests at a Sikh wedding. That food was not supposed to contain meat, fish or eggs, but in fact, a particular dish did contain egg. Bringing any such food into the Sikh temple was contrary to the rules of that temple.

In *Bhamra v Dubb (t/a Lucky Caterers)*,[345] Kuldip Singh Bhamra, C, attended as a wedding guest at a Sikh Temple at Forest Gate. Mr Dubb, D, provided the wedding feast, and served the dish, ras malai, which happened to contain some egg. C was allergic to eggs, and after eating the ras malai, suffered an anaphylactic reaction, and died. **Held:** D owed C a duty of care. Any person who provides food on a commercial basis for consumption by others owes a duty to take reasonable care to ensure that it does not contain harmful substances and is thus fit for human consumption. Eggs are not normally harmful, but D, himself a Sikh, understood that the food to be served at the wedding should not contain any ingredients of that kind. D also knew that some people are allergic to eggs; that any guests at this wedding would expect the food to be completely free of eggs and would feel confident that no harm would come from eating it; and C was entitled to rely on D to serve food which did not contain egg at a Sikh occasion.

iv. **A request for emergency services, and an undertaking to provide same.** Regardless of whether a healthcare practitioner (or an 'extension' of the medical services industry such as an ambulance service) had any antecedent relationship with a person in need of medical assistance, C, a duty of care will arise on D's part towards C where C specifically *requests* medical assistance from D, and there is a reciprocal and affirmative *undertaking* given by D to provide that assistance *to that C*. D acts in the capacity of a 'Good Samaritan' rescuer in such cases, and induces in C the expectation that 'the rescue' would be forthcoming.

In *Kent v Griffiths*,[346] facts previously, **held:** the ambulance service, D, owed a duty of care to assist C (the claim in negligence against C's GP was dismissed), because there was a legal assumption of responsibility on D's part. There was no pre-existing relationship between C and D before the 999

---

[344] [2014] EWHC 222 (QB) [47]–[48].   [345] [2010] EWCA Civ 13.
[346] [2001] QB 36 (CA), with quotes at [18]–[19], [45], [49] (emphasis added) (Lord Woolf MR).

call was placed, but a legal relationship between them 'crystallised' when the first 999 call was accepted: 'The *acceptance of the call* in this case established the duty of care'. The 'assumption of responsibility' was bolstered because the ambulance service should be treated as 'part of the health service ... providing services of the category provided by hospitals'. The ambulance service could not be considered as a 'volunteer' who did not have to assist (under the 'Bad Samaritan' rule above) either, because it undertook 'at least a public law duty', whereby '[t]he provision of ambulances is its statutory function. The London Ambulance Service and its crews are paid out of public moneys to provide their services. It is wholly inappropriate to regard the LAS and its employees as volunteers'.

It will be recalled (from previous discussion[347]) that the *undertaking* 'element of the equation' was precisely what could **not** be proven in the case of the fire brigade in *Capital and Counties*. The property owners, whose properties were destroyed by fire sought to argue that the fire brigade, D, had assumed responsibility to protect their property – but this failed, because there was no assumption of responsibility on the fire brigade's part towards any *one* property owner, but rather, to the public at large; and merely by taking control of the fire-fighting operations, the fire brigade was 'not to be seen as undertaking a voluntary assumption of responsibility to the owner of the premises on fire'.[348] (However, in the 'Hampshire case', the fire brigade created a *new or different danger* for the claimant property owners by a positive act of misfeasance – turning off the sprinkler system – which is why a duty of care was ultimately created.)

v. **Where C engaged in inherently-risky and dangerous activity.** It may seem counter-intuitive – indeed, downright odd – that, where C has voluntarily chosen to put himself into harm's way by engaging in a dangerous, even foolhardy enterprise, D could have legally assumed responsibility to exercise reasonable care to protect C from suffering injury. However, a legal assumption on D's part may still be held to apply (as evident in, e.g., *Barrett* and *Radclyffe*), although it will **not** be commonly-held. As Coulson J pointed out in *Geary v JD Wetherspoon plc,* 'only the existence of particular facts or specific reliance will lead to a finding that [D] assumed a responsibility to [C]. Generally, the cases show that [D] does not owe a duty to regulate [C's] activities for [C's] own benefit'.[349]

In *Geary v JD Wetherspoon plc*, facts previously, **held:** D owed C no duty of care, as there were no facts to support an assumption of responsibility by the pub owners towards C, nor any reliance by C either. (To reiterate, the case proceeded on common law negligence, and not under the Occupiers' Liability Acts, given that the premises were not defective.)

§2.33 Any disclaimer of D's assumption of responsibility must be made in very clear terms, and must comply with the Unfair Contract Terms Act 1977.

The terms and conditions under which D performs its activities may displace any assumption of responsibility towards C – although that exclusion must be in the clearest language.

In *Wattleworth v Goodwood Road Racing Co Ltd*,[350] facts previously, C was killed at a non-MSA event. **Held:** no disclaimer operated to exclude the MSA's liability: 'given the wide advisory role adopted by the MSA with regard to the Goodwood circuit, far clearer and more explicit wording was needed to bring home that no responsibility was to be taken as accepted by the MSA, save for the

---

[347] Cross cite pp 85–89.   [348] [1997] QB 1004 (CA) 1036 (Stuart-Smith LJ).
[349] [2011] EWHC 1506 (QB) [57]–[58].   [350] [2004] EWHC 140 (QB) [124] (Davis J).

MSA event in question'. Further, had any disclaimer been given by the MSA in respect of non-MSA events, then the race track owner/occupier, Goodwood, probably would have sought safety advice from some other source for non-MSA events. They never considered doing so, indicating that MSA did not intend to disclaim responsibility to any user of the race circuit, such as C.

Proving reliance

The second component of the *Hedley Byrne* test is equally as important. As pointed out in *Vicario v Commr of Police*, 'reliance by [C] on that assumption of responsibility … is a key part' of the test[351] (and it failed there). In the personal injury context, it means that D has placed himself in a relationship with C, whereby C's 'physical safety becomes dependent upon the acts or omissions' of D (per *Watson v British Boxing Board of Control Ltd*[352]).

Detrimental, versus non–detrimental, reliance

§2.34 Reliance is proven where C can show that he adjusted his position in reliance on D's exercising care, skill or expertise – such that C would have acted differently, if he had *not* relied upon D. However, this requirement may be applied fairly weakly, especially where C suffers personal injury.

A change of position. Lord Bingham observed, in *Customs and Excise*, that, 'reliance in the law is usually taken to mean that if A had not relied on B, A would have acted differently'.[353] The test is proved, if C adjusted his position, either by doing something or foregoing some opportunity, as a result of which he is worse off than he would have been, had he not relied on D.

> In *Kent v Griffiths*,[354] C's reliance was proven because, but for operator D's acceptance of the 999 call, her husband would have driven C to casualty, precluding her respiratory arrest: 'if an ambulance service is called and agrees to attend the patient, those caring for the patient normally abandon any attempt to find an alternative means of transport to the hospital'. C had a choice open to her, which she forewent, when D promised that an ambulance was coming – a clear case of detrimental reliance.

If C cannot show some adjustment in his position because of the care, judgment or skill which he expected D to exercise, in doing or not doing something, then 'detrimental reliance' will be absent. However, that has not proven to be particularly crucial.

Some courts have fairly briefly stated that C reasonably relied on D to look after his safety, without articulating quite *how* C changed his position. In the sporting contests of *Vowles v Evans*[355] and *Watson v British Boxing Board*[356] – where a duty of care was owed – the participants were said to rely upon the referee to enforce the rules of the game, and the Board to provide adequate medical assistance to injured boxers, respectively. The option for the participants, presumably, was not to participate in the contests at all, although that was not expressly stated. It had been submitted, in *Watson*, that the boxer relied on the Board because, otherwise, he could have employed his own doctor to sit ringside (some boxers did), but Lord Phillips MR considered that to be an 'unrealistic' submission. Nevertheless, a duty was owed, because C's physical safety was 'dependent' upon the Board's arranging appropriate ringside medical

---

[351] [2007] EWCA Civ 1361, [27].   [352] [2001] QB 1134, 1149 (Lord Phillips MR).   [353] [2006] UKHL 28, [14].
[354] [2001] QB 36 (CA) [9].   [355] [2003] EWCA Civ 318, [25] (Lord Phillips).   [356] [2001] QB 1134 (CA) [84]–[85].

attention. Undoubtedly, though, that sort of argument – that C would have engaged his own assistance – is the clearest way of establishing detrimental reliance on C's part.

No change of position. Where C realistically had **no** alternative course of action open to him to protect himself in some other way, but to place his trust in D to act carefully and competently, then can this constitute legally-recognised 'reliance'? It is a more problematical scenario. Inevitably, it will be difficult to prove the 'direct and substantial reliance' on C's part which the law requires (per *Capital and Counties*[357]). The Irish Law Reform Commission[358] called this 'non-detrimental reliance', and gave the example of C who relies on a medically-qualified person to help him where no-one else can, due to the remote location in which C finds himself, but where that person drives on by – D's conduct simply 'speeds up the inevitable consequence, i.e., illness, injury or death' for C. As the Commission noted, whether non-detrimental reliance legally suffices may be doubtful.

A similar problem arises where D may have assumed responsibility for C's safety in some way, but C did not rely on D to do so (in fact, C may have thought the conduct of D unnecessary or uncritical to C's safety, and would have done nothing differently, whether or not D was involved). Proving reliance in such a scenario is perplexing.

In such cases, the better view is that, even if C cannot point to some change of position in reliance upon his expectation that D would conduct himself with reasonable care and skill, the *Caparo* test may still be met, in an appropriate scenario, if there were sufficient proximity and policy reasons to warrant the imposition of a duty of care on D. That approach has been adopted recently.

> In *Biddick v Morcom*,[359] Mark Morcom, C, a DIY handyman, was engaged by Cyril Biddick, 80, D, to fix insulation material in the loft of D's house. The hatch cover in the loft ceiling could be locked by turning a long pole with a hook at the end in the lock. During the work, D offered to stand underneath the hatch and hold the lock in place with the pole, because of the danger of the lock working itself loose, and the hatch opening, from the vibration from C's drill. C agreed, but did not consider the measure to be critical to his safety or necessary to reduce the risk of his falling through the hatch. Whilst the insulation was being fitted, D's phone rang, and D answered it. Whilst away, the latch cover opened (probably because of the drilling vibrations), and C fell through to the floor below, suffering serious injuries. **Held:** D owed C a duty of care (subject to 67% CN). D involved himself to a limited, but important, extent in the potentially hazardous activity being carried out by C, *viz,* to keep the hatch door latched. There was no 'reasonable reliance' by C. However, it was entirely foreseeable that, if D did not keep the lock fixed, the hatch door might open, through vibration or pressure; there was requisite proximity, because once D took that task upon himself, he assumed a duty to perform it carefully, even if C did not see D's role as an element in his own safety; and it was fair, just and reasonable to impose a duty.

Other requirements

§2.35   Any reliance on C's part must have been both reasonable and limited. On D's part, he must have known, or should have known, that his undertaking to assume responsibility would be relied upon by C. On C's part, his reliance upon D's assumption of responsibility may be express or implied.

---

[357] [1997] QB 1004 (CA) 1034 (Stuart-Smith LJ).
[358] *Civil Liability of Good Samaritans and Volunteers* (Rep 93, 2009) [3.29].   [359] [2014] EWCA Civ 182.

i. **Reasonable.** C may fail to prove that he reasonably relied upon the care, skill or expertise of D, where C had feasible options to preserve his own interests (e.g., by seeking help from a source other than D), and neglected to do so. The reality is that, where D involves himself 'in an activity which gives him a measure of control over and responsibility for a situation which, if dangerous, will be liable to injure [C]', then reliance is likely to be reasonable (per *Perrett v Collins*[360]).

This has been exemplified where: D was in a position to control or regulate C's activities (as in *Perrett* itself); D entered the fray to assist C who was in peril or need (per *Kent v Griffiths*); C was trained or expected to follow D's instructions or permissions (per *MOD v Radclyffe*,[361] where the fact that C asked his superior-ranked officer whether he might jump from the bridge into the reservoir 'predicate[d] reliance sufficient for a duty of care'); or D undertook to assist C in a particular task that meant that C's physical safety became dependent on D's conduct (per *Biddick v Morcom*).

ii. **Limited.** C's reliance on D must be *limited*, not general. Essentially, this means that D's exercise of reasonable skill and care was relied upon by C, or by members of a class of whom C was one, rather than by the general public as a whole. It is, in some ways, a cross-check of the floodgates policy factor – too large a class which ostensibly relies upon D, and there will be no reliance at law.

The distinction especially arises in the case of emergency services. In *Kent v Griffiths*, Mrs Kent specifically relied upon the ambulance turning up, given that the service undertook to respond to the 999 calls placed to them by particular callers in need. By contrast, the police and fire brigade services have the role of protecting the public in general against risks which could spread quickly, affecting persons and property; and whilst there is a general reliance by the public on the fire service and the police to reduce those risks, there is no reliance necessary to make out the test. The distinction was pointed out in *Watson v British Boxing Board*, where the fact that Mr Watson was 'one of a defined number of boxing members of the Board' meant that those members, including Mr Watson, 'could reasonably rely upon the Board to look after their safety'.[362]

iii. **Knowledge.** In *Hedley Byrne & Co Ltd v Heller & Partners Ltd*[363] (arising in the context of pure economic loss, discussed in Chapter 4), D's actual or constructive knowledge that C, or a class of persons of whom C was one, was relying upon him, was essential. This requirement has not typically been an issue in personal injury litigation.

For C's part, he may rely upon D as a known entity (as occurred, e.g., in *Watson* and *Kent v Griffiths*, where the boxer and the expectant asthmatic mother were well aware of their respective D's activities, and relied upon D to perform those activities carefully and competently). However, there may be nothing on the facts to show that C specifically knew of, or relied upon, D's undertaking his activities responsibly, e.g., in the case of certifiers or inspectors, who have no contact with C at all. Nevertheless, reliance may still be proven by implication. In *Wattleworth v Goodwood Road Racing Co Ltd*,[364] Davis J remarked that there was no evidence that

[360] [1998] 2 Lloyd's Law Rep 255 (CA) 262.   [361] [2009] EWCA Civ 635, [21] (Sir Anthony May).
[362] [2001] QB 1134 (CA) [87] (Lord Phillips MR).
[363] [1964] AC 465 (HL) 497, 503 (Lord Morris), 510 (Lord Hodson), 529 (Lord Devlin).
[364] [2004] EWHC 140 (QB) [118].

Mr Wattleworth, the deceased racing driver, 'relied on the existence of any MSA licence (even though ... he must have thought that the MSA would have had some involvement in regulatory terms with regard to the circuit) ... [but] in using the circuit, Mr Wattleworth was entitled to assume and would have assumed that all due care had been exercised by the persons – whoever they be – who had undertaken responsibility for safety matters'.

THE INCREMENTAL TEST

§2.36 The incremental test acts as a 'cross-check' on the circumstances in which a duty of care is imposed, albeit that it has been somewhat inconsistently applied in English negligence law.

As an analytical tool, the incremental test is not especially useful. Approved in *Caparo* itself (and derived from Brennan J's judgment in *Sutherland SC v Heyman*[365]), the incremental test occupies a fairly obscure status in English law. In novel or unusual cases of alleged negligence, D will customarily argue that the absence of any closely analogous cases or direct precedent indicates that no duty of care should be found – whilst C will contend that there 'has to be a first time', that the common law develops incrementally, and that there is at least one reasonably analogous case which satisfies the test.

Appellate courts do, however, continue to endorse its relevance. In *Customs and Excise*, Lord Bingham emphasised that the incremental test is not a stand-alone test in its own right, but must be used in combination with the other tests discussed earlier in this chapter: '[t]he closer the facts of the case in issue to those of a case in which a duty of care has been held to exist, the readier a court will be ... to find that there has been an assumption of responsibility, or that the proximity and policy considerations of the threefold test are satisfied. The converse is also true'.[366] In *Islington LBC v Univ College London Hosp NHS Trust*, Buxton LJ acknowledged that the status of the test 'is not easy to discern', but probably only means that if C 'could demonstrate that his case did no more than incrementally extend an already recognised head of liability, that was a good indication that his claim met the *Caparo* requirements'.[367] Both of these were pure economic loss cases, and it is apparent that the incremental test has been the subject of far more explicit consideration in that context (as discussed in Chapter 4).

Even so, where there have been no close analogies, courts have still been prepared to take a fairly significant incremental step to impose a duty in novel personal injury scenarios. *Watson v British Boxing Board of Control Ltd*[368] was one such example. Lord Phillips admitted that no case provided any close analogy to 'advance this case by a small incremental step' (the crashed kit aircraft case of *Perrett v Collins* was not a close analogy) – but the Court of Appeal was prepared to uphold a duty, although at pains to emphasise that the outcome in *Watson* did **not** mean that other sporting regulatory bodies for dangerous sports (e.g., for rugby, speedway, racing cars) owed duties of care to the participants in their sports ('[i]t does not follow that the decision in this case is the thin end of a wedge. The facts of this case are not common to other sports'[369]). However, the whole point of the incremental test is that the 'boundary rope' for sporting regulators **was** moved a little further towards liability, by virtue of *Watson*.

---

[365] (1985) 60 ALR 1 (HCA) 43–44.   [366] [2006] UKHL 28, [2007] 1 AC 181, [7].
[367] [2005] EWCA Civ 596, [25], [27].   [368] [2001] QB 1134 (CA) [86] (May and Laws LLJ concurring).
[369] *ibid*, [91].

No such incremental step was taken in *Michael*, however. Whilst Lord Toulson remarked that the 'established method of the court involves examining the decided cases to see how far the law has gone, and where it has refrained from going',[370] an incremental movement, from the 999 call in *Kent v Griffiths*, to the scenario that befell Joanna Michael, was not one which the majority was prepared to take. Similarly, in a recent case of alleged medical negligence, *ABC v St George's Healthcare NHS Trust*[371] (which is considered in detail in Chapter 3, under 'pure omissions'), Nicol J was confronted with an entirely novel claim in English law: that the medical Ds should have informed C, a non-patient, that her father, D's patient, had Huntington's Disease. C claimed that she would have terminated her pregnancy, had she known of her father's diagnosis, and that various economic and psychiatric consequences had followed from D's failure to inform C of the genetic condition to which she was at risk. The claim was struck out. To impose this duty would (said Nicol J) be a 'giant step' from established authority: 'this is not a case where [C] can show that a novel duty of care would be but an incremental development from some well established duty. It would, on the contrary, be a radical departure to impose liability in circumstances such as these'. Hence, these recent authorities confirm that the incremental test may still have a considerable impact in personal injury cases, in precluding a duty of care.

---

[370] [2015] UKSC 2, [102].   [371] [2015] EWHC 1394 (QB), quote at [27].

3

Duty II – Particular duty scenarios

This chapter applies many of the principles discussed in Chapter 2, but considers four controversial and problematical scenarios involving a duty of care, *viz*, where:

- statute has precluded a duty of care, primarily for reasons of policy;
- D has failed to warn of material risks associated with a medical operation or treatment;
- D has committed a so-called 'pure omission'; and
- D has failed to manage, control or supervise third parties who injure or kill C.

Dealing with the four conundrums in turn:

STATUTORY PRECLUSIONS OF A DUTY OF CARE

There are two specific scenarios, arising under the Congenital Disabilities (Civil Liability) Act 1976 ('the 1976 Act'), in which a duty of care has been barred by statute. Both are entirely policy-driven.

A mother's immunity

§3.1 The 1976 Act confers an immunity upon C's mother, D, in respect of any of D's acts or omissions which occurred during D's pregnancy (i.e., *in utero*) or pre-conception which affected her ability to have a healthy child (per s 1(1)). However, D loses that immunity if her child, C, is injured *in utero* due to D's negligent driving (per s 2).

No negligence action is possible by a child, C, against his or her mother, D, for acts or omissions which cause damage to that child, such as the following, committed during or prior to the pregnancy:

i. if D participates voluntarily in sporting activity, and suffers an injury during that activity because of her own carelessness or lack of reasonable attention;

ii. if D smokes, drinks, takes drugs, or ingests something else, which affects the foetus adversely in some way and results in C's being born injured, disabled, drug-dependent or otherwise afflicted (in the recent case of *CP (A Child) v First-Tier Tribunal (Criminal Injuries*

Compensation),[1] where a child was born with Foetal Alcohol Spectrum Disorder as a direct consequence of her mother's excessive drinking while pregnant, the Court of Appeal confirmed, in dicta, that s 1 would preclude that child from being able to sue her mother in these circumstances);

iii. if D refuses medical intervention, and delivers a handicapped child (a hypothetical example suggested in *Re MB*,[2] where D refused blood samples, surgical procedures, etc, during her pregnancy, as she was frightened of needles). As Lady Justice Butler-Sloss noted in *MB*, the 1976 Act has a certain, perhaps illogical, ramification: '[a]lthough it might seem illogical that a child capable of being born alive is protected by the criminal law from intentional destruction; and by the Abortion Act from termination ..., [but that child] is not protected from the (irrational) decision of a competent mother not to allow medical intervention to avert the risk of death, this appears to be the present state of the law'.[3]

No equivalent immunity is available to the child's *father*, in respect of any acts or omissions which he may commit against his child, C, during the mother's pregnancy (e.g., the father's act of hitting the mother of his child in the stomach during her pregnancy) that may cause C to be born alive and disabled. In that event, the usual claim by a child may be brought under the 1976 Act (as discussed in Chapter 2).

An exception to the mother's immunity, per s 2 of the 1976 Act, applies where a mother is 'driving a motor vehicle', and in consequence of her failing to exercise reasonable care when driving, C 'is born with disabilities which would not otherwise have been present'. Note that the mother only loses her immunity if she knows, or should have known, that she was pregnant at the time of her negligent driving. However, a mother has immunity from her child's suit where she is not *driving* the motor vehicle, but is merely a passenger in it and has behaved negligently (e.g., failed to wear a seatbelt).

The mother's immunity, and the exception to it, adopted the recommendation of a 1974 English Law Commission report, *Injuries to Unborn Children*.[4] The reasons were complex, and policy-driven:

The law reform corner: The mother's immunity

Reasons for the mother's immunity:
- it reflected that such allegations could be difficult, unseemly, prone to create bitterness, and hard to prove, such that a child should not be able to sue his mother for pregnancy-related activities;
- if C could sue his mother for her negligence, that liability could 'easily' be used by the father as a 'weapon' in custody disputes;
- it is unlikely that the mother would be insured for any activities which caused harm to her child whilst *in utero* – in which case, any successful suit by C against his mother might result in a redistribution of family wealth and assets, in the child's favour (to be held on trust), and diverted away from the mother (who, herself, might be injured).

---

[1] [2014] EWCA Civ 1554, [2015] 1 QB 459, [47].   [2] [1997] EWCA Civ 3093, (1997) BMLR 175 (CA) [31].
[3] *ibid*, [50].   [4] (Rep 60, 1974) pp 21–6, 35.

Doesn't extend to the father:

The EWLC recommended that no immunity should extend to C's father, for any acts or omissions committed by the father against C, whilst *in utero* or pre-conception. The Pearson Committee thereafter recommended, in 1978, that C's father **should** have an immunity (because 'the danger of disrupting family life also applies to the father') and the 1976 Act be amended, but this has never occurred.[5]

Why abolish the immunity for driving?

This was for solely pragmatic reasons. The mother will be compulsorily insured for any negligent driving, and hence, any payout by the mother to her child will be paid by an insurer, and not by the mother herself. Hence, the suit will not result in a distasteful redistribution of the family's wealth in favour of the child. In fact, the Pearson Committee recommended that no immunity should apply to either parent in the case of negligent driving, or, where C's ante-natal injury arose from any other parental activity for which insurance was compulsory, but that has never been enacted.

Notably, however, a parental D does not enjoy any immunity from a child's action against him/her in negligence in other scenarios (as discussed in Chapter 2).

'Wrongful life' claims

§3.2   A wrongful life claim arises, when a child, C, who suffers from some naturally-occurring disability, alleges that it was D's legal obligation to bring about, or facilitate, the destruction of C's life prior to his birth. Such a claim is unlawful under English common law, as being contrary to public policy. Separately, by virtue of the Congenital Disabilities (Civil Liability) Act 1976, s 1(2)(b), it has been stated, in dicta, that wrongful life claims are abolished by that statute also.

Under a wrongful life claim, a disabled child, C, alleges that, in the absence of D's negligence, he would not have been conceived; or that the pregnancy would have been terminated – and, either way, C would not have been born in a disabled state.

The scenario entails that C's mother was under medical treatment during her pregnancy by her treating doctors, D; that D negligently failed to diagnose or detect the existence or likely prospect of C's naturally-occurring disability; at the time of D's negligent act or omission, an abortion would have been lawfully available to C's mother; C's mother would have aborted C, had she known of the existence or likelihood of the disability; and C's mother did not abort C, thus giving rise to C's disabled birth.

Note that D's acts or omissions do not **cause** C's disability, for a 'wrongful life' claim – if that scenario arises, and C argues that, but for D's negligence which injured the child, C would have been born healthy, then C's appropriate action is to sue under s 1(1) of the 1976 Act. That claim is perfectly permissible (as discussed in Chapter 2). By comparison, C's claim in a wrongful life claim is that, but for D's negligence, C *would not have been born at all*. D negligently failed to avert C's birth (e.g., by failing to inform C's mother that she was carrying a disabled child following a scan, or failing to competently conduct a test for rubella symptoms, or failing to advise C's parents, pre-conception, that they had a risk of chromosome incompatibility). This claim by the child is, in fact, the mirror version of the parent's 'wrongful birth' claim (also discussed in Chapter 2).

[5] Lord Pearson *et al.*, *Royal Comm on Civil Liability and Compensation for Personal Injury* (Cmnd 7054–1, 1978) 309.

At common law

In *McKay v Essex AHA*,[6] the child, C, was born on 15 August 1975, and hence, the common law applied to her claim, and not the 1976 Act (which only applies to births on or after 22 July 1976).

> In *McKay v Essex AHA*, Mary McKay, C, was born disabled as a result of an infection of rubella suffered by her mother in the third month of her pregnancy. Mrs McKay presented at her GP practice, D, with concerns that she had been exposed to a relative with rubella, and a blood test was taken, but the test result was mislaid. A second blood test was taken, and it is not entirely clear why the results of that test were mis-communicated to Mrs McKay. Mary was born in 1975, with very serious disabilities. She alleged that, but for the negligence of D, her mother would have had an abortion to terminate C's life. **Held (at trial):** C had a reasonable cause of action in negligence, and a strike-out application failed. **Held (CA, 3: 0):** C had no cause of action recognisable at law.

According to the English Court of Appeal, wrongful life claims are barred for **three** reasons of public policy:[7]

Why policy reasons preclude a wrongful life claim

- no duty can be owed by a healthcare practitioner D to the child, C, where the central argument was that D was under a duty to bring about C's destruction. That was contrary to public policy, 'as running wholly contrary to the concept of the sanctity of human life.' Plus, to uphold C's claim would endorse the view that a disabled child's life was of such lesser value than a normal child's life, that it was worth destroying – which the Court could not support (it might also have the effect of increasing the rate of abortion). Importantly, where would the line be appropriately drawn, to permit C to bring a claim against D for failing to advise C's mother, so as to provide her with an opportunity to abort – could C, a child with very minor disabilities (e.g., a squint), sue for wrongful life?

- the fact of birth is not an 'injury' to C that is recognisable at law. As the Irish LRC said, '[l]ife itself is said to be the injury' in such actions,[a] and it cannot be construed as such. (Cf: the birth of a disabled child can be construed as an injury for C's parent/s under a 'wrongful birth' action, because an abortion is lawfully available to them.)

- the assessment of C's harm or damage would be impossible, given that the court's task is to put C in the position as if the tort had not been committed – if the tort had not been committed, C's claim is that he would not exist at all. Hence, a court would have to compare the state of C's existence with his non-existence – of which the court can know nothing. Also, the court cannot compare 'the injured child's life in this world and determine that the child has lost anything, without knowing what, if anything the child has gained [from living]' (per Stephenson LJ). To assess damages would be to enter the realms of theology and speculation, leaving 'judges striving to solve the insoluble.'

[a] *Bioethics: Advance Care Directives* (CP 51, 2008) [5.29].

However, not all jurisdictions share the English court's abhorrence of the wrongful life claim, although many do. The contrary viewpoint is interesting to consider:

[6] [1982] QB 1166 (CA).
[7] *ibid*, with quotes in box locatable at: 1181 (Stephenson LJ), 1181, 1188 (Ackner LJ), 1193 (Griffiths LJ).

The comparative corner: Other jurisdictions on wrongful life claims

In some jurisdictions, the claim for wrongful life has been barred (e.g., in South Africa, per *Stewart v Botha*[8]; in Canada, per *Mickle v SA Grace Hosp*,[9] or abandoned, per *Arndt v Smith*;[10] in Scotland, per *P's Curator Bonis v Criminal Injuries Comp Bd*;[11] and in Singapore, per *Ju v See Tho Kai Yin*[12]).

Elsewhere, there has been some judicial support for the claim (e.g., in France, where the claim was permitted, per *Perruche*;[13] in Australia, where the claim was barred by the HCA in *Harriton v Stephens*,[14] but in the NSWCA below, Mason P dissented and would have allowed it;[15] and in US, a mix of judicial views and results have emerged (e.g., *Procanik v Cillo*,[16] *Harbeson v Parke-Davis Inc*,[17] *Speck v Finegold*[18] and *Turpin v Sortini*[19]).

Where wrongful life claims have been permitted in other jurisdictions, some salient points were that:

- the view that birth or life is deemed incapable of being a legal 'injury' was inconsistent with the principle of corrective justice (*Harriton*, Mason P);
- pragmatically, funds for the lifelong care of a profoundly-injured child are better protected in the hands of the Public Trustee, rather than treating damages as the parents' property in a wrongful birth claim (*Harriton*, Mason P);
- if wrongful life claims were permitted, then that would 'foster the societal objectives of genetic counselling and prenatal testing, and will discourage malpractice' (*Harbeson v Parke-Davis Inc*);
- a proper measure of damage (to counter the difficulty of assessment) is either: (1) by assessing the difference between the value of C's life as a healthy normal child, and the value of C's life as an injured child (*Harriton*, Mason P); or (2) restricting C's damages to medical/care expenses, excluding general damages (*Turpin v Sortini*);
- there are 'incalculables' in the parental wrongful conception claim too, where the 'benefits' of having the joys of a healthy child in the family are non-assessable – but that damages claim is assessable, the incalculable offset does not destroy the cause of action. Hence, why should courts be markedly more sympathetic to parental claims than to those of the children themselves? (*Harriton*, Mason P).

There has never been a wrongful life claim brought in England since *McKay*, so far as the author's searches can ascertain. Indeed, subsequent case law has approved of the *McKay* view that no wrongful life action exists in English common law: per *Hibbert Pownall & Newton v Whitehead*[20] (where the child, born with undiagnosed spina bifida, could not bring a personal action against his doctors). Nevertheless, it has occasionally been mentioned, judicially (see, e.g., Lord Steyn in *McFarlane v Tayside Health Board*[21]), that a parental claim for wrongful conception or wrongful birth also depends upon the court's assessing the parents' position with

---

[8] [2008] 1 LRC 370 ((HC (Cape of Good Hope Provincial Div).   [9] (1998), 166 DLR (4th) 743.
[10] (1995), 126 DLR (4th) 487 (BCCA), rev'd [1997] 2 SCR 539, (1997), 148 DLR (4th) 48 (SCC).
[11] 1997 SLT 1180 (OH).   [12] [2005] 4 SLR 96 (HC).   [13] (Cass ass plén, 17 Nov 2000).
[14] [2006] HCA 15, (2006) 226 CLR 52 (HCA).
[15] [2004] NSWCA 93, with Mason P's observations in the Table at [130]–[162].
[16] 478 A 2d 755 (1984).   [17] 656 P 2d 483, 496 (SC Wash, 1983) (Pearson J).   [18] 408 A 2d 496 (1979).
[19] 643 P 2d 954 (SC Cal, 1982).   [20] [2008] EWCA Civ 285, [2009] WLR 549, [3], [19].   [21] [2000] 2 AC 59 (HL).

The relevant cause of action

§3.4   Where non-disclosure of inherent risks is concerned, the relevant cause of action is negligence, and not assault and battery.

Provided that patient C knows, 'in broad terms', about the nature of the operation and consents to it, then the fact that C is not fully informed as to the risks associated with the operation does not vitiate his consent, so as to render the healthcare professional, D, liable in assault and/or battery. Negligence is the appropriate cause of action for most failure-to-warn cases; whereas an action in battery is appropriate where there was a lack of consent, whether express or implied, to the relevant procedure (and will require quite different matters to be dealt with at trial, as noted in *Border v Lewisham and Greenwich NHS Trust*[28]). That proposition, explicitly made in *Chatterton v Gerson*,[29] was later affirmed in *Sidaway*[30] and in *Hills v Potter*.[31]

For that reason, the phrase, 'informed consent', will be avoided in this chapter, for as May J noted in *The Creutzfeldt-Jakob Disease Litigation*, '[t]here is no English law doctrine of informed consent, and a person may succeed in a claim for failure to inform or warn only if the failure alleged amounts to negligence. To frame such a claim in battery is not only deplorable, but insupportable in law'.[32] Although the phrase, 'informed consent', continues to be used by the highest appellate courts in England (e.g., in *Chester v Afshar*[33]), it is potentially misleading. A lack of consent is certainly very relevant to torts of trespass to the person (see Chapter 14), but if there is a *general consent* to the procedure, then C cannot sue D in assault and battery. The action will have to be brought in negligence, for failure-to-warn.

Inherent risks

§3.5   Inherent risks which the law requires to be disclosed may be either objectively-significant, or subjectively-significant to C, or both.

The map of inherent risks is shown in the Diagram below:

The categorisation of inherent risks

All inherent risks associated with a procedure

significant risks that have to be disclosed

risks that don't have to be disclosed

objectively-significant risks   subjectively-significant risks   therapeutic privilege   unimportant risks

---

[28] [2015] EWCA Civ 8, [26].   [29] [1981] QB 432, 443 (Bristow J.)

[30] [1985] AC 871 (HL) 894–95 (Lord Diplock), 898–99 (Lord Bridge).

[31] [1984] 1 WLR 641 (QB) 647, (Hirst J.).

[32] (1995) 54 BMLR 1 (QB) 7, citing the views in: *Sidaway* [1985] AC 871 (HL) 885 (Lord Scarman).

[33] [2004] UKHL 41, [2005] 1 AC 134, [14] (Lord Steyn).

Objectively-significant risks are those risks which are significant and important, having regard to objective factors; whereas subjectively-significant risks are those which are important to *that particular patient*, because of his particular needs, concerns or circumstances. When considering the question of 'objectively-significant risks', it is perhaps helpful to remember that it is the procedure rather than the patient which bears closest scrutiny; whilst the converse is true for subjectively-significant risks. Both types of risk must be disclosed at law.

Risks which are either unimportant, or subject to therapeutic privilege, do not have to be disclosed at law. The risks under therapeutic privilege are those which should be disclosed, but which can lawfully be held back from the patient where their disclosure could harm the patient's health and welfare (a defence discussed in Chapter 10). The unimportant risks fall into that residual basket of risks which are so trivial, so obvious, or so rare, that they can safely be ignored.

Objectively-significant risks

In English law, there used to be a real disparity as to how to assess an objectively-significant risk, due in no small part to the obscure language and divisions in opinion which occurred in what must rank as one of the most unenlightening House of Lords' judgments, in *Sidaway*.[34] Certainly, the judicial assertions in *Chester v Afshar* (Court of Appeal) that, '[t]he relevant law on the duty to warn is not controversial',[35] and in *Moy v Pettmann Smith (a firm)* that the principles 'are now relatively well understood',[36] were very doubtful – and difficult to reconcile with the (more accurate) remarks in *Birch v UCL Hospital NHS Foundation Trust* that, 'the matter is not as straightforward as it could be'![37]

Thankfully, this uncertainty has been swept aside by one of the most welcome Supreme Court decisions of recent times, *Montgomery v Lanarkshire Health Board*.[38]

§3.6   The test by which to determine whether an inherent risk is objectively significant is whether a reasonable patient would consider that the risk was significant enough that it ought to have been disclosed. An objectively-significant risk is not to be determined by what risks 'reasonable medical opinion' assesses should have been disclosed to the patient; the sole application of the *Bolam* test in this context has been rejected.

Under the 'reasonable patient' test, the court must put itself in the shoes of a reasonable person in the patient's position, and assess whether that patient would regard the risk as being significant. That significance is to be determined according to a range of objective factors, of which the magnitude of the risk is but one factor. Under a so-called *Bolam*[39]-type assessment, however, a risk is not relevant to disclose if D, in not disclosing it, acted in accordance with a practice accepted at the time as proper by a responsible body of medical opinion, even though other Ds might adopt a different practice about disclosure. Although the 'reasonable patient' and the *Bolam* tests will, frequently, give rise to the same answer to the question – should the risk have been disclosed? – that will not always be the case.

---

[34] [1985] AC 871 (HL).   [35] [2002] EWCA Civ 724, [2002] 3 WLR 1195, 67 BMLR 66, [14] (Sir Dennis Henry).

[36] [2005] UKHL 7, [28] (albeit that '[i]t took the law some time to work out the principles governing what the patient is entitled to be told before deciding whether or not to agree to intrusive medical treatment: see *Sidaway*').

[37] [2008] EWHC 2237 (QB), (2008) 104 BMLR 168 (Cranston J) [73].

[38] [2015] UKSC 11, [2015] 2 WLR 768.

[39] Per *Bolam v Friern Hospital Management Committee* [1957] 1 WLR 582 (QB).

that significant risk, if the information is needed so that the patient can determine for him or herself as to what course he or she should adopt'.

> In *Pearce*, Mrs Pearce, C, was expecting her sixth child. She consulted with her treating obstetrician, D, when she was 14 days over term in her pregnancy. She was very upset, and requested the birth to be induced or to have a caesarean section, but was advised that both courses presented risks, and that it would take her longer to recover from a caesarean, and that it was better that she should wait. C was not advised of any increased risk (0.1–0.2%) of the baby being stillborn if the pregnancy continued. The baby later died *in utero*, and was stillborn. **Held:** no duty to disclose the risk. The medical opinion was that it should not have been disclosed, and it was so low that a reasonable patient would not have attached significance to it.

Subsequently, the *Pearce* approach received some strong appellate endorsement. In *Wyatt v Curtis*, Sedley LJ confirmed that Lord Woolf's formulation in *Pearce* 'refine[d] Lord Bridge's test by recognising that what is substantial and what is grave are questions on which the doctor's and the patient's perception may differ, and in relation to which the doctor must therefore have regard to what may be the patient's perception.'[52] Further, in *Chester v Afshar*,[53] Lords Steyn and Hope (of the majority) approved Lord Woolf's view in *Pearce* (albeit that it was common ground that the risk *should* have been disclosed, and the appeal turned on the question of causation there,[54] as discussed in Chapter 8). Several first-instance decisions also adopted the 'reasonable patient' test.[55]

> In *Poynter v Hillingdon HA*,[56] C, a child of 15 months, required heart transplant surgery. There was a 1% risk that, though he might survive the surgery, he might suffer permanent brain damage, but this was not disclosed to his parents. Unfortunately, brain damage occurred when C's heart stopped whilst C was under anaesthetic. **Held:** no duty to warn of brain damage. There was a reasonable body of medical opinion that the risk would not have been disclosed; and the court considered that view to be rational, given the low probability of risk and the gravity of the scenario in which the child was involved.

The *Montgomery* clarification

In *Montgomery v Lanarkshire Health Board*, the Supreme Court explicitly adopted the views of Lord Woolf MR in *Pearce* and of Lord Scarman in *Sidaway*. Lords Reed and Kerr put the position thus:[57]

> The doctor is ... under a duty to take reasonable care to ensure that the patient is aware of any material risks involved in any recommended treatment, and of any reasonable alternative or variant treatments. The test of materiality is whether, in the circumstances of the particular case, a reasonable person in the patient's position would be likely to attach significance to the risk, or the doctor is or should reasonably be aware that the particular patient would be likely to attach significance to it.

That 'reasonable patient' test now represents the modern approach to the duty-to-warn issue in English law, and has usurped the *Bolam* 'peer professional medical opinion' test.

---

[52] [2003] EWCA Civ 1779, [16].   [53] [2004] UKHL 41, [2005] 1 AC 134, [15], [86], respectively.

[54] [2002] EWCA Civ 724, [2002] 3 WLR 1195, [15].

[55] e.g., *Jones v North West Strategic HA* [2010] EWHC 178 (QB) [24]; *Birch v UCL Hospital NHS Foundation Trust* [2008] EWHC 2237 (QB) [73].

[56] (1997) 37 BMLR 192 (QB).   [57] [2015] UKSC 11, [87].

This switch from *Bolam* has occurred hand-in-hand with the greater importance of human rights jurisprudence. As Lord Walker stated in *Chester v Afshar*, 'during the 20 years which have elapsed since *Sidaway*, the importance of personal autonomy has been more and more widely recognised'.[58] In *Montgomery*, the Supreme Court agreed, noting the rights-based approach which now pervades patient care, 'under the stimulus of the Human Rights Act 1998' (which, of course, post-dated *Sidaway*).[59] As a result, 'patient autonomy' is frequently cited in this sort of litigation nowadays.[60] Further, as discussed in Chapter 7, a modified *Bolam* approach applies where patient C alleges medical *mistreatment or misdiagnosis*, per the decision in *Bolitho v City and Hackney HA*[61] – although the House of Lords expressly noted, in *Bolitho*, that it was *not* considering questions of disclosure of risk. Nevertheless, there is now a pleasing symmetry of legal attitude, across treatment, diagnosis *and disclosure*.

As well as these factors, the *Montgomery* Supreme Court pointed out that the decrease in 'medical paternalism'; the wider availability of public information about risks; the modern guidance given by the General Medical Council to doctors which reflected a 'reasonable patient' approach to risks-disclosure; the difficulties which English courts had experienced in applying (or departing from) *Sidaway*; and the successful adoption of a 'reasonable patient' test in other jurisdictions (e.g., in Australia, by virtue of the 1992 High Court of Australia decision in *Rogers v Whitaker*,[62] which was extensively cited in *Montgomery*, and whose test of materiality of risk was closely adopted in *Montgomery*), all contributed to a view that any continued application of the *Bolam* test in English law to risks-disclosure was 'unsatisfactory'.[63]

It is worth noting that the change of attitude in English law is not merely an academic nicety. *Bolam*, and the 'reasonable patient' test, may indeed give differing answers:

In *Birch v UCL Hospital NHS Foundation Trust*,[64] Mrs Birch, C, was a Type-1 diabetic, with a long history of serious health problems. One morning, she woke up with a bad headache, blurred vision, a turned left eye, nausea and vomiting. At UCL Hospital, D, a cerebral catheter angiogram was performed, to rule out the possibility of an artery aneurysm. The angiogram involved inserting a catheter at the groin, and then working it up through the vascular system to the area of the brain to be scanned. It was a potentially life-threatening procedure, which carried a 1% risk of stroke. The risk of stroke from a cerebral angiogram **was** discussed with C and was properly disclosed. However, C was not informed that an investigation of her condition could have been undertaken by non-invasive magnetic resonance imaging (MRI), which did not entail any risk of stroke. **Held:** D should have discussed with C the different imaging methods – the catheter angiogram and the MRI – so as to provide C with comparable risks, even though the *Bolam* opinion had not considered that necessary. In *Montgomery v Lanarkshire Health Board*, Mrs Montgomery, C, gave birth to her first baby at D's hospital. The baby was born with severe disabilities, because of the condition of shoulder dystocia (where the baby's shoulders become stuck behind the mother's pelvis) which caused severe hypoxic injury. C was particularly at risk (a 9–10% risk), given that she was diabetic and small in stature, and that women with diabetes were more likely to have larger babies. **Held:** C ought to have been advised about the risk of shoulder dystocia associated

---

[58] [2004] UKHL 41, [2005] 1 AC 134, [92].   [59] [2015] UKSC 11, [75], [80].
[60] e.g., *A v East Kent Hospitals Univ NHS Foundation Trust* [2015] EWHC 1038 (QB) [20].
[61] [1997] 3 WLR 1151 (HL) 1160.   [62] (1992) 175 CLR 479 (HCA) 490, and cited in *Montgomery* at [72].
[63] [2015] UKSC 11, [75–[86], quote at [86].   [64] [2008] EWHC 2237 (QB), (2008) 104 BMLR 168.

not particularly helpful on its own. Serious harm may, arguably, not be only physical, but also emotional (brought about, e.g., from lifestyle changes forced upon C).

> The following serious injuries **were** significant: disabling stroke in *Birch v UCL Hospital Foundation NHS Trust*; *cauda equina* syndrome in *Chester v Afshar*; cerebral palsy suffered as a result of shoulder dystocia during delivery in *Jones v North West Strategic HA*. **However**, the following were **not** significant risks, notwithstanding their great severity: brain damage in *Poynter v Hillingdon HA*; stillbirth in *Pearce v United Bristol Healthcare NHS Trust*; and permanent paralysis in *Sidaway*.

Injury to the mother, where C is her gravely-disabled baby who was damaged by D's negligence, may also 'count' towards the overall seriousness of the injury, should the undisclosed risk manifest. This was plain in *Montgomery*, where the major obstetric emergency which shoulder dystocia represented to the mother too, was significant.

iii. *Bolam* peer professional opinion: as discussed above, medical opinion as to what should be disclosed by way of risks is *no longer* determinative nor conclusive of what D ought to have disclosed by way of risks, under the 'reasonable patient' test. However, it is unlikely that *Bolam*-type evidence will entirely lose its relevance, in the post-*Montgomery* landscape. Interestingly, since *Rogers v Whitaker* was handed down by the High Court of Australia, the practice of other experts in D's field of expertise as to whether or not warnings should have been provided prior to C's medical treatment has been judicially regarded as being useful and of great assistance, regarding the question of materiality in that jurisdiction.[70] It is foreshadowed that, similarly in English law, evidence of professional practice or guidance will remain relevant to the objective test. Meanwhile, it is worth noting that, even pre-*Montgomery*, there were cases in which the 'reasonable patient' test and the *Bolam* test were perfectly aligned.

> In *Jones v North West Strategic HA*, Jack Jones was born brain-damaged and severely disabled, due to the condition of shoulder dystocia, whereby Jack's shoulder got stuck behind his mother's pelvic bone during the course of delivery. It took 15 minutes to deliver Jack, by which time he was severely brain-damaged. Mrs Jones, C, claimed that she should have been advised, as part of her ante-natal care, of the risk of shoulder dystocia (assessed as being in the region of 1–2%), and that a caesarean section would avoid the risk associated with a natural birth. One of her previous two children, Rebecca, had suffered the same problem, but it had been resolved satisfactorily during the birth. **Held:** a duty to warn C of the risk of shoulder dystocia with a vaginal birth was owed. An expert witness accepted that he would have expected a consultation between D and C to have included a discussion of the advantages and disadvantages of doing a caesarean section rather than a vaginal birth, 'even if it was only to put it on one side'. The then-current Royal College of Obstetrician and Gynaecologist Guidelines also stated that, where there had been previous history of shoulder dystocia, then although a caesarean was not the routine course to be recommended, the option should be discussed between the mother and her doctors.

iv. Comparative risks: where C is proposing to undergo a medical treatment which carries a particular risk, and another avenue of treatment is available which does not, then the comparable risks may become significant, legally-speaking. Comparable procedures which entail different risks render those comparable risks legally significant. A reasonable patient would want to

---

[70] As discussed by the author in: 'Twelve Tests to Identify whether a Medical Risk is "Material"' (2000) 1 *National L Rev* 1, [64]–[67].

weigh up the pros and cons of the two treatments (one of which he will have to undergo) to make an informed choice about which of the two procedures was preferable, and that would require disclosure of the comparable risks.

> In *Birch v UCL Hospital NHS Foundation Trust*, facts previously, **Held:** D should have discussed with C the different imaging methods – the catheter angiogram and the MRI – so as to provide C with comparable risks, and the lack of stroke risk with an MRI. In *Jones v North West Strategic HA*, facts previously, **Held:** not only was there was a duty to warn C of the risk of shoulder dystocia with a vaginal birth, but also mention should have been made of the comparative risks of a Caesarian, especially given C's previous history of shoulder dystocia. In *Montgomery*, the facts were notably similar to *Jones*, and the extremely small risk of a major obstetric emergency with a caesarean, should have been disclosed.

As affirmed subsequently in *Meiklejohn v St George's Healthcare NHS Trust*,[71] the problem in *Birch* was that the risk of one procedure (angiogram) was explained, but a less risky alternative procedure (the MRI) was not. *Jones* was a somewhat different case, because the risks of **both** alternatives (natural and Caesarian births) were not disclosed to C. However, these cases are as far as English law goes at this stage. The duty to warn of comparative risks does **not** extend to a scenario (as occurred in *Meiklejohn*) where D did not even contemplate the alternative diagnosis or treatment, and failed to give a risks assessment of the treatment. That is too onerous a position for the law to adopt.

v. **Essential versus elective procedure:** for elective surgery, it is easier to prove that a non-disclosure was a significant risk in the legal sense, because C will reasonably attach greater significance to risks that are purely a matter of his choice to undertake.

> In *Chester v Afshar*, Miss Chester, C, a journalist, had suffered various episodes of back pain for several years, and had to have an epidural injection to tide her over on a work trip. On her return, she saw a specialist, and had an MRI scan, which showed a prolapsed disc high in the spine (the higher the prolapse, the riskier is surgery to correct it). The specialist referred C to Dr Afshar, a neurosurgeon, with instructions that C was 'anxious to avoid surgery if at all possible'. The surgery (which carried with it a 1–2% risk of damage to the spinal cord) was elective, rather than necessary. Three days after the consultation, C had a lumbar surgical operation, and suffered from *cauda equina* syndrome, leading to leg paralysis. **Held:** it was common ground that the risk should have been disclosed. At CA level,[72] Sir Deny Henry noted that C's surgery was elective, and not an emergency, which helped to render risk of this sort 'significant'.

vi. **D's own experiences:** where the risk was not one which had ever manifested in D's extensive personal experience, then it is justifiable that D would not have considered that C would attach significance to it, and hence, the risk is less likely to be legally significant. However, the converse view – that a risk could still be material, notwithstanding that D had never witnessed that risk in a long career of medical practice – prevailed at trial in *Chester v Afshar* (and thereafter, it was conceded that the risk should have been disclosed).

> In *Chester v Afshar*, facts previously, C told neurosurgeon Dr Afshar, D, that she had heard a lot of horror stories about surgery, and that she wanted to know about the risks. She did not specifically mention paralysis as one of the risks that she wanted to be told about, and this

---

[71] [2014] EWCA Civ 120, [62].

was not mentioned as a risk of surgery by D – but D did say that he had performed about 300 similar operations per year, and that he 'had not crippled anybody yet'. D had never caused any nerve damages in the many hundreds of operations he had carried out over 20–25 years, and he considered the risk very small. **Held:** the risk should have been disclosed: 'however understandable such a response may have been in psychological terms, it was not an adequate response in legal terms'.

vii. The use of medical booklets/literature: any warnings about material risks contained within literature which is given by D to patient C forms part of the total evidentiary package. Whilst written material does not discharge the duty to warn of itself, it can assist D to defeat an allegation of failure-to-warn. Of course, handing to C voluminous lists of remote risks is hardly likely to impress an already-nervous patient, and the larger the volume of risks literature, the less likely the reasonable patient will read it. Lords Reed and Kerr emphasised this in *Montgomery*, noting that a doctor's duty to disclose material risks 'is not therefore fulfilled by bombarding the patient with technical information which she cannot reasonably be expected to grasp, let alone by routinely demanding her signature on a consent form'.[73]

> In *Birch v UCL Hospital NHS Foundation Trust*,[74] facts previously, Mrs Birch, C, signed the standard consent form prior to the cerebral angiogram being performed. It read, 'I have explained the procedure to the patient/parent ... [under] 'Serious or frequently occurring risks': bleeding. renal damage. 1% stroke'. The form also stated that, 'I have also discussed what the procedure is likely to involve, the benefits and risks of any available alternative treatments and any particular concerns of those involved'. It was signed by both D and C. The risk of stroke was disclosed and manifested, but the alternative treatment of an MRI was not discussed, despite the form's content. **Held:** the alternative should have been discussed, under the duty to warn.

The problem of an undisclosed risk is more likely to arise where the literature does **not** contain any information about the risk that patient C alleges was significant. On one potential view, the fact a booklet omits mention of a risk that ultimately eventuates does not mean that it cannot be material in the legal sense. It may behove D to draw that omitted risk to C's attention, so that the omission imposes a *more* onerous duty on D. On the other possible view, the fact that the risk was not mentioned in a pamphlet may contribute to the finding that it must have been too remote and insignificant a possibility to be 'material' in the legal sense. There is yet to be any decisive authority on this point in English law (although the point has proven contentious in Australia, under *Rogers v Whitaker*[75]).

Subjectively–significant risks

§3.7   There are two indicators that a risk is subjectively-significant to *that particular patient*, C: first, where C asks of D specific questions which highlight the particular significance of a risk *for him*; and secondly, where C presents with a highly idiosyncratic medical history, set of needs, or unusual concerns.

---

[72] [2002] EWCA Civ 724, [2003] QB 356, [5], [17].   [73] [2015] UKSC 11, [90].
[74] [2008] EWHC 2237 (QB), (2008) 104 BMLR 168, [20]–[24].
[75] Mulheron, 'Twelve Tests to Identify Whether a Medical Risk is "Material"' [2000] *National L Rev* 1, Factor 9, [68]–[74].

The relevance of questions

When discussing the subjective limb of its newly-proposed test in *Montgomery*, the Supreme Court remarked that '[e]xpressions of concern by the patient, as well as specific questions, are plainly relevant'.[76] Earlier, in *Sidaway*,[77] Lord Diplock remarked that, 'if the patient manifested this attitude by means of questioning, the doctor would tell him whatever it was the patient wanted to know', while Lord Bridge noted that, 'when questioned specifically by a patient ... about risks involved in a particular treatment proposed, the doctor's duty must ... be to answer both truthfully and as fully as the questioner requires'. Subsequently, in *Poynter v Hillingdon HA*,[78] Sir Maurice Drake stated that the duty to disclose must be considered, 'in the context of what the particular patient wanted to know. That is to say, I would consider [the duty] subjectively'.

Hence, where the patient, C, incessantly and worriedly questions about an aspect of the operative procedure or medical treatment, the subjective limb will be triggered (evident in *Chester v Afshar*, where the patient was very nervous and anxious to avoid surgery). Asking questions is legally significant (albeit that the court must be satisfied that such questions were, *in fact*, asked).

But what if C asked **some** questions indicating concern, but did not ask the 'right questions', i.e., questions that would have elicited precisely the information about the risk that, ultimately, was not disclosed? Prior to *Montgomery*, there had been very little direct authority on this in English law, but what there was had tended to suggest that C **had** to ask the right question – failing which D would not be liable for failing to disclose. As Sedley LJ remarked in *Wyatt v Curtis*, that situation is unrealistic: 'there is arguably something unreal about placing the onus of asking upon a patient who may not know that there is anything to ask about'.[79]

> In *Wyatt v Curtis*, Miss Wyatt, C, presented to her locum GP, D1, with chickenpox in her 14th week of pregnancy. D1 did not advise C of the risk of serious abnormalities to her child. Four and a half weeks later, C went to Kings Mill Hospital for an ante-natal check-up, and the senior house officer, D2, learned that she had just had chickenpox, and likewise, did not advise C of the same risk. D2 had asked C whether she had been made aware of the rare problem of chickenpox in pregnancy, and had been told that she had been. C had already asked D1, 'Will the baby be all right?', and was told he would be. C did not put the same question to D2, probably because of the 'false sense of security' created by D1's answer. C's son Luke was ultimately born severely disabled. **Held:** D2 was not negligent, as the relevant question had not been asked by C. In *Poynter v Hillingdon HA*, facts previously, **Held:** no duty to warn. The parents did ask concerned questions about the transplant procedure, but did not ask any questions about the risk of permanent brain damage resulting from the operation.

However, in *Montgomery*, the Supreme Court took a more sympathetic line, noting that, 'courts should not be too quick to discard the second limb [i.e., that the risk was subjectively-significant] ... merely because it emerges that the patient did not ask certain kinds of questions'.[80]

> In *Montgomery*, facts previously, C was concerned about the size of the baby and whether she would be able to deliver the baby naturally. However, C did not ask her obstetrician, D, 'specifically about exact risks', otherwise D stated that she would have advised of the risk of shoulder dystocia. **Held:** even though C did not ask the right question, her personal circumstances of her own small

---

[76] [2015] UKSC 11, [73].   [77] [1985] AC 871 (HL) 890 (Lord Diplock), 898 (Lord Bridge).

[78] (1997) 37 BMLR 192 (QB), 193, 205–6 (where no particular questions were addressed to D).

[79] [2003] EWCA Civ 1779, [19].   [80] [2015] UKSC 11, [73].

size, her diabetes, the risk of a larger baby for a diabetic mother, a natural anxiety about a first-time birth, all contributed to this risk as being one that should have been disclosed.

Again, previous cases which indicated that, where C enquired about risk, D was only required to answer that question by reference to how a reasonable body of medical opinion would have answered it (i.e., a *Bolam*-type assessment), must now be taken to no longer apply. In *Blyth v Bloomsbury HA*,[81] Neill LJ remarked that, where questions are asked by a patient, then, 'as a general proposition it is governed by ... the *Bolam* test'. However, *Montgomery* confirmed that the duty to give full and honest answers to specific questioning is **no longer** to be assessed against *Bolam*-type evidence as to what medical practice deems sufficient to disclose, but goes beyond that.

The comparative corner: *Rogers v Whitaker*, and asking the 'right sort of question'

In *Rogers v Whitaker*,[82] Mrs Whitaker, C, had lost the sight in one eye, as a 9-year-old school girl in England, when she ruptured it in a collision with a paling fence which penetrated the eye socket. C emigrated to Australia, and lived a full life, and had a family. Several years later, advances in ophthalmic surgery meant that the restoration of sight in that eye was feasible. Dr Rogers, D, an ophthalmic surgeon, performed the surgery carefully, competently and without negligence. However, disaster befell C, because not only was sight not restored, but her good eye suffered a rare condition that can arise in this type of surgery – sympathetic ophthalmia – which rendered her blind in her good eye, and hence, totally blind. She was not warned of the risk of sympathetic opthalmia (which did not always lead to loss of vision in any case), and which occurred in approximately 1: 14,000 procedures, with a slightly higher risk where there had been an earlier penetrating injury to the eye operated upon. **Held**: there was a duty to warn of this remote complication in ophthalmic surgery, and a breach in not disclosing it. C has 'incessantly questioned [D] as to, amongst other things, possible complications. She was, to [D's] knowledge, keenly interested in the outcome of the suggested procedure, including the danger of unintended or accidental interference with her 'good', left eye. On the day before the operation, [C] asked [D] whether something could be put over her good eye to ensure that nothing happened to it ... [C] may not have asked the right question, yet she made clear her great concern that no injury should befall her one good eye'. Hence, whilst C did not ask D the specific query as to whether her good eye could be adversely affected, her questions clearly conveyed utmost concern that nothing bad happened to that eye.

Where patient C has idiosyncratic history/needs/circumstances

Any relevant physical or mental characteristics of patient C, of which D was (or should have been) aware, are also relevant, where it means that D ought to have reasonably been aware that, for that C, the risk information would matter. The scenario may arise where, say:

i. **C's own historical experiences:** Where a repeat of an event, unpleasant in the past, made C particularly anxious and concerned, that may render a risk significant.

---

[81] [1993] 4 Med LR 151 (CA).
[82] [1992] HCA 58, (1992) 175 CLR 479, with quote at 491. See also: *Johnson v Biggs* [2000] NSWCA 338.

In *Jones v North West Strategic HA*,[83] facts previously, 'Mrs Jones recalled her experience when Rebecca experienced shoulder dystocia as very traumatic, dramatic and scary. The risk of a repetition of that type of experience (even if ultimately the chances were good that the baby would be safely delivered) can ... properly be taken into account in deciding whether the risk was significant'.

ii. Any pre-existing medical condition on C's part: If C's particular medical history and/or health indicated that there was an elevated concern about the non-disclosed risk manifesting, then the risk is likely to be significant, legally-speaking (as illustrated, again, by the facts of *Jones v North West Strategic HA*, and in *Montgomery* itself, where the fact that C was small, and concerned about being able to deliver the baby naturally, were oft-expressed to D).

iii. C had an aversion to operative procedures: This was evident in *Chester v Afshar*, with medical notes confirming that C was 'anxious to avoid surgery, if at all possible'. Although a duty was conceded, this factor undoubtedly assisted to prompt that concession, as it demonstrated a subjectively-significant risk.

Other subjectively-significant factors have arisen in the extensive failure-to-warn jurisprudence in Australia (as part of *Rogers v Whitaker* jurisprudence), which is of comparative interest:

The comparative corner: Additional factors of subjective risk

- Special family needs. In *Burke v Humphrey*,[84] C underwent a laparoscopy, and sued for her gynaecologist's, D's, failure to disclose that, notwithstanding the tubal ligation, there was a risk of pregnancy (she fell pregnant 13 months later). **Held:** the risk was subjectively-significant, because D knew that C had a family of three boys <2 years due to an unplanned pregnancy: 'it was incumbent upon [D] to have alerted [C] to the possibility of the procedure failing, for he had ample reason to suppose that if warned of the risk she would be likely to attach significance to it'. On the facts, however, such a warning was indeed given.
- Irrational belief giving rise to extreme anxiety. In *Di Carlo v Dubois*,[85] barrister C had convinced himself that he had a brain tumour. His friend, a neurosurgeon, arranged for a scan to be done by another neurosurgeon, D. C was not warned of the risk involved in the administration of a scan enhanced with a non-ionic contrast agent, namely an allergic (anaphylactic) reaction, which is what he suffered. **Held:** the allergic reaction was a subjectively-significant risk, because D knew that C was 'particularly anxious' about the scan, in case it showed that he had a tumour, and that with an irrational anxiety, an adverse reaction was several times more likely.
- Religious/cultural concerns. In *Hassan v Minister for Health*,[86] C was admitted to hospital for a uterine evacuation following a foetal death *in utero*. Unfortunately, the placenta had adhered to the scar tissue from four prior caesareans, and removal of it caused abnormal blood loss, and C had to undergo a complete emergency hysterectomy to stop the ongoing blood loss. She was not warned of the risk of a hysterectomy prior to the

---

[83] [2010] EWHC 178 (QB). However, the claim ultimately failed on causation.   [84] [2001] TASSC 133, [20].

[85] [2004] QCA 150 (Davies JA and McMurdo J, Williams JA dissenting), and especially [77].

[86] [2005] WADC 182, and especially [132]–[133], [149].

procedure being undertaken. C gave evidence that, due to the importance of retaining fertility in her Arabian culture, she would have 'preferred death' to a hysterectomy, that 'the womb for the woman was everything, and without it, she was nothing at all' and 'incomplete', and that it had rendered her marital relationship difficult and insecure. **Held:** D knew that C, if fully warned of the risk of hysterectomy, would have attached great significance to it in view of her culture. A failure-to-warn was proven.

Timings

§3.8   Whether D was under a duty to warn of material risk must be assessed at the time when D is giving the pre-operative advice, and not at a subsequent time (e.g., when the risk crystallises into injury, or even later at trial).

As one court pithily noted, in this context: '[a]ny fool can be wise after the event. That is not the test. The Court must be careful to judge the conduct of [D], where negligent failure to warn is asserted, by reference to what [D] reasonably knew at the relevant time'.[87] In *Jones v North West Strategic HA*,[88] the allegedly negligent failure-to-warn occurred 18 years prior to the trial – and the obstetrician D's disclosure had to be judged according to the standards of what ought to have been disclosed 18 years ago, a tricky task when medical research and knowledge about shoulder dystocia had moved on considerably since. This is an issue relevant to breach, rather than the duty itself, but is worth reiterating at this juncture.

As to when the warning of risk must be given, the timing must enable a reasonable patient to digest and evaluate the risks information. As the Irish Supreme Court remarked in *Fitzpatrick v White*, 'an invalid warning, i.e., one which [patient C] could neither assimilate nor act upon, would be equivalent to no warning' (albeit that C there could digest the warnings as to risks, a mere 30 minutes before his eye operation). Several matters would be relevant on this issue: was the surgery elective only? Was it major and perhaps life-threatening? Was C stressed, medicated, or in pain, and less likely to take on board the risks and make a calm and reasoned decision? Had C been evaluated pre-operatively, with many chances to discuss risks then?[88a]

PURE OMISSIONS

The general rule

§3.9   The law of negligence does not, as a general rule, impose a duty of care on D for 'pure omissions'. That is, D is not legally required to take positive steps to protect C's person or property from suffering foreseeable injury or harm. This general rule applies, regardless of whether C's injury emanates from the acts of third parties, or from natural causes.

Legal policy

Simply put, omissions are treated more leniently by English negligence law than positive acts are, as Lord Hoffmann explained in *Stovin v Wise*:

---

[87] *Capital Brake Service Pty Ltd v Meagher t/as Sparke Helmore* [2003] NSWCA 225, [30] (Ipp JA).
[88] [2010] EWHC 178 (QB), [2010] Med LR 90, [27].   [88a] [2007] IESC 51 (Kearns J).

> It is one thing for the law to say that a person who undertakes some activity shall take reasonable care not to cause damage to others. It is another thing for the law to require that a person who is doing nothing in particular shall take steps to prevent another from suffering harm from the acts of third parties ... or natural causes.[89]

The frequently-cited reference to 'mere' or 'pure' omissions, as used by the House of Lords in, e.g., *Smith (or Maloco) v Littlewoods Organisation Ltd*,[90] is a deliberately diminutive term, reducing their importance in the eyes of the law. The general principle has been approved by several appellate courts,[91] and ranks as one of the more immutable common law negligence principles. As Lord Reed said, in *Mitchell v Glasgow CC*, 'it is usually considered worse to do harm than to fail to help'.[92]

Various policy reasons which support the principle have already been canvassed, in the context of 'Bad Samaritans' who fail to intervene/rescue/assist C (discussed in Chapter 2). While it is in that sphere that these policy justifications have been most clearly stated, they apply to omissions more generally.

It is legally irrelevant that D's failure to assist is either contrary to what a reasonable body of peer professional opinion considered that D should have done (under the *Bolam* test of breach[93]), or otherwise plainly demonstrates a lack of reasonable care. In other words, it does not assist to prove a duty of care, that breach may be made out. Moreover, the mere fact that D's omission to take a step could foreseeably result in C's injury or even death does not create a legal duty either, for foreseeability of harm is only **one** element necessary to establish a duty on D's part under the three-fold *Caparo* test. The omissions principle is, as Sedley LJ noted in *Bishara v Sheffield Teaching Hosp NHS Trust*,[94] essentially a question of legal policy.

However, the general rule notwithstanding, there are recognised exceptional categories in which D owes a duty to C to take positive steps to protect C's person or property.

Acts versus omissions

Before considering those exceptions, it must be admitted that the line between an act (where a duty may arise) and an omission (where, generally speaking, it does not) can be very finely-drawn. Of course, where D watches a blind man walk over the edge of a cliff, that is clearly a complete failure to act and can easily be treated as an omission.

However, take an example from *Mitchell v Glasgow CC*[95] – where driver D hits C's car from the rear, while it is stopped at a red light, D having been distracted by something happening in the car, and C is injured in the collision. D's positive act of driving has brought about the harm; but D has clearly failed to keep a proper lookout, failed to pay due care and attention, and failed to brake in time. How should D's conduct be characterised? These omissions will be actionable, as part of a course of conduct or activity. In *Stovin v Wise*, Lord Hoffmann remarked that, 'the conditions necessary to bring about an event always consist of a combination of acts and omissions', but that the law of negligence 'distinguish[es] between regulating the way in which

---

[89] [1996] AC 923 (HL) 943–45 (Lord Hoffmann).   [90] [1987] AC 241 (HL) 261, 272 (Lord Goff).

[91] e.g.: *Gorringe v Calderdale MBC* [2004] 1 WLR 1057 (HL) [17] (Lord Hoffmann); *Customs and Excise Commrs v Barclays Bank plc* [2006] UKHL 28, [2007] 1 AC 181, [39]; *Mitchell v Glasgow CC* [2009] UKHL 11, [2009] 1 AC 874, [15] (Lord Hope), [39] (Lord Scott).

[92] [2008] CSIH 19, [89] (Lord Reed, dissenting), citing: *Yuen Kun-Yeu v A-G of Hong Kong* [1988] AC 175 (PC) 19.

[93] Per *Bolam v Friern Hospital Management Committee* [1957] 1 WLR 582 (QB).   [94] [2007] EWCA Civ 353, [11].

[95] [2009] UKHL 11, [76], and earlier: [2008] Scot CS 19 (CSIH) [88].

an activity may be conducted, and imposing a duty to act upon a person who is not carrying on any relevant activity [at all]'.[96] The reality is that the line can be distinctly blurred at times, because most omissions occur in a wider context, whereby D is engaging in some activity. A case of motor-racing, and a recent novel case of medical negligence, illustrate this well.

In *Wattleworth v Goodwood Road Racing Co Ltd*,[97] C was killed at a motor-racing circuit, when his vehicle collided with an earth bank. The motor-racing regulator, the FIA, submitted that it could not owe a duty of care because its FIA inspectors who visited the racing circuit never advised on the installation of the earth bank. The earth bank was installed by the owner/occupier of the track to meet local authority noise requirements, even before the FIA inspected the track. **Held:** this was not an example of a 'pure omission'. The FIA inspector had inspected and made recommendations on all parts of the circuit, including the earth bank. It was all part of the one activity which he carried out, for the purposes of making specific recommendations for improving racing safety (nevertheless, the FIA owed C no duty of care, for other reasons, discussed in Chapter 2). In *ABC v St George's Healthcare NHS Trust*,[98] ABC's father was diagnosed with Huntington's Disease in 2009, which is genetic in origin, and which a child has a 50% chance of inheriting if one of her parents has the disease. At the time of the diagnosis, ABC (C, in this case) was in fact pregnant. C's father was subject to hospital and restriction orders, having killed his wife and been convicted of manslaughter a couple of years prior to this diagnosis. He refused to allow his treating healthcare professionals, D, to inform C or his other daughter out of concern for their welfare. Although D questioned the wisdom of that decision, the wish for confidentiality expressed by their patient was respected. However, in 2010, the information about her father's medical condition was accidentally disclosed to C by one of his doctors, and a subsequent test confirmed that C also had the disease. C claimed that she would have terminated her pregnancy, had she known of her father's diagnosis, and that various economic and psychiatric consequences had followed from D's failure to inform C of the genetic condition to which she was at risk. **Held:** the claim was struck out as disclosing no cause of action. Nicol J classified D's failure to inform C of her father's genetic condition as a 'pure omission', arising in circumstances where there was no 'special relationship' or any assumption of responsibility towards C as a family member (daughter). There was no duty of care imposed upon D to inform C directly of information about her father's genetic condition that would have enabled her to test herself and terminate her pregnancy. An alternative claim in negligence, that D failed to counsel and advise C's father to persuade him that his daughters should be told, was not helpful to C either, as it was not alleged that, had her father received such counselling, he would have either told C directly, or permitted D to do so. Hence, in the absence of any consent from the patient himself, there was no overriding duty of care imposed on D to fix the omission and to inform C, as non-patient, of the genetic condition.

Some of the circumstances in the next section also demonstrate the difficulty.

Exceptional scenarios

§3.10   There are limited exceptions where English common law *does* recognise a duty on D's part to protect C's person or property, where there is some 'additional feature' which imposes a duty on D to take positive steps to prevent harm to C. Thus far, that additional feature has arisen

---

[96] [1996] AC 923 (HL) 945.   [97] [2004] EWHC 140 (QB), [2004] PIQR P25.
[98] [2015] EWHC 1394 (QB) [27]–[28]. Cf: *Pate v Threlkel*, 661 So 2d 278 (Fla Sup Ct, 1995), and *Safer v Pack*, 677 A 2d 1188 (Super Ct App Div, 1996), and the analysis in: Mulheron, *Medical Negligence: Non-Patient and Third Party Claims* (Ashgate, 2010), ch 4.

where: (1) an occupier D owes positive duties to protect a lawful visitor; (2) D creates an inherent danger on or near a roadway; (3) D knows, or ought to know, that a third party has created, or interfered with, a hazard on D's property which could harm C's adjoining property; (4) D assumes responsibility to protect C's person or property by contract or by some closely proximate relationship between C and D; or (5) D owes a duty to C to supervise/control/detain a third party who harms C, by virtue of a 'special relationship' between D and the third party.

As Lord Goff pointed out in *Smith v Littlewoods Organisation Ltd*,[99] affirmative duties to step in and prevent harm to C are 'likely to be strictly limited'. Nevertheless, the exceptional circumstances have been described by Lord Goff in *Smith*, and endorsed by Lord Scott in *Mitchell v Glasgow CC*,[100] as, respectively, 'special cases' and as having an 'additional feature' which transforms an omission into a duty. Further, Lord Goff noted that a legal duty to perform positive acts may often be imposed on D by *Contract law*, but it is rarely done in Tort.

Each of the following instances represents an established, and exceptional, basis upon which D is under an obligation, in negligence law, to take reasonable and positive steps to protect C from harm to his person or property:

Exception #1. A duty to exercise reasonable care to protect or avert harm to C is imposed upon occupiers towards visitors and trespassers, by virtue of positive duties to protect entrants from dangers posed by the occupier's land which are imposed by statute[101] (as discussed in Chapter 12).

Exception #2. A duty to exercise reasonable care to protect C, a road user, is imposed upon D who is in control of a dangerous thing on or near the roadway, and which harms C. D must create the source of danger, and that danger must be *inherently* dangerous. On this point, two cases can usefully be contrasted:

In *Haynes v Harwood*,[102] a delivery person, Mr Bird, D, left a horse-drawn van unattended and untethered in a crowded street in Rotherhithe, to visit a wharf and collect his receipt. Whilst he was in the wharf, children threw stones at the two horses, which then bolted down the street. PC Harwood, C, a police officer, saw a woman and child in the path of the bolting horses, and suffered injury when he tried to stop the horses. **Held:** D owed C a duty of care. D had created a source of danger by leaving his horses unattended in a busy street. The noise and movement in the street, and the propensity to unnerve or spook inherently-dangerous animals such as horses, were all reasonably foreseeable. D, the driver, was well aware of the neighbourhood, as he frequently delivered there, and knew that there were three schools in the area. The accident happened between 4.00–5.00pm, when children were likely to frequent the streets, and the deliberate actions of mischievous boys were foreseeable.

But contrast:

In *Topp v London Country Bus (South West) Ltd*,[103] London Country Bus, D, had a system of leaving some of their buses parked in the public street, in a lay-by outside a pub, with the keys in the ignitions and unlocked, to facilitate the changeover of drivers. Normally, there was an 8–10 minute interval between shifts, but one night, a bus had been unlocked for over 9 hours, because a driver

---

[99] [1987] AC 241 (HL) 272–75; *Home Office v Dorset Yacht Co Ltd* [1970] AC 1004 (HL) 1060 (Lord Diplock).

[100] [2009] UKHL 11, [2009] 1 AC 874, [40], with Lord Goff's opinion also endorsed by Lord Rodger, [56].

[101] Contained in the Occupiers' Liability Act 1957 and Occupiers' Liability Act 1984, respectively.

[102] [1935] 1 KB 146 (CA). Also known as *Hynes v Harwood* in some case reports.

[103] [1993] 1 WLR 976 (CA).

called in sick. At 11.15pm, the bus was stolen, and five minutes later, it struck Mrs Topp, C, who was riding home from work. C was killed. The hit-and-run driver was never identified, and her husband and 9-year-old daughter brought actions under the FAA 1976 and on behalf of her estate. (The Motor Insurers' Bureau pays compensation for untraced drivers, but the amount was limited, and the MIB required Mr Topp to sue D, to seek to recoup some of that payment.) **Held:** D did not owe a duty of care to C. It was distinguishable from *Haynes v Harwood*, because there, horses were inherently dangerous to road users, given their unpredictable nature. However, a bus was not inherently dangerous – it required human intervention to be dangerous. Furthermore, to leave a vehicle unlocked with the keys in the ignition on a highway, near a pub, did not create a 'special risk' category necessary to give rise to a duty of care either.

The decision in *Topp* suggests that the exceptional scenarios are indeed of limited application, and will not easily be extended, such as to give rise to a duty on D for his failure to act. Furthermore, there were certain floodgates concerns, for if a duty were imposed on the bus company, then it could equally be imposed in 'very many different circumstances in which a private car, standing unlocked and with its ignition key in the switch, might be stolen, and then driven negligently so as to cause injury or damage ... Is it material or crucial if the vehicle is left outside a pub? And what if the car is left for several weeks in an airport long-term carpark?'[104]

The blurred line between acts and omissions is readily apparent in this exceptional scenario. For example, in *Mitchell v Glasgow CC*,[105] the Scottish Inner House remarked that *Haynes v Harwood* was not, strictly speaking, an 'omissions case' at all, but rather, one where D acted positively (leaving the horses untethered), in such a way as to create a risk of causing injury to the policeman as rescuer. By contrast, in *Chubb Fire Ltd v Vicar of Spalding*,[106] the Court of Appeal described *Haynes* as a case of omission, in that D failed to tie up the horses properly so that they did not run amok.

Exception #3. Where D knew, or should have known, that a third party was positively creating, or interfering with, a hazard on his property (especially by means of fire), D will be under a duty to take reasonable steps to abate that danger himself before it spreads to C's adjoining property. The principle especially arises wherever the danger is a 'natural nuisance' which has a 'known risk of [causing] damage or injury to one's neighbour or to his property' (per *Stagecoach South Western Trains Ltd v Hind*[107]).

Unlike under the previous exception, the source of the danger here does not need to be **inherently** dangerous (i.e., combustible – although the principle could certainly be invoked in that scenario, according to Lord Goff in *Smith v Littlewoods Organisation Ltd*,[108] giving the example of fireworks stored in a garden shed awaiting Guy Fawkes night which a third party interferes with). Again, two cases may be contrasted:

In *Goldman v Hargrave*,[109] Mr Goldman, D, the occupier of a West Australian wheat station, noticed that a 100 ft high redgum tree on the property was struck by lightning during an electrical storm on 25 Feb 1961. D arranged for a contractor to cut down the tree on 26 Feb. D left the tree to burn out, instead of watering it down. On 1 Mar, a strong hot wind blew up, and the fire spread out of control to the farm of his neighbour, Mr Hargrave, C, causing extensive damage. The natural windy

---

[104] *ibid*, [16], and citing the trial judge, May J, with approval.

[105] [2008] CSIH 19, 2008 SC 351, [97].   [106] [2010] EWCA Civ 981, [2010] 2 CLC 277, fn 35.

[107] [2014] EWHC 1891 (TCC) [65], citing: *Leakey v National Trust* [1980] 1 QB 485 (CA) 524.

[108] [1987] 1 AC 241 (HL) 273.   [109] [1967] 1 AC 645 (PC).

conditions and tinder-dry land were the most immediate causes of property damage suffered by C, but C sued D in negligence and in nuisance. **Held:** D was liable in both negligence and in nuisance. D owed C, his neighbour, a duty of care to make the tree safe, by watering the trunk down, which was easily and cheaply within the resources of D.

In *Smith v Littlewoods Organisation Ltd*,[110] the department store, Littlewoods, D, bought a disused cinema in Dunfermline, planning to demolish the cinema and build a supermarket. The cinema was left generally unattended for six weeks, except for some minor foundation work, and was set on fire by some teenage vandals. The fire spread to neighbouring buildings, seriously damaging C1's neighbouring church, and destroying C2's café. C1 and C2 alleged that D owed a duty to them, as neighbouring property owners, to take reasonable care against vandals gaining entry and setting fire in the old cinema. D were not on notice of any dangerous activity by trespassers, or that there had been any attempts to start fires in the past. It was commonly-accepted that only a 24-hour guard could have prevented the fires from being started. **Held:** no duty of care was owed by D to C. This case was distinguishable from *Goldman*, because here, D had no specific knowledge about the activities of trespassers and vandals on their property (the police, fire brigade and neighbours had passed on no information about previous vandalism). Also, the 'omission' here was the failure to install a 24-hour guard – substantially more onerous than watering down a tree.

Hence, both the level of knowledge which D possessed about the source of danger, and the expense or ease with which the omission could be corrected to secure the reasonable protection/rescue of C's person or property, are relevant to this exceptional scenario. As with the *Haynes* scenario, the possibility of floodgates of suits is also something to be guarded against. In *Smith*, Lord Goff pointed out that every house contains 'possible sources of fire if interfered with by third parties, ranging from matches and firelighters to electric irons and gas cookers and even oil-fired central heating systems'.[111] He did not regard it to be justifiable that those householders should be liable in negligence if a third party interfered with those implements.

Exception #4. A duty of care may be imposed on D to take reasonable care to protect C's person or property, where D is under a responsibility to protect C's person or property by virtue of a contract or other closely-proximate relationship between C and D.

In *Stansbie v Troman*,[112] Mr Stansbie, D, a decorator, was left alone on Mrs Troman's, C's, premises to undertake his work. He left the premises to buy some wallpaper, and went out leaving the door on the latch. Whilst he was absent, a thief entered the house and stole property (including a diamond bracelet. **Held:** D owed C, with whom he had a contract to decorate the place, a duty of care, and was liable for the lost property.

Exception #5. Where a special relationship exists between D and a third party, and that third party causes injury or harm to C because of D's omission to supervise or control that third party, then D may be under a duty of care to take positive steps to control, supervise or detain the third party (per *Home Office v Dorset Yacht Co Ltd*[113]). This complex area is the subject of discussion in the next section.

Do these exceptions still retain relevance? It was suggested by the Court of Appeal in *Selwood v Durham CC*[114] that these types of circumstances in which that 'additional something' could be established – and thereby transform an omission to act into a duty to protect/

---

[110] [1987] 1 AC 241 (HL).   [111] *ibid*, 274.   [112] [1948] 2 KB 48 (HL).
[113] [1970] AC 1004 (HL).   [114] [2012] EWCA Civ 979, [2012] WLR(D) 231, [49]–[50].

supervise/control – no longer assumed the same importance, and that the establishment of any duty of care revolved around the tri-partite *Caparo* test.

However, given the continued relevance of the incremental test by virtue of *Caparo* and *Customs & Excise* (as discussed in Chapter 2), the exceptional categories listed above surely serve tangible ongoing importance, in demarcating the circumstances in which C can overcome the general rule that no duty attaches for pure omissions. Furthermore, these exceptional categories have been endorsed by the House of Lords in *Mitchell* (a post-*Caparo* case), including the *Haynes v Harwood* scenario.[115] Also, the Irish High Court recently noted, of the English cases, that the exceptions were justified, for 'it has been judicially recognised that the actions of troublesome children and delinquent juveniles often present a special case' (per *Ennis v HSE*[116]). For these reasons, the categories are still important precedents in negligence law.

THE FAILURE TO CONTROL, SUPERVISE OR DETAIN THIRD PARTIES

The area of negligence, in which liability is sought to be imposed on D for the consequences of the acts or omissions of a third party (TP), whom D did not control, supervise or detain, has been rightly described by the Court of Appeal, in *K v Sec of State for the Home Dept*, as a 'situation which has called for particular attention by the common law courts',[117] and in which, as the Supreme Court recently noted in *Michael v CC of South Wales Police*, liability is not imposed on D in English law 'as a general rule'.[118]

Introduction

A novel scenario

§3.11 Where a third party who is 'dangerous' does harm to C, and where D had some means of control or supervision over that third party, D may owe a duty of care to C to prevent that harm from occurring. In such cases, D does not directly harm C, but has created the opportunity for the third party to harm C.

It is a tragic reality that C may be harmed by the acts of the psychiatrically-disturbed, the murderously-inclined, the violently-disposed, or the youthfully-ignorant. In such cases, where some degree of control or supervision was being exercised over that third party (TP) by D, then a duty of care may be owed by D to C.

As a novel non-traditional duty of care scenario, it will be governed by the assumption of responsibility, and/or *Caparo*,[119] tests (as discussed in Chapter 2) – and it is the **latter** test which has been the principal one by which the modern cases have been analysed (and earlier authorities which eschewed such a detailed analysis may not be decided the same way now[120]). In the TP case of *Mitchell v Glasgow CC*, Lord Hope stated that *Caparo* 'was currently the most favoured test of liability'.[121] It has been applied, too, in several other TP cases, such as *Merthyr*

---

[115] [2009] UKHL 11, [2009] 1 AC 874, [23] (Lord Hope).   [116] [2014] IEHC 440, [63].

[117] [2002] EWCA Civ 775, [13], [16] (Laws LJ).   [118] [2015] UKSC 2, [97].

[119] [1990] 2 AC 605 (HL) 617–18 (Lord Bridge).

[120] e.g., *Holgate v Lancashire Mental Hosp Bd* [1937] 4 All ER 19 (Liverpool Summer Assizes), the correctness of which was doubted by Lord Diplock in *Home Office v Dorset Yacht* [1970] AC 1004 (HL) 1062–63.

[121] [2009] UKHL 11, [2009] 1 AC 874, [21].

Tydfil County BC v C,[122]*Webster v Ridgeway Foundation School,*[123] and *K v Sec of State for the Home Dept.*[124] The relevant questions under that test, of course, are whether it was reasonably foreseeable that C would suffer damage if D failed to control/supervise TP, whether there was a relationship of sufficient proximity between C and D, and whether it was fair, just and reasonable to impose a duty of care on D to avoid the damage of which C complains. The assumption of responsibility test has only been applied in the occasional TP case – e.g., it was relied upon in *Selwood v Durham CC*[125] (although the *Caparo* test figured largely in that case too).

It has become clear that establishing a duty of care in third party cases is problematical, and the decisions are, at times, difficult to reconcile. There are several legal difficulties with these cases. First, the allegation of breach levelled against D is frequently of an *omission* to act, and allegations of 'pure omission' are difficult to substantiate in English law (as considered earlier in this chapter[126]). Secondly, English courts have developed distinct policy reasons against a duty being held, for certain categories of D, such as the police who are investigating or seeking to suppress crime (discussed in Chapter 2). Thirdly, several of these TP cases involve public authorities (apart from the aforementioned police, the leading cases entail government departments, health authorities and local authorities), which may entail greater hesitation to impose a duty of care (a point acknowledged in *K*[127]). Fourthly, causation can be difficult to establish, given that it is the TP's intervention that has been the direct and immediate cause of C's harm (a point dealt with in Chapter 8). Fifthly, the problem of just how many exist in the class of whom C is one is an oft-recurring theme which gives rise to policy difficulties Sixthly, the scenario inevitably throws up a key question: how is the duty to be cast? Is it a duty to control, supervise or take some other step in relation to TP in order to protect C against harm, or is it a wider duty to take some direct step in relation to C (e.g., to warn C of the threat posed by TP)?

In combination, these factors mean that it is a challenging area of negligence liability. It is worth noting that these types of suits commonly arise because any action against TP would be futile, either legally or practically. Commonly, TP will be too young to owe C any duty of care, or TP will be 'shallow-pocketed' (i.e., uninsured), and hence, not worth suing, whereas D will be an insured party.

Not a derivative duty

§3.12   D's liability towards C is not derivative from, or dependent upon, any duty which D may owe to the third party. It is an entirely independent, or separate, duty of care which D may owe to C.

C's claim against D, where TP has wrought havoc against C's person or property, does not stand or fall upon whether D has any liability towards TP. It will certainly **not** assist C to prove that, just because D was negligent towards TP, then it would be 'fair, just and reasonable' that he should be found to owe a duty to C too – that argument was specifically put, and rejected, in *West Bromwich Albion Football Club Ltd v El-Safty.*[128] Conversely, even if D did not (indeed, could not) owe a duty of care to TP, a duty may still be owed by D to C (a possibility acknowledged in *Hill v CC of West Yorkshire Police*[129]).

---

[122] [2010] EWHC 62 (QB) [12], [30]–[36].   [123] [2010] EWHC 157 (QB), [2010] ELR 694, [118]–[119],
[124] [2002] EWCA Civ 775, [11]–[14], [30]–[36], with reference to *Caparo's* test at [12].
[125] [2012] EWCA Civ 979, [2012] WLR(D) 231, [52].   [126] Cross cite pp 146–48
[127] [2002] EWCA Civ 775, [20].
[128] [2005] EWHC 2866 (QB) [67] (Royce J), and aff'd on appeal: [2007] PIQR P7 (CA).
[129] [1989] AC 53 (HL) 62–63.

Hence, it follows that any duties owed by D to C and to TP are entirely independent of each other. The existence (or non-existence) of one does not influence a finding of the other. As will be seen in Chapter 5, this reflects the legal position where a secondary victim, C, brings a claim for negligently-inflicted pure psychiatric injury against D, for negligent acts visited upon the immediate victim. C's claim does not have to be derivative upon a successful claim being instituted by the immediate victim who was put in the 'zone of physical danger' by D's negligence – the House of Lords (per Lord Oliver) made this plain in *Alcock v CC of the South Yorkshire Police*.[130]

The leading cases

This section outlines the key scenarios, and leading cases, which illustrate the problem of suits against D for harm done by TP, whether they be violently-disposed, mentally-ill, or too young to know any better. Many of them conflict in outcome, for reasons which will be considered in the legal analysis which follows (albeit that a couple of them are difficult to reconcile, as noted below).

- Prison authorities – where D is a prison authority, TP a prisoner and C a person injured by TP:

   In *Dorset Yacht Co Ltd v Home Office*,[131] prison officers employed by the Home Office, D, took a group of young boys from the Borstal youth detention centre to Brownsea Island in Poole Harbour, under the supervision and control of three Borstal officers. Due to inadequate supervision, seven of the youths escaped one night, and boarded a yacht, *Diligence of Marston*, and got that yacht moving. It collided with C's yacht, *Silver Mist*, which was moored off the island. The youths boarded C's yacht and wrecked much of it. C sued D in negligence for failing to adequately control, supervise and discipline the youths. **Held:** the Borstal officers, D, owed a duty of care to C, as they had created a potential situation of danger for C, the owner of a nearby yacht at risk of damage.

But contrast:

   In *K v Sec of State for the Home Dept*,[132] Rashid Musa, a citizen of Kenya, was granted limited leave to remain in the UK. During his stay, he was arrested and charged with the buggery of a 15-year-old girl and was sentenced to 18 months jail. After release, Mr Musa was arrested and sentenced for burglary, and a court recommended his deportation. He was detained under the Immigration Act 1971 for that purpose. Due to lack of resources, Mr Musa was released from detention, by order of the Secretary of State, D. Mr Musa then raped Miss K, C, at knifepoint, and raped a boy on a train the following day. He was sentenced to life imprisonment. C sued D in negligence for the harm (including psychological harm) suffered as a result of the rape, on the basis that D released Mr Musa into the community when it knew, or should have known, that he was a very dangerous individual, liable to commit crimes of sexual violence; and that he ought to have been detained until he could be deported. **Held:** D did not owe C a duty of care. In *Thomson (AP) v Scottish Ministers*,[133] Ann Thomson, C, was the mother of Catherine Thomson, who was murdered by John Campbell, at C's house in Moodiesburn, while Mr Campbell was on a short period of 'home leave' from prison. Shortly after his arrest for the murder of Ms Thomson, Mr Campbell committed suicide. Ms Thomson had been a friend of the Campbell family – she had known Mr Campbell himself since childhood, had been his brother's girlfriend for five years, and knew his mother well too. C argued that Ms Thomson, the deceased, was within that group of persons that Mr Campbell was likely to 'have dealings with', during his weekend leave, should Mr Campbell become violent during his home release. **Held:** D did not owe C a duty of care.

---

[130] [1992] 1 AC 310 (HL) 412.   [131] [1970] AC 1004 (HL).
[132] [2002] EWCA Civ 775.   [133] [2013] CSIH 63.

- The police – where D are the police, TP a violently-inclined criminal and C the unfortunate victim of TP's violence. Of course, in leading cases in which the police were alleged to have failed to apprehend or adequately investigate/suppress the activities of those criminals who proceed to injure or kill C – e.g., the dreadful cases of *Hill v CC of West Yorkshire Police*,[134] *Osman v Ferguson*,[135] *Van Colle v CC of the Hertfordshire Police; Smith v CC of Sussex Police*[136] and *Michael v CC of South Wales Police*[137] – then (as examined in Chapter 2), many policy reasons preclude a duty of care on the part of police (under the so-called *Hill* principle). However, proximity was also at issue in each of those cases, and this aspect of the decisions is examined below.

- Educational authorities – where D is a school or kindergarten, TP a pupil, and C is injured by that pupil (whether C is another pupil, or a complete stranger to the school):

  In *Carmarthenshire CC v Lewis*,[138] 3-year-old David wandered out of his 'play pen' at a nursery school owned/operated by D, whilst the nursery teacher, Miss Morgan, was attending to another child from the play pen who had a cut knee. At the time, David was dressed up in coat and scarf and was waiting to go for a walk with Miss Morgan and another nursery mate, as a treat. Unexpectedly, David did not wait for his teacher, but left the room, went through a gate that was supposed to be locked, out into a main road. Mr Lewis, C, was driving his lorry down that street, saw David in the middle of the road, swerved his heavy vehicle to avoid David, and hit a lamppost. C was killed in the accident, and his widow sued the kindergarten for negligence (and vicariously), and the supervising teacher in negligence. **Held:** Miss Morgan was not negligent (in leaving the classroom for 10 minutes to bandage up the hurt child); but the nursery school did owe a duty of care to C, an adjacent road-user. In *Webster v Ridgeway Foundation School*,[139] Henry Webster, C, had arranged to have a 'one-on-one' fight with another student, MM, at his school, Ridgeway School, D. The fight was to be conducted at the school's tennis courts when the school day finished. Unbeknown to him, MM arranged for some older friends and relations to turn up too, and some of these (including Wasif Khan, a non-pupil, who wielded the most serious weapon) attacked C, using a claw hammer, and kicking and striking C whilst he lay on the ground. C sustained serious brain damage from the injuries inflicted in the fight, and sued the school in negligence, on three bases, that D: (1) failed to take reasonable care to keep the school premises secure, and should have fenced the site so as to keep intruders out, and had a staff member on duty at day's end; (2) failed to establish better discipline in the school and deal better with racial tensions there (C was white, and his attackers were Asians); and (3) should have done more to protect C, and failed to exercise management responsibilities for the safety and security of its pupils while on school premises, including during their departure at the end of the day. **Held:** D owed C a duty to take reasonable care to see that C was reasonably safe during school hours, and for a reasonable period after the end of the school day while he was still on the school's premises (however, both breach and causation failed).

- Health authorities (and healthcare practitioners who work there) – where D is a healthcare professional or a health authority, TP a mentally-ill patient who wreaks havoc, and C the unfortunate victim of that patient's harmful behaviour:

  In *Palmer v Tees HA*,[140] the patient, Shaun Armstrong, was released from a mental facility on an out-patient basis on 21 June 1993, having disclosed to a psychiatrist before his release that he

[134] [1989] AC 53 (HL). Subsequently: *R v Coonan (formerly Sutcliffe)* [2011] EWCA Crim 5.
[135] [1993] 4 All ER 344 (CA). Application for leave to appeal to HL was refused.
[136] [2008] UKHL 50, [2009] 1 AC 225 (HL).   [137] [2015] UKSC 2.
[138] [1955] AC 549 (HL).   [139] [2010] EWHC 157 (QB), [2010] ELR 694.
[140] [1999] EWCA Civ 1533. Mrs Palmer's claim for pure psychiatric illness is considered in Chapter 5.

harboured sexual feelings towards children. On 30 June 1994, he abducted, assaulted, killed and mutilated a 4-year-old neighbour, Rosie Palmer, C, who lived in the next street. C's estate sued the health authority, D, which operated the hospital at which Mr Armstrong was treated, for failing to provide him with adequate treatment, and for failing to diagnose that there was a real, substantial and foreseeable risk of his committing serious, sexual offences against children. **Held:** no duty of care was owed to C by the health authority; the claim was struck out as disclosing no cause of action.

But contrast:

In *Selwood v Durham CC*,[141] Claire Selwood, C, was a senior social worker employed by the Durham CC, D1, in their Children in Need team, and was the designated social worker for a daughter of Graham Burton, in family proceedings relating to Mr Burton's children. The Tees, Esk and Wear Valley NHS Trust, D2, operated a Community Mental Health Team and a Crisis Resolution Team, staffed by health workers and social workers employed by D1 and D2. Both signed a protocol, 'Working together in the delivery of services to adults and children', which applied to Mr Burton's circumstances, due to his mental health problems. D2 operated a mental health ward at Cherry Knowle Hospital, to which Mr Burton was admitted as a voluntary patient. During his stay, Mr Burton said that he was 'not pleased' with one of the social workers – the 'nastiest one' – but he did not name C specifically. At an assessment meeting by the CRT, Mr Burton again said that there was someone involved in the court case 'who I dislike and wish to harm, but I am trying to avoid her'. For a case review to be held at the hospital, the managing psychiatrist asked Mr Burton whether C could attend that meeting, but he refused, saying that he would 'kill her on the spot' if he saw her. None of these threats were passed on to C or to her employer, D1. C attended the case review, where Mr Burton attacked her, causing very serious injuries (for which he was sentenced to life imprisonment for attempted murder). D1 conceded that it owed C, its employee, a duty of care, but D2 denied that. **Held:** D2 owed C a duty of care.

- Social housing landlords – where D is a local authority/council, TP is ostensibly under the control of that local authority, and C is injured or killed by TP.

  In *Mitchell v Glasgow CC*,[142] James Drummond (TP) and James Mitchell, C, lived in D's social housing, and the two got along very badly, due to TP's anti-social behaviour (e.g., playing loud music during the night, smashing C's windows with an iron bar), and TP was arrested and jailed for his behaviour. TP regularly threatened to kill C, and said that he would be 'dead meat'. Other tenants heard TP threaten C in this way. D warned TP that if he persisted, they would take action to recover possession of his house. However, TP's threats towards C and other neighbours continued at least once a month. D then invited TP to a meeting to discuss another violent incident involving TP, and about a notice of proceedings for recovery of possession that had been served on him. TP attended the meeting, lost his temper and became abusive. After it, he went straight home, and battered C with an iron bar or stick, causing serious injuries from which C died 10 days later in hospital. C's estate sued D, alleging that it did not warn C that it had summoned TP to the meeting nor of any possible risk of retaliation against C, and that if the warning had been given, C would have kept out of TP's way and would not have been attacked. **Held:** no duty was owed by D to prevent the risk of harm to C.

---

[141] [2012] EWCA Civ 979.   [142] [2009] UKHL 11, [2009] 2 WLR 481 (HL).

But contrast:

> In *Merthyr Tydfil County BC v C*,[143] C and her two children, A and B, lived in social housing provided by Council, D. C reported to D that a young boy, X, in a neighbouring house had sexually abused her two children on two different occasions, in 2002 and in 2004. When C complained to D about the boy X's behaviour in 2002, she was told to keep her children indoors, but no further support was provided. C followed that advice but, over time, as X did not appear to be playing outdoors, C allowed A and B to play outside, but the sexual abuse again allegedly occurred in 2004. D allocated a social worker to C and her family, a person who was also the social worker allocated to X's family. X was later removed from his family by D, and placed with foster parents. C suffered psychiatric injury, allegedly arising from the way in which her complaints about X's abuse of her children had been dealt with. **Held:** it was arguable that D owed a duty to C; the claim could not be struck out.

Depicting the successful cases diagrammatically:

A nutshell of the successful cases where a duty of care was owed

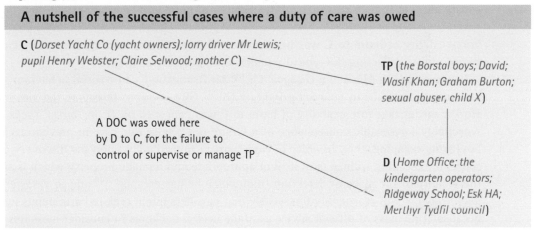

C (*Dorset Yacht Co (yacht owners); lorry driver Mr Lewis; pupil Henry Webster; Claire Selwood; mother C*)

TP (*the Borstal boys; David; Wasif Khan; Graham Burton; sexual abuser, child X*)

A DOC was owed here by D to C, for the failure to control or supervise or manage TP

D (*Home Office; the kindergarten operators; Ridgeway School; Esk HA; Merthyr Tydfil council*)

– and the unsuccessful cases:

A nutshell of the unsuccessful cases where a duty of care was not owed

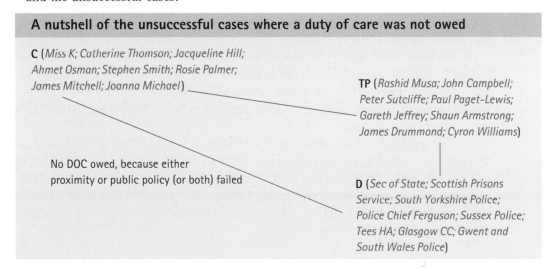

C (*Miss K; Catherine Thomson; Jacqueline Hill; Ahmet Osman; Stephen Smith; Rosie Palmer; James Mitchell; Joanna Michael*)

TP (*Rashid Musa; John Campbell; Peter Sutcliffe; Paul Paget-Lewis; Gareth Jeffrey; Shaun Armstrong; James Drummond; Cyron Williams*)

No DOC owed, because either proximity or public policy (or both) failed

D (*Sec of State; Scottish Prisons Service; South Yorkshire Police; Police Chief Ferguson; Sussex Police; Tees HA; Glasgow CC; Gwent and South Wales Police*)

Notwithstanding that some of the leading cases are difficult to reconcile, the next section teases out the leading grounds on which these decisions have turned.

[143] [2010] EWHC 62 (QB) [30]–[36].

The legal analysis of the leading cases

As Laws LJ remarked in *K*, third party cases 'is the paradigm instance ... where issues of proximity and fairness are acute, and not merely given, in the law of negligence.'[144] As previously noted, the *Caparo* three-part test is customarily used in such cases. This is especially so where (as is frequently the case) C and D are not known to each other, for as Lord Bingham stated in *Customs & Excise Commr v Barclays Bank plc*,[145] to speak of an 'assumption of responsibility' where it does not actually reflect the actions and intentions of the actual D is to render the concept fairly 'notional', whereupon the *Caparo* test is more applicable.

Reasonable foreseeability of harm

§3.13   Where D knows, or should have known, of the 'dangerous' propensities of the third party who causes harm to C, then reasonable foreseeability of harm will be easily established.

Foreseeability of harm to C was uncontroversial in **all** of the leading third party cases mentioned above, reflecting the typically undemanding nature of the test.

For example, in *Mitchell v Glasgow CC*,[146] Mr Drummond's anti-social behaviour was well-known to Council D; in *Selwood v Durham CC*,[147] GB's previous threats to the 'nastiest' social worker meant that foreseeability of harm to C was conceded by D; in *Dorset Yacht*, it was 'a reasonably foreseeable consequence of a failure to exercise due care in preventing [a Borstal boy] from escaping, that, in order to elude pursuit immediately upon the discovery of his absence, the escaping trainee may steal or appropriate and damage property which is situated in the vicinity of the place of detention from which he has escaped';[148] and in *Webster v Ridgeway School*, it was reasonably foreseeable that outsiders might seek to harm pupils in a school, because '[t]he mass of official advice as to the need for schools to consider measures to secure their sites is premised on that reality.'[149]

Alternatively, even where D did not know beforehand of TP's propensities to do harm, the allegation may be that D did not respond adequately to risk of harm, once it was armed with that knowledge (in *Merthyr Tydfil v C*,[150] this was conceded to be reasonably foreseeable).

On the other hand, where TP had no history of prior dangerous conduct that would have alerted D to the foreseeability of harm to another such as C, then the element may conceivably fail – but that scenario has not arisen in any of the leading English cases considered above. Indeed, it would be most unlikely to, given the close relationship between D and TP which exists in these types of cases.

In some third party cases, foreseeability of harm to C may be the **only** element of *Caparo's* tri-partite test which C proves (as, e.g., in *Hill v CC of West Yorkshire Police*). Of course, the enquiry does not, and cannot, end there. As Stocker LJ stated in *Jones v Wright*, '[s]ome limitations must be put upon what is reasonably foreseeable if a duty of care is not to be owed to the whole world at large'[151] – and the 'proximity' and 'policy' limbs of the test certainly serve that vital purpose in third party cases.

---

[144] [2002] EWCA Civ 775, [16].   [145] [2006] UKHL 28, [2007] 1 AC 181, [6].   [146] [2009] UKHL 11.
[147] [2012] EWCA Civ 979, [2012] WLR(D) 231, [19].   [148] [1970] AC 1004 (HL) 1070.
[149] [2010] EWHC 157 (QB), [2010] ELR 694, [118].   [150] [2010] EWHC 62 (QB).
[151] [1991] 3 All ER 88 (CA) 114.

The requisite proximity

§3.14   When searching for the requisite nexus, or proximity, between C and D in third party cases, that may ultimately depend upon the circumstances as between C and the third party, and as between the third party and D, but it is the overall quality of the relationship between C and D which determines the issue.

To reiterate, it is the legal proximity *between C and D* of which the court must be satisfied – but in seeking to establish that, the relationship between the 'sides of the triangle', i.e., D's relationship with TP, and TP's closeness with C, will be relevant. The following proximity factors have been regarded in the leading cases as being relevant, although none of them is conclusive or definitive – it is a 'balancing act':

i.   **The degree of control.** The control that D can feasibly exercise over TP's actions is highly relevant to the establishment of a duty of care.

On the one hand, where TP is *detained* or within D's physical control, and then harms C, that is more likely to give rise to a duty of care on D's part. In *Dorset Yacht*, the relationship of D and C was jailor–custodian, and entailed one of close supervision and control over TP, the Borstal boys.

   On the other hand, if TP is living in the community, or was never within D's detention in the first place, then the degree of D's control over TP lessens considerably, and a duty of care is less likely. In *Palmer v Tees HA*, the involuntary detention of murderer Shaun Armstrong (TP) was not an option, given the 'considerable restrictions' which applied to the procedure – and it would have had 'doubtful effectiveness' in any event, given the time that elapsed between the confessions by TP of his violent fantasies and the murder of Rosie Palmer, C. This indicated that it would be 'unwise to hold that there is sufficient proximity'. In *Hill v CC of West Yorkshire Police*, it was a key factor, against a duty of care, that the control over TP that was evident in *Dorset Yacht* was 'lacking. Sutcliffe was never in the custody of the police force',[152] and a similar point was made, of Miss Michael's killer, in *Michael v South Wales Police*, that he was never in the police's control.[153] In *Thomson v Scottish Ministers*[154] too, Mr Campbell was on home leave from prison and not in custody at the time of C's murder, reducing the extent of D's control.

ii.   **The capacity to warn or protect C.** If D could reasonably have warned C directly, to safeguard C against the resultant harm that befell him at the hands of a dangerous TP, but D failed to take any such steps, that will be highly relevant to the duty of care enquiry.

On the one hand, in some cases, the threat has been a long-standing one, and proximity is more likely then. In *Van Colle v CC of Hertfordshire Police; Smith v CC of Sussex Police*, the police were in a legally proximate relationship with Mr Smith, C, given that the police were aware of the repeated threats of serious violence which had been made by Gareth Jeffrey, TP, towards C. An arguable relationship of proximity was also present in *Osman v Ferguson*, on much the same basis. In both cases, however, no duty of care was upheld, for policy reasons. In *Michael v South Wales Police*, the threat to Miss Michael, C, was much more immediate, following the 999 call that was misdirected; but the majority was not prepared to accept that the police's capacity

---

[152] [1989] AC 53 (HL) 62.   [153] [2015] UKSC 2, [99], [131] (Lord Toulson, for the majority).
[154] [2013] CSIH 63, [52].

to protect C generated a proximate relationship (although it must be said that the majority's core reasoning was based upon policy reasons, and a lack of an assumption of responsibility, both of which were considered in Chapter 2).

On the other hand, wherever C was a member of the public who happened to be in the wrong place at the wrong time, then the ability for D to provide warnings to C is likely to have been practically impossible, and this will militate against a duty of care being imposed. In *Mitchell*,[155] the Council had no duty to warn Mr Mitchell of the dangers posed by Mr Drummond, his co-tenant, for policy reasons (Lord Hope remarked that C 'very properly accepted that he could not present his argument on this basis'). The inability of the Tees HA's psychiatrists to warn C was also a significant factor that precluded a duty of care in *Palmer v Tees HA*: Stuart-Smith LJ asked,'what [could D] ... have done to avoid the danger?'.[156] They could not have warned the family of every child living in the vicinity of where Shaun Armstrong lived; and once released into community care, then any form of warning to potential victims ranged between 'doubtful effectiveness' and utterly infeasible: 'the most effective precaution cannot be undertaken as [D] does not know who to warn'.

The lack of any capacity on D's part to warn C will not automatically preclude a duty of care, however – e.g., in *Carmarthenshire CC v Lewis*, lorry driver Mr Lewis was the unlucky and courageous driver who took action to avoid hitting David in the street, and yet he was owed a duty of care by the kindergarten.

iii. **The knowledge of TP's propensities.** Where D has an information monopoly about TP, which C could not possibly know about, then that factor *may* render C 'vulnerable' – both because TP had that particular propensity, and D was aware of it and was in a position to do something about curtailing it. In *Dorset Yacht*, the Borstal officers' knowledge of the propensities of the Borstal boys to seek to escape, and of the damage that they might do to property during that escape, has already been adverted to.[157] A close knowledge of the various threats posed by TP also existed, on D's part, in *Selwood v Durham CC*, *Osman v Ferguson* and *Van Colle/Smith*. Proximity was made out in all three cases.

However, just because D did have some sort of information monopoly about TP – about which the unsuspecting C knows nothing, and simply cannot ascertain for himself from any other source – is not, by any means, conclusive. For example, the admission by Shaun Armstrong to his psychiatrist that he felt driven to sexually abuse a young child in an interview prior to his release was known only to D, yet no duty of care was owed in *Palmer*. The very nature of several of the relationships in third party cases – prison authority, healthcare, educational authority – will inevitably mean that D holds information about the propensities to violence or unpredictability of TP which were not known to external parties, including C. Hence, argu-ably D's monopoly on information about TP should not be a weighty factor in the matrix of proximity factors.

Where D knew nothing of TP's propensities at all, then most likely that will preclude any proximity arising – demonstrated, e.g., in *Hill v West Yorkshire Police*, where Lord Keith noted that, 'the identity of the wanted criminal [Peter Sutcliffe] was, at the material time, unknown, and it is not averred that any full or clear description of him was ever available'.[158]

---

[155] [2009] UKHL 11, [29].
[156] [1999] EWCA Civ 1533, [32], cf. the mechanic who fails to fix brakes, per Stuart-Smith LJ at [24]–[25].
[157] See above, under 'reasonable foreseeability'.   [158] [1989] AC 53 (HL) 62.

iv. **Temporal and geographic proximity.** A lack of temporal proximity between D's alleged breach, and the harm suffered by C, has proven to be a fairly significant factor against a duty of care – especially in those cases in which TP wreaks havoc and causes tragedy some considerable time after D's alleged breach. Moreover, the fact that the harm done by TP occurred at a place which was geographically remote from D's province of control has been specifically noted in some third party cases to militate against any duty of care being owed. For example, in *Palmer* (where the murder of Rosie Palmer occurred just over a year after D's release of Shaun Armstrong), Pill LJ observed that 'the passage of time and distance' between the two events meant that no duty of care could be owed.[159]

In *Lewis*, Mr Lewis's accident occurred on a road adjacent to the kindergarten, whose breach of perimeter security arrangements had allowed little David to 'escape' onto the road. In *Dorset Yacht*, too, the damage to C's yacht happened in close temporal proximity to the alleged breach (of failing to supervise adequately the Borstal boys), and in close geographical proximity too – albeit that Lord Pearson remarked, '[i]n other cases, a difficult problem may arise as to how widely the "neighbourhood" extends, but no such problem faces [C] in this case'.[160] The temporal and geographic proximity between attack and school hours was also significant in *Webster v Ridgeway Foundation School*, in upholding a duty of care: 'the attack on Henry took place after the end of the school day, but that is not necessarily decisive as to the end of a school's duty towards its pupils, particularly as [C] was still on school premises at the time'.[161]

Even so, in *Thomson v Scottish Ministers*,[162] John Campbell murdered C within three days of his release, but that close temporal proximity was not sufficient to fix D with a duty of care.

v. **Relational proximity.** In some third party cases, there is a close relational proximity between C and D – and where existing, this **may** assist to prove a duty of care.

In *Webster*, the relationship between pupil Henry Webster, C, and his school, D, justified that outcome in part – '[t]here is a relationship of proximity in the school/pupil relationship, at least while the pupils are on the school's premises'.[163] Similarly, in *Merthyr Tydfil County BC v C*,[164] the mother of children A and B had contacted the Council, D, twice, to report of the suspected abuse, and that report assisted to support an arguable duty of care on D's part. Even in *Mitchell v Glasgow CC*, the House of Lords accepted that there was a relationship of proximity between Mr Mitchell, the murdered Council tenant, and the Council itself, given that he was their tenant, and so too was Mr Drummond, who lived next door. D accepted that they had a responsibility for the situation that had arisen, being landlord to both C and TP, and that they had taken steps to address TP's anti-social behaviour. All of this gave rise to an arguable relational proximity between C and D – but policy reasons precluded a duty of care there, ultimately.

vi. **Knowledge of C's identity.** If D knows the identity of C who is at risk from TP's acts before the threat materialises, that is not sufficient, *of itself*, to fix the relationship between D and C with the requisite proximity to base a duty of care. It is not an automatic proposition of law that D owes a duty to a pre-identified victim.

This is clearly illustrated by several appellate decisions: by *Michael v South Wales Police*, where Miss Michael's identity could not have been plainer, given her 999 call; by *Mitchell v Glasgow*

---

[159] [1999] EWCA Civ 1533, [2000] PIQR P1, 19.   [160] [1970] AC 1004 (HL) 1055.
[161] [2010] EWHC 157 (QB), [2010] ELR 694, [116].   [162] [2013] CSIH 63, [45]–[50].
[163] [2010] EWHC 157 (QB), [118].   [164] [2010] EWHC 62 (QB), [2010] PIQR P9, [36].

CC, where the public housing authority well knew of Mr Drummond's long-standing hatred for Mr Mitchell; by *Osman*, where the police knew of the deep resentment felt by Mr Paget-Lewis towards the Osman family; and by *Van Colle* too, where the police knew of the dangerous threats made by Gareth Jaffrey to Stephen Smith. In *Palmer v Tees HA* also,[165] Pill LJ posed the hypothetical example, that a psychotic patient says, 'after release from this mental facility, I will kill Y'. His Lordship 'saw force' in the argument that whether the identity of a victim 'is known *ought not* to determine whether the proximity test is passed' – and so subsequent decisions have demonstrated.

However, just because D does not know the identity of C, as a pre-identified individual, does not preclude a duty of care from being owed in third party cases. *Dorset Yacht* is a prime example: the Borstal officers did not know the identities of the yacht owners whose property the Borstal boys trashed, and yet, the officers owed a duty of care to them.

In any event, proximity is a nuanced enquiry. Even if TP were to say to D, 'I'm going to kill Y after I'm out of here', other factors – geographic and temporal proximity, the degree of control over TP, the ability to take precautions to prevent the harm to C, or to warn C – will also be highly relevant to the proximity enquiry. Some of these may well offset the fact that the identity of the unfortunate victim was known to D. In *Palmer*, Pill LJ's example may have been only hypothetical, but in each of *Osman*, *Van Colle/Smith* and *Mitchell*, the victims were killed by TPs whose propensities for violence were well known to relevant public authorities, and where the victims were also well known to D before the horrific events occurred. Ultimately, no duty of care was owed in any of them.

vii. **An identifiable class, or 'at special risk'.** Even where D did not know of C as a pre-identified victim, D may owe a duty of care, if C was one of an identifiable class *at special risk* from TP.

In *Osman v Ferguson*, the Osman family were exposed to a special risk from Mr Paget-Lewis, TP, over and above that of the public at large (said the court), thereby giving rise to 'an arguable case' that there was a 'very close degree of proximity, amounting to a special relationship', between the Osman family and the police investigating officers (albeit that policy reasons militated against a duty of care). In *Dorset Yacht*, the owners whose yachts were moored off Brownsea Island were in a class that was considered to be at special risk too. In *Selwood v Durham CC*,[166] the Court of Appeal was not prepared to hold that C, the stabbed social worker, was a member of the general public *per se*: she 'was not one of the world at large; she was one of a small group of social workers, working in close proximity and cooperation' with both local authority and health authority (plus she was the one who was the subject of TP's threats, and hence, was in a 'special position'). That also pointed (said the Court of Appeal) to an assumption of responsibility on the health authority's part towards C, because it had, via the joint protocol, assumed responsibility to do what was reasonable to reduce or avoid any foreseeable risk of harm to which an employee of those co-signatories was exposed, in the course of dealing with patients of the Crisis Resolution Team (such as Mr Burton). In some respects, C was almost treated as a 'quasi-employee', because of the joint protocol.

On the other hand, if C was merely one of the vast public who was at risk from TP, with no distinguishing feature separating C from the public (apart from the fact that C was the one

---

[165] [1999] EWCA Civ 1533, [2000] PIQR P1 (CA) P19.   [166] [2012] EWCA Civ 979, [54] (Dame Janet Smith).

harmed), then no requisite proximity will be found. Being in the wrong place at the wrong time does not put C at special risk. As admitted in *Hill v CC of West Yorkshire*, 'Miss Hill was one of a vast number of the female general public who might be at risk from TP's activities but was at no special distinctive risk in relation to them, unlike the owners of yachts moored off Brownsea Island'.[167] In modern case law, proving that C was at 'special risk' has become seemingly more difficult. In *Thomson v Scottish Ministers*,[168] C sought to argue that she was at special risk, precisely because she was within the group of persons that Mr Campbell was likely to 'have dealings with' during his home leave, given her close association with his family. However, she was not – and the Scottish Inner House was at pains to distinguish that other leading prisons case of *Dorset Yacht*, noting that it may have been from another era, and that 'the law has moved on' since that 1970 decision; that *Dorset Yacht* was a product of the wider 'foreseeability + no public policy reasons' test of *Anns v Merton London BC*;[169] and that it may be that the decision is limited to those persons 'having property in physical proximity to the place where the prisoners were confined'. Yet, however, neither the victims in *Hill* nor in *Palmer* knew their attackers; Catherine Thomson did, but that was not sufficient to fix proximity either, as she was treated as being a member of the general public. On the *Thomson* court reasoning, the only party likely to have been at special risk was Mr Campbell's mother, with whom he was residing. This grouping of cases does not favour a wide construction of 'at special risk'.

Certainly, it is *Palmer's* ongoing legacy that any 'special risk' that turns upon a targeted demographic is going to be difficult to establish. The class of children, of whom Rosie Palmer was one, did not constitute sufficient 'at special risk' status for that victim – notwithstanding that she lived in close geographic proximity to Shaun Armstrong and closely fitted the profile of those at risk from his violent sexual fantasies. In this regard, the hypothetical example provided by Cory J in the Canadian case of *Smith v Jones* ('it may be sufficient to engage the duty to warn if a class of victims, such as little girls under five living in a specific area, is clearly identified [rather than a specific individual]'[170]) is entirely distinguishable from, and does not represent, current English law. In fact, many other proximity factors counted against Rosie Palmer's claim too – the outpatient setting, the lack of temporal or physical proximity, the lack of control over TP Shaun Armstrong and the inability to warn the Palmers. Also, the class of whom the little girl was one was too large to sit comfortably with most other English jurisprudence concerning third party claims – *K* and *Hill* being other leading examples.

The notable exception – where a wider view was adopted – is the pre-*Caparo* decision of *Lewis v Carmarthenshire CC*.[171] Mr Lewis was a member of the public who was at no special risk from David's wanderings, and yet a duty of care was owed to him. That decision rested on the test of reasonable foreseeability, well before proximity and public policy were adopted as such strong 'control mechanisms' in *Caparo*. Nowadays, *Lewis* would probably be considered to be at the very limits of third party liability. However, the decision may be reconciled on the basis that Mr Lewis fell within an identifiable class of persons (nearby road-users to the kindergarten), and furthermore, he was within close temporal and physical proximity to TP *at the time of the kindergarten's breach*, and on that basis too, he was distinguishable from the general public because he was in heightened danger.

---

[167] [1989] AC 53 (HL) 62.   [168] [2013] CSIH 63, [45]–[58].   [169] [1978] AC 728 (HL) 751.
[170] [1999] 1 SCR 455, [59].   [171] [1955] AC 549 (HL).

To summarise the proximity factors in some leading third party cases:

Factor	Dorset	Lewis	Hill	Palmer
degree of control which D exercised over TP	yes	yes	no	no
those Cs within geographical proximity to D	yes	yes	–	no
D's knowledge of TP's propensities	yes	yes	no	yes
temporal proximity	yes	yes	–	no
C at special risk	yes	?	no	no

Additionally, if C is harmed or killed by TP, a number of policy reasons may negate a duty of care too.

Whether policy favours, or disfavours, a duty of care

§3.15   Policy reasons may preclude any duty being cast on D, to avoid or to minimise injury to C caused by a dangerous or unpredictable third party.

In *Mitchell v Glasgow CC*,[172] Lord Brown noted that, 'there will be very few occasions on which a bare duty by A *to warn* B of possible impending violence by C will arise'. Even where *a failure to control* is the central allegation of breach, there have been many policy reasons raised against that type of duty too.

There are, of course, exceptional cases where a duty of care was held to be owed by D to C, for the criminal acts of TPs – *Dorset Yacht*[173] being one example. However, there were strong proximity factors in favour of imposing a duty (e.g., geographical and temporal proximity between Brownsea Island and the moored yachts, a close jailor–custodian relationship of control between D and TP), and in addition, it was another of the pre-*Caparo* decisions where the focus was on the requirement of reasonable foreseeability, rather than the other *Caparo* requirements which have become more prominent in third party cases since.

Notably, the many and varied policy reasons as to why no duty of care was imposed upon the Council in *Mitchell* are powerful indicators as to why English law is arguably becoming far more conservative (and pro-D), in respect of third party cases, than was the case pre-*Caparo*.

Before turning to these, however, it is worth noting one factor that is completely **irrelevant** to the duty of care analysis – and that is the gravity of injury that C suffers at the hands of TP. The very fact that C suffers death or some terrible personal injury does not assist to impose a duty on D. Both *K*[174] and *Palmer*[175] confirmed that proposition.

i.   An omission to act. As discussed in Chapter 2, English law is notoriously hesitant to impose a duty, where the rubric of the allegation is that D failed to act to prevent harm befalling C. The alleged wrong on D's part in many of these third party cases is an omission – and some cases have made something of that, in denying that any duty of care was owed. For example, Lord

---

[172] [2009] UKHL 11, [2009] 2 WLR 481, [81], [83] (emphasis added).
[173] [1970] AC 1004 (HL).   [174] [2002] EWCA Civ 775, [29]–[30].   [175] [2000] PNLR 87 (CA) 108.

Brown remarked, in *Mitchell*,[176] that 'the contention that the Council was under a positive duty to warn [Mr Mitchell], and that the Council is liable for [Mr Mitchell's] death because of a mere omission to do so, appears to me plainly unsustainable'.

Obversely, D's positive acts are often referred to, to support a duty of care. For example, in *Merthyr Tydfil County BC v C*,[177] the court noted that C, the mother of the abused children A and B, 'relies upon failings by the Council of commission as well as omission', *viz*, that the Council assigned the same social worker to her family as to the abuser's family, and denied that any report was made following the 2002 complaint. These positive acts assisted to find a duty of care, sufficient to deny a strike-out application.

ii. The practical problems of imposing a duty to warn. In *Mitchell*, Lord Hope set out many policy grounds militating against a duty to warn being imposed upon the Council[178] (drawing on *Van Colle*[179] and others[180]).

The policy reasons against a duty to warn, in third party cases

- *the beneficiaries of the duty?* To whom would the duty to warn be owed? Others in the neighbourhood (other than Mr Mitchell) had complained to the Glasgow CC about D's behaviour too. Any duty would be owed to all of them – or none. The size of the class of threatened potential victims could be problematical;
- *a burdensome duty:* a duty to warn is not necessarily a one-off message – D, as landlords, would need to decide whether, and when, a warning should be given. Paradoxically, 'the more attentive they were to their ordinary duties [regarding the dangerous TP], the more onerous the duty to warn others would become' for D; as intervening would bring about awareness and control;
- *defensive practices and delay:* D might have to defer taking protective steps until the warning had been received by everyone, and an opportunity given for it to be acted on. Also, D 'would be likely to create a practice of giving warnings as a matter of routine. Many of them would be for no good purpose, while others would risk causing undue alarm'. They could also risk losing their effect, if given widely.

---

iii. Resource diversion. The problem of resources being diverted to deal with, prepare for, and defend litigious proceedings, was raised in the context of the *Hill* core principle concerning suits against the police (per *Hill v CC of West Yorkshire Police*) (as discussed in Chapter 2).

The same policy reason has arisen in third party cases too – re health practitioners who deal with mentally-ill and violently-inclined patients (per *Palmer v Tees HA*[181]), and re a Council's

---

[176] [2009] UKHL 11, [2009] 2 WLR 481, [83].   [177] [2010] EWHC 62 (QB), [2010] PIQR P9, [36].

[178] [2009] UKHL 11, [2009] 2 WLR 481, [27]–[28], with other members agreeing: [44] (Lord Scott), [72] (Lord Rodger), [73] (Baroness Hale), [83] (Lord Brown).

[179] [2008] UKHL 50, [2009] 1 AC 225.

[180] e.g., *Hill v CC of West Yorkshire* [1989] AC 53 (HL) 63, 65; *Phelps v Hillingdon LBC* [2001] 2 AC 619 (HL) 672–74; *McFarlane v Tayside Health Board* [2000] 2 AC 59 (HL) 83; *X (Minors) v Bedfordshire CC* [1995] 2 AC 633 (CA) 661–63, and on appeal: [1995] 2 AC 633 (HL) 749–51; *Alexandrou v Oxford* [1993] 4 All ER 328 (CA).

[181] (1998) 45 BMLR 88 (QB) 101–2 (Gage J) (aff'd: [1999] EWCA Civ 1533).

responsibility as a public housing authority: '[it is] desirable too that social landlords, social workers and others who seek to address the many behavioural problems that arise in local authority housing estates and elsewhere, often in very difficult circumstances, should be safe-guarded from legal proceedings arising from an alleged failure-to-warn those who might be at risk of a criminal attack in response to their activities. Such proceedings, whether meritorious or otherwise, would involve them in a great deal of time, trouble and expense which would be more usefully devoted to their primary functions in their respective capacities' (per *Mitchell v Glasgow CC*).

iv. **Conflicts of duties.** If to owe a duty of care to C would actually or potentially conflict with D's existing duty to TP, then that conflict of duties will likely preclude a duty to C.

However, if whatever is required of D to discharge his duty to TP would **also** discharge any duty to C, the duties are coincident, and no conflict arises. The case of *Merthyr Tydfil County BC v C*[182] illustrates – Council, D, owed a concurrent duty of care to the mother, as well as to her children A and B; because 'her interests, and the interests of the children, are consonant. Whilst matters may conceivably have proceeded so that there could possibly have arisen a conflict of interest between mother and children – if, e.g., as a result of the alleged failings of the Council, C had been unable to cope with looking after her children, triggering the Council having to consider steps protective of the children – there was not in this case the same poten-tial for conflict'. The court made the point that the mere existence of *potential* conflict 'is not a trump card' in determining whether a duty is owed; 'it is simply one factor which the court must take into account'.

The tactic of proving coincidental duties to C and to TP does not always work, however. The English Court of Appeal was invited to follow this line of reasoning in *Palmer v Tees HA* too[183] – but with a notable lack of success. Mrs Palmer argued that the duty imposed on Tees HA was, not to warn her and Rosie *per se* of the dangers posed by Mr Armstrong, but to provide adequate medical treatment for that TP to reduce the risk of his killing a child, and/or to stop him from being released whilst he posed a risk – which duty *coincided* with the Tees HA's duty to Rosie Palmer to prevent a mentally-ill person in TP's position from murdering her. However, the Court declined to accept this line of argument, and no such duty was owed.

Similarly, where a healthcare practitioner owes a duty of confidentiality to his patient (TP), then any duty to warn C of the potential threat posed by that patient would likely conflict with this duty of confidentiality. In some cases (*viz*, *W v Egdell*[184] and *R v Crozier*[185]), the scenarios have concerned psychiatrists who *voluntarily* acted to give information about a mentally-ill pa-tient to another, in order to protect the public against that dangerous patient – quite a different context from any legally-imposed **duty** to give that information to protect C. The courts in both *Egdell* and *Crozier* did **not** suggest that a psychiatrist who was treating a violent patient was under *any duty* to inform or protect a potential victim. The issue arose again, however, in the recent case of *ABC v St George's Healthcare NHS Trust*.[186] One of the reasons for denying the existence of any duty of care owed by the medical Ds to ABC, the daughter of their patient who had been diagnosed with Huttington's Disease, was that there was a potential for conflicting

---

[182] [2010] EWHC 62 (QB), [2010] PIQR P9, [36].
[183] [1999] EWCA Civ 1533, (1998) 39 BMLR 35, [5], [32].   [184] [1990] 1 Ch 359 (CA).
[185] (1990) 8 BMLR 128 (CCA). Cf: *X (HA) v Y* [1988] 2 All ER 648 (QB).
[186] [2015] EWHC 1394 (QB) [26].

duties owed by doctors to patients and to non-patient claimants – for if a duty were upheld, then doctors could be sued by their patient if they disclosed information to aggrieved family members which should have remained confidential. As Nicol J put it,[187] the 'starting point' is that medical D are obliged to respect a patient's confidential information, albeit that this is 'a qualified duty' (given the statutory requirement to report notifiable diseases, e.g.[188]).

v. **The size of the class.** Where C was not 'at special risk', then by corollary, it is likely that the class of persons of whom C was one was too large for a duty of care to be owed to any member of that class. It raises the spectre of indeterminate liability – derived from Cardozo CJ's famous dicta, 'liability in an indeterminate amount for an indeterminate time to an indeterminate class', per *Ultramares Corporation v Touche*.[189]

Hence, wherever C was in the wrong place at the wrong time, and was genuinely a random member of the public, policy will generally preclude a duty of care – as illustrated, e.g., in *Hill*, *K v Sec of State*, and *Palmer*.[190] In *Dorset Yacht* too, Lord Diplock suggested, dicta, that a prison authority would not owe a duty of care to a member of the public who was the victim of crime from a 'habitual criminal' whom the Home Office had negligently permitted to escape and who caused damage to persons not in close proximity of the escape, but 'in further pursuance of his general criminal career'.

In that regard, in *Caparo*, Lord Oliver distinguished TP cases from cases of negligent driving or product liability: it is 'enough that [C] chances to be (out of the whole world) the person with whom [D] collided, or who purchased the offending ginger beer' – whereas, for TP cases, even where TP causes C physical harm, the requisite 'nexus' between C and D is not obvious.[191] Of course, the exception is the road user class in *Lewis*, which virtually equated to the general public, and yet the unlucky Mr Lewis was owed a duty by the kindergarten. However, *Lewis* was a pre-*Caparo* case which rested upon the principle of reasonable foreseeability – and C was in close temporal and geographic proximity with D at the time of breach.

Notably though, even where C was a pre-identified victim and, hence, within a tiny class of those at risk from TP's conduct, a duty may still be precluded for policy reasons (as, e.g., in *Van Colle* and *Osman*).

The comparative corner: The *Tarasoff* doctrine

In *Tarasoff v The Regents of the University of California*,[192] Prosenjit Poddar (P), a graduate student at University of California (Berkeley campus), had formed a friendly relationship with a fellow student which he took to be a serious romance, but which the young woman, Tatiana Tarasoff (T), did not. As a result, upon learning of T's true feelings, P underwent a severe emotional crisis. He eventually became a voluntary outpatient at the defendant hospital, and confided to the defendant psychotherapist Dr Moore that he intended to kill a friend 'when she returns from Brazil' (T spent the summer in Brazil). From the conversation, T was an unnamed but identifiable person. The therapist and his superiors decided that P should be confined by police. Later, the campus police at Berkeley interviewed P and were

---

[187] ibid, [17].   [188] e.g., Public Health (Control of Diseases) Act 1984, ss 10,11.
[189] 174 NE 441, 444 (1931).   [190] [1999] EWCA Civ 1533.
[191] [1990] 2 AC 605 (HL) 632, citing the lower court: [1989] QB 653 (CA) 686 (Bingham LJ).
[192] 17 Cal 3d 425, 551 P 2d 334, 343, 131 Cal Rptr 14 (Cal 1976).

satisfied that P was rational, could not be involuntarily detained, and released him, on his promise to stay away from T. Neither T nor her parents were informed of the threat made by P. Two months later, P went to T's house and shot and fatally stabbed her. T's parents sued the hospital, doctors and police on behalf of their daughter's estate. **Held:** the actions in negligence could proceed, as a duty of care was arguable.

Comment: It is unlikely that English law would follow *Tarasoff*, where TP, who was known to D to present a threat to C, 'made good' that threat. Dicta in *Palmer*; the outcome of *Osman v Ferguson*; and the policy reasons put forward by the House of Lords in *Van Colle/Smith*, in *Mitchell* and in *Michael*, all strongly point to that outcome, even where the victim was an identified (or a clearly identifiable) individual. The fact that there may be a real risk, a foreseeable risk, of harm to [C] if [D] does not warn [C] is, of course, not conclusive – 'the question is one of fairness and public policy' (per *Mitchell*[193]). This difficulty in even casting the duty (to protect, to warn, or both), and the continuing influence of the 'mere omissions' rule in English law, add to the problem.[194]

vi. Compensation for C via other means. The point was made, in *Webster v Ridgeway Foundation School*, that the Criminal Compensation Fund is a state-provided financial source to provide compensation for those injured by TP's criminal acts – but that does not absolutely preclude a duty of care being owed to C. Otherwise, 'there would never be a duty of care to protect against possible criminally-caused personal injury'.[195]

However, the availability of other avenues of redress was certainly adverted to in *Michael* as one reason not to find a duty of care (the majority referred to the criminal injuries compensation scheme, and actions against the police under the Arts 2, 3 or 8 of the ECHR), with a suggestion that if further redress was required for C, it was up to Parliament, rather than the common law, to provide it.[196]

vii. The implications for other sectors. In *Mitchell v Glasgow CC*,[197] one of the reasons that a duty of care was denied was that the implication of a duty for other cases was 'complex and far reaching' – if a social landlord could be liable to warn a potential victim, then so could a social worker, or any person, who heard threats issued by D against C. Who would not be subject to the duty?

By contrast, in *Selwood v Durham CC*,[198] one of the reasons in favour of a duty towards social worker Mrs Shelwood, C, was that the proceedings in which social workers become involved is inevitably multi-disciplinary, and that 'it was important that social workers who undertook difficult and sometimes dangerous work should be protected, so far as was practicable'. However, the same sympathy is not extended to some vulnerably placed victims of crime whose paths unfortunately crossed with a violently disposed perpetrator – and for whom the *Hill* core principle remains firmly-entrenched. This aspect of *Selwood* is difficult to reconcile with other third party cases in which a duty of care was most assuredly denied.

---

[193] [2009] UKHL 11, [26] (Lord Hope).
[194] See further: Mulheron, *Medical Negligence: Non-Patient and Third Party Claims* (Ashgate Publishing, 2010) ch 3.
[195] [2010] EWHC 157 (QB) [118].   [196] [2015] UKSC 2, [130].
[197] [2009] UKHL 11, [27].   [198] [2012] EWCA Civ 979, [54].

The incremental test

§3.16 The fact that D has not previously been liable to that category of C for the acts or omissions of TP does not preclude a duty of care from arising, but it will invoke the incremental test.

In *Webster v Ridgeway Foundation School*,[199] the court acknowledged that there had not previously been a case in which a school, as D, had been liable to a pupil for personal injury caused by an attack by an outsider on the school premises, and that this 'does bring into operation the injunction that courts should take care to extend duties of care only incrementally'. The closest type of cases had occurred where D had been liable to pupils for harm caused by bullying co-pupils (per *Bradford-Smart v West Sussex CC*[200]), or where pupils were harmed by dangerous drivers outside the school premises. However, to hold that the school owed a duty of care to Henry Webster to protect him from attack by outsiders was sufficiently analogous to uphold a duty on the school's part to take reasonable care to see that Henry was reasonably safe during school hours, and for a reasonable period after the end of the school day, while he was still on the school's premises.

The ECHR angle

Some of the post-2000 cases explored in this section evidenced a multi-pronged type of claim – in negligence, and under the ECHR, for infringement by D of C's Convention rights (e.g., in *Thomson v Scottish Ministers*,[201] both negligence and a claim for infringement of Art 2, the right to life, were instituted – and both failed). Consideration of the ECHR Convention rights, where D is a public authority, is developed in Chapter 13.

Recent cases have shown a possible change of tack by C in third party cases, by eschewing a claim in negligence altogether, and pursuing a claim solely under the ECHR instead. For example, in *Bedford v Bedfordshire CC*,[202] C was brain-damaged by injuries inflicted by children who were in the care of Council D, under the 'looked after child' regime. In an interesting comment, Jay J noted that, '[t]his action is brought solely under the HRA; there is no claim at common law. [C] have taken the view that no duty of care is owed by the defendant local authority in these circumstances ... I should not be interpreted as disagreeing with him. I should add that, in any event, the Claimant would have been in no better position at common law, even had a duty of care been owed, because he would have had to demonstrate that the Defendant took decisions of a policy nature which were wholly unreasonable. The outcome would have been the same, although the route to it would have deviated slightly'. C brought his claim under Art 8 of the ECHR (right to private life), unsuccessfully, as it turned out. More recently, in *DSD v Commr of Police*,[203] C, two victims of the 'black cab rapist', successfully sued under Art 3 (the right not to be subject to inhuman or degrading treatment or punishment) of the ECHR, where the sole allegation was that the police failed to investigate the rape claims to the standard required by Art 3, given a vast array of systemic and operational failings during the long-running investigation of the case.

---

[199] [2010] EWHC 157 (QB) [118], [121].   [200] [2002] EWCA Civ 7.
[201] [2013] CSIH 63, [36]–[41].   [202] [2013] EWHC 1717 (QB) [12].
[203] [2014] EWHC 436 (QB), aff'd: *Commr of Police v DSD and NBV* [2015] EWCA Civ 646.

4

Duty III – Pure economic loss

INTRODUCTION

Liability for negligently-inflicted financial losses is both complex and challenging. This is due, in part, to the reluctance of English appellate courts to settle upon any **one** test by which to establish whether D owed C a duty of care to avoid the pure economic loss which C suffered.

It is also due, in part, to the sophisticated and 'broad network of economic links that exist in any developed society' (as the Court of Appeal put it in *Conarken Group Ltd v Network Rail Infrastructure Ltd (Rev 1)*[1]). The Scottish Inner House spoke for English law too, when it stated that, '[negligently-inflicted pure economic loss] is a difficult area of the law … which continues to develop … as a process of incrementalism' (per *Hines v King Sturge LLP*[2]).

Recovery for pure economic loss also tends to be an area of negligence which is governed to a large extent by policy – which calls to mind that 'unruly horse' of public policy that Burroughs J spoke of in *Richardson v Mellish*,[3] that 'once you get astride it, you never know where it will carry you'. Part of the challenge, in this chapter, is to provide some defined tracks upon which that horse may predictably pass! It should also be mentioned, at the outset, that English law has not adopted a sympathetic approach to pure economic loss claims. Just as with pure psychiatric injury claims (see Chapter 5), casting any duty of care on D's part to avoid such injury can be very challenging.

This chapter explores **four** principal categories of pure economic loss claims:

- negligent misstatements (also called the 'narrow principle in *Hedley Byrne*'[4]);
- the negligent provision of services (also known as the 'extended principle in *Hedley Byrne*');
- pure relational economic loss (also known as the 'exclusionary rule'); and
- pure economic loss arising from defective buildings (an online section).

Before turning to each in turn, it is important to reiterate a couple of preliminary points.

§4.1 Pure economic loss is financial loss which is *not* consequential upon either personal injury or property damage being suffered by C. The only loss suffered by C is the financial loss of which he complains.

Where C suffers some physical injury because of D's breach, then financial expenses may be incurred by C (e.g., loss of earnings in the future, out-of-pocket transport costs to attend

---

[1] [2011] EWCA Civ 644, [2011] BLR 462, [95].   [2] [2010] CSIH 86, 2011 SLT 2, [45], [50].
[3] (1824) 2 Bing 229, 252.   [4] [1964] AC 465 (HL).

medical appointments), which are consequential economic losses. Similarly, where C's property (say, a car) is damaged by D's negligent driving, then repair costs and the hiring costs of another vehicle may be incurred by C – which, again, are consequential.

These types of economic losses are simply added to C's claim, as heads of damage flowing from the original physical or property damage suffered by C. They are not difficult or controversial to recover, provided that they are causally linked to the breach and are not too remote at law. Pure economic losses, however, are stand-alone losses, incurred by C as a result of D's breach.

§4.2   The duty of care owed by D to avoid pure economic losses on C's part is a duty to exercise *reasonable* care. D does not guarantee, nor give a warranty for either a perfect financial outcome for, or the avoidance of economic harm to, C.

In *Patchett v Swimming Pool and Allied Trades Assn*,[5] Lord Clarke MR reiterated that, even if a duty of care were owed by SPATA, D, to an aggrieved pool-owner, C (which was **not** held in that case), D did not make any warranties about the creditworthiness of that Association's members – '[n]o warranty was given. SPATA was saying that, before each member joined, checks were carried out on its financial record and on its experience in the trade, and there were inspections of its work'. Hence, even where a duty is owed, the standard of care is, as always in negligence, merely one of reasonableness, not perfection (per Chapter 6).

NEGLIGENT MISSTATEMENT

Introduction

§4.3   A negligent misstatement means either information or advice given by D, the statement maker, which (1) was inaccurate, (2) was made without a reasonable degree of skill and care about its accuracy, (3) caused C financial loss, (4) was within the province of D's special skill to provide and (5) D undertook to provide for C's benefit, who he knew, or ought to have reasonably foreseen, would be likely to rely upon D's exercising reasonable care in providing that information or advice.

This is known as the *Hedley Byrne* principle (or the 'narrow application of *Hedley Byrne*'[6]).

Elements (1) and (2) of the abovementioned principle pertain to breach (as discussed in Chapter 7), whilst element (3) pertains to causation (Chapter 8). Elements (4) and (5) pertain to the duty of care question, and will comprise the focus of this chapter.

Whether or not a duty of care arises on D's part to avoid economic loss being suffered by C, where C acted on information or advice conveyed by D, does **not** depend upon whether the parties shared a particular formalised relationship, such as solicitor–client, or banker–customer. A duty of care may not even arise in such a case; or conversely, it may arise in relation to a transaction which falls well outside those recognised relationships. Lord Devlin made that plain in *Hedley Byrne & Co Ltd v Heller & Partners Ltd*,[7] and many of the cases in this chapter bear out that sentiment. Indeed, Lord Mance's statement, in *Customs and Excise Commrs v Barclays Bank plc* – that *Hedley Byrne* is 'the fountain of most modern economic claims' in negligence[8] – sets the scene. Its importance in this area of negligence cannot be overstated.

The reference to 'skill', in the abovementioned principle, does **not** necessarily require that D possessed some particular *professional* qualification or expertise. The term is widely construed, and embraces circumstances where D had particular knowledge by virtue of his occupation

---

[5] [2009] EWCA Civ 717, [29].   [6] Per, e.g., *McLaughlan v Edwards* [2004] Scot SC 31, [7].
[7] [1964] AC 465 (HL).   [8] [2006] UKHL 28, [2007] 1 AC 181, [85].

or position. As Lord Goff remarked in *Henderson v Merrett Syndicates Ltd*,[9] the term 'must be understood broadly, certainly broadly enough to include special knowledge'.

Ancillary causes of action

Several other causes of action may be pleaded, simultaneously with negligently-inflicted pure economic loss. For example, breach of contract may be sought, if the negligent provision of advice or information has occurred within the context of a contractual undertaking on D's part which was supported by consideration from C.

Alternatively, if a pre-contractual misstatement induced a contract between C and D, then an action under s 2(1) of the Misrepresentation Act 1967 may be more attractive than an action in negligence, given that there is no need for C to prove the intricacy of the duty of care analysis which follows in this chapter. This advantage was noted recently, by the Supreme Court, in *Cramaso LLP v Ogilvie-Grant, Earl of Seafield (Scotland)*,[10] that s 2(1) was 'a complex provision, which has the effect of dispensing with the need to establish a duty of care in English law'. The statutory misrepresentation only requires that C prove: the representation was made by D; it was intended to be relied upon; it was in fact relied upon; it was untrue; C entered into a contract in reliance upon the representation; and C suffered loss as a result. C does not need to prove that the representation was made negligently either – it is for D to prove that he had reasonable grounds for believing that the representation was true (per *Laws v Socy of Lloyd's*[11]), thus reversing the burden of proof. Damages awarded are likely to be better under the Act too, given that all actual loss directly flowing from the transaction induced by D is compensable (i.e., the measure of damages in deceit, rather than the measure of damages in negligence which is discussed in Chapter 11) (per *Pankhania v Hackney*[12]).

Rarely, and only where the evidence supports the allegation, false statements by D may give rise to a claim for fraudulent misrepresentation (i.e., deceit).

> In *Derry v Peek*,[13] C sued the directors of a company, D, in respect of false statements in a prospectus for fraudulent misrepresentation. **Held:** the action failed. D believed that their statements were true, although they had no reasonable grounds for their belief. That could not amount to fraud, as fraud requires dishonesty; mere credulity was not dishonesty.

Breach of fiduciary duty may also arise, where a negligent misstatement occurred (pleaded, but not proven, in the client's action against a solicitor in *Nocton v Lord Ashburton*[14]). However, it does not follow that, just because a fiduciary relationship exists, there necessarily would be a parallel tortious duty of care imposed on D (per *BP plc v AON Ltd*[15]). A fiduciary relationship does not import an assumption of responsibility on D's part sufficient to found a duty of care in tort.

Breaking new ground

The decision in *Hedley Byrne v Heller* in 1964 'broke new ground' for creating liability in negligence for pure economic loss (per *Spring v Guardian Assurance plc*[16]). There could be a 'duty to take care in word, as well as in deed', extending *beyond* scenarios in which C and D were in a contractual or a fiduciary relationship (per *Nocton v Ashburton*), or scenarios of fraud (per *Derry v Peek*).

In *Hedley Byrne*, a claim arose from an *innocent* negligent misrepresentation, involving no privity of contract at all.[17] Lord Devlin described the circumstances which could give rise to a duty of care as 'special relationships' – i.e., those which were 'equivalent to contract', and in which D assumed responsibility to avoid economic loss being suffered by C, as a result of negligent information or

---

[9] [1995] 2 AC 145 (HL) 180.   [10] [2014] UKSC 9, [2014] 1 AC 1093, [37].   [11] [2003] EWCA Civ 1887, [86]–[87].
[12] [2004] EWHC 323 (Ch) [17].   [13] (1889) 14 App Cas 337 (HL).   [14] [1914] AC 932 (HL).
[15] [2006] EWHC 424 (Comm).   [16] [1994] UKHL 7, [1995] 2 AC 296, 317 (Lord Goff).
[17] [1964] AC 465 (HL) 528–29 (Lord Devlin), with quotes in Table at 488–89 (Lord Reid), 509 (Lord Hodson).

advice. It is clear, though, that this area of liability has since actually extended well **beyond** where C and D were in a relationship 'equivalent to contract' – i.e., where factors have indicated that the law recognises a duty of care, but where there are very little indicia of a contractual relationship at all.

Actually, prior to *Hedley Byrne*, English law had taken several twists and turns. The 1893 decision in *Le Lievre v Gould*[18] was called, about a century later in *Caparo Industries plc v Dickman*,[19] a 'wrong turn'. In *Hedley Byrne*, though, 'the law was once more set on the right path'.

The legal landmarks achieved in *Hedley Byrne*

1888	a requirement that a contractual or a fiduciary relationship was required, for a misstatement to give rise to an action by C, was **not** part of English law. In *Cann v Willson*[a] (where valuer, D, was engaged by the mortgagor to provide a valuation, and the mortgagee, C, relied upon it to his detriment), D was negligent – because D sent the valuation directly to C, to induce C to lend the money, and D 'knowingly had placed themselves in that position'. But twists followed:
1889	in *Derry v Peek*,[b] the court held that '[t]o found an action for damages [for misrepresentation], there must be a contract and breach, or fraud'
1893	in *Le Lievre v Gould*,[c] the court held that, 'in the absence of contract, an action for negligence cannot be maintained when there is no fraud'. However, both statements in *Derry v Peek* and *Le Lievre* were bad law, according to *Hedley Byrne* – as Lord Reid put it baldly, *Le Lievre* was 'wrong in limiting the duty of care with regard to statements to cases where there is a contract';
	Mr Gould, D, a surveyor, provided stage-of-completion certificates about a building project to lenders, C, who, relying on these, advanced monies to a builder, their mortgagor. The certificates contained negligent statements. D was not appointed by lenders C, so there was no contractual relationship between them. In fact, D knew nothing about the lenders or the terms of their mortgage with the builder. **Held:** D owed no duty to C to exercise care in giving his certificates. No liability arose for negligent misstatement, in the absence of a contract between them.
1914	in *Nocton v Ashburton*, Lord Haldane stated that 'a special duty [of care, re misstatements] may arise from … an implied contract at law or a fiduciary obligation in equity'[d]
1916	in *Robinson v National Bank of Scotland*, Lord Haldane seemed to retreat from *Nocton*: 'I should be very sorry if any word fell from me which should suggest that courts are in any way hampered in recognising that a duty of care may be established when [special cases] really occur'[e]
1951	the majority decision in *Candler v Crane Christmas*[f] was also overruled in *Hedley Byrne*:
	C proposed to invest in a company, and asked to see the company accounts. The company's accountants, D, were requested by the company to prepare accounts, so that they could be shown to C. The accounts, which contained some negligent and misleading statements, were provided to C. **Held (majority):** no duty of care was owed by D to C (following *Le Lievre v Gould*). Given that the contract was between D and the company, and not with C, there could be no liability for the negligent misstatement. Nor was there any fiduciary relationship between them. **Denning LJ (dissenting):** *Le Lievre* was distinguishable, because here, D knew that C was relying on its skill and judgment, and why C wanted to see the accounts. In *Le Lievre*, the lender's existence/identity was not known to surveyor, Mr Gould. In *Hedley Byrne*, Lord Hodson noted that Denning LJ's dissenting judgment 'was to be preferred to that of the majority, although the opinion of the majority was undoubtedly supported by the ratio of *Le Lievre*, which they could not be criticised for following'.

[a] (1888) 39 Ch D 39, 42 (Chitty J).   [b] (1889) 14 App Cas 337 (HL) 347 (Lord Bramwell).
[c] [1893] 1 QB 491 (CA) 498 (Lord Esher).   [d] [1914] AC 932 (HL) 955.   [e] 1916 SC (HL) 154, 157.   [f] [1951] 2 KB 164.

---

[18] [1893] 1 QB 491 (CA).   [19] [1990] 2 AC 605 (HL) 619.

Framework

A convenient framework for an analysis of this area of negligence law is as follows:

> ### Nutshell analysis: Negligent misstatement
>
> Identify whether C and D are in a bi-partite scenario, a tri-partite scenario, or a victim scenario
>
> **Proving a duty of care – a checklist:**
>
> 1 Reasonable foreseeability of economic loss
> 2 An assumption of responsibility by D/a reciprocal reliance by C (the *Hedley Byrne* test); OR sufficient proximity and public policy to found a duty of care (the *Caparo* test)
> 3 The incremental test justified a duty of care being owed by D
> 4 Factors which do not preclude a duty of care
>
> **The rest of the negligence action, as per usual**

Dealing with each in turn:

Reasonable foreseeability of economic loss

§4.4   D must have actually foreseen (i.e., appreciated) – or alternatively, should have reasonably foreseen – that his failure to exercise reasonable care and/or skill when giving information or advice could cause economic loss to C.

Proving reasonable foreseeability of the financial loss suffered by C is 'fundamental' to liability (per *McCullagh v Lane Fox & Partners*[20]), but it is **not** sufficient to establish a duty of care to avoid such damage. In *White v Jones*,[21] Lord Browne-Wilkinson stated that, '[t]he law of England does not impose any general duty of care to avoid negligent misstatements or to avoid causing pure economic loss, even if economic damage to [C] was foreseeable'.

In this context, the meaning of loss being 'reasonably foreseeable' is precisely the same as under the general principles of duty of care (see Chapter 2).

Indeed, it is difficult to identify a case in which the economic loss suffered by C was held to be unforeseeable (particularly given the importance of choosing the relevant D appropriately, as the facts of *Islington LBC v UCL Hosp NHS Trust*,[22] discussed in Chapter 2, demonstrated). Even in cases where proximity was doubtful, and policy dictated against a duty of care being owed, foreseeability was confidently proven (per, e.g., *Arrowhead Capital Finance Ltd v KPMG LLP*[23]). For example, in *Caparo Industries plc v Dickman*,[24] the House of Lords held that it may have been highly foreseeable that a potential bidder for a company might rely on audited accounts prepared by D – but that 'did not suffice to found a duty of care' (and indeed, both lack of proximity and policy precluded a duty of care there). Lord Oliver, in particular, thought the criterion almost useless, in economic loss cases, as placing any restrictions on a

---

[20] [1995] EWCA Civ 8, (1995) 49 Con LR 124, 225.   [21] [1995] 2 AC 207 (HL) 274.
[22] [2005] EWCA Civ 596, [15]–[16].   [23] [2012] EWHC 1801 (Comm) [59].
[24] [1990] 2 AC 605 (HL), with quotes at 643.

duty of care from arising: 'it is almost always foreseeable that someone, somewhere and in some circumstances, may choose to alter his position upon the faith of the accuracy of a statement or report which comes to his attention and it is always foreseeable that a report – even a confidential report – may come to be communicated to persons other than the original or intended recipient'. It followed that, to rely only on a test of reasonable foreseeability of possible economic damage, 'without some further control, would be to create a liability wholly indefinite in area, duration and amount and would open up a limitless vista of uninsurable risk for the professional man'.

Hence, proximity, assumptions of responsibility, reliance, and policy reasons, all combine to circumscribe D's liability in this area of negligence.

The *Hedley Byrne*, *Caparo* and incremental tests

Inter-relationship between the three tests

§4.5   The same three broad approaches, or 'tests', as for personal injury or property damage, have been adopted, in order to assess whether a duty of care is owed by D in respect of negligent misstatement. They are generally assessed in the following order of analysis: (1) the *Hedley Byrne* test; (2) the *Caparo* test; and (3) the incremental 'cross-check' test.

Where negligent misstatement is concerned, the House of Lords has opined – in *Henderson v Merrett Syndicates Ltd*,[25] and subsequently in *Customs and Excise Commrs v Barclays Bank plc*[26] – that the *Hedley Byrne* assumption of responsibility/reliance test is the primary test, rather than the tri-partite *Caparo* test.[27] Where D assumed responsibility in providing advice or information to an identified (or identifiable) party who relied upon D's skill and expertise, it is generally unnecessary to consider the *Caparo* test, because the requisite relationship necessary to give rise to a duty of care will already exist between D and C. Lord Goff pointed out, in *Henderson*,[28] that satisfying the *Hedley Byrne* test will not expose D to liability to the whole world, or to an indeterminate (i.e., open-ended) class of Cs. Such policy reasons fall away. In *Customs and Excise*, Lord Hoffmann also noted that the assumption of responsibility test suited best where D provided the information or advice, knowing that it would be relied upon by someone else (whether the immediate contracting party or some identifiable third party).

However, where C is not an identified or identifiable party – and the *Hedley Byrne* test becomes more difficult to meet, other than in a 'deemed' or 'notional' fashion – then the *Caparo* test should be applied, including a detailed assessment of its third, policy-based, limb. To instance, the prospect of indeterminate liability will figure large, in precluding a duty of care, where D's statement or advice has been put into general circulation, and could be relied upon by numerous strangers to D and for many purposes, all of which D 'had no specific reason to anticipate' (per Lord Bridge in *Caparo*[29]). (In this chapter, 'indeterminate liability' will be used in circumstances where that one D could be exposed to an unknown number of Cs arising from D's act or omission, whereas the 'floodgates' problem will be used to denote the situation where, because of the 'precedential effect' of a finding of negligence against D, then so too could many others, in similarly-instituted suits in the future.)

Under this approach, the order is quite clear-cut: 'one may seek assumption of responsibility and, if it is not found, go back to the *Caparo* tripartite test'.[30] The most authoritative statement

---

[25] [1995] 2 AC 145 (HL).   [26] [2006] UKHL 28, [2007] 1 AC 181.   [27] [1990] 2 AC 605 (HL) 617–18 (Lord Bridge).
[28] [1995] 2 AC 145 (HL) 180–81.   [29] [1990] 2 AC 605 (HL) 620–21.
[30] *Hines v King Sturge LLP* [2009] Scot CS (OH) 96, [44], but outcome overturned on appeal: [2010] CSIH 86.

of this analysis, whether for negligent misstatement or negligent provision of services, was set out in *Customs and Excise*.[31] To summarise:

Per Lords Bingham, Mance and Hoffmann in *Customs and Excise v Barclays Bank* (2007):

The test:	Comments about the test:
The **assumption of responsibility test** – has D (the statement maker) assumed responsibility for exercising care and skill in saying what he said, and did C (the loss sufferer) reasonably rely on D so assuming that responsibility?	• the *Hedley Byrne* test is the 'first port of call' – proof of assumption of responsibility, and corresponding reliance, is sufficient for a duty of care to arise (Lord Bingham); • the test is objective, not subjective – it is not what D intended in making the statement, but what the surrounding circumstances (e.g., a professional relationship) and D's conduct indicate, as to whether D assumed responsibility for its reasonable accuracy (Lord Hoffmann); • however, notions of 'deemed' assumption of responsibility stretch the test to 'breaking point' and render the test entirely artificial (Lord Bingham) – this will occur, e.g., where D has no knowledge or awareness of C's existence, let alone identity; and/or where C did not rely on D, because he did not know that D was rendering the service for his benefit; • the absence of any real and true assumption of responsibility does not necessarily disprove a duty of care, but it is then necessary to consider the *Caparo* test (Lords Bingham and Hoffmann).
The *Caparo* test – (a) Was economic loss to C a foreseeable consequence of D's statement? (b) Were C and D legally proximate? (c) Is it fair, just and reasonable to impose a duty on D?	• this test is to be used when there is no real and true assumption of responsibility on the facts; • in that event, the task is to analyse whether 'the features of different specific situations [is one] which, on a detailed examination of all the circumstances, the law recognises pragmatically as giving rise to a duty of care of a given scope' (per Lord Bridge[a]).
The **incremental test** – the law should develop novel categories of negligence by analogy with established categories/cases, rather than by massive extension of principle	• the test has little value as a 'stand-alone' test, but is to be used as 'an important cross-check', to verify whether the proposed result is fairly close to an already-decided scenario regarding pure economic loss (Lord Mance); • the closer the facts of the case are to one in which a duty of care has been already held to exist, the more likely a duty, and vice versa (Lord Bingham). Courts prefer to 'hug the coastline' of previously-decided cases.

[a] [1990] 2 AC 605 (HL) 618.

---

[31] [2006] UKHL 28, [2007] 1 AC 181, with points in the Table locatable at: [4]–[8] (Lord Bingham), [36]–[37], (Lord Hoffmann), [87]–[88], [93] (Lord Mance).

However, the three tests are not, strictly speaking, easily distinguishable from each other – and nor should they be. There can feasibly be a great deal of overlap. In earlier cases (e.g., in *Henderson v Merrett Syndicates Ltd*[32]), it was suggested that if the *Hedley Byrne* 'special relationship' was established, then 'there should be no need to embark upon any further enquiry whether it is "fair, just and reasonable" to impose liability for economic loss'. However, since then, and even in the intervening period since *Customs and Excise* was decided, the tests tend to be discussed, and applied, quite interchangeably by first-instance courts (per, e.g., *Khambay v Nijhar (t/a Gravitas Consulting)*[33]). What may show a strong degree of reliance by C under the *Hedley Byrne* test also assists to prove the requisite proximity between C and D under the second limb of *Caparo*. Lord Mance noted, in *Customs and Excise*, that '[t]he concept of assumption of responsibility ... may effectively subsume all aspects of the threefold [*Caparo*] approach', and that 'there is no single common denominator, even in cases of economic loss, by which liability may be determined'.[34] In *Merrett v Babb*,[35] May LJ also acknowledged that the two tests relevant to proving a duty to avoid causing foreseeable economic loss were not necessarily distinct:

> two strands of consideration emerged. These may for convenience be called the *Caparo* strand and the *Henderson [adopting the Hedley Byrne]* strand. The *Caparo* strand asks whether, in addition to foreseeability, there is a sufficient relationship of proximity and whether the imposition of a duty of care is fair, just and reasonable. The *Henderson* strand asks whether [D] is to be taken to have assumed responsibility to [C] to guard against the loss for which damages are claimed. The difficulty with the *Caparo* strand is that it is sometimes seen as being unhelpfully vague. The difficulty with the *Henderson* strand is that it was originally often expressed in terms of 'voluntary assumption of responsibility' which tended to import a degree of subjectivity. *Henderson* itself put paid to that ... that responsibility is recognised or imposed by the law. Thus, the *Caparo* strand and the *Henderson* strand, in reality, merge. In my view, it is very often a helpful guide to ask whether [D] is to be taken to have assumed responsibility to [C] to guard against the loss for which damages are claimed. But I also think that it is reaching for the moon – and not required by authority – to expect to accommodate every circumstance which may arise within a single short abstract formulation.

Very rarely will D give an **express** undertaking, written or oral, to C, to exercise reasonable care and skill to protect C against any economic loss arising from D's endeavours ('extremely unlikely in the ordinary course of events': said Lord Griffiths in *Smith v Eric S Bush*[36]). Of those cases, Lord Devlin noted, in *Hedley Byrne*, that 'there can be little difficulty. The difficulty arises in discerning those cases in which the undertaking is to be *implied*'.[37] The most important task, regardless of whether it is the *Caparo* or the *Hedley Byrne* test which is being applied, is to search for **facts and circumstances** which would show that such an undertaking (and concomitant reliance) were implied.

Notably, Lord Hoffmann reiterated in *Customs and Excise* that labels are often bandied about, when discussing whether an 'assumption of responsibility', 'reliance', or 'fair, just and reasonable', are proven. However, the **only** way to properly assess that question is to

---

[32] [1995] 2 AC 145 (HL) 181 (Lord Goff).

[33] [2015] EWHC 190 (QB) [96]–[99]. Also: *Barclays Bank v Grant Thornton UK LLP* [2015] EWHC 320 (Comm) [49]; *Sebry v Companies House (Rev 1)* [2015] EWHC 115 (QB) [110].

[34] [2006] UKHL 28, [2007] 1 AC 181, [93].   [35] [2001] EWCA Civ 214, [2001] QB 1174, [41].

[36] [1990] 1 AC 831 (HL) 862.   [37] [1964] AC 465 (HL) 528–29.

descend to a close examination of the facts, and to infuse the assessment with policy considerations too:

> There is a tendency ... for phrases like 'proximate', 'fair, just and reasonable' and 'assumption of responsibility', to be used as slogans rather than practical guides to whether a duty should exist or not. These phrases are often illuminating but discrimination is needed to identify the factual situations in which they provide useful guidance ... Because the question of whether D has assumed responsibility is a legal inference to be drawn from his conduct against the background of all the circumstances of the case, it is by no means a simple question of fact. Questions of fairness and policy will enter into the decision, and it may be more useful to try to identify these questions than simply to bandy terms like 'assumption of responsibility' and 'fair, just and reasonable'.[38]

Lord Bingham noted, similarly, that it requires 'attention on the detailed circumstances of the particular case, and the particular relationship between the parties in the context of their legal and factual situation as a whole'.[39]

In that regard, in the following section of scenarios, the leading cases are each accompanied by a 'factors box', which draws out the salient factors which were used to assess whether the *Hedley Byrne* and *Caparo* tests were proven, on the particular facts in question. The cases have been chosen to demonstrate a wide array of salient factors. As always, the court must undertake a balancing exercise of 'key competing factors' (as the court stated, and tackled recently, in *Barclays Bank plc v Grant Thornton UK LLP*[40]). In most difficult and novel scenarios giving rise to pure economic loss, not all of the relevant factors will point one way or the other; not all of them are to be given the same weight in every scenario; and none is necessarily conclusive.

As a final note on the incremental test, novel cases in pure economic loss still arise. In 2009, in *Patchett v SPATA Ltd*,[41] the Court of Appeal considered, for the first time, whether D could owe a duty of care, with respect to statements put up on a trade association website; while in 2012, a case was brought by a police informant for pure economic loss (*An Informer v Chief Constable*[42]) which had never been considered by an English court before, and where, as Toulson LJ reiterated, '[t]he fact that this is a novel claim is not necessarily fatal because the categories of negligence are never closed'. In neither case could C point to any case reasonably analogous in which a similar duty had been imposed on D (and, hence, no duty arose).

§4.6 An action for pure economic loss arising from negligent misstatement can come about via three different scenarios: (1) bi-partite relationships, where D provides the information or advice to C directly, and C relies on that information or advice to his detriment; (2) tri-partite relationships, where D provides the information or advice to X, and C relies upon that information or advice to his detriment; or (3) 'victim' scenarios, where D provides the information or advice to X, and X (and not C) relies upon that information or advice to C's detriment.

Notably, it is not necessarily easier to prove a duty of care in a bi-partite scenario, versus a tri-partite scenario – even where there is no third party intermediary X, the factors may comprehensively

---

[38] [2006] UKHL 28, [35]–[36].   [39] *ibid*, [8].

[40] [2015] EWHC 320 (Comm) [91] (no duty of care owed to Barclays Bank by auditors Grant Thornton).

[41] [2009] EWCA Civ 717, [2010] 2 All ER (Comm) 138.

[42] [2012] EWCA Civ 197, [2013] QB 579, [59], citing his own views in: *Glaister v Appleby-in-Westmoreland TC* [2009] EWCA Civ 1325, [55].

point away from the existence of a duty of care owed to C. Moreover, many of the same duty-of-care-factors arise across these categories; there is no mutual exclusivity about them.

Outlining each category in turn, and by reference to leading illustrative cases:

The bi-partite relationship

Most commonly, D makes some statement directly to C which is inaccurate, and upon which C relies, to his detriment. No other (third) party is involved; C and D deal directly with each other. There may be a contract between C and D, but not necessarily; a duty of care may arise, regardless.

The bi-partite relationship in negligent misstatement

Information passes from D to C in a direct relationship — but is a duty of care owed along the dotted line too?

C (*Mr Evatt; informer; Mr and Mrs Patchett; Miss Chaudhry*)

Information passing

DOC owed?

D (*MLC, the police; SPATA; Mr Prabhakar*)

Dealing with the leading bi-partite cases:

> In *Mutual Life and Citizens' Ass Co Ltd (MLC) v Evatt*,[43] Mr Evatt, C, was a policy-holder of the insurance company, MLC, D. He sought advice from D's officer as to the financial stability of Palmer Ltd, one of D's related companies. C was told that Palmer Ltd was a safe vehicle for the investments which he had in mind. That advice turned out to be inaccurate, and C suffered a significant loss of value in his investments with Palmer Ltd. **Held (PC, 3:2):** no duty of care owed by D to C. D's officer's duty was merely to give C an honest answer to his enquiry (which he did).

The factors in play

- *scope of expertise:* D, as an insurance company, did not carry on the business of giving advice on investments, nor did it hold itself out as possessing the necessary skill and competence (any greater than C himself possessed) in assessing the safety of a company as an investment opportunity;
- *payment:* the fact that no fee was charged by D, or paid by C, did not preclude a duty of care from arising.

The decision in *MLC v Evatt* was strongly criticised by both the Court of Appeal in *Esso Petroleum Co Ltd v Mardon*,[44] and by the House of Lords in *Spring v Guardian Assurance*,[45] on the basis that the majority's decision meant that, to be actionable as a negligent misstatement, D's information or advice must have been provided in the course of a business or profession which involved D's giving information or advice of that kind. Both *Esso* and *Spring* considered that to be far too narrow a proposition, and preferred the dissenting view (of Lords Reid and Morris) in *Evatt*, that it was sufficient if the hallmarks of a 'special

[43] [1971] AC 793 (PC, on appeal from New South Wales). Lords Reid and Morris dissented.
[44] [1976] QB 801 (CA).   [45] [1995] 2 AC 296 (HL) (Lord Goff).

relationship' between C and D were proven, no matter whether or not the information was given in the course of D's business or profession. However, this disagreement notwithstanding, the basic tenets of *Evatt* – that D's acting within his skill and expertise (and not outside that realm) is an important factor in assisting to prove a duty of care, and that a duty of care may attach, even to gratuitously-given information or advice – remain good law.

> In *An Informer v Chief Constable*,[46] C, a police informer, supplied information about X to the police, D. C had two 'contact handlers', H1 and H2, who explained how they would protect C's identity, and that C had no authority to engage in any form of criminal activity, but there was no discussion about C's financial welfare. H1 and H2 were not part of the team who investigated X. During the investigation, police listened to X's conversations with other people, including C. C told H1 and H2 that X wanted to talk to him about some money laundering activities. A few weeks later, X was arrested and charged, and confiscation orders were put in place re X's property and assets. C's own records were investigated too (via his bankers, solicitors and accountants), and he was arrested on suspicion of money laundering, and released on bail. H1 and H2 knew of C's arrest from the investigating team, but no officer involved in the investigating team was aware that C was an informer. A restraint order was obtained against C's assets, and the judge who made the order was told nothing about C's role as an informer either. Eventually, the CPS decided not to prosecute C, and the restraint order against him and his assets was formally discharged. C claimed that his arrest and the restraint order put him in dire financial straits, and should never have happened, given that he was an informer. **Held (2:1):** no duty of care owed by D to C.

The factors in play

- *conflict of duties:* until the CPS decided not to prosecute C, there was a conflict between his financial interests and the public interest in preserving property reasonably suspected of being the proceeds of crime. It would not be just or reasonable to place the police, D, under a duty to give priority to supporting C's financial welfare, over the public interest in having crime, and the proceeds of crime, detected (Toulson LJ);
- *parliamentary intent:* the Regulation of Investigatory Powers Act 2000, s 29(2), refers to the police, D, having responsibility for an informer's 'security and welfare' or 'safety and welfare'. Those phrases are not defined, but would cover an informer's exposure to risks of death, injury, harassment and risks of a physical nature – but nothing in the statute indicated that Parliament intended an informer's financial well-being to be safeguarded, and hence, no duty of care of that scope could be owed to C (Toulson LJ);
- *incremental test:* the application of the *Hill* principle (see Chapter 2), which forbade a duty of care arising on the police's part re investigations into crime, applied to economic loss cases too. Each act complained of by C (his arrest and subsequent interview, obtaining restraint orders against him, and failing to apply for the restraint order to be lifted) was carried out in the course of investigating crime. The police had reasonable grounds to suspect that C had committed an offence, which was precisely when the *Hill* principle applied (Arden LJ). Moreover, C 'was not able to cite any case reasonably analogous to the facts of the present case in which a duty to prevent purely economic loss has been recognised' (Toulson LJ).

[46] [2012] EWCA Civ 197, [2013] QB 579, quote in Table at [57] (Pill LJ held that a duty of care to reasonably protect C's financial welfare was owed; but ('with some reluctance') that there had been no breach; hence, C's claim failed 3:0).

In *Patchett v Swimming Pool and Allied Trades Assn (SPATA) Ltd*,[47] Mr and Mrs Patchett, C, wished to have a swimming pool built in the garden of their home. They perused the website of SPATA, D, a trade association made up of most of the major swimming pool installers trading in the UK. C engaged a SPATA-advertised member company, Crown Pools Ltd, to build the pool, but Crown only half-finished the job due to financial difficulties. Although C paid instalments due under the contract, work stopped, and Crown ceased trading. C engaged other contractors to complete the job, and claimed £44,000 as their economic damage caused by the collapse of Crown. In fact, Crown was not a full member of D, but only an affiliate member, and hence, was not subject to D's bond and warranty scheme. C claimed that they were misled by D's website about that. **Held (2:1):** no duty of care owed by D to C.

The factors in play

- *independent enquiry:* D's website may not have given the impression to readers that there were different types of members (full and affiliate), and what the difference meant, but the website plainly urged C to make further enquiries, referring to an 'information pack': 'SPATA supplies an information pack and members lists which give details of suitably qualified and approved installers in the customer's area. The pack includes a Contract Check List which sets out the questions that the customer should ask a would-be tenderer, together with those which must be asked of the appointed installer, before work starts and prior to releasing the final payment'. D could expect that a potential customer would obtain the information pack (it might be different if a website was interactive, so that C could obtain all the information from the website, but this was not that type of website). Had C asked for the information pack, and the list of members referred to on the website, it would have become immediately apparent that Crown was not covered by the bond and warranty scheme;
- *voluntarily given:* the statements on D's website were put into general circulation, for those interested in having a pool built. It was not a case where C requested specific information which was duly provided in response. C was not entitled to rely on a bit 'here and there' on that website; it had to be taken as a whole. D could reasonably expect potential customers to have regard to all, not part, of the information on the website;
- *incremental test:* there was no closely analogous case to warrant a duty being upheld in this scenario.

In *Chaudhry v Prabhakar*,[48] Miss Chaudhry, C, 26, having just passed her driving test, asked her close friend, Mr Prabhakar, D, to find her a second-hand car that 'had not been in an accident'. C knew very little about cars, whereas D, whilst not a mechanic, 'knew something about cars'. He found C a 1-year-old Volkswagon, of low mileage, from a panel beater. C paid £4,500 for it, but then discovered that it had been in a serious accident, had been poorly repaired, and was unroadworthy. C sued D for the costs of replacing the car, hence the claim for pure economic loss. **Held:** D owed C a duty of care (the panel beating firm was also held liable, in contract, for breach of merchantible quality).

---

[47] [2009] EWCA Civ 717, (Lord Clarke, Scott Baker LJ; with Lady Justice Smith dissenting).
[48] [1989] 1 WLR 29 (CA).

- *no independent enquiry:* Heller, D, knew, or should have realised, that the information about Easipower's creditworthiness was likely to be acted upon without independent enquiry being made by Hedley Byrne, C;
- *the purpose test:* the specific purpose for which the information was requested by D (a credit reference re Easipower) closely matched the purpose for which the information was used (D's extending credit to Easipower);
- *an ascertainable class:* Hedley Byrne, C, as one of NPB's customers, was one of a limited ascertainable class, which was sufficient, even though C was not specifically identified (it did not need to be);
- *source of information:* Heller, as Easipower's bankers, was almost the sole repository of information about Easipower's creditworthiness. It would have been almost impossible for C to obtain that information elsewhere;
- *scope of expertise:* assessing the creditworthiness of a business was within the scope of the bank's skill;
- *disclaimer:* Heller did effectively disclaim any assumption of a duty of care for the credit reference which it gave: '[i]f the enquirers chose to receive and act upon the reply, they cannot disregard the definite terms upon which it was given. They cannot accept a reply given with a stipulation, and then reject the stipulation': Lord Morris. (This case was decided in 1964, prior to the enactment of the Unfair Contract Terms Act 1977, and hence, the disclaimer did not have to satisfy any test of reasonableness.)

The provision of advice on valuation and structural soundness of a house. Two cases may be usefully contrasted on this type of alleged negligent misstatement – the key question being whether a valuer/surveyor can owe a duty of care to a prospective mortgagor–purchaser of a house/flat:

In *Smith v Eric S Bush (a firm); Harris v Wyre Forest DC*,[52] Mrs Smith, C, applied to Abbey Building Socy for a mortgage to help her buy a house. She paid an inspection fee of £38.89. Abbey, as mortgagee, was under a statutory duty to obtain a written valuation on the house, and instructed a firm of surveyors and valuers, Eric S Bush, D, to inspect/value the house. The report contained a disclaimer that neither Abbey nor D warranted that the report and valuation would be accurate, and that it was supplied without any acceptance of responsibility. C received a copy of the report, which valued the house at £16,500, and which stated that no essential repairs were required. Without obtaining an independent survey, C purchased the house for £18,000. In fact, the first-floor chimney breasts had been removed, but D had not checked to see whether the chimneys above were adequately supported, and 18 months later, the chimney collapsed, and the house was much-devalued. **Held:** a duty of care was conceded on appeal (unless the disclaimer protected D from liability). In the other case, Mr and Mrs Harris, C, applied to the council, D1, for a mortgage to help them buy a house. They too paid an inspection fee. D1 instructed Mr Lee, D2, a valuer employed by the council, to carry out an inspection and to report. His report was not shown to C, but they were subsequently offered a mortgage by D1. The report was negligently prepared, failing to flag up possible settlement. The house subsequently needed structural repairs (£12,000) and its value fell considerably. **Held:** a duty of care was owed by D1 and D2 to C.

[52] [1990] 1 AC 831 (HL), with quotes in Table at 850, 865, 857–60, 870.

The factors in play

- *payment:* in both cases, C paid an 'inspection fee', which defrayed the valuers' fee (and which was billed to the mortgagee). Hence, C had some relationship 'akin to contract' with the valuer (Lord Templeman);
- *no independent advice:* valuer, D, was well aware that, if C were to buy a modest house, they would probably rely on D's valuation, without an independent survey. 90% of mortgagors relied on the valuation obtained by their mortgagees without obtaining their own valuation, and hence, the chances of C's obtaining independent advice was very low (and D knew that this was the norm for house purchases in English conveyancing). It was also unrealistic to expect purchasers of modest houses to pay for their own valuation (having already paid a fee to the valuer) (Lord Templeman). It might be different, if the transaction concerned a very large block of flats, industrial property, or a very expensive house, where a purchaser might be expected to obtain his own structural survey to 'guide him in his purchase' (Lord Griffiths);
- *size of the transaction:* although a 'modest house', the purchase was nevertheless a very significant purchase for these purchasers C, so that any loss in value was likely to cause significant hardship to them, and their reliance on D was likely to be all the more acute (Lord Griffiths);
- *an identified C:* in both cases, the valuers, D, knew of the mortgagors' identities, as they had signed the application forms for the valuations;
- *the intended recipient:* in the case of Mrs Smith, D knew that the valuation report would be passed on to her by Abbey (that was not the case for Mr and Mrs Harris, but other factors pointed to a duty owing);
- *availability of insurance to D:* the availability (and cost) of insurance was relevant when considering which of two parties should bear a financial loss, and in this case, the surveyor, D, will be insured against this loss;
- *ineffective disclaimer:* the disclaimers of liability by the valuers, D, did not satisfy the requirement of reasonableness provided by s 11(3) of UCTA 1977, and were ineffective. D was a professional person (whether acting independently as for Mrs Smith, or as an employee of the mortgagee as for Mr and Mrs Harris), and whose services were paid for by the mortgagor;
- *scope of expertise:* valuer, D, is typically a chartered surveyor who, by training and experience, will recognise defects and be able to assess value (Lord Templeman);
- *no floodgates concerns:* to hold that valuer D owed a duty of care to the prospective purchasers whose houses D valued, at the request of the purchaser's mortgagee, would not expose D to indeterminate liability – any repairs related to a modest house only; and duties would only arise where D knew that there was a *high degree of probability* that some other identifiable person, C, would act upon the advice.

However, not every purchaser who received an inaccurate valuation report and completed the purchase of a property in reliance upon it is owed a duty of care in negligent misstatement:

In *Scullion v Bank of Scotland plc (t/as Colleys)*,[53] Mr Scullion, C, decided to use some of his pension to participate in a buy-to-let scheme. Bank of Scotland, BOS, specialised in buy-to-let mortgages, and

---

[53] [2011] EWCA Civ 693, [2011] WLR 3212, with quotes in the Table at: [49], [57].

- *independent advice:* one of the key differences from *Smith v Eric S Bush* was that the purchaser there would probably rely on the valuation without independent advice, whereas for Caparo, a large company, to proceed with a takeover bid without 'independent verification' was unlikely, and put the case at odds with *Smith*;
- *unascertainable class:* if D was to be liable to Caparo, as a shareholder who was interested in launching a take-over bid, then so, too, a company could be vulnerable to such a bid from any investor of the public. D had no way of knowing of C's identity, or the terms of its likely takeover bid or intentions. The class of potential Cs was not only the current shareholders of Fidelity, but also *any other party* who could be interested in investing in Fidelity, on reading D's accounts. The class was too large and indeterminate to justifiy a duty of care;
- *no gap in redress/lacuna in the law:* where an auditor, D, negligently prepares end-of-year accounts, then it is not for individual shareholders, such as Caparo, to sue D. Rather, the company itself will bring a claim against D, and any loss suffered by an individual shareholder could be recouped in this way, rendering C's action unnecessary;
- *no payment:* in *Smith*, Mrs Smith paid a fee to defray the valuer's expenses in preparing the valuation, whereas Caparo, as a shareholder, was entitled to be given company accounts prior to the AGM. Hence, Caparo was a 'free-rider' (although Lord Bridge did not place much, if any, emphasis upon this point, other than to note it).

It is notable, however, that a takeover bidder **can** establish that he was owed a duty of care, by the auditors who prepared the company accounts, where the facts are distinguishable from *Caparo*.

> In *Morgan Crucible Co plc v Hill Samuel Co Ltd*,[57] Morgan Crucible, C, who was not an existing shareholder, made a takeover bid for another company, First Castle Electronics plc, and initially made the bid in reliance on the audited company accounts prepared by Judkins & Co, D, First Castle's auditors. However, in seeking to defeat C's takeover bid, the directors of First Castle, and Judkins, made certain statements in 'defence documents', referring back to those company accounts. Ultimately, C increased its bid for First Castle, and achieved the takeover. C then alleged that both the audited company accounts and the post-bid statements were negligently-prepared, so that First Castle was worth much less than C had paid for its shares. **Held:** the claim could proceed; a duty of care was arguably owed.

The factors in play

- *the purpose test:* although the audited statements in *Caparo* were prepared for a different purpose (the supervisory function in the AGM) from the purpose which C relied upon (to launch a takeover), the facts were distinguishable here. When making their defence statements, both directors and auditors were fully aware that C, in particular, would rely on them for the purpose of deciding whether or not to make an increased takeover bid for First Castle, and in fact, made those statements for the purpose of C relying on them, as they were seeking to defeat C's bid;

---

[57] [1991] Ch 295 (CA).

- *source of the information:* although C had its own independent advisers, much of the information on which the accounts and profit forecast was based was information that only D could have possessed;
- *the intended recipient:* where auditor D approves a statement which confirms the accuracy of its previous audited accounts, or which contains a forecast of future profits, and D has been told that C, a bidder, will rely on the accounts and forecast for the purpose of deciding whether to make an increased bid, then C is an intended recipient.

However, undoubtedly the line between a *Caparo* and a *Morgan Crucible* scenario is not always easy to draw. Subsequently, in *Galoo Ltd v Bright Grahame Murray (a firm)*,[58] Glidewell LJ noted that the distinction 'is inevitably a fine one', while Evans LJ remarked that, while it would be 'tempting' to attribute the difference merely to the fact that Morgan Crucible's identity was known to the auditors as a takeover bidder, whereas Caparo's identity was not known to Touche Ross as a takeover bidder, that is perhaps too simplistic. What of the case of an existing shareholder who is known to auditor D as one who is interested in making a takeover bid – a scenario that falls somewhere between *Caparo* and *Morgan Crucible*? Evans LJ expressed the view, in dicta, that a duty of care would not automatically apply, just because C's identity was known. Rather, it would depend upon other factors too – as it was unlikely that D would have intended C to rely on the audited statements, without any independent enquiry being undertaken. This example demonstrates the nuanced enquiry that a duty of care ultimately requires in this area.

Of course, some cases will be at the other end of the spectrum from *Caparo*, where audited statements were intended for C alone, and where D must have intended for C to rely upon them:

In *Law Society v KPMG Peat Marwick*,[59] KPMG, D, were retained by a firm of solicitors, Durnford Ford, to prepare their annual reports for y/e 31 May 1990, as required by s 34 of the Solicitors Act 1974. DF paid D's auditing fees. Shortly afterwards, the Law Society, C, investigated DF for fraud and embezzlement of client trust funds, and the firm ceased practice. Eventually, £8.5m had to be paid out to about 300 defrauded clients from C's Compensation Fund. The Solicitors Act 1974, s 36, required C to maintain and administer that Fund, so as to make grants to relieve loss or hardship suffered in consequence of dishonesty on the part of a solicitor, in connection with that solicitor's practice. C argued that, when preparing DF's reports, D had missed signs of fraud, and that if D had qualified the reports as it should have done, then C would have exercised its statutory powers of intervention in DF's practice much earlier, and put an end to the activities, thereby reducing the amount which was paid out of the Compensation Fund. **Held:** D owed C a duty of care.

The factors in play

- *no indeterminate liability:* if a duty was found, the size of the class would be limited to DF's clients whose money had been wrongly misappropriated from their accounts; and time was limited too, because C requested a report every year, so any continued damage after C's receipt of an accurate report could not be attributed to D;

[58] [1993] EWCA Civ 3, [1994] 1 WLR 1360, 1382 (Glidewell LJ), 1388 (Evans LJ).
[59] [2000] EWCA Civ 5563, [2000] 1 WLR 1921.

- *the intended recipient:* the primary beneficiary of D's audit was not DF's clients, but the Law Society, C, as trustee of the Compensation Fund, because it was on the Law Society that the burden lay. C's function was to protect both the public and the Fund, and accurate audited reports were necessary for protective steps to be taken. KPMG knew that its report had to be passed to the Law Society, C, under s 34 of the Solicitors Act 1974, and that in some cases where the report was adverse on key points, C was the intended recipient;

- *the purpose test:* D's audited report was required under the Solicitors Act 1974, precisely to protect the Compensation Fund, if financial wrongdoing was detected. Hence, the purpose for which it was prepared, and the purpose for which C relied on it, were entirely coincidental;

- *parliamentary intent:* KPMG argued that, since the Fund was financed by the solicitors' profession (by virtue of premiums), then the policy of Parliament was that losses caused by dishonest members of the profession should be borne by the solicitors' profession as a whole, rather than for one accounting firm, D (or its professional indemnity insurer) to bear that loss. KPMG also argued that the sole purpose of suits such as this was, 'through the medium of expensive and time-consuming litigation, to move losses from the solicitors' profession to the accountants, and then back to the lawyers in costs'. However, that did not preclude a duty. It was for C to decide whether it wanted to take the risks of suing, and if so, then it was not for D to complain about the expense involved;

- *no disclaimers:* it was always open for auditors D to seek to disclaim responsibility for any lack of care in the preparation of the audit, which D had not done (and any disclaimer might have been disputed by C, on the basis of lack of reasonableness, anyway);

- *no payment:* if the fee for KPMG's, D's, report had been paid by the Law Society, C, there would have been a contract between C and D. The fact that the fee was paid by DF did not preclude a duty of care from arising.

This sample of cases gives a detailed indication of the factors which are legally relevant, as to whether or not a duty of care will be owed by D, in the case of negligent misstatement (whether bi-partite or tri-partite in nature). Similar factors may apply in the so-called 'victim' scenario.

The 'victim' scenario

It will be recalled that 'victim' scenarios occur where D provides information or advice to X, and X relies upon that, to C's detriment. These scenarios are characterised by the fact that it is another person, X, *and not* C, who has relied upon the information or advice – but it is C who ends up suffering the economic detriment from D's inaccurate statement.

This category is clearly not a *Hedley Byrne* situation, as the statement is not aimed at C who relied upon it – but it is a viable extension of the *Hedley Byrne* principle, as re-affirmed in *McKie v Swindon College*.[60] Further, D may not have exercised 'skill' in the narrow sense, but rather, applied his 'special knowledge' (i.e., his exclusive knowledge) about C, and to C's detriment – that is hardly the exercise of 'skill', but it does draw upon *Hedley Byrne* nevertheless (per *Paros plc v Worldlink Group plc*[61]). C's reliance on D is certainly indirect, in victim cases, but nevertheless, that can suffice for a duty of care to be owed to C.

---

[60] [2011] EWHC 469 (QB) [44].   [61] [2012] EWHC 394 (Comm) [103].

The same factors pointing in favour of, or against, a duty of care, as itemised in negligent misstatement scenarios above, are equally as relevant to the imposition of a duty of care in the 'victim' scenario. It involves, inevitably, a tri-partite relationship:

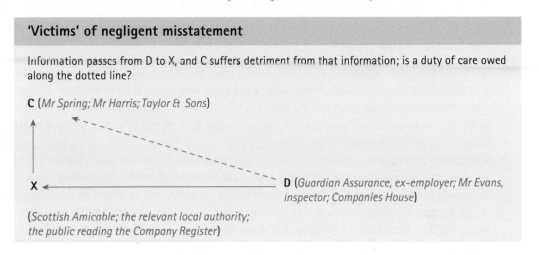

'Victims' of negligent misstatement

Information passes from D to X, and C suffers detriment from that information; is a duty of care owed along the dotted line?

C (*Mr Spring; Mr Harris; Taylor & Sons*)

X ← D (*Guardian Assurance, ex-employer; Mr Evans, inspector; Companies House*)

(*Scottish Amicable; the relevant local authority; the public reading the Company Register*)

Dealing with the leading cases in this area:

The provision of references. Given that references are supplied to X, and are written about C, they are the paradigm 'victim-of-misstatement' scenario.

> In *Spring v Guardian Assurance plc*,[62] Mr Spring, C, was employed by Corinium, estate agents and sellers of insurance policies issued by Guardian Assurance, D, as sales director. Then, the major shareholder in Corinium sold the company to D, and C was dismissed by D without explanation. C sought a job selling insurance policies with Scottish Amicable Life Assurance Society. A positive reference was required, under the regulatory rules governing insurance selling. The reference provided by D was quite negative, including that C 'consistently kept the best leads for himself with little regard for the sales team that he supposedly was to manage', that 'we have found a serious case of mis-selling where the concept of "best advice" was ignored and the policies sold yielded the highest commissions', and that 'there have been other cases where there has been bad advice, but there is no current evidence to indicate whether it was deliberate or through ignorance'. Consequently, Scottish Amicable did not appoint C, nor did other prospective employers. C then sued D for a number of actions (e.g., malicious falsehood, breach of contract and negligence). **Held:** D owed C a duty of care in preparing the reference.

In *Customs and Excise*,[63] Lord Rodger noted that, in the circumstances of *Spring*, it was unrealistic to consider that D *assumed responsibility to* C for the preparation of the reference: the case 'does not readily yield to analysis in terms of a voluntary assumption of responsibility ... I see no reason to treat these cases as exceptions to some over-arching rule that there must be a voluntary assumption of responsibility before the law recognises a duty of care. Such a rule would inevitably lead to the concept of voluntary assumption of responsibility being stretched beyond its natural limits – which would, in the long run, undermine the very real value of the concept as a criterion of liability in the many cases where it is an appropriate guide'. Again, a

---

[62] [1994] UKHL 7, [1995] 2 AC 296 (Lords Lowry, Goff, Slynn and Woolf; Lord Keith dissenting).
[63] [2006] UKHL 28, [2007] 1 AC 181, [52].

descent into the particular factors that arose on the facts of *Spring*, rather than the application of mere labels, was necessary – and, in the House of Lords' view, a duty of care was owed for the following reasons:

The factors in play

- *source of the information:* the relationship between a former employer, D, and an ex-employee, C, was founded on a contractual relationship, and hence, very close. The ex-employer is in the best, and sometimes the only, position to write about C. Given their former relationship, D is possessed of 'special knowledge', uniquely derived from his experience of the employee's character, skill and diligence in the performance of his duties;

- *analogous to a request:* although it is the prospective employer, and not ex-employee C, who actually requests the reference, the position is analogous to *Hedley Byrne*, in that a reference is provided for the conjoint assistance of C, given how necessary references are to obtaining fresh employment in the modern employment market. It may even be C, rather than a prospective future employer, who asks D to provide the reference; and even where the approach comes from the prospective future employer, it will be made with either C's express or tacit authority;

- *no conflict of duties:* it did not necessarily follow that, because D owed a duty of care to his employee, C, in writing a careful reference, that there was any conflict in any duty of care owed to the recipient of the reference (and whether D owed a duty to the recipient of the reference was not necessary to decide here);

- *scope of expertise:* the skill of preparing a reference for an employee fell as much within the expertise of an employer as the skill of preparing a bank reference was within the expertise of Easipower's bank in *Hedley Byrne*;

- *no defensive practices likely:* just because a duty of care was owed, re the writing of references, did not mean that those asked to give them should be inhibited from speaking frankly or from writing what they thought, or writing one at all, lest they were liable in damages through not taking sufficient care in its preparation. It did not follow that bland and meaningless reference-writing would follow from this case;

- *parliamentary intent:* there were regulatory requirements to protect the public from exposure to the activities of company representatives selling insurance policies and who may be dishonest or incompetent, given many examples of mis-selling. Public interest required that suspicions be communicated.

The principle in *Spring v Guardian Assurance* has since been extended, where a bank provides a negative credit reference about a bank client, which damages the spouse of that client who was both a joint holder of the same account with her husband, and a co-director of the family business which largely depended on her husband's credit-rating (per *Gatt v Barclays Bank plc*[64]). That was considered to be an incremental development of the principle in *Spring* – albeit that no breach on the part of the bank was proven there.

Spring does not, however, impose a universally-applicable duty on D for all forms of reference of whatever kind, where public policy reasons dictated against any such duty arising, as

---

[64] [2013] EWHC 2 (QB).

in, e.g., the supply by the police of a clear criminal record certificate in *Desmond v Nottinghamshire Police*,[65] or in the supply of a reference for a teacher in *Camurat v Thurrock BC*.[66] In both cases, alternative remedies for the victim C were available, and the statutory frameworks under which the references were supplied also disinclined any duty of care from arising.

Certification or status of C's business. A business operator, C, may be a victim of a negligent misstatement, if inaccurate statements are made about that business upon which others rely.

> In *Harris v Evans*,[67] Mr Harris, C, started a bungee jumping business, using a mobile telescopic crane, for public use, at various sites around south-west England, including Devon. C contacted the Health and Safety Executive (HSE) to obtain and comply with the safety requirements for using cranes that way. After the business started, Mr Evans, D, a HSE inspector, inspected C's business, and wrongly concluded that C's equipment required adjustment. C was told that he needed further certification before the cranes could be used for this business. Consequently, C's business was shut down by the relevant local authority, relying on that advice. This led to financial losses for C. Later, the Dept of the Environment concluded that D's advice was erroneous and was not in line with HSE policy. C claimed damages for his economic loss, flowing from the local authority's reliance on the inspector's, D's, negligent advice. **Held:** no duty of care was owed by D to C. In *Sebry v Companies House*, a winding-up order was made against the company, Taylor & Son Ltd, in Jan 2009. A copy of that order was received by the Companies House, D, where an employee accidentally noted the winding-up order against the wrong company, Taylor & Sons Ltd, C. As a result, C was described as a company being in liquidation, when it was not, and several suppliers and creditors found out the information by word-of-mouth. **Held:** a duty of care was owed by D to C.

The factors in play

- *defensive practices:* in *Harris*, any duty imposed on inspectors such as D, which rendered them liable for economic damage to the business enterprise they were inspecting, would be likely to cause utmost cautiousness and a desire to postpone making a decision until more concrete facts were found, which could place public safety at risk. However, in *Sebry*, this was a very unusual error, and would not create any undue defensive practices other than to cast a duty on D and its employees to exercise reasonable care to ensure that the information was accurately recorded on the Company Register; it was not the type of case where society should expect D to exercise a judgment without fear of litigation;

- *parliamentary intent:* in *Harris*, the statutory duties of an inspector under the Health and Safety at Work Act 1974 were designed to protect public safety, that was D's paramount consideration – so the freedom to act as D saw fit must prevail over C's individual economic losses. Hence, 'if steps which they think should be taken to improve safety would have an adverse economic effect on the business enterprise in question, so be it ... It would ... be seriously detrimental to the proper discharge by enforcing authorities of their responsibilities in respect of public health and safety if they were to be exposed to potential liability in negligence, at the suit of the owners of the businesses adversely affected by their decisions'. However, in *Sebry*, imposing a duty on Companies House, D, would only require D to do exactly what was required by the Companies Act 2006, i.e., that information about a company such as C was complete, accurate and easily retrievable;

[65] [2011] EWCA Civ 3, [2011] 1 FLR 1361.   [66] [2014] EWHC 2482 (QB).
[67] [1998] EWCA Civ 709, [1998] 1 WLR 1285, with quotes in Table at 1298, 1301–2.

- *other avenues of redress:* the 1974 Act itself contemplated that economic losses could result to business proprietors, as a result of erroneous inspections, and provided remedies for such errors. 'It is implicit in the 1974 Act that Improvement Notices and Prohibition Notices may cause economic loss or damage to the business enterprise in question. [It] provides remedies against errors or excesses on the part of inspectors and enforcing authorities. I would decline to add the possibility of an action in negligence to the statutory remedies' (per Sir Richard Scott V-C). There was no lacuna in the law, given the remedies in the Act (*Harris*). However, in *Sebry*, C, a company damaged in that way, had no other remedy, unless it was provided by the tort of negligence;

- *the incremental test:* in *Sharp v Ministry of Housing and Local Govt,*[a] a clerk at the Land Registry produced a land certificate that omitted to mention a claim which the Ministry had against the vendor, and this mistake extinguished the right of the Ministry to pursue its claim against the purchaser. The clerk was liable to the Ministry for that error. Hence, there was a close analogy, whereby false information on an official register could give rise to a duty of care in favour of one who relied on the accuracy of that information;

- *distributive justice:* in *Sebry*, the effect of finding D liable was that the loss would be ultimately borne by either the business community (limited companies and users of the Register who paid fees) or by the public at large (via an increase in budgetary allocation to that government entity to cover the loss or via insurance). That result was fair and just, given that the compulsory registration system was designed to benefit the business community and the public.

[a] [1970] 2 QB 223 (CA).

Summary of salient factors

Having regard to the exhortations by the appellate courts in this area to avoid the use of labels and to descend to the particular facts and circumstances, the following list, together with supporting authorities derived from the aforementioned discussion, summarises those which the leading cases have demonstrated to be important, when upholding a duty of care:

	A duty of care is more likely (although not necessarily mandated) if …	Relevant case, e.g. …
1	the statement prepared by statement-maker D was in response to a **request for information or advice** from C who suffered the loss, rather than given voluntarily	*Chaudhry v Prabhaker*
2	the **purpose for which the statement was prepared** by statement-maker D, **and** the purpose for which C who suffered the loss relied on that statement, were the same, or very similar, rather than entirely mismatched	*Caparo Industries v Dickman*
3	the statement was passed on by X (the initial recipient of the information) to C who suffered the loss (the ultimate recipient), and D **knew that the information would be passed on** to that ultimate intended recipient	*Hedley Byrne v Heller*

	A duty of care is more likely (although not necessarily mandated) if …	Relevant case, e.g. …
4	C, who suffered the loss, was specifically known to statement-maker D, or was one of **a small or ascertainable class of persons** known to D, rather than one of a large and unascertainable class of persons who might rely on D's statement	*Caparo Industries v Dickman*
5	statement-maker D knew, or should have known, that the information prepared by him would be relied upon by C who suffered the loss, without any **independent enquiry** being made by C – and it was reasonable, in all the circumstances, that C would rely upon D's statement without independent enquiry being made by C (having regard to the type of transaction, and the type of C, etc)	*Smith v Eric S Bush*
6	statement-maker D was **likely to be insured** or **ought to have been insured** against the loss (as opposed to where C ought to have insured himself against the risk of economic loss), a relevant factor as to where, as between C and D, the loss should fall	*Smith v Eric S Bush*
7	the **transaction was a large and significant one**, where inaccurate information would have costly ramifications for C, and for which the law of tort might provide some protection (it was not a 'run of the mill' transaction, where C's reliance on the statement would not be quite as crucial or even likely)	*Smith v Eric S Bush; Caparo Industries v Dickman*
8	the **information was within the scope of D's skill and expertise** to give	*MLC v Evatt*
9	statement-maker D was the sole, or one of **the primary sources, of the information,** which increased C's reliance on the need for accuracy in the statement given by D	*Spring v Guardian Assurance*
10	C, who suffered the loss, **paid D for the statement**, or D had some other financial interest in C's acting on the statement	*Smith v Eric S Bush*
11	statement-maker D did not (or could not) effectively **disclaim any responsibility** for the accuracy of the statement (or service)	*Hedley Byrne v Heller*
12	the statement was provided by D in a **commercial or professional setting,** rather than in a social setting	*Chaudhry v Prabhaker*
13	C, who suffered the loss, had **no other avenue of redress** (by virtue of statute, self-help, common law rights, or otherwise), thus emphasising the need for a duty of care to be upheld in negligence, so as to preclude a **lacuna in the law**	*Harris v Evans; Caparo v Dickman*
14	statement-maker D had **a protective function re the public safety** which would conflict with any duty of care owed to C as an individual	*Harris v Evans*
15	the **parliamentary intent** was that a duty of care was not precluded by the statutory obligations cast on statement-maker D	*Caparo Industries v Dickman*

	A duty of care is more likely (although not necessarily mandated) if …	Relevant case, e.g. …
16	no **conflict of interest** between a duty to C and a duty to another (e.g., the public interest, or another party) would occur, if a duty of care was upheld	*An Informer v Chief Constable*
17	no **prospect of indeterminate liability** was likely to result from the imposition of a duty of care on statement-maker D (i.e., where D's exposure to liability, arising from that one statement, was limited)	*Law Society v KPMG*
18	no **prospect of floodgates** was likely to result from the imposition of a duty of care on statement-maker D (i.e., where the case could set a precedential effect for later Cs who were similarly-situated)	*Smith v Eric S Bush*
19	as a **matter of fairness**, a duty of care should be imposed on statement-maker D	*Scullion v Bank of Scotland*
20	**defensive practices** across an industry were not likely to flow from upholding a duty of care against statement-maker D	*Spring v Guardian Assurance*
21	according to **distributive justice**, liability should be imposed on D, rather than requiring an uncompensated C to bear the loss himself	*Sebry v Companies House*
22	there was a **close temporal proximity** (or, at least, not a long gap) between the making of D's statement and the damage suffered by C	*Goodwill v BPAS (discussed below)*

Matters which do *not* preclude a duty of care from arising

§4.7   The following matters do not preclude a duty of care from arising on D's part, in respect of pure economic loss suffered by C: the lack of detrimental reliance by C; either the presence, or absence, of a contractual relationship between C and D; and where information or advice is given by a managing director, shareholder or representative of a company, D (provided that D may only be liable where he assumed personal liability to C and where there was the requisite reliance by C on D *personally*).

Certain issues are worth stating, as they have tended to provoke much judicial discussion:

No detrimental reliance. In *Caparo*,[68] Lord Oliver, when describing the circumstances giving rise to the necessary relationship of proximity between C and D, noted that the information should have been 'acted upon by the advisee to his detriment'. However, in some cases in which a duty of care has been imposed on D, who has provided negligent information, advice or services, detrimental reliance on C's part has **not** been necessary to prove, i.e., C has not changed his position at all, in reliance on D's acting with reasonable care and skill, and yet, a duty has been upheld.

This feature is particularly apparent where, although D may have known that C's economic well-being depended upon his acting with careful skill and expertise, and D may have assumed a responsibility to act in C's best economic interests, C had no choice to place his affairs with

---

[68] [1990] 2 AC 605 (HL) 638, and cited, e.g., in *Law Society v KPMG* [2000] EWCA Civ 5563, [2000] WLR 1921, [13].

anyone else (*White v Jones*[69]). Consequently, C did nothing different in reliance on D's professional services being administered reasonably – there has been no change of position. Yet, a duty in C's favour has been found. This lack of detrimental reliance is one reason as to why the whole area is far from straightforward.

Similarly, whilst reliance may be possible where C and D had direct dealings with each other (where there was 'mutuality of dealing', as Lord Browne-Wilkinson described it in *White v Jones*[70]), tri-partite relationships are different. C and D may **never** have had any direct dealings at all, so that no express reliance by C can be proven. Yet that is not fatal to a duty to avoid pure economic loss either (as *Hedley Byrne* itself showed). Plainly, D can be liable to C for negligent misstatement under the *Caparo* test, where proximity of relationship, rather than reliance *per se*, characterised their relationship.

The presence, or absence, of a contractual relationship. As discussed in Chapter 1, concurrent duties in Contract and in Tort are permissible at law. In *Henderson v Merrett Syndicates Ltd*,[71] Lord Goff said that 'an assumption of responsibility [by D], coupled with the concomitant reliance [by C], may give rise to a tortious duty of care, irrespective of whether there is a contractual relationship between the parties'. A contractual duty of care between C and D does not preclude a concurrent tortious duty of care. Further, the fact that D owes a contractual duty to X, and a tortious duty of care to C, is perfectly permissible at law – the first duty is defined by the terms of the contract, and the second duty by the general law (as Lord Nolan noted in *White v Jones*[72]).

However, merely because C and D are in a contractual relationship does not **automatically** mean that there is an assumption of responsibility by D, and reliance on C's part, necessary to give rise to a duty of care on D's part to avoid C's financial losses. The court must ask what, precisely, D has contracted to do. According to Lord Goff in *Henderson*,[73] that is a two-stage process: (1) has D undertaken to provide relevant advice, information or services, and if so, did the contract expressly or impliedly provide that D was to exercise reasonable skill and care in so doing? If so, then a duty of care in tort is potentially owed; (2) do the terms of the contract exclude or limit D's liability for failure to perform such obligations, either carefully or at all?

Obversely, the fact that, as between C and D, there is no direct contract, does not necessarily preclude a duty of care from being imposed on D. That argument was raised, and rebutted, in *Henderson*, where D (the managing agents) sought to deny any duty of care in tort to C (the indirect Names in an insurance syndicate), by arguing that they had direct contracts with some Names, but not with the indirect Names, depending upon which contractual chain governed the relationship. Hence, D argued that, by structuring their contractual relationship in that way, C and D had deliberately excluded any assumption of responsibility arising towards the indirect Names. However, a duty of care was nevertheless upheld.

The appropriate D. This issue will become particularly important, if a company has been wound up, and the director, shareholder or employee, D, carried professional indemnity insurance. It must be D who assumed responsibility in law, for the task at hand. Otherwise, the undertaking of responsibility may be attributed to the corporate entity – or to no party at all. In *Williams v Natural Life Health Foods Ltd*,[74] where that precise scenario occurred, Lord Steyn

---

[69] [1995] 2 AC 207 (HL).   [70] *ibid*, 272.   [71] [1995] 2 AC 145 (HL) 194.   [72] [1995] 2 AC 207 (HL) 293.
[73] [1995] 2 AC 145 (HL) 197, and also 206 (Lord Browne-Wilkinson).   [74] [1998] 1 WLR 830 (HL) 837.

noted that the relevant test is whether C, 'could reasonably rely on an assumption of personal responsibility by the individual who performed the services on behalf of the company' (and, in that case, C could not). His Lordship also approved of the reasoning of the Supreme Court of Canada, in *Edgeworth Construction Ltd v MD Lea & Ass Ltd*,[75] that to successfully sue an employee, D, C 'would have to show that it was relying on the particular expertise of an individual engineer, without regard to the corporate character of the engineering firm'.

> In *Williams v Natural Life Health Foods Ltd*,[76] Mr Mistlin, D1, was managing director and controlling shareholder of Natural Life Health Foods, D2. Mr Williams and Mrs Reid, C, entered into a franchise contract with D2 to open a health food shop in Rugby, relying on D1's financial projections for the health food business. The turnover from C's shop was substantially less than predicted, and after 18 months, it ceased trading. D1 had no direct dealings with C, but he played a prominent role in preparing the financial projections, and D2's brochure advertised D1's experience in the health food trade. The franchisor company D2 was wound up, and as a result, C's action proceeded against D1 alone, alleging that C had been given negligent advice. **Held:** D1 did not owe a duty of care to C. D1 did not objectively assume personal responsibility for the accuracy of the statements in the brochure, nor had C relied upon D1 so as to create a special relationship between D1 and C: (1) while the brochure claimed that D1 had expertise in the retail health foods industry (via personal experience in operating a shop at Salisbury), his earlier experience fell a long way short of amounting to an assumption of responsibility to franchisees as to the accuracy of the projections contained in the brochure; (2) a managing director cannot be personally liable to the franchisees, simply because, in a small one-man company, he is the one who will possess the qualities essential to the running of the business; (3) there were no personal dealings between D1 and C – no exchanges, personal dealings, requests for information, conversations, oral assurances, etc – which could have conveyed to C that D1 assumed personal responsibility to them. In *Riyad Bank v Ahli United Bank (UK) plc*,[77] the Fund, C, had a contract with an investment bank, and claimed that it sought technical advice as to its investments from an adviser, D, who was a subcontracted technical adviser to the bank. C suffered loss when those investments failed. There was no direct contractual relationship between C and D, C's contract was with the investment bank. **Held:** D owed a duty of care to the Fund, C: (1) there were close dealings, in that, to provide specialist advice, D regularly attended board meetings of the Fund; and (2) the technical advice was given directly to the Fund by D, and was intended to be relied and acted upon by C, all parties had that expectation.

NEGLIGENT PROVISION OF SERVICES

Introduction

§4.8 According to the 'extended *Hedley Byrne* principle', D who provides professional services within the scope of his skill and expertise, and who causes economic loss to C who relied on the reasonably careful performance of those services, owes a duty of care to C to avoid that economic loss.

The very reason that it is called the 'extended *Hedley Byrne* principle' is because the assumption of responsibility principle has been extended to the provision of professional services, and is

---

[75] [1993] 3 SCR 206 (SCC) 212 (La Forest J).   [76] [1998] 1 WLR 830 (HL) 830.
[77] [2006] EWCA Civ 780, [2006] 2 Lloyd's Rep 292.

no longer confined to information or advice (per Lord Goff in *Henderson v Merrett Syndicates Ltd*[78]). *Hedley Byrne* concerned advice about creditworthiness – and anything which sought to extend it wider than that (as Lord Devlin foreshadowed in *Hedley Byrne* itself, referring to so-licitors' professional services[79]) was dicta only. However, the extended *Hedley Byrne* principle was 'the rationalisation, or technique, adopted by English law, to provide a remedy for the re-covery of damages in respect of economic loss caused by the negligent performance *of services*' (per Lord Steyn in *Williams v Natural Life Health Foods*[80]).

Of course, many scenarios involve D's providing **both** statements and services, within the one transaction. Not a great deal turns on that, as the extended *Hedley Byrne* principle enables li-ability to be imposed in respect of any negligence which can be proven in respect of the service too. The categorisation of economic loss claims is much more difficult, however, in cases such as *Smith v Eric S Bush*, where C ended up with a defective structure, but was able to bring the claim in negligent misstatement (with all the assistance which the *Hedley Byrne/Caparo* tests provided). C would not have been nearly so fortunate, had that case been considered as a defec-tive structure, against which English law has rather turned its face (as discussed in 'Defective buildings', online).

The two cases commonly attributed with the development of this area are *Henderson v Mer-rett Syndicates Ltd*[81] and *White v Jones*.[82] By coincidence, both were heard by an identically-constituted House of Lords. Although *Henderson* was heard subsequent to the case of *White v Jones*, the latter was delayed some six months after *Henderson* was handed down. As Lord Goff admitted in *White v Jones*, a **strict** application of *Hedley Bryne* could **not** give rise to any li-ability for pure economic loss in that case. Of course, at a very elementary level, *Hedley Byrne* concerned statements, whereas *White v Jones* concerned a solicitor's professional services. However, and significantly, there was detrimental reliance on D's part in *Hedley Byrne* (i.e., the advertising agency could have withheld placing the advertisements on Easipower's part), whereas there was no detrimental reliance in *White v Jones* (as noted above, C had no choice but to rely on D's professional services) and yet, a duty of care was upheld in *White*, because the court was prepared to 'fashion a remedy to fill a lacuna in the law' (per Lord Goff[83]), and because 'the law in this area has not ossified' (as Lord Browne-Wilkinson put it[84]).

Hence, the goal-posts moved considerably, in light of both decisions. That has subsequently been judicially admitted – e.g., in *BP plc v AON Ltd*,[85] Colman J remarked that it was clear from *White v Jones* that the majority, 'appreciated that they were recognising a **new** set of circum-stances in which there could be an undertaking of responsibility which gave rise to liability for pure economic loss'.

Any duty of care requires that C and D be in a 'special relationship', according to Lord Browne-Wilkinson in *White v Jones*[86] – a label that, with respect, means very little, without descending into a close analysis of the facts and circumstances (a point emphasised by Lord Hoffmann in *Customs and Excise*, a case regarding the negligent provision of banking services). Notably, that 'special relationship' can exist, even where D assumes responsibility for C's affairs **but** where there was no contractual relationship between C and D at all (i.e., where D was acting pursuant to a contract with another party, X).

---

[78] [1995] 2 AC 145 (HL) 180 (Lord Goff).   [79] [1964] AC 465 (HL) 530–32, cited *ibid*.
[80] [1998] 1 WLR 830 (HL) 834 (emphasis added).   [81] [1995] 2 AC 145 (HL).   [82] [1995] 2 AC 207 (HL).
[83] *ibid*, 268, and 275 (Lord Browne-Wilkinson).   [84] *ibid*, 276.
[85] [2006] EWHC 424 (Comm) [75] (emphasis added).   [86] [1995] 2 AC 207 (HL) 275–76.

Relevant scenarios and legal reasoning

§4.9 Under the extended *Hedley Byrne* principle, the same tests apply to negligent provision of services as applied to negligent misstatement – the *Hedley Byrne* voluntary assumption/reliance test; the *Caparo* test; and the incremental test. The extended *Hedley Byrne* principle has been applied to the provision of services relating to, e.g.: insurance underwriting; legal; building security; banking; and medical.

The same tests as applied in the case of the narrow *Hedley Byrne* negligent misstatement principle, and all of the salient factors outlined above, apply to the establishment of a duty of care under the extended *Hedley Byrne* principle too. Just as with the narrow *Hedley Byrne* principle, in very few cases will the factors all point unambiguously in one direction (and dissenting judgments are fairly frequent too!).

The tri-partite relationship in negligent provision of services

Is a duty of care owed along the dotted line?

C (*two daughters; Commr of Customs and Excise; the indirect Names; the franchisee; Islington LBC; West Bromwich Albion Football Club*)

X

D (*solicitor Mr Jones; Barclays Bank; the managing agents; Mr Mistlin, director; UCL NHS Trust; surgeon Dr El-Safty*)

(*testator, Mr Barrett;
the two companies, Brightstar and Doveblue;
the intermediary agent; the company, Natural Health Foods;
Mrs J; Michael Appleton*)

Leading cases

- Insurance underwriting services:

  In *Henderson v Merrett Syndicates Ltd*,[87] D was a managing agent at Lloyd's Insurance, and offered underwriting services to a syndicate of, first, direct names (i.e., those who entered into an underwriting agency agreement with the managing agent), and secondly, indirect names (i.e., those who entered into an underwriting agency agreement with a 'names agent', who had, in turn, entered into a managing agency agreement on behalf of those names with the managing agent, D). Hence, there was no privity of contract between the indirect names and D, and the underwriting services were delegated by the indirect names, via their names agent, to D. Both direct names and indirect names, C, suffered financial losses, when unprecedented claims were made on Lloyd's underwriters because of expensive natural disasters, especially in the US. The forms of agreement used by C and D were pro forma standard agreements which could not be negotiated. **Held:** a duty of care was owed by D to both sets of names, direct and indirect. D assumed a responsibility to take reasonable care of their choice of insurance risk, and their reliance was an 'inseparable facet' of their relationship with D, as they entrusted D with the conduct of their underwriting business.

[87] [1995] 2 AC 145 (HL).

The factors in play

- *the incremental test:* in *Punjab National Bank v de Boinville*,[a] a duty of care was owed by an insurance broker, D, not only to his client, but also to a specific person whom he knew was to become an assignee of the insurance policy. By analogy, a duty of care could likewise be owed by managing agents at Lloyd's to a name who was a member of a syndicate under the management of agents;
- *scope of expertise:* managing agents, D, held themselves out as possessing a special expertise to advise C on the suitability of risks to be underwritten;
- *significance of the transaction:* C was giving authority to D to bind them to sometimes large contracts of insurance and reinsurance, and to the settlement of claims.

[a] [1992] 1 Lloyd's Rep 7 (CA).

- Legal services:

    In *White v Jones*,[88] Mr Barrett, 78, quarrelled with his two daughters, C, and he executed a new will, cutting them out of his estate. In June, they made up, so Mr Barrett instructed his solicitor, Mr Jones, D, to draft a new will, giving each daughter a legacy of £9,000. Those instructions were received by D in July, but due to holidays, workload, etc, the next available appointment to meet with Mr Barrett was for 17 September. Mr Barrett went on holiday in the meantime, and he fell and hit his head, from which he died on 14 September, before the new will was executed. C were 'disappointed beneficiaries', and sued D for negligence. **Held (3:2):** a duty of care was owed by D to C, to act with expedition and care in relation to drawing up the new will and having it executed. In *Carr-Glynn v Frearsons (a firm)*,[89] another disappointed beneficiary case, Mrs Larder, the testator, was joint tenant with her brother, in the property, 'Homelands'. That joint tenancy was not effectively severed by the solicitor acting for the testator, D, and converted to a tenancy in common. Hence, the testator's share in the property passed to her joint tenant on her death, and not to her financially hard-up niece, Helen, C, via her will, for whom the testator wanted to make specific provision. **Held:** a duty of care was owed by D to C, and C recovered the loss.

The factors in play

- *a lacuna in the law:* there was a gap (of 'cardinal importance', per Lord Goff), because if D was negligent in carrying out the instructions, and that did not come to light until after the testator's death, then the disappointed beneficiaries, C, would have no remedy for obtaining their legacies, unless D owed them a duty of care. Once the testator had died, any alleged negligence could not be fixed for C's benefit – whereas if the mistake was evident before the testator died, then he could insist to D that his instructions were carried out or sue if he did not. Also, the Contracts (Rights of Third Parties) Act 1999 did not apply here, so C could not take advantage of its provisions either. The testator's estate could sue D for failing to carry out his instructions in a timely manner – but

---

[88] [1995] 2 AC 207 (HL) (Lords Goff, Browne-Wilkinson and Nolan; with Lords Keith and Mustill dissenting), and with quotes in the Table at: 254, 275–76.

[89] [1998] EWCA Civ 1325.

the testator did not suffer any loss from D's failing to put his instructions into effect. Hence, the persons who suffered the loss (the daughters, C) had no claim, and the person who had the claim (the testator) suffered no loss;

- *no conflict of duties:* D owed a duty to the testator, when asked by him to draft the will, and D also owed a simultaneous duty to the intended beneficiaries, C. That co-existence of duties was recognised in New Zealand for 15 years in *Ross v Caunters*,[a] and 'we can say, with some confidence, that a direct remedy by the intended beneficiary against the solicitor appears to create no problems in practice'. Besides, where the testator gave D instructions to convey legacies to C, then there could be no realistic conflict of interest between the testator and C: 'the duties owed by the solicitors to the testator and to the specific legatee are not inconsistent. They are complementary' (per Chadwick LJ in *Carr-Glynn*);

- *the intended recipient:* D's assumption of responsibility to the testator was to be treated, legally, as if it were an assumption of responsibility to C – '[i]t is not to the point that the solicitor only entered on the task pursuant to a contract with the third party (i.e. the testator)';

- *sole repository:* where the testator gave instructions to D about changing his will, D knew that Cs' economic well-being was wholly dependent upon his carefully carrying out his function. No-one else could do that: D was the sole repository of the responsibility for performing the professional services for the testator;

- *scope of expertise:* D had the skill and expertise to carry out the testator's task of drafting the will;

- *the incremental test:* in cases in which *a fiduciary*, D, is liable to a beneficiary, C, any liability arising from that relationship is not dependent upon actual reliance by C on D's actions, but rather, on the fact that the fiduciary, D, 'is well aware [that C's] economic well-being is dependent upon the proper discharge by the fiduciary of his duty'. Incrementally, then, D could be liable to the disappointed beneficiaries here;

- *no indeterminate liability:* given the limited number of designated beneficiaries in the will (i.e., two here), there could be no prospect of any duty of care being owed to the whole world. Plus the principle would be applied very narrowly – there would be very few cases where a testator died prior to his instructions being given effect to, meaning that the mistake could not be rectified, and thus requiring a duty of care to be imposed on D.

[a] [1980] Ch 297.

In *Vinton v Fladgate Fielders (a firm)*,[90] the court acknowledged that *Carr-Glynn* was an extension of the principle in *White v Jones*, because it did not concern 'pure will-making', but extended to the solicitor D's failure to advise the testator of the need to serve a notice of severance to her joint tenant, to ensure that her share actually could be passed on by her will. It concerned legal services, in a wider context than in *White v Jones*, but in a similar scenario where D's error could not be fixed.

- Building security systems (e.g., fire alarm):

   In *Hines v King Sturge LLP*,[91] Vancouver Muffin Co, C, a tenant, sued King Sturge, D, a commercial property management company, for a fire at a Glasgow property where D was property manager. By

[90] [2010] EWHC 904 (Ch) [24].
[91] [2010] CSIH 86, 2011 SLT 2 (Lords Osborne and Emslie; Lord Carloway dissenting).

the time that the fire was brought under control, much of the building had been destroyed. It had a fire alarm system fitted, which relied upon an alarm signal being transmitted, by way of a dedicated telephone line, to the Strathclyde Fire & Rescue Service; but the telephone line linking the alarm system to the monitoring control room had been disconnected. D was aware that this was because the building owners had not paid their British Telecom accounts. D (although not responsible for that non-payment) knew of that position, and suggested to the fire authorities that they (D) would attend to the reconnection of the telephone line. That never happened, and at the time of the fire, the monitoring element of the system was not operational. C alleged that D, as managing agents, owed a duty of care to all tenants of the building to exercise reasonable care in the maintenance of the fire alarm system (although C's losses were not specified, the case proceeded on the basis that they were 'financial losses'). **Held (2:1):** a duty of care by D to C was arguable, and the claim could not be struck out.

The factors in play

- *sole repository:* the building's tenants, including C, had no way of knowing that the dedicated telephone line had been disconnected on account of unpaid British Telecom accounts. They assumed that they were paying a service charge which met the costs of the fire alarm system. They could not know of the disconnection via any source other than D, which helped to prove a degree of reliance by C upon D to perform their duties with reasonable care;
- *incremental test:* the Occupiers Liability (Scotland) Act 1960 recognised the potential for landlords to owe tortious duties of care to tenants – and a landlord's agent could owe duties of care to those tenants by analogy;
- *identified C:* C was one of a finite class of tenants of that building, whose properties and businesses were at risk if the alarm monitoring device was not working properly.

- Banking services:

  In *Customs and Excise Commr v Barclays Bank plc*,[92] two companies, Brightstar Systems Ltd and Doveblue Ltd, held accounts with Barclays Bank, D. Both owed the Commr, C, large sums of unpaid VAT. The Commr obtained freezing (Mareva) injunctions[93] against each company, to stop them transferring £1.8m for Brightstar, and almost £4m for Doveblue, from specified accounts out of the jurisdiction, to defeat any judgments that the Commr might obtain against them. The injunctions were served on D by fax, but two to three hours later, D authorised payments out of these accounts at the companies' requests. There was no prospect of the VAT sums ever being recovered by C. It was assumed that D negligently permitted the payments. **Held:** D did not owe C a duty of care. The *Hedley Byrne* test could not be met – and neither could the *Caparo* test (foreseeability and proximity were met, but the third limb, *viz* policy, was not).

---

[92] [2006] UKHL 28, [2007] 1 AC 181, with quotes in the Table at: [17]–[18], [21], [23], [39], [61], [74], [102].
[93] Per CPR 25.1(f).

The factors in play

- *no assumption of responsibility by D:* when this Mareva injunction was granted, Barclays Bank, D, was restrained from disposing of, or dealing with, the bank accounts. However, this did not equate to D's assuming any responsibility towards C. D was legally obliged to comply with the injunction, it had no choice about the matter, and if it did not, it was exposed to a contempt of court order (the bank 'has not, in any meaningful sense, made a voluntary assumption of responsibility. It has, by the freezing order, had responsibility thrust upon it': per Lord Walker). D did not assume responsibility, as the Bank assumed responsibility to the advertising agency in *Hedley Byrne*, or the reference-writer assumed responsibility to Mr Spring in *Spring v Guardian Assurance*, or the valuers assumed responsibility towards the mortgagor–prospective purchaser in *Smith/Harris* (Lord Bingham CJ);
- *no reliance:* there was no detrimental reliance either. Reliance at law usually meant that, if A had not relied on B, he would have acted differently. However, C could not have acted any differently, since it had sought a Mareva injunction and availed itself of the only remedy which the law provided;
- *lack of fairness:* Mareva injunctions were relatively common – and although banks were the usual recipients of the orders, sometimes a garage which is looking after X's car might be 'startled to receive notification of a freezing order. This puts him in essentially the same position as a bank which is notified of an order. Usually, he will do his best to respect the order and to hold on to the car. Should the law add to his burdens, however, by exposing him to an uninsured liability in damages, if he fails to take the care which is ultimately considered to be reasonable and the addressee makes off with the car?' (Lord Rodger);
- *the intended recipient:* once ordered, the intended recipient of D's compliance with a Mareva injunction could only be the court, not C. The Mareva jurisdiction was judicially developed in the 1970s, enforceable only by the court's power to punish those who broke the injunction via contempt of court. There had never been any suggestion of another remedy being available to C, for whose benefit the injunction was granted: '[t]his regime makes perfect sense on the assumption that the only duty owed by a notified party [D] is to the court' (Lord Bingham CJ);
- *an omission:* this failure to comply with a court order is analogous to a failure to comply with a statutory duty imposed upon D. In neither case can the mere failure to comply give rise to an actionable duty of care in negligence (absent some assumption of responsibility on D's part, which was missing here). 'The question of whether the order can have generated a duty of care is comparable with the question of whether a statutory duty can generate a common law duty of care. The answer is that it cannot (per *Gorringe v Calderdale MBC*[a]). The statute either creates a statutory duty or it does not … you cannot derive a common law duty of care directly from a statutory duty. Likewise, … you cannot derive one from an order of court. The order carries its own remedies, and its reach does not extend any further' (Lord Hoffmann);
- *the prospect of indeterminate liability:* it would be unjust and unreasonable for the bank D to be notified of an order that it had no opportunity to resist, and that it could then be liable for a judgment like this – in this case, 'for a few million pounds only, but might, in another case, be for very much more' (Lord Bingham CJ);
- *the incremental test:* C could not show any analogous case to support their argument that a duty was owed to them; no case 'on examination, reveal[ed] any real similarity' (Lord Bingham CJ);
- *the availability of insurance:* it was likely that this D would be covered under D's blanket insurance policy, 'the terms of which are typically of extreme width' – but if third parties (other than banks) breached a Mareva injunction, it was 'not so obvious that they will have, or could obtain, insurance to cover the risk of negligent release' of assets or monies (Lord Mance).

[a] [2004] 1 WLR 1057 (CA).

- Medical services: In most cases, medical services negligently undertaken by D will cause personal injury to the patient, but in less common cases, that negligence will visit pure economic losses on a connected third party, C.[94] The three cases below demonstrate different ways that such loss can come about, *viz*, where employer C is financially affected by D's medical treatment of D's employee; where institutional carer D is put to the costs of caring for D's negligently-treated patient; or in cases of failed sterilisation affecting the patient's partner, and not the patient himself.

  > In *West Bromwich Albion FC Ltd v El-Safty*,[95] professional footballer Michael Appleton signed a 3.5-year contract with football club, WBA, C, in Jan 2001. In Nov 2001, the player suffered a serious injury to his right posterior cruciate ligament in training, and he was referred to Dr El-Safty, D, for surgery. Reconstruction of the player's knee was unsuccessful, and he was forced to retire. It was conceded that D's advice to the player was negligent, and that had he been treated conservatively, he would have recovered within four months, and returned to professional football. C suffered economic loss, because the player's value in the transfer market was considerably reduced, and C was put to the cost of replacing him ('potentially several million pounds'). D had treated over 30 players for C. **Held:** D did not owe C a duty of care. In *Islington LBC v Univ College London NHS Trust*,[96] Mrs J, the patient, was advised by a receptionist employed by the NHS Trust, D, not to recommence taking Warfarin, after her heart operation was postponed. Ten days later, Mrs J suffered a serious and disabling stroke. Thereafter, Mrs J required institutional care, funded by her local authority, Islington LBC, C, who was under a statutory duty to provide care accommodation for Mrs J. That care was provided for five years, but because of relevant legislation governing the NHS, D could not recover the costs of care from Mrs J, who was unable to pay due to lack of personal resources. Hence, C sought to recover those costs from D, whose employee's negligence had caused the stroke. **Held:** no duty of care was owed by D to C. In *Goodwill v British Pregnancy Advisory Service*,[97] Mr McKinlay, the patient, underwent a vasectomy, and was then advised by the BPAS, D (a charity which arranged the operation and counselling) of 'permanent sterility'. He was not warned of the risk of spontaneous reversal which occurred. Ms Goodwill, C, entered into a relationship with Mr McKinlay, and ceased other forms of contraception, in reliance on the vasectomy, but conceived a child three years after her partner's vasectomy operation. C sued D for expenses re her daughter's birth, and for the costs of raising her. **Held:** no duty of care was owed.

The factors in play

- *lack of temporal proximity:* C's forming a relationship with Mr McKinlay and conceiving three years after the negligence in not warning about the spontaneous reversal (*Goodwill*), and any costs of care incurred for a negligently-treated patient 'some substantial time' later (*Islington*), were significant in precluding proximity;
- *no knowledge of C's identity:* Ms Goodwill was not in a 'known or identifiable' category of partners, except for the class of 'future sexual partners' when the vasectomy was performed (*Goodwill*), while the Islington LBC was in the class of 'potential carers' of Mrs J (*Islington*), creating

---

[94] See: Mulheron, *Medical Negligence: Non-Patient and Third Party Claims* (Ashgate, 2010), ch 7.

[95] [2006] EWCA Civ 1299, affirming: [2005] EWHC 2866. The player himself recovered £1.5m in damages in his personal action against D: *Appleton v El-Safty* [2007] EWHC 631 (QB).

[96] [2005] EWCA Civ 596, [2006] LGR 50.   [97] (1996) 31 BMLR 83 (CA) 91.

insufficient proximity (whereas WBA was known, as a specific entity, to Dr El-Safty, but that was insufficient to establish a duty of care in *WBA*);

- *lack of independent enquiry:* in *Goodwill*, C should not have been content with 'receiving [BPAS's] advice at second hand', but should have made some independent enquiry about contraceptive measures;

- *absence of reliance:* in *WBA v El-Safty*, WBA's reliance on D was not financial (i.e., to protect their financial well-being), but rather, was medical (i.e., to look after the health of their employee, Michael Appleton). The Court of Appeal did not explore the proposition that these interests could be entirely coincident, from WBA's perspective, i.e., whilst interested in his medical welfare, it was also vitally interested in its investment!

- *conflicts of interest:* any risk that surgeon D would place a duty to avoid causing financial loss to C above his already-existing duty towards his own patient, had to be precluded, by not finding a duty of care (*WBA v El-Safty*) – although it was difficult to see how those duties could have been at odds here (e.g., there was no suggestion that D's medical treatment of Michael Appleton would be compromised by a short-term gain to C in getting him back onto the field more quickly);

- *floodgates concerns:* if medical staff, D, were liable to Islington, as an institutional carer, for the costs of caring for a negligently-treated patient, then so too, many others in the same boat of outlaying costs for patient care could claim similarly (*Islington*), and if WBA was entitled to a claim against D, then other employers would similarly be able to sue doctors who negligently-treated their employees and caused the employer financial loss (*WBA*);

- *parliamentary intent:* in *Islington*, it was two public authorities in dispute (an NHS Trust and a local authority), both with different sources of public funding, and it was wrong to use the law of negligence to shift the loss away from where it lay (i.e., on the local authority): 'the sorting out of the present position, accidental or not, would seem to be essentially a matter for Parliament, or at least for political decision, rather than for a court deciding a particular case';

- *insurance availability:* in *WBA*, it was unreasonable to expect a surgeon to insure against additional loss of an economic kind, suffered by someone other than his patient; that insurance against financial loss 'naturally lies with the employers'. This helped to preclude any duty of care being owed to employer C;

- *disclaimer of liability:* in *WBA*, Dr El-Safty had no contract with WBA, C, and could not disclaim liability; had WBA indicated that it wanted D's advice for the purposes of looking after its own interests, then D would have been in a position where he could charge for that advice and disclaim liability;

- *lack of fairness:* under the 'artificial' principle in *Hunt v Severs*, D does not owe a duty of care to a private carer. Rather, D owes a duty of care to the injured party, and the law imposes a 'notional payment in respect of that liability by the injured party to that carer'. Hence, if institutional carers were owed a duty of care by D, then it would create a different entitlement as between institutional carer and private carer (*Islington*).

White v Jones: testamentary versus *inter vivos* transactions, and other extensions

§4.10   The extended *Hedley Byrne* principle is being cautiously extended on a case-by-case basis. For example: *White v Jones* concerned a testamentary disposition, i.e., a transaction (will) which was to take effect upon death. However, its principle has since been extended to include *inter-vivos* transactions (i.e., those intended to take effect during the life of the contracting parties).

The fact that *White v Jones*[98] concerned a will was very important, in upholding the duty of care to the disappointed beneficiaries – the 'lacuna in the law', in that the testator could not fix any negligence on D's part so as to rectify the disappointment of his daughters, was clearly evident. It was Mr Barrett's incapacity to remedy matters which brought the daughters and Mr Jones, the solicitor, within the realms of a 'special relationship'. For *inter vivos* transactions, however, any mistakes on D's part can, arguably, be fixed during the client's lifetime (should the client wish to fix the mistake). Lord Browne-Wilkinson drew this distinction:

> in transactions *inter vivos*, the transaction takes immediate effect, and the consequences of solicitors' negligence are immediately apparent. When discovered, they can either be rectified (by the parties) or damages recovered by the client. But in the case of a negligently drawn will, the will has no effect at all until the [testator's] death. It will have been put away in the deed box, not to surface again until the testator either wishes to vary it, or dies … the negligence will lie hidden until it takes effect on the death of the testator, i.e. at the very point in time when normally the error will become incapable of remedy.

– as did Lord Goff:

> take the example of an *inter vivos* gift where, as a result of the solicitor's negligence, the instrument in question is for some reason not effective for its purpose … I do not think that the intended donee could, in these circumstances, have any claim against the solicitor. It is enough, as I see it, that the donor is able to do what he wishes to put matters right.

However, in *Richards v Hughes*,[99] the court noted that anything said on that point in *White v Jones* was dicta only, and the remarks had never been applied directly to a case. Since *White v Jones*, there have been several attempts to extend the principle to other contexts too (such as the provision of tax advice) – strongly resisted by D, on the basis that they constitute unwarranted extensions of what was a novel development of the law in any event. However, some courts have been prepared to extend the boundaries of the *White v Jones* principle, by denying D's strike-out application.

The *White v Jones* principle, applied and extended

Legal or other professional services are given by D to X. C was intended to benefit from the services, but does not, because of some act or omission by D. Is a duty of care owed along the dotted line?

C *(the two daughters; Ms Vinton; the Hughes children; Mrs Gorham and her two children)*

X ← ──────────────────── D *(Mr Jones, solicitor; Fladgates; Mr Richards; Standard Life pension advisor)*

(Mr Barrett; Mrs Dugan-Chapman; Mr and Mrs Hughes; Mr Paul Gorham)

Summarising the leading cases, with reference to their illustration in the diagram above:

---

[98] [1995] 2 AC 207 (HL), with quotes respectively at 276 and 262.   [99] [2004] EWCA Civ 266, [27].

In *Vinton v Fladgate Fielder (a firm)*,[100] the law firm, Fladgates, D, provided tax advice to Mrs Dugan-Chapman. She was shareholder in a family company, Wilton, and at a time when she became seriously ill, the company needed an injection of funds. D advised Mrs Dugan-Chapman to reorganise her shareholdings so that her residuary beneficiaries (including Ms Vinton, C) would not have to pay inheritance tax upon her death. However, the advice turned out to be inaccurate because of how the shares had been acquired. According to HMRC, the residuary beneficiaries had to pay significant sums (approx. £360,000). **Held:** a duty of care was arguably owed by D to C; the strike-out application failed. In *Richards v Hughes*,[101] Mr and Mrs Hughes asked Mr Richards, D, a chartered accountant, to set up a trust fund for the benefit of their children's future education expenses. The trust fund ended up having little capital value. The children, C, sued D in negligence, alleging that he had failed to monitor the performance of the trust fund, and had failed to inform their parents of the erosion of capital value by charges and other outgoings. **Held:** a duty of care was arguably owed by D to C; the strike-out application failed. In *Gorham v British Telecom plc*,[102] Mr Gorham, as an employee of BT, was eligible to join the BT occupational pension scheme, but he did not join it, nor did he send back the opting-out form either (nor were any deductions being made from his payslips). He also had pension rights with his ex-employee, Cable & Wireless, with Standard Life. Mr Gorham ceased making contributions to the Standard Life scheme that would have entitled his wife and two children, C, to extra benefits when he died (Mr Gorham died at just 35). C sued Standard Life, alleging that Standard Life owed them a duty of care, as potential beneficiaries of the arrangements for insurance cover which had been advised to Mr Gorham by Standard Life, and they also sued BT for failing to make the situation about pension entitlement plainer to Mr Gorham. **Held (first instance):** both Ds owed C a duty of care, but causation failed, because of the inactivity of Mr Gorham to follow advice and to follow up gaps in information. **Held (CA, 3:0):** both D's owed C a duty, per *White v Jones* (but causation again failed, by majority).

In *Vinton v Fladgate Fielder*,[103] Norris J stated that, 'the implications of *White v Jones* are being explored case by case' (citing *Richards v Hughes*[104] in that regard). Clearly, the above-mentioned body of case law supports an extension of the ratio in *White v Jones*, notwithstanding that:

i. the transaction extends beyond legal services, and may concern professional tax, pensions or insurance advice, and where D is someone other than a solicitor (e.g., accountants, pension advisers);

ii. there may be an actual, or even a potential, conflict between D's client on the one hand, and the intended beneficiary, C, on the other – but D may still owe a duty of care. There was no conflict of interest in *White v Jones*, of course, because Mr Barrett wanted to give his two daughters the legacies. However, in some cases, it may not be so clear-cut. In *Vinton*, it was conceivable that what was in C's best tax interests might not precisely coincide with the interests of Mrs Dugan-Chapman or the company – that would not be totally clear until trial, but in any event, even a potential conflict of interest did not preclude a duty of care from arising. In *Gorham*,[105] it was mentioned that a conflict was possible, because insured employees may wish to maximise the benefits to themselves during their lifetimes (by less premium deductions per pay packet), whereas other employees may wish to do the best they can for the interests to their dependants – but

---

[100] [2010] EWHC 904 (Ch).   [101] [2004] EWCA Civ 266.   [102] [2000] EWCA Civ 234.
[103] [2010] EWHC 904 (Ch) [24].   [104] [2004] EWCA Civ 266, [25] (Peter Gibson LJ).
[105] [2000] EWCA Civ 234, [2000] 1 WLR 2129, 2141–42.

even so, a potential conflict of interest was no obstacle to the recognition of a potential duty of care in C's favour. If there is a conflict of duties on the facts, though, then it may be more difficult to say that D assumed any responsibility to the intended beneficiary, and on that point, no duty to C may be feasible (per *Steven v Hewats*[106]);

iii. the intended beneficiary may have been **both** the giver and receiver of information. The beneficiaries in *White v Jones* were entirely 'passive recipients' of the transaction (the solicitor D was given the names by the testator and needed to make no further enquiry) – but not all intended beneficiaries will be entirely passive, some instructions may be needed from them. In *Vinton*, Mrs Dugan-Chapman and the residuary beneficiaries were all interested in raising capital in an 'inheritance tax efficient way', and gave instructions to that effect; and in *Gorham*, Mrs Gorham had received personal correspondence from D and was asked to confirm that recommendations made by D had been received and understood;

iv. the intended beneficiary, C, may have been advised by solicitor D to obtain separate legal advice for the transaction for which D was advising his client (as noted, e.g., in *Steven v Hewats*[107]);

v. the error on D's part may be discovered during the client's lifetime, enabling that client to instruct D to fix the problem, or to sue D himself for at least some of the loss – all of which was impossible in *White v Jones* itself. However, wherever the mistake cannot be rectified, that leaves a gap in redress, for which the *White v Jones* principle can apply. For example, in *Richards*, the problem was that 'the consequences were not immediately apparent, but only emerged several years after the scheme which the parents intended to enter into was implemented; only then was the loss of the investment discovered'.[108]

Hence, given the numerous features which distinguish these cases from the *White v Jones* scenario (1995), it is evident that the 'extended *Hedley Byrne* principle' is constantly evolving. As commented by the Court of Appeal in *Richards v Hughes*, the area is one which is 'still subject to some uncertainty and developing', and hence, it is more difficult to strike out a claim in that circumstance, where 'any development of the law should be on the basis of actual, and not hypothetical, facts'.[109] Notwithstanding, however, a recent attempt to extend *White v Jones*, and to bring a novel case of alleged negligence within the extended principle of *Hedley Byrne*, failed, with a categorical finding that the third limb of *Caparo* had failed, and that no useful purpose would be served by the continuation of the litigation (per *James-Bowen v Commr of Police*[110]). Even so, claimants are constantly pushing at the boundaries of *White v Jones's* principle, and for every strike-out application which fails, the door is opened just a little further ajar, in the field of professional negligence liability.

PURE RELATIONAL ECONOMIC LOSS

The scenario

§4.11 Under the exclusionary rule, where D negligently causes damage to property owned by a third party (TP), C cannot recover any pure economic loss (i.e., lost profits) which he suffers as a result of that damage to TP's property, where C possesses (at most) a contractual right to use that property, falling short of a proprietary or possessory interest in that property. For policy reasons, English law does not regard C's pure economic loss as being recoverable damage.

---

[106] [2013] CSOH 61, [13].   [107] [2013] CSOH 61, [6].   [108] [2004] EWCA Civ 266, [27].
[109] *ibid*, [30].   [110] [2015] EWHC 1249 (QB).

The exclusionary rule actually originated in the negligence/*Rylands v Fletcher* case of *Cattle v Stockton Waterworks Co*[111] (as described in Chapter 17). It has been applied consistently since then, in the context of both of these torts (and in private nuisance, of which *Rylands v Fletcher* is a subspecies, discussed in Chapter 16). This chapter will concentrate upon the manifestation of the principle in negligence.

What C is seeking to claim here is a form of pure economic loss (also called 'relational economic loss'), but it cannot be recovered in English law for policy reasons. To clarify, it is properly classified as 'pure economic loss', because C himself has suffered no property damage. Significantly, C possesses no proprietary or possessory interest in TP's property (per *The Aliakmon*[112]). It is TP's property which was damaged, and hence, any economic losses claimed by C must be 'pure', and not consequential. C's economic losses may be caused because he had contractual relations with TP which entitled C to use TP's property to earn income; or C's economic losses may arise regardless of any contractual relations with TP. Either way, C cannot recover those losses.

The scenario is summarised in the Diagram below (with key cases italicised for convenience):

The exclusionary rule (*aka* relational economic loss) in negligence

Imagine that an essential facility (e.g., an electricity cable, bridge, telephone line, oil supply line, seawater farms) is owned by **TP** (*Midlands Elec Board; oil pipeline owned by WLPS/UKOP; Public Works Canada; AOR; various salmon farmers; livestock farmers affected by FMD*) —

D negligently damages/destroys that essential facility
(*Martin; Total, the owners of the Buncefield oil depot at Hemel Hempstead; the tug operators Norsk; the dredge operators; Braer Corp; DEFRA*)

C uses the facility owned by TP (*Spartan Steel; fuel company Shell; Canadian National Rwy; Caltex Oil; Landcatch, the grower of salmon smolt; livestock farmers*)

• C usually has a contract with TP for use of TP's facility or property, for C's business or profit-making endeavours. C relies upon that facility or property to be undamaged, for his economic welfare, and his economic welfare suffers a downturn because the essential facility is out of action or the property is damaged;

• TP can sue D for his *own* property damage. But TP won't be either able or willing to sue D for C's economic losses (claiming them as his own consequential losses)

• hence, for C, the financial loss which he suffers is *pure* (and not consequential) economic loss;

• C cannot sue D in contract for the financial losses suffered, because there is no contract between them. Hence, there is a 'lacuna in the law' – TP, as owner of the facility or property, has the potential to claim, but has not suffered the particular economic loss suffered by C; whereas C has suffered the economic loss, but does not have any claim (unless the law of tort steps in to impose a duty of care on D in C's favour);

• for this particular lacuna, English law has not created a right of remedy for C. Tort law will not assist C.

---

[111] (1874–75) LR 10 QB 453 (Div Ct).
[112] *Leigh & Sillivan Ltd v Aliakmon Shipping Co Ltd* [1986] AC 785 (HL) 809 (Lord Brandon).

The governing policy reasons

The *Spartan Steel* analysis

C's problem, in this scenario, is that he has suffered a type of loss which falls outside the boundaries of what English law regards as being recoverable damages – strictly for policy reasons. Indeed, in *Spartan Steel and Alloys Ltd v Martin & Co (Contractors) Ltd*, Lord Denning MR candidly admitted that, 'the question of recovering economic loss is one of policy. Whenever the Courts draw a line to mark out the bounds of duty, they do it as matter of policy, so as to limit the responsibility of [D]'.[113]

> In *Spartan Steel v Martin & Co*, Spartan Steel, C, manufactured stainless steel in a Birmingham factory which was powered via an electricity cable from a power station of the Midlands Electricity Board. Martins, D, roadworking contractors, were doing roadworks about 0.25 miles away from C's factory, digging up the road with a power-driven excavating shovel. D enquired about where the cables, mains, etc were under the road, and were given plans showing their location. Unfortunately, D damaged the cable which supplied electricity to C's factory. The Electricity Board shut down the power for the 14.5 hours during C's nightshift, whilst they repaired the cable. At that time, metal was in an arc furnace, being melted in order to be converted into ingots. Electric power was needed throughout, to maintain the temperature and melt the metal. When the power failed, and to avoid the metal solidifying in the furnace and damaging the lining of the furnace, C used oxygen to melt the material and pour it out of the furnace. The loss of the melted material was £368 (loss #1, property damage). The profit that would have been made on that particular melt was £400 (loss #2, consequential economic loss on the property damage). However, during the hours when the power was cut off, C would have been able to put four more melts through, and being unable to do so, they lost a profit of £1,767 (loss #3, pure economic loss). D admitted breach. **Held (2:1):** C could recover losses #1 and #2 (i.e., damages of £768), but D owed C no duty of care to avoid loss #3.

In *Conarken Group Ltd v Network Rail Infrastructure*, Moore-Bick LJ remarked that the fact that the exclusionary rule still applies in English law, more than a century after *Cattle v Stockton*, owes everything to 'reasons of policy rather than principle'.[114] The Table below summarises those reasons, as derived from Lord Denning MR's judgment in *Spartan Steel*:[115]

The factors in play

- *parliamentary intent:* if the Midlands Electricity Board did not maintain the cable or shut it down for repairs, then under the governing legislation, Parliament did not intend to expose the Board to liability for damages to the citizens whose lives could be disrupted by the interruption to electricity supply and who suffered financial losses as a result. If the Electricity Board could not be sued for financial losses, then by analogy, 'it would seem right for the common law to adopt a similar policy in regard to contractors [who cause economic loss]';

- *no lacuna in the law/insurability:* interruptions to electricity supply could arise from a number of sources, apart from an excavating shovel severing a cable: a short circuit, a flash of lightning, a tree falling on the wires. Supply is usually restored within hours, so that inconvenience and economic losses to C may not be very large. There are three options available to C: either put up with it and

---

[113] [1973] QB 27 (CA) 36 (Lord Denning MR and Lawton LJ; Edmund Davies LJ dissenting).
[114] [2011] EWCA Civ 644, [95].   [115] [1973] QB 27 (CA), with quotes in Table at 38.

work harder to make up the losses ('they do not go running around to their solicitor'); or install a back-up generator; or take out insurance against the interruption of supply. Consumers and businesses should anticipate, and take on, the risk themselves, rather than seek to place full liability on the contractor, D;

- *the prospect of indeterminate liability/'floodgates':* an interruption to electricity supply could give rise to 'no end of claims' – some genuine, some inflated and some made-up. It would be difficult to check the validity and quantum of claims made;

- *distributive justice:* where electricity supply is cut, then it is fairer that the consequences are sustained by the whole community who suffer small individual losses, rather than casting the entire loss onto contractor, D;

- *physical damage is deemed more 'deserving' of compensation:* where the severance of electricity supply causes actual physical damage to person or property, that physical damage can be recovered at law (and any consequential economic losses, as per, e.g., *British Celanese Ltd v Hunt[a]*). Not only will there be fewer of them, but they are 'readily capable of proof and will be easily checked'.

[a] (1969) 1 WLR 959 (CA).

The last policy reason was aptly demonstrated in a case which was almost identical to *Spartan Steel*, but for one important difference: **all** of C's damages were judicially treated as either property damage or consequential economic loss, and that was recoverable:

> In *SCM (UK) Ltd v WJ Whittall and Son Ltd,*[116] D's employees damaged an electric cable which serviced C's typewriter factory, and the electricity was cut off for several hours. The molten material in C's machines solidified, and the machines were extensively damaged. C lost one day's production. **Held:** D was liable for the costs of repairing the machines, and also for the loss of production on the day of the power failure. This was treated as physical damage to C's property, and the day's lost production as 'economic loss consequent on it'.

As clarified by Jackson LJ in *Conarken Group v Network Rail*, the decision in *SCM* is only explicable on the basis that C could recover damages for loss of production if it were treated as being consequential on damage to the machinery, and not consequential upon the power cut.[117]

One factor which did **not** particularly feature in *Spartan Steel* (because the governing statute ruled out any compensation payable by the electricity supplier TP to Spartan Steel C) – but which **has** been mentioned in other cases, e.g., in the Canadian case of *Canadian National Rwys v Norsk Pacific Steamship Co*[118] – is the so-called 'contractual allocation of risk'. The argument goes that C, the entity using the essential facility owned by TP, will usually (but not always) have a contractual relationship with TP for the use of that essential facility. In that case, C has an opportunity to negotiate with TP the terms of compensation, if C's business is damaged because the essential facility is not available. La Forest J (dissenting) remarked that C and D ought to have considered (or perhaps did consider, as in that case) the issue of allocating the risk of the essential facility's closing or being rendered useless, as a result of D's negligence. In that event, it is unnecessary for tort to step in, to uphold a duty of care in C's favour, because C had a prior opportunity to define where the loss should lie, if D did put the essential facility 'out of action'.

---

[116] [1971] 1 QB 337 (CA).   [117] [2011] EWCA Civ 644, [132]–[134].
[118] (1992), 91 DLR (4th) 289, with quotes at 336–37, and 343, respectively.

Hence, there was no gap in redress, for the opportunity for redress lay entirely in C's control. However, the majority in *Norsk Pacific* (per McLachlin J) considered that the opportunity (or even achievement) of a contractual allocation of loss as between C and D should not deny a duty of care in C's favour. This was because, e.g., 'the parties who control the situation (e.g., the owners of the [essential facility, a bridge in that case]', may have superior bargaining power compared with C; and the argument also tended to ignore the essential concept of negligence, *viz*, to curb negligent conduct by placing liability on the wrongdoer, D. These diverse lines of reasoning have not, as yet, particularly featured in English law, perhaps because of the sparse regard which has been given to this type of pure economic loss since *Spartan Steel*.

The exclusionary rule has been an immutable rule in the context of negligence (as well as for both private nuisance and *Rylands v Fletcher*). In *Shell UK Ltd v Total UK Ltd*, the Court of Appeal noted that it was plain that, in *Cattle v Stockton*, 'the judges were not particularly enamoured of the law that they were laying down', and that, even in 2010, '[d]iffering views about the wisdom of the exclusionary rule are widely held'.[119] Nevertheless, the rule has been frequently applied/upheld in a number of contexts, e.g.:

- the exclusionary rule applies, even where C's pure economic loss was suffered because of damage to TP's property, but where C had **no** contractual relations with TP at all – in such a scenario, C's claim appears even weaker than where C had a contract with TP by which to make a profit or run a business:

  In *D Pride & Partners v Institute for Animal Health*,[120] 14 owners and/or occupiers of livestock farms, C, alleged that DEFRA, D, caused, or failed to prevent, the escape of the foot and mouth disease from its animal research facility at Pirbright in 2007. C's properties were not affected by the virus, but TP's farms were. A prohibition on any livestock movement was imposed, and C lost the chance to take their livestock to market at the most profitable time, had to feed and maintain livestock when otherwise they would have been sold; and some of the stock that would have been sold for breeding had to be sold for meat at a lower price. **Held:** C's claim in negligence failed, as it concerned relational economic loss. Tugendhat J noted that it was a weaker type of claim than usual, because farmers C had no contractual relations with TP, the affected farmers, nor expected to make any profits from their dealings with TP. The relation between C and TP was very slight indeed.

- however, C's scenario will fall outside of the exclusionary rule, if C actually owns the essential facility itself (in a beneficial capacity) – which means that C's claim is not pure economic loss at all, but can be considered to be consequential upon the damage to C's property which D inflicted on the essential facility:

  In *Shell UK Ltd v Total UK Ltd (formerly, Colour Quest Ltd v Total Downstream UK plc)*,[121] explosions at the Buncefield Oil Storage Depot at Hemel Hempstead were caused by an enormous vapour cloud igniting, which had developed from 300 tons of petrol spilling from a storage tank. From the consequent fire, which burned for a long period, there was a substantial impact on the adjacent industrial estate. Total, D, was the joint venturer which owned the Buncefield site. Shell, C, a major fuel company, claimed that significant damage was done to the West London Pipeline System as a result of the explosion, which C did not own, but which C was unable to use, to supply both aviation and ground fuels to customers, except in reduced volumes and/or at increased costs to

---

[119] [2010] EWCA Civ 180, [2011] QB 86, [134], [143].   [120] [2009] EWHC 685 (QB).
[121] [2010] EWCA Civ 180, [2011] QB 86, overruling: [2009] EWHC 540 (QB (Comm) [409], [471]–[472].

itself. **Held (first instance):** C failed on the basis of the exclusionary rule. **Held (CA):** although the exclusionary rule was recognised, this case fell outside it, as C had a (shared) equitable ownership of the pipelines, which was enough to give C title to claim for property damage and consequential economic loss.

- the exclusionary rule applies in English law, even where the class of potential Cs is a small and finite class. The prospect of indeterminate liability (or 'floodgates') – which was given as an important policy reason in *Spartan Steel* – cannot arise in such a scenario, but nevertheless, the rule applies. This was confirmed in two shipping cases decided in 1986, and in a Scottish case (specifically approved in *D Pride & Partners*[122]), in all of which the affected class comprised just a single C, but where C could not recover, because of the rule:

    In *Landcatch Ltd v Intl Oil Pollution Compensation Fund*,[123] Landcatch, C, ran a farm, on which it reared salmon eggs to smolt (juveniles up to two years of age) in freshwater conditions, and then sold them to other farmers, TP, who grew the salmon to maturity in seawater conditions, mostly around Shetland. As a result of an oil spill in the sea off Shetland, caused by the grounding of a vessel by D, the Secretary of State for Scotland designated the affected area an exclusion zone, which included TP's farms to which C contracted to sell their smolt. C suffered economic loss, but this entailed 'nothing more than relational economic loss', notwithstanding that there could only be one C affected in this scenario. In *Candlewood Navigation Corp Ltd v Mitsui Lines Ltd*,[124] D collided with TP's ship, causing it to undergo repairs in dock. C was a time charterer of the vessel, and sued for the profit that it would have made, during that period that TP's vessel was out of operation. No recovery was possible.

The rejection of the principle of 'transferred loss'

§4.12 The principle of 'transferred loss' has not been accepted as part of English law, by which to provide C, who suffers pure economic loss, an avenue of redress by which to avoid the operation of the exclusionary rule.

In *Leigh & Sullivan Ltd v Aliakmon Shipping Co Ltd (The Aliakmon)*,[125] Goff LJ (as he then was, of the Court of Appeal), proposed what he called 'the principle of transferred loss', as an exception to the exclusionary rule, drafted in 'deliberately narrow terms' (D, C and TP are inserted in the following passage as appropriate):

    Where D owes a duty of care in tort not to cause physical damage to TP's property, and D commits a breach of that duty in circumstances in which the loss of or physical damage to the property will ordinarily fall on TP but (as is reasonably foreseeable by D), such loss or damage, by reason of a contractual relationship between TP and C, falls on C, then C will be entitled, subject to the terms of any contract restricting D's liability to TP, to bring an action in tort against D in respect of such loss or damage to the extent that it falls on him, C.

However, that proposal was rejected by the House of Lords. In the view of Lord Brandon,[126] the exclusionary rule was 'simple to understand and easy to apply, [and] has been established by a long line of authority over many years'. No exception could be created for commercial

---

[122] [2009] EWHC 685 (QB) [95].
[123] [1998] 2 Lloyd's LR 552 (OH) (Lord Gill), aff'd: [1999] 2 Lloyd's LR 316 (IH).
[124] [1986] 1 AC 1 (PC).   [125] [1985] 2 WLR 289 (CA) 330.   [126] [1986] AC 785 (HL) 816–17.

contracts of sea carriage, as otherwise the certainty of the exclusionary rule 'would be seriously undermined'.

As Lord Goff himself later pointed out in *White v Jones*,[127] this principle of transferred loss did not apply to that case, given that the lost expectation of the two legacies, due to D's negligence, could **never** have been suffered by the testator, but only by C, the disappointed legatees, albeit that there was a 'close analogy'. In any event, the principle has not achieved recognition at the senior appellate level (as noted, e.g., in *Smith v Littlewoods Organisation Ltd*[128]).

Exceptions to the exclusionary rule

§4.13   There are some recognised exceptions to the exclusionary rule, where D negligently causes damage to property owned by a third party (TP), and C can recover pure economic loss which he suffers as a result of that damage to TP's property, because in those particular instances, C and D have sufficient proximity, and policy reasons favour a duty of care.

There are some limited exceptions to the exclusionary rule in negligence, which Tugendhat J noted, in *D Pride & Partners v Institute for Animal Health*, to be case-specific, and not standing for any particular general principle of, say, C's loss being 'analogous to physical damage'.[129] They turn on their own facts.

For example, in *Morrison Steamship Co Ltd v Greystoke Castle (Cargo Owners)*,[130] Lord Roche gave the example of C's goods being loaded onto the back of TP's lorry; and due to D's negligent driving, TP's lorry runs off the road and is damaged; C's goods are not damaged, but the lorry is so badly damaged that the goods have to be unloaded, reloaded and carried on, which may cause C economic loss, if he has to pay for the costs of unloading and reloading. Inevitably, it must be pure economic loss, because the goods themselves were not damaged and, as with the exclusionary rule, it was TP's property that was damaged, and which caused C's loss. But C could recover those losses in that scenario (said Lord Roche). Similarly, in *Greystoke* itself, it was held that, where cargo owners, C, had their goods loaded for transport at sea in TP's ship, and those cargo owners paid in advance a proportion of any damage done to the goods during transit (a form of pooled insurance), and D damaged TP's ship (but not C's own cargo), then each C could recover any pure economic loss arising from unloading, reloading and relating to that undamaged cargo.

The reasoning in *Greystoke* was that, under this arrangement of a 'general average contribution', TP and C were engaged in a relationship of 'joint adventurers at sea'. In *Murphy v Brentwood DC*,[131] the House of Lords reiterated that *Greystoke* turned on the 'specialties of maritime law', and that it was not an assumption of responsibility/reliance scenario as between C and D (hence the reference to proximity and policy, a *Caparo*-type analysis, in the principle above).

Conclusion

The stark refusal of English law to depart from the exclusionary rule is particularly difficult to countenance, when the House of Lords was prepared to step in on behalf of the disappointed beneficiaries in *White v Jones*, so as to recognise a newly-constructed duty of care, precisely to fill a 'lacuna in the law'. The problem was that the only persons who might have a valid claim

---

[127] [1995] 2 AC 207 (HL) 216.   [128] [1987] 2 AC 241 (HL) 280 (Lord Goff).
[129] [2009] EWHC 685 (QB) [83], [120].   [130] [1947] AC 265 (HL) (decided by a narrow majority).
[131] [1991] 1 AC 398 (HL) 406.

(the testator, Mr Barrett, and his estate) had suffered no loss, and the only persons who had suffered a loss (the two daughters, as 'disappointed beneficiaries') had no claim, but for the law stepping in to create a tortious duty of care. The same lacuna is evident under the exclusionary rule, but for which the law will offer C no assistance. Some types of Cs are seemingly more deserving of compensation than others!

A comparative perspective

In other key Commonwealth jurisdictions, the exclusionary rule in English law **has** been departed from, at the highest appellate level.

The comparative corner: **Canada and Australia**

Canada: In *Canadian National Rwy v Norsk Pacific Steamship Co*,[132] a barge was being towed down the Fraser River by a tug owned by Norsk, D. The barge collided in heavy fog with the New Westminster railway bridge, which caused extensive damage to the bridge. That bridge, owned by Public Works Canada (PWC), was closed for several weeks. It was used by four railway companies, including CNR, C, who was the bridge's main user. PWC recovered compensation for the property damage from D, but PWC could not sue for C's lost profits during the period that the bridge was closed. Hence, C sued D in negligence for those losses. **Held (4:3):** C was owed a duty of care by D, and was able to recover its pure economic loss.

- *physical proximity:* by damaging the bridge, D caused the risk of physical injury to CNR's property, because its trains were frequently on the bridge and could have been damaged during a bridge accident. That danger indicated the closeness between C and D, which was not determinative, but relevant;
- *vulnerability and reliance:* CNR's property could not be enjoyed without the link of the bridge because it was an integral part of its railway system; CNR supplied materials, inspection and consulting services for the bridge; and CNR was included in the periodic negotiations surrounding the closing of the bridge;
- *a common venture (relational proximity):* PWC and CNR were so closely assimilated that they were in a joint or common venture to use the bridge. CNR could be considered as a joint venturer with PWC as the owner of the property. To deny recovery for CNR would be to deny it to a party who, for practical purposes, was in the same position as if it owned the bridge;
- *no floodgates possible:* only four possible Cs existed here. To allow C to recover would not open up the prospect of floodgates to 'casual users of the property'. Also, where contractual relations were in place between TP and C, then potential tortfeasors such as D could gauge in advance the scope of their liability, and insure for it.

Australia: In *Caltex Oil (Aust) Pty Ltd v The Dredge, 'Willemstad'*,[133] an underwater pipeline (four pipes) owned by Australian Oil Refining Ltd carried oil from AOR's refinery on

---

[132] [1992] 1 SCR 1021 (SCC) (L'Heureux-Dube, Cory, McLachlin, and Stevenson JJ; La Forest, Sopinka and Iacobucci JJ dissenting).
[133] (1975) 136 CLR 529 (HCA).

the southern shore of Botany Bay to Caltex Oil's Banksmeadow oil terminal on the northern shore. That pipeline was negligently severed by the dredge Willemstad, D, while it was deepening a shipping channel in the bay. There were errors recorded on Decca's track plotter chart of D's proposed route in the bay, but D's navigators did not notice the error, which constituted negligence on their part. Caltex Oil, C, had to arrange alternative methods of transporting the oil to its terminal while the pipeline was being repaired. **Held (5:0):** C was owed a duty of care by D, and was able to recover those losses.

- *no floodgates possible:* D's navigators knew that the pipeline led directly from the refinery to C's terminal, and that it was not like a water main or electric cable serving the public generally – C was foreseeable as the entity which would probably suffer economic loss if the pipes were broken, hence, a class of one;
- *close proximity:* D's navigators were obliged to take care to avoid damage to the pipeline, which was shown on the drawing supplied to them for the very purpose of enabling them to avoid it whilst dredging. Hence, they had a close relationship with C;
- *vulnerability:* C could not readily avoid the risk of incurring alternative costs of transportation of the oil awaiting transfer to its terminal;
- *fairness:* to uphold a duty of care by D to C would not curb D's freedom of action, because it already owed a duty of care to AOR, the TP, as the owner of the relevant property (the pipelines).

5

Duty IV – Pure psychiatric injury

INTRODUCTION

Uncertainties and problems

Judicial consternation

It is an unfortunate truism that the topic of negligently-inflicted pure psychiatric illness is afflicted with many vagaries and complexities.[1]

That has been openly admitted, judicially. In *Tredget and Tredget v Bexley HA*,[2] the court described the law, in something of an understatement, as 'by no means straightforward', and that 'the arguments must have seemed to the parents as they listened, to have an air of unreality, but unsatisfactory as the legal frame-work has ... been shown to be, the court can only act within its constraints' – while, in *Taylorson v Shieldness Produce Ltd*, Ralph Gibson LJ remarked that the relevant principles are 'as unconvincing as they are surprising'.[3] Soberingly, even the House of Lords has admitted, in *White v CC of South Yorkshire Police*,[4] that, in this area of law, 'the search for principle has been called off' (per Lord Hoffmann), while in the same case, Lord Steyn despaired that the law 'is [neither] coherent [n]or morally defensible'. Earlier, in *Alcock v CC of South Yorkshire Police*, Lord Oliver stated that the law 'is not wholly logical'.[5]

All of this is, indeed, an unpromising start. The special rules governing whether D owes C a duty of care in this area are among the most judicially-criticised of any area of Tort law.

Law reform consideration

As a hallmark of its controversy, the issue has been the subject of frequent law reform consideration, e.g., by the English Law Commission in 1998,[6] the Australian Ipp Commit-

---

[1] The author has discussed several of the issues in this chapter elsewhere, from which some of this chapter is drawn, *viz*: 'Rewriting the Requirement for a "Recognized Psychiatric Injury" in Negligence Claims' (2012) 33 *OJLS* 1; *Non-Patient and Third Party Claims* (Ashgate, 2010), ch 5; 'The "Primary Victim" in Psychiatric Illness Claims: Reworking the "Patchwork Quilt"' (2008) 19 *KCLJ* 81; 'Medical Negligence, Secondary Victims and Psychiatric Illness: Family Tragedies and Legal Headaches' in R Probert (ed), *Family Life and the Law* (Ashgate, London, 2007), ch 5; 'Secondary Victim Psychiatric Illness Claims' (2003) 14 *KCLJ* 213.

[2] [1994] 5 Med LR 178 (Central London CC) 179.   [3] [1994] PIQR P329 (CA) 336.

[4] [1999] 2 AC 455 (HL) 511, and with Lord Steyn's quote at 500.   [5] [1992] 1 AC 310 (HL) 417.

[6] *Liability for Psychiatric Illness* (Rep 249, 1998) ('*English Report*'), and the draft Negligence (Psychiatric Illness) Bill.

tee in 2003,[7] the British Columbia Commission in 1992,[8] and the Scottish Law Commission in 2004.[9]

Close to home, both the English and Scottish Commissions recommended statutory reform, such is the disarray in which the case law finds itself, but both remain unenacted. The Department for Constitutional Affairs stated, in 2007, that it rejected the English Law Commission's recommendation to legislate: 'the Government considers it preferable to allow the courts to continue to develop the law in this area'.[10] More recently, the Scottish Government has also rejected the Scottish Law Commission's recommendations for legislative reform.[11] Hence, both the English and Scottish attempts to clarify the law have, so far, fallen upon deaf legislative ears, and that position is unlikely to change.

Nevertheless, some judges have been adamant that Parliament **should** get involved to legislate in this area. In *Walters v North Glamorgan NHS Trust*,[12] the Court of Appeal remarked that if the law needed to be changed to narrow the scope for recovery, then 'Parliament must do it' – a notion that has been repeated by the House of Lords, in *White (Frost) v CC of South Yorkshire Police*,[13] and in *Rothwell v Chemical and Insulating Co Ltd*.[14] More recently, in *Taylor v A Novo (UK) Ltd*,[15] the Court of Appeal also called for legislative intervention – albeit that 'the case law shows that some modest development by the courts may be possible'.

Where appropriate, some law reform insights will be referred to throughout this chapter, to indicate how some of these Commissions considered that the law *could* be clarified and improved.

Practical considerations

In the scenario of negligently-inflicted psychiatric injury, there is the potential, of course, for numerous claims of large amounts, or 'indeterminate liability',[16] arising out of D's negligence. Not only may C himself suffer some pure psychiatric illness as a result of D's act or omission, but also, C's *relatives and friends* may bring claims for pure psychiatric injury, thereby comprising a class of Cs, the identities of whom D may have no knowledge at all. Hence, this is an area rife with 'third party' claims, and is certainly a well-established one in which healthcare professionals can owe a duty of care to persons who are not their patients.[17] The House of Lords acknowledged this explicitly in *JD v East Berkshire Community Health NHS Trust*:[18]

> [D] may owe a duty of care, not only to the person whom he injures [the immediate victim], but also to that person's parents or spouse who suffer nervous shock through seeing or hearing the event or its immediate aftermath. Medical mishaps can give rise to such a duty.

---

[7] 'Mental Harm' in *Review of the Law of Negligence: Final Report* (2002) ('*Ipp Report*') ch 9.

[8] *Pecuniary Loss and the Family Compensation Act* (WP 69, 1992).

[9] *Damages for Psychiatric Injury* (Rep 196, 2004) ('*Scottish Report*'), and the draft Reparation for Mental Harm (Scotland) Bill.

[10] *Law on Damages* (CP 9, 4 May 2007), ch 3, [97].

[11] *Civil Law of Damages: Personal Injury* (2013) 21, cited in: *Young v MacVean* [2014] CSOH 133, [40].

[12] [2002] EWCA Civ 1792, [2003] PIQR P16, 250.　　[13] [1999] 2 AC 455 (HL) 500 (Lord Steyn), 504 (Lord Hoffmann).

[14] [2007] UKHL 39, [54].　　[15] [2013] EWCA Civ 194, [2014] QB 150, [24].

[16] A phrase derived from Cardozo CJ in *Ultramares Corp v Touche*, 174 NE 441, 444 (1931): 'liability in an indeterminate amount for an indeterminate time to an indeterminate class'.

[17] As discussed in: Mulheron, *Non-Patient and Third Party Claims* (Ashgate, 2010), ch 5.

[18] [2005] UKHL 23, 2 AC 373, [107].

The number of claims for negligently-inflicted psychiatric illness has markedly increased over the last decade – a point noted by the Court of Appeal in *Leach v Gloucestershire Constabulary*.[19] Hence, this type of lawsuit presents particularly topical concerns for Ds and their insurers. Sensible limits need to be imposed.

As a further problem, many claims brought for negligently-inflicted psychiatric injury do not bear much resemblance to those brought by victims of the Hillsborough stadium disaster out of which the modern framework for 'nervous shock' law in England arose. At an FA Cup semi-final on 15 April 1989, at the Hillsborough Stadium in Sheffield, between Liverpool and Nottingham Forest, overcrowding and crushing in two spectator pens resulted in 96 dead, 400 injured, and numerous psychiatric illness claims brought by relatives, friends, and police officers, who witnessed the horrific crushing and the aftermath. The disaster spawned significant psychiatric illness claims against the Chief Constable, e.g.: *Alcock*,[20] *Hicks*,[21] *McCarthy*,[22] *White (Frost)*[23] and *Hugh v Gray*.[24] English law has struggled, at times, to apply the relevant principles to more drawn-out scenarios.

Pure versus consequential mental injury

§5.1   'Pure' psychiatric injury is a mental injury that is *not* consequential upon personal injury of any type to C. However, where C's property is damaged and C suffers consequential mental injury, then that has been judicially regarded as being a 'pure' mental injury.

Personal injury

'Pure' psychiatric injury occurs where that is the **all and only** personal injury that C suffers as a result of D's negligence. Those sorts of cases raise 'unusual difficulty for the court'; whereas consequential mental distress claims are reasonably 'commonplace in personal injury cases', and do not raise the same types of difficulty (per *McCafferty v Scott's Caravans*[25]).

Where psychiatric injury is negligently-inflicted and consequential upon physical injury, then it is much easier for C to recover damages by way of compensation. That is because the cause of action is complete upon proof of the immediate physical damage, and damages are then recoverable for any consequential mental injury, anxiety, worry, etc, associated with that physical damage. That mental harm forms one of the heads of non-pecuniary loss (i.e., pain, suffering and loss of amenity, or PSLA). By contrast, the cause of action is only complete, for negligently-inflicted pure psychiatric injury, when C has suffered a recognised psychiatric injury. Damages for a lesser form of mental harm, such as worry, anxiety, etc, can be recovered by C if the claim is for consequential mental harm, but that lesser form of harm will not do, for claims of negligently-inflicted pure psychiatric injury. Hence, the distinction between consequential and pure mental harm is very important in English common law.

To give a couple of examples of consequential mental injury: in the *Guidelines for the Assessment of General Damages in Personal Injury Cases*, it is noted that, if C suffers from a negligently-inflicted physical injury or disease which will lead to death, then a component will be permitted for mental suffering, if C knows that death is approaching and is suffering during

---

[19] [1998] EWCA Civ 1368, [1999] 1 WLR 1421, 1433.   [20] [1992] 1 AC 310 (HL).   [21] [1992] 2 All ER 65 (HL).
[22] (QB, 11 Dec 1996).   [23] [1999] 2 AC 455 (HL).   [24] [2006] EWHC 1968 (QB).   [25] [2011] CSOH 16, [30].

the course of it.[26] Negligently-caused disfigurement can also entail consequential psychological damage:

> In *Johnson v Le Roux Fourie*,[27] Penny Johnson, C, 42, a successful businesswoman with family and active social life, consulted a plastic surgeon, D, for advice as to minor plastic surgery to her nose and dark circles under her eyes. D proposed (and C agreed to) more radical plastic surgery, including replacement of pre-existing breast implants, and a type of facelift. The surgery had serious consequences, e.g., C's right facial nerve was permanently damaged, causing an abnormal grimace and twitching; her right eye had to be taped shut as she could not shut it herself; her breast was left lopsided, oddly-shaped, excreting blood and pus, and with unsightly lumpy scarring; and C suffered from depression. **Held:** the psychiatric consequences of C's physical injuries were taken account of, in assessing PSLA at £80,000.

However, some cases appear to treat psychiatric injury as 'pure', when it actually appeared to be consequential upon personal injury (e.g., a mother's pain and suffering during a difficult birth).

> In *Farrell v Merton, Sutton and Wandsworth HA*,[28] Mrs Farrell, C, gave birth to her son Karol at D's hospital, but due to D's negligence, Karol was born with severe and irreversible brain damage, and suffered from cerebral palsy. C was not allowed to see Karol until he was one day old, and was not told about his grievous injuries. Instead, C was shown a photograph of Karol lying on a mattress shortly after he was born, and was told that he 'had had a hard time with the caesarian'. **Held:** C recovered £75,000.

The principles governing recovery of pure psychiatric injury (e.g., the 'immediate aftermath' doctrine) were applied in *Farrell*; whereas in other cases, the death *in utero* and stillbirth of a baby has been regarded as an injury to the mother to which additional physical or psychological damage could be appended, i.e., treating her claim for 'psychological injury' as a consequential claim (as in, e.g., *Wild v Southend Univ Hosp NHS Foundation Trust*,[29] in which *Farrell* was not cited). Such inconsistencies do not aid the clarity of the law.

Property damage

Where C's cherished property is damaged or destroyed, and from which C suffers mental injury as a result of witnessing it, then somewhat confusingly, that does **not** appear to have been treated as a consequential mental injury, but instead, invokes the principles of pure psychiatric injury (per *Attia v British Gas plc*[30]). In fact, the treatment of psychiatric injury arising from property damage has become more acute, as a result of recent cases involving the destruction of sperm in fertility banks (e.g., *Yearworth v North Bristol NHS Trust*,[31] and *Holdich v Lothian Health Board*[32]), and is discussed later in the chapter. Indeed, in *Holdich*, the Scottish Outer House aptly described the type of psychiatric injury claim arising from property damage as being 'less pure' than the traditional type of case where C suffers no damage at all, other than psychiatric injury.[33]

---

[26] Judicial College (12th edn, 2013) 1.   [27] [2011] EWHC 1062 (QB).
[28] (2001) 57 BMLR 158 (QB), quotes at 158, 164.   [29] [2014] EWHC 4053 (QB) [1].
[30] [1987] EWCA Civ 8, [1988] QB 304, especially 320.   [31] [2009] EWCA Civ 37, [2010] 1 QB 1, [55].
[32] [2013] CSOH 197, 2014 SLT 495.   [33] *ibid*, [89].

The framework

A convenient framework for an analysis of this rather complicated area of the law is as follows:

Nutshell analysis: Pure psychiatric injury

Pre-conditions:

#1 proof of a recognised psychiatric injury
#2 the type of C must be identified – whether C is a primary victim; a secondary victim; an elevated primary victim; a fear-of-the-future C; a residuary C; or a stress-at-work C

Proving duty of care (for *that particular* category of C) – a checklist:

the 'primary victim' claimant

- for *Page v Smith*-type Cs, reasonable foreseeability of psychiatric *or* physical injury; for other primary victims, reasonable foreseeability of psychiatric injury
- legal proximity, according to the usual proximity factors
- the 'normal fortitude' rule does not apply
- whether shock is required is unclear
- public policy considerations may apply to preclude a duty from being owed

the 'secondary victim' claimant

- reasonable foreseeability of psychiatric harm
- relational proximity: close ties of love and affection
- spatial and temporal proximity
- direct perception of events
- the 'normal fortitude' rule applies
- proof of 'shock', in the legal sense, *is* required
- public policy considerations may apply to preclude a duty from being owed

the 'elevated primary victim' claimant

- not a *Page v Smith*-type claimant
- the 'normal fortitude' rule does not apply
- otherwise, refer to the 'primary victim', above

the fear-of-the-future claimant

- not a *Page v Smith*-type claimant
- the 'normal fortitude' rule applies
- otherwise, refer to the 'primary victim', above

the residuary category of claimant

- reasonable foreseeability of psychiatric harm
- legal proximity (depending on an assumption of responsibility by D to avoid psychiatric harm to C, and reliance by C upon D's exercising that responsibility)
- public policy considerations may apply

> **the stressed-at-work claimant**
>
> * reasonable foreseeability of psychiatric harm
> * legal proximity, by virtue of employment relationship (but not every employer will be liable for an employee's psychiatric injury)
> * the normal fortitude rule applies to the psychiatrically-vulnerable employee
>
> The rest of the negligence action, as per usual

Occasionally, other aspects of the negligence action can also be in issue, when C is pursuing a negligently-inflicted psychiatric injury claim. For example, fixing the relevant standard of care, and proving breach on the part of D, must be undertaken in the usual way (per Chapters 6 and 7). The usual principles of causation (per Chapter 8) apply – and notably, whether D's breach caused C's psychiatric injury may be just as much at issue as in the case of physical injuries to C (e.g., in the leading case of *Page v Smith (No 2)*,[34] the causal connection between D's breach and C's psychiatric injury was ultimately upheld, having been referred back to the Court of Appeal for decision). The principles of remoteness of damage, as discussed in Chapter 9, also apply – with the noteworthy exception that, in *Page v Smith*, physical injury to C was foreseeable, but the psychiatric injury that actually occurred, whilst unforeseeable, was compensable. This exceptional scenario to the *Wagon Mound* principle,[35] which states the damage suffered must have been of a foreseeable type, is the only instance in English law where C can recover, in negligence, for a type of damage that was unforeseeable. However, in respect of all other types of victims and scenarios described in this chapter, the ordinary *Wagon Mound* principle applies – C, who has suffered psychiatric injury, must show that such injury was reasonably foreseeable.

However, it is in proving a duty of care that most problems arise in negligently-inflicted psychiatric injury suits, and is where this chapter will be focused.

Dealing with each aspect of the abovementioned framework in turn:

PRECONDITION #1: A RECOGNISED PSYCHIATRIC INJURY

The threshold principle

§5.2 As a threshold principle, D cannot be liable to C for negligently-inflicted pure psychiatric injury, unless C suffered a recognisable psychiatric injury. Three different reasons have been judicially given for this principle: legal policy; remoteness of damage; and *de minimis* damage.

Some judges may have differed in the labelling – i.e., a 'genuine psychiatric injury' (per the *Creutzfeldt-Jakob Disease (CJD) Litig, Andrews v Sec of State for Health (Damages Assessments)*[36]); a 'recognised psychiatric injury' (per *White (Frost) v CC of South Yorkshire Police*[37]);

---

[34] [1996] 1 WLR 855 (CA). Note, too, the unsuccessful '*novus actus interveniens*' argument by D in *Farrell v Merton, Sutton and Wandsworth HA* (2000) 57 BMLR 158 (QB).

[35] *Overseas Tankship (UK) Ltd v Morts Dock & Eng Co Ltd (Wagon Mound (No 1))* [1961] AC 388 (PC) 426.

[36] (1998) 54 BMLR 111 (QB) 113.

[37] [1999] 2 AC 455 (HL) 500. Also: *North Glamorgan NHS Trust v Walters* [2002] EWCA Civ 1792, [12], [20]; *Page v Smith* [1996] AC 155 (HL) 167, 190.

or even a 'recognizable psychiatric injury' (per the EWLC, to take account of future psychiatric diagnoses[38]) – but it all represents the same threshold requirement for the level of injury which is compensable.

The principle was established by Lord Bridge in *McLoughlin v O'Brian*,[39] who said that 'the first hurdle which [C] claiming damages of the kind in question must surmount is to establish that he is suffering, not merely grief, distress or any other normal emotion, but a positive psychiatric illness'.

> In *McLoughlin v O'Brian*, Mrs McLoughlin's, C's, husband and three of her children were seriously injured in a car accident, shortly after leaving home. C was at home when the accident happened, about 2 miles away. C was told about the accident by a friend, about an hour after it happened, and she rushed to hospital. C saw her husband and children about two hours after the accident, in a bloodied and badly-injured state. C's daughter later died in hospital. C suffered from depression and personality changes after the accident. **Held:** C suffered a compensable recognised psychiatric injury.

The requirement of a recognised psychiatric injury, as opposed to something less, has been confirmed at the highest English appellate level several times since,[40] and currently represents an incontrovertible dogma of negligence law in this jurisdiction. The position is different, if proof of damage is **not** an ingredient of the tort, such as in assault. In that scenario, mental distress, anger and upset is sufficient to constitute compensable damage (per *RT v CC of the Police Service of Northern Ireland*[41]).

Undoubtedly, the threshold principle acts as an important ring-fence (a 'powerful control mechanism', per *CJD Litigation; Group B Plaintiffs v UKMRC*[42]) for these types of claims. Three reasons have been given for the principle.

i. **Policy reasons.** The requirement is directly attributable to policy (indeed, 'reasons more to do with policy than logic', admitted the Court of Appeal in *White v London Fire & Civil Defence Athy*[43]).

The main policy reason is 'floodgates' concerns, for as Lord Wilberforce remarked in *McLoughlin v O'Brian*: '"shock", in its nature, is capable of affecting so wide a range of people, [so there remains] a real need for the law to place some limitation upon the extent of admissible claims'.[44] That is, the principle ring-fences the potential number of Cs (arising, say, out of a large group of spectators who witness an horrific accident). A number of other policy reasons have been put forward in relevant case law:[45]

---

[38] *English Report*, [2.3].   [39] [1983] 1 AC 410 (HL) 431.

[40] *Calveley v CC of Merseyside Police* [1989] AC 1228 (HL) 1029; *Alcock v CC of South Yorkshire Police* [1992] 1 AC 310 (HL) 422; *Page v Smith* [1996] AC 155 (HL) 167, 171, 181, 189, 197; *White (Frost) v CC of South Yorkshire Police* [1999] 2 AC 455, (HL) 469, 491, 501; *Barber v Somerset CC* [2004] UKHL 13, [2004] 1 WLR 1089 [6]–[7]; *Hicks v CC of South Yorkshire Police* [1992] PIQR P433 (HL) P436; *R v Ireland* [1998] AC 147 (HL) 156; *Wainwright v Home Office* [2003] UKHL 53, [2003] 2 AC 406 [45]–[47], [62].

[41] [2011] NIQB 13, [22].   [42] [2000] Lloyd's Rep Med 161 (QB) 163 (Morland J).   [43] [1999] PIQR P314 (CA) P316.

[44] [1983] 1 AC 410 (HL) 421. Also: *White v CC of South Yorkshire Police* [1992] 2 AC 455 (HL) 493–94; *Page v Smith* [1996] AC 155 (HL) 197; *JD v East Berkshire NHS Trust* [2005] 2 AC 373 (HL) [133] (Lord Brown).

[45] Derived, variously, from: *McLoughlin v O'Brian* [1983] 1 AC 410 (HL); *White (Frost)* [1999] 2 AC 455 (HL) 493–94; *Creutzfeldt-Jakob Disease (CJD) Litig, Andrews v Sec of State for Health (Damages Assessments)* (1998) 54 BMLR 111 (QB); *Hinz v Berry* [1970] 2 QB 40 (CA); and cited also in Mulheron (*OJLS*) 6–7.

- the prospect of disproportionate burdens being imposed on D are correspondingly reduced;
- mental injury is easier to 'fake' or to exaggerate than physical injury, and hence, more deserving of a higher threshold of injury;
- conflicting witness and expert evidence as to the nature, or existence, of mental harm is more likely than in the case of physical injury, so that a reference point based upon external classifications of disorders is more objectively verifiable for a court;
- permitting C to recover for mere mental injury may either act as a disincentive to rehabilitation, or may actually create/prolong that type of mental harm;
- it is not in the best societal interests to permit claims for distress only, given that a certain level of mental fortitude is expected and required;
- from a distributive justice view, physical harm is more important than psychological injury; and
- abusive or vexatious claims are less likely, if the law insists upon C's proving that he has suffered a genuine psychiatric illness.

ii. **Damages too remote.** Alternatively, it was suggested, by Evans LJ in *Vernon v Bosley (No 1)*,[46] that damages for feelings of grief, anxiety, bereavement, etc, are too remote to be compensable in law, and that the principle is 'not [a] policy-induced rule ... but rather, a restriction on the heads of damage which may be recovered by a successful [C].'

However, this observation does not sit comfortably with other judicial observations that mental harm of whatever description is of a 'type' or 'kind' of injury that is foreseeable under the ordinary *Wagon Mound* principle. For example, even in the odd case of *Attia v British Gas plc*,[47] where C suffered an anxiety-based disorder from witnessing the destruction of her home, Bingham LJ was satisfied that when 'applying the ordinary test of remoteness in tort, ... [D] should reasonably have contemplated psychiatric damage to [C] as a real, even if unlikely, result of careless conduct on his part'. In *Alcock* too, Lord Ackner expressly acknowledged that '[m]ere mental suffering' was reasonably foreseeable.[48] Hence, it is submitted that the better view is that grief, anxiety, etc, is not a type of injury that is too remote in law to be recoverable.

iii. **The *de minimis* principle.** It was suggested by Lord Bingham, in *Watkins v Home Secretary*,[49] that distress, anxiety, etc, do not meet the *de minimis* threshold of damage which the law will compensate in negligence (per the principle of '*de minimis non curat lex* – the law does not take account of trifles). *Watkins* was an alleged misfeasance in public office case, but any torts which are not actionable *per se* will require some 'material damage' to be proven: 'an expression understood to include recognised psychiatric illness, but not distress, injured feelings, indignation or annoyance'.

Of the three, the policy justification is by far the most judicially-cited and accepted.

The diagnostic classifications

§5.3   To determine the threshold requirement of a recognised psychiatric injury, English courts typically have regard to two international classifications for psychiatric injury, DSM-V and ICD-10.

---

[46] [1997] PIQR 255 (CA) 313.   [47] [1987] EWCA Civ 8, [1988] QB 304 (CA) 319.
[48] [1992] 1 AC 310 (HL) 401.   [49] [2006] UKHL 17, [2006] 2 AC 395, [7].

The Court of Appeal observed, in *Sutherland v Hatton*,[50] that there was a 'considerable degree of international agreement on the classification of mental disorders and their diagnostic criteria' in English law, by reference to the following two classifications:

- the American Diagnostic and Statistical Manual of Mental Disorders (DSM-V), i.e., the 5th edition of the Manual, produced by the American Psychiatric Assn;[51] and
- the International Statistical Classification of Mental and Behavioural Disorders (ICD-10), i.e., the 10th revision of the classification by the World Health Organisation.[52]

Under each classification, each recognised mental disorder is given a unique reference code. It was said, in *Dickie v Flexcon Glenrothes Ltd*, that there was 'no suggestion that one was better than the other, although DSM-IV covers a wider range of symptoms and is more prescriptive than its ICD counterpart'.[53] Certainly, from a psychiatrist's perspective, DSM-V is more-developed than ICD-10, given its exclusive focus on mental health.

The use of these diagnostic classifications in the medico-legal context has given rise to four particular dilemmas, *viz*, (1) the classifications were never designed or intended for legal use, and hence, the several caveats and qualifications that exist in both DSM-IV and ICD-10 for diagnostic purposes are routinely overlooked, and are rarely mentioned in judgments; (2) there is continuing uncertainty as to whether the classifications are *a*, or *the*, reference point for a recognised psychiatric illness at law;[54] (3) whether judges, and not expert psychiatric witnesses, should (or can) decide whether the criteria in the classifications are satisfied, or whether deference to the psychiatrist experts is always required, remains uncertain;[55] and (4) a court's reliance on the classifications can be problematical, where changing diagnostic criteria have not been incorporated.[56] These difficulties have been analysed by the author in further detail elsewhere.[57]

What is excluded

§5.4 A number of emotional manifestations or reactions are not compensable injuries, where pure mental injury is claimed. These include: grief, distress, apprehension, annoyance, worry, sorrow, fear, anxiety, outrage, shame, horror or despondency.

For a claim for pure psychiatric injury, '[e]motional responses to unpleasant experiences of even the most serious type do not found a claim for damages' (as the court put it in *RK v Oldham NHS Trust*[58]). It follows that a number of Cs have been unable to advance their claims, as this sample shows:

---

[50] [2002] EWCA Civ 76, [5] (Hale LJ), aff'd on appeal: *Barber v Somerset CC* [2004] UKHL 13.

[51] Published in May 2013 (see: http://www.dsm5.org/Pages/Default.aspx). DSM-IV-TR, was published in 1994, and revised in 2000.

[52] Published 1992. The 11th revision is due by 2017 (see: http://www.who.int/classifications/icd/revision/en/).

[53] [2009] Scot (D) 3/11 (Sheriff Court, Kircaldy, 4 Sep 2009) [129].

[54] Contrast: *CJD Litigation; Andrews v Sec of State for Health (Damages Assessment)* (1998) 54 BMLR 111 (QB) 113, with *Hussain v CC of West Mercia Police* [2008] EWCA Civ 1205, [16], and see too: *Wild v Southend Univ Hosp NHS Foundation Trust* [2014] EWHC 4053 (QB) [3].

[55] See, e.g.: *Calvert v William Hill Credit Ltd* [2008] EWHC 454 (Ch) [134], point not considered on appeal: [2008] EWCA Cvi 1427.

[56] See, e.g.: *Murtagh v MOD (Ireland)* [2008] IEHC 292 (re PTSD).

[57] 'Rewriting the Requirement for a "Recognized Psychiatric Injury" in Negligence Claims' (2012) 33 *OJLS* 1, 10–19 (sources and citations mostly omitted).

[58] [2003] Lloyd's Rep Med 1 (QB) [20].

In *Reilly v Merseyside HA*,[59] Mr Reilly, C, a hospital visitor, was trapped in a jammed hospital lift for a considerable time, and suffered an anxiety disorder; 'here there was no recognisable psychiatric injury, but only normal emotion in the face of a most unpleasant experience'. The temporary physical manifestations of vomiting and sweating were not sufficient to constitute physical damage either. In *RK v Oldham NHS Trust*,[60] baby MK, C, suffered a spiral fracture of her leg when two months old, and a paediatrician, D, wrongly diagnosed the injury as 'non-accidental'. MK was removed from her parents' home. After brittle bone disease was correctly diagnosed, MK was returned to her parents' care, after a separation of eight months. MK displayed behavioural disturbances and reduced development of 'the attachment dynamic' between parents/child. The medical evidence was that MK had suffered a psychological injury, but not a genuine psychiatric illness (the extreme youth of MK making a diagnosis of the latter very difficult).

In neither of the above did C meet the threshold pre-requisite of a genuine psychiatric disorder.

One exceptional case in which damages were awarded for 'ordinary shock' (*Whitmore v Euroways Express Coaches Ltd*[61]) was described by the EWLC as 'an aberration';[62] and the author's searches have not revealed any case in which *Whitmore* has been either cited or followed since, apart from a very brief reference in *Ravenscroft v Rederiaktiebølaget Transatlantic*.[63]

Perhaps more significantly, though, it was suggested by Maurice Kay LJ, in the misfeasance case of *Hussain v CC of West Mercia Constabulary*,[64] that English law may have set the bar too high, in requiring proof of a recognised psychiatric injury for negligently-inflicted mental harm. Rather, his Lordship used the terminology of 'a grievous non-physical reaction' to describe the threshold which could give rise to a claim for pure mental injury arising from misfeasance. Additionally, he said (dicta) that: 'what Lord Bridge was concerned to discount in *McLoughlin v O'Brian* was "normal human emotions", not significantly abnormal manifestations of non-physical sequelae. If my approach does not live easily with the established approach in cases of negligence resulting in personal injury, I would strive to treat misfeasance in public office exceptionally'.[65] However, this view that something lesser will (and should) constitute compensable harm has not received other English judicial support – although it does enjoy considerable support in some other jurisdictions.

The comparative corner: Something lesser will do

New Zealand: in *J&P Van Soest v Residual Health Management Unit*[66] (a case concerning fatal medical mistreatment of patients by a cardiac surgeon at the Christchurch Public Hospital), Thomas J (in the minority of the NZCA) held that 'mental suffering ... of the order, or approaching the order, of a psychiatric illness and therefore plainly outside the range of ordinary human experience' should be compensable. The majority disagreed, as assessing what suffering fell outside 'ordinary human experience' would make the test unworkable, and floodgates problems may arise, 'to throw the courts open to everyone caused distress by the negligent injuring of a loved one'.

---

[59] (1994) 23 BMLR 26 (CA) 30. See, for similar facts: *AD v Bury MBC* [2006] EWCA Civ 1.
[60] [2003] Lloyd's Rep Med 1 (QB) [20].   [61] *The Times*, 4 May 1984.
[62] *English Report*, [2.3], fn 15.   [63] [1991] 3 All ER 73 (QB) 80.
[64] [2008] EWCA Civ 1205. Sir Anthony Clarke MR preferred to leave the issue on another occasion.
[65] *ibid*, [19] and [20].
[66] [1999] NZCA 206, [2000] 1 NZLR 179, [83] (Thomas J), [69] (Blanchard J, giving the majority judgment).

Canada: in *Mustapha v Culligan of Canada Ltd*[67] (a case concerning dead flies in an unopened bottle of drinking water), McLachlin CJ (writing for the court) suggested that something less than a recognised psychiatric injury could suffice for negligently-inflicted mental harm: '[t]he law does not recognize upset, disgust, anxiety, agitation, or other mental states that fall short of injury. I would not purport to define compensable injury exhaustively, except to say that it must be *serious and prolonged and rise above the ordinary annoyances, anxieties and fears that people living in society routinely, if sometimes reluctantly, accept* ... minor and transient upsets do not constitute personal injury, and hence do not amount to damage.' In *Healey v Lakeridge Health Corp*,[68] the Ontario CA said that, '[t]he precise manner in which the threshold is defined or identified is a matter of legitimate debate'.

United States: the tort of negligent infliction of emotional distress requires 'mental anguish', which can comprise a spectrum of emotional disturbances, from a recognisable psychiatric injury, to lesser emotions of, say, grief, embarrassment or anger (per *Renville v Fredrickson*[69]).

Hence, clearly there is some level of judicial unease – both with the English and overseas judiciary – about the delineation between **degrees** of compensable mental damage.

Subtle distinctions abound

Much will depend upon the psychiatric evidence adduced – and the delineations between compensable and non-compensable injuries can appear, at least to the lay-person, to be very fine indeed.

In *Ward v Leeds Teaching Hosp NHS Trust*,[70] Mrs Ward's, C's, daughter, Katherine, entered hospital to have her wisdom teeth removed, but failed to regain consciousness after the operation, and died two days later. The NHS Trust, D, denied that any duty of care was owed to C in respect of her claim for PTSD. **Held:** C failed, because (inter alia) C suffered 'a severe and prolonged bereavement reaction', described by the court in terms that cast doubt on whether it was a recognised psychiatric illness worthy of compensation. In *Tredget and Tredget v Bexley HA*,[71] Mrs Tredget, C1, gave birth to her son amid chaos and pandemonium in the delivery theatre. Mr Tredget, C2, was present at the delivery, and was asked to encourage his wife during the delivery. The baby, severely asphyxiated, died of his injuries when 48 hours old. Both Cs sued for pathological unresolved mourning caused by their child's death. **Held:** C could recover for pure psychiatric injury (£32,500 for C2, and £17,500 for C1).

So, in legal terms, pathological unresolved mourning was deserving of compensation, but a severe bereavement reaction was not. On such fine delineations turn the success of C's claim.

Another subtle distinction is that C may try to circumvent the need to prove a recognised psychiatric injury, by establishing some actionable physical injury which would enable C to

[67] [2008] SCC 27, (2008), 293 DLR (4th) [9].   [68] [2011] ONCA 55, (2011), 328 DLR (4th) [43], [66] (Sharpe JA).
[69] 324 Mont 86, 89 (Mont SC 2004).   [70] [2004] EWHC 2106 (QB) [18].
[71] [1994] 5 Med LR 178 (Central London CC) 181.

recover some lesser psychological injury as being consequential upon that physical injury. Not only does this tactic obviate the need to bring a claim for **pure** psychiatric injury, but it would also render engagement with the arbitrary rules governing primary–versus–secondary–victim recovery unnecessary. There are **three** possible ways in which proof of some physical injury may permit a route to the recovery of a lesser type of mental harm, such as distress, worry, etc:

i. the psychological disturbance may, medically-speaking, arise directly from a physical impairment that is, itself, non-observable (e.g., a disturbance in C's central nervous system), but which constitutes a physical impairment, in itself, that is compensable;

ii. in reverse, C's psychological damage may have translated into some actionable physical damage. In *Morris v KLM Royal Dutch Airlines*,[72] C's peptic ulcer disorder was brought about by a psychological disturbance, and he could recover for that ulcer. By contrast, in *Hussain*,[73] C argued that he had physical symptoms of anxiety (*viz*, discomfort and numbness in his left arm and leg when 'under stress') which amounted to physical injury, but it was held that these physical manifestations were simply not significant enough to cross the *de minimis* threshold to be recoverable at law; and

iii. if D's act or omission causes C some physical injury, then the cause of action is complete upon proof of immediate physical damage, and damages are then recoverable for any consequential anxiety, worry, etc, associated with that physical damage, as PSLA heads of damage. As Lord Steyn stated in *White (Frost) v CC of South Yorkshire Police*, '[t]here are those whose mental suffering was a concomitant of physical injury. This type of mental suffering is routinely recovered as "pain and suffering", where "mental suffering" was said to include either a recognised psychiatric illness or something lesser such as "extreme grief"'.[74] For this reason, it would be helpful for C to construe physiological changes as 'physical damage', to which anxiety-based damages can 'tag' or attach. To date, English authority does not support either symptomless physiological change to the human body, or the inhalation, ingestion or absorption of chemical compounds, as constituting 'physical injury' upon which anxiety-based damages could be grafted.

In the *Pleural Plaques Litig*,[75] arising from wrongful asbestos exposure in the workplace, 9 of the 10 test Cs had not suffered any recognised psychiatric illness as a result of their developing pleural plaques from that wrongful exposure. (The 10th victim, Mr Grieves, was the only C to suffer a recognised psychiatric injury, *viz* depression, and hence, his claim was legally treated differently, discussed later.) All nine test Cs had each suffered anxiety and a physiological change, caused by the presence of symptomless pleural plaques in their lungs. The crucial question for these Cs was whether that physiological change amounted to physical *damage*. **Held (CA, 2:1, HL, 5:0):** the pleural plaques were not physical damage, and hence, any claims for 'tagged-on' anxiety-based damages could not succeed. An earlier line of authority,[76] upholding that pleural plaques were actionable physical damage, was overruled.

---

[72] [2001] EWCA Civ 790.   [73] [2008] EWCA Civ 1205.   [74] [1999] 2 AC 455 (HL) 491.

[75] *Grieves v Everard & Sons* [2006] EWCA Civ, aff'd: *Johnston v NEI Intl Combustion Ltd* [2007] UKHL 39.

[76] i.e., cases against the MOD: *Church* (1984) 134 NLJ 623 (QB); *Sykes* (1984) 134 NLJ 783 (QB); *Patterson* [1987] CLY 1194, all noted in *Pleural Plaques*, [3]–[6].

The law reform corner: The threshold damage

The English Comm:[77] the Negligence (Psychiatric Illness) Bill required a 'recognizable psychiatric illness'.

The Scottish Comm:[78] although the law was right to impose the threshold principle, there will be cases 'in which drawing the line between a recognised psychiatric injury or disorder, and mere stress or anxiety, may not be easy.'

The Ipp Committee:[79] despite the widespread reliance of C's experts on DSM-IV in seeking to prove a recognisable psychiatric illness, such reliance may be misplaced, given that the Manual warns against its use in legal contexts, and that it was developed as a tool for clinical, not legal, purposes. It recommended, instead, that a panel of experts develop guidelines for compensable psychiatric illnesses for use in litigious contexts.

PRECONDITION #2: THE TYPE OF CLAIMANT

§5.5   The requirements for establishing that D owed C a duty of care to avoid C's psychiatric injury differ, depending upon the type of C.

The establishment of a duty of care in this area of negligence depends very much upon the type of claimant – some types have a far easier job of proving the criteria than others. There are *six* possible categories of C who may suffer from pure psychiatric injury, which categories are not mutually exclusive. To summarise:

the 'primary victim' C	EITHER a person who is directly involved in a traumatic or dangerous event as a participant, and in the zone of physical danger, but who, although not physically harmed, suffers from a psychiatric injury, OR a guilt-ridden person
the 'secondary victim' C	a person who is a spectator to a traumatic or dangerous event which injures or kills a loved one, and who suffers from a psychiatric injury as a result of what he witnessed
the 'elevated primary victim' C	a person who appears to be a secondary victim, but who is 'elevated' to fulfil the role of primary victim, given that there is no-one who is ultimately killed or injured
the stressed-at-work C	a person who suffers from a psychiatric injury in the workplace, from undertaking the ordinary tasks which form part of that employee's job description
the fear-of-the-future C	a person who is exposed to a disease-causing agent, and who suffers no immediate physical injury, but who develops a psychiatric injury from the despair and worry that the disease will manifest in the future ('the worried well')
the residuary category of C	the person who develops a psychiatric injury as a result of the negligent act or omission of D, and who does not fit within any of the abovementioned categories, but obtains compensation nevertheless

---

[77] *English Report*, [5.3], [5.5]–[5.6].   [78] *Scottish Report*, [2.3].   [79] *Ipp Report*, [9.6], and Rec #33.

The law's recognition of an entitlement to recovery for pure psychiatric injury is usually traced to *Dulieu v White & Sons*,[80] and *Bourhill v Young*,[81] for primary and secondary victims, respectively. However, the differing duty of care criteria, depending upon the type of victim – and the expansion of the categories beyond the primary/secondary victim dichotomy – is primarily why the category of C must be correctly identified at the outset. The existence of a duty of care is the *principal* battleground for C's alleging pure psychiatric injury.

Dealing with each category in more detail:

Primary victims

The changing definition

§5.6   The *main* type of primary victim is where C is in the range of foreseeable physical injury from D's act or omission, as a participant who was in the 'zone of danger', and who suffers no physical injury as a participant, but who suffers psychiatric injury instead. The 'zone of danger' may constitute either physical injury/death or a loss of bodily integrity (e.g., imprisonment). Alternatively, a primary victim is one who genuinely believes that he has been the unwitting cause of, or a contributing factor in, another's injury, death or imperilment.

In *North Glamorgan NHS Trust v Walters*, a primary victim was defined as 'one who was *involved, either mediately or immediately as a participant*, as opposed to one who was no more than a passive or unwilling witness or spectator to the injury caused to another'.[82] This was a paraphrase of the House of Lords definition in *Alcock v CC of Yorkshire Police* (the relatives' claim in Hillsborough).[83]

However, and to contribute some considerable confusion to the issue, the House of Lords has subtly varied the definition of the primary victim since *Alcock*, as the following Table shows:

The changing primary victim definition		
Case	about ...	The evolving PV definition ...
Alcock v CC of South Yorkshire Police (1992)	Hillsborough stadium disaster (relatives' claims)	someone 'involved, either mediately or immediately, as a participant' in the event which gave rise to his psychiatric illness – such 'participants' would include (a) those who feared for their own safety; (b) rescuers who go to the assistance of others; and (c) 'unwilling participants in the event', including guilt-ridden parties (Lord Oliver)
Page v Smith (1996)	car accident	someone who was 'a participant' – i.e., someone 'directly involved in the accident' and 'well within the range of foreseeable physical injury' – 'someone who is in the range of foreseeable physical injury flowing from an event, even though he suffers no actual physical injury, provided that he was in fact exposed to a risk of physical injury, or reasonably believed that he was so exposed' – i.e., within the 'zone of danger' (Lord Lloyd)[a]

[a] [1996] AC 155 (HL) 184. The expression, 'zone of danger', was used by Henry LJ in *Frost* (CA) to describe the *Page* test. It was sourced to US authority in *Grieves* [2006] EWCA Civ, [88].

[80] [1901] 2 KB 669 (KB).   [81] [1943] AC 92 (HL) 103.   [82] [2002] EWCA Civ 1792, [12] (emphasis added).
[83] [1992] 2 AC 310 (HL) 407–8 (Lord Oliver).

White (Frost) v CC of South Yorkshire Police (1999)	Hillsborough stadium disaster (police claims)	someone within the range of foreseeable risk of injury (i.e., within the 'zone of physical danger') – as a 'threshold requirement', he must have objectively been exposed to danger and a risk of physical injury, or reasonably believed that he was so exposed (Lord Steyn)[b]
W v Essex CC (2001)	child abuse by foster child	someone who (a) is himself in the range of foreseeable physical injury/zone of physical danger; or (b) believes that he has been the unwitting cause of, or a contributing factor in, another's injury, death or imperilment – the primary victim is an 'unwilling participant in the event' (Lord Slynn)[c]
Rothwell v Chemical and Insulating Co (Pleural plaques litigation (2007)	asbestos exposure causing pleural plaques	someone who was himself in the range of foreseeable physical injury/zone of physical danger ('who suffers psychiatric injury caused by fear or distress resulting from involvement in an accident caused by [D's] negligence or its immediate aftermath') (and W v Essex CC was not referred to) (Lord Hope)[d]

[b] 1999] 2 AC 455 (HL) 499 (Lord Steyn).
[c] [2001] 2 AC 592 (HL) 601 (Lord Slynn, with whom the other members of the House agreed).
[d] [2007] UKHL 39 (a conjoined appeal from: Grieves v FT Everard & Sons [2006] EWCA Civ 27).

It is evident that *Alcock's* definition of 'primary victim' – which has never been explicitly overruled – was much wider than **any** of the definitions that followed it. The definition of primary victim in *Page v Smith*, *White (Frost)*, and *Pleural Plaques*, all closely resemble each other, and posit the primary victim as one in the zone of physical danger. *W v Essex CC* was significant, because it drew the 'guilt-ridden' participant back into the primary victim definition, as an 'involuntary participant', **and** it circumvented the requirement that the primary victim must have been within the range of foreseeable physical injury: that is a sufficient, but not a necessary, pre-requisite for a primary victim. The *W v Essex* line of authority has been approved by the House of Lords since (in *JD v East Berkshire Community Health NHS Trust*[84]). In *Pleural Plaques*, however, the House of Lords did not refer to *W v Essex* at all, citing only the 'zone of physical danger' definition. Indeed, *Pleural Plaques* (2007) was itself a difficult decision, given that (as the author has noted elsewhere):

> the five speeches created a myriad of difficulties for primary victim analysis: Lord Hope and Lord Mance thought it doubtful whether the leading case on primary victims, *Page v Smith*, had been correctly decided, and said that it should be reviewed on another occasion; in contrast, the other three members of the court either stated or assumed that *Page* was correct. Only Lord Hope offered any definition of the primary victim, and none of their Lordships made any reference to the various (and differing) primary victim definitions that have been given by the House of Lords since *Page*.[85]

[84] [2005] UKHL 23, [2005] 2 AC 373, [27].
[85] 'The "Primary Victim" in Psychiatric Illness Claims, etc' (2008) 19 *KCLJ* 81, 83 (footnotes omitted).

Hence, the whole landscape of just who is a primary victim remains somewhat murky and confused.

Furthermore, the policy of the House of Lords in the area of negligently-inflicted psychiatric injury has been difficult to discern. On the one hand, it contemplated, in *W v Essex*, the ongoing development of rather loose boundaries for those who may constitute a primary victim C, with Lord Slynn remarking that the categorisation of primary/secondary victims was not 'finally closed. It is a concept still to be developed in different factual situations'.[86] On the other hand, in *White*, Lord Steyn said that the *Alcock* definition was deliberately couched to limit the 'ever widening circle of plaintiffs'. Yet it seems that the courts' desire to limit the number of potential primary victim claims has wavered, for *Essex* clearly contemplates a larger number of potential primary victims than *White* did. Given all this development post-*Alcock*, it is somewhat surprising that the Court of Appeal in *Walters*, in 2003, chose to paraphrase *Alcock's* relatively distant definition of primary/secondary victims delivered back in 1992, and omit the developments in between!

Those included within primary victim status

The abovementioned refinements and adjustments in legal position mean that, essentially, a primary victim can take two forms: the 'zone-of-danger' primary victim, and the 'guilt-ridden' primary victim. Expanding upon each category in turn:

'Zone-of-danger' primary victims. This type of victim has featured in the following scenarios:

- where C was involved in a car accident, due to D's negligent driving:

  In *Page v Smith*,[87] Mr Page, C, was involved in a relatively minor car accident, due to the negligent driving of Mr Smith, D, who turned right immediately into C's path. C's previous myalgic encephalomyelitis (ME) (or CFS), which he had suffered for some 20 years, became chronic and permanent. That type of injury was deemed to be unforeseeable, arising from a minor car accident. **Held (3:2):** C was a primary victim, and could recover for his pure psychiatric injury. He was in the zone of physical danger, as the victim of a car accident. In *Boumedien v Delta Display Ltd*,[88] Mr Boumedien, C, was in bed asleep in his ground floor bedroom in the middle of the night, when D's car crashed into the front garden wall of his property. C was not physically injured, but was very shocked and frightened, and thought that his house was falling down or that there had been an earthquake. C suffered a psychiatric illness. **Held:** C was a potential primary victim, being within the range of foreseeable physical injury.

- where C was involved in a workplace accident or incident, due to employer D's negligence:

  In *Donachie v CC of the Greater Manchester Police*,[89] Mr Donachie, C, a police officer with the Crime Squad, had to undertake nine separate and highly-risky trips by foot to tag the underside of a criminal gang's car, due to a faulty battery in the tagging device. C was subjected to the fear of serious injury or death if observed by the gang during a tagging operation. C had a particular vulnerability to stress because of a pre-existing hypertension condition, and this eventually led to a stroke. **Held (trial):** C lost his claim, given his pre-existing vulnerability to psychiatric injury. **Held (CA):** C could recover for his psychiatric injury, as he was a *Page*-type primary victim, in the zone of

---

[86] [2000] UKHL 17, [2001] 2 AC 592, 601.
[87] [1996] AC 155 (HL) (Lord Lloyd gave the majority speech, Lords Ackner and Browne-Wilkinson agreeing).
[88] [2008] EWCA Civ 368, [6].   [89] [2004] EWCA Civ 405.

danger. In *Young v Charles Church (Southern) Ltd*,[90] Mr Young, C, a construction worker, handed a scaffold pole to his co-employee, who accidentally brought it into contact with live overhead power lines. The co-employee was killed instantly, and another employee nearby suffered burns. C was not physically injured, but suffered psychiatric illness. **Held (trial):** C lost his claim, because he was not a 'participant in the accident', but merely very close to it. **Held (CA):** C was a primary victim, as he was in the area of physical danger created by D's negligent system of work in allowing scaffolding to be erected near 'live' powerlines.

- where C was the victim of medical misdiagnosis or mistreatment by D:

  In *RK v Oldham NHS Trust*,[91] facts previously, baby MK was in the zone of physical danger, because she was a sufferer of undiagnosed brittle bone disease, but did not suffer the requisite psychiatric injury.

- where C was in the vicinity of a violent person or a violent act, because of D's negligence:

  In *A v Essex CC*,[92] adoptive parents, Mr and Mrs A, C, were not told by the council, D, that their adopted son, William, was extremely disturbed and violent. D was aware, before the placement, that William had a history of aggression towards family members, and that Mr A was mentally fragile. William caused psychiatric injuries to both parents, as a result of his bad behaviour (which included throwing an iron at their natural child). **Held:** D owed C a duty of care to avoid psychiatric injury, as C were within the range of foreseeable physical injury (the 'zone of danger') from William's behaviour. In *Burns v Boots UK Ltd*,[93] Margaret Howieson, C, went shopping in Dundee with her family, including Alyssa, 20 months, who was in a child buggy. Whilst other family members went into a Boots (D's) store, C stayed with the children outside. A rolling pin fell from a third floor window of D's store, striking Alyssa on the head as she sat in her buggy, fracturing her skull. C took the screaming infant into her arms, and suffered psychiatric injury. **Held:** C was a primary victim, for standing right beside Alyssa, she was also within the range of foreseeable physical injury.

However, in *McLoughlin v Jones*,[94] Hale LJ took a different tack regarding 'physical injury', holding that 'loss of liberty is just as much an interference in bodily integrity as is loss of a limb' (Brooke LJ considered that it was an 'interesting point ... clearly worthy of full argument on some other occasion'). Clearly, that concept of what amounts to 'physical injury' goes well beyond the *Page v Smith* scenario of potential broken bones, etc, in the eyes of some judicial opinion.

In *McLoughlin v Jones*, Mr McLoughlin, C, was charged with grievous bodily harm and robbery. At his trial, he was represented by a firm of solicitors, D. C was convicted and sentenced to four years' imprisonment. After serving three months, C was acquitted at a retrial, because of new witness evidence which had not previously been available. C alleged that D had conducted his defence negligently, and that he suffered serious depression as a result of his wrongful imprisonment. **Held:** D owed C a duty of care to avoid the psychiatric injury. C was a primary victim, arguably 'the same sort of primary victim as in *Page v Smith*', because conviction and imprisonment was an interference with his bodily integrity.

---

[90] (1997) 39 BMLR 146 (CA) (C was not a secondary victim either).   [91] [2003] Lloyd's Rep Med 1 (QB) [20].
[92] [2003] EWCA Civ 1848, [2004] 1 WLR 1881.   [93] [2011] CSOH 182.
[94] [2001] EWCA Civ 1743, with quotes in text and case description at [49] (Brooke LJ) and [57] (Hale LJ).

'Guilt-ridden' primary victims. This was clearly an additional category to the 'zone of danger' primary victim, given that, in *W v Essex CC*,[95] Lord Slynn expressly acknowledged that, 'it is beyond doubt that [C] were not physically injured by the abuse and ... it does not seem reasonably foreseeable that there was a risk of sexual abuse of the parents [by G]'.

Although the 'guilt-ridden' C was approved as a potential primary victim in *W v Essex CC* (as discussed above), the 'survivor guilt' victims have actually had a very chequered history, insofar as recovery for psychiatric injury is concerned. That a person who is the unwitting cause of another's peril could be a primary victim has some early precedence (in *Dooley v Cammell Laird & Co Ltd*[96]), but this was described in less-than-endorsing terms by Lord Jauncey in *Alcock* as a 'very special case'.[97] The category, however, certainly was encompassed within Lord Oliver's description, in *Alcock*, of an 'involuntary participant'. The possibility was then directly canvassed, but *failed*, in *Hunter v British Coal Corp*[98] – which was decided in 1999, post *Page v Smith* in 1996, and pre-*W v Essex* in 2001. Subsequently, of course, the guilt-ridden primary victim was approved in *W v Essex CC*[99] – without the inconsistency with *Page v Smith* being explained or reconciled. Additionally, *Hunter* was only briefly referred to in *Essex*, but without any detailed discussion. Then, in the *Pleural Plaques* litigation, the primary victim was again expressed solely in *Page v Smith*-type terms, and *W v Essex*, and the guilt-ridden victims, were (confusingly) not referred to at all.

Hence, whilst the guilt-ridden victim is endorsed as a primary victim at the highest appellate level in English law, all of this represents a chequered and unsatisfactory history. Be that as it may, the 'guilt-ridden' primary victim scenarios have included (but with very mixed success):

- parents whose children were sexually abused:

   In *W v Essex CC*,[100] Mr and Mrs W, C, were approved adolescent foster carers. They accepted G, 15, into their home as a foster-child. C had taken steps to ensure that the council, D, would not place any sexual abuser with them, given that they had four children (aged 8–12) of their own. Unknown to C, but known to D's social worker, G had a history of serious sexual misconduct. G had been cautioned by the police for an indecent assault on his own sister, and was being investigated for an alleged rape. During the month that G stayed with the family, it was alleged that he systematically abused each of C's children. C suffered psychiatric injuries, their marriage broke down, and Mr W was unable to work for long periods. **Held:** the claim could not be struck out; C could proceed to trial as potential primary victims. C were 'unwilling participants', having brought their children and G together under the one roof, and feeling responsible for failing to recognise the seriousness of their children's plight more quickly. In *Merthyr Tydfil County BC v C*,[101] C lived in an area in which the Council, D, was obliged to provide social services. C became aware that her two children had been subjected to inappropriate sexual behaviour by a neighbour's child, X, and C reported the abuse to authorities, who passed on the complaint to D. D advised C to keep her children indoors, but over time, given that X did not appear to be playing outdoors, C allowed her children to play outside again. Two years later, X abused the children again, which C reported to D. D denied that C had ever reported a previous incident; and then allocated the same social worker to both C's and X's families. C suffered psychiatric injury, due to suffering 'irrational guilt feelings that she has been unable to protect her children, and that she felt tormented by uncertainty about how she could protect them

---

[95] [2001] 2 AC 592 (HL) 600–1.   [96] [1951] 1 Lloyd's Rep 271 (Liverpool Assizes).
[97] [1992] 1 AC 310 (HL) 420.   [98] [1999] QB 140 (CA).   [99] [2001] 2 AC 592 (HL).
[100] [2001] 2 AC 592 (HL).   [101] [2010] EWHC 62 (QB) [5].

in the future'. Later, X was removed from her family by D, and placed in foster care. **Held:** C's claim could proceed, given her potential primary victim status as a guilt-ridden C.

• employees who are involved in mishaps and accidents with fellow employees in the workplace:

In *Hunter v British Coal Corp*,[102] Mr Hunter, C, suffered from depression stemming from his (incorrect) belief that he brought about the death of a work colleague who was killed by an exploding water hydrant. C had accidentally backed into the hydrant when operating a forklift, and as he drove away, it exploded. C was at least 30 metres away when the hydrant exploded, and never saw the body of his dead colleague. **Held:** C's claim failed. C was not 'an actor' in the tragic incident, and was not in the zone of physical danger himself: 'the law requires a greater degree of physical and temporal proximity than was present in this case before Mr Hunter could properly be treated as a direct, or primary, victim'. In *Monk v PC Harrington Ltd*,[103] Mr Monk, C, was working at Wembley Stadium, when a temporary platform fell about 20 metres onto two fellow construction workers. C did not observe the accident, but heard about it on his portable radio. C rushed over to both men to assist them. One was very seriously injured and non-responsive and died at the scene, and the other suffered a badly broken leg. C suffered PTSD, and sued his employer in negligence for an unsafe system of work. **Held:** C could not be a primary victim founded on being a guilt-ridden victim because he was unable to save his injured co-employee, because C's psychiatric injury was not induced by a genuine belief that he had caused his co-employee's death.

Those excluded from primary victim status

i. Rescuers. Rescuers (i.e., those who provide medical or other assistance of a type that is neither trivial nor peripheral, per *Monk v PC Harrington Ltd*[104]) are in a much worse position now, post-*White/Frost*, than was the position under Lord Oliver's definition in *Alcock*.

§5.7 Where C rescues X, where the rescue was necessary because of D's negligent act or omission, and where C was in danger during that rescue attempt, then that rescuer qualifies as a primary victim. However, if C as rescuer is *never* in the zone of danger when effecting the rescue, then C is not a primary victim.

Rescuers were expressly classified as primary victims under the *Alcock* definition, but the subsequent *Page v Smith* definition was much narrower. Subsequently, in *White (Frost)*, a bare majority of the House of Lords[105] considered that rescuers should **not** be in a 'special category', for the purposes of recovering for psychiatric injury. The dissenters[106] had considered that rescuers **should** remain in the 'special category' that previous decisions such as *Alcock* had placed them, but this view did not prevail.

Rescuers will not always be at risk of physical injury when involved in, or attending to, an accident or its aftermath – and if they are not, then they will not be primary victims. Hence, where C provides rescue services in a particularly grievous accident, and where 'justice may cry out for compensation for the psychiatric harm he suffers in consequence' (to quote a

---

[102] [1999] QB 140 (CA) 149 (Brooke LJ) 154.   [103] [2008] EWHC 1879 (QB), [2009] PIQR P3.

[104] [2008] EWHC 1879 (QB).

[105] [1999] 2 AC 455 (HL) 497, 499 (Lord Steyn), 509–11 (Lord Hoffmann), Lord Browne-Wilkinson agreeing with both.

[106] Lords Goff and Griffiths.

submission in *Greatorex v Greatorex*[107]), C cannot recover, unless he, himself, *was exposed to physical danger*. On that basis, the following did **not** fall into that category:

> In *White (Frost) v CC of South Yorkshire Police*,[108] six police officers, C, who were involved in various forms of post-accident rescue and assistance at the Hillsborough disaster, brought a test case against their employer, D, in negligence, alleging inadequate training. All Cs suffered PTSD, having witnessed gruelling and horrible scenes; one had set up a makeshift morgue; and others had helped the injured and carried the dead from the spectator pens to the middle of the ground. **Held (3:2):** no C could recover damages for psychiatric injury. They were never actually in the zone of physical danger themselves or 'personally threatened'; all danger had passed by the time they arrived. In *Monk v PC Harrington Ltd*,[109] facts previously, **held:** C was not in the zone of danger during/after the scaffolding collapse, and nor was it reasonable for C to think that he was risking his own physical safety in assisting his colleagues.

However, where the rescuers **were** in the zone of danger, they can be classified as primary victims in modern law, post *White/Frost*:

> In *Chadwick v British Transport Comm*,[110] in the Lewisham train disaster of 1957, two trains collided in bad weather, and 90 people were killed. Mr Chadwick, C, lived about 200 yards from the scene, and went to offer assistance. He spent over 7 hours continuously pulling the dead and injured from the train wreckage, and returned to his house covered in mud and blood. Following the accident, C changed from a productive worker, and cheerful man, to a depressed person, unable to work. C died before trial, and his estate sued for C's psychiatric injuries. **Held:** C's estate could recover. The case was explained *ex post facto*, in *White*, on the basis that C, as rescuer, was a primary victim, because he was in danger of the roof collapsing throughout the long night in which he helped pull the dead and injured from the wreckage.

§5.8   However, where rescuer C assists victim D who *self-inflicted* his injuries due to his own negligent or deliberate act, and C suffers a psychiatric injury in effecting that rescue, D does not owe C a duty of care to avoid that psychiatric injury for policy reasons.

This principle stems from *Greatorex v Greatorex*,[111] for two policy reasons:

> In *Greatorex v Greatorex*, Mr Greatorex Jnr was involved in a car accident, after he had been drinking. He was trapped in the car with grievous injuries, and emergency services were called. Coincidentally, the Leading Fire Officer who attended was Mr Greatorex Snr, C, who was the father of the driver. C was nowhere near the scene of the accident when it happened; he attended the accident solely in the course of his employment. C suffered severe PTSD afterwards. **Held:** C could not recover damages as a primary victim, as he was never in any physical danger, nor in fear of any danger, from the car accident.

As a first policy reason, this scenario, whereby a rescuer assists a victim who brought about his own peril, will often (but not always) occur in a family situation. 'Home life may involve many instances of a family member causing himself injury through his own fault'[112] – and it would be contrary to public policy for one family member, who had injured himself, to owe a duty of care to another family member who sought to help and rescue him, and suffered psychiatric injury from what he witnessed. The following examples were provided in *Greatorex*: a father commits suicide and his body is found by his son; or a husband negligently wounds himself

---

[107] [2000] 1 WLR 1970 (QB) 1976.   [108] [1999] 2 AC 455 (HL).   [109] [2008] EWHC 1879 (QB).
[110] [1967] 1 WLR 912 (CA).   [111] [2000] EWHC 223 (QB), [2000] 1 WLR 1970, [66]–[81].   [112] *ibid*, [72].

with a kitchen knife in front of his wife; or a son has extensive loss of blood from a fall caused by his own negligence and is found by his mother. Should the son, the wife and the mother, C, respectively, suffer psychiatric injury, public policy should prevent that psychiatrically-injured relative from suing their injured relative, or the relative's estate, D.

Secondly, for D who self-inflicts an injury to owe a duty of care to his rescuer C would be a serious imposition upon D's right of self-determination. D injures himself – whether negligently or deliberately – but he should not owe a duty to someone who then comes to rescue him. Any such duty should be for Parliament to impose, via legislation (which has never occurred). It is a difficult field of law, and 'Parliament is the best arbiter of what the public interest requires'.[113]

ii. **Fear-of-the-future victims.** The fear-of-the-future victim is distinguishable from the *Page v Smith*, zone-of-physical-danger primary victim.

§5.9 Those who have been exposed to a disease-causing agent, and worry about contracting a disease in the future, are not primary victims under the *Page v Smith* category, notwithstanding that the very fact that C has been exposed to that dangerous agent has put C in the 'zone of danger'.

The leading case sets this principle:

> In *Creutzfeldt-Jakob Disease Litig; Group B Plaintiffs v UKMRC*,[114] several young children, C, who had shown signs of stunted growth, were injected with human growth hormone (HGH) as part of a clinical trial. Studies then suggested that this type of HGH was capable of infecting injectees with Creutzfeldt-Jakob disease, a brain-wasting and untreatable condition that consigned its sufferers to 'unimaginable suffering and certain death'. By 1 Jul 1977, information received by the Dept of Health, D, was that it would be unsafe to continue with the HGH clinical trials. That was forwarded to key Committees with advice to immediately withdraw HGH supplies for clinical use. This was not done. Later, C (the Group B claimants) were informed of the risk of their developing the horrible and incurable CJD, and developed psychiatric injuries. **Held:** Cs were not primary victims. (However, they could recover for their psychiatric injuries, on a separate basis.)

There were **two** principal distinguishing features, according to Morland J, which meant that fear-of-the-future victims were not primary victims:

i. The triggering event for Mr Page's shock was the involvement in the car accident. There was a close temporal proximity between D's breach and C's onset of injury. By contrast, the triggering event for the HGH recipients' distress was from learning, *several years after the treatment*, through medical advisers, friends, family and the media, that they were at risk of developing the disease. Their realisation was also exacerbated by sensationalist media coverage. Hence, the breach in administering the injections when they ought not to have been given was not at all contemporaneous with the onset of C's psychiatric injury. Hence, for primary victims in the zone of danger, they must be within the zone of *immediate* physical danger (i.e., with close temporal proximity to D's act or omission), in order to claim primary victim status. A long gap between D's negligence, and C's psychiatric injury, will not give the immediacy and proximity that a primary victim needs. C's psychiatric injury must be an immediate response to physical danger or to some traumatic event, to constitute a primary victim.

ii. For Mr Page, all the physical danger had passed by the time that his psychiatric injury manifested. However, for the HGH recipients, the physical dangers that they faced were entirely in the future.

---

[113] *ibid*, [77].   [114] (1997) 41 BMLR 157 (QB) 164.

The injection itself was no physical danger – but the contracting of a ghastly terminal disease in the future certainly was. Hence, the *CJD Litigation* was not the same type of case as was *Page v Smith*.

Hence, even though those who are exposed to a disease-causing agent are ostensibly in the zone-of-physical-danger, they are **not** primary victims in the *Page v Smith* sense, in English law. However, whilst they were not treated as primary victims *per se*, they are treated, in English law, as a residuary category of Cs who may prove a duty of care under the *Caparo* test. This avenue is considered later in the chapter.

Secondary victims

Physical injury

§5.10   A secondary victim, C, is a spectator or bystander to the death or injury of an immediate victim which was caused by D's negligence, and who suffers psychiatric injury as a result.

This description was posed by Lord Lloyd in *Page v Smith*;[115] alternatively, it is someone who was a 'passive and unwilling witness of injury caused to others' (per Lord Oliver in *Alcock*[116]).

> In *Alcock v CC of South Yorkshire*, a test case was brought by a range of relatives and friends of the dead and injured in the Hillsborough disaster – brothers, sisters, fiancés, parents, children of the injured and dead, and in a variety of locations – in the ground itself, outside the ground, some at home watching the game on TV in Liverpool. Some had seen the dead bodies at the ground and the makeshift morgue approximately 8 hours after the disaster happened; some saw TV broadcasts; and some saw the events unfold from within the stadium itself from another stand. **Held:** all test Cs failed to recover as secondary victims, because all failed one or more of the criteria for secondary victim recovery.

There is inevitably a tri-partite relationship arising in secondary victim scenarios, as the diagram below shows (with reference to some of the leading cases, discussed in this chapter):

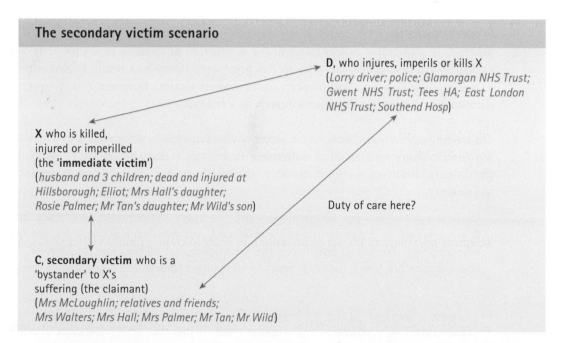

The secondary victim scenario

D, who injures, imperils or kills X
(*Lorry driver; police; Glamorgan NHS Trust; Gwent NHS Trust; Tees HA; East London NHS Trust; Southend Hosp*)

X who is killed, injured or imperilled (the '**immediate victim**')
(*husband and 3 children; dead and injured at Hillsborough; Elliot; Mrs Hall's daughter; Rosie Palmer; Mr Tan's daughter; Mr Wild's son*)

Duty of care here?

C, secondary victim who is a 'bystander' to X's suffering (the claimant)
(*Mrs McLoughlin; relatives and friends; Mrs Walters; Mrs Hall; Mrs Palmer; Mr Tan; Mr Wild*)

---

[115] [1996] AC 155 (HL) 184.   [116] [1992] 1 AC 310 (HL) 407.

Two of these cases concerned fathers, each of whom was present when his child, who died *in utero* due to D's medical negligence, was delivered as a stillbirth. The foetus itself does not have a separate legal personality (unless born alive, as per Chapter 2), and neither father witnessed the actual or threatened death or injury of the child's mother prior to, or at, the stillbirth. Hence, in order to avoid a type of 'legal black-hole', the Court of Appeal confirmed recently, in *Wild v Southend Univ Hosp NHS Foundation Trust*,[117] that *the mother* is to be considered as the immediate victim, to whom the father is a potential secondary victim.

§5.11 The duty of care which D owes to a secondary victim, C, is not derivative from, or reliant upon, legal liability being owed by D to the immediate victim whose peril C witnessed. A duty may be owed to C, even if no liability arises from D to the immediate victim.

D may not be liable to the immediate victim for a number of reasons (e.g., because of some defence), or because there was **no** breach of duty by D towards the immediate victim, or because no damage was proven (e.g., because the immediate victim is not **actually** harmed). Legally-speaking, D may be found to have been negligent towards secondary victim C, without the immediate victim having any cause of action against D at all. Hence, any duty owed to the secondary victim is independent, distinct and separate.

The English Law Commission,[118] together with other law reform bodies,[119] have reiterated this point. The House of Lords has approved of that proposition too. For example, suppose that a parent sees his child in peril, but the child skips away from the incident unharmed – in *Alcock*,[120] Lord Oliver remarked that the parent could be a secondary victim, even though there was no immediate victim existing. Although some courts since have suggested, in dicta, that any duty to the secondary victim is derivative (per *Farrell v Merton, Sutton and Wandsworth HA*,[121] *Hall v Gwent Healthcare NHS Trust*,[122] and in *Storey v Charles Church Developments plc*[123]), both precedent and logic suggest that this is incorrect. There **can** be a secondary victim, without any immediate victim existing.

Property damage

§5.12 Where C is a spectator or bystander to the destruction or damage of C's property which was caused by D's negligence, and who suffers psychiatric injury as a result, C cannot be regarded as a secondary victim to that property as 'immediate victim'. However, C may nevertheless be permitted to recover for psychiatric injury, as a residuary C.

The leading case where C's cherished property was damaged or destroyed, and where C suffered psychiatric injury as a result of witnessing it, is *Attia v British Gas plc*,[124] which pre-dated the primary/secondary victim dichotomy. The treatment of such a C has become increasingly obfuscatory.

In *Attia v British Gas plc*, Mrs Attia, C, lived in a house in Greenford, Middlesex. British Gas, D was engaged to install central heating. When C returned home about 4 pm, she saw smoke billowing from the loft. C telephoned the fire brigade, but by the time they arrived, the whole house was on fire, and it took four hours to bring under control. The house and its contents were

---

[117] [2014] EWHC 4053 (QB) [20]–[22].   [118] *English Report*, [2.22]–[2.24].   [119] *Ipp Report*, [9.31].
[120] *Alcock* [1992] 1 AC 310 (HL) 412.   [121] (2000) 57 BMLR 158 (QB) 161.   [122] [2004] EWHC 2748 (QB) [16].
[123] (1995) 73 Con LR 1, 19.   [124] [1987] EWCA Civ 8, [1988] QB 304.

extensively damaged whilst C watched. D conceded negligence, and settled the property damage aspect of C's claim. However, C also claimed for psychiatric/mental injury, from the shock of seeing her home and its contents ablaze. **Held:** C's claim was permitted to proceed to trial; D owed C a duty to avoid causing psychiatric damage from witnessing the destruction of cherished property.

Bingham LJ gave an example, in *Attia*, of where C may have a similar claim, i.e., where 'a scholar's life work of research or composition was destroyed before his eyes as a result of [D's] careless conduct'.[125] In any event, the injury flowing from property damage was regarded, in *Attia*, as needing to be a recognised psychiatric injury.

In both of these examples, C sustained psychiatric injury, as a result of *witnessing* damage to cherished property. Would the situation be the same, if C did not witness it, but merely was told about the damaged/destroyed property and suffered psychiatric injury as a result? That distinction, between what is and is not directly perceived, is crucial in the law governing recovery by secondary victims of damages for psychiatric injury arising from physical injury, whereby direct perception is a necessary pre-requisite to recovery (as discussed later in the chapter). In *Yearworth v North Bristol NHS Trust*,[126] the English Court of Appeal did not need to decide this issue and left the question open for another day.

In *Yearworth*, six men, Cs, underwent chemotherapy for cancer. Due to the risk that such treatment could damage or remove Cs' fertility, they elected to produce samples of their semen for storage at D's hospital's fertility unit. Prior to the sperm being used, the amount of liquid nitrogen in the storage tanks fell below the requisite level, the automated system for topping up the levels did not work, and they were not manually topped up either. The semen samples thawed and perished. Five Cs suffered psychiatric injuries upon being told that news (the other suffered mental distress). **Held:** the sperm was Cs' property for the purposes of their tort claims; but these Cs were only told of the destruction of their property, they did not witness it. However, they were permitted to proceed with their claims under the law of contract (bailment), which enabled them to recover damages for mere mental distress,[127] as well as for psychiatric injury. In *Holdich v Lothian Health Board*,[128] Mr Holdich, C, elected to have sperm samples stored at D's cryogenic storage facility, prior to receiving treatment for testicular cancer. The liquid nitrogen in the storage vessel in which the sperm was stored leaked, and the temperatures in the vessel raised, rendering the samples unusable. C claimed damages for depression, as a result of the loss of a chance of fatherhood. **Held:** C's claim could proceed in tort.

The Scottish Outer House recently stated, in *Holdich*, that the *Yearworth* Court of Appeal assumed, without deciding, that the primary/secondary classification applied to such cases, that Mrs Attia was considered as a 'primary victim', and that the cancer victims in *Yearworth* were analysed as secondary victims.[129] (However, rather than categorising those Cs as secondary victims, arguably all that the *Yearworth* court was doing was to point out that *direct perception* of the property's destruction may be required for policy reasons, to circumvent the number of potential claims, just as the requirement applies to secondary victims.)

However, in this author's view,[130] these cases of property damage giving rise to psychiatric injury are 'special cases' which fall into the residuary basket, and which do not involve any

---

[125] *ibid*, 320.   [126] [2009] EWCA Civ 37, [2010] 1 QB 1, [55].

[127] Per: *Jarvis v Swans Tours Ltd* [1973] 1 QB 233 (CA).   [128] [2013] CSOH 197, 2014 SLT 495.

[129] *ibid*, [87].   [130] Mulheron, 'The "Primary Victim" in Psychiatric Illness Claims, etc' (2008) 19 *KCLJ* 81, 99–105.

necessity to descend to the primary/secondary victim classification at all. That view is supported by the Court of Appeal in *Boumedien v Delta Display Ltd*,[131] where D negligently crashed his car into C's front garden wall. Smith LJ noted that, 'if this [C] was a victim of [D's] negligence, it was as a primary or ordinary victim; no question arose of his being a secondary victim. He could not claim to be a secondary victim caused by seeing or hearing damage to a wall'. In *Holdich* itself, the Outer House also preferred the view that the primary/secondary classification 'should not arise in sole victim cases, where the allegation is of wrong done directly to [C's] interests, where [C's] identity, as an individual or possibly as a member of a class, is known in advance to [D], and where [D] has a duty of care by virtue of pre-existing legal proximity to safeguard the interest in question'.[132]

To conclude, whether the property is a house, a wall, or sperm, C **may** potentially recover damages for psychiatric injury arising from the destruction of that property, but that will be analysed under the ordinary principles of negligence as residuary Cs (per the *Caparo* and *Hedley Byrne* tests). The better view is that there is **no** question of C's constituting a 'secondary victim', where the property was the 'immediate victim'.

The elevated primary victim

§5.13 Elevated primary victims occur where a would-be secondary victim, C, is not a bystander to any immediate victim (because there is no immediate victim of D's act or omission), and hence, C is treated as a primary victim.

In the typical secondary victim scenario, C is a bystander, and D imperils the immediate victim by his act or omission, which C witnesses and suffers psychiatric injury as a result. However, what if there is no immediate victim at all? Legally speaking, how should C be legally treated then – as a secondary victim for whom there is no immediate victim? Or as a primary victim, because there is no immediate victim to whom he could be a secondary victim?[133]

Controversially, it is the **second** of these options which has been adopted in the key English cases to date. English courts have been reluctant to designate C as a secondary victim, where there is no immediate victim existing. In effect, C has been 'promoted' to the status of primary victim, even though C does not satisfy the definition of primary victim (i.e., C was not in the 'zone of danger', and was not 'guilt-ridden' either). Two cases are illustrative:

In *AB v Leeds Teaching Hosp NHS Trust*,[134] this group litigation[135] arose out of an enquiry into paediatric cardiac surgery at the Bristol Royal Infirmary, which revealed that various babies who had died at, or soon after, birth had had their organs (e.g., brains, lungs, spinal cords and hearts) removed and retained for histopathological examinations, without their parents' consent. The parents, C, alleged that learning of this unauthorised organ retention caused them psychiatric injuries. Lead Cs, Mrs Shorter, Mrs Carpenter, and Mr and Mrs Harris, C, claimed damages for psychiatric injury. **Held:** Cs were classified as primary victims, principally because their children were not immediate victims to whom a duty could

---

[131] [2008] EWCA Civ 368, [6].   [132] [2013] CSOH 197, [88].

[133] This section is partly derived from the analysis in Mulheron, 'The "Primary Victim" in Psychiatric Illness Claims, etc' (2008) 19 *KCLJ* 81, 93–94.

[134] [2004] EWHC 644, [2005] QB 506, especially at [252]–[253], [279].

[135] Certified as a Group Litigation Order under Pt 19.III of the Civil Procedure Rules, and entitled, *Nationwide Organ Retention Group Litigation*.

have been owed post-mortem. However, two of the three Cs failed, because they failed one or more of the duty of care criteria. In *Farrell v Avon HA*,[136] Mr Farrell, C, excitedly attended D's hospital to see his newborn son Jordan (J), who was born of a brief relationship with J's mother (C and the mother were not a couple at the time of J's birth). Upon arriving, C was told that the baby had died, and he was given a corpse to cradle. Twenty minutes later, C was then told that there had been a terrible mistake, and that this was someone else's baby who had died, and that J was alive. C suffered PTSD, and relapsed into previous alcohol and drug dependency. **Held:** C was a primary victim, and recovered £10,000.

These parental Cs were not participants in these incidents; they were not guilt-ridden in the *W v Essex* sense, because they did not cause or contribute to the decision to harvest the organs or imperil their children; and they were not in the zone of physical danger from the hospitals' activities. However, in *AB*, Gage J said that, if there was no immediate victim in respect of whom the parents could be secondary victims, then if they 'are victims at all, they must be primary victims'.[137] One of the most interesting aspects of *Farrell* (and there were many!) was that Mr Farrell would not have satisfied the various secondary victim pre-conditions for recovery. It was fortunate, then, that he was decreed to be a primary victim, as there was no other primary victim – 'the only victim of the incident was [C] himself'; no other person was 'physically involved in the incident as a potential victim'; and '[h]ow can there be a secondary victim if there is no other person who was physically involved in the incident as a potential victim?'[138] However, Mr Farrell clearly did not fit any of the definitions of primary victim.

The elevated primary victim cases

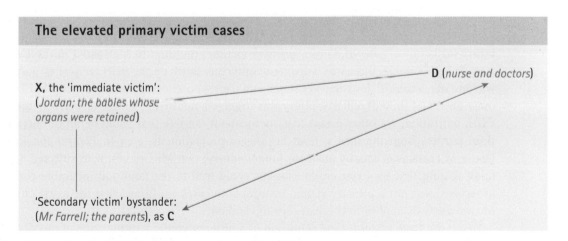

There is a certain logic in *AB's* and *Farrell's* outcomes. A secondary victim imputes, 'secondary to someone' – and without an immediate victim, the secondary victim should be elevated. Otherwise, the definition of Lord Lloyd in *Page v Smith*, of a secondary victim 'in the position of a spectator or bystander', is impossible to apply, in these rather odd cases. In addition, in *AB* and *Farrell*, the secondary victim is the **only** (i.e., the primary) victim of D's negligence. Hence, the case for applying the various control mechanisms that are pertinent to secondary victims do not apply with nearly the same force, in that there will be very few Cs who are psychiatrically injured in a scenario where their immediate victim was not injured or killed.

---

[136] [2001] Lloyd's Rep Med 458 (QB).   [137] [2004] EWHC 644, [2005] QB 506, [199].
[138] [2001] Lloyd's Rep Med 458 (QB) 466, 471.

However, instead of elevating the parents and Mr Farrell to primary victim status, it is strongly arguable that they **ought** to have been treated as secondary victims, with no immediate victim existing. This would enable the primary victim definitions couched by the House of Lords to be applied consistently and meaningfully, rather than departing from those definitions because of the coincidental matter that *the immediate victim* did not happen to be the subject of any actual negligence. Also, given the easier task which primary victims face in establishing a duty of care, a bright-line division between the categories is all the more important to maintain. Finally, to hold that the parents and Mr Farrell must have been primary victims suggests that any duty to a secondary victim must be *derivative* (i.e., that it can only be established if there was some negligence towards the immediate victim) – but as discussed above, the duty to the secondary victim is entirely separate from, and independent of, any duty of care owed to/ negligence toward/harm suffered by the immediate victim. The parents and Mr Farrell would equate to Lord Oliver's example, in *Alcock*, of the child who walked away unharmed from the situation of peril, leaving his psychiatrically-injured parents to claim as secondary victims.

Notably, the decision in *Farrell* has been doubted (in *Walters v North Glamorgan NHS Trust*[139]), but never overruled.

Fear-of-the-future claimants

§5.14   A fear-of-the-future victim of psychiatric injury is not a 'zone of danger' primary victim, despite having been in the zone of danger in contracting a disease later in life. For that C who suffers pure psychiatric injury, the analysis of a duty of care adheres to the tri-partite *Caparo* test.

To reiterate, there were several reasons as to why a fear-of-the-future victim of psychiatric injury (C) is not a 'zone of danger' primary victim, according to Morland J in the *CJD Litigation*.[140] For example, there was no contemporaneous shock on the HGH recipients' part, as there was in *Page v Smith*[141] – whatever shock and distress occurred, happened well after D's acts or omissions; and their psychiatric injury was triggered, not by the wrongfully-given injections of HGH, but rather, via other means (e.g., news about the fate that could befall C, obtained from third parties, from the media, from healthcare professionals, etc). In *Pleural Plaques*,[142] the House of Lords was equally adamant (unanimously) that Mr Grieves, who suffered depression upon fearing that his exposure to asbestos could lead to the fatal and incurable condition of asbestosis, was not a primary victim. Instead, both cases confirmed that the usual *Caparo* duty of care analysis applies to this category of claimant.

Under the *Page v Smith*-type definition of a primary victim – in the zone of physical danger, a participant in the event and not a bystander, someone who did not develop physical injury as a result of D's breach, but who suffered psychiatric injury instead – it is difficult to conceive of how these HGH recipients were not primary victims. The lack of temporal immediacy between their injury and the breach is the only important aspect in which they differed from Mr Page's situation, and on this point, *W v Essex CC*[143] did not require a close contemporaneous link between the Council's breach and the parents' psychiatric injury either.

---

[139] [2002] EWHC 321 (QB) [23].   [140] [2000] Lloyd's Rep Med 161 (QB), (1998) 41 BMLR 157, 163–64.

[141] [1996] AC 155 (HL).

[142] *Johnston v NEI* [2007] UKHL 39, [33] (Lord Hoffmann), [54] (Lord Hope), [77] (Lord Scott), [95] (Lord Rodger), and [104] (Lord Mance). The CA, by majority, had earlier reached the same view: *Grieves* [2006] EWCA Civ 27, [89]–[91] (Lord Phillips (CJ)).

[143] [2001] 2 AC 592 (HL).

Residuary claimants

§5.15 In limited circumstances, C can recover damages for negligently-inflicted psychiatric injury, without establishing primary or secondary victim status at all. Nor is there any question of C's being a stress-at-work or a fear-of-the-future victim. Nevertheless, C is permitted to recover, as a residuary C.

It was suggested by Gage J, in the organ retention case of *AB v Leeds Teaching Hosp NHS Trust*,[144] that those claiming for pure psychiatric injury must be placed in **either** primary **or** secondary victim categories – 'the House of Lords has made it clear that those claiming solely for psychiatric injury must be placed in one or other category'. The majority of English cases have made an earnest attempt to adhere to this viewpoint.

However, the House of Lords has not limited itself in this way. In *Barber v Somerset CC*, the employees' claims for free-standing psychiatric injury, brought about by excessive workloads, were permitted. Not one of their Lordships mentioned *Alcock*, *Page v Smith*, *White*, or *Essex*; and the terminology of primary and secondary victims was not used at all. Fear-of-the-future victims, whilst permitted, have not been treated under the primary/secondary victim framework either. This class of residuary claimant imbues the area with even further uncertainty. The limited circumstances giving rise to the basket of residuary claimants are outlined later in the chapter.

Stress–at–work claimants

§5.16 Workplace stress claims, by employee against employer, have been treated separately from, and outside of, the primary victim/secondary victim classification.

Even though the 'stressed-at-work' employee C has been described as a 'primary victim' in some cases (per *White v CC of South Yorkshire Police*[145]) clearly they are not within the zone of physical danger, nor feel the type of guilt that the primary victim definition requires. No attempt has been made, judicially, to fit them within a *Page v Smith*-type analysis. Also, there is no question of secondary victim status for these employees.

In fact, entirely different principles have been developed by English courts to permit recovery in these types of cases.[146] The 'stressed-at-work' C, for whom the employer has assumed a responsibility to avoid or minimise psychiatric injury, has been able to recover, but only in certain defined circumstances.

In *Johnstone v Bloomsbury HA*,[147] a junior doctor, C, had a breakdown after being required to work at D's hospital, the University College Hospital, as a senior house officer, for excessive hours without rest. His contract of employment provided that he had a standard 40-hour working week, and that, in addition, he would be available on call for a further 48 hours a week on average. On some weeks, C was required to work >100 hours, with inadequate periods of sleep. As a result, C suffered from depression, lethargy, diminished appetite and suicidal feelings. **Held:** C was owed a duty of care to avoid his foreseeable psychiatric injury. This duty was owed, irrespective of the

---

[144] [2004] EWHC 644 (QB), [2005] QB 506, [197].

[145] [1999] 2 AC 455 (HL) 506. Also: *Hatton v Sutherland* [2002] EWCA Civ 76, [21]; *McLoughlin v Jones* [2001] EWCA Civ 1743, [55].

[146] Especially: *Hatton* (*ibid*); *Barber v Somerset CC* [2004] UKHL 13, [2004] 1 WLR 1089.

[147] [1991] IRLR 118.

contractual terms in the employment contract which required him to work overtime. In *Walker v Northumberland CC*,[148] Mr Walker, C, a social worker employed by D, was under an excessive workload, and had a mental breakdown in 1986, for which he had four months of leave. The nature of the work (especially child abuse cases) was inherently very stressful. C was reassured by his superiors that he would receive an assistant and a lower case load when he returned. However, when C returned, he had to deal with the case backlog created whilst he was away, plus a considerable new case load, and had a second breakdown. C was dismissed. C sued D, for failing to take reasonable steps to avoid exposing him to a health-endangering workload. **Held:** C was owed a duty of care. By 1985/86, there was no evidence that those in C's position were particularly vulnerable to stress-induced mental illness, and it was not reasonably foreseeable to D that the workload to which C was exposed gave rise to a material risk of mental illness. However, when C returned to work after his first breakdown, a repetition of illness was reasonably foreseeable, if C was again exposed to the same workload, and C's duties were not alleviated by effective additional assistance.

Conclusion

The categorisation outlined above matters enormously to the legal analysis required to establish a duty of care. As discussed below, primary victims who fall within the *Page v Smith* category possess certain legal advantages over secondary victims. For example, the secondary victim is subject to the 'normal fortitude' rule, whereas a primary victim does not have to cope with the restrictions of that rule. Also, the test of 'reasonable foreseeability' for a primary victim is wider (i.e., **either** physical or psychiatric injury to C must have been foreseen or reasonably foreseeable) than it is for a secondary victim (i.e., it must have been reasonably foreseeable that C would suffer psychiatric injury). Moreover, secondary victims must prove that their psychiatric injuries were induced by 'shock', probably unlike other Cs.

Turning now to the criteria governing the duty of care which each category of C requires:

PRIMARY VICTIM CLAIMANTS

A primary victim C must prove the relevant test of reasonable foreseeability (albeit that the type of test depends upon the type of primary victim at issue); that there was a sufficient legal proximity between wrongdoer D and C who suffered the psychiatric injury (either established by the usual factors of spatial and temporal proximity, or by the proof of an assumption of responsibility by D towards C to avoid causing psychiatric injury); and that public policy favoured the imposition of a duty of care.

Duty of care requirements

Reasonable foreseeability

§5.17 For the 'zone of danger' primary victim who was within the range of foreseeable physical injury, C's psychiatric injury does not have to be foreseeable. As an exception to the usual *Wagon Mound* principle of foreseeability, it is sufficient if there is some foreseeable *physical* injury to C (or to a class of persons of whom C is one) as a result of D's negligence.

---

[148] [1995] 1 All ER 737 (QB).

The *Page v Smith* anomaly. For the 'zone-of-danger' primary victim, *physical* injury will be foreseeable, given that C was in the zone of physical danger – but psychiatric injury may be so unlikely and far-fetched as to be unforeseeable. Nevertheless, the zone-of-danger C can prove the requisite test of foreseeability, according to *Page v Smith*.[149] This is the sole instance, in English law, where C can recover for a type of injury (i.e., psychiatric injury) which was not reasonably foreseeable. This category of C thereby represents a rare exception to the general *Wagon Mound* principle[150] of remoteness, which provides that the damage suffered must have been of a reasonably foreseeable type in order to be compensable.

> In *Page v Smith*, Mr Page's chronic and permanent CFS, arising from his involvement in a minor car accident, was a type of injury which was unforeseeable, but physical injury in a car accident was entirely foreseeable. In *A v Essex CC*,[151] it was 'difficult to accept' that the parents could foreseeably suffer from psychiatric injury as a result of D's placing William, the violent child, with them – but it was certainly foreseeable that William might assault them and damage their property, hence, *Page v Smith* applied.

The justifications for this wide test of foreseeability were put by Lord Lloyd in *Page v Smith*[152] on two bases – first, as a matter of medical diagnosis ('[i]n an age when medical knowledge is expanding fast, and psychiatric knowledge with it, it would not be sensible to commit the law to a distinction between physical and psychiatric injury, which may already seem somewhat artificial, and may soon be altogether outmoded. Nothing will be gained by treating them as different "kinds" of personal injury, so as to require the application of different tests in law'); and secondly, there was no prospect of floodgates of claims, even if a wide test of foreseeability was applied. Lord Lloyd described the foreseeability of physical injury in *Page v Smith* as a 'limiting factor', so that there could be 'no question' of D being liable to the whole world. Merely 'bumping the neighbour's car while parking in the street', where no physical injury to the neighbour was remotely foreseeable, would not render D liable, should the neighbour develop (unforeseeable) psychiatric injury.

In fact, the test of foreseeability is even more claimant-friendly, given that (as discussed in Chapter 2) the correct legal question to ask is, not whether injury to that particular C was foreseeable, but whether injury to *a class of persons of whom C was one*, was foreseeable. Hence, if C's injury arises out of road accident, then the correct question is – should D have reasonably foreseen injury to another road user of any kind. It is **not** correct to ask whether D should have foreseen physical injury to that particular road-user C.

> In *Smith v Co-op Group Ltd*,[153] Joshua Smith, D, 13, was a paper-boy employed by the Co-op, D. He was riding his bike and delivering newspapers to houses in a relatively quiet street, when he rode straight out into the street without looking, and into the path of a lorry being driven by Mr Hammond, C. D was very seriously-injured, and C suffered psychiatric injury as a result of hitting the boy. **Held (trial):** C could not recover: 'I just cannot see that someone of that age [13] would foresee that if he cycles into the road, and is hit by a lorry, that he could foresee physical injury to the lorry driver'. **Held (CA):** C could recover for his psychiatric injury because the correct test was wider: 'it would have been obvious to a boy of 13 that the risk of causing personal injury to another road

---

[149] [1996] AC 155 (HL). Lord Lloyd gave the majority's speech (Lord Ackner and Lord Browne-Wilkinson agreeing).

[150] *Overseas Tankship (UK) Ltd v Morts Dock and Engineering Co Ltd (Wagon Mound (No 1))* [1961] AC 388 (PC) 426.

[151] [2003] EWCA Civ 1848, [2004] 1 WLR 1881, [71].

[152] [1996] 1 AC 155 (HL), with quotes at 188, and 189–90, respectively.

[153] [2010] EWCA 725, [20] (Moore-Bick LJ).

user by cycling across the road without warning would have been great ... he would have realised that the driver (even of a car) might brake violently, swerve or skid, collide with other vehicles or a stationary object and suffer injury as a result'.

Judicial uncertainty about *Page v Smith*. Some senior appellate judges have openly questioned whether the wide test of foreseeability in *Page v Smith* should be reviewed for zone-of-danger primary victims. In *Johnston v NEI Intl Combustion Ltd*,[154] Lords Hope and Mance thought it doubtful whether *Page v Smith* had been correctly decided, and stated that it should be reviewed on another occasion. In *White (Frost)*, Lord Goff also questioned the correctness of *Page v Smith*.[155] In *Corr v IBC Vehicles Ltd*,[156] Lord Neuberger called *Page v Smith* 'somewhat controversial', and foreshadowed that it may come up for challenge before the Supreme Court at some point.

However, as Lord Walker noted in *Corr*, whilst *Page v Smith* 'has attracted adverse comment from some legal scholars', it serves as 'a much simpler test for judges trying personal injury cases, even if it sometimes results in compensation for damage in the form of psychiatric sequelae which might not, on their own, have been reasonably foreseeable by [D]'.[157] In *Johnston*, Lord Hoffmann also supported the principle in *Page v Smith*, opining that it had not given rise to any difficulties in application.[158]

In any event, the ratio of *Page v Smith* remains in place for now.

> ## The law reform corner: Reasonable foreseeability
>
> The Scottish Comm:[159] recommended that the law would be more coherent and principled if there was only liability for negligently-inflicted psychiatric injury when that injury was a reasonably foreseeable consequence of D's actions, so as not to depart from the *Wagon Mound* principle.

§5.18   For the 'guilt-ridden' primary victim, however, the *Wagon Mound* principle applies, i.e., C's psychiatric injury must have been reasonably foreseeable.

For the guilt-ridden primary victim, C **must** prove foreseeability of psychiatric injury, in order to recover for precisely that type of injury, thus complying with the *Wagon Mound* principle (per Lord Slynn in *W v Essex CC*, who considered the parents' psychiatric injury as a result of bringing their children and boy G under the one roof was reasonably foreseeable – it was certainly not foreseeable that the parents would suffer any physical injury, i.e., sexual assault, from G, but the key point was that the type of injury for which the parents were claiming had to be foreseeable, *viz*, psychiatric injury).

Proximity

§5.19   If D has placed C in a zone of physical danger via his acts or omissions, then proximity will customarily be established by the parties' physical and temporal closeness. However, C must have been, in fact, exposed to a risk of physical injury, or reasonably believed that he was so exposed.

Where psychiatric injury occurs from C being placed by D in the zone of physical danger, that is *prima facie* sufficient to fix proximity, as it follows from the immediacy of the physical danger to C.

---

[154] [2007] UKHL 39, [52] and [104], respectively.   [155] [1999] 2 AC 455 (HL) 473–76.
[156] [2008] UKHL 13, [2008] 1 AC 884, [54].   [157] *ibid*, [40].
[158] [2007] UKHL 39, [32].   [159] *Scottish Report*, [1.10], [3.32].

However, if C cannot prove that he was, in fact, exposed to a risk of physical injury, or reasonably believed that he was exposed to that risk, then the requisite proximity will be lacking, and no recovery will be permitted. In *McFarlane v EE Caledonia Ltd*,[160] Stuart-Smith LJ considered that the notion of a primary victim could be expanded somewhat, to include not only a C who is in the actual area of danger created by the event, but also a C who is never in danger, but who reasonably thinks that he is, 'because of the sudden and unexpected nature of the event'. Any belief by C, that he was within the danger zone, must not be 'genuine but irrational': it must be reasonable in all the circumstances – and this is harder to prove, if C was never actually in physical danger. To contrast some cases:

> In *Young v Charles Church (Southern) Ltd*,[161] facts previously, **held (CA):** Mr Young, C, was a primary victim, because he was in the area of physical danger created by D's negligent system of work in allowing scaffolding to be erected near 'live' powerlines. In *McFarlane v EE Caledonia Ltd*, Mr McFarlane, C, a painter on an Alpha Piper oil rig, was near to the rig when it exploded in 1988, and 164 men died. C was on a support vessel, 550 metres away, at the time of the explosion. The closest that he got to the flames was 100 metres, when the support vessel sought to render assistance to fight the fire, but C could still hear the screams of the men who were in the midst of the fire. **Held:** C could not recover for his psychiatric injury, as he was not genuinely in fear of his own safety, nor objectively was he endangered whilst on the support vessel. In *Fagan v Goodman*,[162] Ms Fagan, C, witnessed an accident whilst driving on a motorway. Another car driver, Mr Goodman, D, changed lanes, without seeing a police motorcyclist in his 'blind spot'. The policeman swerved and crashed into the central road barrier, and died at the scene. C saw the horrific fatal injuries that the policeman sustained, including a severed arm, and suffered psychiatric injury. **Held:** C could not recover, as she did not need to take emergency action to avoid being caught up in the accident, nor was she at any risk of colliding with the policeman, his out-of-control motorcycle, or D's car. 'The fact that a (near) collision involving vehicles in another lane of a major road may have led to one of the vehicles losing control and thus immediately ... in an accident does not give rise to a foreseeable risk that a person in the general vicinity of where the negligence takes place is ... involved in that accident ... The result for [C] would have been otherwise if she had been forced to take emergency action to avoid the results of [D's] negligence'.

Undoubtedly, fine factual distinctions are raised by the 'close-to-physical-danger-but-not-in-fact-injured' type of case. Arguably, Mrs Fagan was as much in the zone of danger created by D's negligent driving, as was Mr Young by his employer's negligent system of scaffolding; and Mr Young did not need to take 'emergency action' to avoid the electrocution that struck his workmate dead. Yet Mr Young could recover as a primary victim, and Mrs Fagan could not. Thus, much depends upon how the court chooses to define the 'zone'. Obviously, the wider that 'zone', the better for the primary victim C.

§5.20 If C is a guilt-ridden primary victim, proximity may be established where there was a sufficient closeness in time and space with the immediate victim, or where D legally assumed a responsibility for C's well-being. Additionally, C must have a genuine belief that he caused the immediate victim's injury or death.

Again, the borderline between the recoverable scenarios, and those which do not suffice for primary victim status, can be very finely-drawn, as the two contrasting cases below demonstrate:

[160] [1994] PIQR 154 (CA) 162, citing the lower court: [1993] PIQR 241 (QB) 249 (Smith J).
[161] (1997) 39 BMLR 146 (CA). [162] QBD, 30 November 2001, quotes at [25]–[26].

In *Hunter v British Coal Corp*,[163] facts previously (re the exploding fire hydrant), C suffered from guilt-induced depression after the death of his colleague. **Held:** C was not a primary victim, because of a lack of proximity: 'the law requires a greater degree of physical and temporal proximity than was present in this case before Mr Hunter could properly be treated as a direct, or primary, victim'. In *W v Essex CC*,[164] parents Mr and Mrs W, C, suffered from guilt, for bringing boy G and their children under the one roof. **Held:** C could proceed as potential primary victims. D knew that G was known to be or suspected of being a sexual abuser; and it was impossible for C to verify that from any other source. Hence, C were in a very vulnerable position, once D chose not to disclose that information.

While *Hunter* was only briefly cited in *Essex*, the cases are difficult to reconcile. *Hunter* did not have sufficient physical proximity, whereas, in *Essex*, no such physical proximity to danger *for parents* C was present on the facts, for all the parents did was to 'bring the abused and the abuser together'. Hence, the reasoning in *Hunter* (where guilt was not sufficient) and *Essex* (where it was) is distinctly at odds. However, the parents in *Essex* could point to another proximity factor, *viz*, that D withheld information which could not be ascertained or verified elsewhere, and knew that supplying the information to C would have prompted C to act differently.

§5.21 Where C is temporally and physically proximate to horrifying events caused by D's negligence, and suffers psychiatric injury from what C witnessed, that is not sufficient, of itself, to establish C as a primary victim.

The wider *Alcock* definition of the primary victim[165] – i.e., 'one who was involved, either mediately or immediately as a participant' in events – has *not* been literally applied, in circumstances where C was closely proximate to and involved in very upsetting events, but was not in the zone of physical danger himself. That close proximity is simply insufficient to prove primary victim status.

In a trio of cases involving three mothers – who brought claims for pure psychiatric illness arising out of the death of their children, allegedly as a result of the acts or omissions of the relevant health authorities – each mother was closely exposed to the events surrounding her child's death; and each lost her primary victim claim.

In *North Glamorgan NHS Trust v Walters*,[166] Ms Walters', C's, son, Elliot, developed acute hepatitis and liver failure which treating doctors, D, failed to diagnose. Elliot suffered a seizure in front of C in hospital, and also lost the opportunity to undergo a liver transplant because of the misdiagnosis. He was then transferred to another hospital, where C was told that Elliot had been severely brain-damaged by the seizure, would never recognise her, and would have practically no quality of life. C stayed with her son, or close by, for the 36 hours of his medical treatment, witnessing the events first-hand, and turned off Elliot's life support machine at the end. **Held (trial,[167] and CA):** C was not an 'unwilling participant' in the events which brought about Elliot's death, because she was not within the range of foreseeable physical injury herself, nor did she play any causative role in Elliot's death for which she could feel guilty. In *Hall v Gwent Healthcare NHS Trust*,[168] Karen Hall's, C's, mentally disturbed husband, Andrew Hall, had been under the care of health authority, D, for serious mental illness since 1992. For his family, certain care orders were in place (e.g., all sharp knives had to be removed from the home). In 2000, Mr Hall was the target of a cruel hoax played

[163] [1999] QB 140 (CA) 149 (Brooke LJ) 154.   [164] [2001] 2 AC 592 (HL) 601 (Lord Slynn).
[165] [1992] 1 AC 310 (HL) 407.   [166] [2002] EWCA Civ 1792, [12].
[167] [2002] EWHC 321 (QB), [21]–[22].   [168] [2004] EWHC 2748 (QB) [16]–[17].

by his work colleagues, in which he went to India for a 'business trip' which was non-genuine. The hoax mentally destabilised C, and he showed disturbed behaviour on the return flight to England, suffering a 'florid psychotic state' in which he developed the belief that 15 Christian families were going to be killed because of him, and to avoid this, he would have to kill his 12-year-old daughter, Emma. He acted upon this belief soon after (having purloined a knife from his sister's house during a brief visit there on his return to England). C was in the house at the time of the fatal attack on Emma, and took the knife from her husband after the stabbing. Mr Hall was confined to Broadmoor, following trial. **Held:** C was not a primary victim, as she was not herself at risk of physical injury, nor had she unwittingly contributed to her daughter's peril (quite the opposite, she had ensured that no knives were kept in the home). In *Palmer v Tees HA*,[169] Sean Armstrong was released from D's mental facility, having disclosed to a psychiatrist before his release that he harboured sexual feelings towards children. About a year later, he abducted, assaulted, killed and mutilated a 4-year-old girl, Rosie Palmer, who lived nearby. Rosie's mother, Ms Palmer, C, suffered psychiatric illness, and alleged that D failed to provide adequate treatment for Mr Armstrong, failed to prevent his release, and failed to diagnose that there was a substantial risk of his committing serious sexual offences against children. **Held:** C was not a primary victim – for the same reasons as Ms Hall and Ms Walters after her. 'Although at one stage [counsel] suggested that [C] was a primary victim, he did not seriously argue the point; in my judgment, she clearly was not.'

Of the trio, only Ms Walters managed to prove that she was, in the alternative, a secondary victim (but for reasons that have attracted controversy). Both Mrs Hall and Ms Palmer also failed in their secondary victim claims, for reasons considered in the next section.

These cases give rise to an odd anomaly. Where parents (such as Mr and Mrs W) are 'guilt-ridden' victims, they are candidates to be treated as potential primary victims, whereas the law treats parents whose children are imperiled or killed by D's negligence far less sympathetically, where those latter parents do nothing for which they subsequently experience feelings of guilt or responsibility – even though they may have been closer in space and time to the tragedies that enveloped their children. This is one reason why *W v Essex CC* represents (in the author's opinion) a 'legal wrong-turn'.[170]

Public policy considerations

§5.22   Policy reasons such as 'floodgates concerns' and 'distributive justice' may preclude any finding of primary victim status.

The Group B victims in the *CJD Litigation* were distinguished from the 'zone of danger' primary victims for various reasons, one of which was 'floodgates' public policy concerns:

> if they were [primary victims], the ramifications would be incalculable. If they were primary victims, so would be those exposed to asbestos or radiation where primary liability may depend not upon common law negligence but on statutory duty or even strict liability, even if they became aware of the risk of physical injury years later and consequently developed psychiatric injury. The potentiality of a huge number of claims in similar situations would arise, making insurance difficult or impossible. It could involve all manner of products and a huge range of potential tortfeasors. It could inhibit the producers, prescribers and suppliers of a product from warning the public of the danger of a product. For example, if a potentially lethal substance had been negligently

[169] [1999] Lloyd's Rep Med 351 (CA), [35]–[37], quote at [35] (Stuart-Smith LJ).
[170] 'The "Primary Victim" in Psychiatric Illness Claims, etc' (2008) 19 *KCLJ* 81, 90.

introduced into a production batch of canned food, it would be disastrous if a supplier or producer were inhibited from warning the public of danger for fear that, among those who had already eaten the canned food, some might bring a claim as a primary victim for psychiatric injury triggered by the warning.[171]

Further, whereas the number of potential secondary victims is circumscribed by a number of 'control mechanisms' and by the normal fortitude rule (described in principle §5.33), those factors do not operate in primary victim claims. Hence, floodgates concerns were real, and not fanciful, in Morland J's view, if the CJD claimants were to be treated as zone-of–physical-danger primary victims.

The policy factor, 'distributive justice', has also figured in the primary victim context. It will be recalled (from Chapter 2) that this factor requires judges to determine whether they reasonably believe that ordinary people in the community ('commuters on the Underground', per *McFarlane v Tayside Health Board*[172]) would consider it just and fair to compensate C, in light of what those people would consider to be a just distribution of burdens and losses among members of a society.

In *White (Frost) v CC of South Yorkshire*,[173] facts previously, the police officers who performed rescue and other services during the Hillsborough stadium disaster were unable to recover damages as primary (or secondary) victims – partly because ordinary citizens would think it unfair if the police received damages, after the relatives had received nothing in *Alcock* seven years earlier. The ordinary citizen would think that this was, at best, not treating like cases alike, and at worst, favouring the less deserving against the more deserving.

Other features of note

The 'normal fortitude' rule is inapplicable

§5.23 As a primary victim, C can recover for his psychiatric injury, even if it was sustained because C lacked the mental fortitude or 'natural phlegm' of an ordinary person. That is, a pre-existing vulnerability may render C's psychiatric injury unlikely, but nevertheless, it may be foreseeable, given that the 'normal fortitude' rule does not apply to C.

The source of the principle. According to Lord Lloyd in *Page v Smith*,[174] a primary victim is **not** subject to the 'normal fortitude' rule. Hence, for a primary victim with a so-called 'egg-shell skull personality', he can establish that D owed him a duty of care to avoid his psychiatric injury, even if that injury would only have been foreseeable in a person of vulnerability.

This principle means that C's past history of mental illness or instability is no bar to his recovering for psychiatric injury which a negligent D may inflict upon him.

In *Page v Smith*, facts previously, Mr Page, C, had suffered from CFS in the past, and was vulnerable to a relapse – but could still recover damages for psychiatric injury, even if it was sustained because C lacked the fortitude of an ordinary person to withstand the tribulations of a minor car accident. In *Donachie v CC of Greater Manchester Police*, facts previously, police officer Mr Donachie, C, had a particular vulnerability to stress by reason of his pre-existing hypertension, but that pre-existing susceptibility could be taken into account when assessing whether his psychiatric injury was

---

[171] [2000] Lloyd's Rep Med 161 (QB) 165.   [172] [2000] 2 AC 59 (HL) 82 (Lord Steyn).
[173] [1999] 2 AC 455 (HL) 510 (Lord Hoffmann).   [174] [1996] AC 155 (HL) 197.

foreseeable, as he was a *Page*-type victim. Had C been a secondary victim, any pre-existing vulnerability could **not** have been taken into account, when assessing whether his psychiatric injury was reasonably foreseeable.

In *Page*, Lord Lloyd remarked that the lack of a normal fortitude requirement for a primary victim was defensible in that, 'liability depends on foreseeability of physical injury, [and so] there could be no question of [D] finding himself liable to all the world'.[175] However, as demonstrated in this chapter, primary victims can seemingly also encompass Cs who were not in the zone of physical danger at all (but were 'guilt-ridden'), and hence, the field of potential Cs is not as ring-fenced as Lord Lloyd perhaps envisaged. Whatever its justification, the Court of Appeal remarked, in *Greatorex v Greatorex*, that the consequence of the distinction between primary and secondary victims is that a primary victim does have that advantage, of recovering damages, notwithstanding that he could not have met the normal fortitude rule.[176]

Contrasts with other areas. By contrast, for a secondary victim, it is assumed, at law, that a person of normal fortitude should be able to withstand the ordinary jolts and jogs of life without succumbing to psychiatric injury. In *Page v Smith*,[177] Lord Lloyd remarked that this is one of the advantages that primary victims enjoy over secondary victims – D has to take a primary victim exactly as D finds him. By contrast, a secondary victim must prove that D should have reasonably foreseen psychiatric injury to *a person of normal fortitude* before he can recover. As Otton LJ reiterated in *Bridges v P&NE Murray Ltd*, in the case of a primary victim:

> D must take C as he finds him, it will avail D nothing that C has a psychologically vulnerable egg-shell personality. This is in contrast to those cases involving secondary victims, where it must be established that the defendant should have foreseen injury by shock to a person of normal fortitude.[178]

In this respect, primary victims claiming for pure psychiatric injury **also** have a distinct advantage over victims who are claiming damages for *physical* injury, because in physical injury cases, D is entitled to require foreseeability of harm in a person of normal physical robustness, and the test of foreseeability of harm (at the remoteness of damage stage) is based upon that assumption. Once an egg-shell claimant proves that some physical harm, even for a person of normal physical vulnerability, was foreseeable, then D must take C as he finds him and compensate him for *all* his losses, even if his injury was particularly grave because of some pre-existing vulnerability (see Chapter 9).

Hence, the law associated with primary victim recovery on this point is an oddity, in comparison with other areas of negligently-inflicted injury.

A change in the law needed? As pointed out in *White*,[179] it was the assumption that the normal fortitude rule applied to both primary victims and secondary victims, up until *Page v Smith* in 1996. The requirement for primary victims was dropped in that case – to Mr Page's great advantage, for he did not have to prove that it was reasonably foreseeable that a person of ordinary fortitude would have suffered chronic fatigue syndrome as a result of the minor car accident in which he was involved.

This case effected a turnaround in the law, as prior to that, any C, whether primary or secondary victim (i.e., 'the ordinary frequenter of the streets'), could only recover for psychiatric

---

[175] [1996] AC 155 (HL) 189.　　[176] [2000] 4 All ER 769 (QB) 773.

[177] [1996] AC 155 (HL) 189, 197. Also: *AB v Leeds Teaching Hosp NHS Trust* [2004] EWHC 644, [190]; *McLoughlin v O'Brian* [1983] 1 AC 410 (HL) 429; *Bourhill v Young* [1943] AC 92 (HL) 110, 117.

[178] (CA, 21 May 1999).　　[179] [1999] 2 AC 455 (HL) 476.

injury if it was reasonably foreseeable that a person of ordinary fortitude or robustness would have suffered the same injury as a result of D's breach (per *Bourhill (or Hay) v Young*[180]).

There is a strong case for returning the law to the pre-*Page v Smith* position, so as to ensure that the normal fortitude requirement is re-established for primary victims. For one thing, the reason given by Lord Lloyd for dropping the normal fortitude requirement has fallen away as this area of the law has developed (the inclusion of the 'guilt-ridden primary victims' has already been noted above, not to mention the elevated primary victim). Hence, D can be liable to a larger cohort of potential Cs than the zone-of-danger primary victims which Lord Lloyd envisaged. Hence, the restriction on liability provided by the normal fortitude requirement may be worth reinstating, to 'ring-fence' D's liability to psychiatrically-vulnerable Cs.

Moreover, the law would certainly be simplified if this distinction between the primary and secondary victim was eliminated. Notably, Lord Ackner remarked, in *Page v Smith*, that 'normal fortitude' is an 'imprecise phrase'.[181] Also, for the elevated primary victim cases, it appears that the normal fortitude requirement is also disapplied, although the requirement certainly applies to the secondary victim before he is 'elevated' (a point that was evident, e.g., in *AB v Leeds*[182]).

The law reform corner: Commentary on this requirement

Scottish Law Comm:[183] that a primary victim is not assumed to be a person of normal fortitude is asymmetrical with both secondary victim, and physical victim, recovery. The rule of normal fortitude 'stalks the current law' on recovery for pure psychiatric injury. It should be revised, so that D could assume ordinary mental robustness on the part of all primary or secondary victims.

English Law Comm:[184] described the normal fortitude rule as a 'deceptively difficult issue', and a 'blunt and arbitrary control device', so that the rule should be 'best interpreted as meaning nothing more than that ... in deciding whether psychiatric illness was reasonably foreseeable (and analogously to reasonable foreseeability in physical injury cases), one can take into account the robustness of the population at large to psychiatric illness'.

Ipp Committee:[185] the normal fortitude rule should be abolished for *all* Cs seeking damages for pure psychiatric harm. Such revision would bring the law on psychiatric and physical harm into parallel.

Requirement of shock

§5.24   It is unsettled as to whether the psychiatric injury incurred by the primary victim must have been induced by a 'shock', in the legal sense, in order to be compensable.

The term, 'shock', means (per *Alcock*[186]), 'a sudden assault on the nervous system' (Lord Keith), 'the sudden appreciation of a horrifying event, which violently agitates the mind, [as opposed to] the accumulation over a period in time of more gradual assaults on the nervous system'

---

[180] [1943] AC 92 (HL) 110, 117.   [181] [1996] AC 155 (HL) 170.
[182] [2004] EWHC 644 (QB), [2005] QB 506, [259], [268], [279] (Gage J).
[183] *Scottish Report*, [2.16]–[2.20], [3.19].   [184] *English Report*, [5.21], [5.26].
[185] *Ipp Report*, [9.16] and [9.19].   [186] [1992] 2 AC 310 (HL), with quotes at, respectively, 396–98, 401, 411.

(Lord Ackner), and 'a sudden and unexpected shock to [C's] nervous system' (Lord Oliver). Lord Ackner's has been particularly endorsed as being 'generally accepted as the correct formulation' of the requisite shock (per *Wild v Southend Univ Hosp*[187]).

For secondary victims, it is a limiting criterion. However, there is uncertainty as to whether shock is a requirement for primary victims, which arises for various reasons:

- undoubtedly, in *Page v Smith*, Mr Page **did** suffer a shock when colliding with Mr Smith's car – but none of the Lords stated shock to be a criterion for a primary victim who was in the zone of danger;
- in *W v Essex CC*, the parental C's were potential primary victims, albeit that they suffered no shock which was contemporaneous with G's abuse of their children;
- in the employment context, English (and Scottish[188]) case law has doubted whether shock is a requirement beyond the secondary victim scenario. Indeed, in *Alexander v Midland Bank plc*,[189] the Court of Appeal was adamant that shock did **not** apply, because *Alcock* was 'concerned with secondary victims, where the law has restricted liability to those who were closely related to the primary victim and who witness through sight and sound an horrific event which causes shock. The rule has nothing to do with primary victims'. However, that was dicta only, given that 'stress-at-work' cases have always been governed by different rules;
- in the fear-of-the-future *CJD Litigation*,[190] the lack of contemporaneous shock was also problematical for the HGH recipients – and partly for this reason, they were not *Page v Smith*-type primary victims.

Given these precedents in combination, the better view seems to be that the primary victim does **not** need to prove psychiatric injury by shock.

The law reform corner: Commentary on this requirement

English Law Comm:[191] whether shock applies to primary victims was, at the time of the report, an open question – but in any event, the requirement should be abolished for all victims. The full extent of any injury might only become obvious to C over a period of time, so that rather than becoming 'suddenly aware of the full horror, [C] learns of the severity of the injuries after a number of ... years'. Moreover, 'the fixing of any cut-off point for "suddenness" will be essentially arbitrary'. It would be better to exclude the requirement altogether.

Scottish Law Comm:[192] it is not a pre-requisite for some so-called primary victims, such as work stress claims. In any event, the shock requirement should be entirely done away with.

Hence, to conclude: although the law associated with secondary victims is frequently perceived to create the most difficulties in negligently-inflicted psychiatric injury law, in many respects the primary victim is the more troublesome twin. All too frequently, the courts have chosen to sacrifice doctrinal clarity to help an unfortunate C, acknowledging that C is not in the 'secondary victim' category, and yet finding for C nevertheless, by 'finessing' the primary victim definition.

---

[187] [2014] EWHC 4053 (QB) [26].   [188] *Cross v Highlands & Islands Enterprise* 2001 SLT 1060 (OH) [61].
[189] [1999] IRLR 723 [50].   [190] [2000] Lloyd's Rep Med 161 (QB) 165.
[191] *English Report*, [2.62], [5.29(4)].   [192] *Scottish Report*, [2.5].

Contrary to the primary victim scenario, thankfully the definition of a secondary victim has remained fairly static over the years. It is the application of the duty of care criteria to different scenarios which has proven problematical.

SECONDARY VICTIM CLAIMANTS

Duty of care requirements

The secondary victim C has a number of hurdles to overcome, if he is to prove that D owed him a duty to avoid his psychiatric injury. Amongst other pre-requisites, secondary victims have to satisfy the legal loopholes known as the '*Alcock* control mechanisms' (named after the case in which they were most notably couched by the House of Lords[193] – although their actual origin was earlier, in *McLoughlin v O'Brian*[194]). They are known colloquially[195] as 'dearness, nearness and hearness', respectively, and will be considered shortly.

These control mechanisms provide a considerable bulwark against the prospect of indeterminate liability on D's part. This is important, where one highly-distressing event may be witnessed by many – precisely the context of *Alcock* itself.

Of course, even where one traumatic incident afflicts only one or two people with psychiatric injury, the *Alcock* control mechanisms have posed significant barriers to that secondary victim recovery too.

Dealing with each duty of care requirement in turn:

Reasonable foreseeability

§5.25   A secondary victim, C, must prove that his psychiatric injury was a reasonably foreseeable consequence of D's acts or omissions.

Whereas, for the *Page v Smith*-type primary victim, **either** physical **or** psychiatric harm must have been foreseeable, the position for secondary victims is more onerous. According to Lord Lloyd in *Page v Smith*, as a control device, '[f]oreseeability of psychiatric injury remains a crucial ingredient when [C] is the secondary victim, for the very reason that the secondary victim is almost always outside the area of physical impact, and therefore outside the range of foreseeable physical injury'.[196] More recently, in *Taylor v A Novo (UK) Ltd*,[197] Lord Dyson MR reiterated that, as the 'starting point' for secondary victims, C's psychiatric injury must have been a reasonably foreseeable consequence of D's negligence.

Typically, it has not been particularly difficult for a secondary victim to prove that test of foreseeability, where a traumatic event has occurred. Psychiatric evidence is frequently called in aid.

In *Tredget v Bexley HA*,[198] facts previously, psychiatric harm on C's part (the parents involved in the chaotic birth of their deceased child), was reasonably foreseeable, because the psychiatric evidence was that neonatal death is more difficult to bear, where birth and death are wrapped up in the same moment.

---

[193] *Alcock v CC of Yorkshire Police* [1992] 2 AC 310 (HL).   [194] [1983] 1 AC 410 (HL) 421–23 (Lord Wilberforce).

[195] See, e.g., the reference to American commentary's use of these terms, noted in: *Frost v CC of South Yorkshire Police* [1996] EWHC Admin 173 (CA) [70] (Henry LJ).

[196] [1996] AC 155 (HL) 184 (Lord Lloyd).   [197] [2013] EWCA Civ 194, [5].

[198] [1994] 5 Med LR 178 (Central London CC) 183.

However, if the secondary victim's psychiatric injury is extreme and idiosyncratic, then the law of negligence will not require a reasonable D to avoid it. That scenario has occurred, but rarely.

> In *Powell v Boldaz*,[199] Mr and Mrs Powell, C, were the parents of Robert, 10, who died of un-diagnosed Addison's disease. Robert's treating GPs, D, admitted negligence. C brought a disciplinary complaint against D, and learnt, during these proceedings, that false documents (a clinical summary sheet and letter) had been substituted for the originals. Mr Powell claimed that he suffered psychiatric injury as a result of learning of the substitution of the documents ('my head exploded'), and Mrs Powell also claimed for psychiatric injury arising from both Robert's death, and then the substitution. **Held:** neither C recovered. It was not reasonably foreseeable that a parent in this position would suffer such injury because of the substitution, or that this could invoke in both Cs such a reaction, when it was 'far from clear that the substitution ... made any material difference to the medical history'.

Relationship proximity: close tie of love and affection

§5.26 As a secondary victim, C must prove that he shared a 'close tie of love and affection' with the immediate victim of D's negligent act or omission (i.e., the first *Alcock* control mechanism). Close ties may be rebuttably presumed in some types of relationship between C and the immediate victim, but in other cases, that tie must be established by evidence.

In *Alcock*, Lord Keith stated that close ties between the secondary victim, C, and the immediate victim were essential for the secondary victim's recovery, precisely because it was 'the existence of such ties which leads to mental disturbance when the loved one suffers a catastrophe'.[200] This is the first *Alcock* control mechanism.

In some types of relationship, close ties may be presumed – in *Frost (White) v CC of South Yorkshire Police*, Lord Hoffmann put husband and wife, parent and child, and engaged couples, into this category; 'otherwise, they must otherwise be established by evidence'.[201] All of this constitutes a distasteful exercise in 'proving (and disproving) the love', according to some.[202] Even where a close tie of love and affection was presumed, that can be rebutted on the evidence. Indeed, sometimes, a close tie cannot be established at all, e.g.:

- long-standing workmates and friends were not close enough in *Gregg v Ashbrae Ltd*;[203]
- cousins employed as army officers in a war-zone were not close enough in *Bici v MOD*;[204]
- strangers involved in a car accident will always fail the criterion, per *Fagan v Goodman*.[205]

On the other hand, even a mother and child relationship of only a few hours can suffice (per *Farrell v Merton, Sutton and Wandsworth HA*[206] – in circumstances where a birth went badly, and baby Karol was born with severe and irreversible brain damage, his mother could recover damages for depression and anxiety as a secondary victim, because the fact that the child was 'only hours old' did not diminish the close emotional tie which existed between Mrs Farrell and her child as the immediate victim).

---

[199] [1998] Lloyd's Rep Med 116 (CA), with quotes at 124 and 122 (the case is also reported as *Powell v Boladz*).
[200] [1992] 1 AC 310 (HL) 397. Also, 411 (Lord Oliver).   [201] [1999] 2 AC 455 (HL) 502 (Lord Hoffmann).
[202] Most oft-cited is the criticism of J Stapleton, 'Restraint of Tort' in P Birks (ed), *Frontiers of Liability* (1994) 95 ('Is it not a disreputable sight to see brothers of Hillsborough victims turned away because they had no more than brotherly love towards the victim?'), cited, e.g., in: *Van Soest* [1999] NZCA 206, [118] (Thomas J).
[203] [2005] NIQB 37.   [204] [2004] EWHC 786 (QB).   [205] (QB, 30 Nov 2001).
[206] (2000) 57 BMLR 158 (QB) 163.

It is the lack of these ties between rescuer C and the immediate victim being rescued that precludes C from claiming secondary victim status. None of the police officers in *White* had any such ties with the victims of the Hillsborough disaster; nor did the rescuer co-employee in *Monk v PC Harrington Ltd.* Hence, if the rescuer is not in the zone of danger himself, and suffers psychiatric injury from what he witnesses or endures during the rescue operation, then that injury will go uncompensated.

The criterion becomes particularly acute where C, as secondary victim, and the immediate victim, do fall within one of the presumed relationships of close love – but all the evidence points to the fact that no such close tie was ever maintained. That will harm a secondary victim's prospects of recovery, but not an elevated primary victim's, as demonstrated by the following leading case:

> In *Farrell v Avon HA*,[207] facts previously, Mr Farrell, C, did not maintain any close tie of love and affection with the mother of his child before Jordan's birth, or with Jordan following his birth. D sued for PTSD and for subsequent alcohol and drug dependency. **Held:** C recovered £10,000 for the injury.

Had Mr Farrell been legally treated as a secondary victim, it is questionable whether he would have recovered any damages, as he maintained no close tie of love or affection with the mother or the child, either before or after the birth of Jordan. Mr Farrell's lack of close ties surely would have rendered that criterion very difficult to satisfy, *ex post facto*.

The law reform corner: Commentary on this requirement

English Law Comm:[208] 'relational proximity' was the one *Alcock* control mechanism that the Commission thought should be retained, and this requirement for a close tie between C and the immediate victim could be satisfied either at the time of D's act or omission or at the onset of C's psychiatric illness. It also recommended that the legislation stipulate a fixed list of relationships where a close tie would be presumed, i.e., spouse; parent; child; brother or sister; a partner who had lived with the immediate victim for at least two years. In other cases, C would need to prove the close tie of love and affection by evidence.

Ipp Committee:[209] re a close tie of love and affection, it 'necessitate[s] the forensic examination and assessment of the nature and quality of intimate human relationships in a way that may bring the law into disrepute'. If (1) C was assumed to be a person of normal fortitude, and (2) the test of reasonable foreseeability of mental harm were properly applied, then sufficient restrictions on recovery would exist, without need to resort to this *Alcock* criterion.

Scottish Law Comm:[210] a list of relationships in which persons were presumed to have a close relationship should be stated – plus it favoured the use of the slightly wider term, 'close relationship', in order to give those with feelings of 'personal responsibility' (say, a nanny toward a child) or loyalty (say, employees or neighbours towards each other) an opportunity to prove that sufficient ties existed to justify secondary victim status.

---

[207] [2001] Lloyd's Rep Med 458 (QB).
[208] *English Report*, [6.10], [6.26]–[6.34]; and cll 1(3)(b), 3 of the Draft Negligence (Psychiatric Illness) Bill.
[209] *Ipp Report*, [9.25]–[9.26].   [210] *Scottish Report*, [3.54]–[3.55], and cl 5.

Spatial and temporal proximity

§5.27 A secondary victim, C, must have been present at the accident involving the immediate victim, or at the immediate aftermath of the accident. With respect to temporal proximity, it is apparent that the immediate aftermath is approximately two hours only.

The event, or the immediate aftermath. This is the second *Alcock* control mechanism. The requirement for spatial and temporal proximity has been articulated in several House of Lords' decisions; and in *Alcock* itself, Lord Oliver noted that Cs in earlier successful cases were:

> either personally present at the scene of the accident, or [were] in the more or less immediate vicinity and witnessed the aftermath shortly afterwards; ... there was not only an element of physical proximity to the event but a close temporal connection between the event and [C's] perception of it.[211]

Similarly, in *AB v Leeds Teaching Hosp NHS Trust*, Gage J reiterated that, as a control mechanism, secondary victim C 'must be close in time and space to the event caused by [D's] breach'.[212]

Even if C is not present at the accident itself which was brought about by D's negligence, the immediate aftermath is sufficient to render C in close proximity in time and space to the accident. The period is rather artificially and arbitrarily construed. Two hours after the negligence/injury was acceptable in *McLoughlin v O'Brian*, although it was right 'on the margin of what the process of logical progression would allow' (said Lord Wilberforce[213]). Two hours and 10 minutes was also within it:

> In *Galli-Atkinson v Seghal*,[214] C's daughter, Livia, 16, was killed at 7.05pm, when D's car mounted a footpath and hit her. Livia died at the scene. C saw the accident site, not aware that anything was wrong, but then attempted to cross the police cordon to look for Livia, who was late returning from a ballet lesson. At that point, one hour after the accident, C learnt that her daughter had been killed (a police officer described her screaming as 'unforgettable'). C and her husband then went to the mortuary and viewed Livia's body at 9.15 pm. C suffered psychiatric illness. **Held:** C could recover, as the mortuary visit was within the requisite immediate aftermath. That period 'extended from the moment of the accident until [C] left the mortuary: there was an uninterrupted sequence of events'.

On the other hand, 8–9 hours after the negligence/injury was outside the 'immediate aftermath' in *Alcock* (re the Hillsborough accident),[215] and three hours was also too long in *Hevican v Ruane*[216] (another car accident).

Hence, although different Courts of Appeal have stated that the 'immediate aftermath' is a 'flexible idea ... not confined to what happens "immediately" upon the termination of the relevant physical acts' (per *RS v Criminal Injuries Compensation Authy*[217]), and that 'a somewhat more relaxed approach to what constitutes the immediate aftermath' has been adopted in case law (per *Taylor v Novo*[218]), the reality is that the dividing line is entirely arbitrary.

---

[211] [1992] AC 310 (HL) 411. See too, 402, 404 (Lord Ackner), 422 (Lord Jauncey); *Page v Smith* [1996] AC 155 (HL) 189 (Lord Lloyd); *Frost/White* [1999] 2 AC 455 (HL) 502 (Lord Hoffmann), 477 (Lord Goff).
[212] [2004] EWHC 644 (QB) [190].   [213] [1983] 1 AC 410 (HL) 419.   [214] [2003] EWCA Civ 679.
[215] [1992] 1 AC 310 (HL).   [216] [1991] 3 All ER 65 (QB).
[217] [2013] EWCA Civ 1040, [11].   [218] [2013] EWCA Civ 194, [34].

§5.28 C must be physically and temporally proximate to either D's act or omission which gave rise to the accident or to the immediate aftermath. It is *not* sufficient if C is proximate *only* to the immediate victim's death, where that death occurred some time after D's act/omission and injury to the immediate victim, and outside the immediate aftermath of the accident.

In the paradigm scenario, D's negligent act or omission may cause the almost simultaneous death or injury of the immediate victim. The whole event is the accident. But what if C did not witness the negligently-caused accident itself, but was only present at the death of the immediate victim, some time later, and well outside the immediate aftermath? That is not sufficient proximity, according to the Court of Appeal in *Taylor v A Novo (UK) Ltd*[219] – a case which was not the usual kind of secondary victim dispute (said that court).

> In *Taylor v Novo*, Cindy Taylor was injured in a work accident, when a fellow employee caused a stack of racking boards to tip over on top of her. Her employer, D, admitted breach. She suffered injuries to her head and left foot, and seemed to be making a good recovery when, 21 days later, she suddenly collapsed and died at home, due to deep vein thrombosis and consequent pulmonary emboli from her injuries. Her daughter, Crystal Taylor, C, had not witnessed the accident, but did witness her mother's death at home, and suffered PTSD. **Held:** C was not sufficiently proximate, because she was not present at the scene of the accident, nor involved in its immediate aftermath. Witnessing the death 21 days later was not sufficient to prove this criterion.

The death of the immediate victim was not a part of the 'event' to which secondary victim C had to be proximate. After all, if a death (witnessed by C) which occurred some 21 days after D's negligence was to be regarded as part of the event, then why not a death months or even years later? The Court of Appeal considered that the *Alcock* control mechanisms had to be applied with rigour and restriction. As Lord Dyson MR stated, if the death were part of the 'event', then that would 'potentially extend the scope of liability to secondary victims considerably further than has been done hitherto ... these same policy reasons militate against any further substantial extension. That should only be done by Parliament.'[220] Clearly, the necessary ring-fencing of secondary victim claims (as rightly occurred in this case) is continuing to drive legal analysis in this unsatisfactory area of negligence.

However, the fact that, in *Taylor v Novo*, C did not witness the negligence itself – but was removed from the scene and only witnessed the **effects** of D's negligence – aligns the situation with many medical negligence scenarios. The problem is that secondary victim C is often physically or temporally remote from the medical negligence 'event' – the medical mistreatment or misdiagnosis occurred behind closed doors, in operating theatres, recovery rooms, or in doctors' surgeries. Often, all that the secondary victim witnesses is the effects of the negligence on the immediate victim afterwards, in the hospital ward or later at home. Although the House of Lords stated, in *JD v East Berkshire Community Health NHS Trust*, that medical mishaps can give rise to a duty of care owed by a healthcare professional/hospital towards one who 'suffer[ed] nervous shock through seeing or hearing the event or its immediate aftermath',[221] that does not apply in medical negligence scenarios, as a general rule, where the effects of the negligence take hours, days, weeks, or even months, to manifest (and which secondary victim

[219] [2013] EWCA Civ 194.　[220] *ibid*, [31].　[221] [2005] UKHL 23, [10].

C witnesses). That delay will result in C **not** having the requisite proximity with D's breach to satisfy the *Alcock* requirement of spatial and temporal proximity.

> In *Taylor v Somerset HA*,[222] Mr Taylor's heart disease went misdiagnosed by treating doctors, D, for many months. Mr Taylor then suffered a fatal heart attack at work. Mrs Taylor, C, was told her husband was ill at hospital, and she visited within the hour. Twenty minutes later, C was told of her husband's death. She could not believe the fact of Mr Taylor's death, and viewed his body as 'proof'. C sued D for the shock and distress caused by her husband's death. **Held:** C failed, as the news of her husband's death was not within the 'immediate aftermath' of D's original medical negligence of failing to diagnose and treat. Mr Taylor's death at work, and the transfer of his body to hospital where Mrs Taylor saw him, was not part of the relevant 'event' – it was far too removed in time. In *Palmer v Tees HA*,[223] facts previously, **held:** Mrs Palmer, C, was never within the aftermath doctrine in respect of the alleged negligence of the treating psychiatrist, D, who released Sean Armstrong into the community, despite his confessions beforehand of his evil intentions towards young children, and of the ongoing lack of supervision. The effects of that negligence – Rosie Palmer's murder, almost a year after Mr Armstrong's release – was far too removed in time from the alleged negligence.

Taylor v Novo sits comfortably with this general rule, i.e., witnessing *the effects* of negligence is not 'good enough'. However, it does not necessarily sit well with the exceptions that have been judicially crafted in that area. This rather messy scenario is described below.

    Exceptions to the immediate aftermath. In medical negligence scenarios, English courts have compromised (softened) the spatial and temporal proximity requirement in **two** respects:

§5.29   As exceptions to the immediate aftermath doctrine: (1) if the failure of secondary victim C to fit within the immediate aftermath was brought about, in part, by D's *own preventative actions*, then the doctrine will be more sympathetically construed in favour of C; and (2) witnessing the *effects* of the negligence can, exceptionally, be held to be within the aftermath doctrine, even if outside the immediate aftermath.

Alcock was a disaster scenario – an accident, quickly followed by the immediate victim's injury or death, and where an immediate aftermath could feasibly (albeit artificially) apply. However, the corollary of more drawn-out affairs which do not neatly fit the *Alcock* pattern is a real inconsistency in the manner in which claims for pure psychiatric illness are treated at law.

    Any deliberate attempts by D to prevent the secondary victim from witnessing the effects of D's negligent act or omission may assist the prospects of the secondary victim's recovery.

> In *Farrell v Merton, Sutton and Wandsworth HA*,[224] facts previously, where Mrs Farrell, C, gave birth to a son, Karol, who suffered severe and irreversible brain damage, **held:** C recovered. What C witnessed was within the 'immediate aftermath' of the trauma of the birth, because 'the unusual delay of just over a day between [C] giving birth and first seeing her son was wholly attributable to [D], who had chosen not to take her to the hospital to which her baby had been sent and not to tell her of the injury and difficulties which had occurred'. C's ignorance of Karol's condition was solely due to the hospital staff's conduct.

Additionally (and somewhat inconsistently with *Taylor v Novo*, where the collapse and death of Mrs Taylor was not within the immediate aftermath), there have been cases in which all that C witnessed was the effects of D's negligence, well outside the immediate aftermath of the

---

[222] [1993] 4 Med LR 34 (QB).   [223] [1999] EWCA Civ 1533.   [224] (2001) 57 BMLR 158 (QB), quotes at 158, 164.

negligence itself, or of the injury inflicted on the immediate victim – and yet, the second *Alcock* control mechanism **was** met.

> In *Froggatt v Chesterfield and North Derbyshire Royal Hosp NHS Trust*,[225] Mrs Froggatt, 28, underwent a mastectomy, following D's misdiagnosis that she was suffering from cancer. Three weeks later, she was informed of the misdiagnosis. When Mr Froggatt, C1, saw his wife undressed for the first time, 12 days after the operation, he suffered a shock; as did her son, C2, when he overheard his mother telling her friend on the phone that she had been diagnosed with cancer. **Held:** C1 recovered £5,000 for his psychiatric injury, and C2 recovered £1,000. There was 'closeness in time' between the misdiagnosis and the shock which C1 and C2 received (although the term, 'aftermath doctrine', was not referred to). They suffered an 'affront to the senses'. In *W v Essex CC*,[226] facts previously, Mr and Mrs W, C, did not witness any sexual assaults perpetrated by G upon their children, and had not come across the children or G in their 'immediate aftermath'. Rather, C were told about the abuse some time after the final abuse, and four weeks after the abuse started. **Held:** C could proceed to trial as potential secondary victims: '[w]hilst there has to be some temporal and spatial limitation on [C] who can claim to be secondary victims, ... it seems to me that the concept of "the immediate aftermath" of the incident has to be assessed in the particular factual situation. I am not persuaded that, in a situation like the present, the parents must come across the abuser or the abused "immediately" after the sexual incident has terminated'.

This exceptional line of authority has received endorsement in some Commonwealth jurisprudence:

The comparative corner: Spatial and temporal proximity

Singapore: in *Pang Koi Fa v Lim Djoe Phing*,[227] secondary victim C was the mother of a patient for whom a medical operation went wrong. C was told of the need for her daughter to have an operation to remove a tumour from her pituitary gland. She recommended that course to her daughter; was at her daughter's bedside in intensive care after the operation, was present when her daughter was negligently discharged whilst still sickly, brought her daughter back to hospital as her condition worsened, and was there when her daughter died. **Held:** C could recover for psychiatric injury. Amarjeet JC noted that medical negligence is far removed from the accident which plays out over a few minutes only, and causes calamitous shock as it unfolds – operative procedures, by contrast, will occur behind closed doors, and the results of negligently-administered medicine may take some time to manifest.

These exceptions vest the law of secondary victim recovery with inconsistency. Plenty of secondary victims have witnessed the 'effects' of D's alleged negligence, and that has simply not been sufficient to base recovery for pure psychiatric illness (e.g., Mrs Palmer, Mrs Hall, Mr Tan, Mrs Taylor and Mr Sion, to name a few who are considered in this and the following section), as they have not been able to take advantage of the exceptional scenarios. Also, the exceptional cases do not sit well with the *Alcock* authority on what constitutes the 'immediate aftermath',

---

[225] [2002] All ER (D) 218 (QB) [78].   [226] [2001] 2 AC 592 (HL) 601.
[227] [1993] 3 SLR 317 (HC, Amarjeet JC), quote at 329.

nor do they sit easily with the Court of Appeal's view in *Taylor v Novo* that a restrictive attitude towards secondary victim recovery is warranted for policy reasons. Further, the correctness of *Froggatt* was doubted in *Wild v Southend Univ Hospital*,[228] while *W v Essex CC* was a strike-out application, and as such, the weight of its authority was questioned ('or limited value') by Lord Dyson in *Novo*.[229] All of this vests the law with a messy appearance.

Clearly, the immediate aftermath/spatial and temporal proximity criterion has been watered-down, both by exceptions and by its inconsistent application. Unsurprisingly, some law reform opinion is to the effect that secondary victim recovery would be better off without the criterion altogether.

The law reform corner: Commentary on this requirement

English Law Comm:[230] this second *Alcock* control mechanism should be abolished. In addition to the unsatisfactory tensions in case law as to what constituted a compensable 'immediate aftermath', the most important factor both to ring-fence the number of secondary victims, and to explain the aetiology of psychiatric injury, is a close tie of love and affection, and not the fact of how close to the event was the secondary victim.

Scottish Law Comm:[231] the 'immediate aftermath' requirement was a blunt instrument which discriminated against those who were simply too far away from the scene to make it in time to obtain compensation for their psychiatric injuries. Also, the 'immediate aftermath' varied, from 20 minutes, to a few hours, to several days.

Direct perception

§5.30 As a secondary victim, C's psychiatric injury must have been caused by direct perception of the accident or of its immediate aftermath, with C's own eyes and ears, and not by hearing about it from a third party.

This third and final *Alcock* control mechanism, reiterated by Lord Hoffmann in *Frost (White)*,[232] was affirmed earlier in *Alcock*, by several of the Law Lords,[233] and even earlier in *McLoughlin v O'Brian*.

> In *McLoughlin v O'Brian*,[234] facts previously, it was not Mrs McLoughlin's friend telling her the bad news about her family's car accident that C was entitled to recover for. It was the sight and sound of her loved ones in pain and distress which C witnessed at the hospital. In *Tredget and Tredget v Bexley HA*,[235] facts previously, the 'chaos' and 'pandemonium' of the birth in the delivery theatre happened 'in full sight' of Mr Tredget, C1. Mrs Tredget, C2, was sedated and suffering from exhaustion and not fully conscious of what was happening around her, but had sufficient senses and instinct during the course of labour and birth to know that something was terribly wrong. Direct perception was made out for both Cs.

---

[228] [2014] EWHC 4053 (QB) [51].   [229] [2013] EWCA Civ 194, [2014] QB 150, [34].
[230] *English Report*, [6.10]–[6.16], and citing: *Jaensch v Coffey* (1984) 155 CLR 549 (HCA) 600.
[231] *Scottish Report*, [2.23].   [232] [1999] 2 AC 455 (HL) 502 (Lord Hoffmann).
[233] [1992] 2 AC 310 (HL) 398 (Lord Keith), 405 (Lord Ackner), 411 (Lord Oliver).
[234] [1983] 1 AC 410 (HL) 422–23.   [235] [1994] 5 Med LR 178 (Central London CC) 183.

The requirement, however, does not square with medical science. The medical testimony in *Ravenscroft v Rederiaktiebolaget Transatlantic*[236] was that there is no diagnostic or medical difference in the triggers for psychiatric injury for a person who has witnessed an accident, or a person who was present at the aftermath, or a person who simply is told about the accident from another person. Furthermore, it is difficult to reconcile that recovery should be denied to a wife who is told on the phone that her husband has been killed in a negligently-caused accident, whereas a wife who sees her husband with serious but not fatal injuries can recover, merely due to a rule based on public policy (per *Ravenscroft*[237]). Nevertheless, current English law does not reflect that medical or policy view.

Again, secondary victims may find this criterion difficult-to-impossible, where much of what happened was behind closed doors, out of sight, or at some place geographically removed from C.

§5.31   If C receives bad news about the immediate victim orally in person, by phone or in writing, then as a general rule, the direct perception requirement will not be satisfied (even where C witnesses that victim's dead body). However, recovery of damages for pure psychiatric injury may exceptionally be achieved by C by some other legal avenues.

Receiving bad news – no recovery. Direct perception is very difficult to establish, where C was merely told of the effects of D's negligence towards the immediate victim, without witnessing those acts or omissions first-hand. As the Court of Appeal recently put it, in *Brock v Northampton General Hosp NHS Trust*, '[i]t is one of the fine distinctions which have been made in the cases, that a telephone call giving bad news cannot found liability to secondary victims, whereas seeing someone can in appropriate cases'.[238] The problem is particularly acute in medical negligence cases. **None** of the following could meet 'direct perception':

In *Tan v East London and the City HA*,[239] Mrs Tan attended D's hospital to give birth, but due to D's negligent treatment, the baby girl died *in utero*. Mr Tan, C, who had been eagerly looking forward to the birth, was told of the death by D's staff by phone, about 20 minutes after it occurred. C immediately visited the hospital, was present during the stillbirth, held his dead daughter after delivery and during the night, and saw her placed in a metal coffin box the following day. C suffered severe depression, contributing to his loss of employment. C was unable to directly perceive of the negligence that occurred, even though he was intimately involved in events thereafter. That involvement was insufficient for direct perception. In *Wild v Southend Univ Hosp*,[240] Mr and Mrs Wild were expecting the birth of their child, when Mrs Wild had a show of blood, and attended hospital. No foetal heartbeat could be detected, and the death *in utero* of the baby was diagnosed. Mr Wild, C, was devastated and horrified. C and his wife went home overnight, and attended next day for the stillbirth. Thereafter, C suffered PTSD. However, C was held to suffer from a 'growing and acute anxiety' that successive medical staff could not find a heartbeat, and looked and sounded as if something was terribly wrong, after which point C realised that his baby had died. 'But none of that ... equates to actually witnessing horrific events leading to a death or serious injury'. In *Taylor v Somerset HA*,[241] facts previously, Mrs Taylor, C, received the phone call with the

---

[236] [1991] 3 All ER 73 (CA) 79.   [237] *ibid*, and see too: *Jaensch v Coffey* (1984) 155 CLR 549 (HCA) 608 (Deane J).
[238] [2014] EWHC 4244 (QB) [84].   [239] [1999] Lloyd's Rep Med 389 (Chelmsford CC).
[240] [2014] EWHC 4053 (QB) [47].   [241] [1993] 4 Med LR 34 (QB) 37.

bad news that her husband had become ill at work and had been taken to hospital, and she thereafter saw his body at the mortuary. Direct perception was absent, as the law could not compensate for shock brought about by communication of the bad news by the doctor. In *Palmer v Tees HA*,[242] facts previously, the dreadful news communicated to Mrs Palmer, C, that they had found Rosie's mutilated body, and her observance of that body a few days later, was not sufficient to constitute 'direct perception'. In *Brock v Northampton General Hosp NHS Trust*, Rachel Brock took an overdose of paracetamol and required urgent hospital treatment. To relieve intra-cranial pressure, a bolt was inserted into Rachel's head, but it was inserted too deep into her brain, causing a brain haemorrhage, and she died two days later. Her parents, Mr and Mrs Brock, C, were with their daughter often during the medical treatment, and saw the bolt (but did not know, at that time, that it had been inserted negligently). C were living close-by on-site at the hospital, and received a call that their daughter's condition had greatly deteriorated. They realised, from that call, that Rachel was going to die. Following a further brain scan showing irretrievable bleeding on the brain, the life support machine was turned off. The news conveyed by the call could not found liability in these circumstances.

It follows that C's viewing the dead body of a loved one, however traumatic, is not sufficient for direct perception. Furthermore, earnest efforts by D to minimise the trauma of the events surrounding a relative's extremely grave situation may reduce the 'direct perception' of events. It seems that it is within D's power to reduce the opportunities for C, the distressed relative, to claim as a secondary victim, by instigating suitable systems by which to reduce the causes of distress – a point which is presumably well-practised by hospital administrative and clinical staff.

In *Ward v Leeds Teaching Hosp NHS Trust*,[243] facts previously, Mrs Ward, C, observed her daughter, Katherine's, poor health following the wisdom teeth extraction, but lacked sufficient direct perception of the distressing events. D's nurses and medical staff 'were careful to keep [C] informed of the gravity of Katherine's condition, without alarming her unduly or exposing her to any sights or sounds which might cause her distress. Even the viewing of Katherine's body at the mortuary, assuming for these purposes it was sufficiently proximate in time, did not take place without [C's] nephew first taking the trouble to view the body, to ensure that nothing untoward would be seen'. Hence, the 'overwhelming factor' in C's psychiatric injury was that her cherished daughter had died, rather than the events at the hospital.

Receiving bad news – allowing recovery. Exceptionally, where bad information about D's negligence has been conveyed to C orally in person, or by phone, or in writing, at some point thereafter, on only rare occasions has C been owed a duty of care:

• that duty was conceded:

In *AB v Tameside and Glossop HA*,[244] a former healthcare professional involved in obstetric treatment tested HIV-positive. His employer, D, had to inform women, C, who were under treatment from that health worker, of the very slight risk of HIV infection, and letters were sent advising C of the availability of 'further advice, counselling, and possibly a test'. **Held:** a duty to take care when conveying accurate, but distressing, news was *conceded* by D (but D successfully defended the negligence claim on the basis that breaking the news to C in that way was not negligently done).

---

[242] [1999] EWCA Civ 1533.

[243] [2004] EWHC 2106 (QB) [20], [2004] Lloyd's Rep Med 530, 535.

[244] [1997] 8 Med LR 91 (CA), quote at 92, and also: 94 (Brooke LJ), 101 (Kennedy LJ), with Nourse LJ agreeing with both judgments (the CA overturned the trial judge who had permitted recovery: French J, 31 Jan 1995).

- C sued in negligent misstatement:

  In *Allin v City and Hackney HA*,[245] Mrs Allin, C, gave birth to a baby, but was told that the baby had died. About six hours later, Mrs Allin discovered that the baby was alive. Mrs Allin sued for PTSD, as a result of receiving this inaccurate information, and for D's failure to refer her for psychological treatment afterwards. **Held:** C recovered £10,000 for psychiatric injury.

- C was treated as an elevated primary victim, and not a secondary victim. Communication of bad news (inaccurate information that Mr Farrell's baby son had died, **plus** the sight of the 'dead' body of his son) grounded recovery for Mr Farrell in *Farrell v Avon HA*[246] (facts previously). However, Mr Farrell was ultimately treated as a **primary** victim, and that allowed him to tiptoe around this common law rule of 'direct perception' governing secondary victim recovery which Mrs Taylor, Mrs Ward, Mr Tan and Mrs Palmer were unable to surmount;

- C was told the information (about the death of a close relative, say) at the scene of the accident, within the immediate aftermath of D's negligence, and when experiencing the sights and sounds associated with a very serious accident.

  In *Galli-Atkinson v Seghal*,[247] facts previously, the combination of the limited scenes which C saw at the accident site, together with the mortuary visit (also within the immediate aftermath), was sufficient to amount to direct perception. In *Young v MacVean*,[248] Martha Young's, C's, son David was hit whilst walking on the footpath, due to D's negligent driving. C came across the crash scene on her way to a gym visit without knowing that David was involved, but it brought back memories of her husband's death in a North Sea helicopter crash. C saw the car wreck, knew that David was in the vicinity, started to be very concerned that David was involved, and was frantic even before the police attended the gym to inform her of her son's death. C's psychiatric injury was caused by the shock of coming upon the aftermath of the crash scene, rather than as a result of the shock of being told that David had been killed.

- C was treated outside the primary victim/secondary victim classification altogether, so as to recover under the *Caparo* test (per *Creutzfeldt-Jakob Disease Litig; Group B Plaintiffs v UKMRC*[249]).

  Hence, there are legal avenues open to the recipient of bad news which causes psychiatric injury, by which that C can recover compensation – but they have been fairly sporadic, and **not** via the secondary victim route.

§5.32 Where secondary victim C directly perceives the *effects* of D's negligence, the better view appears to be that English law will not consider that C has satisfied the direct perception requirement, although exceptions to the contrary do exist.

Quite apart from the other avenues for recovery referred to above, some authority has (confusingly) supported the notion that C's direct perception, by sight or by ear, of the *consequences or effects* of D's negligence upon a loved one, can adequately satisfy this pre-requisite for a secondary victim.

---

[245] [1996] 7 Med LR 167 (Mayor's and City of London Court).   [246] [2001] Lloyd's Rep Med 458 (QB).
[247] [2003] EWCA Civ 679.   [248] [2014] CSOH 133.   [249] [2000] Lloyd's Rep Med 161 (QB).

In *Froggatt v Chesterfield and North Derbyshire NHS Trust*,[250] facts previously, both Mr Froggatt and his son, C, had directly perceived the effects of the medical negligence perpetrated by D upon Mrs Froggatt, seeing the disfigurement of the mastectomy, and overhearing the news being discussed on the phone, respectively. In *North Glamorgan NHS Trust v Walters*,[251] facts previously, Ms Walters, C, witnessed, not the medical acts or omissions perpetrated on her son Elliot *per se*, but the *effects* of that negligence. However, being told information about Elliot's condition as events were unfolding in, and between, hospitals, together with her own observations, were sufficient for direct perception. In *Galli-Atkinson v Seghal*,[252] facts previously, Mrs Galli-Atkinson, C, viewed Livia's body at the mortuary, but was kept away from the actual scene of the accident by police cordon. Nevertheless, she could recover, as her psychiatric injury was not only sustained by what she had been told about the accident; she was around the scene, which was obviously a very serious accident, where she experienced mounting panic; and the injuries to Livia's body, which C saw at the mortuary, were horrific.

In *Froggatt*, a passage from *Sion v Hampstead HA*,[253] by Peter Gibson LJ, was quoted with approval (and had more impact on the result in *Froggatt* than it did in *Sion* itself!):

> I can see no reason in logic why breach of duty causing an incident involving no violence and suddenness, such as where the wrong medicine is negligently given to a hospital patient, could not lead to a claim for damages for nervous shock, e.g., where the negligence has fatal results and the visiting close relative, wholly unprepared for what has occurred, finds the body and thereby sustains a sudden and unexpected shock to the nervous system.[254]

That legal view would go some way to reducing the importance of the direct perception requirement for secondary victims (although the 'immediate aftermath' doctrine could still prevent such actions).

However, this strand of reasoning has neither been developed nor applied consistently, rendering the criterion uncertain. It certainly sits uncomfortably with cases such as *Taylor v Somerset HA* and *Ward v Leeds Teaching Hospital*. Even more recently, in *Brock v Northampton General Hosp NHS Trust*,[255] parents who witnessed the effects of a bolt being inserted too far into their daughter's brain was insufficient to base recovery (it may have been different, said the court, if their daughter had collapsed in front of them, after undergoing such a procedure). Moreover, the passage of Peter Gibson LJ was dicta (the ratio of *Sion* being that C, the secondary victim, had not suffered from a shock-induced psychiatric injury, discussed below) – and in *Taylor v Novo*,[256] Lord Dyson MR disapproved of the passage in *Sion*, and regarded it as not binding on the Court of Appeal.

The law reform corner: Commentary on this requirement

English Law Comm[257] and Ipp Committee:[258] both regarded the requirement of direct perception as giving rise to distinctions which were arbitrary and artificial, and that it should be abolished. The secondary victim's proximity to the event or its aftermath was not always a relevant factor in determining how the person would react.

[250] [2002] All ER (D) 218 (QB) [78]-[80].   [251] [2002] EWCA Civ 1792, [35], [40] (Ward LJ).
[252] [2003] EWCA Civ 679.   [253] (1994) 5 Med LR 170 (QB) 174, 176, appeal dismissed: [1994] 4 Med LR 170 (CA).
[254] [2002] All ER (D) 218 (QB) [78].   [255] [2014] EWHC 4244 (QB) [93].
[256] [2013] EWCA Civ 194 [33].   [257] *English Report*, [6.10]-[6.16].   [258] *Ipp Report*, [9.24].

> Scottish Law Comm:[259] was critical of the ungenerous attitude which the law took towards those who were told of the death of a loved one but who were too distraught, or coincidentally too far away, to directly perceive of the negligence or of its immediate aftermath. It also recommended that the rule be abolished.

'Normal fortitude'

§5.33   D is not liable for a psychiatric injury that a secondary victim, C, has suffered only because C is abnormally susceptible or vulnerable to such injury. D is only liable to C if a person of ordinary fortitude would foreseeably have suffered some psychiatric injury. Once that is proven, then C can recover for the full extent of his psychiatric injury.

The requirement of normal fortitude appears to emanate from the early (1942) case of *Bourhill (or Hay) v Young*,[260] and was confirmed by Lord Lloyd, in *Page v Smith*, as being one of the important control mechanisms applicable to secondary victim recovery.[261]

> In *Bourhill v Young*, C, a pregnant lady, heard a motor accident in which a motorcyclist was killed, saw the scene afterwards (but not the accident itself), and the bloodstains on the road from where the motorcyclist had eventually come to rest. She suffered a psychiatric illness from what she had seen and heard, and also gave birth to a stillborn child. **Held:** C was not permitted to recover compensation.

The following statement explained, in part, the reasons for the decision:

> The driver of a car or vehicle, even though careless, is entitled to assume that the ordinary frequenter of the streets has sufficient fortitude to endure such incidents as may from time to time be expected to occur in them, including the noise of a collision and the sight of injury to others, and is not considered negligent to one who does not possess the customary phlegm.[262]

It is important to note that the principle does not require the secondary victim himself to be a person of normal fortitude. As the Ipp Committee noted, 'being a person of normal fortitude is not a precondition of being owed a duty of care' as a secondary victim.[263] Rather, it must be foreseeable that a person of normal fortitude or 'customary phlegm' would have suffered some psychiatric injury. If that is proven, then an emotionally fragile secondary victim can recover for the full extent of his psychiatric injury (an application of the 'egg-shell skull' rule). On the other hand, if the secondary victim is an 'egg-shell skull personality', and the psychiatric injury sustained was *only* foreseeable in a person of vulnerable tendencies, the secondary victim will not recover.

In that respect, the principle of normal fortitude operates, for secondary victims, much the same as for C's recovery for physical injury – a vulnerable C can recover for the full extent of his injuries, but only if some physical injury would have been sustained by the notional person of normal fortitude. D is not expected to foresee injury to 'egg-shell psyche' persons, when no injury would have been suffered by anyone else.

> In *Powell v Boldaz*,[264] facts previously (re the substitution of one page for another), the normal fortitude rule was an insurmountable barrier for both secondary victim parental Cs. Mrs Powell had 'an

---

[259] *Scottish Report*, [2.23]–[2.24].   [260] 1942 SC (HL) 78.   [261] [1996] AC 155 (HL) 197.
[262] [1943] AC 92 (HL) 117 (Lord Porter).   [263] *Ipp Report*, [9.13].
[264] [1998] Lloyd's Rep Med 116 (QB) 123–24.

innate pre-disposition to develop an anxiety disorder', while Mr Powell was 'still grieving' about son Robert's death at the time when the substitution occurred. It seemed likely that normally robust Cs would have withstood news of the alleged substitution without succumbing to psychiatric illness; or, in other words, it was most unlikely that the same injury would have been sustained by persons of normal fortitude. In *Farrell v Avon HA*,[265] Mr Farrell, C, had a pre-existing psychological problem which rendered him more at risk than others of developing PTSD. As a primary victim, this did not preclude C's recovery for psychiatric injury. However, even had C been considered a secondary victim (with no immediate victim existing, as discussed previously), being given a corpse to hold in the mistaken belief that it was his son was surely the type of exceptionally catastrophic event that could foreseeably cause psychiatric injury in a person of normal fortitude. However, C would likely have failed the 'close tie' requirement (above). In *Tredget and Tredget v Bexley HA*,[266] Mr and Mrs Tredget, C, could recover for their 'pathological unresolved mourning', following the death of their son Callum at two days old. The medical opinion was that each parent 'had a prior susceptibility towards an aggravated reaction to Callum's birth and death. There had been the prior loss or termination of pregnancies'. However, presumably a person of normal fortitude would foreseeably have suffered some psychiatric injury as a result of the circumstances of this tragic birth.

The law reform corner: Commentary on this requirement

English Law Comm:[267] the normal fortitude rule should be implemented as part of the usual test of foreseeability – i.e., the rule is 'best interpreted as meaning nothing more than that ... in deciding whether psychiatric illness was reasonably foreseeable (and analogously to reasonable foreseeability in physical injury cases), one can take into account the robustness of the population at large to psychiatric illness'.

Scottish Law Comm:[268] the normal fortitude rule, which 'stalks the current law', as it applies to secondary victims, has distinct problems in the way in which it seeks to limit liability – partly because 'there is a wide range of susceptibility to mental harm among the general population. Thus, *ordinary* fortitude is difficult to assess'. Also, the rule can hardly mean, 'average fortitude', because most people do not suffer psychiatric injury at all, as a result of witnessing negligence to loved ones. Overall, the Commission called the rule 'a legal construct which is difficult to evaluate'. Instead, it favoured a rule that, for both primary and secondary victims, there should be no recovery if the injury was of the type that C could reasonably be expected to endure without seeking compensation, because it either represented one of the vicissitudes of life or a normal bereavement.

Shock

§5.34 For secondary victims, the psychiatric injury must be induced by shock – a concept which constitutes 'a sudden assault on the nervous system'. Whether C suffered a shock is to be judged objectively.

Alcock was the first occasion in English law in which 'shock' emerged as an independent criterion for liability governing secondary victim recovery (the meaning of 'shock', in the legal

---

[265] [2001] Lloyd's Rep Med 458 (QB) 462.   [266] [1994] 5 Med LR 178 (London CC) 181.
[267] *English Report*, [5.21], [5.26].   [268] *Scottish Report*, [1.5], [3.18]–[3.19], [2.20], [3.30].

sense, has been described previously in this chapter[269]). Without an 'assault on the senses' or a 'violent agitation of the mind', C will be vulnerable to the finding that his injury should be borne without compensation.

When deciding whether the event was 'horrifying' or capable of constituting a 'violent agitation of the mind' is to be determined 'by objective standards, and by reference to persons of ordinary susceptibility', and not by reference to how much medical knowledge that particular C may have possessed (per *Liverpool Women's Hospital NHS Foundation Trust v Ronayne*[270]).

Several would-be secondary claimants have had difficulty in proving the requisite shock – and this is especially so, if they have also failed the 'direct perception' requirement. The shock criterion **precludes** secondary victim recovery in a number of scenarios:

- where C suffers a psychiatric injury caused by a gradual wearing-down by giving long-term care to the immediate victim:

    In *Alcock*,[271] Lord Oliver ruled out a secondary victim recovering because of caring for loved ones who had suffered injury or misfortune – that had to 'be considered as ordinary and inevitable incidents of life which, regardless of individual susceptibilities, must be sustained without compensation';

- where C has a dawning or gradual realisation that things are not going to turn out well for the immediate victim (as all of the following cases demonstrated, in none of which could C recover):

    In *Sion v Hampstead HA*,[272] Mr Sion Snr's, C's, son was injured in a motorcycle accident and taken to D's hospital. D's staff failed to diagnose substantial and continuing bleeding from Mr Sion Jnr's left kidney, and he fell into a coma from which he never recovered, dying 14 days after admittance. C maintained a bedside vigil throughout this time, witnessing his son's deterioration and eventual death, and suffered psychiatric injury. C could not recover. Whilst it was not necessary that medical negligence be sudden and violent, it was still necessary that C sustained a 'sudden and unexpected shock to the nervous system'. Within a week of hospitalisation, C realised that it was almost certain that his son would not survive, and when death came, 'he was not surprised, and felt that, in a way, he had been preparing himself for this to happen'. That did not satisfy the 'shock' requirement. In *Ward v Leeds Teaching Hosp NHS Trust*,[273] facts previously, Mrs Ward, C, had not suffered a sudden shock with the death of her daughter Katherine after the wisdom teeth operation. C suffered '[a]n event outside the range of human experience, [which] sadly, does not ... encompass the death of a loved one in hospital unless also accompanied by circumstances which were wholly exceptional in some way so as to shock or horrify'. In *Brock v Northampton General Hosp NHS Trust*,[274] facts previously, there was nothing 'wholly exceptional' to shock or horrify Mr and Mrs Brock, C, 'dreadful as it may have been'. A nurse's call made them realise that daughter Rachel was going to die, and their sight of her, when told that she was brain-dead, was not a shocking event, but rather, a confirmation of the terrible realisation.

---

[269] See pp 254–55.

[270] [2015] EWCA Civ 588, [13] (Tomlinson LJ), citing with approval: *Shorter v Surrey & Sussex NHS Trust* [2015] EWHC 614 QB, [214] (Swift J).

[271] [1992] 1 AC 310 (HL) 416 (Lord Oliver).

[272] (1994) 5 Med LR 170 (QB) 174, 176, appeal dismissed: [1994] 4 Med LR 170 (CA).

[273] [2004] EWHC 2106 (QB) [21] (HHJ Hawkesworth QC).   [274] [2014] EWHC 4244 (QB) [95]–[96].

- where C has already received notice of bad news about the immediate victim, and hence, seeing the immediate victim later on does not involve shock (in neither of the following could C recover):

  > In *Tan v East London and City HA*,[275] Mr Tan, C, was told of the death of his unborn daughter over the phone, and he travelled straight to the hospital, and was present during the operation. His visit to the hospital was made in the full knowledge that his baby had died, and hence, he did not suffer a shock in the legal sense. In *Taylor v Somerset HA*,[276] Mrs Taylor, C, insisted upon seeing her husband's body in the mortuary after being informed of his death, but that did not constitute a 'shocking event', because the purpose of the mortuary visit was only to 'settle her disbelief'. Plus the body 'bore no marks or signs to her of the sort that would have conjured up for her the circumstances of his fatal attack'.

- where C may have been present at a shocking and horrifying event, and suffered psychiatric injury as a result of grief and bereavement, but not as a result of an 'assault' in the *Alcock* sense. Naturally, these cases are very much 'at the borderline' of what is, and is not, permissible by way of recovery:

  > In *Less v Hussain*,[277] on 4 May, Ms Less, who was pregnant, realised that she could not feel foetal movement, and went to the hospital, accompanied by her partner, Mr Carter, C. Death *in utero* was diagnosed. Ms Less was given tablets to induce labour, and C stayed with her. On 6 May, baby Luis was delivered stillborn, C held him, and Luis' body was taken away and brought back dressed in a dress ('because, despite his sex, that was all that could be found'). C suffered a bereavement reaction. **Held:** C could not recover, as his injury did not arise from shock, i.e., the sudden appreciation by sight or sound of the hugely distressing events he witnessed.

However, the criterion of 'shock' has suffered from two grave inconsistencies, since *Alcock* made the requirement mandatory for secondary victims.[278]

Problem #1: A drawn-out and 'seamless' shock

§5.35 The shock requirement has been held, on occasion, to constitute a series of events and assaults on C's nervous system which, although separate, can comprise *one* shocking and seamless event.

This interpretation, where it applies, enables the scenario to play out over several hours – and, clearly, what one judge may consider to be a 'dawning realisation' of the fate to befall an immediate victim may comprise a drawn-out, yet sudden and violent agitation of the mind, to another.

> In *North Glamorgan NHS Trust v Walters*,[279] facts previously, Mrs Walters, C, succeeded in proving one shocking event. It was 'an inexorable progression from the moment when the fit occurred as a result of the failure of the hospital properly to diagnose and then to treat the baby, the fit causing the brain damage which shortly thereafter made termination of this child's life inevitable and the dreadful climax when the child died in her arms. It is a seamless tale with an obvious beginning

---

[275] [1999] Lloyd's Rep Med 389 (Chelmsford CC).   [276] [1993] 4 Med LR 34 (QB) 37–38.

[277] [2012] EWHC 3513 (QB).

[278] Some of this analysis is drawn from Mulheron, 'Secondary Victim Psychiatric Illness Claims' (2003) 14 *KCLJ* 213.

[279] [2002] EWCA Civ 1792, [2003] Lloyd's Rep Med 49, with quotes at [34], [40] (Ward LJ).

and an equally obvious end. It was played out over a period of 36 hours, which for her both at the time and as subsequently recollected was undoubtedly one drawn-out experience'; and 'the assault on [C's] nervous system had begun and she reeled under successive blows as each was delivered'. In *Tredget and Tredget v Bexley HA*,[280] Mr and Mrs Tredget, C, recovered, because their full appreciation of their newborn's condition after the pandemonium birth 'only came with time', and it was 'unrealistic to separate out and isolate the delivery as an event, from the other sequence of happenings from the onset of labour to Callum's death two days later ... although lasting for over 48 hours from the onset of labour to the death, this effectively was one event'. In *Galli-Atkinson v Seghal*,[281] facts previously, *Walters* was expressly relied upon, such that the events following Livia's accident were an uninterrupted sequence that constituted the aftermath of D's negligent driving which killed Livia, and which retained sufficient proximity to that initial event.

In *Walters*,[282] Ward LJ considered that the verdict for Mrs Walters had not achieved any change in the law; Clarke LJ expressly observed that, *if* the Court of Appeal's finding in favour of Ms Walters did mean that an incremental step in the law needed to be taken, 'I for my part would take that step on the facts of this case'; and Sir Anthony Evans agreed with both judgments.

Walters has received some judicial endorsement since. In *Galli-Atkinson v Seghal*, the court noted that the law is not 'restricted by what Lord Ackner said in *Alcock* to a frozen moment in time ... an event itself may be made up of a number of components; this was accepted by this court in *Walters*'.[283] Even more significantly, in *JD v East Berkshire Community Health NHS Trust*, the House of Lords described the *Walters/Tredget* decisions as a 'distinct line of authority'[284] in the field of pure psychiatric injury and secondary victim recovery.

It comes as no surprise that Cs, in drawn-out negligence scenarios, have sought to expand the 'seamless tale' to something longer than 36 hours, and that courts have had to draw arbitrary lines in the sand, where that has been attempted. However, the *Walters* line of authority has not enjoyed much success in recent English case law; it has been distinguished, or restricted to its facts. Indeed, in a quartet of cases over the course of 2014–15, none of the following Cs could recover as secondary victims (with *Walters* being cited, but distinguished, in each of them[285]):

In *Taylor v Novo*,[286] facts previously, the death of Mrs Taylor, some 21 days after she was injured at work, was 'certainly not part of a single event or seamless tale'. Her injury at work, and her death at home, were 'distinct events'. In *Wild v Southend Univ Hosp*,[287] facts previously, the court noted that, in *Walters*, the sequence started with the very serious illness of Elliot, and with various good and bad news and diagnoses, until he died 36 hours later in his mother's, C's, arms, whereas in *Wild*, the sequence started with C's realisation that his child had died *in utero*, and then C and his wife had to endure the agony of waiting until the next day until the stillbirth: 'this case is materially different from the facts in *Walters*, being based on an "event" which starts with the realisation that Matthew has already died'. In *Liverpool Women's Hosp NHS Foundation Trust v Ronayne*,[288] Mrs Ronayne entered D's hospital to undergo a hysterectomy, but suffered septicaemia when a suture was inadvertently misplaced in her colon. She was re-admitted to hospital, and her husband,

---

[280] (1994) 5 Med LR 178, with quote at 183–84.   [281] [2003] EWCA Civ 697.

[282] [2002] EWCA Civ 1792, with quotes at [43], and [51].   [283] [2003] EWCA Civ 697, [25].

[284] [2005] UKHL 23, [2006] 2 AC 373, [107] (Lord Rodger).

[285] To this quartet must be added a very recent decision: *Owers v Medway NHS Foundation Trust* [2015] EWHC 2363 (QB), where again, *Walters* was distinguished, and the husband's claim for pure psychiatric injury failed.

[286] [2013] EWCA Civ 194, [2014] QB 150, [35].   [287] [2014] EWHC 4053 (QB) [48], [53].

[288] [2015] EWCA Civ 588, [35]–[41] (Tomlinson LJ).

Edward Ronayne, C, suffered PTSD upon seeing the deterioration in his wife's condition and appearance over two days following her re-admittance, which he described as like 'the Michelin Man'. Mrs Ronayne eventually recovered, after a lengthy hospital stay. The claim failed, as there was no 'inexorable progression', and nor was it 'seamless'. Rather, it was 'a series of events over a period of time', and a 'dawning realisation' that his wife's life was in danger, plus this was told to C orally by the treating doctors before C saw his wife in a swollen condition; there was no 'sudden appreciation of an event'. In *Shorter v Surrey & Sussex HC NHS Trust*,[289] Mrs Sharma had a brain aneurysm on 5 May, which went undetected from a CT scan. She was re-admitted to hospital a week later, after the CT scan was interpreted correctly, but suffered a fatal re-bleed that night, and died the following day (negligence towards Mrs Sharma was conceded). Julie Shorter, C, was Mrs Sharma's sister, and thereafter suffered depression. C submitted that there was a seamless tale of events, from when the incorrect diagnosis was conveyed to her on 12 May, to when Mrs Sharma passed away on 13 May. C's claim failed, as she lacked physical proximity to her sister throughout these events. C received four phone conversations which increased her fears as to her sister's welfare; and her sight of her sister was not of the same category of unpleasantness as Mrs Walter's view of her baby suffering from an epileptic fit, rigid and convulsing and with blood pouring from his mouth. The facts of *Walters* were distinguishable.

This cadre of recent cases precluding family members as secondary victims is undoubtedly a welcome trend by the NHS Litigation Authority, and serves notice that *Walters* will be very strictly construed.

The comparative corner: The treatment of *Walters* elsewhere

Hong Kong: In *Wong Fung Sze v Tuen Mun Hosp*,[290] Mr Sze was operated on by the treating doctors, D, for oesophageal cancer. Mr Sze and his wife, C, were told in May 2001 that relevant CAT and MRI tests were negative. They were then told, on 21 July, that the cancer had spread to Mr Sze's skull, brain and upper neck. C claimed that she suffered shock on receiving that news; or alternatively, that she received a series of shocks between when she thought that her husband was clear of cancer, to the point at which he died on 22 Sep. C argued that her husband was destined to die of cancer, but that the quality of his end-of-life would have been better, and her psychiatric injury would have been prevented, if D had not negligently misdiagnosed his cancer. **Held:** C could not recover. The series of events, May–Sep, could not constitute one horrifying event; and C did not suffer the requisite shock. Whilst acknowledging that *Walters* represented a 'very realistic approach' in medical negligence cases, there were three key points of distinction between this case and *Walters* (said the court):

(1) it would be a 'quantum leap' from a 36-hour horrifying event to one lasting four months;

(2) Mrs Walters was given high hopes of baby Elliot's likely recovery by the hospital, whereas Mrs Sze realistically must have harboured doubts about her husband's prospects of survival; and

---

[289] [2015] EWHC 614 QB.

[290] [2004] HKDC 154, quotes at [25]–[29], leave to appeal denied: Judge To in Chambers, 11 Oct 2004.

(3) in *Walters*, D initially gave a very positive assurance that Elliot had suffered no brain damage, whereas no such positive statement was made by D here, meaning that, '[t]he psychiatric illness of [C] was therefore the result of gradual assaults on her mind during this period of four months', because of her worry and gradual realisation of her husband's true condition.

Singapore: In *Pang Koi Fa v Lim Djoe Phing*,[291] facts previously, **held:** C could recover. C witnessed gradual deterioration of her daughter's condition for about three months, compounded by D's neglect or refusal during that time to attend to her daughter: 'the dicta of Lord Ackner no doubt left open the inclusion of situations of psychiatric illness in the appropriate and abnormal case where the elements of suddenness may not be present, and where psychiatric illness assaults the nervous system, builds up, and manifests itself over some short period of time'.

The author has criticised the lack of consistency displayed by the decision in *Walters* elsewhere (and some other academic commentary since has not been particularly kind to it either[292]):

Mrs Ward and Mr Sion would no doubt argue that their experiences in hospital were equally as seamless as Mrs Walters', with an initial expectation that their children were ill, but then gaining the realisation that their lives were ending. Furthermore, the psychiatric evidence given in *Walters* suggested that it was the *longer* duration of events surrounding Elliot's death, rather than his sudden death, which resulted in Ms Walters' shock: 'the psychiatric impact is more severe than if the child had died suddenly, as it was compounded by uncertainties over the diagnosis and re-admission to various hospitals'.[293] Surely the protracted experiences of Mr Sion and Mrs Ward were just as capable of producing that type of shock? The inconsistencies in outcome are obvious, despite Ward LJ's assertion in *Walters* that *Sion* was 'a very different case'.[294] The Scottish Commission's semantic discussion[295] of how the cases differ – that *Walters* demonstrates that the 'sudden realisation of danger within a continuing process' is compensable whereas *Sion's* 'continuing process [of realisation]' is not – only serves to emphasise the difficulties inherent in the reasoning of the two decisions ... In that respect, the law may well have moved on to embrace what Lord Ackner envisaged in *Alcock* – that shock 'has yet to include psychiatric illness caused by the accumulation over a period of time of more gradual assaults on the nervous system'.[296] That position, it seems, *has* been reached in English law, and an explicit acknowledgment of that fact should have been made in *Walters*.[297]

Problem #2: Witnessing a body

§5.36   Whether viewing an immediate victim's body in order to fully comprehend the consequences of D's negligence can give rise to a shock has not been treated entirely consistently either.

---

[291] [1993] 3 SLR 317 (HC) 334.

[292] e.g.: V Chico, 'Saviour Siblings: Trauma and Tort Law' (2006) 14 *Med L Rev* 180, 211; Editorial, 'Clinical Negligence: Secondary Victims and Recovery for Nervous Shock' (2003) 11 *Med L Rev* 121, 124; M Puxon, 'Comment' on *Tredget* [1994] 5 Med LR 184, and a similar observation at: [1994] 5 *Med LR* 177; S Allen, 'Post-traumatic Stress Disorder: The Claims of Primary and Secondary Victims' (2000) 2 *JPIL* 108, 109.

[293] [2002] EWCA Civ 1792, [10].   [294] [2002] EWCA Civ 1792, [29].

[295] *Scottish Report*, [2.4].   [296] [1992] 2 AC 310 (HL) 400.

[297] Mulheron, 'Pure Psychiatric Injury Claims by Third Parties Associated with the Patient' in *Medical Negligence: Non-Patient and Third Party Claims* (Ashgate Publishing, 2010) 291.

In *Taylor v Somerset* and *Tan v East London*, C's viewing of the immediate victims' dead bodies was merely for confirmation, and did not constitute a 'shocking event' in either case. The purpose was to grieve, to settle disbelief, and the like.

However, against these decisions must be contrasted the husband's recovery of £5,000 for psychiatric damage in *Froggatt v Chesterfield and North Derbyshire Royal Hosp NHS Trust*.[298] Mr Froggatt knew that his wife had undergone a (needless, as it turned out) mastectomy. Yet, the court was willing to hold that, 'when he saw [his wife] undressed for the first time after the mastectomy, he was quite unprepared for what he saw and he was profoundly and lastingly shocked by it.'[299] Mrs Taylor witnessed her dead husband; Mr Froggatt witnessed his disfigured wife; and yet only the latter could recover at law.

It will be recalled that the direct perception requirement was 'watered down' in *Froggatt* – as was the shock requirement. All of this renders the application of the shock requirement very uncertain.

Conclusion. More than for any other secondary victim criterion, the requirement for a 'sudden shock' is the most problematical. It tends to be applied either strictly or in a distinctly watered-down version, with little consistency demonstrated in the case law. The concept is artificial, for something that 'violently agitates the mind' may occur over a fairly lengthy period.

The expert medical report given in *White (Frost) v CC of South Yorkshire Police*, cited in the Court of Appeal, was that, '[i]n fiction, and perhaps in a layman's view of shock as a psychological event, the individual experiences a grossly untoward event or situation with one or more sensory modalities but almost always vision, and is instantaneously "shocked" or traumatised. In practice, this almost never occurs'.[300] Indeed, as a psychiatric expert pointed out in *North Glamorgan v Walters*, the protracted nature of the immediate victim's decline may be the very reason that the secondary victim sustained 'shock'.[301] It also leads to factual lotteries, for if C happens to have been told something that raises his hopes but those hopes prove false (as in *Walters*), it may be easier to prove the requisite shock. Moreover, the Court of Appeal was invited to take a 'small incremental step ... to replace the shock requirement and substitute a requirement that the psychiatric illness need only be caused by directly witnessing or experiencing some trauma'.[302] Ultimately, this step was not directly taken – but C could prove a 'series of assaults' equating to shock in any event.

The law reform corner: Commentary on this requirement

English Law Comm:[303] given all of its problems, the requirement of shock for secondary victims should be abolished by statute. As a control mechanism, it was blunt and crude. It excluded those worn down by a lifetime of caring for the immediate victim, whom society may feel most worthy of compensation. Also, to retain the shock criterion emphasised the requirement of proximity of time and space, itself a problematical control mechanism. The *only* control mechanisms that ought to be retained for secondary victims of any type were proof of a recognisable psychiatric illness, reasonable foreseeability of pyschiatric harm to a person of normal fortitude, and a close tie of love and affection between C and the immediate victim.

---

[298] [2002] All ER (D) 218 (QB).   [299] *ibid*, [79].   [300] [1997] 3 WLR 1194 (CA) 1207.
[301] [2002] EWCA Civ 1792, [10].   [302] *ibid*, [19(iv)].
[303] *English Report*, [5.29], and expressly abolished in: Draft Negligence (Psychiatric Illness) Bill, cl 5(2); and [5.6], [5.10], [5.27], [6.16].

> Scottish Law Comm:[304] the shock requirement should be abolished, as it represented an outdated mode of medical and judicial understanding as to how mental injury was incurred. Some psychiatric injury for which shock is a precursor to diagnosis, such as PTSD, are inherently more compensable, in comparison to depression, for which shock is not necessarily a precursor. Plus, shock has not been applied to work-related stress claims.

Can C be *both* 'primary' and 'secondary' victim?

§5.37 English case law demonstrates that, despite the different duty of care requirements which attach to each type, C can indeed be *both* a primary victim and a secondary victim.

The House of Lords has appeared to vacillate as to whether C had to be either/or, or whether he could be both, primary victim and secondary victim.

In *Alcock*,[305] Lord Oliver described primary victims, and 'on the other hand', secondary victims. It seemed to be a definition of two halves. In *White*,[306] Lord Steyn described primary victims, and said that 'all other victims, who suffer pure psychiatric harm, are secondary victims.'

However, in *Page v Smith*,[307] Lord Lloyd rationalised some earlier cases as examples of where C was 'both primary and secondary victim of the same accident'. In *W v Essex CC*[308] too, Lord Slynn allowed the parental Cs to take both primary **and** secondary victim claims to trial.

Lower level cases have also adhered to this view that C can be both primary and secondary victim, with a lack of clear demarcation. For example, in *Farrell v Merton, Sutton and Wandsworth HA*,[309] (where C's son, Karol, was born with irreversible brain damage), the court made no bold statement as to what type of victim Mrs Farrell was, but hedged its bets. It held that Mrs Farrell was either a primary victim, directly involved in the events (the trauma of the birth), or a secondary victim, who witnessed the aftermath of the medically-caused injury suffered by Karol. In *Tredget v Bexley HA*,[310] Judge White was not conclusive as to whether the parents were primary or secondary victims either. At one point, the parents were described as 'directly involved in and with the event of the delivery' ... and 'each principals rather than passive witnesses'; whereas earlier, the legal criteria for the parents to fulfill were described in secondary victim-type terms.

The lack of a clear-cut distinction between the two categories has been confusing and problematical, given that different rules apply to each category, which the author has criticised elsewhere:

> no clear-cut distinction between [primary and secondary victim definition] has been maintained. Yet surely how we define a primary victim is a matter of law. Once a definition has been laid down, it is then a question of fact whether [C] falls within it. To treat secondary victim status as a 'fallback position' into which [C] might fall if he does not 'make it as a primary victim', is symptomatic of the courts' inability to produce a stable definition of the primary victim.[311]

To summarise, the following Table sets out why the secondary victim has a 'harder job' of proving a duty of care was owed to him than the primary victim does:

---

[304] *Scottish Report*, [2.4]–[2.5].   [305] [1992] 1 AC 310 (HL) 407–8.   [306] [1999] 2 AC 455 (HL) 496–9.
[307] [1996] AC 155 (HL) 190.   [308] [2001] 2 AC 592 (HL).   [309] (2001) 57 BMLR 158 (QB) 164.
[310] [1994] 5 Med LR 178 (Central London CC), with quotes at 183 and 182 respectively.
[311] 'The "Primary Victim" in Psychiatric Illness Claims, etc' (2008) 19 *KCLJ* 81, 87.

A comparison of primary and secondary victims	
Primary victim	**Secondary victim**
The *Page v Smith* primary victim may recover for either a foreseeable psychiatric injury, or for an unforeseeable psychiatric injury if some *physical* injury was foreseeable but did not actually occur	A secondary victim must prove that his *psychiatric* injury was reasonably foreseeable
Primary victims are not subject to the control mechanisms emanating from *Alcock*	Secondary victims must satisfy the three '*Alcock* control mechanisms' (however interpreted)
Some types of primary victim are definitely not subject to the shock requirement; and whether a *Page v Smith* primary victim is subject to the requirement is unclear	Secondary victims must prove that they suffered a 'sudden shock', a sudden appreciation of a horrifying event, as opposed to a dawning and gradual realisation of pending tragedy or misfortune
D must take a primary victim just as he finds him	Secondary victims must prove that pure psychiatric injury was foreseeable in a person of 'normal fortitude'

Primary victims have access to several advantages over their secondary victim counterparts – but neither type of C enjoys an easy time of proving that a duty of care was owed. The definition of the primary victim has changed over time; and the rules governing the imposition of a duty of care towards secondary victims are littered with inconsistencies. Certainly, it is useless to base any outcome upon whether C is 'deserving' of compensation. In *Walters*, Elliot's fit occurred before Mrs Walters' eyes because she happened to be in the same hospital room as he was; whereas in *Taylor*, Mr Taylor died of his undiagnosed heart condition at work, and so Mrs Taylor lost her claim. In *Farrell v Merton*, Mrs Farrell was only vaguely aware of son Karol's damaged condition following his birth (due, in part, to the hospital's removal of Karol to another treatment site), and she could recover; whereas Mr Sion, who maintained a vigil beside his dying son's bedside in hospital for two weeks, failed in his claim. *Walters* states that the *Alcock* control mechanisms should not be applied 'too rigidly or mechanistically',[312] whereas in *White*, Lord Steyn conceded that 'the only sensible general strategy for the courts is to say thus far and no further'.[313] And many unsuccessful secondary victims, including Mrs Ward, Mrs Taylor, Mrs Palmer, Mrs Hall, Mr Tan and Mr Sion, would no doubt say that an overly-mechanistic application of the legal criteria was exactly why they lost their claims.

Given the disarray in secondary victim law, it is unfortunate that EWLC's recommendations by which to simplify this area of the law have not been adopted in England, nor has their draft Bill been enacted. The area will inevitably have to develop incrementally, on a case-by-case basis.

ELEVATED PRIMARY VICTIM CLAIMANTS

Whether D owes an elevated primary victim, C, a duty of care, has followed a fairly abbreviated pattern of primary victim analysis. As dealt with in the leading cases of *AB v Leeds* and in *Farrell v Avon HA*:

[312] [2002] EWCA Civ 1792, [48] (Clarke LJ).   [313] [1998] UKHL 45, [1999] 2 AC 455 (HL) 500.

Reasonable foreseeability of psychiatric injury

§5.38   For the elevated primary victim, the wide test of reasonable foreseeability, relevant to the 'zone of danger' primary victim, is not applicable. Rather, C must prove that the risk of psychiatric injury was foreseen or reasonably foreseeable.

Occasionally, an elevated primary victim will *not* be able to prove that his psychiatric injury was a foreseen or reasonably foreseeable consequence of D's wrongdoing. The claim will fail at that point.

> In *AB v Leeds Teaching Hosp NHS Trust*,[314] facts previously, the parents of the babies whose organs were harvested and retained post-mortem were treated by Gage J as primary victims, but two out of the three Cs (Mrs Harris and Mrs Carpenter) failed to prove that it was either foreseen or reasonably foreseeable that they would suffer psychiatric injury when they discovered that their dead children's organs had been retained. Mrs Harris 'was a robust person and someone whom Dr Clifford would have regarded as unlikely to collapse under the strain'. Mrs Carpenter 'was a well-adjusted, practical and sensible woman. It was foreseeable that she would be angry and distressed by the knowledge of organ retention, but not that she would suffer psychiatric injury'.

Proximity

§5.39   In the case of an elevated primary victim, the usual proximity factors (i.e., geographic, temporal and relational) have, to date, been assumed.

Given that, in both *AB v Leeds* and *Farrell v Avon HA*, the mishaps occurred in a hospital setting, and by healthcare professionals who were operating in that environment in their professional capacity, some degree of relational proximity towards the more vulnerable C was inevitable. There was no discussion of proximity in either case, indicating how obvious the proposition was in those scenarios.

The 'normal fortitude' rule

§5.40   An elevated primary victim C can recover for his psychiatric injury, even if it was sustained because C lacked the mental fortitude or 'natural phlegm' of a person of normal fortitude.

This is a significant advantage which an elevated primary victim enjoys over secondary victims – and a prime reason for the importance of the *AB v Leeds/Farrell v Avon* line of authority.

> In *AB v Leeds Teaching Hosp NHS Trust*,[315] it was not fatal to Mrs Shorter's claim that she was an 'emotionally fragile person' who was in a very distressed state following the birth of her daughter, and then her death at a very early stage. Gage J concluded that 'the reasonable consultant obstetrician would have reasonably foreseen that this event would result in some psychiatric injury in Mrs Shorter'. C recovered £2,750 for her psychiatric injury. In *Farrell v Avon HA*,[316] Mr Farrell, C, was not a person of normal fortitude; according to the psychiatric evidence, C 'was probably always going to react badly to death', given his previous psychological history, treatment of his heroin addiction with a methadone programme, and alcohol dependency. Hence, C was more at risk of developing

---

[314] [2004] EWHC 644 (QB), [2005] QB 506, [253] (Mrs Harris), [279] (Mrs Carpenter), [268] (Mrs Shorter).
[315] [2004] EWHC 644, [2005] QB 506, [268].   [316] [2001] Lloyd's Rep Med 458 (QB) 464.

PTSD than the general population. Perhaps a father of normal fortitude may have withstood the shock of what was undeniably a terrible incident without suffering psychiatric injury, but this question was legally irrelevant. As a primary victim, D had to take Mr Farrell, C, exactly as they found him.

Shock

§5.41   It is unclear whether an elevated primary victim needs to prove that his psychiatric injury was caused by a 'shock' in the legal sense.

The criterion is not explicitly discussed in either *AB* or in *Farrell*. Undoubtedly, both sets of parental Cs did suffer trauma upon learning bad news about their children (false bad news, in Mr Farrell's case), but the relevant courts did not clarify whether a shock-induced injury was a pre-requisite to recovery.

FEAR-OF-THE-FUTURE CLAIMANTS

It will be recalled that 'fear-of-the-future' claimants are **not** primary victims *per se* (per the *CJD Litigation*), but have nevertheless been permitted to recover for psychiatric injury under the tri-partite *Caparo* test.

Reasonable foreseeability, and the normal fortitude rule

§5.42   For a fear-of-the-future C, his psychiatric injury must have been reasonably foreseeable. C must prove that a person of 'normal fortitude' would foreseeably suffer from some psychiatric injury, in which event C can recover for the full extent of his injury.

Notwithstanding that fear-of-the-future victims were in the zone of physical danger by being exposed to a disease-causing agent, they are not primary victims in the *Page v Smith* sense. Hence, they cannot take advantage of the wider test of foreseeability which applies to *Page v Smith*-type claimants – instead, their *psychiatric* injury must be foreseeable. This may be difficult to prove. On this point, the two leading English fear-of-the-future cases can be usefully contrasted.

> In the *CJD Litigation*,[317] facts previously, **held:** the illnesses suffered by the various HGH recipients, C, were reasonably foreseeable to the treating doctors, D, especially when there was a real prospect that C would learn of the dire consequences possibly awaiting them, not only from doctors and counsellors, but from angry, ill-informed, relatives and from sensational media reports which would tend to highlight or sensationalise the risk of the potential terrible outcome. In the *Pleural Plaques Litig*,[318] facts previously, **held:** Mr Grieves', C's, psychiatric injury was not reasonably foreseeable. C had a long-standing fear of developing asbestos-related illness. Medical evidence described C's condition as 'relatively unique' among those workmen who had been exposed to asbestos dust. Also, C was not alarmed by the actual inhalation of asbestos fibres or by anything else done by the employer D, but by information given to him some 20 years later, following an X-ray. All of this rendered his psychiatric injury unforeseeable.

---

[317] [2000] Lloyd's Rep Med 161 (QB).

[318] [2007] UKHL 39, [2008] 1 AC 281, [30] (Lord Hoffmann), [57]–[58] (Lord Hope), [77] (Lord Scott), [100] (Lord Rodger), and [104] (Lord Mance). In the CA: *Grieves* [2006] EWCA Civ 27, [76] and [94] (Lord Phillips CJ).

Just as with secondary victims, the normal fortitude rule applies, in that C must establish that a person of reasonable fortitude and 'customary phlegm' would foreseeably suffer from some psychiatric injury. This proposition was confirmed in the *CJD Litigation*, where Morland J stated that, '[i]t was reasonably foreseeable that, if the worst fears were realised and deaths from CJD occurred, Hartree HGH recipients, both *those of normal fortitude* and those more vulnerable, might suffer psychiatric injury'.[319]

The same proposition was applied in *Pleural Plaques*. Mr Grieves was not a person of normal fortitude – he suffered from an irrational fear of developing a terminal illness resulting from asbestos exposure. However, Lord Hoffmann stated that he must nevertheless be taken to be subject to the rule of normal fortitude, given that 'the employer would be unlikely to have any specific knowledge of how a particular employee was likely to react to the risk of asbestos-related illness more than 30 years after he had left his employment. An assumption of ordinary fortitude is therefore inevitable'.[320]

Proximity

§5.43   Given that temporal proximity between C's psychiatric injury and D's acts or omissions may be absent (if the injury manifests well after the breach occurred), legal proximity will usually depend upon whether D assumed a legal responsibility toward C to avoid his psychiatric injury.

Proximity requires, as always, a close examination of the circumstances and relationship between C and D. On this point, the two leading cases were in sympathy.

> In the *CJD Litigation*,[321] an assumption of responsibility was proven, from the following factors: D treated, diagnosed or otherwise cared for the HGH recipients of the clinical trial, as identifiable Cs; D's clinical trial entailed highly skilled and specialist treatment, rendering the recipients of the clinical trial vulnerable, and reliant upon D; in arranging the clinical trial, D constituted monopolistic providers of the medical services or were otherwise in a powerful position vis-a-vis the recipients, such that the recipients were vulnerable; the relationship between the clinicians, D, and the recipients was 'akin to that of doctor and patient, one of close proximity. But they were all children. They themselves did not choose to receive the treatment. They were selected for the treatment by clinicians at growth centres', i.e., relational proximity; D withheld information which could not be ascertained or verified elsewhere, and knew that supplying the information to the recipients would have prompted them to act differently. These factors, in combination, established that D assumed a responsibility toward the recipients to avoid causing them psychiatric harm in the conduct of the trial. In *Pleural Plaques*, Mr Grieves, C, was in a sufficiently-proximate relationship with D, his ex-employer. There was no debate about that point in the case.

Public policy

§5.44   No policy reasons have precluded recovery for psychiatric injury by a fear-of-the-future C to date.

In *Pleural Plaques*, there was no public policy reason precluding an ex-employee's recovery; and in the *CJD Litigation*,[322] Morland J noted that D 'committed a wrong upon the Group B

---

[319] [2000] Lloyd's Rep Med 161 (QB) 168 (emphasis added).   [320] [2007] UKHL 39, [2008] 1 AC 281, [25]–[26].
[321] [2000] Lloyd's Rep Med 161 (QB) 165.   [322] [2000] Lloyd's Rep Med 161 (QB) 168–69.

[Cs], by imperilling their lives from a terrible fatal disease', but that there was nothing 'in the facts and circumstances of this litigation why public policy, including social and economic policy considerations, should exclude them from compensation'. Policy reasons may preclude these types of Cs from being *primary victims*, but those reasons have not been transposed into an analysis under the *Caparo* test.

RESIDUARY CLAIMANTS

§5.45   The primary victim/secondary victim classification has been departed from in limited circumstances, *viz*, where: (1) inaccurate medical advice was given by D which gave rise to psychiatric injury on C's part, and where negligent misstatement was relied upon; or (2) C was not in the zone-of-danger by reason of the acts or omissions of D, but for whom psychiatric injury was reasonably foreseeable, and towards whom D assumed responsibility to avoid causing such psychiatric injury.

 i. Negligent misstatement. Framing the cause of action in this way has been (rarely) employed, to enable C to avoid classification as either primary or secondary victim (as discussed previously under the heading, 'Receiving bad news').
 ii. Assumption of responsibility/reliance. Alternatively, courts have found for C by invoking the 2-part *Hedley Byrne*-type assumption of responsibility/reliance test and/or the 3-part *Caparo* test, which govern novel duty of care scenarios. This type of residuary C, whilst infrequently-occurring, has featured in some quite differing scenarios:

The residuary C category: examples

- a claim against the Home Office:
  In *Butchart v Home Office*,[a] Mr Butchart, C, was a prisoner on remand at Winchester Prison. C was earlier in a mental health facility; had self-harmed whilst in police custody; and once in prison, was put under supervision and regular watch because his legal representatives were concerned about his suicide risk. C was placed with a cellmate who also had suicidal tendencies. C woke up early one morning to discover that his cellmate had strangled himself, and C suffered a severe shock. Later, C was told that 'if the suicide was anyone's fault, it was his', and was allocated a cell with another suicidal prisoner. **Held:** C could recover, as he was psychiatrically injured by breach of a 'primary duty of care owed to him'.
- a claim against a utilities supplier:
  In *Attia v British Gas plc*,[b] facts previously, Ms Attia, C, could recover for her psychiatric injury, for the destruction of her home, albeit that she was neither a primary nor a secondary victim.
- a claim against the police (and two cases can be usefully contrasted):
  In *Swinney v CC of Northumbria Police*,[c] Mrs Swinney, C, a pub landlady, supplied information to police about the identity of driver X, a hit-and-run driver who had killed an off-duty police officer, which she had overheard in pub conversation. The information, along with C's contact details, was then stolen from a police vehicle, due to the police, D's, negligence, and fell into X's hands. Subsequently, C was threatened with violence and arson, and suffered psychiatric injury. C alleged that

[a] [2006] EWCA Civ 239.
[b] [1988] QB 304 (CA).
[c] [1997] QB 464 (CA).

D owed her a duty of care with respect to the storage and safe keeping of the information, given that the police knew of X's violent character and that any informant's information was given in the strictest confidence. **Held:** C's claim was permitted to proceed. In *Leach v CC of Gloucestershire Constabulary,[d]* Mrs Leach, C, a voluntary worker on the Young Homeless Project at Cheltenham, was appointed to assist the notorious serial murderer Frederick West in his police interviews, in her capacity as an 'appropriate adult'.[e] C had to listen to harrowing and traumatic accounts in approximately 40 interviews, to accompany Mr West to the murder scenes, and to remain alone with him in a locked cell. During the interviews, Mr West admitted to 30 murders, and was charged with 11, and hanged himself while in remand in 1995. Mrs West was tried a few months later, and found guilty of 10 murders. C suffered PTSD, and sued the police, D, in negligence for failing to provide her with counselling. **Held:** C's action was struck out.

[d] [1998] 1 WLR 1421 (CA).
[e] Pursuant to the Police and Criminal Evidence Act 1984.

These cases proceeded upon a duty of care analysis of foreseeability; an assumption of responsibility/reliance; and no public policy precluding a duty of care (below).

The treatment of cases in which C suffers damage to his 'cherished property', and from which C suffers mental injury, has already been adverted to in this chapter.[323] It is not treated as a consequential mental injury, but instead, invokes the principles of pure psychiatric injury (per *Attia v British Gas plc*[324]). Notably, if these property damage cases are treated according to the residuary category of C, then the 'direct perception' requirement does not apply – which is significant, where C's property is destroyed, but C does not witness that destruction. In *Attia*, C did witness her house burning. However, in the sperm wastage cases of *Yearworth* and *Holdich*, no such direct perception occurred. As noted previously,[325] the *Yearworth* Court of Appeal queried whether recovery of psychiatric injury should only arise where C's property is destroyed and is observed by C, as a policy ring-fencing upon the number of potential claims, but without deciding the question. In *Holdich*, the Scottish Outer House permitted the claim in tort to proceed, without addressing that issue explicitly.

Expanding upon each duty of care limb in turn:

Reasonable foreseeability

§5.46 For a residuary C, his psychiatric injury must have been reasonably foreseeable (reflecting the *Wagon Mound* principle). The normal fortitude rule applies.

In *McLoughlin v Jones*,[326] the court remarked that, if it were wrong in holding that C was a *Page v Smith*-type primary victim (discussed previously[327]), then in the alternative, the 'ordinary [*Wagon Mound*] principle should apply: psychiatric injury to C should be the reasonably foreseeable result of [D's] negligence' (and, in that case, psychiatric injury resulting from a wrongful imprisonment was foreseeable). The important point is that foreseeability of psychiatric injury is necessary to give rise to a duty of care, in these types of residuary cases. For example:

[323] See pp 240–42.   [324] [1987] EWCA Civ 8, [1988] QB 304, 320.   [325] See pp 241–42.
[326] [2001] EWCA Civ 1743, [59] (Hale LJ).   [327] See pp 231–33.

In *Butchart v Home Office*,[328] Mr Butchart, C, was known to the Home Office, D, to have been psychiatrically vulnerable before the suicide of his cellmate occurred, self-harming, and on suicide watch; it 'knew, or ought to have known, that [C] was a prisoner vulnerable to psychiatric harm'. In *Swinney v CC of Northumbria Police*, C's psychiatric injury was held to be foreseeable, given the campaign of terror from a criminal gang.

The comparative corner: A Canadian example

In *Mustapha v Culligan of Canada Ltd*,[329] Mr Mustapha, C, sued for psychiatric injury sustained as a result of seeing the dead flies in a bottle of water supplied by Culligan of Canada, D. C was replacing an empty bottle of drinking water with a full one when he saw a dead fly and part of another dead fly in the unopened replacement bottle. He became obsessed with the event, considered that it had 'revolting implications' for the health of his family, which had been consuming water supplied by D for the previous 15 years, and developed a major depressive disorder with associated phobia and anxiety. **Held:** C's damage was too remote to be compensable. Such a psychiatric reaction would not have been reasonably foreseeable in a person of ordinary fortitude (and there was no evidence that D had special knowledge of C's peculiar sensibilities). The medical evidence was that C's reaction was 'highly unusual' and 'very individual', and flowed in part from 'cultural factors' such as C's unusual concern over cleanliness, and the health and well-being of his family.

Assumption of responsibility/reliance

§5.47   A number of factors have indicated that D must have assumed a responsibility to minimise the risk of C's suffering psychiatric injury, and that C exercised a reciprocal reliance upon D.

If the primary victim/secondary victim categorisation is not to apply (nor the elevated primary victim, nor the stress-at-work categories), and if C is nevertheless permitted to recover for negligently-inflicted psychiatric injury, then C's claim has generally been analysed under an 'assumption of responsibility' test. The following factors have been used to separate the deserving cases from those that should fail:

- if D could identify C before the event, then a special relationship between them is easier to establish:

  In *Swinney*, the police, D, assumed responsibility for preserving the confidentiality of information about illegal activities which C supplied. D was the only recipient to whom C could have given that information. If disclosed, then that was likely to expose C to a greater risk than the ordinary risk to the general public. She was in an entirely different category from the vast class of potential female victims of the 'Yorkshire Ripper', distinguishing the case from *Hill v CC of West Yorkshire Police* (per Chapter 2).

- if D performed professional services entailing highly-skilled and specialist work on C's behalf (albeit that a mere contract of engagement, without more, could not give rise to a duty of care):

---

[328] [2006] EWCA Civ 239, [20] (Latham LJ).   [329] [2008] SCC 27, quote at [18].

In *McLoughlin v Jones*, solicitors, D, were engaged by client, C, to exercise reasonable skill and care in preparing his case for trial in such a way as to minimise the risks of a wrongful conviction, and of his suffering false imprisonment and psychiatric injury, should he be convicted. On that basis, D 'should be deemed to have assumed responsibility for those consequences' (by contrast, where solicitors D, were not engaged by C at all, but the outcome of the litigation turned out to be detrimental for C, *McLoughlin* will be distinguished, as in *James-Bowen v Commr of Police*[330]). In *Attia v British Gas*, British Gas, D, assumed responsibility to C to perform the specialist hazardous activity of installing central gas heating with skill and care, a task for which she had to rely upon their professional competence.

- if D is in a powerful position vis-à-vis C, so that C is vulnerable and exposed:

    In *Butchart*, the custodial relationship placed Mr Butchart, C, in a vulnerable position; and the assumption of responsibility which D undertook towards C was heightened by the fact that C was known to have been psychiatrically vulnerable before the suicide of his cellmate occurred. 'The [Home Office] knew or ought to have known that [C] was a prisoner vulnerable to psychiatric harm. In those circumstances it [is] ... inevitable that the duty of care ... included a duty to take reasonable steps to minimise the risk of psychiatric harm'. In *Swinney*, the police, D, were the repositories of information about X's illegal activities, and the only recipients to whom Mrs Swinney, C, could give such information. Hence, they wielded considerable power *vis-à-vis* the Swinneys, and assumed a responsibility toward them to keep the informant's information safe. In *McLoughlin*, the fact that C's liberty could be lost, if D's conduct was negligent, put C in a position of real vulnerability, and helped to contribute to an assumption of responsibility.

- if D has not assumed legal responsibility towards a third party that would conflict with a legal responsibility towards C (any such conflict will rule out an assumption of responsibility):

    In *Leach*, this factor was significant in striking out Ms Leach's, C's, claim against the police, D: 'the whole essence of [C's] relationship to the police is that they did not assume responsibility towards her in relation to her duties as appropriate adult. She was there at the police station to be of assistance to Mr West, and the police might not be able to do their job of interviewing Mr West effectively if they were under a concurrent legal duty to be protective of [C's] psychological well-being'.

STRESS-AT-WORK CLAIMANTS

The employment relationship, of itself, does **not** entail an automatic duty on the employer's part to avoid psychiatric injury on the employee's part (otherwise, the police officers in *White* should have established a duty owed to them by their employer, the Chief Constable, for their psychiatric injuries, which they certainly could not). English precedent clearly demonstrates that the employment contract gives rise to an automatic duty of care to avoid *physical* injury to an employee – but it does **not** prescribe that the employer is liable for **all** types of injuries suffered by the employee.

To reiterate, employees may have **other** avenues for recovering damages for psychiatric injuries sustained in the workplace. For the employee who is in the zone-of-danger himself (per *Page v Smith*), or who is guilt-ridden at a co-employee's injury or death (per *Monk v*

---

[330] [2015] EWHC 1249 (QB) [60]–[62].

Harrington), the relevant principles discussed earlier in the chapter apply.[331] However, secondary victim claims are most unlikely for an employee who witnesses a work accident, as rarely will work colleagues have shared the requisite ties of love and affection required.

For the stress-at-work employees, important guidance was provided by Lady Justice Hale in the leading case of *Hatton v Sutherland*[332] (reversed on another point, but the guidance was affirmed on appeal to the House of Lords, where the case is known as *Barber v Somerset CC*[333]). Employees who are overworked to the point of mental illness have been permitted to recover damages for their injury, on the basis that responsibility for causing the psychological risks faced by an employee must be borne, at least in part, by the employer. However, it is **not** an all-encompassing duty to avoid an employee's mental injury, whatever the circumstances, as Hale LJ's propositions demonstrate:

[*Principles relevant to duty of care*]:

(2) The threshold question is whether this kind of harm to this particular employee was reasonably foreseeable: this has two components (a) an injury to health (as distinct from occupational stress) which (b) is attributable to stress at work (as distinct from other factors).

(3) Foreseeability depends upon what the employer knows (or ought reasonably to know) about the individual employee. Because of the nature of mental disorder, it is harder to foresee than physical injury, but may be easier to foresee in a known individual than in the population at large. An employer is usually entitled to assume that the employee can withstand the normal pressures of the job unless he knows of some particular problem or vulnerability.

(4) The test is the same whatever the employment: there are no occupations which should be regarded as intrinsically dangerous to mental health.

(5) Factors likely to be relevant in answering the threshold question include:

(a) The nature and extent of the work done by the employee. Is the workload much more than is normal for the particular job? Is the work particularly intellectually or emotionally demanding for this employee? Are demands being made of this employee unreasonable when compared with the demands made of others in the same or comparable jobs? Or are there signs that others doing this job are suffering harmful levels of stress? Is there an abnormal level of sickness or absenteeism in the same job or the same department?

(b) Signs from the employee of impending harm to health. Has he a particular problem or vulnerability? Has he already suffered from illness attributable to stress at work? Have there recently been frequent or prolonged absences which are uncharacteristic of him? Is there reason to think that these are attributable to stress at work, for example because of complaints or warnings from him or others?

(6) The employer is generally entitled to take what he is told by his employee at face value, unless he has good reason to think to the contrary. He does not generally have to make searching enquiries of the employee or seek permission to make further enquiries of his medical advisers.

---

[331] See pp 233–36   [332] [2002] EWCA Civ 76, [43]. Hale LJ wrote the judgment for the court.

[333] [2004] UKHL 13, [2004] 1 WLR 1089, [5] (Lord Scott) (one of the conjoined appeals). Hale LJ's 16 propositions have been much-cited since.

[*Principles relevant to proving breach*]:

(8) The employer is only in breach of duty if he has failed to take the steps which are reasonable in the circumstances, bearing in mind the magnitude of the risk of harm occurring, the gravity of the harm which may occur, the costs and practicability of preventing it, and the justifications for running the risk.

(9) The size and scope of the employer's operation, its resources and the demands it faces are relevant in deciding what is reasonable; these include the interests of other employees and the need to treat them fairly, for example, in any redistribution of duties.

(10) An employer can only reasonably be expected to take steps which are likely to do some good: the court is likely to need expert evidence on this.

(11) An employer who offers a confidential advice service, with referral to appropriate counselling or treatment services, is unlikely to be found in breach of duty.

(12) If the only reasonable and effective step would have been to dismiss or demote the employee, the employer will not be in breach of duty in allowing a willing employee to continue in the job.

This section sets out some summary propositions pertinent to the establishment of a duty of care (readers are referred to detailed works for further analysis regarding stress-at-work claims[334]).

Reasonable foreseeability

§5.48   An employer D's duty to avoid psychiatric injury on the employee's, C's, part arises where either (1) D *knew* that a particular employee was vulnerable to stress-induced illness; or (2) it was objectively foreseeable, to a reasonable employer, that psychiatric injury could foreseeably result from a particular task or tasks.

The abovementioned test of foreseeability, derived from *Hatton v Sutherland* (CA) and also from Brown LJ in *Bonser v UK Coal Mining*,[335] reflects the fact that, in most cases, employer D will know his employee C.

Employer D must have foreseen that its employee would suffer *illness*; foreseeability that C would suffer stress in his work environment is **not** sufficient. As Brown LJ stated, '[o]verwork, of itself, is likely to lead to stress. It is altogether less likely to lead to the breakdown of the stressed employee's health. For that to be foreseen, [C] will generally need to establish, not only that the employer knew that he or she was being overworked, but, in addition ... either (i) that the employer knew that the individual employee was, for some reason, particularly vulnerable to stress-induced illness; or (ii) that the [employee] was manifesting clear signs of some impending harm to health before eventually illness followed'.[336]

Stress-at-work claims must arise from circumstances in which 'the stresses inherent in [the] employment' have put the employee at risk of psychiatric illness, and where he has done precisely the work which the employer required him to do. In other words, the employer's assumption of responsibility arises from the employee performing the very tasks required of his employment.

---

[334] e.g., I Smith and A Baker, *Employment Law* (11th edn, Oxford University Press, 2013); S Honeyball, *Honeyball and Bowers' Textbook on Employment Law* (13th edn, Oxford University Press, 2014).
[335] [2003] EWCA Civ 296, [30].   [336] *ibid*.

These cases are very fact-specific, but a couple of examples will suffice to illustrate:

In *Melville v Home Office*,[337] Mr Melville, C, was employed by the Home Office, D, as a health care officer at HMP Exeter. His duties included recovering the bodies of prisoners who had committed suicide. He attended eight suicides between 1981 and 1988. In the last, he helped to cut down the body, remove a ligature, and attempt revival. C subsequently suffered from nightmares and flash-backs, developed a stress-related illness, and retired on grounds of ill-health early the following year. Before he stopped work, C gave no indication that he was developing a stress-related illness; but D's documents recognised that persons who were called on to deal with traumatic incidents in prisons (e.g., suicides), might suffer health problems, and that they should receive support from the prison care team. **Held:** C could recover. Even though C had not shown troubles in his health, D foresaw that employees who were exposed to particular traumatic incidents might suffer psychiatric injury.

But contrast:

In *Pratley v Surrey CC*,[338] Miss Pratley, C, was employed by Surrey CC, D, as a care manager. The demands of the work and a lack of funding made it a pressurised job (which D knew). However, C gave no indication that she felt pressurised, and deliberately withheld information about the fact that she took time off for stress (the doctor's certificate indicated 'neuralgia'), nor did she use the occupational health and counselling services which were available to D's employees. C spoke to her line manager prior to going on holiday, in which it was 'promised' that a new stacking system would be introduced to ease her workload – but when C returned from holidays and found that it had not been implemented, she suffered psychiatric illness, and was subsequently dismissed. The line manager had not taken immediate steps to implement that system, deciding rather to wait to see how things were and how C felt when she returned from holiday. **Held:** C could not recover. Her psychiatric injury (immediate collapse, following the disappointment of a 'cherished idea' about the stacking system, arising from the conversation about workload) was not a reasonably foreseeable psychiatric injury. In *Yapp v Foreign and Cth Office*,[339] the FCO, D, withdrew Mr Yapp, C, from his post without his having had the opportunity to state his case, and C suffered a psychiatric illness. **Held:** C could not recover. C was an 'apparently robust employee, with no history of any psychiatric ill-health'. A major setback to his career was foreseeably likely to cause C distress and anger, but it was not a dismissal, a disciplinary sanction, or based on any established misconduct. D could not have reasonably foreseen, in the absence of any sign of special vulnerability, that C might develop a psychiatric illness as a result of its decision.

In *Yapp*, Davis LJ pointed out that the second limb of the principle – whereby psychiatric injury resulting from a breach of duty by an employer will be assessed as reasonably foreseeable, even if there was no awareness of a prior relevant susceptibility or vulnerability on the part of that employee – will 'likely be very unusual', and will probably require 'appropriately special facts' of the type in *Melville*. Hence, the legal principles in this area are not particularly sympathetic towards the C employee.

The normal fortitude rule

§5.49 For employee C whom employer D knows to be particularly vulnerable to stress-related illness, D must take C as he finds him. Otherwise, D is entitled to rely on the normal fortitude rule.

---

[337] [2005] EWCA Civ 6, [133]–[134].   [338] [2003] EWCA Civ 1067.   [339] [2014] EWCA Civ 1512, [155]–[156].

The interplay of the normal fortitude rule and stress-at-work claims has been somewhat controversial. It will be noted that, in proposition (3), Hale LJ opined that an employer was usually entitled to assume the employee could withstand the normal pressures of the job, unless he knew of some particular problem or vulnerability. In other words, any pre-existing disposition to mental injury may be taken into account. Hale LJ justified that view thus: '[t]he question is not whether psychiatric injury is foreseeable in a person of "ordinary fortitude". The employer's duty is owed to each individual employee, not to some as yet unidentified outsider ... The employer knows who his employee is [and whether he has a pre-existing vulnerability to stress]'.[340]

In *Daniel v Dept of Health*,[341] Patricia Daniel, C, a cancer research network manager employed by D, alleged that she suffered psychiatric injury, arising from bullying by a senior colleague and serious overwork. C had a history of bipolar disorder (which has a very high rate of recurrence), but C's condition was unknown to D, and C did not mention it in her liaisons with work colleagues. **Held:** C could not recover, as no duty of care owed. D did not know that a risk of occupational stress and subsequent mental injury existed for those in C's position; and there were no signs that others doing the same work, in a pressured job, had suffered injury to their health. The focus must then turn to the individual employee, but there were no individual indications or signs from C herself of impending mental injury (C mentioned stress, insomnia and losing weight to a senior colleague, but he was unable to observe those changes himself). C was reticent about her health problems, 'consistent not only with her desire not to appear weak to her employer, but also her desire to remain at all times professional in her conduct and approach'. In *Croft v Broadstairs Town Council*,[342] Mrs Croft, C, was D's town clerk. C received a warning letter about her conduct, and there were follow-up meetings and correspondence. The letter was unexpected, and C was shocked and distressed to receive it. She then suffered depression as a result of the letter, rendering her unfit for work. Two town councillors knew that C had been undergoing counselling when the letter was received. **Held:** C could not recover, as no duty was owed. D did not know of C's psychiatric vulnerability to depression (despite the knowledge about the counselling). Absent actual knowledge, D was entitled to expect C to be a person of ordinary robustness, including in dealing with disciplinary matters. Her breakdown was not reasonably foreseeable.

However, although that notion was approved by Lord Hoffmann in the *Pleural Plaques Litig*,[343] it was with the caveat that an assumption of ordinary fortitude on the employee's part was necessary, where employee C was long-departed from employer D's workplace. Although Mr Grieves was not a person of normal fortitude (he suffered from an irrational fear of developing a terminal illness resulting from asbestos exposure), Lord Hoffmann stated that the rule must apply to him, given that 'the employer would be unlikely to have any specific knowledge of how a particular employee was likely to react to the risk of asbestos-related illness more than 30 years after he had left his employment. An assumption of ordinary fortitude is therefore inevitable'.[344] Presumably, where the workforce is very large, an assumption of ordinary fortitude may also be appropriate.

---

[340] [2002] EWCA Civ 76, [23].   [341] [2014] EWHC 2578 (QB) [177]–[186].   [342] [2003] EWCA Civ 676.
[343] *Grieves v FT Everard & Sons Ltd* [2007] UKHL 39, [25]–[26].   [344] *ibid*, [25]–[26].

The law reform corner: The 'normal fortitude' rule

Scottish Law Comm:[345] the normal fortitude rule should be applied to all occupational stress claims: '[p]ersons who have responsible jobs are expected to accommodate the stress inherent in their work and can reasonably be expected to endure any resultant mental harm without seeking reparation. Similarly, there are professions, the armed forces, firemen and the police for example, which involve exposure to personal danger and participation in horrifying situations'. However, that should not rule out occupational stress claims altogether (said the Commission), as such professionals, 'will be able to do so when the mental harm is a consequence of an event that goes well beyond what can usually be expected to occur in the ordinary course of their jobs.'

Proximity

§5.50   The relationship of employment gives rise to the requisite proximity.

Where an employer, D, employs an employee, C, who sustains a psychiatric injury as a result of D's acts or omissions at the workplace, the question of proximity tends to be enmeshed with that of reasonable foreseeability (as Lady Justice Hale's propositions demonstrate). Hence, this element has not attracted much discussion in the context of 'stress-at-work' claims.

The rest of the cause of action

Breach of duty must be proven in the usual way, as noted in *Hatton*. Hence, the principles in Chapter 7 are pertinent. For example, in *Daw v Intel Corp*,[346] Pill LJ remarked that the provision of counselling services would not automatically preclude a finding of breach (although such a step will always be relevant, per *Hartmann v South Essex Mental Health NHS Trust*[347]). The usual principles of causation (per Chapter 8) and remoteness (per Chapter 9) will also apply.

---

[345] *Scottish Report*, [3.25]; also [3.30] and Recommendation 5(b), Draft Bill, s 3(2).
[346] [2007] ICR 1318 (CA) [45].   [347] [2005] EWCA Civ 6.

6

Breach I – The standard of care

Under the second element of the tort of negligence, the relevant question is whether the conduct of D fell below the standard of care which the law expects of D, and so constitutes negligent behaviour. This enquiry necessarily involves a two-stage analysis: (1) setting the standard of care against which D's behaviour should be judged (a question of law); and (2) deciding whether D's conduct met, or fell below, that standard (a question of fact). This chapter considers the first enquiry, while Chapter 7 considers the second.

INTRODUCTION

Reasonableness, not perfection

The requisite legal standard

§6.1   The law of negligence imposes a reasonable standard of care on D, and not a standard of perfection (the latter would, if permitted, impose a form of strict liability). Fixing the requisite reasonable standard of care in any given case is a question of law.

That proposition was espoused in the seminal judgment of Lord Atkin in *Donoghue v Stevenson*: '[y]ou must take *reasonable care* to avoid acts or omissions which you can reasonably foresee would be likely to injure your neighbour'.[1] In *Bolton v Stone* too,[2] the House of Lords remarked that, '[t]he standard of care in the law of negligence is the standard of an ordinarily careful man' – or an ordinarily careful cricket club, in that case. The synonymous phrases of 'ordinary care', 'proper care', or 'prudent care', were all used in *Bolton v Stone* to describe the standard which the law expects of D. That ordinary careful adult has traditionally been equated to the person 'on the top of the Clapham omnibus' (per *Bolam v Friern Hosp Management Committee*[3]).

What the law of negligence does **not** impose upon D is a requirement that he meet a standard of perfection, i.e., a level of conduct which is so unattainably high that breach is inevitable, because even reasonable conduct could not satisfy such a standard. The reality is that mistakes, errors of judgment, and acts and omissions falling short of perfection, commonly **do** occur in

---

[1] [1932] AC 562 (HL) 580 (emphasis added).
[2] [1951] AC 850 (HL), with quotes respectively at: 863 (Lord Oaksey), 865 (Lord Reid), and 868 (Lord Radcliffe).
[3] [1957] 1 WLR 582 (QB) 586 (McNair J).

any endeavour of life – but they do not represent breach, and negligence, **unless** they fall below what would be expected of a reasonable person in D's position. As the Privy Council endorsed, in *Hamilton v Papakura DC (NZ)*,[4] the law does not impose 'an unattainable standard that guarantees against all harm and all circumstances'.

There is an important distinction to be drawn here, as the Court of Appeal noted in *Barrie v Cardiff CC*: '[t]he standard of care is a question of law; but whether or not, in any given case, that standard has been attained is a question of fact for the judge to decide, having regard to all the circumstances of the case'.[5] It follows that any error in setting the standard of care too high (or too low) will be an appealable error of law – and, in that regard, first-instance courts must resist the temptation to set the bar *too high*. Additionally, if a first-instance court takes into account a characteristic or circumstance which is legally irrelevant to the question of standard, that will be an error of law too. Appellate courts can readily interfere with an assessment of the standard of care, given that it is a question of law.

> In *Barrie v Cardiff CC*,[6] Sam Barrie, C, aged 6, tripped over protruding concrete edging at her school playground in Cardiff. The edging was about 15 mm higher than the surrounding area of tarmac. The Cardiff Council, D, as the local education authority, owed a duty of care to C; but setting the standard, and whether D was in breach of that standard, were at issue, because of the playground's condition. C had brittle bone disease, but that did not play any role in her tripping. The playground was commonly used by children 4–7 years old. **Held:** the requisite standard of care was a school playground which was reasonably (not perfectly) safe for a school for ordinary infants of 4–7 years: 'a playground is ... not to be criticised by the standards of a bowling green'. The standard was not to be elevated because of C's brittle bone disease. The standard set by the trial judge was too high. No breach occurred here, as D had met the reasonable standard of care.

> In *Penney, Palmer and Cannon v East Kent HA*,[7] cytoscreeners employed by health authority D reported four cervical smears taken from various patients, C, as being negative, which meant that there was no timely follow-up or diagnostic or therapeutic interventions. Each C went on to develop invasive adenocarcinoma of the cervix. **Held (trial):** D was negligent. However, D appealed on the basis that the case set a dangerous precedent 'by requiring inappropriately high standards of care by those responsible for primary screening' under the national cervical screening programme. **Held (CA):** the standard was properly set (i.e., 'a reasonably competent screener exercising reasonable care at the time when the screening took place'). Breach was also proven, given that, on each slide, there was a small number of inflamed groups of endocervical cells showing changes in nuclear and cytoplasmic morphology, such that the smears should have been classified as at least 'borderline'.

§6.2   An unattainable standard of care – i.e., one which D *cannot* achieve because of D's particular characteristics or circumstances – is nevertheless lawful.

Albeit that the standard of care is to be set at a reasonable, rather than a perfect, level of care and/ or skill, there will still be some circumstances (discussed below) in which it may be impossible for D to meet even that reasonable standard of care – because of D's own frailties, inexperience,

---

[4] [2002] 3 NZLR 308, [2002] UKPC 9, [31], endorsing the comments of the NZCA in the court below.

[5] [2001] EWCA Civ 703, [19]. Although this quote is commonly attributed to Lord Wilberforce in *Goldman v Hargrave* [1967] 1 AC 645 (PC) 663, it does not seem to appear anywhere in Lord Wilberforce's judgment.

[6] [2001] EWCA Civ 703, [2002] ELR 1, quote at [23].

[7] (2000) 55 BMLR 63 (CA), quotes at [3], [22] and [34].

or circumstances. Nevertheless, an unattainable standard of care is not unlawful, merely by virtue of the fact that it is out of reach for D. English law is content to set artificially high standards of care for some categories of D, for policy reasons, as discussed later in the chapter. Principally, in such cases, D is an insured party, such that if D falls below that unattainable standard of care, then C is enabled to obtain compensation for his injury – a 'better' result, concludes the law of negligence, than suppressing the standard and thereby perhaps precluding any finding of breach.

No average or team standard

§6.3 There is no concept of an '*average* standard of care' in English law; every single act or omission by D is assessed against the reasonable standard. There is no concept of a '*team* standard of care' either; the acts/omissions of each member of a team will be assessed separately, against the level of skill expected of a reasonable person in that team member's position.

Importantly, *every single act or omission* by D is to be judged against the reasonable standard of care. There is no legal recognition of D's achieving an average – or even a higher-than-average – standard of care on a regular basis (whether as a driver, a doctor, or otherwise), so as to compensate for one momentary lapse of care, amounting to negligence. In other words, it is **not** possible for D to allege that, 'so long as he had provided an adequate service on average, he should not be held liable for the very odd occasion when his performance fell below the norm' (per *Wilsher v Essex AHA*[8]). All that matters is whether, *at any particular instance* when dealing with a specific activity, D's conduct dropped below the reasonable standard.

Additionally, there is **no** concept of 'a *team* standard of care', whereby the standard of care which the law requires of each person operating within a team, is set at the standard which an ordinarily competent team, as a whole, has provided to C. A 'team standard of care' – whether that team consists of professional or non-professional members – is not a tenable proposition in English law. That was also made plain by *Wilsher v Essex AHA*,[9] in which the Court of Appeal held that it would not be right to expose a nurse to an action in negligence for failing to possess the skill and experience of a specialist consultant who worked in such a unit, by applying some artificial and over-arching 'team standard of care' (although it must be emphasised that the early mistakes made in treatment of this baby were not made by the nurses involved in his care).

In *Wilsher v Essex AHA*, Martin Wilsher, C, was born very prematurely, and was cared for in a special care baby unit at Princess Alexandra Hospital, Harlow, by a team of senior and junior doctors and nurses. The trial judge accepted that the fact that C survived at all and without brain damage 'is due both to the remarkable advances of medical science ... and to the treatment he received in the [hospital]'. However, within the first 36 hours of his life, C was super-saturated with oxygen, due to a mistake by two members of the team. **Held:** breach proven. Just because the unit was a very specialised one did not necessarily mean that all members working in the unit held themselves out as capable of undertaking the specialised procedures which that unit set out to perform. Furthermore, the fact that C only survived his very premature birth because of the extremely high and dedicated level of care that he received throughout his 6 month stay at the hospital did not preclude a finding of breach, regarding what occurred during the first 36 hours. (Ultimately, though, causation failed.)

---

[8] [1987] QB 730 (CA) 747 (Mustill LJ) (the case went to the HL only on causation; statements by the CA regarding standard and breach were not the subject of appeal).

[9] [1987] QB 730 (CA) 749–50 (Mustill LJ), 775 (Glidewell LJ), quote in text by Lord Bridge (on appeal to HL).

An objective standard, subject to exceptions

§6.4   The standard of care set by the law is, with limited exceptions, an objective standard, i.e., the standard is not ordinarily dependent upon the particular characteristics of, or circumstances affecting, D.

An objective standard – assessed according to the conduct expected of an ordinary reasonable adult – 'eliminate[s] the personal equation ... [and is] independent of the idiosyncrasies of the particular person whose conduct is in question' (per *Glasgow Corp v Muir*[10]).

This approach has two advantages. First, it standardises how citizens of society are expected to behave (i.e., to act as a person of ordinary prudence would behave) and omits any enquiry as to how reasonable D, himself, believed his conduct to be; and secondly, it more easily permits the court to adjudge D's acts or omissions as negligent or not – 'the spokesman of the fair and reasonable man, who represents after all no more than the anthropomorphic conception of justice, is and must be the court itself' (per Lord Radcliffe in *Davis Contractors Ltd v Farnham UDC*[11]). The court has a far more successful prospect of setting the reasonable standard, if the law eliminates the personal angle.

However, as with most matters in law, the general rule is proven by the exceptions thereto. Sometimes the 'personal equation' does matter, in that there are several factors which do impinge upon the reasonable standard of care, whereby the court must set the standard according to the particular idiosyncrasies of D, or according to the particular circumstances in which D operates. In other words, the law does not always insist upon a purely objective standard. However – and the law is not entirely consistent on this point – there are several idiosyncrasies or circumstances, about which D can do nothing, of which the law takes no account at all. These various factors and disparities are explained in the following sections. By way of summary of this chapter's content, the following nutshell analysis may assist (where ↑ denotes an elevated standard; ↓ denotes a suppressed standard; and ↔ denotes that the standard does not change at law):

Nutshell analysis: Fixing the standard of care

Check for any of the following, and assess its impact on the reasonable standard of an ordinary adult:

CHARACTERISTICS:

Specialism ↑
Age ↓
Disability depends: ↔ (where known) or ↓ (where unknown)
Inexperience ↔
Parents ↑
Gender ↔

---

[10] [1943] AC 448 (HL) 457 (Lord Macmillan).

[11] [1956] AC 696 (HL) 729, noted in the context of frustrated contracts, not negligence, but the sentiment is equally applicable. See too: *Badger v MOD* [2005] EWHC 2941 (QB), [9].

CIRCUMSTANCES:

'Agony of the moment' or 'battle conditions' ↓
'Diagnosis with a focus' ↑
Locality perhaps ↓, but scant authority
Dangerous or fast-moving recreational or sporting contests ↓ to some extent (except for promoters and organisers, for which ↔)
Available resources and facilities perhaps ↓, but divided views
Local practices ↔

It is important to appreciate that, should the law elevate the standard of care for any reason, breach is more likely, because the mistake/error complained of is more likely to fall below that elevated standard. Obversely, if the standard of care is suppressed because of some characteristic or circumstance, then breach is less likely, as whatever happened is less likely to fall below such a suppressed standard of care. It may be useful to consider the standard of care as a 'floating level' – whatever the conduct of D, it cannot be changed, but the standard of care at law can vary, up or down, depending upon either D's characteristics or the surrounding circumstances.

THE IMPACT (IF ANY) OF D'S CHARACTERISTICS

Specialism

§6.5　For D who has a particular profession or specialism, the requisite standard is 'the ordinary skill of an ordinary competent man exercising that particular art'.

This so-called *Bolam*-standard of care – named after the seminal case of *Bolam v Friern Hospital Management Committee*[12] – is set neither by the unskilled person (i.e., the 'ordinary person on the London underground'), nor by reference to the person holding the highest degree of skill. As McNair J said, when instructing the jury in this medical negligence action brought by Mr Bolam against his psychiatrist (in respect of electro-convulsive therapy which went badly), where D exercises some special skill or competence, the test:

> is not the test of the man on the top of the Clapham omnibus, because he has not got this special skill. The test is the standard of the ordinary skilled man exercising and professing to have that special skill. A man need not possess the highest expert skill; it is well-established law that it is sufficient if he exercises the ordinary skill of an ordinary competent man exercising that particular art.

Hence, if D, who is exercising a professional or specialist calling, makes an error which any similar professional, 'acting with ordinary care, might have made too', then no breach will lie, for the legal standard of care will have been met (per *Whitehouse v Jordan*[13]).

Graduated specialisms

§6.6　Within one type of profession (say, legal, medical, engineering, etc), the degree of specialism possessed by D determines the requisite standard of care. However, even at a lower specialism,

---

[12] [1957] 1 WLR 582 (QB) 586 (McNair J).　　[13] [1981] 1 WLR 246 (HL) 263 (Lord Fraser).

D may fail to meet the relevant standard of care, by failing to refer C to a more specialist or expert environment, which could have provided better resources and expertise for C.

Given the graduated levels of knowledge, skill and expertise within a profession, the standard of care necessarily will vary across those levels. The Table below illustrates, by reference to the *medical* profession. As Lord Scarman stated, in *Maynard v West Midlands Regional HA*, 'a doctor who professes to exercise a special skill must exercise the ordinary skill *of his specialty*'.[14]

Graduated specialisms within the medical profession

The type of specialist	Illustrative case
A *tertiary specialist*, who accepts referrals from other specialists, will be judged against the ordinary standard of care and skill in that tertiary specialism.	In *De Freitas v O'Brien*,[a] D was a spinal specialist who took referrals from orthopaedic and neuro-surgeons who were engaged in a wider field of surgical practice. **Held:** D was judged against (the limited number of) tertiary specialists in his field (no breach proven).
A *specialist doctor* must meet the ordinary skill of his speciality.	In *Lillywhite v University College London Hosp NHS Trust*,[b] D was a professor of obstetrics and gynaecology who was experienced at reading and interpreting foetal ultrasound scans. His conduct, in examining a foetal scan, was examined against 'the ordinary skill of his speciality, i.e., a consultant sonologist at a tertiary referral centre' (breach proven).
A *general practitioner (GP)* must meet the standard of general practice, but nothing higher than that.	In *Holt v Edge*,[c] the patient, C, slipped and fell in the shower, and complained of neck cramp, breathing difficulties, and pins and needles in her arms. Her husband phoned D, a GP at the local medical centre, and C was told to rest; a night doctor visited and detected high blood pressure and recommended further rest; but feeling no better three days later, C was admitted to A&E, where she was diagnosed with an atypical brain haemorrhage. She was operated on, suffered a stroke, and was left disabled. **Held:** the standard expected of a conscientious and competent GP, who was not expected to know of these unusual symptoms of a brain haemorrhage, was met. The usual symptoms of pounding headaches and vomiting were entirely absent in C's case. In *Stockdale v Nicholls*,[d] a GP sent a practice nurse to check on an ill baby at the baby's home. The nurse diagnosed 'nose infection and snuffles'. The baby later suffered septicaemia. **Held:** the GP met the standard of a reasonably competent GP in sending the practice nurse, rather than attending himself.

[a] (1995) 25 BMLR 51 (CA).
[b] [2005] EWCA Civ 1466, [22], [84] (condition of holoprosencephaly).
[c] [2006] EWHC 1932 (QB) [75], aff'd: [2007] EWCA Civ 602. Also: *Hardman v Riddell* [2004] EWHC 1691 (QB).
[d] [1993] 4 Med LR 191 (QB) 199.

[14] [1985] 1 WLR 634 (HL) 648 (emphasis added).

A *medical practitioner working in a prison hospital* has been the subject of somewhat contrary authority. On the one hand, the medical practitioner is not required to meet as high a standard of care as that which must be provided in a civilian hospital – given the different functions that these hospitals perform (lawful detention versus seeking a cure) (per *Knight v HO*[e]). On the other hand, a prisoner, while detained in prison, is legally entitled to expect the same level of medical care, as if she was at liberty, subject to the constraints of having to be escorted to a general hospital (per *Brooks v HO*[f]).

In *Knight v Home Office*, medical staff working in the hospital psychiatric wing of Brixton prison were caring for C, a prisoner at suicide risk. Only 15-minute inspections were possible, rather than continuous observation of C, and C committed suicide in between two inspections. **Held:** no breach proven. The higher patient/staff ratio at Brixton was appropriate for the different function which the prison hospital served. D's hospital met the standard of a reasonable institution whose primary function was detention.

In *Brooks v Home Office*, C, a female prisoner on remand, and in the stages of a high-risk pregnancy, had a scan which indicated potential difficulties with both twins (one was eventually stillborn, and the other suffered from considerable disabilities). C was not immediately referred from the mother-and-baby unit at Holloway Prison to a maternity hospital. **Held:** breach proven. C, while detained, was entitled to expect the same level of ante-natal care, for herself and her children, as if at liberty, subject to the constraint of having to be escorted to hospital.

A *medical practitioner in a military environment* will be judged according to the standard accepted by a reasonable and responsible body of military psychiatrists or nurses (which takes account of any additional training or instruction given to doctors or nurses practising in the military environment).

In *Multiple Claimants v MOD (Pt I)*,[g] Cs were former members of the Armed Forces who allegedly suffered psychiatric injury as a result of combat exposure during service for their country. The case was not about exposure to the stress and trauma of combat, but rather, that the MOD were negligent in failing to take any adequate steps to prevent the development of psychiatric illness, and in failing to detect, diagnose or treat such illness. **Held:** the MOD had committed systemic breach in three limited respects.

A *practitioner of alternative medicine* will be judged against two standards: (1) the reasonable standard of skill and care appropriate to traditional Chinese herbal medicine, which had a long and distinguished history; and (2) given that D operated alongside orthodox medicine, D had reasonably to satisfy himself that the remedy was not actually or potentially harmful; and that there was no adverse report in orthodox medical journals re the remedy.

In *Shakoor v Situ*,[h] Mr Situ, D, a practitioner of Chinese herbal medicine, treated Mr Shakoor, C, for fatty lumps of tissue beneath the skin, by prescribing a herbal remedy containing 12 different herbs. After taking 9 doses, C fell ill with nausea, yellowing of the eyes and skin, and heartburn. C's liver turned necrotic, and despite an urgent liver transplant, C died. The treatment was considered safe in Chinese medicine, although some letters and articles in *The Lancet* had queried the safety of one particular herb in the medicine. D had not read those articles. **Held:** no breach proven. D met both standards.

[e] [1990] 3 All ER 237 (QB) 243.
[f] (1999) 48 BMLR 109 (QB) 114–15.
[g] [2003] EWHC 1134 (QB) [2.D].
[h] (2000) 57 BMLR 178 (QB) 185–86.

Those who offer *voluntary first-aid services* must meet the standard of the ordinary skilled first-aider exercising and professing to have the skill of a first-aider trained in accordance with the First Aid Manual.	In *Cattley v St John Ambulance Brigade*,[i] Sean Cattley, C, a young motorcross rider participating in a motor scrambling event at Bedford, was injured when he was thrown off his bike and hit his head directly on the trackside bank and came to rest on his back. He lost consciousness, could not move his legs, was treated trackside by voluntary St John Ambulance officers, D, and taken to hospital. Although C recovered the ability to walk, he suffered permanent spinal damage and residual disabilities. C alleged that D treated him negligently at the scene. **Held:** the standard of care was set by the First Aid Manual, and was met.
A *midwife* must meet the standard of a reasonably competent midwife carrying out the functions expected of the post-natal ward of a district general hospital.	In *Spencer v NHS North West*,[j] C alleged that the midwifery staff at the hospital where she was born failed to suspect that she was developing a streptococcal infection on her first night. Her condition was picked up too late to avoid very serious long-term disability. **Held:** the standard of care was met. The fact that C was unsettled and crying, when less than a day old, was not a reason to suspect serious infection.
A person who *undertakes medically-related tasks, but who does not hold himself out as having any medical qualifications or expertise*, will be judged according to the standard of a reasonable person without medical qualifications or expertise who undertakes such a task.	In *Philips v William Whiteley Ltd*,[k] a jeweller, D, conducted an ear-piercing operation for Ms Philips, C, at a department store's jewellery department. A septic abscess formed on C's ear. D had cleaned his instruments before he arrived, and then passed them through a flame to disinfect. His instruments were found to be in a septic condition. **Held:** D met the standard of a reasonable jeweller undertaking a minor surgical operation within the limitations of what antiseptic measures could be taken in a department store, and was not required to meet the standard of a doctor or surgeon. Goddard J said: '[i]f a person wants to ensure that the operation of piercing her ears is going to be carried out with that proportion of skill that a Fellow of the Royal College of Surgeons would use, *she must go to a surgeon*'.

[i] (QB, 25 Nov 1988, Judge Prosser QC).
[j] [2012] EWHC 2142 (QB) [17]. See too: *Croft v Heart of England NHS Fndn Trust* [2012] EWHC 1470 (QB) [22].
[k] [1938] 1 All ER 566 (KB), quote at 569 (emphasis added).

The notion of graduated specialisms applies equally in other professional contexts. For example, in *Fraser v Bolt Burdon Claims*, the court noted that, 'in the legal context, it is no proper criticism of a solicitor in general practice that he has not the advocacy skills or specialist experience of a barrister', and that '[e]ach professional person falls to be judged by the standards of his fellows in his particular profession, not by the standards of ... a more specialised branch of his profession than that of which he is part'.[15]

[15] [2009] EWHC 2906 (QB) [52].

A caveat

The fact that D does not need to attain the standard of care expected of a more skilled part of his profession may be offset by the fact that those of more limited expertise may be required to refer C to one with greater expertise, in order to attain the requisite standard of care (per *Hardman v Riddell*[16]).

> In *Brooks v Home Office*,[17] facts previously, **held:** breach proven. Given that the consultant in charge of the obstetric unit at Holloway was away at the time that the pregnancy scan was done, and given that the doctor left in charge had limited expertise in reading scans, 'the only prudent course ... was to refer [C] to a specialist so as to provide the obstetrical expertise which should have been available to her'. A civilian hospital would have had greater resources to deal with the problem. (However, causation failed, and so negligence ultimately failed.)

Whilst the medical environment in which D's conduct is being performed has, occasionally, given rise to a lower standard of care than would apply in a 'superior' environment, that variation in the standard can also be overcome by C, by relying upon a duty-to-refer, under the so-called 'locality rule' (discussed below).

A tension between judicial viewpoints?

Several English judges have exhorted that a check **must** be kept on the standard of care in the professional context, so as not to move the law of negligence towards strict liability, by treating any less-than-perfect conduct by a professional D as a breach.

For example, as Bingham LJ reiterated in the auditing case of *Eckersley v Binnie & Partners*, '[t]he law does not require of a professional man that he be a paragon, combining the qualities of polymath and prophet'.[18] In general terms, the classic statement by Taschereau J from the Supreme Court of Canada continues to resonate: '[c]ases necessarily occur in which, in spite of exercising the greatest caution, accidents supervene and for which nobody can be held responsible ... Perfection is a standard required by law no more for a doctor than for other professional men, lawyers, engineers, architects, etc' (per *Cardin v La Cité de Montréal*[19]). Professional Ds 'are not insurers' of a good outcome (per *Bull v Devon AHA*[20]), and they do not 'warrant a perfect result' (*Wilsher v Essex AHA*[21]). In *Phelps v Hillingdon LBC*, the House of Lords too recognised the care that should be taken, when adjudging whether a standard of care was breached: '[t]he recognition of the duty of care does not of itself impose unreasonably high standards ... The difficulties of the tasks involved, and of the circumstances under which people have to work in this area, must also be borne fully in mind. The professionalism, dedication and standards of those engaged in the provision of educational services are such that cases of liability for negligence will be exceptional'.[22]

Nevertheless, some judicial statements, especially in other jurisdictions, have cast the standard imposed upon a professional D very highly indeed.

---

[16] [2004] EWHC 1691 (QB) [64] (no breach).   [17] (1999) 48 BMLR 109 (QB) 114–15.

[18] (1988) 18 Con LR 1 (CA) 80 (Bingham LJ). Applied since, to hold a professional D not negligent, e.g.: *Barings plc (in liq) v Coopers & Lybrand (a firm)* [2003] EWHC 1319 (Ch) [578]–[579].

[19] [1961] SCR 655 (SCC), 29 DLR (2d) 492 (SCC) 494 (Taschereau J).

[20] (1989) 22 BMLR 79, 113, [1993] 4 Med LR 117 (CA) (Dillon LJ).

[21] [1987] QB 730 (CA) 747 (Mustill LJ).   [22] [2001] 2 AC 619 (HL) 655 (Lord Slynn).

> ## The comparative corner: Vignettes from other jurisdictions
>
> **Ireland:** in *Dunne v National Maternity Hosp*,[23] the standard of care applying to doctors was said to be very high, for two reasons: '[t]he complete dependence of patients on the skill and care of medical attendants, and the gravity from their point of view of a failure in such care, makes it undesirable and unjustifiable to accept as a matter of law a lax or permissive standard of care for the purpose of assessing what is and is not medical negligence'.
>
> **Australia:** in *Bankstown Foundry Pty Ltd v Braistina*,[24] McHugh JA remarked that, '[t]hroughout the common law of negligence ... the standard of care required of a defendant has moved close to the border of strict liability'. This statement drew criticism from the High Court of Australia, on appeal, for its 'tendency to mislead',[25] but it was subsequently approved by a differently-constituted NSWCA (in *Inverell MC v Pennington*[26]).

The limits of the *Bolam* standard of care

§6.7 The *Bolam* standard of care does not apply where a professional D commits an act or omission in circumstances where he is exercising *no* professional judgment and skill whatsoever. The concept of the 'professional D' extends beyond 'the learned professions'.

Where D's task is not one which requires some special skill, then the standard required of D must accord with that which would be reasonably expected of 'the person on the Clapham bus'. However, the line between professional and non-professional judgment can be quite blurred.

> In *Kelly v Board of Governors of St Laurence's Hospital*,[27] nurses employed at the hospital, D, failed to accompany an epileptic in-patient, C, to the toilet, at a time when C was taken off all medication preparatory to tests. The question arose as to whether that decision not to accompany C was a matter of professional judgment, or a custodial matter 'where the standard of care is much more the standard of the ordinary individual than such as might be dictated by medical practice'. **Held (2:1):** the *Bolam* medical standard was applicable.

The application of the *Bolam* standard depends upon D's exercising a 'special skill', albeit that just who possesses special skill has been the subject of some division of judicial opinion. According to *Carty v Croydon BC*, '[t]he phrase "professional person" is not a term of art'.[28] To fall within that phrase, the guidance in *M v Newham LBC*[29] was cited in *Carty* as relevant: '[t]hose who engage professionally ... bring to their task skill and expertise, the product partly of training and partly of experience, which ordinary uninstructed members of the public are bound to lack'.[30] Apart from medical Ds (the subject of *Bolam* itself), some callings in life comfortably fit within that phrase, for example:

---

[23] As observed in: [1989] IR 91 (SC) 110 (Finlay CJ).   [24] [1985] Aust Torts Reports ¶80–713 (NSWCA) 69,127.

[25] *Bankstown Foundry Pty Ltd v Braistina* (1986) 160 CLR 301 (HCA) 307 (Mason, Wilson and Dawson JJ).

[26] [1993] Aust Torts Rep ¶81–234 (NSWCA) 62 406 (Clarke JA).   [27] [1988] IR 402 (SC).

[28] [2005] EWCA Civ 19, [2005] 1 WLR 2312, [45].

[29] Reported as part of the litigation: *X (Minors) v Bedfordshire CC* [1995] 2 AC 633.

[30] [1995] 2 AC 633 (HL) 666 (Sir Thomas Bingham MR).

- architects (*Nye Saunders & Partners (a firm) v Alan E Bristow*[31]);
- chartered surveyors and property consultants who perform valuations and give property investment advice (*Capita Alternative Fund Services (Guernsey) Ltd v Drivers Jonas (a firm)*[32]);
- project managers of a construction project (*Royal Brompton Hosp NHS Trust v Frederick A Hammond*[33]);
- educational psychologists, teachers and those who provide special educational needs for vulnerable children (*Barrett v Enfield BC*[34]);
- social workers (per *M v Newham LBC*[35]);
- education officers who decide whether a child is to be kept at a school or moved to another educational environment (*Carty v Croydon BC*[36]).

However, the *Bolam* standard applies more widely than just to the 'learned professions', for example:

- tree inspectors who inspect premises to ensure that trees are reasonably safe for visitors (*Bowen v National Trust*[37]);
- football referees (*Vowles v Evans*[38]);
- window lock installers and technicians (*Adams v Rhymney Valley DC*[39]).

In *Adams*, this issue split the members of the Court of Appeal. The key question was whether it was negligent to provide a tenanted property with lockable windows with removable keys, rather than with push-button locks which could be opened by a child. Question – was that issue to be determined in accordance with what 'the person on the Clapham bus' would regard as reasonable, or by what a window lock designer would regard as reasonable? In other words, were the characteristics of the particular D to be taken into account? According to the majority, the *Bolam* standard of care applied. Morritt LJ said that the *Bolam* standard 'does not depend on the actual possession of the relevant qualification. Emergencies apart, if the act in question can only safely be done by a person with the necessary skill to do it, then the standard of care to be shown is that appropriate to one possessing that skill'; whilst Sir Christopher Staughton agreed that: '[t]he key question is whether the *Bolam* test still applies, although the particular D did not in fact have the qualifications of a professional in the relevant field of activity ... [however] the *Bolam* test is not the monopoly of the expert'.[40]

However, Sedley LJ dissented, and considered that the *Bolam* standard had no application in the case: 'no design skills at all were applied to the choice of window lock ... The reason why the test [and *Bolam* standard] has no relevance to this case is that its purpose is to enable the court to determine whether a person professing and purporting to exercise a particular skill has exercised it with sufficient competence to escape a charge of negligence. In the present case, the problem is that nobody in the council purported to exercise the relevant design skill ... [D], which has failed altogether to set about exercising a professional skill, cannot expect to be judged by the court as if it had exercised it: the court cannot proceed as if an educated choice was made, when it knows that it was not'.[41]

---

[31] (1987) 37 BLR 97 (CA) 103 (Stephen Brown LJ).   [32] [2011] EWHC 2336 (Comm).
[33] [2000] EWHC Technology 39.   [34] [2001] 2 AC 550, [1999] 3 WLR 79 (HL).
[35] See: *X (Minors) v Bedfordshire CC* [1995] 2 AC 633 (HL) 666 (Sir Thomas Bingham MR).
[36] [2005] EWCA Civ 19, [2005] 1 WLR 2312.   [37] [2011] EWHC 1992 (QB).   [38] [2003] EWCA Civ 318.
[39] [2001] PNLR 4 (CA).   [40] *ibid*, [42] and [57].   [41] *ibid*, [15]–[16].

Although the *Adams* principle has not been widely applied since, and the division in the Court of Appeal's reasoning notwithstanding, Mackay J noted, in the tree inspector case (*Bowen v National Trust*), that the principle 'is now well established'.[42] The issue is equally significant when the *Bolam* test of proving breach is called upon – as discussion in Chapter 7 will demonstrate.

Age

§6.8   The standard of care which the law imposes upon a child, D, is suppressed to the standard expected of a reasonable or 'ordinary' child of the same age as D.

The relevant standard, where a child's behaviour is under scrutiny for negligence, is that of 'an ordinarily prudent and reasonable child' of the same age (per *Mullin v Richards*[43]). The relevant standard is not that of either a 'paragon of prudence' or a 'scatterbrained child' (per Salmon LJ in *Gough v Thorne*[44]).

A child, for this purpose, is anyone below the age of majority – in *Mullin* itself, the child was 15 years old; and in *Foskett v Mistry*,[45] the child was 16.5; and a somewhat suppressed standard of care was still applied in both cases.

It will be recalled from Chapter 2 that very young children do not owe any duty of care to D (per *Carmarthenshire CC v Lewis*[46]), nor to themselves where contributory negligence is at stake ('a judge should only find a child guilty of contributory negligence if he or she is of such an age as to be expected to take precautions for his or her own safety': per *Gough v Thorne*[47]). Hence, the principle under discussion in this section is only pertinent to those children who are of sufficient age to be found liable in negligence.

It follows that, for a child to fall below the suppressed standard of care and to be found negligent, that child's conduct 'must be careless to a very high degree' (per *Mullin*). That degree of carelessness might be shown by the child's breaking the rules or acting beyond the norms of a game; or acting quite recklessly towards C (in the sense of showing a very high degree of carelessness) (per *Orchard v Lee*[48]). However, in these leading cases, there was **no** breach of duty in either, given where the standard of care was set.

In *Mullin v Richards*,[49] two 15-year-old school friends, Teresa Mullin (C) and Heidi Richards (D), were sitting side by side at a desk at their school in Birmingham, and were playing around at the end of their maths class, hitting each other's white plastic 30 cm rulers as though in a play sword fight. One of the rulers snapped, a sharp piece of plastic went into C's eye, and she lost all sight in that eye. C sued D and the Birmingham CC (as the relevant education authority) in negligence. The maths teacher was held not liable in negligence for any failure to supervise. Re the claim against D, the standard against which D's behaviour should be judged was that of an ordinary, reasonable 15-year-old schoolgirl, who would have appreciated that there was some risk of injury involved in using plastic rulers as though they were swords – and Heidi met that standard. In *Orchard v Lee*,[50]

---

[42] [2011] EWHC 1992 (QB) [7].

[43] [1997] EWCA Civ 2662, [1998] 1 WLR 1304, 1308–9, and affirmed in: *Dunnage v Randall* [2015] EWCA Crim 673, [123].

[44] [1966] 1 WLR 1387 (CA) 1391.   [45] [1984] RTR 1 (CA).   [46] [1955] AC 549 (HL).

[47] [1966] 1 WLR 1387 (CA) 1390 (Lord Denning MR).   [48] [2009] EWCA Civ 295, [2009] PIQR P16, [10]–[11].

[49] At first instance, the trial judge held Heidi, D, liable in negligence, but that Teresa, C, was liable for 50% CN.

[50] [2009] EWCA Civ 295, quote at [19].

Mr Lee, 13, D, and his friend, 13, were playing a game of tag in a courtyard and in part of a walk-way reserved for a playing area, when D, running back and taunting his friend, collided with Miss Orchard, C, a lunchtime assistant supervisor at the school, causing C injury. D was playing a game of tag within a designated play area; he was not breaking any rules in playing the game, because running in those areas was not prohibited; and he was not acting to any significant degree beyond the norms of that game. Hence, D met the standard of care required: '13-year-old boys will be 13-year-old boys who will play tag. They will run backwards and they will taunt each other. If that is what they are doing and they are not breaking any rules, they should not be held liable in negligence. Parents and schools are there to control children, and it would be a retrograde step to visit liability on a 13-year-old for simply playing a game in the area where he was allowed to do so'. It might have been different if D had been 'playing tag close to traffic in the street'.

Reasons for, and ramifications of, the legal approach

In *Mullin*,[51] the justifications for a suppressed standard for children were derived from the High Court of Australia's majority decision in *McHale v Watson*:[52]

i. children often behave in unpremeditated and impulsive ways, and are not yet of an age to have an adult's realisation of danger or wariness – that requires 'a degree of sense and circumspection which nature ordinarily withholds till life has become less rosy';

ii. children may consider something to be an interesting and exciting activity, but which is in fact dangerous (in *McHale*, e.g., the court took judicial notice 'that the ordinary boy of 12 suffers from a feeling that a piece of wood and a sharp instrument have a special affinity');

iii. it is always open to Parliament to overrule the common law on this point, and raise the standard of care expected of children – but unless it does, children (and adults) 'must accept, as they go about in society, the risks from which ordinary care on the part of others will not suffice to save them. One such risk is that boys of 12 may behave as boys of 12; and that, sometimes, is a risk indeed'.

In *McHale v Watson*, D was a 12-year-old boy who sharpened a metal instrument, and then later threw it at a post, expecting it to embed in the post. The metal shard glanced off the post, or else missed it altogether, and hit C, a young girl, in the eye. C lost her eye as a result. **Held (3:1):** no breach occurred.

In addition, the lower standard of care to be applied to a child accords with the lower standard which also applies to recreational endeavours involving horseplay between participants (discussed shortly) – and, in that regard, the law achieves a welcome consistency. This was pointed out in *Orchard v Lee*,[53] where Waller LJ discussed the case of *Blake v Galloway*,[54] in which two 15-year-olds, C and D, engaged in some 'mucking around', eventually causing injury to C's eye. The standard of care imposed in such cases is suppressed, such that only conduct that amounts to 'recklessness, or a very high degree of carelessness' will amount to a breach. Whilst the child cases of *McHale* and *Mullin* were (somewhat surprisingly) not cited in *Blake v Galloway*, it was entirely coincidental with *Blake* that a lower standard of care should be applied to children's acts or omissions – because those cases 'demonstrate consistently with *Blake* that, for a child to be held culpable, the conduct must be careless to a very high degree' (according to *Orchard v Lee*[55]).

---

[51] [1997] EWCA Civ 2662, [1998] 1 WLR 1304 (CA).   [52] [1996] HCA 13, (1996) 115 CLR 199, [9]–[10].
[53] [2009] EWCA Civ 295, [10].   [54] [2004] EWCA Civ 814.   [55] [2009] EWCA Civ 295, [2009] ELR 178, [11].

The legal ramification, of course, is to render it less likely that C, the person injured by the child's acts or omissions, will recover compensation. The young girl who lost her eye in *McHale* could not recover damages for her injury, and nor could the teaching supervisor in *Orchard* – despite the courts' expressed 'sympathy' for their predicaments. Should the law change, in that regard?

The law reform corner: A vignette from Ireland

Recognition that children may escape liability: The Irish LRC[56] considered that the suppressed standard of care that applied to children would make a difference to the legal outcome (i.e., child D would not be negligent, whereas an adult D would be) in limited cases – and asked whether the lower standard of care should be changed by statute:

> 'Our [common] law could, of course, impose an adult standard of care in such instances and hold the child liable. But it may be argued that to do so would offend against the principle of justice, since the law would thus require the child to act according to a standard beyond his or her capacities. However attractive this may be as a pragmatic solution, we consider that it should not be accepted because of its injustice.'

Redress by statute? The Irish LRC considered that Parliament should intervene, and create a legislative remedy for the unfortunate road-user C who is injured by a child D, in the case of that child's *negligent driving*:

> 'society as a whole should bear the responsibility of compensating victims of injury involving motor vehicles on the roads where the driver of the car causing the injury is a child, and by reason only of his or her particular age, mental development and experience is free from liability which would otherwise attach if the adult standard of care were to apply. For this very small band of cases, we recommend that there be established a fund for compensation to be paid for by the State.'

Conditions for liability: The Fund would apply to provide compensation to C where three conditions were met:

(a) The Fund would relate only to injuries on the road where the driver of a motor vehicle was < 16;

(b) Recourse to the Fund would not be possible where the child was found liable in negligence or, conversely, where the child was found not to have been liable in negligence in cases where, applying the adult standard of care, no liability would have been involved;

(c) If someone other than child D is liable for C's injury, that party, and not the Fund, should compensate C.

Outcome: This legislative proposal was never enacted by the Irish Parliament.

Objective or subjective?

§6.9   English law is presently unsettled as to whether child D's behaviour is to be compared with that of an ordinary child of similar age – or with a child who has a similar experience, development and intelligence to that child D.

---

[56] *Liability in Tort of Minors and the Liability of Parents for Damage Caused by Minors* (Rep 17, 1985) 58.

Of course, the latter option would render the enquiry a subjective, rather than an objective, test – and indeed, the subjective approach was suggested by the Australian case of *McHale v Watson*.[57] Owen J stated that, 'the standard by which [the child's] conduct is to be measured is ... that reasonably to be expected of a child of the same age, intelligence and experience' – which certainly imputed a subjective component.

However, that notion has seemingly been dismissed in English law. In *Mullin v Richards*,[58] Waller LJ specifically 'questioned' (i.e., doubted) the use of the term, 'intelligence', in Owen J's statement in *McHale*, and thereafter referred to the requisite standard as being that of 'an ordinary, reasonable 15-year-old schoolgirl' – with no reference to D's intelligence or experience at all. This construction in *Mullin* of the relevant standard applicable to child D was consistent with earlier English authority, which had appeared to endorse the objective approach too. As the Irish LRC explained,[59] in *Yachuk v Oliver Blais Co Ltd*, the Privy Council (on appeal from Canada) favoured 'the objective view of the child's age alone (rather than his intelligence and experience as well)', and that objective approach was favoured in other cases such as *Gough v Thorne* ('the court, in exempting [the child] from any fault under this test, had no need to consider the subjective approach').

Hence, the subjective approach towards the standard of care expected of a child appears to have no modern support in English case law. However, the Commonwealth position is mixed, or to the contrary.

The comparative corner: Relevant Commonwealth vignettes

Australia: subsequent to *McHale v Watson*[60] (where a subjective approach appeared to be contemplated), there was division of opinion in some lower courts, as to the appropriate standard which the majority's judgment represented. In judicial consideration of the subject in 2012, the Western Australian Court of Appeal said somewhat confusingly, in *Town of Port Hedland v Hodder*,[61] that, '[t]he decision of the majority in *McHale v Watson* might be summarised (with some risk of generalisation) in the proposition that the standard of care expected of children ... is subjective in the sense that it takes account of their age and development, and the degree of foresight and prudence that might be expected of a child of like age, but objective in the sense that the child is expected to conform to the standards of behaviour reasonably expected of children of that age and development generally'.

Canada: the subjective approach appears to have been favoured in Canada. In *McEllistrum v Etches* (SCC),[62] Kerwin CJ stated that, 'it is a question for the jury in each case whether the infant exercised the care to be expected from a child of like age, intelligence and experience'. In *Ottosen v Kasper*,[63] this was described as a 'foundation case' for the principles for assessing the negligence of a child. More recently, in *Hixon-Gause v Roberts*,[64] the subjective approach was again preferred, endorsing the comments in *Bourne v Anderson*:[65] 'in referring to the care to be expected "from a child of like age, intelligence

---

[57] [1996] HCA 13, (1996) 115 CLR 199 (HCA) [6].   [58] [1997] EWCA Civ 2662, [1998] 1 WLR 1304 (CA) 1309.

[59] *Liability in Tort of Minors and the Liability of Parents for Damage Caused by Minors* (Rep 17, 1985) fn 61.

[60] [1996] HCA 13, (1996) 115 CLR 199 (HCA).   [61] [2012] WASCA 212, [193].   [62] [1956] 5 SCR 787 (SCC) 793.

[63] [1986] BCJ No 139, [4].   [64] [2003] BCSC 874, [40].   [65] [1997] BCJ No 915, [59]–[60].

and experience", *McEllistrum* was referring to the reasonable or prudent child, and to an objective standard of care. The subjective factors, of the particular child's age, intelligence, and experience, are only relevant to the fixing of that standard of care [which is] the conduct to be expected of a 7 year and 4 month old child having the same intelligence and experience as Geordie'.

The standard, whether C or D

§6.10   Whether the child's behaviour is being judged as one who has been contributorily negligent, or as one who has negligently inflicted injury upon C, the same suppressed standard of care applies.

Very frequently, it is the child's behaviour as *claimant*, where the standard of care is most relevant, i.e., where an allegation of the defence of contributory negligence has been made against that child, for being careless of his own well-being, and for bringing about his own injuries in some way (per Chapter 10). The same suppressed standard of care continues to apply. In determining whether the child was contributorily negligent, it was necessary to judge what he did against the standards to be expected of a similarly-aged child.

> In *Toropdar v D*,[66] a child, 10, C, was playing a game with friends in which they tried to find a hidden object. He found the object and ran excitedly out into the road, from behind a bus, and collided with Mr Toropdar's, D's, car, which was being driven within the speed limit down the street. C suffered serious injuries when flung onto the bonnet and then onto the road. C had not stopped or looked in D's direction from his concealed position behind the bus. **Held:** C was contributorily negligent (33%). Being 10, C was of an age where he could be reasonably be expected to take precautions for his own safety; and to appreciate the dangers involved in running from behind a bus into a city street, in contravention of road rules – but, '[a]t the same time he could not be expected to have the same ingrained approach to safety and self-preservation as an adult or even a teenager'.

Of course, anything said about a suppressed standard of care, in relation to a child who is contributorily negligent, is dicta only, where the standard of care expected of *a child D* is concerned. Nevertheless, there is a clear alignment in English law between the standard of care expected of a child, whether C or D.

Disability (physical or mental)

The standard of care expected of D at law depends upon whether or not D was aware of his disability.

Non-awareness of the condition

§6.11   Where D suffers from a disability (e.g., a medical condition) of which he was unaware, and of which he could not reasonably have been aware, the standard of care is suppressed to that of a reasonable D who is unaware that he was suffering from that condition.

---

[66] [2009] EWHC 2997 (QB), quote at [13] (Clarke J).

This proposition has been set, in English law, by *Mansfield v Weetabix Ltd.*[67] The justification is that to apply a purely objective standard (e.g., the ordinary reasonable driver) that does not take account of a medical condition of which D was unaware, would render D strictly liable. That was not a fair or just outcome. In such cases, given the suppression of the standard of care, D is unlikely to be found liable for breach.

Hence, what matters is whether D knew, or ought to have known, of his disability. If not, the standard is reduced. If so, the standard is the usual objective standard of a reasonable driver, etc. The infirmity that gives rise to D's loss of control or incapacity may be sudden, or it may be gradual – either condition suffices to invoke the *Mansfield* principle, provided that D is unaware of it, and should not reasonably have been aware of it.

> In *Mansfield v Weetabix*, Mr Tarleton, D, was a lorry driver for Weetabix. On the day of the accident, he was driving a 38-ton lorry, and failed to take a sharp bend in the village near Stoke-on-Trent, and crashed into a shop belonging to Mr and Mrs Mansfield, C, causing extensive damage. D did not know that he suffered from the condition, but he had malignant insulinoma which resulted in a hypoglycaemic state in which the brain is starved of glucose and unable to function properly. D had a propensity to suffer from blackouts; he would recover from the blackouts but was completely unaware of anything having happened; D's wife knew of his condition, but had concealed it from her husband because she did not wish to worry him. D did not have much to eat on the day, which probably helped to induce that state by lowering his blood sugar level. D had been driving errati- cally before the accident happened, and he could not remember anything of the journey between 1.00pm when he started off, and at 3.40pm when the accident happened. D had died prior to trial. **Held:** no breach proven. A person with D's condition commonly did not appreciate that his ability was impaired, and D was no exception. The standard of care which D was obliged to show was that of a reasonably competent driver unaware that he was or might be suffering from a condition that impaired his ability to drive.

Prior to *Mansfeld*, there had been another example of the standard of care being suppressed where D was not aware of his infirmity, and nor could he reasonably have suspected that he was afflicted with that infirmity (*Jones v Dennison*[68]), where negligence was not proven either.

The reasoning, and the ramifications. To apply the objective standard of the ordinary rea- sonable driver to Mr Tarleton's grave situation, of which he had no knowledge, 'would be to impose strict liability. But that is not the law' (held Leggatt LJ in *Mansfield v Weetabix*).[69]

Of course, if 'strict liability' means that D should not be liable for a condition of which he is unaware, then that is a supportable proposition. On the other hand, if 'strict liability' means to impose a standard of care upon D which is impossible for him to achieve, and which is unattainable in all the circumstances, then the law regularly imposes such a form of strict li- ability – inexperienced Ds may often find themselves in that position (discussed below). Yet, in *Mansfield*, the Court of Appeal firmly approved of the proposition that an inexperienced D should not benefit from a suppressed standard, because there, an inexperienced D is aware of his limitations. Mr Tarleton was not.

The suppression of the standard of care, per the *Mansfield* principle, means that C will likely not recover. Hence, unless C is insured for the damage or injury that he suffers at D's hands, C will go uncompensated. As in other instances in which the standard of care has been suppressed (see discussion of D's age, above), the idea was floated by Leggatt LJ that it was always open

---

[67] [1998] 1 WLR 1263 (CA) 1267–68.   [68] [1971] RTR 174 (CA).   [69] [1998] 1 WLR 1263 (CA) 1268.

to Parliament to reverse the law and hold D to a reasonable standard of care. In the meantime, however, D 'was in no way to blame, he was not negligent'.[70] The Irish High Court agreed with this view, in *Counihan v Bus Atha Cliath-Dublin Bus*. It noted that most drivers are insured, and a state compensation fund is available for harm done by the uninsured driver, so that 'it is, perhaps, somewhat surprising that a category of persons [C, in a *Mansfield* scenario] who are injured due to no fault of their own are, as a result of the state of the law, deprived of appropriate compensation ... [but] a change in that law is a policy decision which is a matter for the Oireachtas'.[71]

Awareness of the condition

§6.12   Where D suffers from a disability (physical or mental), of which he is aware, then the standard of care expected of D is not suppressed at law.

Although this proposition has been stated in the context of D as a road-user, there is no reason that it should be restricted to that scenario.

Essentially, if D was indeed alert to the fact that his ability was impaired, or if he ought to have known of his infirmity, but continued to act anyway, then the *Mansfield* principle has no application to D at all. Just because D may have been impaired mentally or physically, or have lost some partial control of his movements and/or judgment at the time of the accident, is not enough to bring D within the protection of that principle.

> In *Das Intl Ltd v Manley*,[72] D suffered a serious car accident, in which he suffered a mild concussion. D could not remember much of what happened after his accident (including his own subsequent actions towards C, another road-user). That scenario was expressly distinguished from *Mansfield*, and D's actions towards C were negligent because they fell below the standard of a reasonable road-user (albeit, a road-user acting in emergency conditions). In *Roberts v Ramsbottom*,[73] D was involved in a car accident when he suffered a cerebral haemorrhage/stroke. D had awareness of his surroundings and of the traffic conditions during the episode, and tried to manipulate the car's controls, but collided with a stationary van. D drove off and then crashed into C's vehicle, causing injury. The Court of Appeal in *Mansfield* endorsed the outcome in *Roberts* that D was negligent, noting that the standard of a reasonable driver should apply, if D continued to drive when he was unfit to, and when he should have appreciated his unfitness to drive, but deliberately decided to continue. D's actions fell below that standard.

If a driver injures a pedestrian or passenger, because he lacks good eyesight or hearing, or has some other physical infirmity that affects his capacity to drive, the law still insists that D meet the standard of a reasonable driver. The infirmities do not suppress the standard expected of D in any respect. That much was made plain, in dicta, in *Nettleship v Weston*,[74] and has been applied in tragic case law since.

> In *C v Burcombe*,[75] Mr Burcombe, D, aged 70, had stopped his car at a layby to fix a flat tyre. At the time, D was under medication for heart disease, and though declared fit to drive, he had been warned by his GP not to attempt strenuous activity. In changing the wheel on his car, this degree

---

[70] *ibid*, 1268.   [71] [2005] IEHC 51, [2005] 2 IR 436. The Oireachtas is the legislature of the Irish Republic.
[72] [2002] EWCA Civ 1638.   [73] [1980] 1 WLR 823 (QB).
[74] [1971] 2 QB 691 (CA) 699, citing: *Richley v Faull* [1965] 1 WLR 1454 (QB) and *Watson v Whitney* [1966] 1 WLR 37 (CA).
[75] [2003] CLY 3030 (CC Watford, 27 May 2002).

of activity brought on a severe heart attack. Nevertheless, he got back into the car and drove off, pulling away from the layby very slowly in first gear, with his hazard lights flashing and wearing no seatbelt. D then lost control, and veered onto the opposite side of the road, and collided with two vehicles in succession, killing both drivers and one passenger, C. D also died of the heart attack. His estate denied liability. **Held:** breach proven. Having driven off with at least some awareness that he was very unwell and unfit to drive, that meant that D was aware of his condition, and could not rely on *Mansfield*. D also failed to heed his GP's advice, another instance of not meeting the standard of reasonable care.

Inexperience

Professional and non-professional Ds treated alike

§6.13   The inexperience of D, who is undertaking a *non-professional* activity, does not suppress the standard of care which the law expects of D ('the *Nettleship* rule'). The inexperience of D, who is undertaking a *professional* activity, does not suppress the standard of care either; D's conduct is to be compared with the standard of an ordinary skilled and experienced D who is professing to exercise that professional skill ('the *Wilsher* rule').

The '*Nettleship* rule' stems from *Nettleship v Weston*,[76] where it was held that a learner driver was held to the same standard of care as that of a reasonably competent driver.

> In *Nettleship v Weston*, Mr Nettleship, C, agreed to give a friend's wife, Mrs Weston, D, some driving lessons. Before taking on the responsibility, C satisfied himself that the car was insured against risk of injury to a passenger. They negotiated two lessons successfully. However, during the third, D was holding the steering wheel and controlling the pedals, whilst C was moving the gear lever. D failed to straighten up after turning left, and panicked. The car mounted the kerb and collided with a lamp post. D was convicted of driving without due care and attention. C was injured in the collision. **Held (at trial):** D not negligent, on the basis that the defence of *volenti* applied. **Held (CA, 2:1):** breach/negligence proven. *Volenti* could not apply, given the check that C carried out before doing the lessons, that showed expressly that he did not consent to run the risk of injury which might occur through D's lack of skill. Further, D did not meet the standard of a reasonable driver.

As Lord Denning MR, of the majority, memorably put it, '[t]he learner-driver may be doing his best, but his incompetent best is not good enough'. (Salmon LJ dissented, preferring the view that a learner driver should be judged by the standard of a reasonable learner driver.) Although subsequent cases (such as *Das Intl Ltd v Manley*[77]) have noted that the *Nettleship* rule applies '[i]n the context of driving', there is no rational basis for limiting the rule to inexperienced drivers alone. Essentially, this is an instance where the law imposes a standard of care which the inexperienced D may not possibly be able to achieve.

The professional D is in the same position. Although stated much earlier (in 1952, per *Jones v Manchester Corp*),[78] the principal authority for that proposition is the 1987 Court of Appeal decision in *Wilsher v Essex AHA*.[79] Both cases concerned medical Ds, but again, as with the inexperienced D, the principle appropriately extends to all professional Ds.

---

[76] [1971] 2 QB 691 (CA) 699.   [77] [2002] EWCA Civ 1638, [15].
[78] [1952] 2 QB 852 (CA), with quotes in the following case description at 871 and 867 (Denning LJ).
[79] [1987] QB 730 (CA), with quotes in the following case description at 773–74 (Glidewell LJ).

In *Wilsher v Essex AHA*, a doctor, D, 'a fairly junior doctor of limited experience',[80] mistakenly inserted a catheter into a vein, instead of in the umbilical artery, of Martin Wilsher, C, who was born a very premature baby. The aim had been to measure arterial blood oxygen levels. The mistake meant that the monitor gave a lower reading of blood oxygen levels (reading venal blood), so that, as a result, C was 'supersaturated' with oxygen for up to 8–12 hours. It was not actually the insertion of the catheter into a vein instead of an artery which was alleged to be negligent ('it was an error which competent doctors could and from time to time did commit'), but rather, the failure to pick up, from an examination of an X-ray, that the catheter was in the wrong place. C ultimately developed the incurable eye condition, retrolental fibroplasia (RLF), which resulted in blindness, for which super-saturation of oxygen was a possible cause. After inserting the catheter, the junior doctor asked the senior registrar to check what he had done. The registrar did so and failed to see the mistake, he inspected the X-ray with the junior doctor and failed to detect that it was misplaced, and some hours later, when replacing the catheter, did exactly the same thing. **Held:** the junior doctor committed a breach of duty, in mis-reading the X-ray, but not in placing the catheter.

Wilsher went up to House of Lords,[81] but only on the question as to whether the super-saturation of oxygen in the first 30 hours of the patient's life caused or materially contributed to his injury, i.e., blindness (ultimately, it did not). The standard of care expected of the junior inexperienced doctor was not revisited on appeal, and hence, the Court of Appeal approach governs the legal position on this issue.

The justifications for the *Nettleship/Wilsher* rules

Several reasons underpin the view that inexperienced Ds should be held to an often unachievable standard of care, according to judicial reasoning:

i. the rule avoids the haphazardness that could arise if courts had to take the particular experience of D into account. One standard is legally more convenient. In *Nettleship*, Megaw LJ remarked that '[t]he disadvantages of the resulting unpredictability, uncertainty and, indeed, impossibility of arriving at fair and consistent decisions outweigh the advantages [of a variable standard]. The certainty of a general standard is preferable to the vagaries of a fluctuating standard';[82]

ii. as the Singapore High Court has since observed in *Ng Keng Yong v Public Prosecutor*,[83] if the 'indulgence' of a lower standard of care is to be extended to trainees in one area of life, then how can those limits properly be circumscribed? If extended to learner drivers (or a trainee navy officer in that case), why not to every other field of endeavour where trainees operate? Also, why should the standard not also be variable, depending upon 10-years' post-qualification experience, 20-years' experience, etc? The High Court refused to countenance such a variable standard of care, as a matter of policy;

> In *Ng Keng Yong v Public Prosecutor*, the acts and omissions of a trainee navy ship officer, D, resulted in a collision and the death of four crew members. The inexperienced navigator had taken control

---

[80] The trial judge's description, cited at: [1987] QB 730 (CA) 748.

[81] [1988] AC 1074 (HL).

[82] [1971] 2 QB 691 (CA) 707. His Lordship dissented on the issue of quantum, but not on this point of law. More recently, see: *Das Intl Ltd v Manley* [2002] EWCA Civ 1638, [15].

[83] [2004] SGHC 171, [2004] 4 SLR 89, [78]–[79]. The court was certainly not attracted to D's argument that the standard to which she should be held was that she 'took her training seriously'.

of a vessel that was plying in open waters with heavy merchant traffic. Furthermore, once she took the control of the Courageous, she was responsible for the lives and safety of the crew on board. **Held:** breach proven. The court expressly approved of the *Wilsher* rule. D had to be held to the same standard as a reasonably competent and qualified Officer-On-Watch. 'This may seem harsh, but to subject her to a lower standard of care would unfairly place the safety of everyone else around her at risk [of not recovering compensation]'.

iii. all young professionals needed to be treated alike, with a uniform standard of care applying to all of them – Mustill LJ made the point, in *Wilsher*, that doctors are not the only professionals who learn their craft, 'not only from lectures or from watching others perform, but from tackling live clients or customers, and no case was cited to us which suggested that any such variable duty of care was imposed on others in a similar position'.[84] Trainees are similarly held to the standard of a reasonable and experienced solicitor;

iv. the rule assists C, who is damaged by an inexperienced D's conduct, to recover compensation. Suppressing the standard of care, in any scenario, compromises the compensatory function, because breach is less likely to be found. This is even more marked where D is compulsorily insured for the harm which C suffers – as in the case of negligent drivers (per Lord Denning MR in *Nettleship v Weston*). For those, like Fleming, who hold the view that the 'paramount social need for compensating accident victims ... clearly outweighs all competing considerations',[85] this is the strongest argument for a fixed standard that disregards inexperience. A similar point was made by Mustill LJ in *Wilsher*, that to depart from a uniform standard of care would mean that the standard of care which a patient was legally entitled to demand would depend upon the fortunes of 'rostering', and that C's chances of recovery would be far more limited if he was entrusted to the care of a 'complete novice ... (unless perhaps he can point to some fault of supervision in a person further up the hierarchy) than if he has been in the hands of a doctor who has already spent months on the same ward';[86]

v. the *Nettleship/Wilsher* rule, insisting upon the standard of the experienced D, certainly does not condemn junior or inexperienced Ds to a finding of negligence. Some inexperienced Ds *will* be able to clamber over the reasonable threshold of care which the law requires of them. It is not always unattainable.

> In *Colwill v Oxford Radcliffe Hosp NHS Trust*,[87] a junior doctor, D, placed an intravenous cannula in the forearm of a patient, C. Unfortunately, a staph infection developed at the site of the cannula, and despite antibiotics, C developed staphylococcal septicaemia and other illnesses which left her hemiplegic, almost blind, and with severe cognitive impairment. The trial judge remarked that this was a case of a junior doctor, 'unschooled in the hospital policy, carrying out a practice to which she had become accustomed on another ward, without any consideration of the discomfort to the patient', a 'poor practice' which a senior doctor at the hospital admitted he was 'not proud' of. **Held:** D's insertion of the cannula at that site, whilst 'undesirable', was not negligent (but breach on the part of another doctor, for failing to administer anti-biotics in a timely manner, was proven). In *Jones v Manchester Corp*,[88] a young and inexperienced house doctor of 5 months post-qualification experience allowed only 10 seconds between injections rather than 30. **Held:** this was 'negligent to a degree which was inexcusable even in an inexperienced person'.

[84] [1987] QB 730 (CA) 750–51.
[85] *Law of Torts* (8th edn, Law Book Co, London, 1992) 111, cited in: *Lindahl Estate v Olsen* [2004] ABQB 639, fn 100.
[86] [1987] QB 730 (CA) 750. [87] [2007] EWHC 2881 (QB), especially, [40] and [60]–[79].
[88] [1952] 2 QB 852 (CA).

The impact of the *Wilsher* rule

§6.14 As a result of the *Wilsher* rule, an inexperienced professional D must seek guidance from a more senior colleague, if he is 'out of his depth'.

In *Wilsher* itself, both Glidewell LJ and Lord Browne-Wilkinson VC held that, had the junior doctor D not summoned the senior registrar to check the position of the catheter and to check the X-ray, but carried on regardless in administering oxygen to the premature baby C, then D would have fallen below the standard. The Court of Appeal has since noted, in *Marwan v Hillingdon HA*,[89] that for a 'senior house officer of limited experience', there are practical and legal protections available: '[i]f [he] had felt himself out of his depth, he had access to the Registrar on duty or by telephone ... The safeguard against the dangers of his inexperience lay in his own commonsense appreciation of when he was out of his depth and needed more experienced guidance'. If a junior professional fails to take advantage of those steps, he will be negligent.

Furthermore, decisions from elsewhere demonstrate that it is not open for D to argue that the operation or transaction for C was particularly difficult for one who was inexperienced *in that particular procedure*.

The comparative corner: Inexperienced surgeons

Scotland: in *Greenhorn v South Glasgow Univ Hosp NHS Trust*,[90] C, a patient, underwent a hysterectomy, and suffered incontinence, due to over-activity of the bladder muscle. C did not respond to physiotherapy, so had a further operation, during which her iliac artery was ruptured by D, a surgeon-in-training, resulting in serious blood loss and neurological injury for C. The evidence was that for obese patients (such as C), the operation was more difficult and hazardous for inexperienced surgeons. **Held**: breach proven. That D was a surgeon-in-training and lacked relevant recent experience did not alter the standard of care; the standard expected of an inexperienced doctor learning a surgical procedure 'was the same as that of an experienced doctor of her grade'.

Canada: in *Miles v Judges*,[91] D, a fully-qualified and experienced surgeon, had performed numerous (about 20) laparoscopic cholecystectomies, mostly by one procedure. D then changed to another procedure for which he was on a 'learning curve'. The operation for patient C went horribly wrong, resulting in C's common iliac artery and iliac vein being pierced. This led to serious irreversible brain damage. **Held**: breach proven. That D was an experienced surgeon who was 'on a learning curve' for this procedure did not reduce the standard of care.

The difficulties with the *Wilsher* rule

Wilsher is a difficult decision. It was a majority decision, in which the two majority members, Mustill and Glidewell LJJ, did not precisely agree what the correct legal effect of inexperience should be, nor did they agree on the outcome of the legal analysis – and where the Vice-Chancellor, Sir Nicolas Browne-Wilkinson, strongly dissented on the legal effect of inexperience altogether. Given these disparities, it is, in hindsight, perhaps a pity that the question of standard of care did not also proceed on appeal to the House of Lords.

---

[89] (CA, 23 May 1996, Waite LJ).   [90] [2008] CSOH 128, [109].   [91] (1997), 72 ACWS (3d) 378 (Ont Gen Div) [62].

	Mustill LJ	Glidewell LJ	Browne–Wilkinson VC
The relevant standard of care applied to the junior doctor	The standard was that expected of a doctor holding *that particular post* at the hospital – 'different posts make different demands. If … the structure of hospital medicine envisages that the lower ranks will be occupied by those of whom it would be wrong to expect too much, the risk of abuse by litigious patients can be mitigated, if not entirely eliminated'.[a]	The junior doctor must be judged by the same standard as his more experienced colleagues. If a lower standard applied, then inexperience would frequently be urged as a defence to an action for professional negligence.	A chief hazard of inexperience is that one does not always know the risks which exist. A doctor who has properly accepted a post in a hospital in order to gain necessary experience should only be held liable for acts or omissions which a careful doctor *with his qualifications and experience* would not have done or omitted.
Applying the standard to the facts, was there a breach by the junior doctor, D?	Yes. In spite of his inexperience, D knew that it was possible for a catheter to be accidentally inserted in a vein, for he himself had diagnosed just such an occurrence about a month previously. D did not do enough to guard against that possibility occurring.	No. D sought the advice and help of his superiors when he considered that he needed it, and that met the standard of care expected, even though he may himself have made a mistake. D was not negligent (by contrast, the senior registrar who checked the X-ray and who failed to notice the mistake was negligent).	No. D failed to identify the wrongly inserted catheter, despite the absence of a 'loop' disclosed on the X-rays, because he lacked the experience to look for such loop. Junior doctors of his experience in special care baby units were, in general, unaware of the significance of such loop. Also, he called in his superior doctor to check what he had done, which met the standard of care expected of D.

[a] [1987] QB 730 (CA) 751, 756 (Mustill LJ); 774 (Glidewell LJ); 777 (Browne-Wilkinson VC).

Mustill and Glidewell LJJ formed the majority in *Wilsher*, because on the question of law posed, neither considered that inexperience should reduce the standard of care expected of a junior physician. Since then, English cases have affirmed that the *Wilsher* rule, denying inexperience as a defence in medical negligence claims, is 'well established' (per *E v Castro*[92]); and it has been oft-cited.[93]

[92] [2003] EWHC 2066 (QB) [100].
[93] e.g., *Ryan v East London and City HA* (QB, 2 Feb 2001) [24]; *Skelton v Lewisham and North Southwark HA* [1998] Lloyd's Rep Med 324 (QB); *Dowdie v Camberwell HA* (QB, 1 Jul 1997).

However, the subtle difference between the majority opinions should not be ignored. Glidewell LJ's view was the most draconian, holding an inexperienced doctor to the standards of his experienced colleagues, whereas Mustill LJ held that the standard of care was to be fixed, not by the level of experience, but by *the post held*. This distinction between the two majority views has, occasionally, been glossed over – in *Djemal v Bexley HA*,[94] the court endorsed the view of Mustill LJ that the standard of care depends upon the particular post held, and stated that 'Glidewell LJ was of the same opinion' (which clearly he was not).

> In *Djemal v Bexley HA*, a senior houseman, D, was acting as an A&E casualty officer, and had four months' experience in that position. C presented in A&E at 9.00pm with a sore throat and swallowing difficulties. A viral upper respiratory tract infection was diagnosed, whereas C had, in fact, an infection of the epiglottis and obstruction of the airway. C's condition later that night deteriorated, which led to an emergency, and subsequently, hypoxic brain damage and a persistent vegetative state. **Held:** breach proven. D had to meet the standard of an experienced A&E physician, and that was not met in the conduct of the initial A&E diagnosis.

Finally, a brief mention should be made of Browne-Wilkinson VC's dissenting judgment in *Wilsher*. To reiterate, his view was that inexperience **should** suppress the standard of care expected of a professional D. If adopted, that would not necessarily preclude an action by C because of that suppressed standard. Rather, C's recourse in negligence would, instead, be two-fold: (1) a systemic claim in negligence against the hospital which permitted or arranged that staffing in the first place; and/or (2) a negligence claim against the inexperienced D's supervisor/superior, for which negligence the hospital would be vicariously liable. That view has been reflected, for example, in some Canadian decisions. Also, there was earlier English authority that suggested that inexperience on the part of a house officer (a newly qualified hospital resident) **would** reduce the standard of care that could legally be expected, because 'such a position was held by a comparative beginner' (per *Junor v McNicol*[95]). The *Wilsher* dissenting view would also recognise the inherent unfairness of the law's setting an artificial standard which it knows may be utterly out of the reach of junior or inexperienced professionals.

The dissenting view re the *Wilsher* rule

- doctors and other young professionals require 'on-the-job training' – for how else are they to acquire the necessary skills, other than by 'practising' their craft upon 'real patients' and 'real clients'? Per Lord Browne-Wilkinson V-C: 'anyone who ... wishes to obtain specialist skills has to learn those skills by taking a post in a specialist unit ... such doctors cannot in fairness be said to be at fault if, at the start of their time, they lack the very skills which they are seeking to acquire';[a]

- it would be fair to suppress the standard for the inexperienced professional D, when C has alternative legal avenues available by which to recover compensation, *viz*, either (1) C may sue D's employer directly for systemic negligence, because that employer failed to provide sufficiently-qualified and competent staff (per Glidewell LJ), or failed to ensure staff of sufficient skill and experience were on hand to treat C (per Browne-Wilkinson V-C), or failed to provide proper supervision for junior staff (per *Jones v Manchester Corp*[b]). As Mustill LJ explained in *Wilsher*,

[a] [1987] QB 730 (CA) 777.
[b] [1952] 2 QB 852 (CA) 871 (Denning LJ).

---

[94] [1995] 6 Med LR 269 (QB), quote at 271.   [95] (*The Times*, 26 Mar 1959, HL, Lord Kilmuir LC).

this allegation would 'not require any consideration of the extent to which the individual doctors measured up to the standards demanded of them as individuals, but would focus attention on the performance of the [hospital] as a whole';[c] or (2) C may sue the senior professional employee under whose supervision D, the junior professional, was acting, in negligence; and pursue the employer for vicarious liability;

- setting a lower standard for inexperience did *not* entail any knowledge or consent of the patient, in acknowledging that a lower standard of care would apply. Instead, that C would be left to his alternative avenues, noted above (per Lord Browne-Wilkinson V-C).

[c] [1987] QB 730 (CA) 747.

As mentioned above, Canadian medico-legal jurisprudence has variously supported a departure from the *Wilsher* rule – for reasons that reflect Lord Browne-Wilkinson V-C's concerns – although more recent Canadian case law supports the uniform standard of care:

The comparative corner: Some vignettes of inexperienced doctors in Canada

There were early dicta, from the Supreme Court of Canada, in *Fraser Estate v Vancouver General Hosp*,[96] that junior doctors learning their craft should be held to a lower, more realistic, standard of care. A lower standard of care was set for two inexperienced interns – but even that lower standard of care was not met. They treated a car accident casualty, C, in hospital, took X-rays, inspected them without realising that C had a dislocated neck, and discharged C. C went home and died of his injuries. The interns' conduct fell below even a low standard of care, for they had failed to consult a skilled radiologist in the reading of X-rays. In Ontario, in *Crits & Crits v Sylvester*, the Ontario CA described the standard for doctors as 'that degree of care and skill which could reasonably be expected of a normal, prudent practitioner of the *same experience* and standing'.[97] However, in her leading treatise, *Legal Liability of Doctors and Hospitals in Canada*, Justice Picard noted that 'there is no authority for the use of this comment to support a lower standard for the inexperienced'; and subsequent Ontario judgments have since held the same (per *Dale v Munthali*: 'the reference to a practitioner "of the same experience" does not appear to be supported by the authorities. The standard to be applied to Dr Munthali should not be lower by reason of his inexperience. The standard which could reasonably be expected of a normal, prudent practitioner must be applied'[98]).

To conclude, English jurisprudence shows no signs of departing from the *Wilsher* rule, which prescribes one uniform standard of care for all professional Ds. The rule is supportable, as a matter of policy, because of the consistency and certainty that it provides to C.

[96] [1952] 2 SCR 36 (SCC) 46.
[97] [1956], 1 DLR 502 (CA) 508, affd: [1956] SCR 991, (SCC) (emphasis added), and cited in, e.g.: *Lindahl Estate v Olsen* [2004] ABQB 639, [100].
[98] (1977), 16 OR (2d) 532 (HC) 538.

THE IMPACT (IF ANY) OF THE CIRCUMSTANCES IN WHICH D IS OPERATING

Back in 1946, Asquith LJ remarked, in *Daborn v Bath Tramways Motor Co Ltd*, '[i]n determining whether a party is negligent, the standard of reasonable care is that which is reasonably to be demanded in the circumstances'.[99] In most cases, the circumstances do not, in fact, impact upon the standard of care expected of D; but exceptionally, some do. This section sets out those exceptions.

Before doing so, it is useful to have brief regard to the recent enactment of the Social Action, Responsibility and Heroism Act 2015 (the 'SARAH Act'),[100] which appears to do no more than to reflect the existing common law (at best), or to infuse that common law with unnecessary confusion (at worst). The Act provides as follows:

> s 2 The court must have regard to whether the alleged negligence or breach of statutory duty occurred when the person was acting for the benefit of society or any of its members.
>
> s 3 The court must have regard to whether the person, in carrying out the activity in the course of which the alleged negligence or breach of statutory duty occurred, demonstrated a predominantly responsible approach towards protecting the safety or other interests of others.
>
> s 4 The court must have regard to whether the alleged negligence or breach of statutory duty occurred when the person was acting heroically by intervening in an emergency to assist an individual in danger.

As evident from the discussion below, the common law already provides considerable protection to those acting beneficially for society, or who act 'heroically'. To what extent this statute amends these common law principles remains to be seen – but as with the (equally unnecessary) enactment of s 1 of the Compensation Act 2006 (discussed in Chapter 7), it is likely to prompt some quizzical discussion from the judges tasked with deciding negligence cases which feature Ds who fit within the parameters of the statute.

'Agony of the moment' scenarios

§6.15   Where D is conducting himself in emergency, or 'agony of the moment', scenarios (i.e., in 'battle conditions'), the standard of care is suppressed (but is never rendered negligible).

The relevant principles

Emergency or 'agony of the moment' scenarios involve a 'sudden and serious difficulty' for D to cope with, hence the sympathetic standard of care (per *The Ariguani*[101]). Typically, resources (whether human or equipment) may be stretched; and/or hasty judgments necessary on D's part; and/or appropriate resources with which to treat the emergency may be entirely lacking.

A suppressed standard of care in such circumstances has extensive English judicial support. As the Court of Appeal noted in *Das Intl Ltd v Manley*: 'the same standard of care is not expected of persons faced with emergency situations. Such people should behave in a way which is not unreasonable, taking into account the exigencies of their situation. Even where the

---

[99] [1946] 2 All ER 333 (CA) 336.   [100] In force on 13 Apr 2015.   [101] [1940] 66 Lloyds' List L Rep 244.

situation allows some time for reflection, but still presents a person with a dilemma, the courts will be prepared to make allowances'.[102] The term, 'battle conditions', was coined by Mustill LJ in *Wilsher v Essex AHA*[103] to describe where a medical emergency may overburden the available resources, where the healthcare practitioners are being forced, by circumstances, to do too many things at once, or where they have to take a difficult decision on the spur of the moment. In these scenarios, mistakes 'should not lightly be taken as negligence', according to the Court of Appeal. The statement was actually dicta (i.e., no 'battle conditions' applied during the treatment of a premature baby there). In *Kent v Griffiths*,[104] Lord Woolf also confirmed that, in battle conditions, a court may be more inclined to find that an 'error of judgment' was made, i.e., a mistake which nevertheless satisfied the reasonable standard of care; whilst in *In Re F*, Lord Donaldson stated that, '[i]n an emergency, a doctor has little time to ponder the choices available. He must act in the best interests of his patient, as he sees them, but he can be more readily forgiven if he errs in his judgment'.[105]

It follows that, the more time there is for considered reflection by D, the less likely that the standard will be suppressed, as it will not be a true emergency or 'agony of the moment' scenario at all.

> In *Davis v Stena Line Ltd*,[106] Stena, D, owned and operated the 'Koningin Beatrix', a roll-on roll-off ferry that plied the southern Irish Sea route. Mr Davis, C, fell overboard from the ferry due to an accident, and through no fault of anyone. The captain employed by D was not aware of a rescue boat's readiness to launch, and so proceeded with his plan to manoeuvre the ferry close to C, who had spent up to 50 minutes in the water at that point, in order to try and retrieve him through the vessel's bunker door. C drowned. **Held:** The captain was negligent in his attempts to save C. No suppressed standard of care, due to 'agony of the moment', could apply, as the captain's decision to rescue C 'was a calculated decision, reached after discussion with another bridge officer ... although [the captain] was faced with an emergency (i.e. a man overboard), he had plenty of time between the commencement of the emergency and the time that Mr Davis was located, in which to decide on his course of action in effecting the actual rescue ... therefore, the decisions that Captain Williams had to and did make in order to rescue Mr Davis were not 'agony of the moment' decisions'.

Relevant scenarios

Emergency, or 'agony of the moment', scenarios – and the ancillary 'tolerance' for a suppressed standard of care – has been particularly evident in **four** scenarios: 'Good Samaritan' interventions; road-users; emergency services; and in fast-moving recreational endeavours. (The principle also applies, where C is put in peril by D, and contributory negligence against C is being assessed, as discussed separately in Chapter 10.)

Dealing with each in turn:

i. **Good Samaritan interventions.** A 'Good Samaritan' D is one who provides assistance voluntarily to C, who is ill, injured or unconscious as a result of an accident or other emergency, where D has no reasonable expectation of compensation or reward, and has no pre-existing relationship with C. Not only will 'battle conditions' suppress the standard of care, but also, D may be operating in circumstances where he does not profess to have the particular skills and expertise which would best suit the emergency.

---

[102] [2002] EWCA Civ 1638, [18].   [103] [1987] QB 730 (CA) 749.   [104] [2000] EWCA Civ 25, [2001] QB 36 (CA) [46].
[105] [1990] 2 AC 1 (HL) 17.   [106] [2005] EWHC 420 (QB), quote at [74].

In *Cattley v St John Ambulance Brigade*,[107] facts previously, **held:** no breach proven. It was conceded that a duty of care was owed to C; but D had acted according to the procedures outlined in the St John First Aid Manual.

Judge Prosser concluded that, although varied, the standard is not negligible: '[a]nyone confronted with an emergency situation is not to be held to the standard of conduct normally applied to one who is not in that situation [although] ... the conduct required is still that of a reasonable person under the circumstances as they would appear to one who was using proper care, and the emergency is to be considered only as one of the circumstances'.

Notably, the standard of care expected of a 'Good Samaritan' was **not** suppressed, in *Cattley*, by either of the following: (1) that D acted voluntarily and without reward, or (2) that D was motivated by altruism and by the best of intentions in seeking to assist C.

ii. **Emergencies for road users.** If D, a road-user, has been placed in an emergency situation because of the actions of another road-user, then D's actions may be hurried, and done without time for the thought or judgment that a reasonable road-user, not afflicted with that emergency, would have shown. However, even then, D may not have done enough to meet the suppressed standard of care. It will depend upon all the circumstances. Two cases may be usefully contrasted.

In *Ng v Lee*,[108] Mr Lee, a coach driver, D, saw a blue car cut suddenly in front of his coach, causing D to brake and swerve suddenly, skidding across the road and colliding with a small bus. Two passengers in the small bus, C, were killed, and many others were injured. The owner/driver of the blue car was never traced. **Held (PC):** no breach proven. D's driving had to be judged in light of the emergency in which he had been placed by the driver of the untraced car: D was 'attempting to extricate himself, his coach and his passengers from a situation ... of extreme danger. The consequences of his action were in fact unfortunate, but that should not be laid at his door. He did what any careful driver would instinctively have done in the circumstances, and we are satisfied that he acted with the alertness, skill and judgment which could reasonably have been expected.'

In *Das Intl Ltd v Manley*,[109] Mr Manley, D, was driving along a motorway at 5 am, in darkness, when he swerved to avoid a pedestrian at the side of the road. He crashed into the central reservation barrier, rebounded back across the carriageway and eventually came to rest in a field. He suffered whiplash and shock, got out of his car, and headed towards the motorway, to get help. Shortly after, Mr Parker, C, driving along the same motorway, suddenly saw D in the cycle lane, waving his arms. C also crashed off the motorway. He was not seriously injured, but his vehicle was written off. Witnesses described D as being shocked and confused in the aftermath of both accidents. D suffered from mild concussion and found it difficult to remember what had happened after his own accident. **Held:** breach proven. Notwithstanding the 'very great sympathy for [D] in the situation in which he found himself, it was an unhappy one indeed', he did not meet the standard of care of a reasonable road user. Even though D had been involved in a serious accident, and needed to attract the attention of other motorists for help, 'it cannot be reasonable to move suddenly from the side of the road straight into the path of a fast moving vehicle when it is pitch dark and one is wearing dark clothing, which makes it even more difficult to be seen'.

---

[107] QB, 25 Nov 1988, Judge Prosser QC.   [108] [1988] RTR 298 (PC, on appeal from the HKCA) 302.
[109] [2002] EWCA Civ 1638, quote at [18].

Notably, in *Das*, Hale LJ commented that, '[t]here are accidents for which no-one can be blamed. That is correct. But I would accept that such situations are comparatively rare'.[110] This observation reiterates that a suppressed standard of care will still not exculpate most D road-users from breach.

iii. **Emergency services scenarios.** Emergency services frequently confront 'agony of the moment' or emergency conditions – and that has judicially been taken into account in leading cases, albeit that professional rescuers, and those professionally trained to cope with emergency situations, will be held to a standard of care higher than that of mere volunteers. Nevertheless, courts have constantly cautioned against setting the bar too high for this class of defendant:

- re ambulances, per *Kent v Griffiths*[111] – Kennedy LJ said that, 'the standard of care owed by the ambulance service was not to be set too high, given that the ambulance service operates in a difficult area, with cash limits, competing claims on limited sources, difficulty in deciding between competing calls for assistance from different locations, and the ever present problems of traffic hazards'; and earlier, the trial judge Turner J had also stated that '[in] a situation of emergency the consequent duty will not be set at an unrealistically or unattainably high level';[112]

- re police, per *Macleod v Commr of Police*[113] – unfortunately, road and other accidents do arise when the police are attempting to apprehend a criminal, or to respond to an emergency summons for help. As noted in *Macleod* (where breach was proven), 'the duty on the driver of the police car is to drive with such care and skill as is reasonable in all the circumstances. He owes C a duty of care, notwithstanding the fact that this was an emergency'. The flashing of the emergency lights by D, so as to give 'conspicuous warning of their presence or approach', must be taken into account too: 'it would inhibit the valuable work done for the community as a whole, if drivers in the emergency services were not allowed to drive their vehicles on the basis that pedestrians [and other road-users] would recognise their warning lights and sirens and give them proper priority by keeping out of their paths'. That standard expected of D would be lower than for a civilian who was driving his child to hospital in an emergency, which emergency was not apparent to any other road user (per *Keyse v Commr of Police*,[114] where no breach was proven). However, just what constitutes police driving sufficient to exceed that requisite standard of care can divide judicial opinion, as aptly demonstrated in *Henry v Thames Valley Police*.[115] The majority of the Court of Appeal held that the police constable, D, had left insufficient room for a suspect, C, to dismount safely from his motorcycle, thereby running over C's leg; whereas the dissenter agreed with the trial judge that C's conduct had 'put the police officers into a very tricky situation in which they had to make judgments in seconds about what he was going to do' and that it was a 'stressful situation' for D, where C had driven at grossly excessive speeds and had sought to evade capture. These are frequently borderline assessments;

110 *ibid*, [16].
111 [1998] EWCA Civ 1941, (1998) 47 BMLR 125, 134; and later: [2000] EWCA Civ 25, [2001] QB 36, [46].
112 [1999] Lloyd's Rep Med 424 (QB).
113 [2014] EWHC 977 (QB) [16], citing: *Marshall v Osmond* [1983] QB 1074 (CA).
114 [2001] EWCA (Civ) 715, [29], [31] (Judge LJ).
115 [2010] EWCA Civ 5, [2010] RTR 14 (Smith and Arden LJJ; with Pill LJ dissenting).

- re fire brigades, per *Capital & Counties plc v Hampshire CC*[116] – Stuart-Smith LJ remarked that, '[i]t seems hardly realistic that a fire officer, who has to make a split second decision as to the manner in which fire-fighting operations are to be conducted, will be looking over his shoulder at the possibility of his employers being made vicariously liable for his negligence. If there can be liability for negligence, it is better to have a high threshold of negligence established in the *Bolam* test, and for judges to remind themselves that fire officers, who make difficult decisions in difficult circumstances, should be given considerable latitude before being held guilty of negligence'; and

- re GP's who confront urgent scenarios in medical surgeries, per *Knight v Home Office*[117] – as Pill LJ said, '[t]he facilities available to deal with an emergency in a general practitioner's surgery cannot be expected to be as ample as those available in the casualty department of a general hospital', so that, 'the standard of care required will vary with the context'.

iv. **Recreational endeavours.** For those involved in hurly-burly sporting or recreational contests, the standard of care will be suppressed, primarily because of the 'agony of the moment' scenarios which often arise in such contests, and which are often an inherent part of the game or competition. This is discussed separately below.

Hence, English courts have endorsed the principle that the standard of reasonable care is suppressed in 'agony of the moment' scenarios; so that the temptation to set the bar too high, when so-called 'battle conditions' are confronted, must be strenuously resisted.

'Diagnosis with a focus' scenarios

§6.16   Where the need for a particular diagnosis is flagged up to D, then that 'diagnosis with a focus' may elevate the standard of care; it must certainly be taken into account when assessing the standard required.

If patient C has been referred by one health care professional to another, D, with concerns noted about the patient's presentation, then a higher standard of care will be required, because D must conduct 'a scan with a focus', as the court put it in *Pithers v Leeds Teaching Hosp NHS Trust*.[118] In both of the following cases, breach was proven on this basis:

> In *Pithers v Leeds Teaching Hosp*, a sonographer at a local hospital was unable to visualise the foetal bladder in a routine abdominal ultra-sound scan, and C, the patient, was referred to Leeds General Infirmary for a further opinion by D, a specialist registrar. D's diagnosis of a further scan noted the bladder to be 'well visualised and appear[ing] normal'. In fact, C was born with a condition, cloacal-exstrophy, in which substantial parts of the abdominal content develop outside the abdominal wall, and for which no bladder can be visualised. The law demanded of D, as a senior physician at a major hospital, 'a high standard of care and skill specifically when focusing on the issue thus raised: "cloacal exstrophy or not"'. It was 'a scan with a focus', so that 'there is a heavy burden on Leeds, when seeking to reconcile its incorrect visualisations, with the exercise of all reasonable care and skill'.
> In *Lillywhite v University College London Hosp NHS Trust*,[119] Alice Lillywhite, C, suffered from the condition of holoprosencephaly, in which her forebrain failed to divide into two early in her foetal

---

[116] [1997] QB 1004 (CA) [87].   [117] [1990] 3 All ER 237 (QB) 243.
[118] [2004] EWHC 1392 (QB), with quote in following case description at [13].
[119] [2005] EWCA Civ 1466, [30] (Latham LJ, with whom Buxton LJ agreed).

development, and no falx was formed by which to divide the forebrain. C was born with quadraple-gia, and profoundly mentally-disabled. The radiographer who initially studied the foetal scan could not detect the falx, and referred the scan, with a note, 'falx?', to D, a professor of obstetrics and gynaecology at D's university hospital, and who was experienced at reading and interpreting foetal ultrasound scans. D diagnosed that the falx was present, and that C's brain development showed no abnormalities. Ultimately, it was concluded that D must have seen 'shadows' on the ultrasound which resembled a falx. In any event, the referral had constituted a diagnosis with a focus, and that scenario 'demanded a high standard of care and skill in the context of a focused referral based upon the concerns of [the radiographer]'.

Although this elevated standard has only arisen for consideration in the medical context (so far as can be ascertained), there is no reason in principle as to why it could not be applied in any other context.

Locality

§6.17   If D is operating in a rural/country environment without access to the resources, equipment or collegiate expertise which would be available to a counterpart in a city/urban environment, then there is a *very limited* recognition in English law that the standard of care may be sup-pressed. As a corollary, D may fail to meet the standard of care if C should have been referred elsewhere, and was not.

The relevant principles

A so-called 'locality' rule – whereby a lower standard of care is legally tolerated of the rural/country D than of the urban/city D – has very limited recognition in English jurisprudence (and it does not go by that name, in any event). The highest that can be said is that, in some rare cases, the court has taken into account the fact that D was operating in a rural environment.

For example, in *Hickey v Marks*,[120] the Court of Appeal approved of the trial judge's deci-sion that D doctor's treatment of his patients 'was to be judged by the standards of a general practitioner working single-handed in a rural area' (and, even so, negligence was held there – although that was actually a libel action brought by the doctor, regarding a TV programme concerning the doctor's treatment of a young drug addict). Similarly, in the employment neg-ligence case of *Yorkshire Traction Co Ltd v Searby*,[121] the locality of where the incident hap-pened had some impact upon the standard of care, and what precautionary steps a reasonable employer needed to have taken.

In *Yorkshire Traction Co Ltd v Searby*, Walter Searby, C, a bus driver, was assaulted by a passenger one night, about 10:50pm. He suffered both physical injury and PTSD. His assailant was never identified. C alleged that there should have been a screen installed by his employer, D, to separate the driver from his passengers. There was evidence of prior assaults by passengers on bus drivers, but these were more prevalent in urban than in rural areas. C had, himself, twice been assaulted; and in the preceding 14 years, an average of 8 assaults a year were of sufficient gravity to require D's drivers to take time off work. In some urban areas, buses had been fitted with screens (as in Cleveland, as a trial), but in other areas, such as in South Yorkshire, they had not. **Held:** no breach proven. The risk of injury to a bus driver in South Yorkshire was very low, which was relevant when

---

[120] (CA, 6 Jul 2000) [31], [53].   [121] [2003] EWCA Civ 1856.

determining what was expected of a reasonable employer. Just because screens had been installed in Cleveland conditions did not mean that it was negligent of D not to have installed them in South Yorkshire conditions.

However, even if the so-called 'locality rule' reduces the standard of reasonable care against which the acts or omissions of D are judged, then C is not necessarily without remedy.

Failure to refer

Even where locality may suppress the standard of care, D may not meet it, if D failed to refer C to another location/venue where more specialist facilities, expertise or more experienced staff existed. If facilities or staffing levels were not adequate to cope with C's problem, then a duty to refer has commonly been upheld.

> In *Gouldsmith v Mid-Staffordshire General Hosp NHS Trust*,[122] Mrs Gouldsmith, C, presented at hospital with a lesion on her left (dominant) hand which caused blockages in arteries. C had previously suffered from arterial thrombosis (blood clotting) and antiphospholipid syndrome (where vessels become narrowed or blocked by blood clots). Within six weeks, all digits on C's left hand had to be amputated. **Held:** breach proven. If the hospital did not have the medical staff qualified to carry out what would have been a complicated and difficult treatment, C should have been 'seen and treated in a tertiary centre of excellence (on the evidence, and for reasons of geography, either Birmingham or Manchester)'.

Thus, on balance, any differential standard of care brought about by locality, and a consequent lack of facilities, equipment and medical staffing expertise, may be 'evened out' by a duty to refer – rendering any so-called 'locality rule' otiose. The fact that D should have referred C on does **not** automatically mean liability in negligence, however, for three reasons:

i. just because D did not refer does not automatically mean that D fell below the standard of reasonable care. The level of performance undertaken by D, in the less-than-ideal circumstances, may have reached the reasonable standard of care in any event, given that perfection is not the touchstone;

ii. any inherent risks to C that were likely to be encountered during C's transfer elsewhere may outweigh the benefits of the treatment which C would have received at the other venue:

> In *Macey v Warwickshire HA*,[123] baby Macey, C, suffered cerebral palsy. He alleged that this was due to his post-natal care, when his mother, presenting with a premature labour at 34 weeks, ought to have been transferred from the local hospital, St Mary's, where there was no special care baby unit, to Walsgrave Hospital, the principal regional maternity hospital, where facilities and staff could have dealt with C's severe respiratory distress, which started 7 minutes after his birth, and carried on for two hours until after C's emergency transferral to Walsgrave. C also alleged that he should have been intubated and ventilated before being transferred. **Held:** breach not proven on these grounds. Although the facilities at St Mary's were 'limited', the standard of care which could be provided there was reasonable for the time (1981). Also, C should not have been intubated and ventilated at St Mary's prior to his transfer, because no-one at St Mary's had expertise to carry out intubation on a newborn infant; it was not a specialist maternity hospital equipped with suitable

---

[122] [2007] EWCA Civ 397, quote at [41] (per Kay LJ, dissenting on causation, but not on breach).
[123] [2004] EWHC 1198 (QB), with quotes at [44]–[51], and [63]–[65] .

staff. Also, there were real risks to C, if intubated and hand-ventilated during an ambulance journey of 20 minutes. (However, breach was proven because of the 45 minute delay following C's birth, before medical attention was drawn to C's respiratory distress.)

iii. if referring C elsewhere to superior equipment, expertise, etc, would probably have made no difference to the ultimate result for C, then there is no causal link between the breach (the failure to refer) and C's damage (per Chapter 8, and illustrated in *Gouldsmith*,[124] where causation was proven).

Thus, to summarise, there is some limited judicial support in England for a suppressed standard of care, depending upon the locality in which D is operating, but any variations in the standard of care are generally 'smoothed out' by a duty to refer in such cases. Even then, failing to refer will not automatically entail a finding of negligence, if a referral probably would not have derived a better outcome for C, or if the failure to refer is supported by a reasonable body of respected medical opinion.

The comparative corner: A snapshot of the locality rule in Canada

The locality rule is particularly rooted in Canadian jurisprudence, in a geographically large country with a dispersed population, albeit that the locality rule has come in for some strident criticism in Canadian case law.

The locality rule: derived from *Wilson v Swanson* (SCC), 'the medical man must possess and use that reasonable degree of learning and skill ordinarily possessed by practitioners *in similar communities* in similar cases.'[125] The rule has been applied to the standard of care expected in the provision of care, diagnosis and treatment, but *not* in respect of the provision of advice and information.[126] The rule has been supported in several provinces in Canada – e.g., in *Challand v Bell*[127] ('From a GP at a rural point, a different standard is exacted than from a specialist at an urban point'); and *Kivisalu v Brown*[128] ('[a]lthough I hesitate to use the word "geographical" when employing this test [for standard of care], there is a measure of geography that enters into the assessment');

Reasons for the rule: rural doctors regularly faced difficulties such as a lack of specialists to refer to, lack of facilities, lack of support staff, long periods of being on-call, and with a general overload of patients to cope with (per *Sunnucks v Tobique Valley Hosp*[129]); as a matter of fairness, a court should not hold a family GP conducting a medical practice in a rural area of Vancouver Island to the same standard as an obstetrician practising in the city of Vancouver (a statement that had as much to do with locality as with specialisation) (per *St Jules v Chen*[130]).

Departures from the rule: more recently in 2007, in *Smith v Liwanpo*[131] (where a CT scan was not performed on a patient, following a difficult colonoscopy), the locality rule was considered not to be a valid reason to suppress the standard of care, for two reasons:

[124] [2007] EWCA Civ 397.

[125] (1956), 5 DLR (2d) 113 (SCC) [43] (emphasis added); *McCormick v Marcotte* (1971), 20 DLR (3d) 345 (SCC) 346.

[126] Noted in the introductory annotations to: *Hopp v Lepp* (1979), 98 DLR (3d) 464 (Alta SC App Div).

[127] (1959), 18 DLR (2d) 150 (Alta TD) 154.   [128] [2002] BCSC 1901, [34].

[129] (1999), 216 NBR (2d) 201 (QB) [179] (Clendening J).   [130] [1990] BCJ No 23 (Gow J).

[131] (SCJ, 23 Apr 2007, Morissette J) [114]–[116], citing: *Crawford v Penney* [2003] OJ No 89 (SCJ).

(1) the community hospital had an arrangement with a nearby major hospital whereby an urgent referral of the patient could have been done; and (2) '[t]he courts have long ago settled the issue of locality. It should be abandoned'. Other provincial Canadian decisions have also expressly refused to follow the locality rule.[132] In their leading medical text, Picard and Robertson considered the rule 'ripe to be buried'.[133]

Reasons given for departing from the rule, and imposing one uniform standard of care: the rule creates a geographic lottery; it defies the national standards of competence set by professional examinations and continuing medical education; rural doctors themselves felt uncomfortable about the rule; so much medical practice was conducted in areas that could be described as 'rural' that a differentiation would be a 'sad comment indeed'; due to technological advances, particularly in communication, consultive help was always relatively near; and the duty of D to refer the patient, if the situation called for it, reduced the significance, and justification, of a locality rule.

Dangerous recreational/sporting pursuits

Participants towards spectators

§6.18   The standard of care expected of a participant in a sporting or recreational activity, D, vis-à-vis a spectator, C, is suppressed, in that D must not act with either a reckless disregard of C's safety or a deliberate intent to cause C harm.

The law clearly sets a suppressed standard of care for the participant in a sporting or recreational activity, where injuries are caused to spectators. It has been called a 'special' relationship, so that this 'different relationship involves its own standard of care' (per *Wooldridge v Sumner*[134]).

The participant, D, must meet the standard of not acting recklessly towards spectators (i.e., acting in disregard of the safety of others); of not acting with deliberate intent to cause them harm; and of complying with the rules of the game. It follows that mere lapses of skill by D, or errors of judgment, may well meet the expected standard of care. In this context, D would act recklessly if he participated in a game or a competition, 'when he knew, or ought to have known, that his lack of skill was such that, even if he exerted it to the utmost, he was likely to cause injury to a spectator watching him' (per Diplock LJ in *Wooldridge v Sumner*[135]). That observation was dicta, because D was an 'exceptionally skilful and experienced' horse-rider there. Nevertheless, the proposition is important – D does not have to be incredibly skilful, but must have adequate competence to take part in the competition without posing a threat to the safety of spectators.

In *Wooldridge v Sumner*, during the 1959 National Horse Show at White City Stadium, London. Mr Wooldridge, C, a professional photographer, attended a competition for heavy-weight hunters (involving the horses demonstrating a walk, a trot, a canter and a gallop). A horse called 'Work of Art', owned by Mr Sumner and ridden by Mr Holladay, D1, collided with C, during the gallop. At the time of the accident, C was not taking any pictures because he had run out of film, but was sitting on a bench seat just beside the racing track, between two planter boxes/tubs. C was not

---

[132] e.g., *Sunnucks v Tobique Valley Hosp* (1999), 216 NBR (2d) 201, [180]; *Skeels v Iwashkiw* [2006] ABQB 335, [76].
[133] *Legal Liability of Doctor and Hospitals in Canada* (4th edn, Carswell, Toronto, 2007) 251.
[134] [1963] 2 QB 43 (CA) 57.   [135] *ibid*, 68.

experienced in regard to horses (and was described as 'unfamiliar with and wholly uninterested in them'). The steward of the course had told C to move off the side of the running track, but C did not heed the warning. C then 'took fright', and stepped or fell into the path of the galloping Work of Art, and was knocked down and severely injured. **Held:** no breach proven. D1, as rider, may have shown 'some errors of judgment' or 'a lapse of skill', in the way that he rode Work of Art around that corner of the track, but he had shown no reckless disregard for C's safety. He was 'riding within the rules [when] he won'. (D2, the British Horse Society, as the promoters of the show, also met the standard of care expected of an occupier, in taking reasonable care to provide a suitable arena for the event.)

It follows that mere 'misfortunes' which spectator C suffered in the 'best tradition of sporting competitive endeavour' (to cite an expression of Sellers LJ in *Wooldridge*[136]) would **not** expose D to any finding of breach, e.g., where at a cricket match, D hits a six, and the ball hits C in the crowd; or a tennis player hits a ball or throws a racket accidentally into the crowd; or at a rugby match, a player dives into a tackle and comes into heavy contact with the surrounding barrier, injuring an adjacent spectator C (hypothetical examples in *Wooldridge*); or at a car rally, a driver collides with another rally car, causing D's car to deviate, jump the barriers, plough into the crowd, and injure C (dicta in *Hall v Brooklands Auto Racing Club*[137]); or D skids on 'black ice' that was unknown to exist on a road during the Monte Carlo Rally, crashes into a tree, badly injuring a spectator crew (an unreported case cited in *Wooldridge v Sumner* – '[i]f the road had been known to be icy, then it would clearly have been reckless or foolhardy for even a skilled driver in the rally to travel so fast; then the decision would, and I think should, have been [negligence]'[138]); or driver D in a Jersey road race crashes at speed due to brake-failure, killing spectator C (per *O'Dowd v Frazer-Nash*[139]).

On the other hand, if participants in a game 'divert clearly from the rules [of the game], there may well be room for liability' towards spectators, precisely because recklessness or a deliberate intent to cause spectator C harm will be easier to prove (per *Wooldridge v Sumner*[140]). To provide some examples cited therein: if ice-hockey players fight off the play well away from the game and injure spectator C during their fight (per *Payne and Payne v Maple Leaf Gardens Ltd*[141]); or a golfer, not in the course of play, swings a club and injures spectator C standing by (per *Cleghorn v Oldham*[142]), or loses his ball, and then plays it against the rules of the game and in disregard for the safety of those in the 'line of danger', and hits a spectator in the eye; or a tennis player hits a ball or throws a racket into the stands in temper or annoyance, when play was not in progress, thereby injuring spectator C (dicta examples in *Wooldridge*).

An alternative test? In a curious twist, the *Wooldridge* test was judicially modified several years later, in *Wilks v Cheltenham Homeguard Motor Cycle and Light Car Club*.[143] That was another suit by injured spectators against a participant (this time a motor-cycle rider). The Court of Appeal cited with approval an academic view[144] that the correct standard to apply was that

---

[136] *ibid*, 54.

[137] [1933] 1 KB 205 (CA). This case concerned the liability of the promotor of the event, not that of the rally car driver.

[138] [1963] 2 QB 43 (CA) 56.

[139] [1951] WN 172 (McNair J), and cited in: *Wooldridge v Sumner, ibid*, 49–50, 56 (Sellers LJ).

[140] [1963] 2 QB 43 (CA) 55–57.   [141] [1949] 1 DLR 369.

[142] (1927) 43 TLR 465, and cited in *Woodridge v Sumner* [1963] 2 QB 43 (CA) 55–56 (Sellers LJ).

[143] [1971] 1 WLR 668 (CA).   [144] A Goodhart, 'The Sportsman's Charter' (1962) 78 *LQR* 490, 496.

D, the participant, must not commit an 'error of judgment that a reasonable competitor, being the reasonable man of the sporting world, would not have made'.

This *Wilks* test imposes a potentially higher standard than not acting with reckless disregard of a spectator's safety. It was admitted by the Scottish Inner House (in *Sharpe v Highland and Islands Fireboard*[145]) that the *Wooldridge* and *Wilks* tests were not precisely the same. Indeed, most recently, in *McMahon v Dear* (where a ball spotter was struck and injured by a golf ball hit by a competitor), the Scottish Outer House refused to follow *Wooldridge's* recklessness test, preferring *Wilks'* test (ultimately, no breach was found, on the basis of that test).[146]

However, insofar as English case law is concerned, the *Wooldridge* and *Wilks* standards of care appear to have been equated as being the same test. In *Smoldon v Whitworth*,[147] Lord Bingham CJ treated them equivalently, but in doing so, plainly reiterated the *Wooldridge* standard, for participants towards spectators, where he said that *Wooldridge* and *Wilks* 'recognised that a sporting competitor, properly intent on winning the contest, was (and was entitled to be) all but oblivious of spectators. It therefore followed that he would have to be shown to have very blatantly disregarded the safety of spectators before he could be held to have failed to exercise such care as was reasonable in all the circumstances'. Hence, whatever difference in view may have been cast by *Wilks*, the *Wooldridge* standard is the prevailing standard, insofar as modern English law is concerned.

Reasons for the suppressed standard. Why is the standard set so low, for participants towards spectators? There are four reasons, according to the case law:

i. a reasonable spectator would expect, and would be entitled to expect, no different, because they are there to watch a sporting spectacle, in which D is a competitor/player who is 'merely seeking to excel and to win, it being the very purpose on which he is engaged, and the very endeavour which people have assembled to witness and applaud' (per *Wooldridge v Sumner*[148]);

ii. even with a suppressed standard of care, it is not a negligible standard, and provides *some* protection for spectator C. The game or tournament must be performed 'within the rules and the requirement of the sport, and by a person of adequate skill and competence' – albeit that C, 'the spectator, does not expect his safety to be regarded by the participant [D]' (per *O'Dowd v Frazer-Nash*[149]);

iii. there is often an element of 'agony of the moment' in these scenarios, which suppresses the standard of care expected at law (discussed above). For example, in *Wooldridge*,[150] Danckwerts LJ pointed out that the rider's duty to his employer, who owned the horse, 'was to utilise the qualities of the horse so as to show it to the best advantage. This involved the horse going at a fast gallop. Decisions have to be taken in a split second'. Diplock LJ agreed: 'a participant in a game or competition gets into the circumstances in which he has no time, or very little time, to think ... If, therefore, in the course of the game or competition, at a moment when he really has not time to think, a participant by mistake takes a wrong measure, he is not, in my view, to be held guilty of any negligence', and that D's decison-making 'had to be made in circumstances in which he had no time to exercise an unhurried judgment';

iv. a suppressed standard of care reflects that it is expected, at some level, that spectators will be versed in the art of self-preservation. In *Wooldridge v Sumner*, Diplock LJ noted that any reasonable competitor 'would be entitled to assume that spectators actually in the arena would be paying attention

---

[145] [2007] CSIH 34, [10].   [146] [2014] CSOH 100, 2014 SLT 823, [209].
[147] [1997] PIQR P133 (CA), quote at P138–P139.   [148] [1963] 2 QB 43 (CA) 52 (Sellers LJ).
[149] [1951] WN 172 (QB, McNair J), cited *ibid*, 156.
[150] [1963] 2 QB 43 (CA) 60 (Danckwerts LJ), 67–68, 70 (Diplock LJ).

to what was happening, would be knowledgeable about horses, and would take such steps for their own safety as any reasonably attentive and knowledgeable spectator might be expected to take'.[151] That assumption can be translated to other stadiums and arenas where other sports are played. A suppressed standard on the competitor's part is an apt recognition that, in dangerous or heated sporting spectacles, the law expects a level of conduct on **both** C's and D's part.

Participants towards participants

§6.19 The standard of care expected of one participant in a sporting contest, D, towards another participant, C, is suppressed somewhat differently, in that D must not act recklessly nor show a high degree of carelessness towards C, where D is conducting himself in the 'hurly-burly' and fast-moving, vigorous contest.

In *Caldwell v Fitzgerald and Maguire*,[152] Tuckey LJ affirmed that, 'there will be no liability for errors of judgment, oversights or lapses of which any participant might be guilty in the context of a fast-moving contest. Something more serious is required'. The Court of Appeal, noting the proposition above, also approved of the trial judge's view that, practically-speaking, 'it may ... be difficult to prove any breach of duty, absent proof of conduct [by D] that ... amounts to reckless disregard for the fellow contestant's safety'. In *Collet v Smith*,[153] the court explained the requisite degree of wrongdoing in these terms, i.e., that participant D knew that there was 'a significant risk of serious injury' to another participant C, if D behaved as he did. The standard expected of a participant towards another probably represents a higher standard than the *Wooldridge* standard, because D can fail to meet the requisite standard, even if he has **not** acted recklessly. None of these cases supports any notion, however, that D's breach of the rules of the game or contest establishes negligence.

Notwithstanding the suppressed standard which operates in these circumstances, breach may nevertheless be proven, in that participant D's conduct fell below that standard – as occurred in the following:

In *Condon v Basi*,[154] C and D were playing for opposing teams in a non-professional football match, when C suffered serious injury (a broken leg) as a result of a dangerous tackle by D. In effecting that tackle, D showed a reckless disregard of C's safety, and his conduct fell far below the standard reasonably expected of any participant in an amateur game. In *Caldwell v Fitzgerald and Maguire*, Mr Caldwell, C, a professional jockey, was injured when he was unseated from his horse, as a result of dangerous manoeuvres by two fellow jockeys, D, for which D were liable in negligence.

Alternatively, the scenario may be mere horseplay between friends – and even that (whilst not an organised regulated sporting contest which is governed by explicit rules) is conducted in accordance with certain tacitly-agreed understandings or conventions. There will be no expectation, in such circumstances, that either skill or judgment will be exercised by D. Among those participants, Lord Dyson MR commented, in *Blake v Galloway*,[155] that they will be required to meet the standard of not acting 'either recklessly or with a very high degree of carelessness'.

---

[151] *ibid*, 71. [152] [2001] EWCA Civ 1054, [2002] PIQR P6, [5], [11], [22].

[153] [2011] EWHC 90208 (Costs) [42]–[43], citing: *Watson and Bradford City AFC v Gray and Huddersfield Town FC* (*The Times*, 26 Nov 1998, Hooper J).

[154] [1985] 1 WLR 866 (CA). [155] [2004] EWCA Civ 814, [2004] 1 WLR 2844, [8], with reasoning at [13], [15]–[16].

In *Blake v Galloway*, Master Blake, C, was practising with a jazz quintet with four friends at a venue in South Devon, when they adjourned for a lunchtime break in the grounds. They all engaged in some high-spirited, good-natured and friendly horseplay, throwing twigs, pieces of bark chipping, and mulch, at each other. C picked up a piece of bark chipping, approximately 4 cm in diameter, and threw it towards the lower part of Master Galloway's, D's, body; and D picked up the same piece of bark and threw it back at C, striking him in the right eye. C lost sight in the eye from the injury. No participant was throwing items towards anybody's head, or picking on another. C was not looking in D's direction when the bark was thrown, otherwise he probably would have taken evasive action. **Held:** no breach proven. There was no reckless disregard or a high degree of carelessness here. D did not depart from the tacit understandings or conventions of horseplay; did not deliberately aim the piece of bark at C's head; and the game was conducted at speed and fairly vigorously.

Reasons for the suppressed standard. In *Blake v Galloway*, Lord Dyson MR drew a close analogy between organised formal sports, and informal horseplay, and considered that the suppressed standard of care applied in both scenarios, for three reasons:

i. the contests or games both involved participation in an activity which involved physical contact, or at least the risk of it, on a consensual basis;

ii. in such contests, decisions are usually expected to be made quickly, and often as an instinctive or urgent response to the acts of other participants – hence, an 'agony of the moment' scenario; and

iii. the very nature of the activity makes it difficult to avoid the risk of physical harm.

Variations in standard? In *Condon v Basi*,[156] which concerned the action between footballers over a dangerous tackle by D against C, the Court of Appeal opined that the standard of care from one participant to another depended upon the level of competence and seniority of the game being played. According to Sir John Donaldson MR, '[t]he standard is objective, but ... there will of course be a higher degree of care required of a player in a First Division football match than of a player in a local league football match.'

The correctness of this proposition was doubted in the Scottish case of *Sharpe v Highland and Islands Fire Board*,[157] but has not, as yet, been considered further in English case law.

Referees towards participants

§6.20   The standard of care expected of a referee, D, towards a player/participant in a game or competition, C, is similarly suppressed, in that D must not act recklessly nor show a high degree of carelessness towards C, where D is conducting himself in the 'hurly-burly' and fast-moving, vigorous contest.

This proposition was enunciated in *Smoldon v Whitworth*,[158] and was confirmed in *Vowles v Evans*.[159] (In both of these tragic cases, C were young men playing games of rugby, who packed into a scrum in the position of hooker, and whose necks were broken when the scrums collapsed.)

In *Smoldon*,[160] the Court specifically rejected the *Wooldridge* standard of care, as being inapplicable to referees. The proposition – that the standard that a referee must meet is that

---

[156] [1985] 1 WLR 866 (CA) 868.   [157] [2005] CSOH 111, 2005 SLT 855, [23].
[158] [1997] PIQR P133, [1997] ELR 249, 256.   [159] [2003] EWCA Civ 318, [2003] 1 WLR 1607, [26].
[160] [1997] PIQR P133 (CA) P139.

he cannot act with **either** a deliberate intention of causing injury to the participant **or** a reckless disregard for the safety of the participant – was unpalatable because (according to Lord Bingham CJ, who gave the judgment of the court) '[t]he position of a referee *vis-à-vis* the players is not the same as that of a participant in a contest *vis-à-vis* a spectator. One of his responsibilities is to safeguard the safety of the players'. For that reason, a **higher** standard of care is imposed on a referee than on a participant.

Nevertheless, referee D operates under a suppressed standard of care at law, in that the circumstances in which D is operating can lawfully and properly be taken into account, when determining the standard of behaviour which the law imposes on him. Those circumstances properly include whether D was required to act in a heated, fast-moving, or rushed context, or whether he had time to come to a considered decision. Two reasons were given by the Court of Appeal in *Smoldon*:[161]

i. 'The threshold of liability is a high one. It will not easily be crossed' (said Lord Bingham CJ). In other words, the lower the standard of care, the more difficult it is to prove D negligent. That lower standard is defensible, because the standard should not be set so high that referees should be fearful of being held negligent for not meeting that standard; and

ii. referees 'could not be properly held liable for errors of judgment, oversights or lapses of which any referee might be guilty in the context of a fast-moving and vigorous contest'. In other words, the 'agony of the moment' scenario can serve to suppress the standard of care expected of referee D.

Naturally, there will be no suppression of the standard of care where, rather than decisions being taken during the heat of play, a referee acted while play was stopped and there was time for considered thought.

In *Vowles v Evans*,[162] Richard Vowles, C, suffered permanent incomplete tetraplegia, when he was injured in a collapsed scrum during an amateur rugby game, which was being refereed by David Evans, D. C was playing as hooker, when his team's loose head prop dislocated his shoulder and had to leave the field. The team did not have a trained front row forward on the bench to replace him (nor anyone else who had that training or experience of playing in the front row). D was aware of this problem, and told the team captain that they could provide a replacement from within the scrum, or opt for non-contestable scrummages – the choice was theirs – adding that, if the team opted for non-contestable scrummages and won the match, they would not be entitled to an award of points in the League competition. Hence, one of the team, CJ, said that he would 'give it a go', and things proceeded uneventfully until injury time, when the other team was aiming for a 'pushover' try. The two sets of forwards scrummaged, and C collapsed, breaking his neck. Rule 3(12) of the Laws of the Game provided:

In the event of a front row forward being ordered off, the referee, in the interests of safety, will confer with the captain of his team to determine whether another player is suitably trained/experienced to take his position; if not, the captain shall nominate one other forward to leave the playing area and the referee will permit a substitute front row forward to replace him ... When there is no other front row forward available, ...then the game will continue with non-contestable scrummages ...

---

161 *ibid*, P139.   162 [2003] EWCA Civ 318, [2003] WLR 1607, [37]–[38].

Held: breach proven. D did not satisfy himself that CJ was suitably trained/experienced for the front row, but left the decision to the team captain. Under the Law, it was not proper to offer the captain that option. D abdicated the responsibility, which was his, of deciding whether the situation had been reached where it was mandatory to insist upon non-contestable scrummages. Hence, D breached his duty to exercise reasonable care for the safety of the players. Also, D's decision was taken while play was stopped, and there was time to give considered thought to it.

Cross-fertilisation. There has been cross-fertilisation of relevant jurisprudence in this context, in that *Caldwell*[163] referred to judicial statements in *Wilks* (re participants towards spectators) and *Smoldon* (re referees towards participants). Indeed, Judge LJ aligned the referee's standard with the participant's standard of care toward other participants, in that both were entitled to a suppressed standard of care, depending upon the circumstances. In *Blake v Galloway*, reference was made to the *Wooldridge* standard, but 'in a slightly expanded form' (per Lord Dyson MR) – a fact that is clear when the principles governing participants to spectators, and participants to participants, are compared; they are not quite the same principle.

Does the grading of the referee matter? Could the 'circumstances', by which the standard is set, include the grade of certificate which D possessed as referee? That notion appeared to gain some support in *Vowles v Evans*,[164] where the Court of Appeal referred to the scenario where, in a low-level amateur game or contest, the designated referee may not turn up, or may be injured, and from the crowd of spectators, a volunteer referee is recruited. Lord Phillips MR stated that 'the volunteer cannot reasonably be expected to show the skill of one who holds himself out as referee, or perhaps even to be fully conversant with the laws of the Game'.

Alternatively, could the 'circumstances' include the grade of match that D was refereeing? In *Smoldon*, this view gained support from Bingham CJ, who preferred that D, as referee, had to reach the level of skill appropriate to that expected of a referee who was refereeing a match of a certain seniority/standard; and that the requisite standard was **not** set by his grade of certified refereeing.

In neither case did the issue require deciding, because both referees were graded appropriately for the level of game that they were refereeing. However, the law is not entirely resolved on these points.

Furthermore, it is unclear as to how the remark (albeit dicta) of Lord Phillips MR in *Vowles v Evans* is to be reconciled with the *Nettleship* rule. According to the latter, any inexperience does not suppress the standard of care expected of D. Yet, a referee plucked from the crowd may be vastly inexperienced, and still can take the benefit of a suppressed standard of care under the *Vowles* dicta. No attempt has been made to reconcile those points of view since.

Promoters towards spectators/participants

§6.21   The promoter or organiser of a sporting event, as occupier of the premises at which the event is held, owes a reasonable standard of care towards spectators and participants, with no suppression of the standard applicable.

The occupier's duty to lawful visitors to his premises is covered in Chapter 12, and readers are referred to that analysis for further detail. For present purposes, it is sufficient to note that, even in the case of dangerous sporting contests or competitions, spectators enjoy seeing competitors taking risks, but 'they expect, and rightly expect, the organisers to erect proper enclosures, and to do all that is reasonable to ensure their safety' (per Lord Denning MR in *White v Blackmore*[165]).

---

[163] [2001] EWCA Civ 1054, [2002] PIQR P6, [17], [20].   [164] [2003] EWCA Civ 318, [2003] WLR 1607, [28].
[165] [1972] 2 QB 651 (CA) 663.

Those who promote sporting events have to be 'mindful' of the dangers presented by the competitors (e.g., of the 'unpredictable conduct of horses, however well-trained and however skilfully ridden, especially in the excitement of competition or when confronted with some unexpected movement on or about their course', per *Wooldridge v Sumner*[166]). But provided that the promoter managed and planned the event with sufficient care, there will be no negligence.

In *White v Blackmore*,[167] Mr White, C, was an experienced 'jalopy' racing driver, and Mr Blackmore, D, organised jalopy races. During one race, C was 'sitting out', and stood next to the spectators' enclosure rope. The rope became entangled in the rear wheel of a racing car, and the stakes attached to the rope were pulled out. C was catapulted into the air, and suffered serious injuries, from which he died. **Held (at trial):** D was negligent, as occupier, in tying all the ropes to one stake, but D prevailed because of the defence of *volenti*. **Held (CA):** negligence was upheld, but *volenti* did not apply where the risk of injury arose, not from participation in the dangerous sport of motor-racing, but from the organisers' failure to take reasonable precautions for the safety of visitors to the meeting. A visitor to a motor race meeting did not willingly accept the risk of injury due to the organisers' defaults in ensuring his safety.

It is also significant that promoters customarily are not acting in the 'agony of the moment' – their safety systems and arena designs are established well before the competition or contest commences. The point was made by the Northern Ireland Queen's Bench recently, in *Browning v Odyssey Trust Co Ltd*,[168] that '[p]romoters and organisers ... are not taking decisions in the excitement of the competition. Their assessments [of appropriate safety precautions for spectators and competitors] should be measured and proportionate to the risk involved'. The legal effect, of course, is that the standard of care applying to this D is not suppressed, by virtue of any 'heat of battle' during which a competitor or a spectator is injured.

In *Browning v Odyssey Trust*, Courtney Browning, 12, C, was hit on the forehead by a puck which left the ice-rink, whilst she was sitting as a spectator at an ice hockey game in Belfast during the warm-up. C claimed that the owners/occupiers of the Odyssey Arena, where the accident happened, breached its duty to her, in failing to provide barriers and netting which would afford sufficient protection for spectators. **Held:** no breach proven, the standard of reasonable care was met by D, in taking the safety precautions (e.g., netting, perspex glass) that were provided at the arena.

In summary

The variable standards of care operating in the context of dangerous sporting or recreational pursuits are illustrated in the following Diagram:

Variable standards of care

the reasonable standard, expected of **promotors/organisers towards spectators** – to act with reasonable care in ensuring their safety

the suppressed standard, expected of **participants towards participants**, and of **referees towards participants** – to act with such degree of care as is appropriate in all the circumstances, including that of the 'hurly-burly' and swift-moving nature of the game/contest

the further suppressed standard, expected of **participants towards spectators** – to not act recklessly or with deliberate intent to do harm and to not breach the rules of the game/contest

---

[166] [1963] 2 QB 43 (CA) 55.   [167] [1972] 3 All ER 158 (CA).   [168] [2014] NIQB 39, [24].

Available resources and facilities

§6.22 Where D has to contend with limited resources and facilities, then 'resource allocation' difficulties may be taken into account when setting the standard of care required of D, only in *very limited* circumstances, *viz*, for occupiers towards neighbouring landowners, and (more controversially) for healthcare authorities.

In an ideal world of 'deep-pocket' monetary resources, D could have implemented a system to prevent C's injury – but the ideal world is too expensive, and unrealistic, to countenance. Where D proves that it has available only limited resources (whether human, monetary or equipment), then – apart from the controversial 'locality rule' which has already been considered – there are two areas in which those scarce resources have been taken into account in setting the standard of care at law: occupiers from whose land something dangerous emanates or from which danger is created to an adjoining landowner; and health authorities.

Notably, this issue is not to be confused with a discretion as to how to deploy resources, which may preclude D from owing C any duty of care whatsoever, either because the issue is non-justiciable or because the third limb of the *Caparo* test fails (as discussed in Chapter 2). The analysis in this section assumes that a duty of care is owed – the only question here is what, if any, effect the scarcity of resources has upon the standard of care which must be achieved by D.

Apart from the two areas noted above, basing a decision in negligence on resource issues has sometimes led to appellate judicial discomfort.

> In *Carty v Croydon LBC*,[169] C suffered a number of physical and developmental problems from a young age, and brought a claim for educational negligence. **Held:** no breach proven. C argued that the trial judge was wrong to take into account a lack of resources available to D, the educational authority, when deciding whether there had been a breach of duty. The trial judge stated that it would be wrong to characterise as negligent a decision 'which, whilst not ideal, was reasonable in the light of available resources', and also that any alternative placement of C would have to be at a specialist school within the borough 'or (subject to ... funding ...) outside the borough'. However, the Court of Appeal held that, on a fair reading of the judgment, 'the judge did not base his conclusion, that the failure to remove [C] from [a school] was not negligent, on the fact that there were no resources available to fund a placement outside the borough'.

Occupiers, and damage to adjoining landowners

§6.23 An occupier of land, D, owes a duty of care to a neighbouring occupier, C, to prevent the spread of a hazard (whether natural or man-made) from his land. The standard of care required of D is to take such steps *as are reasonable in all the circumstances* to prevent or minimise the risk of injury or damage to C caused by that hazard. Hence, the standard is subjectively-assessed, having regard to D's resources.

This section does **not** concern the standard of care which an occupier, D, must meet, when considering his conduct towards either visitors or trespassers to his land. That topic (which

---

[169] [2005] EWCA Civ 19, [2005] 1 WLR 2312, [77].

is governed to large extent by the Occupiers' Liability Act 1957 and the Occupiers' Liability Act 1984, respectively) is considered separately, in Chapter 12. Rather, this section concerns D's conduct towards neighbouring landowners, which is governed entirely by the common law.

D's relevant 'circumstances'. In *Goldman v Hargrave*,[170] Lord Wilberforce referred to D's duty towards neighbouring landowners as being a 'measured duty of care'. To meet that duty, 'if the small owner does what he can, and promptly calls on his neighbour to provide additional resources, he may be held to have done his duty: he should not be liable, unless it is clearly proved that he could, and *reasonably in his individual circumstances should*, have done more'. In *LMS Intl Ltd v Styrene Packaging and Insulation Ltd* too, the court grouped a number of cases together, in which C's injury was caused by a hazard emanating from D's land, and stated three principles:

i. D, the occupier, has a positive duty to take reasonable steps to prevent or minimise the risk of injury or danger emanating from his land, howsoever caused (i.e., whether natural or man-made, and whether made by a lawful entrant or by a trespasser);

ii. D cannot discharge that duty simply by not creating or adding to the source of danger or hazard, the liability can arise from not abating it; and

iii. importantly for the standard of care expected, D is assessed according to the personal resources *of that particular D*, such that 'it will be a matter of fact and degree as to whether what the occupier does in purported compliance with that duty *was reasonable in all the circumstances.*'[171]

The court may take into account the following, regarding D's circumstances:

i. the personal resources of D (whether they are plentiful or modest);

ii. the type (or magnitude) of danger on D's land and how expensive it is for D to abate or remove it;

iii. the time that would be required to abate or remove the hazard;

iv. the physical abilities of D (whether he was able-bodied or infirm); and

v. the comparative means of C and D (the owner of a small property where a hazard arises should not have to do as much as D who owns a larger property and who has greater resources to protect it).

Why does the law take account of D's resources in this type of case? In *Goldman*, it was said to be because D, the occupier, 'has had this hazard thrust upon him through no seeking or fault of his own ... A rule which required of him in such unsought circumstances, in his neighbour's interest, a physical effort of which he is not capable, or an excessive expenditure of money, would be unenforceable or unjust.'[172] That is, fairness requires a modification of the standard of care, so as to be more subjectively-assessed than usually applies.

Applications. The principle has applied, whatever natural nuisances emanate which affect D's neighbour, C (per *Stagecoach South Western Trains Ltd v Hind*[173]). Notably, where D is a public (local) authority, then the reality is that D will have substantial financial resources – and yet, the court must still take into account the competing demands on those resources and

---

[170] [1967] 1 AC 645 (PC, on appeal from the HCA) 663 (emphasis added).

[171] [2005] EWHC 2065 (TCC), [2006] TCLR 6, [46] (emphasis added).

[172] [1967] 1 AC 645 (PC, on appeal from the HCA) 663-64.   [173] [2014] EWHC 1891 (TCC) [65].

the public purposes for which they are held. In other words, it may not be fair to require D to expend those resources on infrastructure works in order to protect a few individuals against a modest risk of property damage (per *Vernon Knight Associates v Cornwall CC*[174]).

- *escape of fire* – occupier D has a continuing duty to abate a fire from spreading from his property to the property of adjoining landowner, C, according to the leading authority of *Goldman v Hargrave*.[175]

> In *Goldman v Hargrave*, a farmer, D, failed to put out a fire in a tall redgum tree which had been struck by lightning in an upper fork, 100 ft above ground. D dealt with the problem by clearing and dampening the area round the tree, and cutting it down. However, D then took no further steps to prevent the spread of fire, which he could readily have done by dousing the burning tree with water. Instead, he let the fire burn itself out. However, a hot dry wind sprang up, revived the fire, caused it to spread rapidly, resulting in extensive damage to C's neighbouring farm. **Held:** breach proven. Although the fire had started by natural causes, D did not meet the standard of care expected. The resources required to extinguish the fire were not excessive – some water and some time on D's part. The fire could be removed with little effort and no expenditure.

The principle has since been affirmed. As the court put it in *LMS v Styrene Packaging*, 'in any such case, it is always necessary to decide how far the occupier needs to go to discharge that duty'.[176]

> In *LMS*, fire broke out in Styrene Packaging's, D's, factory premises in Bradford. The factory was used to make polystyrene blocks for insulation purposes and polystyrene mouldings for use in packaging. The fire started when D's employee cut expanded polystyrene blocks with a hot wire machine – a practice which was liable to cause explosion of the flammable materials. The fire spread to two adjoining factory premises which were leased and occupied by LMS, C. Over £3m worth of damage was caused to C's property, machinery, plant and contents. **Held:** breach proven. D fell below the standard of care required, because prevention measures were possible, *viz*: D should have implemented adequate training and safety systems; following correspondence with the Fire Authority and the Health and Safety Executive, D should have compartmentalised the stored blocks or put in an automatic fire detection system; D should have installed interlocks on the hot wire cutting machine; and D also failed to put out the fire around the hot wire cutting machine, when it was within its capabilities to do so.

- *escape of mosquitoes* – where a public authority, D (Thames Water Utilities) allegedly expended insufficient effort to stop the breeding and escape of mosquitoes from its Mogden Sewerage Treatment Works, D owed the surrounding residents 'a measured duty of care in respect of mosquitoes', whereby 'the standard of care is to be shaped by the personal capabilities and circumstances of Thames Water' (per *Dobson v Thames Water Utilities Ltd (No 2)*[177]). No negligence was proven.

- *loss of support for C's land* – in *Holbeck Hall Hotel Ltd v Scarborough BC*,[178] there was no distinction (said the Court of Appeal) between a hazard caused by loss of support, and a danger on D's land which spread or encroached onto C's land. There did not need to be an encroachment as such – only a danger or hazard to C's land. This has become known as the *Leakey* principle, named after the leading case. Again, in such cases, the standard of care is set, according to the circumstances and resources of D.

---

[174] [2013] EWCA Civ 950, [49(iii)].   [175] [1967] 1 AC 645 (PC).   [176] [2005] EWHC 2065 (TCC), [2006] TCLR 6, [41].
[177] [2011] EWHC 3253 (TCC), 140 Con LR 135, [946].   [178] [2000] 2 All ER 705 (CA).

In *Leakey v National Trust*,[179] the homes of a group of people, C, had been built at the foot of a large mound situated on D's land. Over the years, soil and rubble had fallen from the National Trusts', D's, land onto C's land, due to natural weathering and the nature of the soil. By 1968, D knew that this weathering was a threat to C's properties. After a very dry summer and wet autumn, a large crack opened in the mound above C's house, and C notified D of the danger to their houses, but D denied responsibility. A few weeks later, a large quantity of earth, and some stumps, fell onto C's land. C brought an interlocutory application to seek an order that D urgently carry out the work required to abate the danger. **Held:** D was liable in negligence (and in nuisance, see Chapter 16). The danger resulted from the forces of nature, which constituted a hazard that D was legally required to abate, and it was within its resources to do so. Hence, in this particular case, C did not need to contribute to the repair bill.

- *escape of floodwaters onto C's land* – a public authority may not be required to install very expensive infrastructure works to prevent flooding, where those works were expensive, and its resources did not warrant it. It will all depend upon the circumstances, and the resources available to D.

In *Lambert v Barratt Homes Ltd*,[180] Mr Lambert, C, was one of several householders whose properties were flooded by surface water flowing from land belonging to Rochdale MBC, D. **Held:** D was not in breach of its 'measured duty', because D's duty did not extend to constructing drainage ditches and a catchpit at their own expense. Although D had funds far in excess of those available to householders, C, D was under financial pressure too, especially where its resources were held for public purposes and were not generally available for the benefit of private persons. However, in *Vernon Knight Associates v Cornwall CC*,[181] floodwater escaped from one of D's roads in the county, which flooded C's holiday village in Cornwall, twice. **Held:** breach proven: 'even after making due allowance for the pressures on local authorities, the measured duty on the council did require it to take reasonable steps to keep that drainage installation functioning properly'. D had decided that the risk of flooding from the road was serious enough to justify building special infrastructure works (e.g., installing drains, gullies and a catchpit), but ultimately, these were not maintained as they should have been.

Health authorities

§6.24 English law is presently unsettled as to whether the standard of care required of a health authority *may* be suppressed because of limited or scarce resources, albeit that the standard will never be reduced, at law, to a negligible level of care.

For a Health Authority or hospital, D, English courts have dealt with the application of resources (or the lack of them) to the relevant standard of care in a somewhat inconsistent fashion to date.

This principle is only relevant where systemic negligence on the Health Authority's part is alleged (quite separately from alleged negligent acts or omissions on the part of a healthcare practitioner, for whom the Health Authority is allegedly vicariously liable). 'systemic negligence' – arising from an 'institutional duty of care', or a 'non-delegable duty on the hospital authority toward the patient', as it is otherwise termed – means the failure by the Health Authority to put in place the requisite managerial or operational procedures that reasonably

---

[179] [1980] 1 QB 485 (CA), and applied recently in: *Coope v Ward* [2015] EWCA Civ 30.
[180] [2010] EWCA Civ 681.   [181] [2013] EWCA Civ 950, [58].

would have prevented patient C's harm from occurring. It is an allegation of direct wrongdoing against the governing Health Authority (as discussed in Chapter 7).

Of course, the standard of care must not be set too high – a Health Authority is only required to implement a system 'framed to deal with that which is reasonably foreseeable, [but not a system] framed to deal with the possibility that a rare occurrence will happen' (per *Garcia v St Mary's Trust*[182]). Hence, Health Authorities do not have to meet the very high standard of 'ensur[ing] that proper assistance was readily available' to prevent C's harm that had been the view of the trial judge in *Bull v Devon HA*, but it was disapproved on appeal, because it:

> implies an absolute and unqualified obligation [and] overstated the duty falling on the authority, again having regard to the number of suitably qualified obstetricians available to the hospital on the particular Saturday afternoon … With that limited manpower available, it might have been quite impossible, however diligent the attempt, to secure the attendance of either [obstetrician] within 10–15 minutes, because both of them might have had inescapable other commitments.[183]

However, English case law is somewhat divided, as to whether a Health Authority's resources are legitimately to be taken account of, in reducing the standard required, if resources are scarce and limited.

View #1. On one view, the standard of care should be suppressed, because of the 'logistical constraints' (as the court put it in *Richards v Swansea NHS Trust*[184]) under which a Health Authority operates. The 'limited resources' argument is one factor that a court **can** legitimately take into account, when pitching the standard of care required to be met by the Health Authority. Its relevance is judicially supported for several reasons:

i. a Health Authority owes co-duties to other patients, which may prevent it from giving one patient the treatment or resources that it 'would ideally prefer' (per *Arthur JS Hall & Co v Simons*[185]);

ii. moreover, a Health Authority must manage and provide an effective and careful workplace for its own staff (per *Garcia v St Mary's Trust*[186]);

iii. whether a public authority has 'got its resource allocation right' is not a matter for a judge to adjudicate – rather, it is a parliamentary decision (an argument also made, in the police context, in *Hill v CC of West Yorkshire*[187]).

As always, where a standard is suppressed due to circumstances, then the *practical* effect is that it will be harder – although not impossible – to prove breach.

> In *Hardaker v Newcastle HA*, Mr Hardaker, C, a diver, suffered from symptoms of serious decompression illness ('the bends'), which required treatment in a decompression chamber. C alleged that a decompression chamber available at Newcastle University, adjacent to the hospital there (the Royal Victoria Infirmary, RVI), ought to have been open at all hours. It was closed on the weekends, the time at which C suffered the bends, meaning that he had to be transferred to the police diving school's decompression chamber in Sunderland). The decompression chamber at Newcastle University was under the control of the Newcastle HA, D. **Held:** no breach proven.

[182] [2006] EWHC 2314 (QB) [96].   [183] (1989) 22 BMLR 79 (CA) 83 (Slade LJ).
[184] [2007] EWHC 487 (QB) [31] (no breach proven).
[185] [2002] 1 AC 615 (HL) 690 (Lord Hoffmann, referring to doctors, but of equal application to Health Authorities).
[186] [2006] EWHC 2314 (QB) [95].   [187] [1989] AC 53 (HL) 63–64 (Lord Keith).

> [D's duty of care to C] was qualified by the resources available to them ... They cannot be held to have been negligent for failing to apply sufficient resources to the [Newcastle University] chamber to keep it available at all hours: such an allegation involves an assessment of the priority of allocation of resources which a Court cannot perform ... The suggestion that the RVI should have secured the attendance of a doctor at Sunderland assumes the availability of a suitable doctor who was not otherwise required and the resources to pay him. The evidence came nowhere near to establishing that [D] had been negligent in this regard, quite apart from the fact that issues of resource allocation are not for the Court. On the day in question, Dr Dorani said he could not have left the A&E Department, even to go to the helicopter landing site, without significantly depleting the staff. He was on duty with two junior doctors, and would not have wanted to send either of them to accompany the helicopter. It was reasonably the practice at the RVI to send out medical staff only in the event of a major medical disaster, such as a rail crash or major road crash. Mr Hardaker's case did not come into this category.[188]

Hence, the court was prepared to accept that the Royal Victoria met the standard of care required of it by law, as 'qualified' by its limited resources.

Nevertheless, any suppressed standard of medical care expected of Health Authority D, due to its resource limitations, cannot be reduced to a standard that is manifestly inadequate or absent altogether. Nor can the non-availability of resources, due to governmental budgetary constraints, be used by D as a defence to a negligence claim. In *Knight v Home Office*[189] (the suicide-at-Brixon-prison-case), Pill J provided the following hypothetical example: what if Parliament did not provide any funds to a prison to operate a hospital wing, so that prisoners did not receive any on-site medical care? An ordinary reasonable standard of medical care to those housed in the prison would **still** be operative, and a breach would thus be found if no medical treatment was provided at all. The criticism by Pill J, that any suggestion that a lack of resources could not possibly be a defence, has been endorsed at appellate level (per *Sussex Ambulance NHS Trust v King*[190]). Nevertheless, Pill J confirmed that the allocation of resources by Parliament is 'one factor' which the court must consider when deciding what standard of care the law should demand.

View #2. On the other hand, some cases suggest a harder-line approach, whereby no reduction in the standard of care is appropriate where resources are scant/limited. Two reasons have been cited:

i. many potential Ds face resource problems, and do not benefit from a suppressed standard of care.

> In *Bull v Devon HA*[191] Mrs Bull gave birth to twins at a campus of a hospital which was operated by the Devon HA, D. It was a 'split-site' hospital, constructed over three campuses. First twin, Darryl, was delivered without incident, but an obstetric emergency developed with the birth of the second twin, Stuart, C, who was born 68 minutes later. C suffered brain damage due to hypoxia, causing profound mental disability and spastic quadriplegia. C alleged that D failed to have an adequate system for summonsing an obstetrician, so that all attempts made to summon the registrar between births were unsuccessful, and the pager went unanswered. **Held:** breach proven. The system of summoning the obstetricians on call between campuses was 'precarious', 'unreliable and essentially unsatisfactory', and 'operating on a knife-edge', with no reasonable explanation as to why the system had broken down.

---

[188] QB, 15 Jun 2001, [54]–[56].   [189] [1990] 3 All ER 237 (QB), with example and quote at 243.
[190] [2002] EWCA Civ 953, [45].   [191] (1989) 22 BMLR 79 (CA).

It had been suggested in argument that 'since the small number of consultants and registrars had to deal with three different sites, [t]hey could not be expected to do more than their best, allocating their limited resources as favourably as possible'. Mustill LJ replied that he had 'some reservations' about the argument, and that 'there are other public services in respect of which it is not necessarily an answer to allegations of unsafety that there were insufficient resources to enable the administrators to do everything which they would like to do'. The statement was dicta: because C had not argued that the hospital had been negligent in providing insufficient resources, the court would leave this 'important issue of social policy' to another day.

ii. in *Wilsher v Essex AHA*, Sir Browne-Wilkinson V-C supported the notion that the Health Authority's standard of care should not be reduced (so that it could more easily escape liability) if resources available to it were limited – rather, holding up the standard, and finding direct liability against an under-resourced Health Authority, was preferable to deciding that a doctor was in breach, when he could do nothing about the under-resourced system in which he had to operate:

> Claims against a health authority that it has itself been directly negligent, as opposed to vicariously liable for the negligence of its doctors, will, of course, raise awkward problems ... But the law should not be distorted by making findings of personal fault against individual doctors who are, in truth, not at fault in order to avoid such questions. To do so would be to cloud the real issues which arise.[192]

Although Sir Browne-Wilkinson VC dissented on the issue of the effect of inexperience, his views on resource allocation and its impact on standard of care were not subject to any criticism by the majority in *Wilsher* (and the issue was not dealt with on further appeal to the House of Lords).

Resource allocation is, at the end of the day, a political decision upon which Health Authorities who are sued – and the courts which must determine those suits – have no control. In *Hardaker v Newcastle HA*,[193] it was pointed out that, how Royal Victoria Infirmary spent its not overly-indulgent budget allocation was a question for the NHS Trust, and not for the court to examine and overrule. In *Kent v Griffiths* too,[194] the Court of Appeal concurred that, 'where what is being attacked is the allocation of resources, whether in the provision of sufficient ambulances or sufficient drivers or attendants, different considerations could apply. There then could be issues which are not suited for resolution by the courts'.

Hence, judicially speaking, opinion as to the relevance of the resources available to a Health Authority on the standard of care expected of it, is somewhat divided. However, the better view (on the basis of the abovementioned authorities) is that the standard of care required of a Health Authority *will* be suppressed, where D can show that the harm to C was brought about due to D's limited resources – but having said that, the standard will never be reduced, at law, to a negligible standard.

---

[192] [1987] QB 730 (CA) 778.   [193] QB, 15 Jun 2001, [54].   [194] [2000] EWCA Civ 25, [47].

7

Breach II – Proving negligence

INTRODUCTION

§7.1   Breach is doing something which a prudent and reasonable person would not do, or failing to do something which a prudent and reasonable person would do.

This definition of breach, adapted from Alderson B's 'classic statement'[1] in *Blyth v Birmingham Waterworks Co*[2] back in 1856, highlights the key question: what would a reasonable person have done differently, to avoid the risk of harm or injury occurring to C? If the answer to that is, 'nothing', then breach will fail.

That something has gone wrong is, of itself, absolutely no evidence of breach. Injuries, damage, adverse outcomes, and less-than-desirable results, may all arise from an exercise of reasonable care. Courts have, on occasion, addressed remarks to Cs for whom they obviously felt a great deal of sympathy for their misfortunes, but for whom they could not find in favour, because there was no lack of reasonable care. For example, motor vehicle accidents, and medical mishaps, may ruin young lives, e.g., in *Arnot v Sprake*, where the Court of Appeal held against car accident victim C, concluding that it was 'highly regrettable that unfortunately [C] has suffered serious injury as a result of the impact he sustained'[3]; and in *Nawoor v Barking Havering and Brentwood HA*, where a birth went very badly:

> the family of this child must feel that an injury so severe, with such obvious long-term consequences, could only be the product of something going wrong, and negligently wrong. Understandable that may be, but it is not the appropriate conclusion in this case. I regret to have reached the conclusion I have, because this child is clearly going to be affected in the longer term as a teenager and an adult, but regret it though I do, it is the conclusion I firmly reach.[4]

---

[1] As recently described in: *Dunnage v Randall* [2015] EWCA Crim 673, [123].
[2] (1856) 11 Ct Exch 781, 156 ER 1047–1049.   [3] [2001] EWCA Civ 341, [54].
[4] [1998] Lloyd's Rep Med 313 (QB) [last paragraph].

The framework

The framework of analysis for breach is set out in the following Table:

> **Breach in a nutshell**
>
> **Preliminary matters:**
>
> i   Proving the requisite foreseeability
> ii   Assessing the date of breach
> iii Ruling out 'inevitable accident'
> iv   Potential dual bases of liability: vicarious liability and systemic breach
>
> **Modes of proving breach – where applicable on the facts:**
>
> 1 Testing the precautionary steps against *Bolton v Stone's* 'breach factors'
> 2 Applying the *Bolam* test (as qualified by '*Bolitho's* gloss')
> 3 Other potential tests of breach:
>   - Contravening specific duties of care
>   - Contravening relevant rules/standards
>   - Contravening the 'making it worse' rule
> 4 The doctrine of *res ipsa loquitur*
>
> **What does not prove breach:**
>
> - D's view, pre-event or pre-accident
> - An expert organisation's opinion
> - Changing the system, post-accident
> - Failing to remove an inherent risk in D's conduct
> - And finally, the (ir)relevance of proving 'gross negligence'

A matter of terminology

§7.2   Any distinction between mere 'errors of judgment', and breaches of duty, has proven unhelpful, and is not determinative of the question of breach.

In *Barrett v Enfield LBC*,[5] Lord Hutton stated that 'the court must be satisfied that the conduct complained of went beyond mere errors of judgment in the exercise of a discretion and constituted conduct which can be regarded as negligent'; and, in *Arthur JS Hall & Co v Simons*,[6] Lord Hope noted that, 'a mere error of judgment on [a barrister's] part will not expose him to liability for negligence'.

However, this terminology has proven unhelpful in English cases. An error of judgment, as with any other mistake, **can** constitute negligence. As Lord Fraser said in *Whitehouse v Jordan*,[7] any statement that 'in a professional man, an error of judgment is not negligent' is an inaccurate statement of the law – correctly, it must say that an error of judgment 'is not *necessarily*

---

[5] [1999] UKHL 25, [2001] 2 AC 550 (HL) 591.   [6] [2000] UKHL 38, [2002] 1 AC 615 (HL) 726.
[7] [1981] 1 WLR 246 (HL) 263 (emphasis added).

negligent' – because '[m]erely to describe something as an error of judgment tells us nothing about whether it is negligent or not. The true position is that an error of judgment may, or may not, be negligent; it depends on the nature of the error'. This position was emphasised later in *Davis v Stena Line Ltd*,[8] where Forbes J described an 'error of judgment' as 'ambiguous and not very helpful', and in *Henry v Thames Valley Police*,[9] where Smith LJ remarked that, '[w]hat matters, in a civil action, is whether [D's] actions were negligent, in that they fell below the expected standard of reasonable skill or care. It may be wise to avoid any argument about whether there has been an error of judgment'.

Given this judicial admonishment, the terminology, 'error of judgment', is avoided in this chapter.

PRELIMINARY MATTERS

The test of foreseeability

The general principles, and leading authorities, governing the test of foreseeability of damage were examined in Chapter 2. To reiterate, negligence is concerned with a *reasonable* D, not a highly-anxious, or highly-perceptive or visionary, perfectionist.

In *Jolley v Sutton LBC*,[10] Lord Hoffmann stated that the concept of reasonable foreseeability 'does not denote a fixed point on the scale of probability'. Merely possible (i.e., very small or far-fetched) risks may be foreseeable, but they are not *reasonably* foreseeable; a risk must be likely enough that a reasonable D, careful of the safety of his neighbour, would not think it right to neglect or ignore that risk (per *Overseas Tankship (UK) Ltd v Miller Steamship Co Pty Ltd (Wagon Mound No 2)*[11]). It must be a 'real risk, and not just a mere possibility' (per *Khan v Harrow CC*[12]). To reiterate, and as clarified in *Smith v Littlewoods Organisation Ltd*,[13] whenever the word, 'probable', is used in the context of reasonable foreseeability, it decidedly does **not** entail any proof on the balance of probabilities. Rather, 'it is used as indicating a real risk, as distinct from a mere possibility of danger. It is **not** used in the sense that the consequence must be more probable than not, before it can be reasonably foreseeable.'

A narrower foreseeability test

§7.3 The reasonable foreseeability test, under breach, is a narrower test than that which is applied at duty of care stage. At breach stage, the court is required to assess whether the event or accident was so unlikely (i.e., unforeseeable) as not to require any precautionary steps or alternative course of action to be taken by D.

The enquiry, at breach stage, is quite specific – was the event or accident foreseeable, so that D acted unreasonably in not taking steps to forestall its occurrence? After all, if the event was so remote and so unlikely as to be unforeseeable, then no reasonable D would have taken precautionary steps to guard against the risk of that danger or harm manifesting (even if some steps or alternative course of conduct can be identified, which probably would have precluded the harm from occurring).

---

[8] [2005] EWHC 420 (QB) [11].   [9] [2010] EWCA Civ 5, [2010] RTR 14, [43].
[10] [2000] 1 WLR 1082 (HL) 1091.   [11] [1967] 1 AC 617 (PC) 642–43.
[12] [2013] EWHC 2687 (TCC) [59]–[62] (Ramsey J).   [13] [1987] AC 241 (HL) 269.

However, there is an 'inevitable overlap' between the establishment of a duty of care and the proof of breach, insofar as proving a foreseeable risk of injury is concerned – that was acknowledged, e.g., in *Gabriel v Kirklees MC*.[14] Indeed, in the following, a duty of care was owed to C (hence, that test of foreseeability was upheld), but no breach ensued because the event or accident was unforeseeable, although judicial opinion differed as each case proceeded to appeal, highlighting the difficulty of assessing the issue:

> In *Bolton v Stone*,[15] C, Miss Stone, was hit by a cricket ball while standing on the footpath outside her house at Cheetham Hill. The Cheetham Cricket Ground, owned by the Club, D, was adjacent to the road, and matches had been regularly played there since about 1864. The residential area where C lived was constructed in 1910. The ball had travelled a distance of about 100 yards, over a 7-foot high fence (but, with the upward slope of the ground, about 17 feet above the cricket pitch where the ball exited the ground). The evidence was that hitting a ball onto the road was altogether exceptional, and had occurred about 6 times in 38 years. **Held (CA):** D was not liable in nuisance, but was liable in negligence. **Held (HL):** D was not liable in negligence or in nuisance. Re negligence, the risk of C's injury was too small to be reasonably foreseeable, although it was variously assessed as 'infinitesimal', or 'not far from the borderline'. In *Whippey v Jones*,[16] Mr Jones, 42, C, was jogging along a footpath at Riverside Walk in Leeds when he was accosted by Hector, a fully-grown 2-year-old Great Dane, owned by Christopher Whippey, D, an RSPCA Inspector. After colliding with Hector, C fell down a slope to the river and badly broke his ankle. **Held (trial):** breach proven, because D failed to take sufficient care to ensure that there were no other people about before he let Hector off the lead. **Held (CA):** no breach proven, because the test of foreseeability necessary for proof of breach failed. Hector had no tendency to jump up at other people; at the most, he stopped and barked at people 5–10 feet away. There was no reason why D, as a reasonable dog handler in the park, should have anticipated that if Hector was let off the lead when some other adult was about, that person would be physically harmed from Hector bounding up and colliding with him.

Previous occurrences

§7.4

Where C suffered an injury or harm from an event or accident which had *never* happened previously, that does not, of itself, render the risk unforeseeable. Obversely, if the risk had eventuated prior to C's accident, it does not automatically render the risk *reasonably* foreseeable. In all cases, the question is whether that risk was sufficiently foreseeable to require a reasonable D to take precautionary steps to avert the risk of injury.

It is impossible to draw any clear conclusions, where there is an absence of any previous similar accident. That very fact 'is not conclusive, but it is helpful', in disproving foreseeability (per Swinton Thomas LJ in *McGivney v Golderslea Ltd*[17]) – or, as Waller LJ put it in *Simkiss v Rhondda BC*,[18] no previous incident tends to offset 'to a great extent' an argument that the risk of injury was foreseeable.

> In *Abouzaid v Mothercare (UK) Ltd*,[19] Iman Abouzaid, C, 12, was helping his mother to attach a 'Cosytoes' sleeping bag to a pushchair, manufactured by D, when its elasticised strap slipped from

---

[14] [2004] EWCA Civ 345, [27].

[15] [1951] AC 850 (HL) 860 (Lord Normand), 863 (Lord Oaksey), 867 (Lord Reid), 869 (Lord Radcliffe), on appeal from: [1950] 1 KB 201 (CA).

[16] [2009] EWCA Civ 452.   [17] [1997] EWCA Civ 2656, (2001) 17 Const LJ 454.

[18] (1983) 81 LGR 460 (CA).   [19] [2000] EWCA Civ 348.

his grasp and the buckle hit him in the left eye, causing a detached retina injury. **Held:** no breach in negligence. There had never been any comparable accidents; elastic was a commonly used fabric; and long experience had not shown that its use in children's products was likely to cause injury.

However, it can never be said that, just because something has not occurred before, it is unforeseeable. It may be a matter of sheer good fortune and coincidence that the accident had not happened previously.

In *Bunker v Charles Brand & Son Ltd*,[20] Mr Bunker, C, was an employee of a construction and engineering firm engaged in work in a tube tunnel. It was being drilled out by a machine being used by Charles Brand, D. The normal way to reach the front of the machine was by walking along the angle irons, using a girder as a handhold. As C was doing so, his foot slipped off onto the rollers, which moved, and C fell, suffering serious injury. **Held**: D was liable for breach, under the OLA 1957: '[t]he mere fact that no accident had happened in the past does not absolve [D] from taking further precautions'. D should have put down planks beside or on top of the rollers, to enable a firm walkway for getting up to the front of the machine.

Obversely, just because the incident had occurred previously (without injury) does not, of itself, indicate that the test of foreseeability will automatically be proven. The latest manifestation of the incident may still be reasonably unforeseeable, especially if its past occurrences have been rare (of course, it cannot be totally unforeseeable, as it has happened before!). Two sporting cases provide good illustrations, in which there was no breach:

In *Bolton v Stone*,[21] facts previously, there was no breach, even where the cricket ball had been hit out of the ground on a few occasions previously. In *Horton v Jackson*,[22] a golfer's drive shot hit another golfer, Mr Horton, C, the shot being executed without looking up to see where the injured golfer was located and in plain view. There had been only two proven incidents before this accident at this part of D's golf course in the previous 16 years, with upwards of 800,000 rounds of golf played from this tee. This eventuality was foreseeable – but was not *reasonably* foreseeable, so there was no need for the golf club to institute further precautions. In any event, the golfer 'was so intent on playing his shot and, for some reason, playing it quickly, that he simply did not look, and on his own evidence was not aware of the presence of [C] until after his ball had struck him. No steps could have been taken by the golf club to prevent folly of this kind'.

On the other hand, foreseeability is likely to be proven if previous complaints had been made to D about the very same event/incident – or if the very incident which gave rise to C's injury or harm happened shortly after a similar incident. In the following, breach was proven:

In *Stimpson v Wolverhampton MBC*,[23] Mr Stimpson, C, a member of the public, was hit in the mouth by a golf ball which was played in Council D's public park. The accident was foreseeable, given evidence from a park attendant that people regularly played golf, in spite of being told not to; sometimes by repeat offenders; and some complaints had been made by the public who had been physically struck by golf balls. In *Cunningham v Reading FC*,[24] Mr Cunningham, C, was an on-duty police officer at a football match at D's Reading Football Stadium, when, during a match, there was an outbreak of horrible and terrifying violence, with Bristol City fans attacking Reading fans and invading the pitch. Dangerous missiles were thrown, including lumps of concrete torn up from the

[20] [1969] 2 QB 480, 489.   [21] [1951] AC 850 (HL).   [22] [1996] CLY 4475 (CA) (Douglas Brown J).
[23] CA, 22 May 1990.   [24] [1992] PIQR P141 (QB) P153.

dilapidated terraces, and one of these struck C, injuring him. Concrete had been broken and used as missiles less than four months previously, and hence, D 'had been put on full notice of the potential danger from this state of affairs, and had done nothing whatsoever to remedy it'.

Occasionally, the lack of previous occurrence of the accident is because C's behaviour in the instant case was unusual, almost unprecedented. In that event, it will be difficult to prove that C's injury was reasonably foreseeable.

In *Cornish Glennroy Blair-Ford v CRS Adventures Ltd*,[25] Glenn Blair-Ford, C, suffered permanent tetraplegia when he threw a wellington boot backwards through his legs at D's outdoor pursuits centre at the River Dart Country Park in Devon. C's head was low down by his legs, his hands went through his legs with a lot of force, throwing the welly high into the air, not what was intended; and then C toppled over and fell onto his head and neck, rather than toppling forwards onto his face and chest. **Held:** C's injury was not reasonably foreseeable. The execution of his throw 'could not have been foreseen, namely, considerable force, bending very low, positioning the head almost between the knees, falling forwards when the hands were still between the knees, and striking the ground with his head and neck at such an angle as to cause the catastrophic injury sustained by him. His was no ordinary throw. The fact that the welly went almost straight up in the air rather than being thrown a long distance is powerful evidence that he threw it and fell in an unusual way that was not and could not have been foreseen'.

Known susceptibilities

§7.5   Where D *knows* that C is particularly susceptible to injury, then the test of foreseeability will be proven, as that particular D has *foreseen* the risk.

Where the susceptibility of C to injury is actually known to D, then the risk is foreseen; and the question of breach will then be assessed by reference to what (if any) precautions a reasonable D should have taken to protect **that particular C**. D's knowledge may relate to its systems' or its employees' vulnerabilities, either of which pose a potential risk. For example:[26]

In *Paris v Stepney BC*,[27] Mr Paris, C, was a garage hand employed in D's garage. He had only one functioning eye, due to a war-time injury. C was hammering at a wheel to remove a bolt, when a chip of metal flew up and entered his good (right) eye, blinding him. Goggles were not supplied to the employees in this garage; indeed, there was no evidence that it was customary for employers of garage employees to supply goggles. **Held (3:2):** breach proven. In *AG (British Virgin Islands) v Hartwell*,[28] PC Kelvin Laurent was the sole police officer in charge on the island of Jost Van Dyke in the BVI. He was entrusted with guns and ammunition. One evening, PC Laurent abandoned his post, left the island, taking a gun with him, visited a restaurant at another island where his former partner (Ms Lafond) waitressed, and fired four shots at her and her current partner. Craig Hartwell, C, a pub customer, was caught up in the shooting and suffered serious injuries. C sued the police employer, D, for entrusting PC Laurent with a gun, when he was known to have 'personal troubles', and had

---

[25] [2012] EWHC 2360 (QB) [66].

[26] Also: *Hicks v Young* [2015] EWHC 1144 (QB) (a blind guest fell out of a second-floor open window of a guest-house, suffering grievous injuries), discussed further in Chapter 12, 'Occupiers' Liability'.

[27] [1951] AC 367 (HL) 376. Also: *McDonald v Highlands & Islands Enterprise* 2001 SCLR 547, [2001] IRLR 336, [68].

[28] [2004] UKPC 12, [2004] WLR 1273 (on appeal from the British Virgin Islands).

threatened another companion of Ms Lafond's with a long-bladed knife shortly before this incident. PC Laurent had been visited by a supervisor; that colleague accepted his explanation of events (he was using the knife to peel an orange) and did not question the threatened party; and merely told PC Laurent to sort out his personal problems in a more professional way. **Held:** breach proven. This particular employee posed a real risk to members of the public such as C, with his volatility, access to guns, and past threatening behaviour, i.e., that he would 'lose control of himself over his family problems and find the lure of a gun irresistible'.

The English Court of Appeal has since acknowledged, in *Armstrong v British Coal Corp*,[29] that the 'essence' of *Paris* was that C succeeded, 'because he was known by his employers to have only one sound eye, and they failed to provide him with appropriate goggles. The claim did not succeed on the basis that goggles should have been provided for *anyone* working in the same process as [C], although, obviously, being rendered blind in one eye is a very serious injury even for a man with two sound eyes'.

Hence, it is always relevant to ask: what **actual** knowledge did D have of any particular susceptibility of C to harm? The point is particularly important in the employment context, for as *Paris* and *Hartwell* demonstrate, employers will typically know of the physical infirmities afflicting their employees. The rationale was explained by Lady Justice Hale in *Sutherland v Hatton*:[30] an employer's duty is owed *to each individual employee*, and not to some 'unidentified outsider' – the latter being the usual case where D injures C, and has no knowledge of C's particular susceptibilities to grave injury at all. In an employer's case, C's susceptibilities are typically **known** to D, because '[t]he employer knows who his employee is', and hence, may know of C's 'particular vulnerability' – in which case, both foreseeability, and the precautionary steps that D should have taken as a reasonable employer, may be even more starkly realised.

The date for assessing breach

§7.6   Whether D's conduct met the standard of reasonable care must be assessed at the date that the alleged negligence occurred.

D is not to be judged by the wisdom of hindsight. One Canadian judge aptly stated the challenge thus:

> Hindsight has no role to play in evaluating conduct that is said to fall below a reasonable standard of care. Practices change and standards evolve. As much as possible, one must try to go back and experience the event as it was then.[31]

In *Roe v Ministry of Health*,[32] Denning LJ put it more artistically: that 'we must not look at what happened in 1949 through 1954 spectacles'.

The principle has some very practical consequences. First, it can adversely affect C, where some accident has befallen him, ahead of advances in scientific knowledge – because whatever happened to him may well have been unforeseeable. Scientific knowledge itself may have

[29] [1998] EWCA Civ 1359, [1998] CLY 975 (emphasis added).
[30] [2002] EWCA Civ 76, [2002] IRLR 263, [23].
[31] *Latin v Hosp for Sick Children* [2007] OJ No 13 (SCJ) [30] (Lax J). Also: *Hardman v Riddell* [2004] EWHC 1691 (QB) [61].
[32] [1954] 2 QB 66 (CA) 72.

advanced and later shown up, as disastrous, a practice that could not have been known to be faulty when C's injury or damage happened. The problem has arisen particularly in the engineering, product liability and medical contexts:

In *Williams v Univ of Birmingham*,[33] Michael Williams, C, studied physics at D's university, as an undergraduate, between 1970–74. He died of malignant mesothelioma, aged 54. His estate claimed that C undertook speed-of-light experiments in a 90-foot-long service tunnel, which was not ventilated, and had central heating pipes running through it, which were lagged with asbestos installed in the 1930s or 1940s. D's asbestos dust tests in 2004, 2006 and 2007 on dust residues taken from the tunnel showed all forms of blue, brown and white asbestos present. D argued that C's exposure to asbestos during those tunnel experiments was minimal, and that it was not liable for causing C's fatal mesothelioma. **Held:** no breach. As to what D should reasonably have foreseen about the dangers of asbestos exposure in 1974, the acceptable levels of exposure were contained in the Factory Inspectorate's 'Technical Data Note 13' (1970), which D was entitled to rely on, as recognised and established guidelines. Given the level of exposure to asbestos fibres actually found, D could not have reasonably foreseen that C would be exposed to an unacceptable risk of asbestos-related injury. In *Abouzaid v Mothercare (UK) Ltd*,[34] facts previously, **held (CA)**: no breach proven. Manufacturer D had not equipped his product with a securing device, but in 1990, no manufacturer of childcare products could reasonably have recognised that the elastic attachment straps for a Cosytoes could pose a hazard to the eyes of children or adults. 'We must not look at the 1990 accident with 2000 spectacles.' The fact that D should either give a warning or take steps to eliminate the risk of eye injuries at the time of trial (2000) was irrelevant, when determining negligence against D in 1990. In *Roe v Ministry of Health*, nupercaine, a spinal anaesthetic, was stored in sealed glass ampoules, themselves stored in a phenol solution. Phenol percolated through tiny invisible cracks in the glass contaminating the nupercaine. When injected, it caused paralysis from the waist down for two young labourers, C, who had minor surgery for back pain. Knowledge of cracks in glass was known in 1951, but not in 1947 when the operations on C occurred. **Held:** no breach. The possibility of cracks in glass was not known or foreseeable at the time of the operation, and hence, dyeing the phenol with a colourant, which would have shown any infusion of phenol into the nupercaine, was not required.

Even if D's breach is alleged to have occurred over a lengthy time interval, the court will need to take account of developing knowledge about the particular risk concerned over that **same** time period, but not later.

In *Baker v Quantum Clothing Group Ltd*,[35] employers were sued in negligence and under the Factories Act 1961, s29(1), for hearing loss experienced by employees in the knitting industry of Derbyshire and Nottingham prior to 1990, who suffered noise-induced hearing loss resulting from exposure to noise levels between 85–90dB. **Held (3:2):** no breach proven. The 1972 Code of Practice provided official guidance re the maximum acceptable levels of noise; to comply with 90dB, as the highest acceptable level, met the standard of the reasonable and prudent employer during the 1970s and 1980s, at least until the 1986 Directive became generally known in the industry.

As Lord Saville said, to hold D liable for breach in this case would have been to 'depend, to a significant degree, on hindsight, and consequently place an undue burden on employers'.[36]

---

[33] [2011] EWCA Civ 1242, [2012] PIQR P4, [61].   [34] [2000] EWCA Civ 348, [51]–[52].
[35] [2011] UKSC 17, [2011] 1 WLR 1003.   [36] *ibid*, [136].

Secondly, delay in achieving trial can render the proof of liability very challenging – particularly in professional negligence cases, as pointed out in *Mortgage Express Ltd v Joliffe & Flint (a firm)*:

> to make good a charge of professional incompetence will often involve a fellow professional in the same area of practice, indulging in an attempt to second-guess the judgment of [D], sometimes many years after [D] was called on to express his professional opinion, and in circumstances where neither party is able, with confidence, to replicate the precise circumstances in which the opinion under attack came to be expressed, and where [D] thereby may well find himself seriously disadvantaged. It is for reasons such as these that an allegation of professional negligence should not be lightly made, and that the law requires that such an allegation should be distinctly proved.[37]

The problem manifests acutely where C was injured during birth, because given the suspension of limitation periods until C reaches the age of majority,[38] the court may be asked to determine whether a breach of the reasonable standard occurred, at some point a quarter of a century or more before the trial itself occurs (e.g., there was a 25-year gap between alleged negligence and trial in *Macey v Warwickshire HA*,[39] and an even longer 28-year gap in *C v Cairns*[40]). As one court despaired, the trial was 'long after the facts have faded from recollection' (per *Bull v Devon AHA*[41]). Frequently, D (or D's staff) who was involved in an allegedly negligent event will genuinely have no recollection of the event, and contemporaneous notes, even where they have survived, may be incomplete (per *Macey*[42]). Other documentary evidence may be missing too (e.g., scan photographs, as occurred in *Lillywhite v UCL Hosp NHS Trust*[43]). Key medical witnesses, including D, may have moved jurisdiction (as in *Wisniewski v Central Manchester HA*, where D had moved to work in Australia and did not return for the trial, leading to certain adverse inferences being drawn against him[44]). Also, practices within the medical profession may have significantly changed since the alleged breach – but such advances must be ignored by the trial judge, *viz*: in the provision of ante-natal and neo-natal care (*Macey*), or in cervical screening practices (*Penney, Palmer and Cannon v East Kent HA*[45]), or in the drug treatment available for a medical condition (*Bellarby v Worthing and Southlands Hosp NHS Trust*[46]), or in a hospital's procedures for managing staff (*Bull v Devon AHA*).

The degree of speculation may be just too great for a court, given the gaps in evidence, to find that breach occurred. That is a direct consequence of the difficulty in reconstructing the evidence as to what happened on a fateful day. As the court stated in *Leggett v Norfolk, Suffolk and Cambridgeshire Strategic HA*: '[i]t is ... my sad conclusion that the evidence of what happened on 19 March 1990 to cause kernicterus contains so many gaps, and is now so difficult to reconstruct with confidence, and the degree of speculation has become so great, that I am quite unable to find that there was, on the balance of probabilities, a lack of reasonable care [by doctor D]'[47]. There is also the temptation to adduce evidence, of what competent practice amounted to, from secondary literature published and/or available at some point

---

[37] (QB, 20 Dec 1995).   [38] Per the Limitation Act 1980, s 38(2).

[39] [2004] EWHC 1198 (QB). See too: *Mirza v Birmingham HA* (QB, 31 Jul 2001).

[40] [2003] EWHC 437 (QB).

[41] (1989) 22 BMLR 79 (CA) 116 (Mustill LJ). (The trial judge Tucker J described the 17-year gap there as 'deplorable'.)

[42] [2004] EWHC 1198 (QB) [2]–[3].   [43] [2005] EWCA Civ 1466, [9].

[44] [1998] EWCA Civ 596.   [45] (2000) 55 BMLR 63 (CA) [22].

[46] [2005] EWHC 2089 (QB) [106] (advances in available drugs had occurred since the alleged negligence in 1999).

[47] [2006] EWHC 1238 (QB) [114].

after the alleged negligence occurred, which must be sternly resisted. The court noted in *French v Thames Valley Strategic HA* that, '[i]n determining the state of medical knowledge and practice in 1991, both parties, but in particular [C], referred to and sought to rely on literature significantly later than 1991 ... The use of such literature significantly increases the risk of inappropriate hindsight ... where the conflicts between the experts should be resolved by reference to the literature, I have relied on that which is the most contemporary to [C's] delivery'.[48]

Ruling out 'inevitable accidents'

§7.7   Inevitable accidents occur where a reasonable D could not have taken any precautionary steps to avoid the risk of injury to C; and hence, these accidents cannot constitute negligence.

What it means

An inevitable accident is one which D could not avoid by any reasonable measures (per *The Merchant Prince*[49]). The doctrine has been difficult to prove, in reality. The cases in which D has sought to plead this include the following circumstances:

i.   a natural external event, constituting an Act of God (per *Baldwin v Foy*,[50] due to a hailstorm – but no inevitable accident was proven);

ii. an unexpected medical condition suffered by D, which brought about the injury to C.

> In *Stotardt v Selkent Bus Co*,[51] Michelle Stotardt, C, was seriously injured when a single-decker bus owned by Selkent, D, drove into shop premises in Eltham. The bus stopped at traffic lights, then turned into a road and crossed onto the southbound carriageway, struck a car, demolished three bollards on the pavement, and ended up ploughing into the shop where C was trapped between the bus and the shop wall. The bus driver, Mr Benjamin, claimed that he had post-traumatic amnesia following a blow to the head in the crash, and only recalled what happened when he heard people shouting at him after the collision. **Held:** no inevitable accident proven. MRI scans showed no brain abnormalities; and passengers stated that D's driver was perfectly conscious (and swearing) whilst driving on the wrong side of the road.

iii. a series of circumstances so unexpected that D could not have avoided the outcome (i.e., the harm to C) by any reasonable measures, in 'agony-of-the-moment' scenarios. Provided that there were **some** precautionary measures that D could have undertaken (e.g., changing lanes to avoid a collision, per *Whitehead v Bruce*[52]), then an inevitable accident will be ruled out, as a matter of law. However, even so, C may fail to prove negligence, precisely because a reasonable D would not have taken those precautionary steps which were at least theoretically available – that, however, is a different point, whereby the reasonable standard of care was not met. In cases of inevitable accident, there is nothing that D reasonably *could* have done to avoid C's accident.

> In *Knightley v Johns*,[53] an accident occurred in a one-way tunnel in Birmingham, when Mr Johns, D1, overturned his car, close to a tunnel entrance. Inspector Sommerville, D2, forgot to

---

[48] [2005] EWHC 459 (QB) [12].   [49] [1892] P 179 (CA) 187 (Lord Esher MR).   [50] [1997] IEHC 111.
[51] [2003] EWHC 2135 (QB).   [52] [2013] EWCA Civ 229, [32].   [53] [1982] 1 WLR 349 (CA) 367–68.

close the tunnel immediately, and hence, instructed PC Knightley, C, to ride his motor-cycle the wrong way down the tunnel to close it. C collided with Mr Cotton's, D3's, oncoming car, which Mr Cotton was driving in the correct manner, and C suffered serious injuries. C sued Mr Cotton in negligence, as well as Inspector Sommerville, for instructing him to ride the wrong way, and he sued Mr Johns, because it was his negligent driving in the tunnel 'which was the cause of all the trouble'. **Held:** an inevitable accident proven so that Mr Cotton, D3, was not negligent, for there was nothing that he could reasonably have done to avoid the accident with PC Knightley, riding the wrong way down a one-way tunnel. In *Arnot v Sprake*,[54] Lindsey Arnot, C, was riding his motorcycle in Countryman Lane, a small unclassified rural road in Sussex, when he rounded a bend at 45 mph and collided with a crop sprayer pulling a trailer, driven by D. C suffered very severe injuries. **Held:** no inevitable accident proven. D could have taken a number of precautionary steps, *viz*: stopped at the give way sign at the junction; left his vehicle with its hazard warning lights on and walked up the road and placed a red-coloured warning triangle in the road; switched on the flashing light on his cab; sounded the horn on his vehicle; and flashed the headlights of the vehicle as it pulled out of the junction. (However, D did not need to take any of these steps; he had met the standard of reasonable driving; the sole cause of this accident was C's taking the bend too fast.)

Burden of proof

In *The Merchant Prince*,[55] it was held that, if D was claiming that what happened was an inevitable accident, then D had to show that the accident was inevitable, such that the result (i.e., the accident) could not have been avoided. That is, the burden of proof shifted to D to prove that he was not negligent, on the balance of probabilities.

This shift was confirmed, more recently, in *Stotardt v Selkent Bus Co*, where Brown J noted that it was 'common ground' between C and D that it was for D to displace negligence, and to show on the balance of probabilities that the accident was caused without fault on the part of D.[56]

Potential dual bases of liability: vicarious liability and systemic breach

§7.8 D may be liable to C for direct wrongdoing because of some systemic fault on D's part. Direct liability arises where D owes a personal, non-delegable duty of care to C which D breaches. Additionally, where D's employee injures C, then D may be vicariously liable to C for that wrongdoing. Claims by C against D for vicarious liability and for systemic negligence may be brought concurrently, notwithstanding that the bases for the claims are entirely different.

The distinction

Where C is injured because of some act or omission by D's employee, then D may be vicariously liable to C for that employee's wrongdoing, if the employee's tort was committed in the course of his employment with D. That type of claim entails no corporate failure on D's part, but is a form of strict liability. By contrast, 'systemic negligence' (also called an 'institutional

---

[54] [2001] EWCA Civ 341.   [55] (1892) P 179 (CA) 189–90 (Fry LJ).   [56] [2003] EWHC 2135 (QB) [5].

duty of care', and a 'non-delegable duty' on D's part) means that D failed to have in place management and operational procedures that would reasonably have prevented the injury to C.

This dual basis of liability may be evident where C is *an employee of D*, and is injured in the workplace by a work colleague – as discussed in 'Employers' liability' (an online chapter), employee C may sue his employer both for vicarious liability, and for systemic negligence. This dual basis of liability is reflected more broadly too, where C is **not** an employee injured in the workplace, but an 'outsider' who is injured by D's systemic wrongdoing, and/or by D's employee. Vicarious liability is discussed in detail in Chapter 18. This section deals only with the systemic negligence allegation.

It was noted, in *EL v Children's Socy*,[57] that systemic negligence can entail a much more extensive inquiry than vicarious liability, because it will be the entire systems and organisation which will be under scrutiny. By contrast, vicarious liability for an employee's alleged wrongdoings (e.g., his sexual assaults against C), rather than for systemic negligence in failing to prevent them, will probably involve 'narrower factual disputes' (per *AB v Nugent Care Socy*[58] and *A v Hoare*[59]); and be 'generally more straightforward' (per *NXS v Camden LBC*[60]), rendering vicarious liability easier to prove.

One advantage of systemic negligence (for C) is that an extension to the 3-year limitation period that would apply to systemic negligence claims for personal injuries is possible, under s 11 of the Limitation Act 1980; whereas claims for personal injuries in respect of *deliberate conduct* by an employee are not subject to an extendable limitation period under s 11, but rather, are subject to a non-extendable 6-year limitation period, which can rule out C's claim altogether (per *KR v Bryn Alyn Community (Holdings) Ltd*).[61]

Systemic negligence for medical wrongdoing

A claim of systemic negligence by a patient against the owner/operator of the hospital at which the patient was treated was raised in a line of English cases more than half a century ago, but the authorities were 'weak', in that the judgments were minority opinions in appellate courts. In the modern era, the claim is more viably asserted, but frequently without success.

In *Cassidy v Ministry of Health*,[62] the Court of Appeal unanimously found in favour of the patient – but whilst the majority relied upon vicarious liability, Denning LJ based his view on the proposition that 'the hospital authorities are themselves under a duty to use care in treating the patient'. A year later, in *Jones v Manchester Corp*,[63] Denning LJ followed his earlier decision and held a hospital board *directly* responsible for a man's death under anaesthetic (the other two members of the Court of Appeal again did not support this view). Two years later, in *Roe v Minister of Health*,[64] again one member of the Court of Appeal (Morris LJ) was prepared to at least find a direct breach on the part of the hospital, but none was proven:

---

[57] [2012] EWHC 365 (QB) [72].   [58] [2009] EWCA Civ 827, [2010] 1 WLR 516, [18].
[59] [2008] AC 844 (HL) [85].   [60] [2009] EWHC 1786 (QB) [191]. For the same observation: *Raggett v Soc of Jesus Trust 1929 for Roman Catholic Purposes* [2009] EWHC 909 (QB) [121].
[61] [2003] EWCA Civ 85, [2003] QB 1441, [108].   [62] [1951] 2 KB 343 (CA) 362 (Denning LJ).
[63] [1952] 2 All ER 125 (CA) 133.   [64] [1954] 2 QB 66 (CA) 90.

a hospital might have undertaken to provide all the necessary facilities and equipment for the operation, and the obligation of nursing, and also the obligation of anaesthetizing a patient for his operation. The question ... is whether the hospital undertook these obligations. In my judgment, they did.

The Irish High Court noted, in *Byrne v Ryan*, that these views about a hospital's direct liability were 'somewhat ahead of their time'.[65]

Since then, however, there have been several English medico-legal cases in which the *possibility* of systemic negligence, on the part of a governing Health Authority in conducting a hospital, has been judicially recognised. For example, in *A (a child) v MOD*: '[t]hose responsible for the operation of a hospital offer a medical service to those whom they accept for treatment ... this acceptance for treatment carries with it personal positive duties to the patient which cannot be discharged by delegation ... [including a] duty to use reasonable care to ensure that the hospital staff, facilities and organisation provided are those appropriate to provide a safe and satisfactory medical service for the patient. This is an organisational duty';[66] in *X (Minors) v Bedfordshire CC*: 'those conducting a hospital are under a direct duty of care to those admitted as patients to the hospital';[67] and in *Robertson v Nottingham HA*, a hospital 'has a non-delegable duty to provide a proper system of care, just as much as it has a duty to engage competent staff and proper and safe equipment'.[68]

Nevertheless, the allegation has been rarely upheld. The following Table provides a sample of illustrative cases in the medical context (where C is the patient):

The systemic breach alleged	An illustrative case	The result
Failing to provide adequate staff for posts in a hospital – if doctors did not have sufficient skill or experience to provide the special care demanded by particular patients, then the Health Authority would be at fault in appointing them to the posts which they held	In *Wilsher v Essex AHA*,[a] this claim was not put by C who was a very premature baby being treated in the Special Care Baby Unit, but it was canvassed as a potential allegation of negligence, *against the hospital itself*, by all three members of the Court of Appeal	No breach proven. However, in *Knight v Home Office*,[b] the court said that *Wilsher* 'clearly contemplated that a hospital authority could be held liable if it failed to provide staff of sufficient skill and experience to give the treatment offered at the hospital'
Failing to provide adequate staff training and supervision, particularly for junior doctors	In *Jones v Manchester Corp*,[c] the doctor employee administered anaesthetic to C, who subsequently died	This systemic breach was upheld by Denning LJ

[a] [1987] QB 730 (CA) 747 (Mustill LJ), 778 Browne-Wilkinson V-C), 775 (Glidewell LJ).
[b] [1990] 3 All ER 237 (QB) 242.
[c] [1952] 2 All ER 125 (CA) 133.

[65] [2007] IEHC 207 [no pp].   [66] [2004] EWCA Civ 641, [32].
[67] [1995] UKHL 9, [15].   [68] (1996) 33 BMLR 178 (CA) 197.

The systemic breach alleged	An illustrative case	The result
Failing to provide adequate staffing levels, or to implement a reasonably safe system for summonsing staff in the event of hospital emergencies	This was the allegation of systemic breach in *Garcia v St Mary's NHS Trust*,[d] where C had heart by-pass surgery, and a post-operative bleed several hours later led to brain damage. C claimed that the hospital had a 'crash call' procedure which was deficient in that, even with the speediest arrival from the doctor's home to the operating theatre (here, the response time was 31 minutes), that would *condemn* C to significant brain damage	These systemic negligence allegations failed
The arrangements for the hospital set-up – e.g., if a 'split-site' hospital is constructed over two campuses, and the hospital failed to ensure that an adequate or efficient system was in place for summonsing doctors from one site to the other	In *Bull v Devon AHA*,[e] a mother gave birth at one campus of the hospital, where the second twin, C, was not delivered until 68 minutes after the first twin and as a result suffered brain damage from hypoxia. Urgent attempts were made to summon the registrar from the other campus between births, but he could not be found, and the pager went unanswered	Direct liability on the part of the Health Authority succeeded. This 1970 system was judicially described as 'precarious', 'unreliable and essentially unsatisfactory', 'operating on a knife-edge'
Failing to establish adequate communications systems between hospital staff, e.g., in between change of shifts	In *Robertson v Nottingham HA*,[f] C claimed that the hospital failed to have sufficient systems in place for reliable communication of information between medical staff working on different shifts and, more generally, between medical staff and nursing staff	Systemic negligence proven

[d] [2006] EWHC 2314 (QB) [82], [95].
[e] (1989) 22 BMLR 79 (CA).
[f] (1996) 33 BMLR 178 (CA) 198 (also known as: *Re R (A minor) (No 2)*).

The systemic breach alleged	An illustrative case	The result
Failing to have adequately sufficient or timely assessment procedures for patients in place, or to provide adequate and sufficient opening hours during which specialist medical equipment was available	In *Hardaker v Newcastle HA*,[g] C alleged that the hospital was required to pre-assess a diver for numbness, paralysis, and other symptoms of 'the bends', before invoking treatment in a decompression chamber, which method of pre-assessment meant an in-built delay to treatment; and that the decompression chamber at Newcastle University, next to the hospital, should not have been closed on the weekends, meaning that C had to be transferred to the police diving school's decompression chamber in Sunderland	These allegations of systemic negligence failed

[g] QB, 15 Jun 2001.

Hence, systemic negligence allegations against health authorities are certainly permitted, but breach of that non-delegable duty to the patient has been difficult to prove.

TESTING PRECAUTIONARY STEPS AGAINST THE QUADRANT

§7.9 When assessing breach, a court will consider what precautionary steps D *could* have taken, in order to avoid the injury or harm to C. Whether a reasonable D *ought* to have taken those precautionary steps depends upon an analysis of: the magnitude of the risk; the gravity of the injury, should the risk manifest; the cost of taking those precautionary steps; and the social or economic utility which could be compromised if the precautionary steps were taken ('the *Bolton v Stone* factors'). Although every possible precautionary step, if taken, would have prevented C's injury, the purpose of the law of negligence is not to obliterate all risk of injury arising from D's activities, or to guard C against obvious risks.

Successful negligence suits can only arise in circumstances where some precautionary step was possible. Unavoidable or inevitable accidents cannot, by definition, be instances of negligence, as no reasonable D could have acted differently in avoiding them. Agony-of-the-moment, or emergency, scenarios (as described in Chapter 6) will result in a suppressed standard of care (as in, e.g., *Wooldridge v Sumner*[69]) – but, in addition, it will be difficult to point to a reasonable D as having done anything differently.

The list of precautionary steps represents the acts or omissions which C hopes to prove as being D's breaches. They represent what D *could* have done to avoid the accident. However, whether breach succeeds depends upon whether a reasonable D *should* have undertaken them, which is quite a different question.

[69] [1963] 2 QB 43 (CA).

Take the example of C, who enters an occupier's premises, and suffers some injury due to the state of the premises (per Chapter 12). The precautionary steps commonly alleged in these cases include:

- erecting further and better warning signs;
- removing the danger altogether by taking down the structure which posed the danger to C;
- concealing the source of the danger with a cover of some description;
- making it more difficult (or impossible) for C to gain access, by erecting more physical barriers;
- refusing C permission to enter the premises at all;
- organising security patrols of the premises; or
- providing better education about the dangers to a class of persons of whom C was one.

If every possible precautionary step were taken, then the injury would not have happened. However, as remarked in *Scout Assn v Barnes*,[70] 'it is not the function of the law of tort to eliminate every iota of risk' (per Jackson LJ) and that 'the law of tort must not interfere with activities just because they carry some risk' (per Smith LJ). Unfortunately accidents happen, for which no compensation may be awarded, if the quadrant of factors, discussed in the following section, does not point towards breach.

The quadrant of factors

The four factors derived from the seminal House of Lords' decision in *Bolton v Stone*,[71] and identified in the Table below, govern the breach assessment. This is the primary test of breach.

Quadrant of factors re breach

Magnitude/probability:	Gravity/seriousness:
What was the probability of injury or harm being suffered by C, if the precautionary steps were not taken? The higher the probability, the more arguable it is that a reasonable D would have taken one or more of those steps, and vice versa.	What was the gravity of the injury or harm that could have occurred to C, if the precautionary steps were not taken? The graver the potential injury or harm, the more arguable it is that a reasonable D would have taken one or more of those steps, and vice versa.
The relevant probability relates to that particular injury suffered by C and the way that it happened, and not of accidents generally (per Uren v Corporate Leisure (UK) Ltd[a]). Historical data of accidents can be useful in establishing whether the probability was sufficient to warrant the precautionary steps being taken (per Tomlinson v Congleton BC[b]).	*The gravity of injury has been assessed in various ways: (1) by reference to historical evidence of injuries suffered in similar cases (per Bolton v Stone[c]); (2) by reference to the actual harm suffered by C (per Stimpson v Wolverhampton MBC[d]); and (3) by reference to the probability of potential serious harm to C (per Abouzaid v Mothercare (UK) Ltd[e]). The gravity of injury may be quite differently-assessed, under each of these.*

[a] [2011] EWCA Civ 66, [76], and later: [2013] EWHC 353 (QB).
[b] [2004] 1 AC 46 (HL) [22]–[25].
[c] [1951] AC 850 (HL) 862.
[d] CA, 22 May 1990.
[e] [2000] EWCA Civ 348, [33].

---

[70] [2010] EWCA Civ 1476, [34] and [49], respectively.   [71] [1951] AC 850 (HL).

Cost and practicability of precautionary steps:	Social (including economic) value/utility considerations:
What were the costs, difficulties and in-convenience to D of taking those pre-cautionary steps? The cheaper the cost and less burdensome the task, the more arguable it is that a reasonable D would have taken one or more of those steps, and vice versa.	To what extent (if any) would taking those precau-tionary steps have affected the social utility of D's activities for third parties, other than C? If the social value would not have been affected, or if no third parties would be inconvenienced by those precautionary steps being adopted, then it is arguable that a reasonable D would have taken those precautionary steps, and vice versa.
The costs may be of three types: (1) the monetary expense necessary to under-take the precautionary steps (per Over-seas Tankship (UK) Ltd v The Miller Steamship Co Ltd[f]); *(2) the time required to undertake those steps; and (3) the resources, facilities, and staffing avail-able to undertake the steps (per* Walker v Northumberland CC[g]).	*The social utility of D's activities can be assessed in a variety of ways: (1) re the recreational enjoy-ment which third parties derive from sporting en-deavours, organised games, etc (per* Tomlinson); *(2) re the benefits of the activity to the young, or to some other deserving sector of society (per* Wilkin-Shaw v Fuller[h]); *(3) re the economic ben-efit to the community (per* Latimer v AEC[i]); *and (4) re the value which emergency services provide to society (per* Watt v Hertfordshire CC[j]).

[f] [1967] 1 AC 617 (PC, on appeal from Australia) 642 (Lord Reid).
[g] [1995] 1 All ER 737, [1995] PIQR P521 (CA) P534.
[h] [2012] EWHC 1777 (QB) [98], aff'd: [2013] EWCA Civ 410.
[i] [1953] AC 643 (HL).
[j] [1954] 1 WLR 835 (CA).

The most notable subsequent application of the *Bolton v Stone* quadrant occurred in the tragic case of *Tomlinson v Congleton BC*,[72] but the four factors have been explicitly referred to in a number of other cases too. For example, in *Wilkin-Shaw v Fuller*,[73] the first-instance court re-ferred to the 'balance of risk, gravity of injury, costs and social value'; while recently, when the Scottish Outer House was discussing the English case law on breach, it summarised the balanc-ing act in these terms: 'the likelihood of injury, the seriousness of the injury which might occur, and the social value of the activity giving rise to the risk, and cost of preventative measures must all be balanced' (per *French v Strathclyde Fire Board*[74]).

It is a genuine 'balancing exercise' (per Jackson LJ in *Scouts Assn v Barnes*[75]), because rarely will all the factors either point towards breach, or refute it. It will depend upon all the facts and circumstances. The Court of Appeal spoke for all such cases by stating, in *Allen v Stoke-on-Trent CC*,[76] that '[t]here is clearly a balance which has to be struck between placing burdens on [Ds] which they find it impracticable to fulfil, and allowing [Ds] to ignore their responsibilities'.

[72] [2003] UKHL 47, [2004] 1 AC 46 (HL).
[73] [2012] EWHC 1777 (QB) [44] (Owen J), aff'd: [2013] EWCA Civ 410.
[74] [2013] ScotCS 3 (CSOH) [43].   [75] [2010] EWCA Civ 1476, [30].   [76] CA, 14 Feb 1989, Woolf LJ.

After all, the cost of taking a precaution may be very small – but so may the risk be, and a reasonable person may validly decide to take no steps to eliminate that risk at all (per *Gabriel v Kirklees MC*[77]). The tension among the quadrants was well-illustrated in *Tomlinson*:

> In *Tomlinson v Congleton BC*,[78] Mr Tomlinson, C, injured himself when he went swimming in a lake in a disused quarry in a country park owned and occupied by two local authorities, D. Swimming in the lake was prohibited, and there were prominent notices stating, 'Dangerous water: no swimming'. D was aware that the notices were frequently ignored, that they did not prevent visitors to the park from entering the water, and that several accidents had resulted from swimming in the lake. T stood in shallow water (up to his knees), and from that standing position, dived and struck his head on the sandy bottom, breaking his neck. **Held (by the CA, upheld by HL):** no breach proven. A reasonable occupier would not have done anything different to avoid the risk of injury to C.

The quadrant pulled in entirely different directions. The gravity of harm, should it occur, was immense (death by drowning, or very serious personal injury), whereas the risk of injury was low; some of precautionary steps would have been expensive to implement (at least for these local authorities); and most crucially of all, the social value derived from using the beaches of the lake for purposes of sunbathing, paddling, playing with children ('the harmless recreation of responsible parents and children with buckets and spades on the beaches', said Lord Hoffmann) would have to be prohibited if the beaches were planted up with bushes and shrubs to prevent access to the lake, i.e., 'there is an important question of freedom at stake', in that it was unjust for the 'harmless' activities of responsible third parties to be prohibited by some so-called duty on the occupier's part to safeguard 'irresponsible visitors against dangers which are perfectly obvious'.[79] Indeed, *Tomlinson* (and other cases like it before[80] and since[81]) reflect the modern reality that D does not have to show unreasonably risk-averse behaviour to avoid a finding of breach. Lord Hobhouse put it this way:

> Does the law require that all trees be cut down because some youths may climb them and fall? Does the law require the coastline and other beauty spots to be lined with warning notices? Does the law require that attractive waterside picnic spots be destroyed because of a few foolhardy individuals who choose to ignore warning notices and indulge in activities dangerous only to themselves? The answer to all these questions is, of course, no. But this is the road down which your Lordships, like other courts before, have been invited to travel ... In truth, the arguments for C have involved an attack upon the liberties of the citizen which should not be countenanced. They attack the liberty of the individual to engage in dangerous, but otherwise harmless, pastimes at his own risk, and the liberty of citizens as a whole fully to enjoy the variety and quality of the landscape of this country.

Lord Scott was equally as forceful:

> why should the council be discouraged, by the law of tort, from providing facilities for young men and young women to enjoy themselves in this way? Of course there is some risk of accidents arising

---

[77] [2004] EWCA Civ 345, [25].

[78] [2003] UKHL 47, [2004] 1 AC 46 (HL) [39]–[43] (Lord Hoffmann), [81] (Lord Hobhouse), [94] (Lord Scott), and affirming: [2002] EWCA Civ 309, [2003] 2 WLR 1120.

[79] *ibid*, [27], [46].

[80] e.g., *Simkiss v Rhondda BC* (CA, 22 Feb 1983) ('If the exercise of reasonable care required [D] to fence off this bluff, ... it would also require them to fence every natural hazard in the Rhondda Valley adjacent to housing estates').

[81] e.g., *Evans v Kosmar Villa Holidays* [2007] EWCA Civ 1003, [2008] 1 WLR 297, [41].

out of the joie-de-vivre of the young. But that is no reason for imposing a grey and dull safety regime on everyone.

Indeed, *Tomlinson*, and other cases like it, illustrate that a reasonable D does **not** need to take precautionary steps against obvious risks.

In *Vaughan v MOD*,[82] Spencer Vaughan, C, 22, was a member of the Royal Marines. He participated in a week's Adventure Training Exercise in Gran Canaria, as an opportunity to crew a yacht during off-shore sailing exercises. During a lunch break, C made a shallow dive into the sea, when he was in waist-deep water, hit his head on a concealed object beneath the surface of the water (which may, or may not, have been a sandbank), and suffered tetraplegia. There had been no recorded incident of any injury caused to any Marine by his diving into shallow water, over a 5-year period prior to this accident. **Held:** breach failed against D. Reasonable foreseeability of the accident was proven; but the risk of diving into shallow water was so obvious that D did not need to warn C of those dangers.

The following Table has regard to instructive negligence cases[83] which show the various factors straining in different directions – with those factors which most significantly contributed to the outcome bolded:

Breach: Application of the quadrant test

Case	Nutshell facts	Precautionary steps?	Probability cost	Gravity compromise	Held:
Bolton v Stone (1951)	cricket ball hit Miss Stone, C – it was hit 100 yds, and cleared the fence of cricket club – a similar 'six' had been hit approx. only 6 times in 30 yrs	– erect a higher fence – close cricket club down altogether, to protect surrounding houses	Very low Very costly	Medium to high **Highly compromised**	No breach
Tomlinson v Congleton BC (2003)	C broke his neck in a swimming accident at a lake – disregarded signage forbidding swimming	– plant up beaches with prickly bushes, to stop access – more warning signs – employing full-time lifeguards	Very low Variable, from cheap to very expensive	Very grave **Highly compromised**	No breach
Paris v Stepney BC (1951)	C, a partially-sighted mechanic employee, was hammering at a wheel at D's garage – a chip of metal flew up and entered his good eye, blinding him	– supply goggles to mechanics during work tasks	Low Very cheap	**Very high** –	Breach

---

[82] [2015] EWHC 1404 (QB) [33].

[83] The citations for these cases are located elsewhere in the chapter, and will not be reproduced here.

Case	Nutshell facts	Precautionary steps?	Probability	Gravity	Held:
			cost	compromise	
Latimer v AEC Ltd (1953)	employee C slipped on factory floor during night-shift – factory engaged in post-war construction work – floor flooded during heavy rain storm – some oily coolant was spread from its usual channel to coat the floor – sawdust had been spread, but some areas left untreated	– close down factory, and send night-shift home, until floor was properly cleaned	Very low (no previous accidents)	Medium	No breach
		– spread more sawdust than had been spread, to cover it properly	Varied between low cost and very heavy cost	Very highly compromised (D doing vital post-war manufacturing work)	
Watt v Hertfordshire CC (1954)	car accident in which a woman was pinned under the car; fire brigade was asked to respond – a lifting jack in fire brigade vehicle shifted when braking suddenly, 100 m from the depot – it hit one fireman, C, injuring him	– wait until the correct vehicle arrived back at depot, to which the jack could be fitted properly	Medium to high	Medium to high	No breach
		– further efforts made to restrain jack used, before the vehicle set out to save the victim	Cheap (to fire brigade)	Very highly compromised (when life and limb are at stake, more risk justified)	
Stimpson v Wolverhampton MBC (1990)	C, a visitor to a public park, was hit in the mouth by a golf ball while walking through the park – golf was prohibited in the park	– instruct Council staff to admonish offenders – strictly enforce on-the-spot fines – erect further and more visible notices prohibiting golf	High (people regularly played golf in the park)	Previous injuries had been slight	Breach
			Relatively cheap	–	
Cunningham v Reading FC (1992)	C, an off-duty policeman was injured when football hooligans threw concrete missiles from the delapidated terraces	– repair the concrete on the terraces – fix major cracking and portions of the crumbling concrete	Very high	Very serious	Breach
			Cheap (<£3,000)	–	

Case	Nutshell facts	Precautionary steps?	Probability cost	Gravity compromise	Held:
Collins-Williamson v Silverlink Train Services (2009)[a]	C, a passenger, was mucking around on a train platform late at night, drunk – as train left platform, C was too close, fell between train and platform, and his leg was partially amputated	– employ more staff to see trains off, especially late night trains – CCTV at stations, which are constantly supervised	Extremely low Very costly	Very high Some compromise	No systemic breach
Uren v Corporate Leisure (UK) Ltd (2011, 2013)	C participated in a 'Health and Fun Day' at MOD, his employer – including games of a kind played in, 'It's a Knockout' – C dived headfirst into a pool, and was rendered a tetraplegic, at 21	– give instructions to avoid a head-first entry into the pool, which would have still preserved the 'fun' for the participants – undertake a risk assessment associated with headfirst entry into the pool, and take reasonable steps to eradicate the risks of serious injury	High (trial judge had held, in error, that the risk of spinal injury was low) Very cheap	Very high High – 'some social value' in the game and in the whole afternoon	No breach – but remitted back for trial because of error; on retrial, breach proven

[a] [2009] EWCA Civ 850.

Clearly, the outcome of these cases will sometimes turn on very finely-balanced, intuitive, and difficult-to-predict judgments by the court.

The public employee's dilemma

Undoubtedly, the assessment of *Bolton v Stone* factors sometimes produces 'winners' and 'losers', which may seem to be unjust. For example, private sector employees are arguably better off in seeking to prove breach than their counterparts in emergency services, if injured in the course of their employment – because their employer is predominantly engaged in profit-making activities, and hence, the fourth quadrant is not significant (or as significant) in the balancing exercise, as it is when the employer is an emergency services provider. In other words, private sector employers are not engaged in 'social utility' of the sort that emergency service providers are, and hence, the private employee has a better chance of proving negligence.

In *Sussex Ambulance NHS Trust v King*,[84] Buxton LJ suggested that the reasoning in *Watt v Hertfordshire CC*, which gives rise to this result, should be revisited on appeal, for several reasons:

i. if employees of emergency service providers were exposed to the risk of injury, and were less well-protected by the law of negligence, then that would 'raise considerations of distributive justice ... [because] if employees required to run risks to advance private interests can recover if doing their employer's bidding leads to injury, so employees required to run risks to advance public interests should, by the same token, be able to recover';

ii. in *Ogwo v Taylor*,[85] the House of Lords rejected the 'fireman's rule', under which a public employee could not complain in negligence if that employee is injured whilst engaged in the very hazard (e.g., fire-fighting) that he was employed to deal with. *Watt* is difficult to reconcile with 'the spirit of *Ogwo v Taylor*';

iii. the public interest of emergency service providers helping the community that they serve is treated, under *Watt*, as a matter to do with breach; whereas it should properly be dealt with under the third limb of the *Caparo v Dickman* test, i.e., that it must be fair, just and reasonable to impose a duty of care.

However, to date, the decision and reasoning in *Watt* remains good law, despite these misgivings. As an aside, further discussion of the requirement of employer D to undertake risk assessment of the dangers posed to employee C in the workplace, especially in light of *Uren v Corporate Leisure (UK) Ltd*,[86] is contained in 'Employers' liability' (an online chapter).

The impact of the Compensation Act 2006, s 1

§7.10   According to s 1 of the Compensation Act 2006, the court must take into account whether D was conducting a 'desirable activity', when assessing whether D ought to have taken a precautionary step. However, judicial commentary since the enactment of s 1 suggests that the section adds nothing to the common law.

The purpose of the provision

The Compensation Act 2006, s 1,[87] is a curious provision. It states as follows:

---

s 1 Deterrent effect of potential liability

A court considering a claim in negligence ... may, in determining whether the defendant should have taken particular steps to meet a standard of care (whether by taking precautions against a risk or otherwise), have regard to whether a requirement to take those steps might:

(a) prevent a desirable activity from being undertaken at all, to a particular extent or in a particular way, or

(b) discourage persons from undertaking functions in connection with a desirable activity.

---

[84] [2002] EWCA Civ 953, [2002] ICR 1413, especially [47].   [85] [1988] 1 AC 431 (HL) 438–39 (Lord Bridge).
[86] [2013] EWHC 353 (QB).   [87] In force on date of Royal assent, 25 Jul 2006.

The main concern about this provision is – why enact it at all? The fact that 'desirable activities' by D or by others similarly-situated may be compromised was already 'part and parcel' of the fourth *Bolton v Stone* quadrant (especially in light of the decision in *Tomlinson v Congleton BC*). Perhaps some cases did not always emphasise that fourth quadrant – e.g., in *Stimpson v Wolverhampton MBC*,[88] the Court of Appeal noted that the duty on D 'has to be considered in the light of the frequency and seriousness of the risk in the context of the burden imposed on [D], when considering the measures which should be taken to reduce or prevent the incidence and frequency of the risk', with no reference to the social values that could be compromised – but that fourth quadrant certainly has plenty of judicial authority to support it.

The drafters of the Explanatory Memorandum[89] professed to state that the section did not amend the common law at all, but merely sought to 'clarify' it, and that s 1:

i.   had a community education aspect, i.e., it was 'intended to contribute to improving awareness of this aspect of the law; providing reassurance to the people and organisations who are concerned about possible litigation; and to ensuring that normal activities are not prevented because of the fear of litigation and excessively risk-averse behaviour';

ii. was 'not concerned with, and does not alter, the standard of care ... It is solely concerned with the court's assessment of what constitutes reasonable care in the case before it'; and

iii. provides that a court may, when assessing precautionary steps, 'have regard to whether a requirement to take those steps might prevent an activity which is desirable from taking place (either at all, to a particular extent, or in a particular way), or might discourage persons from undertaking functions in connection with the activity'.

As the Explanatory Notes suggest,[90] taking account of D's desirable activities, when determining whether D complied with the 'standard of reasonable care', was **already** a long-standing part of English law. Indeed, many cases (apart from *Tomlinson*) illustrate that proposition, where D's conduct **was** held to be reasonable – in part because of the socially useful activity which D performed. In none of the following was breach proven:

In *Bolton v Stone*,[91] the cricket club, D, was not negligent in permitting a cricket ball to be hit out of the ground into C's adjoining property, because any further preventative measures could have meant the socially useful activity of cricket ceased at the ground. In *King v Sussex Ambulance NHS Trust*,[92] Anthony King, C, an ambulance officer, suffered injuries when a patient-and-stretcher chair slipped onto him as he and his colleague were negotiating a narrow winding stairway in the patient's cottage. His colleague had to let go of the chair because of sudden pain, and the whole load fell onto C, causing him injury. However, the ambulance service, D, did not have a choice but to respond to the patient's urgent needs. D had limited resources, and there was no other equipment that D could have given its employees to manage patients in houses; and calling upon the fire brigade to do the job for them was not an option. There was simply no alternative equipment for speedy use in this sort of situation, given the 'reasonable despatch' that care for the patient entailed. In *Daborn v Bath Tramways*,[93] D, the driver of a left-hand-drive ambulance during war-time, collided with C

---

[88] CA, 22 May 1990 (Sir Roualeyn Cumming-Bruce).

[89] See: cl 10–13, especially, 'Background and useful information' by the Dept for Constitutional Affairs, available at: <http://www.dca.gov.uk/legist/compensation.htm#c>.

[90] Cl 13 (s 1 'reflects the existing law and approach of the courts as expressed in recent judgments of the higher courts').

[91] [1951] AC 850 (HL).   [92] [2002] EWCA Civ 953, (2002) 68 BMLR 177.   [93] [1946] 2 All ER 333 (CA).

whilst turning, not being used to the left-hand-drive. Driving such a vehicle was a socially necessary duty to assist the injured during a national emergency.

Hence, the social value of D's activities has **long** been a factor in determining what amounts to taking reasonable care, so as to attain the legal standard of care. However, it was felt to be beneficial to non-lawyers, especially, to restate the law in s 1 (assuming that non-lawyers devote time to reading such legislation!).

Political opinion was, however, less-than-convinced about s 1's utility.

The political corner

The House of Commons Select Committee on Constitutional Affairs:[a] the Committee disagreed with s 1, noting that 'it would undoubtedly, at least in the short term, lead to an increase in costly satellite litigation to define what is a "desirable activity". Moreover, the wide breadth of that term (or any alternative, such as "social value" or "utility") ... is not to change the law, [D] would likely ... seek to rely upon [s 1, to obtain] a shield against liability. This could result in possibly inconsistent decisions'.

[a] *Compensation Culture: Third Report* (HC 754-I) (1 Mar 2006) [68].

Judicial consideration

Courts have not been enamoured of s 1 since its introduction either.

In *Wilkin-Shaw v Fuller*,[94] the court stated that, 'it does not seem to me that section 1 adds anything to the common law. Some risk is inherent in many socially desirable activities ... the question in any individual case is whether the social benefit of any activity is such that the degree of risk that it entails is acceptable'. Indeed, Owen J disparaged its enactment, noting that s 1 'appears to have been introduced as a response to the perception of the growth of a "compensation culture". The draft bill was ... accompanied by explanatory notes that asserted that section 1 did no more than "reflect the existing law". In that case, it is somewhat difficult to see why it was felt necessary to enact it, and why, as enacted, it was couched in discretionary terms'. In *Scout Assn v Barnes*[95] too, Jackson LJ reiterated that s 1 merely 'enshrined' the common law principle that it was not negligence's function 'to stamp out socially desirable activities'. Further, in *Uren v Corporate Leisure (UK) Ltd*,[96] Smith LJ noted that it was 'common ground' that s 1 'did not add anything to the common law position ... At least since *Tomlinson*, if not before, the common law has required the court to take such matters into account'. Indeed, in the retrial in *Uren*, Foskett J seemed to question whether the provision was perhaps out-of-step with modern attitudes, noting that, 'rightly or wrongly, and despite the influence of a case such as *Tomlinson* and s 1, we live in a more "risk averse" age now than when those earlier cases were decided'.[97]

The problem is that, far from the provision not adding anything to the common law, its enactment may give **greater** weight to that 'fourth quadrant' than the common law envisaged.

---

[94] [2012] EWHC 1777 (QB) [42], [46], aff'd: [2013] EWCA Civ 410.

[95] [2010] EWCA Civ 1476, [34], citing: D Owen (ed), *The Philosophical Foundations of the Law of Tort* (Clarendon Press, 1995), ch 11.

[96] [2011] EWCA Civ 66, [13].   [97] [2013] EWHC 353 (QB) [75].

Indeed, *Scout Assn v Barnes*[98] illustrates this uncertainty at judicial level. In Jackson LJ's (dissenting) view, the social utility of scouts' training, recreation and health benefits for young people counted for sufficient, in the overall balancing exercise, to negate negligence.[99] However, the majority held that, while the scouts' game in which C was injured 'had some social value; it was a good active competitive game to keep boys occupied on long winter evenings', playing it in the dark did not add to its value but only to its excitement. Yet, it significantly increased the risk of injury to C, and the game was negligently-conducted. Clearly, Ward LJ also had some serious reservations, characteristic of many of the finely-balanced outcomes of the quadrant's application:

> Here was a big strong 13-year-old lad, well-used to rough and tumble, playing rugby with distinction for his county, ever ready to take the bumps and the bruises, ever willingly to put his body on the line for the thrill of his sport. For him, you get hurt, you get up, and you get on with it. He brought the same enthusiasm and competitive instincts to his participation in his local Scout troop. He was the least likely boy to need wrapping in cotton wool. So, is awarding him damages for an injury suffered playing the game, 'Objects in the Dark', not an example of an overprotective nanny state robbing youth of fun simply because there was some risk involved in the exercise? Is this a decision which emasculates those responsible for caring for our children and in so doing, enfeebles the children themselves? Where do you draw the line? I have found that hard to answer.[100]

The answer was (somewhat surprisingly), 'negligence'. In other cases too, the provision, whilst cited, did not save D from a finding of breach.

> In *Sutton v Syston Rugby Football Club Ltd*,[101] a rugby colt player suffered a serious knee injury when he fell and gashed his knee on the broken stub of a cricket boundary marker which (he claimed) a pitch inspection would have detected. The law did not require steps that were too difficult for ordinary coaches and match organisers to meet. 'Games of rugby are, after all, no more than games and, as such are obviously desirable activities within the meaning of s 1 of the Compensation Act 2006', but even so, 'before a game or training session, a pitch should be walked over at a reasonable walking pace by a coach or match organiser, and if that is done, that will satisfy a Club's common law duty of care in relation to such inspection'. However, ultimately causation failed. In *Reynolds v Strutt & Parker LLP*,[102] C, an employee of a real estate firm, D, suffered a very severe head injury when involved in a bike accident, during a 'team building day' organised by D. The 'reward of employees by employers in ways such as that chosen in this case is a desirable activity', but still, D committed a breach, in failing to carry out a risk assessment and communicate better about safety equipment (e.g., helmets).

Nevertheless, in other cases in which D's activities obviously carried a 'social value', there was no breach:

> In *Wilkin-Shaw v Fuller*,[103] Charlotte Shaw, 14, C, drowned whilst on a training exercise on Dartmoor, when she fell into a fast-flowing stream, and was swept away by the strong current. She had been on the Moor with 10 other children from a secondary school, training for the Ten Tors expedition. D was a teacher at the school, and was team manager responsible for the training of the children for the Ten Tors expedition. D argued that C's death was the result of a tragic accident

---

[98] [2010] EWCA Civ 1476.   [99] *ibid*, [29]–[30].   [100] *ibid*, [50].
[101] [2011] EWCA Civ 1182, [13].   [102] [2011] EWHC 2263 (Ch) [46].
[103] [2012] EWHC 1777 (QB) [134]–[135] (Owen J), and on appeal: aff'd [2013] EWCA Civ 410.

when she fell into the stream, whilst being assisted by a well-intentioned scout master unconnected with the school. **Held (trial):** no breach by D. The group was 'cold and wet', but did not appear to be 'completely exhausted', and were capable of continuing: 'some risk is inherent in many socially desirable activities. The Ten Tors event, and the training that those who participate must undergo, is a classic example … the question in any individual case is whether the social benefit of any activity is such that the degree of risk that it entails is acceptable'. **Held (on appeal):** however, in a reframed case on appeal, another teacher, Miss Timms, was held in breach for failing to be at a tor checkpoint when due, because she had overshot and got lost without adequate explanation. Ultimately, however, causation failed. In *McErlean v Rt Rev Monsignor MacAuley*,[104] C slipped on an icy pavement, whilst accompanying school children to choir practice for a forthcoming nativity play. No breach was found. The court noted that, 'practising for a nativity play or taking part in choir practice is a desirable activity', and s 1 'added nothing to the common law'. In *Hopps v Mott Macdonald Ltd*,[105] Graham Hopps, C, an engineer, was travelling in Basrah in a vehicle which crossed an improvised explosive device, and was badly injured. He claimed that the MOD should have provided armed forces with better armoured vehicles which would have provided greater protection to the occupants. No breach was proven. The court held that s 1 could apply just as much to employment activities in the theatre of war, as it could to D who provides public amenities or socially-valuable activities such as the playing of sports. Taking the precautionary step advocated by C (retaining employees at the airport until better vehicles were available) would 'prevent the desirable activity of reconstruction of a shattered infrastructure after a war in a territory occupied by HM forces, particularly when failure to expedite that work would carry with it risks to the safety of coalition forces and civilian contractors in Iraq as a whole'.

Hence, employment activities can well fall within the phrase of 'desirable activities'.

THE *BOLAM/BOLITHO* FRAMEWORK FOR BREACH ANALYSIS

§7.11   The *Bolam/Bolitho* framework establishes a two-step test by which to determine breach, *viz*, to consider: (1) whether D's act or omission was supported by a body of peer professional opinion, i.e., whether D acted in accordance with a practice accepted as proper for an ordinarily competent D by a respectable body of professional opinion ('the *Bolam* test of breach'), and (2) whether that peer professional opinion is defensible/rational/logical ('the *Bolitho* gloss'). Where both limbs of the test are met, D is not in breach.

This two-part test represents the current framework that applies to professional breach (per Beatson J in *French v Thames Valley Strategic HA*[106]).

The *Bolam* test

The test, derived from the direction to the jury given by McNair J in *Bolam v Friern Hosp Management Committee*, a case of alleged medical negligence, states:

[a doctor] is not guilty of negligence if he has acted in accordance with a practice accepted as proper by a responsible body of medical men skilled in that particular art … Putting it the other way

---

[104] [2014] NIQB 1, [12].   [105] [2009] EWHC 1881 (QB) [93].   [106] [2005] EWHC 459 (QB) [9]–[10].

round, a man is not negligent, if he is acting in accordance with such a practice, merely because there is a body of opinion who would take a contrary view.[107]

Also called the test of 'peer professional opinion', the *Bolam* test of breach requires that expert evidence be adduced by D to prove that the act or omission of D met the reasonable standard of care, and did not fall below it. The evidence is to be given by one or more of D's 'peers', who operates in the same broad field of activity.

> In *Bolam*, Mr Bolam, C, a travelling salesman, suffered from mental illness, and attended the Friern Hospital to undergo electro-convulsive therapy. When administered, the electric current passing through the brain caused convulsions. D, the treating psychiatrist, did not warn C of the risk of bodily fracture during the convulsions. During the treatment, C lay in a supine position with a pillow placed under his back, his lower jaw supported by a mouth gag, a male nurse standing at each side of the bed in case he should fall from it, but otherwise no restraints or relaxant drugs were used. During the second treatment, C's hip joints were dislocated, and his pelvis on each side was badly fractured by the head of the femur being driven through the pelvic bone. C claimed that the ECT should have been administered with relaxant drugs (which would have precluded the risk of fracture altogether) and manual restraints, and that he should have been warned of the risk of fracture (1:10,000 probability). C's expert evidence supported the use of relaxant drugs and restraints to reduce or eliminate the risk of fracture. **Held:** no breach. D's expert evidence, which prevailed, was that relaxant drugs carried considerable risks because of the difficulty in getting the dosage right and not inducing heart stoppage; and manual restraints were generally ineffective to eliminate fractures. In *Davies v Univ Hosp of North Staffordshire NHS Trust*,[108] Tracy Davies, C, had a brain tumour, and claimed that, had a scan been carried out in Jan 2001 by her treating doctor, D, the tumour would have been detected. The various diagnoses, of C's recurrent headaches and vomiting, were frontal sinusitis or migraine, with neurological problem 'unlikely'. C suffered loss of vision and other damage. (The tumour was also misdiagnosed as being malignant, which was admitted as a breach.) **Held:** no breach. D's diagnosis of sinusitis or migraine was a reasonable diagnosis, and a reasonable course of action in the circumstances in Jan 2001, and accorded with a responsible body of professional opinion.

This *Bolam* test of breach is not be confused with the *Bolam* standard of care which was addressed in Chapter 6. The two passages of McNair J's instruction to the jury address two different legal matters.

Expanding the *Bolam* test

§7.12 Although both *Bolam* and *Bolitho* were medical negligence claims, the *Bolam* test of peer professional opinion is a test of professional negligence *generally*. More controversially, the *Bolam* test of breach has been applied in the context of the non-professional D too.

The *Bolam* test represents the '*locus classicus* of the test for the standard of care required of a doctor or *any other person professing some skill or competence*' (according to Lord Browne-Wilkinson in *Bolitho v City and Hackney HA*[109]). The Table below sets out authorities that support the application of the test of breach in broader professional contexts:[110]

---

[107] [1957] 1 WLR 582 (QB) 587.   [108] [2014] EWHC 4004 (QB) [62].   [109] [1998] AC 232 (HL) 239.

[110] Note that, although *Bolam* was relevant in each, negligence was not necessarily proven pursuant to that test.

The wider application of *Bolam*

- architects: *Nye Saunders and Partners v Alan E Bristow;*[a]
- building project managers: *Royal Brompton Hosp NHS Trust v Frederick A Hammond;*[b]
- quantity surveyors, and contractual management specialists: *Ampleforth Abbey Trust v Turner & Townsend Project Management Ltd;*[c]
- valuers of shares: *Zubaida v Hargreaves;*[d] or property: *Blemain Finance Ltd v E Surv Ltd;*[e] or precious chattels/paintings/artifacts: *Thomson v Christie Manson & Woods Ltd;*[f]
- chartered surveyors and property consultants: *Capita Alternative Fund Services Ltd v Drivers Jonas (a firm);*[g]
- structural and civil engineers: *Cooperative Group Ltd v John Allen Associates Ltd;*[h]
- educators of children with special needs (say, autistic children): *S v Chapman;*[i]
- geologists: *Mirant-Asia Pacific Ltd v Oapil;*[j]
- general providers of educational services of young pupils: *Phelps v Hillingdon LBC;*[k] educational services for pupils with learning difficulties: *Carty v Croydon LBC;*[l] or as providers of professional training: *Abramova v Oxford Institute of Legal Practice;*[m]
- teachers, specifically: *Liennard v Slough BC;*[n]
- social workers: *MS v Lincolnshire CC;*[o]
- lawyers: *D Morgan plc v Mace & Jones (a firm);*[p]
- traffic engineers/highway authorities: *Lovell (Nee Geraghty) v Leeds CC;*[q]
- chartered accountants: *Goldstein v Levy Gee (a firm);*[r]
- underwriting agents/insurers: *Henderson v Merrett Syndicates.*[s]

[a] (1987) 37 BLR 92 (CA).
[b] [2000] EWHC Technology 39, [26], [34].
[c] [2012] EWHC 2137 (TCC).
[d] [1995] 1 EGLR 127 (CA)
[e] [2012] EWHC 3654 (TCC).
[f] [2005] EWCA Civ 555.
[g] [2011] EWHC 2336 (Comm).
[h] [2010] EWHC 2300 (TCC).
[i] [2008] EWCA Civ 800.
[j] [2004] EWHC 1750 (TCC).
[k] [2000] UKHL 47, [2001] 2 AC 619.
[l] [2005] EWCA Civ 19, [2005] 1 WLR 2312.
[m] [2011] EWHC 613 (QB), [2011] ELR 385.
[n] [2002] EWHC 398 (QB).
[o] [2011] EWHC 1032 (QB).
[p] [2010] EWHC 3375 (TCC).
[q] [2009] EWHC 1145 (QB).
[r] [2003] EWHC 1574 (Ch), [2007] Lloyd's Rep PN 18.
[s] [1995] 2 AC 145 (HL).

In *Nye Saunders & Partners v Alan E Bristow*, Stephen Brown LJ stated that the *Bolam* test 'applied to any profession *or calling* which required special skill, knowledge or experience'.[111] Other judges have applied the *Bolam* test of breach to 'callings' too. Similar phraseology was used by Morritt LJ in *Adams v Rhymney Valley DC*[112] – who stated that

---

[111] (1987) 37 BLR 92 (CA) 103.   [112] [2000] EWCA Civ 3035, [2000] Lloyd's Rep PN 777 (CA) [57].

the *Bolam* test 'does not depend on the actual possession of the relevant qualification', and that it applies wherever 'the act in question can only safely be done by a person with the necessary skill to do it'.

> In *Adams v Rhymney Valley DC*,[113] the Adams family (parents, and three children aged 7, 4 and 3) were tenants of a terrace house in New Tredegar. Shortly before they moved in, the owners of the accommodation, D, had replaced the windows in the terrace with hardwood-framed windows of standard design as part of a refurbishment of all its 9,000 dwellings. The windows were equipped with a key-operated lock. The keys for the windows were hung on a shoelace on the keyrack in the kitchen. The house had no smoke alarms. One morning, Mr Adams awoke to find the staircase on fire. He alerted his wife, who was sleeping upstairs with the children. He could not reach them because of the smoke and flame, and when he went outside for air, the door slammed shut on him and he could not get back in; Mrs Adams tried desperately to save the children, but could not reach the key downstairs, and, unable to unlock the bedroom windows, finally managed to smash a hole in one window. Mrs Adams fell out, suffering severe injuries. The three children all died in the fire. Had Mrs Adams been able to open the window, she and the children would probably have escaped. C claimed that D should have installed push button windows instead of key locks. **Held:** no breach. The decision to provide a lock with a removable key was supported by the evidence of window designers/installers. D was not in breach in not consulting with widespread opinion, and in not installing smoke alarms in the council accommodation.

There was a division of opinion in the Court of Appeal:

- the majority (Morritt LJ and Sir Christopher Staughton): providing safe windows was a 'calling' to which the *Bolam* test applied, because judgments had to be exercised about the conflict between the need to provide a means of escape or rescue in the case of fire, and the need to prevent children climbing or falling out of windows, especially in upper floors. In 1989/90, it was very common for houses to have lockable windows with removable keys on the first and upper floors, and that decision was one that a competent window designer/installer would have made at that time;
- the dissenter (Sedley LJ): the *Bolam* test had no relevance, because nobody in D's office professed to exercise any relevant design skill for windows. Instead, on an assessment of the quadrant of factors (probability; gravity; cost of precautions; third party considerations, such as security from burglary too), push button locks ought to have been provided, instead of locks with removable keys.

Hence, as *Adams* aptly demonstrates, the application of the *Bolam* and *Bolton v Stone* tests of breach **can** result in different outcomes – because where D is undertaking a task requiring specialist skills, and where the *Bolam* test of breach properly applies, the court must accept the opinion of a body of responsible practitioners called by D, unless that opinion contravenes the *Bolitho* test (below).

More recently, in *Bowen v National Trust*,[114] Mackay J went so far as to say that the application of the *Bolam* test of breach to areas beyond the 'learned professions' was 'now well-established'. The Scottish Outer House also observed, in *ICL Tech Ltd v Johnston Oils Ltd*,[115] that the concept of a 'profession' is 'a developing one, and also porous at its boundaries', but it was

---

[113] [2000] EWCA Civ 3035, [48] (Staughton LJ), [58], [60] (Morritt LJ), [16], [28] (Sedley LJ).
[114] [2011] EWHC 1992 (QB) [7].   [115] [2012] CSOH 62, [23].

no longer crucial to the application of the *Bolam* test, precisely because the test was no longer limited to the 'recognised professions'.

In *Bowen v National Trust*, a school group was visiting Felbrigg Hall in Suffolk, owned by D, for outdoor educational activities, and took shelter during some rain under a large beech tree, about 160–180 years old. Without warning, a large branch fractured from the trunk and fell on the group. One child was killed, three were seriously injured and the rest traumatised. The various relatives/injured claimed that D failed to carry out a competent risk assessment of the tree (albeit that it was conceded that no tree is absolutely safe). **Held:** no breach. Tree inspectors giving evidence on behalf of D considered that the risk assessment on an old tree which showed signs of stress and defects was that the affected branches should not be cut out, given the relatively low use of the path beneath; it would have been different, had the tree stood next to a carpark or highway. A responsible body of tree inspector opinion supported not cutting down the branch which caused the fatality and injuries. In *Wattleworth v Goodwood Road Racing Co Ltd*,[116] Simon Wattleworth, C, was driving his Austin Healey car on the Goodwood motor-racing circuit, and lost control of his car, collided with a tyre-fronted earth bank on the inside of the track, and was killed. His estate argued that the owners/operators of the circuit, D, negligently designed or selected the tyre structure fronting the bank at the relevant part of the bend. **Held**: no breach. A responsible body of experts in motor-racing safety supported the particular tyre wall at that bend (earth-filled lorry tyres laid house-brick fashion, fronting the earth bank). D had chosen a reasonable safety barrier, 'whether or not one puts it in precise *Bolam* terms'.

§7.13 Minority peer professional opinion, or such opinion which is drawn from a small body, can still constitute valid *Bolam* evidence so as to refute breach.

Variations in peer professional opinion are expected, indeed common. The House of Lords noted, in *Maynard v West Midlands Regional HA*, that, '[t]here is seldom any one answer, exclusive of all others, to problems of professional judgment'.[117] The fact that there may be a very small body of peer professional opinion to draw upon does not negate *Bolam* evidence on behalf of D. It is not a case of 'counting heads' and coming up short. A small number of tertiary specialists can constitute a 'responsible body of medical opinion', such that any judicial reference to a 'substantial body of medical opinion' (per *Hills v Potter*[118]) is not meant in a 'quantitative sense'.

In *De Freitas v O'Brien*,[119] Patricia De Freitas, C, 37, suffered severe back pain, and scans showed disc degeneration at the L4/5 level. She underwent surgery by D, an experienced spinal surgeon. The surgery was unsuccessful, C suffered a leakage of cerebro-spinal fluid, was transferred to intensive care, and was left with inflammation of a membrane covering the spinal cord. She was left with crippling pain, and virtually confined to bed thereafter. 'No-one reading her case notes could fail to have the deepest sympathy for her'. **Held:** no breach proven. D was a spinal specialist who only took referrals from orthopaedic and neuro-surgeons engaged in a wider field of surgical practice. There were only 11 specialist spinal surgeons in England at the time who could be regarded as constituting peer opinion, as to whether accepted medical practice would have countenanced surgery on C. Two of them supported surgery on C, whereas the other experts would not have recommended surgery.

---

[116] [2004] EWHC 140 (QB).   [117] [1984] 1 WLR 634 (HL) 638 (Lord Scarman).
[118] [1984] 1 WLR 641 (QB) 653.   [119] (1995) 25 BMLR 51 (CA).

That small number of specialists constituted a responsible body of medical opinion, justifying D's decision to operate.

Hence, the *Bolam* test may still be satisfied by the existence of a small number of peers in the field who considered D's conduct as meeting the reasonable standard of care – even if the majority of peers considered that D's practice was negligent. The fact that the *Bolam* evidence may be a minority view does **not** render it 'unreasonable' or 'irrational', pursuant to *Bolitho's* gloss. In *McCallister v Lewisham and North Southwark HA*[120] (where no breach was found in respect of the treatment given), Rougier J stated:

> Even though he may not have been actually acquainted with it, the current literature does not indicate that, in deciding to operate, [D] blundered or went outside a body of respectable medical opinion. This was a borderline case, and although ... [D] can immerse himself in a school of thought which would have condoned intervention here, I am bound to say that I think that school was very much in the minority.

§7.14   Where two bodies of conflicting (but respectable) peer professional opinion are put forward, one for C and the other for D – and where both opinions satisfy the *Bolitho* gloss – the better view is that the court cannot prefer C's body of opinion over D's, by means of a 'superiority analysis'. Breach will be refuted on the basis of the *Bolam* evidence adduced on D's behalf.

i. **The traditional House of Lords' position.** The court's role, when applying the *Bolam* test, is not to venture into a consideration of two contrary bodies of opinion, to select which, of C and D's expert opinion, it prefers. That would require the court to undertake a 'superiority analysis', in what would amount to a 'battle of the experts'. Regardless of the fact that such a battle is frequently played out in the courtroom, the task for the court has been stated in fairly restrictive terms, by the House of Lords:

> It is not enough to show that there is a body of competent professional opinion [for C] which considers that there was a wrong decision, if there also exists a body of professional opinion, equally competent, which supports the decision [by D] as reasonable in the circumstances ... A court may prefer one body of opinion to another: but that is no basis for conclusion of negligence [against D] ... a judge's "preference" for one body of distinguished professional opinion to another also professionally distinguished, is not sufficient to establish negligence in a practitioner [D] (*Maynard v West Midlands Regional HA*[121]).
>
> [the court must] remember that it is no part of its task of evaluation to give effect to any preference it may have for one responsible body of professional opinion over another, provided it is satisfied by the expert evidence that both qualify as responsible bodies of medical opinion (*Sidaway v Governors of Bethlem Royal Hosp*[122]).
>
> it would be wrong to allow such assessment to deteriorate into seeking to persuade the judge to prefer one of two views both of which are capable of being logically supported. It is only where a judge can be satisfied that the body of expert opinion cannot be logically supported at all that such opinion will not provide the benchmark by reference to which [D's] conduct falls to be assessed (*Bolitho v City and Hackney HA*[123]).

---

[120] (QB, 15 Dec 1993) [no pp].   [121] [1984] 1 WLR 634 (HL) 638, 648 (Lord Scarman).
[122] [1985] 1 All ER 643 (HL) 659 (Lord Diplock).   [123] [1997] 4 All ER 771 (HL) 779 (Lord Browne-Wilkinson).

That inability to choose C's evidence over D's has been described by lower English courts as 'uncontroversial' (per *Kingsberry v Greater Manchester Strategic HA*[124]), and the 'correct approach' (per *M v Blackpool Victoria Hosp NHS Trust*[125]), and has been oft-applied where the court expressly admitted that two schools of reasonable thought existed and that it was not permitted to undertake any superiority analysis (per *Tuke v Mid Essex Hosp Services NHS Trust*[126]). As the Court of Appeal noted in *Marriott v West Midlands Regional HA*, 'it is not open to simply prefer the expert evidence of one body of competent professional opinion over that of another, where there was a conflict between the experts called by the parties'.[127]

> In *Bellarby v Worthing and Southlands Hosp NHS Trust*,[128] patient C, 49, suffered from Crohn's disease for almost 25 years. Seriously ill, he was admitted as a hospital in-patient for almost three months, and also suffered deteriorating vision which was eventually diagnosed as candida. C alleged that this condition was mistreated, in that his treating doctors, D, used intravenous Amphotericin instead of Fluconazole. **Held:** no breach proven. Despite the greater use of Fluconazole in later years, the use of Amphotericin in 1999 was not negligent at the time, especially when candida might have seeded elsewhere in C's body. There were two possible approaches to treatment (said the court); each was logical on the evidence; and both were supported by a respectable body of opinion. The question 'was not whether one treatment was to be preferred to another, but whether [D's] treatment was unreasonable as described in *Bolam*, *Maynard* and *Bolitho*.' It was not.

That view, however, has recently been eroded by some significant case law to the contrary, where that is precisely what an adjudicating court *has* done – preferred one body of medical opinion to the other.

ii.   A superiority analysis, nevertheless? The question is whether the test of breach is actually a three-step framework: (1) the *Bolam* test; (2) the *Bolitho* gloss; and (3) a superiority analysis. That would be contentious – but it has some support.

In the 2007 decision of *Smith v Southampton University Hosp NHS Trust*,[129] the trial judge held that both D doctors were not negligent, but her findings were later criticised by the Court of Appeal on this basis:

> She appears to rely exclusively on the *Bolam* test. Thus, she merely says that [Ds' expert] is highly reputable and that it had not been suggested that he did not represent the view of a responsible body of gynoncological surgeons. With great respect to the deputy judge, I do not think this is good enough. Where there is a clear conflict of medical opinion, the court's duty is not merely to say which view it prefers, but to explain why it prefers one to the other. This, in my judgment, is all the more so when the expert whose view is preferred accepts a substantial element of what the less favoured expert describes as basic good practice – in this case, keeping your scissors shut unless you can see what you are doing. In such circumstances, it is not sufficient, in my view, simply to say that [the expert] is representative of a responsible body of medical opinion and that, as a consequence, [D] was not negligent.

This is not an isolated instance. For example, in *Dowdie v Camberwell HA*,[130] the court accepted that the two distinguished expert witnesses for D had testified that D's conduct was 'within the

---

[124] [2005] EWHC 2253 (QB) [11].   [125] [2003] EWHC 1744 (QB) [24].   [126] (QB, 1 May 2003) [32].
[127] [1999] 1 Lloyd's Rep Med 23 (CA).   [128] [2005] EWHC 2089 (QB) [98]–[99], [112].
[129] [2007] EWCA Civ 387, [44].   [130] (QB, 1 Jul 1997) [no pp].

range of acceptable practice', but that 'does not oblige me to accept their evidence and, on this issue, I accept the evidence of [C's] experts'. In *Townsend v Worcester and District HA*[131] too, the court referred to 'choosing between the experts'.

Importantly, however, the rejected opinion adduced for D, in all of these cases, did **not** fail the *Bolitho* threshold, in that it was not considered illogical and unsupportable or indefensible. It was simply not the peer professional opinion which the courts preferred. There is, of course, a world of difference between an opinion that is rejected because it lacks a logical basis (as required by *Bolitho*), and one that is rejected because, whilst logical, another opinion is more plausible. Were a 'preferability' analysis to be incorporated as a *third stage* of the analysis of breach, it would significantly depart from the House of Lords' statements reproduced above. Indeed, it seems that Lord Scarman would (per *Maynard*) describe it as an 'error of law'.[132]

A preferability analysis, of course, does introduce a 'battle of the experts'. The onus upon C's experts inevitably alters – instead of seeking to argue that D's expert opinion was illogical and indefensible due to one of the *Bolitho* reasons (outlined below), C's experts would seek to argue that, whilst a reasonable and logical point of view was adopted by D, their own view was preferable. In that assessment, the wisdom of hindsight would have considerably more room for operation. C's body of peer professional opinion, which proposed a procedure that would have precluded or minimised the adverse outcome for C, would arguably be preferable. In addition, although the medical paternalism signified by the *Bolam* test was rightly tempered by the *Bolitho* gloss, it would surely be incorrect to permit a court (where the judge is a lay person with no formal medical training) to reject a reasonable body of expert opinion adduced on D's part in favour of an expert opinion that it considered preferable. That was never the judicial role envisaged by the House of Lords in *Sidaway*, *Maynard* or *Bolitho*, and to require that third step – a superiority analysis – strains both legal precedent, and the propriety of the court's role in professional negligence suits.

Anticipating the other view?

§7.15   It is not legally necessary that D should have considered and reflected upon the alternative avenues available to him (including the peer professional opinion adduced in C's favour), and made a deliberate choice between those opinions. It is sufficient if D's conduct is supported by a respectable body of peer professional opinion.

The *Bolam* test of breach does *not* require D to 'second-guess' what an alternative peer professional opinion may think, or investigate the alternatives that others with specialist skills might favour, and then conduct a cost–benefit analysis of the various options before coming to his decision, in order to preclude a finding of negligence. It is sufficient that D acts according to *one* body of peer professional opinion – and what matters is the end result, and not the processes by which it came to be given.

This point proved contentious in *Adams v Rhymney Valley DC*,[133] where the Court of Appeal held, by majority, that there was no difference between D, who decided to follow a particular practice because, on the basis of his experience, it was a reasonable and accepted professional practice; and D, who sat down in a chair and mused upon **all** the alternative practices open to him and then consciously selected the one to follow. Both Ds would escape

---

[131] (1994) 23 BMLR 31 (QB) [no pp].   [132] [1984] 1 WLR 634 (HL) 639.
[133] [2000] EWCA Civ 3035, [30], [43] (Sir Christopher Staughton), [59] (Morritt LJ), [19] (Sedley LJ, dissenting).

a finding of breach if their conduct accorded with accepted professional practice. (By contrast, the dissenter, Sedley LJ, considered it to be a 'requirement of the *Bolam* test' that D consider and evaluate the alternatives.) The majority considered Sedley LJ's view to be untenable, as an unacceptable re-writing of the *Bolam* principle, and that it 'would drastically alter the law of negligence'. The very point of *Bolam* was to give D a defence to a claim in negligence if he acted in accordance with a practice that was accepted as proper by a reasonable body of persons who practised the same 'art'. D did not have to anticipate that other body of opinion, and then actively consider and then reject that opinion. What mattered to liability was the act or omission by D, and whether it fell below the standard of reasonable care, and not the thought processes which preceded it. That principle can be applied to D's considerable advantage.

> In *Camerata Property Inc v Credit Suisse Securities (Europe) Ltd*,[134] C, a company owned by a wealthy shipping businessman, invested in a 5-year bond issued by Lehman Bros, on the advice of Credit Suisse, D, for US$12m. On 8 Oct 2008, Lehman Bros was declared bankrupt, and C lost all or most of its investment. C claimed that D's advice was negligent, and that it would have otherwise sold the bond before the investment was lost. D's officer, who was C's relationship manager and adviser, had not properly read the information provided to him by C; and C would naturally and properly assume that his adviser would be aware of such information, and would have it in mind when advising C. **Held:** no breach. Ultimately, D's investment advice was sound; and was not to be condemned as negligent because of failings in the process that led to that advice. In *Smith v West Yorkshire HA (t/a Leeds HA)*,[135] a baby boy, C, suffered from quadriplegic cerebral palsy, allegedly because of the negligent management of his mother's labour by the medical staff at D's hospital. C claimed that D's medical staff mis-interpreted the trace readings on the cardiotocograph ('CTG'), recording the foetal heartbeat and the rate of maternal contractions. C argued that one responsible body of professional opinion took the view that the trace was of a baby who was unwell. Another body of professional opinion took the view that the trace was of a baby who was well (and D himself considered that the CTG was within acceptable limits). **Held:** no breach proven. If there were different bodies holding respectable but significantly different opinions on CTG trace interpretation, D's conduct was not compromised by the fact that he failed to take into account that the other respectable opinion could reasonably take a different view.

Reliance on professional guidelines

§7.16   D's compliance with the protocols and guidelines produced by professional bodies does not, of itself, preclude breach. However, it will constitute very strong evidence of D's adherence with a reasonable body of professional opinion, so as to satisfy the *Bolam* test of breach.

As the High Court was anxious to point out in *Zarb v Odetoyinbo*,[136] professional protocols and guidelines still have to satisfy the *Bolitho* scrutiny – and hence, it must follow that a failure to comply with them cannot, of itself, be regarded as irrational. However (said the court), D's compliance is a 'major obstacle' to any finding of breach of duty (as it was there, where the Guidelines of the Royal College of General Practitioners were complied with by D), and it was 'difficult to envisage' when a set of guidelines would not be *Bolam*-compliant.

---

[134] [2011] 2 BCLC 54 (CA) [199].   [135] QB, 27 May 2004, [27]–[28].   [136] [2006] EWHC 2880 (QB) [110].

Obversely, D's failure to comply with professional guidelines will render it difficult to satisfy the *Bolam* test, and expert evidence notwithstanding, D will find it difficult to justify that non-compliance.

In *Thomson v James*,[137] patient C, a young child, was not given a measles vaccination by D, his GP, because it was contra-indicated in the case of convulsions, which C may have experienced. **Held:** breach proven. D ought to have been aware of the Dept of Health and Social Services (DHSS) advice that, even if a child had a history of convulsions, the vaccination could be administered with special precautions, *viz*, the simultaneous injection of immunoglobulin. Failure to comply with DHSS guidelines on measles vaccination was crucial to that finding.

Where D's expert refers to a 'seminal' article in the area that supported D's conduct, that has also tended to carry great weight when determining *Bolam*-compliance (as it did, for example, regarding an article discussing the treatment of angina, and the utility of heart by-pass surgery, in *Shaw v McGill*[138]).

The *Bolitho* 'gloss'

§7.17 According to the *Bolitho* test, the court is required to disregard peer professional '*Bolam*' opinion, where that professional opinion is not responsible or capable of withstanding logical analysis. However, the *Bolitho* test cannot be used to permit the court to choose, or to prefer, one peer professional opinion over another, where *both* have a logical basis.

The test, and reasons for its introduction

Unsurprisingly, the *Bolam* test of medical breach – whereby D was exculpated if he acted in accordance with a practice accepted as proper by a responsible body of practitioners – was judicially criticised on several counts (and across a range of jurisdictions):

i. it was 'over protective and deferential' toward D (per *Foo Fio Na v Dr Soo Fook Mun*[139]);

ii. it had the potential to be satisfied 'by the production of a dubious expert whose professional views existed at the fringe of medical consciousness' (per *Khoo v Gunapathy d/o Muniandy*[140]);

iii. there was a perception that the medical profession was 'above the law', that the *Bolam* test deprived courts of the opportunity of 'precipitating changes, where required, in professional standards' (per *Hajgato v London HA*[141]), and that the courts were being 'dictated to' rather than exercising their judgment (per *Burne v A*[142]);

iv. the reality was that 'professions may adopt unreasonable practices. Practices may develop in professions ... not because they serve the interest of the clients, but because they protect the interests or convenience of members of the profession' (per *F v R*[143]);

---

[137] (1996) 31 BMLR 1 (QB).   [138] (QB, 31 July 1998).

[139] [2007] 1 MLJ 593, [2006] MLJU 518, (Federal Court of Appeal, 29 Dec 2006) [26].

[140] [2002] 2 SLR 414 (CA) [63].   [141] (1982), 36 OR (2d) 669 (Ont SCJ) [56] (Callagan J).

[142] [2006] EWCA Civ 24, [10].

[143] [1983] 33 SASR 189 (Full Ct) 191 (King CJ) (although this was a disclosure case). Also: *Scott v Lothian University Hosp NHS Trust* [2006] ScotCS (OH) [33], [36].

v. there was a sense that the *Bolam* test did not adequately protect the community against medical practices that could not withstand critical scrutiny, and that more judicial safeguards for the public were necessary (per law reform opinion[144]);

vi. it was contended that a judicial scrutiny of medical expert opinion was no different from the type of careful analysis that a judge must make in respect of other professional evidence, be it 'a judgment by an accountant, lawyer, underwriter or other professional' – if the court was the final arbiter in respect of these professionals, then so too should it be with the medical profession (per *Wisniewski v Central Manchester HA*[145]).

It follows that, pursuant to the now-'commonplace'[146] *Bolitho* test, the court is the final arbiter of breach. In *Bolitho v City and Hackney HA*,[147] Lord Browne-Wilkinson stated the test thus:

> in cases of diagnosis and treatment there are cases where, despite a body of professional opinion sanctioning D's conduct, D can properly be held liable for negligence (I am not here considering questions of disclosure of risk) ... that is because, in some cases, it cannot be demonstrated to the judge's satisfaction that the body of opinion relied upon is reasonable or responsible. In the vast majority of cases, the fact that distinguished experts in the field are of a particular opinion will demonstrate the reasonableness of that opinion. In particular, where there are questions of assessment of the relative risks and benefits of adopting a particular medical practice, a reasonable view necessarily presupposes that the relative risks and benefits have been weighed by the experts informing their opinions. But if, in a rare case, it can be demonstrated that the professional opinion is not capable of withstanding logical analysis, the judge is entitled to hold that the body of opinion is not reasonable or responsible.

It will be very difficult to apply *Bolitho* where a distinguished expert in the field considered D's allegedly-negligent conduct to be reasonable (noted, e.g., in *Cowley v Cheshire and Merseyside Strategic HA*,[148] where *Bolitho's* caveat was rejected by the court). Indeed, more recently, a court was not prepared to invoke the *Bolitho* gloss, holding that it would be a 'very bold and inappropriate step for a court to find, in effect, that the authors of two leading world textbooks on orthopaedic surgery had described a surgical technique which could not be logically supported' (per *Ecclestone v Medway NHS Foundation Trust*[149]).

To hold that the medical opinion proffered by experienced specialists should be departed from has been termed a 'rare' occurrence (*In re B (a child)*[150]), 'very seldom' occurring (*M v Blackpool Victoria Hosp NHS Trust*[151]), and only to apply in exceptional circumstances, where 'the evidence shows that a lacuna in professional practice exists' (*French v Thames Valley Strategic HA*[152]). It has been said that peer professional opinion under the *Bolam* test 'should not lightly be set aside' (*AB v Leeds Teaching Hosp NHS Trust*[153]). It would have to be so

---

[144] See, e.g., *Ipp Report*, [3.10] and [3.24], citing the major enquiry in NZ in: *Committee of Enquiry into Allegations Concerning the Treatment of Cervical Cancer at National Women's Hosp and into Other Related Matters* (1988).

[145] [1998] EWCA Civ 596, [1998] PIQR P324 (CA) P335, citing the trial judge.

[146] *Kingsberry v Greater Manchester Strategic HA* [2005] EWHC 2253, 87 BMLR 73 (QB) [11].

[147] [1998] AC 232 (HL) 243 (Lord Browne-Wilkinson).

[148] [2007] EWHC 48 (QB) [55]. Also: *Ndri v Moorfields Eye Hosp NHS Trust* [2006] EWHC 3652 (QB) [35].

[149] [2013] EWHC 790 (QB) [47].

[150] [2000] 1 WLR 790 (Fam Ct) 796 (Otter LJ). Also: *Calver v Westwood Veterinary Group* [2001] PIQR 168 (CA) [31] (Simon Brown LJ); *E v Castro* [2003] EWHC 2066 (QB) [99].

[151] [2003] EWHC 1744 (QB) [42].   [152] [2005] EWHC 459 (QB) [112].   [153] [2004] EWHC 644 (QB) [226].

irrational that it '[could] not be logically supported at all' (*French*[154]). A degree of '*Wednesbury* unreasonableness' was required in one case (*Kushnir v Camden & Islington HA*[155]), although in *Joyce v Merton Sutton and Wandsworth HA*,[156] that term was disapproved of, given that it is an administrative law concept that was 'directed to very different problems and [its] use, even by analogy, in negligence cases can ... only serve to confuse'.

Further, the fact that the expert evidence adduced on behalf of D is a minority view of accepted medical practice does not, of itself, render that view illogical, irrational or irresponsible. Nevertheless, that may be more likely, if that minority opinion was based on a dubious expert whose professional views existed at the fringe of medical consciousness, or if D's expert adhered to out-of-date ideas (per *McGovern v Sharkey*[157]). However, the expert's competence and 'respectability' matter, for *Bolitho's* gloss. Recently, Green J provided an important vignette, when he remarked that lengthy NHS experience 'is a matter of significance' when considering D's expert to be logical and defensible; that an expert retired for 10 years 'and whose retirement is spent expressing expert opinions, may turn out to be far removed from the fray and much more likely to form an opinion divorced from current practical reality'; and that 'many judges and litigators have come across so called experts who can "talk the talk" but who veer towards the eccentric or unacceptable end of the spectrum. Regrettably there are, in many fields of law, individuals who profess expertise but who, on true analysis, must be categorised as "fringe"' (per *C v North Cumbria Univ Hosp NHS Trust*[158]).

Nevertheless, there is a body of English case law which shows that courts **are** prepared, on unusual occasion, to characterise peer professional opinion as lacking 'logical analysis', or as being 'irresponsible' or 'irrational', per *Bolitho*. These labels are, however, only helpful when 'fleshed out' with examples. Indeed, given the number of occasions upon which *Bolitho's* gloss has been applied, it is doubtful whether the test application quite warrants the moniker of a 'rarity'.

The *Bolitho* factors

The following Table identifies the factors which have indicated to the court that the requisite logical analysis of the body of peer professional opinion was absent:[159]

The *Bolitho* factors	
Factor	Case example/s
I The peer professional opinion has overlooked that a 'clear precaution' to avoid the adverse outcome for C was available, so that the outcome could have been easily and inexpensively	In the pre-*Bolitho* case of *Hucks v Cole*[a] (1968), a patient suffered from septicaemia, causing various sores and yellow spots on her fingers and toes. D, the treating GP, put C on a 5-day course of tetracycline antibiotics, but ceased them when the sores showed signs of improvement, although he knew that the septic spots contained streptococcal infection

[a] [1993] 4 Med LR 393 (CA) (decided in 1968).

---

[154] [2005] EWHC 459 (QB) [9]–[10].

[155] QB, 16 Jun 1995, citing: *Bolitho* [1993] 4 Med LR 381 (CA) 392 (Dillon LJ).

[156] (1995) 27 BMLR 124 (CA) 156.   [157] [2014] NIQB 117, [43].   [158] [2014] EWHC 61 (QB) [25(vi)].

[159] See further, Mulheron, 'Trumping *Bolam*: A Critical Legal Analysis of *Bolitho's* "Gloss"' (2010) 69 *CLJ* 609, from which this section of the chapter is substantially derived.

Factor	Case example/s
avoided – even if a reasonable body of medical opinion would have agreed with D's conduct. The *Bolam* test 'is not a licence for professionals to take obvious risks which can be guarded against'.[b] However, it is unlikely that *Bolitho* will be activated, to render *Bolam* evidence 'illogical', if D's medical conduct under scrutiny involved high complexity and uncertainty, such that there was no 'clear precaution'.	and organisms that could lead to puerperal fever, and that penicillin could kill streptococcal infection. The next day, C contracted puerperal fever. A number of distinguished doctors gave evidence, for D, that they would not have treated C with penicillin either. **Held:** breach proven. Penicillin was a clear precaution. In *Lowe v Havering Hosp NHS Trust,*[c] D left an 8-week gap between consultations with C, a patient, who had dangerously high and uncontrolled blood pressure, and who then suffered a major stroke. D had 'suspicions' that C was not diligently taking his medication, which emphasised the need to see C more frequently; and especially when C was a relatively young man who had a wife and dependent family, and for whom a disabling stroke would be devastating (a social, rather than a medical, consideration, but one which a reasonable D ought to have taken into account). **Held:** breach proven. More frequent appointments were easily arranged.
	In *French v Thames Valley Strategic HA,*[d] C was born prematurely (29 weeks), and suffered from brain damage and cerebral palsy. Her mother suffered from pre-eclampsia, and claimed her obstetrician and gynaecologist, D, delivered C prematurely by caesarean section, and that but for the premature delivery, C's injuries would probably have been avoided. **Held:** no breach proven. This area was vested with technical difficulty; and in the case of pre-eclampsia, literature advised that the best timing of delivery was 'a matter of opinion and judgment, with few facts or absolute guidelines', and where 'the pathological findings are so controversial and contradictory'.
II The peer professional opinion supports a practice that *guarantees* an adverse outcome for C – unless limited resources, and D's co-existing duties towards other parties, render the practice *Bolam*-compliant.	In *Garcia v St Mary's NHS Trust,*[e] patient C underwent heart bypass surgery, completed by 7.00 pm. At 11.53 pm, C coughed, lost consciousness, and suffered an acute post-operative bleed into the chest area, a recognised complication to this surgery. A 'crash call' was placed at 11.54 pm; the anaesthetic team arrived at 11.56 pm; at 11.58 pm, the cardiothoracic registrar on-call was notified at home; he arrived in the recovery room at 00.25 am; and by 00.40 am, the bleeding was under control. C was left brain-damaged. The neurological experts agreed that the length and severity of a period of hypotension/hypoperfusion of 30 minutes meant that there would be severe neurological damage. C claimed that, unless there was

[b] *Adams v Rhymney Valley DC* [2000] EWCA Civ 3035, [2000] Lloyd's Rep PN 777, [40].
[c] (2001) 62 BMLR 69 (QB).
[d] [2005] EWHC 459 (QB) [112].
[e] [2006] EWHC 2314 (QB) [88], [91]–[93].

Factor	Case example/s
	an on-call registrar staying at the hospital overnight to deal with such emergencies, the inevitable delay condemned C to severe brain damage. **Held:** no breach proven. The practice of having no specialist registrar on site was defensible, given the co-existing duties which registrars had to other patients and to co-employees.
III The peer professional opinion failed to weigh, or to properly direct its attention to, the comparative risks and benefits of D's practice. It is the process, rather than the ultimate decision, that activates the *Bolitho* test under this scenario. However, even if an alternative course had a very low risk to C, that does not necessarily activate the *Bolitho* gloss. The law will not insist upon a course of conduct that completely eliminates the risks of an adverse outcome, if that system is not workable.	In *Wiszniewski v Central Manchester HA,*[f] patient C was showing an abnormal foetal heartbeat prior to birth. Ultimately, C suffered irreversible brain damage in the 13 minutes immediately prior to his birth because, as he moved down the birth canal, the umbilical cord wrapped round his neck and had a knot in it, so that he was effectively being strangled. The attending obstetrician, D, adduced evidence that a respectable school of medical practitioners would not have moved immediately to intervene in a birth, at the sign of possible trouble with the foetal heartbeat. **Held:** breach proven. The alternative course of intervening to perform an artificial rupture of the membranes which, whilst itself had a small risk, was preferable to exposing C to the risk of brain damage by not intervening. In *Garcia,*[g] facts previously, no breach proven. The risk of post-operative bleeding into the chest area following heart by-pass surgery was 1 in 1,000. Having a specialist registrar on site for such an event might have reduced/eliminated the risk of C's brain damage. However, the hospital system had to be designed to accommodate the 'reasonably foreseeable' event, and not the 'rare occurrence'. The hospital's practice was *Bolam*-compliant.
IV The peer professional opinion endorses D's practice, but that practice contravenes widespread public opinion. One of the justifications for scrutinising *Bolam* evidence is to safeguard community expectations of acceptable practice.	In *AB v Leeds Teaching Hosp NHS Trust*[h] (the Nationwide Organ Retention Group Litigation), various doctors, D, failed to inform the relatives (mainly parents) of children who had died either at, or shortly after, birth, that a post-mortem examination of their children involved the removal of organs (brains, hearts, lungs) for later scientific examination. The parents had no opportunity for objection and/or refusal. The joint expert report stated that the practice in 1992, when this happened, was not to be explicit with parents about the details of post-mortems, an almost universal practice up to 1999/2000. **Held:** breach proven. Even if the practice was universally accepted, it was 'irresponsible conservatism' on the part of the medical profession, exhibited by the national scandal that gave rise to the group litigation in the first place.

[f] [1998] EWCA Civ 596.
[g] [2006] EWHC 2314 (QB) [96].
[h] [2004] EWHC 644 (QB).

Factor	Case example/s
V The peer professional opinion cannot be correct, when taken in the context of the whole factual evidence, or in the context of advances in scientific knowledge.	In *Tagg v Countess of Chester Hosp Foundation Trust,[i]* patient C suffered a bowel injury during a gynaecological operation. Held: breach proven. D's expert surgeon gave evidence supporting the surgical practice adopted by D. However, that expert opinion was 'neutralised by the unreliability of the factual evidence about what happened and about what was found at the operation'. In *Hucks v Cole,[j]* facts previously, one reason for disregarding the *Bolam* evidence adduced for D was that the peer professional opinion ignored advances in medical knowledge, i.e., the potential use of penicillin.
	In *Lillywhite v UCL Hosp NHS Trust,[k]* although the *Bolitho* test was not expressly applied to discount *Bolam* evidence on behalf of sonologist D, that is effectively what occurred. C, baby Alice, was born with a severe malformation of her brain, caused in the early stages of foetal development by the failure of her fore-brain to divide into two. As a result, she was severely brain-damaged, quadriplegic, and unable to use her limbs or to talk. Held (trial): no breach in failing to identify that three parts of the brain – a cavum septum (CSP), anterior horns from the lateral ventricles, and a falx – were absent. Peer opinion adduced for D was that D must have identified echoes mimicking the brain structures. Held (CA, 2:1): the peer professional opinion was 'neither possible nor plausible ... when looked at in the context of the evidence as a whole; and, in the case of the lateral ventricles, the only suggested explanation indicated negligent unawareness of the-then state of the art'.
VI The peer professional opinion was not internally consistent – in that the expert endorsed D's practice, but then said that peer professional opinion would not have done that, but quite the opposite.	In the *Organ Retention Litig,[l]* facts previously, D's peer professional opinion agreed that parents were entitled to have their wishes in respect of their deceased child's body respected and complied with. Gage J could not perceive how those wishes could be respected, without the parents being told that organs from their children might be kept and not buried with the bodies.
	In *Taaffe v East of England Ambulance Service NHS Trust,[m]* patient C, 50, suffered chest pains, and her son called an ambulance. C had a history of hypertension, a family history of cardiac disease, and no pre-existing history of significant indigestion, which was the nature of the pain she described.

[i] [2007] EWHC 509 (QB) [64].
[j] On this point, see, e.g.: *Khoo v Gunapathy d/o Muniandy* [2002] 2 SLR 414 (CA) [65]–[66].
[k] [2005] EWCA Civ 1466, [106].
[l] [2004] EWHC 644 (QB) [235].
[m] [2012] EWHC 1335 (QB) [69].

Factor	Case example/s
	D, the paramedics, noted that C's pain had eased by the time they arrived, and two ECGs appeared normal. No detailed history was taken, and D did not advise C to attend hospital for investigations, because she was visiting her GP the next day. Five days later, C suffered a heart attack and died. C's estate claimed that D should have taken her to hospital or advised her to attend hospital. Expert evidence supported D's decision not to take her to hospital. **Held:** breach proven. D's expert evidence was internally inconsistent – having said that it was essential for a paramedic 'to look at the full picture', that did not occur here: that evidence was 'not consistent with the need to look at all relevant information in making the decision, nor logical'.
VII The peer professional opinion adhered to the wrong legal test (i.e., referring to the wrong standard of care expected of D); or contended what *that expert* would have done, rather than the view of a respected body of medical experts.	In *Hutchinson v Leeds HA,*[n] surgeon D had allowed faecal impaction to cause the disintegration of patient C's posterior-rectal wall, thereby requiring C, a young woman who was being treated by D for acute myeloblastic leukaemia, to undergo surgery and to have a colostomy. **Held:** breach proven. D's expert adhered to the standard that D had not committed 'an error so gross and/or so crass that no reasonably competent doctor would ever have committed', but that was not the *Bolam* standard of care. Hence, D's expert had 'set a yardstick by which to assess the acts or omissions of [D] and his team, which is unjustified, and which must affect the quality of this part of his evidence, and I do not accept it'.

[n] (QB, 6 Nov 2000) [78].

These factors constitute the grounds, to date, upon which English courts have been prepared to reject peer professional opinion as being indefensible and 'not capable of withstanding logical analysis'.

The effect of the SARAH Act 2015

As discussed in Chapter 6, the implementation of the Social Action, Responsibility and Heroism Act 2015[160] would appear to have no impact upon the standard of care relevant for Ds who engage in heroic or socially-beneficial activities. The common law already views such Ds sympathetically. However, whether s 3 of that Act is quite so benign in its impact upon proof of breach is rather less clear.

---

[160] In force 13 Apr 2015.

> s 3   The court must have regard to whether the person, in carrying out the activity in the course of which the alleged negligence or breach of statutory duty occurred, demonstrated a predominantly responsible approach towards protecting the safety or other interests of others.

As the author has discussed elsewhere,[161] the abovementioned provision suffers from three distinct uncertainties. First, the use of the word, 'predominantly', is odd, because *Bolam* is clearly not a 'numbers game', such a position has been clearly rejected at common law. Secondly, whether the 'responsible approach' is to be assessed by a *Bolam* assessment, as qualified by a *Bolitho* (judicially-undertaken) scrutiny, or whether it is solely to be a judicial assessment which re-introduces the banned-at-common-law superiority analysis, is unclear. Thirdly, the provision appears to apply to any type of D, whether a professionally-qualified party (the traditional, but not exclusive, province of the *Bolam* test) or not. At the time of writing, the SARAH Act has not been judicially considered.

Where the *Bolam/Bolitho* framework does *not* apply

There are some circumstances in which it will be inappropriate for the court to rely upon peer professional opinion at all. In such cases, it is not a question of merely determining whether there was a respectable body of expert opinion to support D's (non-negligent) version of events, but rather, the court will weigh the evidence on both sides, and may properly prefer that of C's expert witness to that of D's. Certainly, expert evidence may not always be a pre-requisite in professional negligence cases, a point reiterated in *Royal Brompton Hosp NHS Trust v Hammond*.[162]

Indeed, in some cases, the battle-lines are drawn thus: D will argue that the alleged breach is a matter of expert judgment that falls within *Bolam*, given that peer professional opinion can then be properly adduced to uphold the practice (subject to the *Bolitho* caveat) – whereas C will argue that the alleged breach does not fall within *Bolam* at all because it involved no expert judgment whatsoever, and hence, it is for the court to form its own view, on all the evidence, and to prefer one expert's opinion to that of the other, as a valid course.

There are **three** scenarios in which the *Bolam* test has no room for application:

No body of peer professional opinion

§7.18   The *Bolam* test does not apply, if there is no evidence of an existing '*body* of *professional practice*' in respect of D's conduct. In that event, the court will hear all the evidence (expert and factual) and form its own view as to breach.

The allegedly-negligent incident may be so unusual or extraordinary that there will be no *Bolam* evidence to adduce, upon which the court could safely rely. In such cases, the court may hear expert evidence adduced by C and D, and decide for itself whether D's conduct fell below the standard of reasonable care. Hence, peer professional opinion may be helpful, but will not be determinative.

---

[161] Mulheron, 'Legislating Dangerously: Bad Samaritans, Good Society and the Heroism Act 2015' (2016) *Modern Law Review* [forthcoming].

[162] [2002] EWHC 2037 (TCC), 88 Con LR 1, [19].

In *Michael Hyde & Assoc Ltd v JD Williams & Co Ltd,*[163] a heating system was installed in C's premises during the conversion and refurbishment of old cotton mills. D was the architect. Six months after completion, textiles being stored at the premises by C showed 'phenolic yellowing', whereby anti-oxidants in plastic packaging can migrate to textiles and be absorbed by the textiles. C alleged that D ought to have been aware of the risk of discolouration and warned C of it. D contended that it was not aware of the process, and that those within the textile industry, such as C, ought to have known about its dangers and C could not blame others for its own shortcomings. **Held:** breach proven. The *Bolam* test of breach did not apply in this case; the court could assess the question of breach for itself. In *AB v Tameside and Glossop HA,*[164] a series of patients, C, allegedly suffered psychiatric illness for the way in which they were informed by the Glossop Health Authority, D, that they might be at risk of infection from contact with a former healthcare worker who had tested HIV-positive at D's clinics. There had been only one broadly similar incident in the whole of England before this litigation, at a time when the public's understanding of HIV/AIDS was far different. **Held:** no breach proven, in selecting the method of communicating the information to C. In *Ampleforth Abbey Trust v Turner and Townsend Project Management Ltd,*[165] new boarding accommodation was built for Ampleforth College, C, a school in North Yorkshire, for which D was project manager. The works were completed much later than expected. The builder claimed extensions of time and additional payments; whereas C sought liquidated damages of £750,000 for the delay. The whole project was carried out by the builder under letters of intent that C issued from time to time; the contract itself was not signed until long after completion, and hence, C never had any entitlement to liquidated damages. C sued D for professional negligence, alleging that D should have had the builder sign the building contract, so that C would have had a right to pursue liquidated damages for delay and would have achieved a better outcome in its dispute with the builder. **Held:** breach proven. However, the court stated that it obtained from the expert evidence very 'limited' assistance, because it was 'extremely rare for construction projects of any significance to be completed under letters of intent', an exceptional case, and there was no 'body of practice' to support it.

In *Hyde*, the *Bolam* test was discounted for two reasons – because the issue involved no *specialist* skill (discussed below); and because the incident was unusual, and the experts' evidence as to whether they would have further investigated the risk of discoloration 'amounted to no more than an expression of personal opinion as to what the witness would or would not have done, thereby falling short of being evidence of a responsible *body* of architects, or a recognised *practice* within the profession ... [there is] little to suggest that there were two recognised but contrary views of an accepted *practice* governing the decision in question'.[166] In *AB*, Brooke LJ noted that D's suggestion that the *Bolam* test governed the case was wrong, 'because there simply was no adequate well of professional experience on which the court could usefully draw in the present case'. Rather, the court 'has to perform the familiar role of considering the factual evidence carefully, listening to the expert evidence, and forming a view as to whether, in all the circumstances, [D] fell below the standards reasonably to be expected of them'.[167] Similarly, *Ampleforth Abbey* was 'not, properly speaking, a *Bolam* case at all' – the experts were merely saying what they would have done in a similar situation if project-managing the contract (e.g., they emphasised the importance of the protection provided by a contract, rather than mere letters of intent; and the nature of the risks and disadvantages if

---

[163] [2000] EWCA Civ 211, [2001] PNLR 8.   [164] (1996) 35 BMLR 79 (CA).
[165] [2012] EWHC 2137 (TCC) [101]–[102].   [166] [2000] EWCA Civ 211, [10] (original emphasis).
[167] (1996) 35 BMLR 79 (CA) 93.

the contractor were to walk off site with no contract in place), in other words, they gave their 'personal opinions or reactions'.

In *Royal Brompton* too,[168] HHJ Lloyd QC rejected *Bolam*-type evidence as being determinative, where 'the purposes or the upshot of the expert's opinion is no more than a statement of belief as to what he would have done in the circumstances, presented as evidence of practice'. Such evidence falls short of being evidence of a responsible *body* of experts, or a recognised *practice* within the profession (per Stephen Brown LJ in *Nye Saunders*[169]). In short, it is of 'little assistance' (per *199 Knightsbridge Development Ltd v WSP UK Ltd*[170]). In such cases, the court is entitled to make up its own mind; but it can certainly use the expert evidence adduced on either side to 'understand what would go through the mind of a professional person in those cases, where what would be common sense to the rest of the world would not, or might not, be sensible in that profession or occupation' (per *Royal Brompton*[171]).

> In *Royal Brompton*, new buildings were constructed for C's Royal Brompton and National Heart and Lung Hospitals in Chelsea, for which D was project manager. C claimed that D and the architect failed to ensure that a contract drawing correctly showed the extent of the land available for site offices and other temporary purposes. **Held:** breach proven. D should have checked the drawing to make sure that C's instructions had been properly interpreted by the architect, and referred the drawing on to C instead of merely filing it. The parties accepted, for this part of the claim, that much of what the experts said about what a project manager should do with a drawing received from an architect, 'was not truly evidence of practice, but of personal reaction'. The court prefaced its decision on this part of the claim, 'if expert evidence was needed', doubting that it was.

Questions of fact

§7.19 Questions of fact are solely for the court to decide, and are not determined by *Bolam* peer professional opinion.

The court adjudicates questions of fact, to which the *Bolam* test does not apply; whereas, regarding whether or not D met acceptable standards of medical practice, *Bolam* certainly applies. Sometimes, a case will involve **both** questions.

> In *Penney, Palmer and Cannon v East Kent HA*,[172] cytology screeners, D, reported four cervical smears taken from patients C as negative. Hence, there was no timely follow-up or diagnostic or therapeutic intervention, and each C went on to develop invasive adenocarcinoma of the cervix. **Held:** breach proven. The question of whether or not cancerous cells were visible on the slides was a question of fact for the court to decide. On the balance of probabilities, cancerous cells were on the slides. By contrast, whether D should have observed cancerous cells on the slides was a question of breach, to be assessed on the *Bolam* test. The conclusion that, in respect of these four slides, the cytoscreeners did not meet the required standard of care, was valid on the face of the expert evidence. Given that, on each slide, there were a small number of inflamed groups of endocervical cells showing changes in nuclear and cytoplasmic morphology, the smears ought to have been classified, at least, as 'borderline'.

---

[168] [2002] EWHC 2037 (TCC), 88 Con LR 1, [20].   [169] (1987) 37 BLR 92 (CA).   [170] [2014] EWHC 43 (TCC) [105].
[171] [2002] EWHC 2037 (TCC) [20], [75], and [104].   [172] (2000) 55 BMLR 63 (CA).

Of course, where the *Bolam* test does not apply, then the court may select one expert's explanation over that of another – because, whilst the court is not supposed to prefer one body of medical opinion to the other, where both represent respected medical practice, experts' explanations *of fact* fall outside the *Bolam* test.

In *Fallows v Randle*,[173] this approach was applied, where contrary explanations occurred, between C's and D's experts, as to why a 'Fallope' ring was not in place when a second operation was carried out, when it ought to have been.

Not matters of 'expert judgment'

§7.20 Given that the *Bolam* test applies to matters requiring 'expert judgment', i.e., matters where special skill or expertise is required and for which the court needs evidence on what constitutes the relevant 'body of practice', matters falling outside 'expert judgment' are not governed by that test. Rather, these matters fall to be determined by the court's forming its own view as to breach.

The *Bolam* test applies 'where the court *cannot answer the question* without expert evidence, as to the body of professional practice prevailing at the time, where the negligence lies in not following established practice' (per *Royal Brompton v Hammond*[174]). HH Judge Lloyd QC outlined the two reasons why *Bolam* evidence is needed: (1) 'the court would not otherwise know of it, as a matter of common sense (or judicial notice), or as a matter of expertise which the court should possess', and (2) 'as a matter of policy, a professional person should not be held liable without the court being satisfied that any competent professional would have done otherwise'. In other words, *Bolam* evidence is required to give the court information as to the relevant 'body of practice' which the court is unable to determine for itself.

Hence, once the expert strays into territory where he simply gives his own personal reaction as to what he would have done in the scenario; or provides an opinion that does not require specialist skill at all, then the court does not need that evidence to determine breach – it makes that assessment for itself (per *Michael Hyde v JD Williams*[175]), albeit that peer professional opinion may still sometimes be helpful on the point.

In *Worboys v Acme Investments Ltd*,[176] Sachs LJ gave the example of where a court could find a breach of duty against the professional D, without resort to *Bolam* evidence – where, say, 'an architect omitted to provide a front door to the premises'. Expert judgment requires the exercise of some special skill or expertise – but providing a visible and accessible means of access to premises does not require architectural skill and expertise, so the court can decide for itself whether the failure to provide such a door is a breach, without recourse to expert *Bolam* evidence. In *Wembridge v Winter*,[177] there was a large explosion of fireworks stored in a steel shipping container on a farm near Lewes in East Sussex. Two people were killed in the explosion.

---

[173] (QB, 7 May 1996), aff'd: [1997] 8 Med LR 160 (CA).   [174] [2002] EWHC 2037 (TCC), 88 Con LR 1, [17], [20].

[175] [2001] PNLR 233 (CA) [25], citing: *Nye Saunders and Partners v Alan E Bristow* (1987) 37 BLR 92 (CA) 103 and *Gold v Haringey HA* [1988] 1 QB 481 (CA) 490.

[176] (1969) 4 BLR 133, 139, and cited in: *Royal Brompton* [2002] EWHC 2037 (TCC) [18].

[177] [2013] EWHC 2331 (QB) [223].

Their estates and various firefighters and police officers sued for injuries sustained. Mr Winter, D1, gave inadequate or misleading information to firefighters at the scene about the contents of the container. East Sussex Fire and Rescue Service, D2, were sued for failing to evacuate the fireground. **Held:** breach proven. The *Bolam* test of breach did not apply to this scenario. There were no different schools of thought about highly technical matters in dealing with fireworks explosions, and whether/when to evacuate the fireground; rather, the 'problem is the speed and complexity of events, rather than making allowance for different intellectual or technical approaches'.

There are numerous facets of professional practice, however, where it is a very finely-balanced judgment as to whether or not the matter truly falls to be determined by *Bolam* evidence. For example, the case law is not always entirely consistent about whether the assessment of risks and benefits is a matter which properly falls within the *Bolam* test of breach. In *Bolitho*,[178] Lord Browne-Wilkinson observed that '[t]he assessment of medical risks and benefits is a matter of clinical judgment which a judge would not normally be able to make without expert evidence'. On the other hand, in *Michael Hyde v JD Williams & Co*[179] (the phenolic yellowing case), the court was of the view that whether D should have further investigated the risk of discoloration did not require any special architectural skills, but was simply an exercise in discounting the risk, and the factors relevant to that risk could be assessed by the court itself. The trial judge held that the factors governing that risk assessment 'are not peculiar to architectural or engineering practice. It was a matter of weighing risk against benefits: the risk was a known risk of some form of discoloration on materials; the potential effect of *any* form of discoloration on garments which were going to be kept in the distribution centre was obviously a matter of great concern ... this had to be weighed against the benefits of lower cost and a more flexible heating system'. Further investigations should have been carried out.

Similarly, whilst only matters of 'clinical judgment' in medical practice fall within the province of the *Bolam* test, the phrase has been widely interpreted, to permit *Bolam* evidence to determine the question (subject to *Bolitho's* caveat). That the following instances were taken to amount to 'clinical judgment' may appear somewhat surprising, but nevertheless, they fell within the *Bolam* test of breach:

- the nature of communications between nursing and physician staff, when a patient is discharged, because any decision about discharge from hospital involves an exercise of professional judgment by the medical professional to either authorise the discharge or to refer the patient to a colleague because of continuing worrying symptoms:

> In *Rehman v University College London*,[180] patient C was discharged following abdominal surgery, but where her bowel had (unknown to staff) been perforated during the operation, and where C later suffered severe peritonitis, her condition became life-threatening, and she required further urgent surgery. C claimed that the hospital discharged her too early, that she was in obvious pain at the point of discharge by the nursing staff who authorised her departure, and that had she not been discharged, the perforated bowel would have been diagnosed and repaired earlier. C argued

---

[178] [1998] AC 232 (HL) 243.   [179] [2000] EWCA Civ 211.

[180] [2004] EWHC 1361 (QB) [72]–[74], citing, e.g.: *Chapman v Rix* [1994] 5 Med LR 239 (HL) 245 (decided 21 Dec 1960) (Keith LJ, dissenting); and M Jones, *Medical Negligence* (3rd edn, Sweet & Maxwell, 2003).

that this case concerned, essentially, a breakdown of communication – the nursing staff ought to have informed the medical staff that C was in pain and did not wish to go home, that this was not a case of clinical judgment, and that a hospital was no different from any other work place where news was not communicated between employees. **Held:** breach proven. *Bolam* applied, so that expert evidence was admissible on how a responsible nurse would act when particular symptoms manifested, and on whether it would be entirely within the nurse's discretion to make up his own mind at the point of discharge.

- managing and organising hospital staff to meet on-call responsibilities – as the court noted in *Garcia v St Mary's NHS Trust*, '[o]bviously, this issue does not relate to medical or surgical diagnosis or techniques. What it relates to is staffing levels. But it has been argued before me on the footing that the *Bolam/Bolitho* principles apply to that question as well',[181] and the court accepted that:

  In *Garcia v St Mary's*, facts previously, the claim concerned whether it was reasonable for the hospital not to make provision for an on-call cardiothoracic registrar to stay overnight in the hospital. Without that measure, patient C claimed (and the court agreed) that there was an inevitable half-hour delay built into the system between the 'crash call and the commencement of a re-sternotomy', which was a system which condemned C to suffer brain damage. **Held:** no breach proven. *Bolam* applied, and the professional practice governing staffing levels survived *Bolitho* scrutiny (as discussed previously).

- acquiring information from a patient about his symptoms – as the court remarked in *Burne v A*, '[t]his skill, while an important aspect of clinical practice, sits at the threshold rather than at the centre of it'.[182]

  In *Burne*, doctor D sought to gain information from a mother over the telephone about what symptoms her child, C, was showing. C was vomiting at school and experiencing headaches. C had been born prematurely, and with a hydrocephalic condition that required him to be fitted at the age of nine weeks with a ventriculo-peritoneal shunt. This device continuously drained excess fluid from the brain cavity, and any blockage of it was potentially critical. This had occurred at least once previously. Following a conversation between mother and D, a diagnosis of upper respiratory infection was made by telephone. The following day, C's condition worsened, he was admitted to hospital, and it was found that the shunt had become blocked, leading to a heart attack and brain damage. **Held:** regarding the information-gathering technique used here, *Bolam* evidence was relevant. D's questioning fell short of the reasonable standard of care, given that 'this was no ordinary patient'. The medical evidence on both sides was that making enquiry about C's condition by a series of 'open' questions, to help with diagnosis, was acceptable professional practice. The trial judge disagreed, holding that, in relation to C whose particular vulnerability was known to D, 2–3 direct, leading, 'closed', questions about C's vomiting and drowsiness would have led to a correct diagnosis of a blocked shunt. (Ultimately, a retrial was ordered, because the medical experts at trial had not been asked to address the *Bolitho* point specifically, i.e., whether their view could be so lacking in logic that it should be rejected by the court.)

---

[181] [2006] EWHC 2314 (QB) [88].   [182] [2006] EWCA Civ 24, [13] (Sedley LJ).

OTHER POTENTIAL TESTS OF BREACH

Contravening specific duties of care

§7.21 The content of the duty of care which D owes C may, in some cases, also define whether D has breached that duty of care.

Where D is under a specific, and more narrowly-focused, duty than the general duty to exercise reasonable care to avoid or to minimise the risk of harm to C, and D contravenes the duty, that will constitute a breach, e.g.:

- a doctor is under a specific duty to warn a patient of material or significant risks associated with an operative procedure or treatment (as examined in Chapter 3). Hence, failure-to-warn of a specific risk of that kind will constitute breach;
- a driver is under a specific duty to exercise reasonable care towards other road-users. Breach may be constituted by, e.g., failing to provide any, or any proper lookout; losing control of the vehicle; failing to apply the brakes in time, or at all; failing to stop, steer, or otherwise control his vehicle so as to avoid a collision.

Contravening relevant standards or rules

§7.22 In determining whether D took all reasonable steps to reduce or eliminate the risk of harm to C, a court may have regard to the governing rules or standards which apply to D's conduct. However, adherence to, or departure from, those rules/standards is *not* conclusive on the question of breach.

Compliance or otherwise with building standards arises particularly in the context of occupiers who are sued for faulty premises. D's failure to comply with industry or professional construction standards (such as the relevant British Building Standard) does not **necessarily** entail a breach, so as to lead to liability under the Occupiers' Liability Act 1957. According to Staughton LJ in *Green v Building Scene Ltd*,[183] 'it is one thing to lay down ... standards, with [the] objective [of avoiding accidents], and another to define what is reasonably safe in all the circumstances of a particular case.' Conversely, the Court of Appeal reiterated in dicta, in *Perry v Butlins*,[184] that compliance with professional standards does not necessarily preclude liability on the part of occupier D (no building regulations directly bore upon the issue there). Nevertheless, compliance with relevant building standards is often referred to as a relevant pointer to the conclusion that occupier D was not in breach of his common duty of care (as occurred, e.g., in *McGivney v Golderslea Ltd*[185]). Further principles, relevant to the standard of care, and proof of breach, on an occupier's part, are discussed in Chapter 12.

The same principle applies, say, where an amateur referee does not comply with the 'Laws of the Game' for rugby union, as issued by the Council of the International Rugby Football Board. Departure from those rules does not **automatically** impute breach by that referee either. It will depend upon the circumstances (see e.g. the discussion of *Vowles v Evans* in Chapter 6).

---

[183] [1994] PIQR P259 (CA) P269.   [184] [1998] Ed CR 39 (CA).
[185] [1997] EWCA Civ 2656, (2001) 17 Const LJ 454.

Contravening the 'making it worse' rule

Scope of application, and derivation

§7.23 The 'making it worse' test of breach provides that breach is proven where D makes C's condition worse than it would have been without D's intervention.

The test has very narrow application – and has been the subject of much criticism in any event. Its application appears to be limited to two fields of endeavour:

- where the 'good Samaritan' D goes to the aid of someone who is injured or imperilled, and in 'wading in' and assisting, makes C's condition worse than it would have been without D's intervention; and
- where D is an emergency services provider (and, in this context, the test is reconsidered under 'Public authority liability', in Chapter 13).

Feasibly, this test may be more difficult for C to prove, because D's conduct may fall below the reasonable standard of care, and yet **not** make the situation for C worse, in that the outcome (e.g., death) was always destined for C in any event. In that event, D will be excused. A rule of breach that is harder to satisfy for C is yet a further bulwark against successful claims being brought against either category of D. This reflects a judicial concern 'not to discourage benevolence and altruism' (as the Court of Appeal put it in *McLoughlin v O'Brian*[186]) or Samaritanesque help.

The making-it-worse test of breach has some scant support at Court of Appeal level in *Kent v Griffiths* where, by its inexcusable delay, the ambulance **did** make the situation for C worse than it would have been, had they not undertaken to intervene.

> In *Kent v Griffiths*,[187] Mrs Kent, C, was pregnant, and became seriously ill at home with a severe asthma attack. Her GP attended C at home, and urgently called an ambulance to transfer her to hospital. A 999 call was placed by the GP and accepted by the ambulance service, with two follow-up calls eliciting assurances that an emergency ambulance was 'on its way'. The ambulance was delayed, and C suffered both a miscarriage and brain damage as a result of the delay in reaching hospital. **Held:** breach proven. An assumption of responsibility/reliance 'crystallised' when the first 999 call was accepted: '[t]he acceptance of the call established the duty of care'. Had the GP who had called the ambulance been told that it would take some 40 minutes to arrive at the patient's house, the patient's husband could have driven her to hospital himself, thereby saving crucial minutes.

Lord Woolf MR cited, with approval, the well-known Canadian case of *Horsley v MacLaren (The Ogopogo)*,[188] where the making-it-worse rule was advocated too – but in that case, the actions of the rescuer, in seeking to save Mr Matthews, C, when he fell overboard from D's cruiser, 'cannot be said to have worsened Matthews' condition'. Some further dicta support for the application of the rule in the good Samaritan context was evident in *Capital and Counties plc v Hampshire CC*, where Stuart-Smith LJ observed that, if a doctor 'volunteers his assistance, his only duty as a matter of law is not to make the victim's condition worse'.[189]

---

[186] [1981] QB 599 (CA) 611 (Stephenson LJ), appeal allowed: [1983] 1 AC 410 (HL), but this point was not criticised.
[187] [2001] QB 36 (CA) [49].   [188] [1972] SCR 441 (SCC) 452, [1971] 2 Lloyd's Rep 410, 412.
[189] [1997] QB 1004 (CA) 1035 (the other members of the CA agreed). For further discussion, and criticisms, of the making-it-worse test, see: Mulheron, *Medical Negligence: Non-Patient and Third Party Claims* (Ashgate Publishing, 2010), pp 207–10.

Criticisms of the test

There are several difficulties with the 'making it worse' test:[190]

i. as a test of breach, it may be inconsistent with the outcome of the *Bolam* test of breach (i.e., peer professional opinion may suggest that whatever D did fell below the standard of care, even if it did not actually make C's condition worse that if he had done nothing). Breach tests which produce different results may lead to a lack of coherency in the law;

ii. as stated, the test seems to have been endorsed specifically where the law is reluctant to find good Samaritans and emergency service providers negligent, and a more difficult test of breach accords with that sympathetic attitude. However, it is highly questionable whether it is needed in those scenarios in any event. It will be recalled, from Chapter 6, that the standard of care applicable to both the good Samaritan and the emergency services provider is likely to be suppressed by two factors – emergency 'battle' conditions, and a *Bolam*-standard that does not attribute to D any skills which he did not profess to have;

iii. the test seems more aligned with causation than it is to breach. If good Samaritan D intervenes to assist C, but C's outcome would have been dreadful (e.g., fatal) anyway, and D's lack of reasonable care did not make C's condition worse than was pre-ordained before D intervened, then D's conduct did not cause C's injury (i.e., death) (per the 'but-for' test explored in Chapter 8). That does not mean that there was no breach – but rather, that there was no causal link established. The same problem was evident, obversely, in *Kent v Griffiths*. The intervention by the ambulance D, 40 minutes late, meant that C's husband did not drive her to hospital; if he had done so, then on the balance of probabilities, C's physical damage and the loss of her baby would have been avoided. However, that is a causal, and not a breach, enquiry;

iv. the principle outlined at the commencement of this section states that D must make the situation worse than if he had done nothing (for that is the interpretation which this author places upon the Court of Appeal statements identified earlier). However, there is another possible interpretation of the 'making it worse' rule which has been suggested academically, i.e., that D made C's condition worse 'than if timely and competent treatment had been provided by [D]'.[191]

Surely, in the good Samaritan or emergency service provider scenarios, the better course is to apply the usual *Bolam* test of breach – as indeed applied in *Cattley v St John Ambulance Brigade*[192] (discussed in Chapter 6), where there was a strong body of evidence from those skilled in first-aiding and other highly-qualified medical specialists, that D's officers treated C's injuries in accordance with the ordinary skills to be expected of a St John Ambulance first-aider trained in accordance with the First Aid Manual.

THE DOCTRINE OF *RES IPSA LOQUITUR*

Setting the context

Meaning, effect and rationale

§7.24   C may seek to rely on the doctrine of *res ipsa loquitur*, wherever difficulty is encountered in proving breach, but C alleges that, nevertheless, it must have been negligence that caused

---

190 Some of these points are also made in, e.g.: A Grubb, 'Medical Negligence: Duty of Care and *Bolam*' (1998) 6 *Medical L Rev* 120; and see too: I Kennedy and A Grubb, *Principles of Medical Law* (Oxford University Press, 1998) 301; M Jones, *Medical Negligence* (3rd edn, Sweet & Maxwell, 2003) 112; K Williams, 'Litigation against English NHS Ambulance Services and the Rules in *Kent v Griffiths*' (2007) 15 *Medical L Rev* 153, fn 34.

191 Williams, 'Medical Samaritans: Is there a Duty to Treat?' (2001) 21 *OJLS* 393, 394.   192 QB, 25 Nov 1988.

his injury or damage – for what other rational and feasible explanation could there be? The accident would not ordinarily occur without negligence.

Literally, the phrase, *res ipsa loquitur*, means that 'the thing speaks for itself'.[193] Whatever else may be said about the doctrine, the notion that it is as simple and transparent as this phrase suggests should be immediately dismissed. As a doctrine, it is not of ancient origin – its source has been traced[194] to an 1863 decision.

> In *Byrne v Boadle*,[195] a flour barrel fell from D's shop window on to C, who was a passerby below. **Held**: '[t]his is one of those cases in which, I think, a presumption of negligence by defendant is raised, and it was for him, who had all the means of evidence and knowledge within his reach, to meet it'.

Two years later, Erle CJ gave what has come to be regarded as the classic exposition of the principle:

> In *Scott v London and St Katherine's Docks*,[196] Mr Scott, C, a customs-house officer, entered D's dock, and while passing under a crane, was injured when some bags of sugar fell onto him from the crane platform. There was no warning of the danger, and no explanation as to how the sugar bags came to fall. **Held:** the doctrine applied.
>
>> where the thing is shewn to be under the management of [D] or his servants, and the accident is such as in the ordinary course of things does not happen if those who have the management use proper care, it affords reasonable evidence, in the absence of explanation by [D], that the accident arose from want of care.

For much of its existence, though, the doctrine has been bedeviled by judicial inconsistency and, at times, barely-concealed antipathy – per such remarks as, 'the one thing that can certainly be said ... is that "it has not been allowed to speak for itself"' (per *Anchor Products Ltd v Hedges*[197]); that if the phrase 'had not been in Latin, nobody would have called it a principle' (per *Fred Ballard v North British Rwy Co*[198]); and that it simply amounts to an 'exotic ... phrase to describe what is, in essence, no more than a common sense approach' (per *Lloyde v West Midlands Gas Board*[199]). Its effect was well-articulated in *MacDonald v York County Hosp*:

> In certain situations, [C's] burden of proving negligence on the part of [D] is difficult, if not impossible, because [C] does not know how his injury or loss occurred and, consequently, cannot plead any act or omission amounting to negligence on the part of [D]. Only in situations where the exact cause of the accident is unknown can the maxim of *res ipsa loquitur* have any application ... *Res ipsa loquitur* is a circumstantial rule of evidence based on the concept that, when an accident occurs under circumstances where it is so improbable that it could have happened without the negligence of [D], the mere happening of the accident gives rise to an inference that [D] was negligent.[200]

[193] *Oxford Dictionary of Law* (6th edn, Oxford) 463.
[194] *Ratcliffe v Plymouth and Torbay HA* [1998] Lloyd's Rep Med 162 (CA) 178 (Brooke LJ).
[195] (1863) 2 H&C 722, 159 ER 299 (Ch) (Pollock CB).
[196] (1865) 3 H&C 596 (Exch) 598, 159 ER 665, 667.
[197] (1966) 115 CLR 493 (HCA) 496, and cited in: *Schellenberg v Tunnel Holdings Pty Ltd* [2000] HCA 18, [121].
[198] 1923 SC (HL) 43, 56 (Lord Shaw).   [199] [1971] 1 WLR 749 (CA) 755 (Megaw LJ).
[200] [1972] 3 OR 469 (HC) 486–87 (Addy J).

In other words, the doctrine's rationale is that, in some cases, 'it would be palpably unfair to require [C] to prove something which is beyond his reach, and which is peculiarly within the range of [D's] capacity of proof' (per *Hanrahan v Merck Sharp & Dohme (Ireland) Ltd*[201]). There is an 'evidential gap' here for C – and the doctrine implies that it would be unfair for the consequences of that 'gap' to rest on C.

There may also be circumstances in which, say, a video recording speaks for itself ('*res ipsa videtur*', as the court termed it in *McKeown v British Horseracing Authy*,[202] but that did not apply in that case). The application of *res ipsa loquitur*, in the particular context of defective products, is considered in 'Defective products' (an online chapter).

Terminology

As a matter of terminology, *res ipsa loquitur* has been called everything, from a 'maxim' to a 'rule of evidence'.[203] Indeed, the topic has descended into jingoistic judicial debate. Some judges have suggested that it indicates 'when a *prima facie* case of negligence is proven' by C (per *Ratcliffe v Plymouth and Torbay HA*[204]) but that it does not raise any presumption (per *Wilsher v Essex AHA*[205]). Others have stated that it **does** raise a 'presumption of negligence', albeit that 'it would be dangerous to allow presumptions to be substituted for ... negligence' (per *Byrne v Boadle*[206]). Some others term it as 'a rule of evidence', but not a rule of law (per *Lillywhite v UCL Hosp NHS Trust*[207]), but some other jurisdictions believe that English judges *have* indeed elevated it to a rule of law (per *Schellenberg v Tunnel Holdings Pty Ltd*[208]). To top it all off, some English judges have refused to call it a 'doctrine' at all (per *Lloyde v West Midlands Gas Board*[209]).

However, in this section, *res ipsa loquitur* is referred to as a 'doctrine', for the sake of convenience.

Raising (and rebutting) the doctrine

To raise the application of the doctrine, C will need to prove the criteria outlined in the following Table (drawn, in most part, from Erle CJ's judgment in *Scott v London and St Katherine's Docks Co*). The doctrine's application can, however, be rebutted by D – or, more colloquially, '[t]he *res* [or thing], which previously spoke for itself, may be silenced, or its voice may, on the whole of the evidence, become too weak or muted' (per *Lloyde v West Midlands Gas Board*).

---

[201] [1988] ILRM 629 (SC) 634–35, cited in: *Lindsay v Mid-Western Health Board* [1993] 2 IR 147 (SC) 168.

[202] [2010] EWHC 508 (Admin) [165].

[203] In the case law, all of the following appear: a 'maxim', a 'rule of law', a 'guide', a 'principle', an 'approach', a 'manner of reasoning', a 'presumption', an 'exotic label', a 'forensic tool', a 'diagnostic theory', a 'brocard', an 'aid' and 'a doctrine'.

[204] [1998] Lloyd's LR (Med) 162 (CA) 177 (Hobhouse LJ).

[205] [1987] QB 730 (CA). Also: *Lloyde v West Midlands Gas Board* [1971] 1 WLR 749 (CA) 755 (Megaw LJ).

[206] (1863) 2 H&C 722 (Exch) 727, 159 ER 299, 301.

[207] [2005] EWCA Civ 1466, [87] (Buxton LJ). Also: *Lindsay v Mid-Western Health Board* [1993] 2 IR 147 (SC).

[208] [2000] HCA 18, [69] (Gaudron J) ('it is, in [Australia], no more than a Latin phrase describing a permissible process of reasoning. The same is true in Canada. However, it may enjoy some higher status as a principle of law or evidence in the UK').

[209] [1971] 1 WLR 749 (CA) 755 (Megaw LJ), cited with approval: *Ratcliffe v Plymouth and Torbay HA* [1998] Lloyd's LR (Med) 162 (CA) 177.

D may do this, via any of the avenues noted by Brooke LJ in *Ratcliffe v Plymouth and Torbay HA*[210]), also outlined in the Table.

C's raising an inference of negligence, via the doctrine:	D's means of displacing an inference of negligence:
• Incontrovertible facts about the act and outcome must 'speak for themselves'; • D had exclusive or sole control over the thing which caused C's damage or injury; • D has no plausible innocent explanation of what caused the accident to occur; **and** • The accident was of a type that does not normally occur in the absence of negligence.	• Too many facts are contested; • D lacked sole or exclusive control over the thing that caused C's damage or injury; • D can offer a plausible 'innocent' explanation of what happened to C, which does not connote any negligence on D's part; or • No rational explanation is possible, but D took all reasonable care and skill and was not negligent.

If any of these four criteria fail for C, then without an inference of negligence to assist him, C must seek to prove that a breach caused the damage of which he complains in the ordinary way – which may be very difficult, if C has no direct evidence by which to substantiate his case.

Dealing with each criterion in turn:

Incontrovertible facts

§7.25   The first criterion of the doctrine is that the incontrovertible facts about the act and outcome must 'speak for themselves'. If there is contested evidence on the very facts said to give rise to the injury, then the doctrine cannot apply.

To invoke the doctrine, C must be able to point to the 'existence of an unchallenged and unchallengeable fact' or facts (per *Doherty v Reynolds*[211]).

> In *Cassidy v Ministry of Health*,[212] Mr Cassidy, C, entered hospital to undergo an operation to repair two stiff fingers, and emerged with four stiff fingers and a 'useless' left hand, which he alleged was due to negligent surgery. **Held:** the doctrine of *res ipsa loquitur* applied.

On the other hand, in circumstances of contested evidence as to what actually happened to C, two factors tend to disprove this criterion for C:

i.   Disputed expert evidence. Wherever the cause of C's injury is contested by expert opinion, than *res ipsa loquitur* is inappropriate – in *Ratcliffe*,[213] Hobhouse LJ said that '[w]here expert and factual evidence has been called on both sides at a trial, [the doctrine's] usefulness will normally have long since been exhausted'.

> In *Croft v Heart of England NHS Foundation Trust*,[214] Arthur Croft, C, suffered an injury during his birth at Solihull Hospital, Birmingham, due to an obstetric brachial plexus injury. C suffered injury

---

[210] See points (4), (5) and (6) in: [1998] Lloyd's Rep Med 168 (Brooke LJ).
[211] [2004] IESC 42, [no pp] (Keane CJ).   [212] [1951] 2 KB 343 (CA).   [213] (1998) 42 BMLR 64 (CA) 85.
[214] [2012] EWHC 1470 (QB). See too: *Doherty v Reynolds* [2004] IESC 42, where the same injury (in an adult) could not give rise to the doctrine's application either.

to the nerves in his neck, and a permanent weakening and loss of function in his right arm, allegedly due to the negligence of the midwifery team. The court noted that, in a previous case in the Chester CC on the same injury in 2009, over 80 pieces of learned literature on the cause of obstetric brachial plexus injuries, plus expert evidence from biomechanical engineers, orthopaedic surgeons, and obstetric experts, were reviewed over a 10-day trial. **Held:** C could not rely on the doctrine, given the disarray of expert evidence on the issue: '[no] conclusion can be drawn as to whether the majority of [obstetric brachial plexus injuries] are probably caused by traction, probably caused by propulsion, or probably caused by a combination of both'. C had to prove his case in the usual way (but failed).

ii. **The procedure was complex and technical.** The more inherently-dangerous or uncertain the procedure, the more difficult is C's task of raising the doctrine – because matters can go tragically amiss, without any negligence at all. Birth is one such procedure, having been described by Denning LJ in *Whitehouse v Jordan* as the 'most dangerous process in the life of anyone'.[215] Complex surgery for gender reassignment is another (per *Bergman v Haertsch*[216]). Indeed, the modern English judicial view is that it is 'doubtful' whether the doctrine has much room to apply in most medical negligence cases (*Thomas v Curley*[217]).

Obversely, the doctrine is more likely to apply where the task was reasonably orthodox, routine and mechanical, but produced an entirely unexpected damage (said Buxton LJ in *Lillywhite v UCL Hosp NHS Trust*[218] – where the doctrine did **not** apply). It can also apply, where a procedure has an excellent safety record (despite its complex and technical nature), because there are so many design and manufacturing protections in place. The maintenance of aircraft is one such category. One time, the 'perils of airflight' would not have permitted the doctrine to apply, but the Privy Council confirmed that those days were well behind:

> In *George v Eagle Air Services Ltd (Saint Lucia)*,[219] Hughes Williams, C, a mechanic working for D, an airline in St Lucia, serviced and repaired D's aircraft. He was flying with a pilot on a flight from St Lucia to Union Island, when the plane crashed as it was about to land at Union Island, and both were killed. C's estate claimed that the pilot must have been negligent. **Held:** the doctrine of *res ipsa loquitur* applied: '[t]his was [D's] aircraft, their flight and their pilot. Aircraft, even small aircraft, do not usually crash, and certainly should not do so. And, if they do, then, especially where the crash is on land as here, ... it is not unreasonable to place on them the burden of producing an explanation which is at least consistent with absence of fault on their part'. However, D did not suggest any explanation for the crash, and hence, failed to displace the inference of pilot negligence.

Sole or exclusive control

§7.26   The second criterion of the doctrine is that the thing which inflicted the damage upon C must have been under the sole management and control of D (or of someone for whom D was responsible).

---

[215] [1980] 1 All ER 650 (CA) 652.   [216] (NSW SC, 22 Jun 2000) [49] (Abadee J).

[217] [2013] EWCA Civ 117, [10], [17], citing: *Ratcliffe v Plymouth and Torbay HA* [1998] Lloyds Rep Med 162 (CA) 177.

[218] [2005] EWCA Civ 1466, [85].   [219] [2009] UKPC 21, [2009] WLR 2133, [13].

According to *Scott v London & St Katherine Docks Co*,[220] the 'thing' under D's control may be, say: the premises where D's activities were conducted and where C suffered injury; the particular activity which D was conducting; or the equipment used by D (i.e., the dock and the crane; or the plane, in *George v Eagle Air*).

> In *Ward v Tesco Stores Ltd*,[221] Ms Ward was shopping at a Tesco's store, when she slipped on some yoghurt which had been spilt on the floor (how it got there was unknown). C sued for the personal injury suffered. C could not prove how long the yoghurt had been there. **Held (2:1):** the doctrine succeeded. The floor was the *res* or 'thing' here, over which D had sole control.

However, if C cannot prove that degree of control on D's part (C squarely bearing the burden of proof), then no inference of negligence is possible. C may confront several problems on this point:

i. Several Ds. If several Ds were involved, then C may be unable to identify which one was responsible for the particular damage (a problem that can often arise where several doctors participated in the operative procedure on C).

> In *Donne Place Investments Ltd v McDonnell*,[222] a dispute arose between developer C, and architect and project manager D, regarding two sites in Chelsea. Their agreement was terminated before the developments were finished. C claimed that D had caused undue delay in performing its obligations under the building contracts, e.g., it took 9 months to obtain awards for three party walls, before construction works could commence. C relied on *res ipsa loquitur* to argue that the delay was negligent. **Held:** *res ipsa loquitur* could not apply. The task of securing the party wall awards was not in D's sole control; rather, a surveyor had been appointed who was responsible for much of that project work. D was not responsible for the appointment of all subcontractors, and hence, the relevant activities were not within D's sole control.

ii. Lack of control over the object/instrument. Another potential complication is whether D had the requisite control, when an object or instrument was in the sole custody or possession of C, the injured party.

Conceivably, this problem could arise in the employment context, when a machine is being operated by employee C, whilst on the employer's, D's, premises. This commonly precludes the doctrine in that context. On the other hand, medical negligence scenarios are quite different. As Hobhouse LJ said in *Ratcliffe*: 'it is commonplace that [patient C] will not have fully known what occurred, particularly if the relevant procedure was an operation carried out under anaesthetic. The procedures were under the control of [doctor D]'.[223]

No innocent explanation

§7.27   The third criterion of the doctrine is that D must have no plausible innocent explanation of why C suffered the injury. D's burden, to rebut an inference of negligence, is *not* to prove an 'innocent' explanation on the balance of probabilities – only that the explanation is 'plausible'.

In seeking to rebut the doctrine, D's plausible innocent explanation may owe a great deal to the uncertainties of the scientific process by which the accident happened, or the inscrutability of

---

[220] (1865) 3 H&C 596, 601, [1861–73] All ER Rep 246, 248.   [221] [1976] 1 WLR 810 (CA).
[222] [2011] EWHC 930 (TCC).   [223] [1998] Lloyd's Rep Med 168 (CA) 65.

the human body, etc. To be 'plausible', D's explanation must be something more than 'theoretically or remotely possible' (per *Smith v Sheridan*[224]), but less than the standard of proof on the balance of probabilities (per *Lillywhite v UCL Hosp NHS Trust*[225]).

This principle has been evident in various contexts – e.g., in product liability, engineering and medical accidents – where a plausible explanation was possible, thus rebutting the doctrine's application:

> In *Carroll v Fearon, Bent and Dunlop Ltd*,[226] a tyre burst on C's car, causing the car to crash. Given that the tyre exploded several years after it left the factory, and had been regularly used since, the tyre's failure 'might have resulted from any one of a number of possible causes, including ... misuse or abuse, or inadequate repair of earlier damage'. In *United Marine Aggregates Ltd v GM Welding & Engineering Ltd*,[227] a serious fire broke out in a large aggregate processing plant owned by UMA, C, situated at Murphy's Wharf on the Thames, near Greenwich. C claimed that the fire was caused by hot work being carried out by contractors, D, who were doing repair work at the wharf, by setting fire to the rubber lining in a steel hopper or chute (the actual cause of the fire was never determined). The same method of working had been used without incident for almost 20 years; so arguably this fire must have had something to do with how the work was being carried out by D. C had changed the lining material in 2006, and it was possible that it was more combustible than the previous materials. That went 'some way to undermining any reliance' on *res ipsa loquitur*. In *Ratcliffe v Plymouth and Torbay HA*,[228] C underwent a successful operation on his right ankle, and received a spinal anaesthetic to relieve post-operative pain. Thereafter, he was left with a serious neurological defect, from his waist downwards. An MRI scan showed a lesion in the thoracic spine. C claimed that this must have been caused by the spinal anaesthetic being administered at the wrong place, and claimed *res ipsa loquitur*. The anaesthetist responsible for the spinal injection, D, stated that he had administered it at the lumbar spine. There was a plausible explanation for the paralysis, i.e., some asymptomatic weakness in C's central nervous system which the stress of the surgery could have 'brought to life'. Hence, *res ipsa loquitur* could not apply.

Hence, providing some sort of plausible innocent explanation is a common 'safety avenue' for D, by which to rebut the doctrine. Uncertainty is a valuable commodity, when it comes to rebutting an inference of negligence. As was memorably put in one Canadian case:

> The human body is not a container filled with material whose performance can be predictably chartered and analysed ... Because of this, medical science has not yet reached the stage where the law ought to presume that a patient must come out of an operation as well as or better than he went into it.[229]

On the other hand, remote and implausible possibilities as to why C suffered the injury will not be good enough to rebut the doctrine. Wherever D's explanation is considered to be 'entirely theoretical and based on speculation' (to quote *Lindsay v Mid-Western Health Board*[230]), then the doctrine cannot be rebutted, and an inference of negligence may arise.

---

[224] [2005] EWHC 614 (QB) [113] (implausible explanation; negligence proven).

[225] [2005] EWCA Civ 1466, [60], citing: *Ratcliffe* [1998] Lloyd's Rep Med 162 (CA) point 5 (Brooke LJ).

[226] [1998] PIQR 416 (CA), cited in: *Divya v Toyo Tire and Rubber Co Ltd* [2011] EWHC 1993 (QB) [69].

[227] [2012] EWHC 779 (TCC) [273].   [228] [1998] Lloyd's L Rep 162 (CA).

[229] *Girard v Royal Columbian Hosp* (1976), 66 DLR (3d) 676 (BCSC) (Andrews J), and cited in, e.g.: *Lindsay v Mid-Western Health Board* [1993] 2 IR 147 (SC) 166–67.

[230] [1993] 2 IR 147 (HC) [6] (Morris J).

In *Lindsay*, patient C, 8, was admitted for an emergency appendectomy under general anaesthetic. After the operation, it appeared initially that C was beginning to regain consciousness in the normal manner, but then she experienced a series of seizures, and sank into a coma. C suffered from irreversible brain damage, and never regained consciousness. By trial, C had been in a deep coma for 18 years. C claimed that her condition was due to a 'hypoxic insult' which she had suffered during the course of the operation, as a result of a reduction in, or withdrawal of, her oxygen supply. Anaesthetist D put forward the explanation that C had suffered from a viral infection. This was rejected; it was not a plausible explanation. The more likely explanation for C's damage (said the court) was the withdrawal of or reduction in oxygen supply.

The accident does not normally occur without negligence

§7.28   The fourth criterion is that the accident must be of a type that does not normally occur in the absence of negligence. Hence, D can rebut the doctrine by proving, not that there was an innocent explanation, but that D was not negligent.

D may rebut any inference of negligence under *res ipsa loquitur* by explaining that, irrespective of the adverse outcome (which cannot be explained by medical science), D exercised all reasonable care and skill during the activity or procedure. The doctrine will then have no room to operate. This acts as an *alternative* avenue to the innocent explanation avenue of rebuttal. This was confirmed by Stuart-Smith LJ in *Delaney v Southmead HA*: 'it is always open to [D] to rebut a case of *res ipsa loquitur*, either by giving an explanation of what happened which is inconsistent with negligence, or by showing that [D] had exercised all reasonable care'.[231]

Where things fall from a height onto C, innocent explanations may be hard to come by; and it will also be difficult for D to show that things fall without negligence (whether that negligence be framed as to how the thing was secured in place, where it was placed, or what security measures were placed around it to stop it falling). Where the flour bag dropped from the shop window in *Byrne v Boadle*,[232] and the sugar bags fell in *Scott v St Katherine Docks Co*,[233] the doctrine was established in each case. Slipping hazards in food halls and in supermarkets ('yoghurt pots and pieces of fruit like grapes and cherries appear to be frequent culprits', per *Bovaird v Westfield Shoppingtowns*[234]), or slipping on water near a drinks dispensing station on a cruise ship (as occurred in, e.g., *Dawkins v Carnival plc (t/as P&O Cruises)*,[235] also give rise to the doctrine – which will be impossible to rebut if D did not have a reasonable system of inspection and frequent cleaning in place which would have detected a spillage sometime before C's accident.

In *Ward v Tesco Stores Ltd*,[236] facts previously, **held:** the doctrine of *res ipsa loquitur* applied. Slipping on yoghurt on a floor was not something that would occur in the ordinary course of things, if floors are kept clean and spillages dealt with as soon as they occur. The incident required some explanation from Tesco, D, to show that the accident did not arise from any want of care on its part. D could not do that. The evidence was that the spillage had been on the floor long enough for it to have been cleaned up by a member of staff. It did not matter that C could not prove that the yoghurt had only been there for a few seconds. Whenever there was slippery liquid on the floor of

---

[231] (1995) 26 BMLR 111 (CA) 118.   [232] (1863) 159 ER 299 (Exch).   [233] (1865) 3 H&C 596, 159 ER 665.
[234] [2007] NIQB 123, [13].   [235] [2011] EWCA Civ 1237
[236] [1976] 1 WLR 810 (CA) (Lawton and Megaw LJJ; Ormrod LJ dissented).

the supermarket, D should know that it was not an uncommon occurrence, and that if it was not promptly attended to, it would cause a serious risk to customers, which was consistent with fault on D's part. In *Saldanha v Fulton Navigation Inc*,[237] Kennedy Saldanha, C, was First Engineer on board D's ship, the *Omega King*. It was lying at anchor off the coast of Wales, when the weather conditions deteriorated and became severe. The vessel began to drag anchor, the master decided to weigh anchor, the anchor would not come up because the locking pin on the chain stopper was jammed, so C was instructed to inspect and fix the pin, to save a potentially dangerous situation for ship and crew. While C was doing that, a large wave broke over the bow, and he fell against a nearby bollard and was injured. C sued D, his employer, in negligence. **Held:** the doctrine of *res ipsa loquitur* applied, because 'there is a very strong inference that ships do not get into this type of situation without negligence having occurred. Either the problems should be sufficiently foreseen so as to be avoided at an early stage [or] it is usually possible to alleviate the effects of wind, waves and current by appropriate engine and rudder manoeuvres short of actually weighing anchor and steaming away'. D could not provide a rational explanation of how the dangerous situation arose without negligence on its part.

On the other hand, D may well succeed in rebutting the doctrine in this way:

In *Lindsay v Mid-Western Health Board*,[238] facts previously, **held:** *res ipsa loquitur* could not apply. Although there was no innocent explanation possible (see above), no negligence could be proven: '[it] was for [anaethesist D] to establish that, from beginning to end of this anaesthetic procedure, there was no negligence on its part. This it did decisively ... and so the case returned to [C's] bailiwick to prove negligence'. Ultimately, C could not prove that D lacked reasonable care, and failed in her claim.

Of course, this element of the doctrine raises a significant issue regarding burden of proof – is it for D to prove he was not negligent on the balance of probabilities where the doctrine is raised, or is it for C to still prove that D was negligent in the usual way? It has been a vexed question, as discussed below.

The burden of proof

§7.29   The applicable burden of proof, where the doctrine of *res ipsa loquitur* is raised by C, is not entirely clear in English law, but the preferential view is that D bears an evidentiary burden, where the doctrine is raised.

It is trite law that C must prove his case of negligence on the balance of probabilities. However, the uncertainty surrounding the burden of proof, where *res ipsa loquitur* is pleaded, is attributable to some judicial language which has been either vague or somewhat inconsistent. **Three possibilities have been raised in the case law.**

Option #1: D cannot rebut the inference, because an irrebuttable presumption arises
The first possibility is that C raises the inference (by establishing the four criteria discussed above), and thereafter, the '*res*' (the thing) speaks for itself. The *res* raises an irrebuttable presumption of negligence to be drawn – and there is no point in D bearing any burden, because

[237] [2011] EWHC 1118 (Admlty), [2011] 2 Lloyd's Rep 206.   [238] [1993] 2 IR 177 (SC), quote at 185.

negligence is made out, and nothing that D could provide by way of evidence could rebut the presumption.

This possibility was noted by the Court of Appeal in *Ratcliffe v Plymouth and Torbay HA*,[239] as being *res ipsa loquitur* in its 'purest form', whereby the thing 'does truly speak for itself'. A couple of examples were given: a surgeon cuts off a patient's right foot, instead of the left: or a swab is left in the operation site.

However, Brooke LJ remarked, in *Ratcliffe*,[240] that this scenario is likely to be **very** unusual, for two reasons: (i) D is likely to bring some factual evidence to bear on the question of what precisely happened: '[i]t is likely to be a very rare medical negligence case in which [D] takes the risk of calling no factual evidence, when such evidence is available to them, of the circumstances surrounding a procedure which led to an unexpected outcome for a patient'; and (ii) once C adduces expert evidence as well, the thing is not 'speaking for itself' any longer, and even if D were not to call any evidence at all, 'the judge would be deciding the case on inferences he was entitled to draw from the whole of the evidence (including the expert evidence), and not on the application of the maxim in its purest form'. Indeed, any suggestion of an irrebuttable presumption of negligence has been strongly disfavoured in English case law since.

Option #2: D bears an evidentiary burden

This second possibility is the mid-spectrum position, whereby D bears an evidentiary burden only. C can use the doctrine to raise a *rebuttable* inference or presumption of negligence on D's part, where the four criteria are satisfied. D must then rebut the presumption (if he can) by either establishing a plausible innocent explanation for what happened to C; or that whatever happened to C cannot be explained, but that no negligence occurred. If D can achieve this, then no inference of negligence can be drawn. The persuasive burden of establishing negligence still (and always) remains with C, and C must prove his claim in negligence in the usual way, 'without that initial advantage' (per *Hussain v King Edward VII Hosp*[241]).

This view was specifically approved by the Supreme Court recently in *David T Morrison & Co Ltd (t/a Gael Home Interiors) v ICL Plastics Ltd (Scotland)*, where Lord Reed noted that the doctrine 'belongs to the law of evidence, and refers to circumstances from the establishment of which an inference of negligence can be drawn, so as to shift the evidential burden of proof to [D]'.[242] Additionally, that D only bears an evidentiary burden has derived much Court of Appeal support too (e.g., in *Lloyde v West Midlands Gas Board*,[243] and *Bhamra v Dubb (t/as Lucky Caterers)*,[244] where the court approved shifting the evidential burden to D as being a concept 'simply ... of common sense', and in *Bull v Devon AHA*[245] too, where the court noted that, 'delays in summoning and securing the attendance of the registrar or consultant were so substantial as to place upon the authority the evidential burden of justifying them', which onus was not discharged).

It follows, under this option, that *res ipsa loquitur* does **not** shift the persuasive (or legal) burden of proof – that always rests on C. Once D has discharged the evidentiary burden which the doctrine raises, it remains for C to prove negligence in the ordinary way.

---

[239] (1998) 42 BMLR 64 (CA) 82–83.   [240] *ibid*, 65–66.
[241] [2012] EWHC 3441 (QB) [35]; and see too: *Hay v Grampian Health Board* (1994) 25 BMLR 98 (CSOH) [202].
[242] [2014] UKSC 48, [4].   [243] [1971] 1 WLR 749 (CA) 755 (Megaw LJ).
[244] [2010] EWCA Civ 13, [31]–[34].   [245] (1989) 22 BMLR 79 (CA) 101 (Slade LJ).

Option #3: D bears the persuasive burden

A third possibility is that the persuasive burden shifts to D under the doctrine, so that, once raised, D must disprove negligence on the balance of probabilities. It is not for C to prove that he was negligent; it is for D to prove that he was not. This would effectively transfer the persuasive onus to D to disprove negligence.

This approach was advocated in *Cassidy v Ministry of Health*,[246] where the Court of Appeal held that the legal burden lay on hospital authority D to prove that there had not been any negligence on its part in the post-operative treatment of C's hand, left useless after the operation (which burden D could not discharge).

However, subsequent English authority strongly suggests that, on this point, *Cassidy* is no longer good law. In *Ratcliffe*,[247] Hobhouse LJ said that '[t]he burden of proving the negligence of [D] remains throughout upon [C]'. This was reiterated recently in *Hussain v King Edward VII Hosp*,[248] where Eady J remarked that, '[o]ne should never lose sight of the simple fact that the burden of proof remains on [C] throughout ... That is why [D] is only required to show a plausible alternative explanation in order to rebut a prima facie case.'

Conclusion on burden

It appears that the more-countenanced view is that D only bears an evidentiary burden, where the doctrine is raised against him. This is entirely defensible, given the point mentioned in the Ontario case of *Phillips v Ford Motor Co*,[249] that shifting the persuasive burden to D 'would come dangerously close to a fictional use of the maxim as a foundation for the doctrine of strict liability', whereby adverse outcome equals liability.

Of course, there is much sympathy for C, in these sorts of cases. The doctrine is said to apply precisely because, in the procedure in question (say, a surgical operation), C 'rarely knows anything; what has happened is known only to the [D]' (per *Lindsay v Mid-Western Health Board*[250]). However, the weight of English authority shows that it is only intermittently effective.

Two concluding notes

Although the doctrine of *res ipsa loquitur* is often considered relevant to proof of breach, it is probably more pertinent to proof of causation. As described in *Lloyde v West Midlands Gas Board*, the doctrine 'enable[s] [C] to succeed because, *although the precise cause of the accident* cannot be established, the proper inference on balance of probability is that the cause, whatever it may have been, involved a failure by [D] to take due care for [C's] safety'.[251] In *Corby Group Litigation v Corby DC* too, the court noted that, '[t]here is also reliance upon the doctrine of *res ipsa loquitur*, so far as causation is concerned'.[252] Hence, arguably it is proof of causation – rather than proof of breach – which is truly at the heart of the doctrine.

Finally, it is perhaps fair to say that, whilst the English judiciary's reception to *res ipsa loquitur* has been mixed, litigants' reliance on it has been equally uncertain. They have sometimes

---

[246] [1951] 2 KB 343 (CA).   [247] [1998] PIQR P170 (CA) P186.   [248] [2012] EWHC 3441 (QB) [12].

[249] [1971] 2 OR 637 (HC) 653.   [250] [1993] 2 IR 147 (SC) 183.

[251] [1971] 1 WLR 749 (CA) 755, cited, e.g., in: *Kyriakou v Chase Farms Hosp NHS Trust* [2006] EWHC 2131 (QB) [52].

[252] [2009] EWHC 1944 (TCC) [702].

taken the unusual step of asking for judicial guidance on the doctrine, because of apparent inconsistencies amongst previous judgments (as occurred in *Ratcliffe v Plymouth and Torbay HA*[253]). Even within cases, confusion can reign supreme. In *Bull v Devon AHA*,[254] while negligence was ultimately proven, only one member of the Court of Appeal (Slade LJ) used *res ipsa loquitur* as the basis for that conclusion. In *Fallows v Randle*,[255] the court noted the utility of the doctrine, but decided in C's favour without relying on the doctrine at all. Courts have also sometimes remarked that the doctrine's application was 'misconceived' by the parties (per *Graham v Watt-Smyrk*[256]), whilst an eye-popping turnaround about the doctrine can be evident on D's part.

> In *Brown v Merton, Sutton and Wandsworth AHA*,[257] patient C underwent an epidural anaesthesia, developed severe pain when receiving second doses, and developed quadraplegia. The anaesthetist D initially denied any application of *res ipsa loquitur*, but then conceded liability on that basis.

The doctrine does indeed have a chequered application in English jurisprudence.

The comparative corner: Some Commonwealth vignettes of the doctrine

British Columbia: In *Rabachuk v Cooke*,[258] patient C had a hernia operation. A plastic sheath was found at the surgical site, and was removed two weeks after the initial operation. **Held:** *res ipsa loquitur* was invoked to infer negligence on surgeon D's part, in failing to detect the loss of the sheath from the operative instrument. The court referred to the following 'incontrovertible facts': that '1. The foreign body was left in the patient and not discovered until after the operation was complete. 2. The sheath was of sufficient size (1cm x 2cm) to be seen and a visible component of the instrument used. 3. There had been difficulty in the operation of the instrument'.

New Brunswick: In *Cosgrove v Daudreau and Hotel-Dieu d' Edmundston*,[259] a surgical sponge was left in C's abdominal cavity, and it was discovered and removed 18 months later. Surgeon D adduced no evidence at trial as to how the sponge came to be left at the surgical site. **Held:** *res ipsa loquitur* applied: 'in the ordinary course of things', a sponge or lap pad is not left behind in the abdominal cavity after surgery, and it was probably left there as a result of D's negligence in not performing an adequate sponge count.

New Zealand: In *MacDonald v Pottinger*,[260] a pair of forceps was left in C's body after a complicated medical operation. Surgeon D, who performed the procedure, had been assisted by several others. **Held:** *res ipsa loquitur* did not apply. The procedure was never under the sole control and management of D.

Alberta: In *Clare v Ostolosky*,[261] C suffered a failed tubal ligation. **Held:** *res ipsa loquitur* did not apply. There was a reasonable explanation as to why a later tubal pregnancy was

---

[253] (1998) 42 BMLR 64 (CA) 73 ('[counsel] told us that there is a good deal of inconsistency as between different judges trying medical negligence cases about the way they should handle the operation of the maxim in these cases (if indeed, contrary to the views ascribed to some judges, it applies at all in this type of litigation). ... he invited us to give some guidance about the appropriate way to approach the maxim in medical negligence litigation').

[254] (1989) 22 BMLR 79 (CA).   [255] [1997] 8 Med LR 160 (CA).   [256] (QBD, 24 Nov 1986).

[257] [1982] 1 All ER 650 (CA).   [258] [2001] BCSC 1349, [8] (Grist J).   [259] (1981), NBR (2d) (QB) [28]–[33].

[260] [1953] NZLR 196.   [261] (2001), 300 AR 341.

possible, and why C's right fallopian tube still remained open; a 'spontaneous reanastomosis does occur without any effect upon the tube or its appearance'.

Malaysia: In *Udhaya Kumar v Penguasa Hosp*,[262] baby C suffered severe brain injury from contracting encephalitis. Held: *res ipsa loquitur* did not apply. D's diagnosis and treatment of C's high fever was plausible.

WHAT DOES *NOT* PROVE BREACH

D's view, pre-accident

§7.30   The fact that D evidenced some intention, prior to the event or accident, to take a precautionary step that would, on the balance of probabilities, have prevented the injury or harm to C, is not, of itself, proof of breach.

Suppose that D was well aware of (i.e., had foreseen) the risk of injury to C, and had some precautionary steps within its contemplation. However, D did not implement these precautionary steps for whatever reason (e.g., lack of time or money or motivation). Then the injury to C occurs.

The fact that D did not implement those steps is no automatic proof of breach. The reasons for not implementing may have been reasonable. Alternatively, D may have, mistakenly, considered the precautionary step to be necessary to meet the standard of reasonable care, whereas such a step was more onerous than the law expected of a reasonable D. Under either scenario, the failure by D to take that step is not conclusive proof of breach, because a reasonable D may have acted no differently to prevent the risk of injury or damage.

In *Tomlinson v Congleton BC*[263] (the diving in the lake case), Council D was aware that its notices forbidding swimming and diving in the lake were commonly ignored, and that several accidents had resulted from swimming. In a meeting prior to C's accident, D resolved to plant vegetation (e.g., prickly bushes) around the shore, to prevent people from entering the water. However, it had not carried this out, due to financial shortages. **Held:** no breach proven.

On the other hand, if D had specifically foreseen that a precautionary step were possible, and with hindsight should indeed have been taken to reach the reasonable standard, then breach will be proven.

In *Reffell v Surrey CC*,[264] a school girl, C, put her hand through a glass plate door at D's school, when it was swinging. Replacement of the panel with toughened glass or with grilles or wooden slats would have prevented the injury. That precaution had been proposed by D's officers before the accident. **Held:** breach proven.

An expert organisation's opinion

§7.31   The fact that an expert organisation advocates that a precautionary step ought to have been taken by D to prevent the risk of injury or harm to C, is not, of itself, proof of breach.

---

[262] [2004] 2 MLJ 661 (HC Muar).   [263] [2003] UKHL 47, [2004] 1 AC 46, [51], [55].
[264] [1964] 1 WLR 358 (QB) 365.

It is always for the court to determine whether a reasonable D should have taken a precautionary step to avoid the risk of injury or harm to C. An expert organisation's opinion as to what D should have done may simply have pitched the required standard of care too high. D must achieve reasonableness, not perfection.

> In *Darby v National Trust*,[265] Mr Darby, C, died by drowning in a pond at Hardwick Hall. A Water and Leisure Safety Consultant to the Royal Society for the Prevention of Accidents gave evidence that, as a minimum, 'No Swimming' notices should be installed around all deep water, given that 450 people die of drowning each year in the UK. **Held**: no breach proven. (This case is discussed further in Chapter 12, regarding occupiers' liability; D was not required to erect a sign for such an obvious danger.)

A change of system, post-accident

§7.32   The fact that D took precautionary steps *after* C suffered the injury or harm which, had they been implemented before the event, would probably have prevented that injury or harm, is not, of itself, proof of breach.

A responsible D may put in place a system, post-accident, that will prevent it from happening again – but that does not enable the court to draw any inference of negligence; after all, D may be 'ultra-cautious' after an accident, without realising that what he believes to be necessary to avoid future liability was not, actually, legally mandated (per *Yates v National Trust*[266]).

In *Staples v West Dorset DC*,[267] the Court of Appeal noted that, once Council D knew that a visitor had slipped off the edge into the sea, 'they posted warning notices. [But] the fact that they took that action after the accident does not enable me to draw the inference that, in order to discharge the common duty of care to the visitor, they should have done so before the accident occurred'. Besides, hindsight is not the prism through which the court must look, when assessing breach. As Lord Pearce was quoted in *Ratcliff v McConnell*,[268] the crucial issue is 'how the matter appeared, *before the accident*, to a reasonable person in [D's] position'.

> In *Ratcliffe*, a student, C, climbed over a pool fence at night, and suffered tetraplegia from diving into the shallow end of the pool. Post-accident, the pool-owner, D, implemented a number of further preventative steps (e.g., marking out the depth of water on the side of the pool, further warning signs in the changing room). In *Orchard v Lee*,[269] an accident happened in the school courtyard and walkway area, when school friends playing a game of tag collided with C, a lunchtime assistant supervisor at the school. Running around the courtyard and walkways was quite common among the young boys before the accident and broke no rules. However, after the accident, the rules were changed and notified to pupils, and the layout of the area was changed to discourage running. **Held, in both cases:** no breach proven.

Nevertheless, the fact that precautionary steps were taken after the accident does have the effect (as pointed out in *Stimpson v Wolverhampton MBC*[270]) of 'clearly show[ing] that there were additional steps which [D] might have taken' – and that some of them may have been cheap to implement, prior to the mishap.

---

[265] [2001] EWCA Civ 189, [2001] PIQR P17, [10].   [266] [2014] EWHC 222 (QB) [72].
[267] [1995] PIQR P439 (CA) 445.
[268] [1999] 1 WLR 670 (CA) [42] (emphasis added), citing: *McGlone v British Rwys Bd* 1966 SC (HL) 1, 17.
[269] [2009] EWCA Civ 295, [2009] PIQR P16.   [270] CA, 22 May 1990.

In *Cunningham v Reading FC*,[271] concrete terraces were repaired within days of a serious hooliganism incident, at a cost of slightly less than £3,000. In *Stimpson*, a large sign was erected after a golfer visiting the premises was hit in the mouth by a golf ball struck by C – the sign prohibited the playing of golf in the park and gave notice of an on-the-spot fine for anyone found to be contravening the notice. **Held, in both cases:** breach proven.

Inherent risks

§7.33 The failure by D to remove an inherent risk cannot amount to a breach, for the nature of an inherent risk is that it cannot be removed through the exercise of reasonable skill and care. However, inherent risks can give rise to breach in one of two ways, *viz*, failure-to-warn, and failure to detect/report.

Inherent risks were defined in *Chester v Afshar*[272] – and the fact that such a risk manifests in a procedure/at a venue/during an event does not prove breach, because no precautionary step could have removed it.

For example, as Hale LJ pointed out in *Sussex Ambulance NHS Trust v King*,[273] employees whose occupations in the public service are inherently dangerous (i.e., fire fighters, police officers, and ambulance technicians) cannot expect their employers to remove those risks, because reasonable care will not remove them – they must be accepted as part of the job. What those employees can expect is that the employer will take reasonable steps to remove the risks which it would be negligent to disregard (by the provision of a safe system of work, safe equipment, etc, as discussed in 'Employers' liability', an online chapter). On that basis, inherent risks share some similarities with inevitable accidents.

Two ways that breach can arise are as follows:

i. C was not warned about material inherent risks, so as to make an informed decision as to whether or not to proceed with the procedure (as discussed in Chapter 3); and

ii. it was D's responsibility to detect, identify, report upon, or guard against any inherent risks that were apparent in a procedure/business, but failed to do so. For example, in the auditing context, the inherent risk that financial accounts may be misstated, due to the nature of the client's type of business, its environment, and the nature of the accounts, may lead to an overly-positive report by the auditor. As stated in *Barings plc v Coopers & Lybrand (a firm)*,[274] '[a]n important part of the process of planning an audit is to identify the inherent risks affecting the client, and to devise procedures which will afford the auditor a reasonable expectation of detecting material misstatements arising from those risks'. Similarly, there is an inherent risk of abuse, as noted by Lord Millett in *Lister v Hesley Hall Ltd*:[275] 'in boarding schools, prisons, nursing homes, old people's homes, geriatric wards, and other residential homes for the young or vulnerable, there is an inherent risk that indecent assaults on the residents will be committed by those placed in authority over them, particularly if they are in close proximity to them and occupying a position of trust'. Those who own/operate such facilities may be in breach for failing to prevent such abuse (although that claim failed in *Lister*).

---

[271] [1992] PIQR P141 (QB) 153.   [272] [2004] UKHL 41, [2005] 1 AC 134, [72].
[273] [2002] EWCA Civ 953, [2002] ICR 1413, [21].   [274] [2003] EWHC 1319 (Ch) [503].
[275] [2001] UKHL 22, [2002] 1 AC 215, [83].

Relevance of 'gross negligence'

§7.34   There is no general requirement in English law that breach can *only* be proven by 'gross negligence'. However, in very limited circumstances, that test of breach is appropriate; and the parties may also agree, via contractual terms, that D's liability will be limited, in that D cannot be liable except for gross negligence.

The suggestion that D should **only** be liable for breach if guilty of 'gross negligence' has been made in a few contexts in which D was sympathetically-placed – but largely without success.

Meaning. The precise meaning of 'gross negligence' is unclear, as case law pertinent to awards of exemplary damages (canvassed in Chapter 11) illustrates. The phrase can carry any one of **three** possible meanings: (1) a grave departure by D from the standard of reasonable care; (2) conduct that amounts to either wilful or reckless disregard for C's welfare (i.e., D possesses a certain intent); or (3) conduct that causes an onerous level of damage to C. In what sense the term is used in the following contexts has often been left quite unclear.

General rule. The contexts in which the need to prove 'gross negligence' have been argued/mooted are multifarious. In the case of the 'good Samaritan' who attempts a rescue or who tries to assist a victim, the ambulance officers argued, in *Cattley v St John Ambulance Brigade*,[276] that the conduct complained of should be 'manifestly short of the standard to be expected', amounting to gross negligence, before they should be held in breach, but that submission was rejected outright by the court. Judge Prosser QC remarked that such a test was not known to English negligence law, and 'would be confusing and ... unnecessary'. (Interestingly, the view that good Samaritans should only be liable for 'gross negligence' has indeed received legislative enactment in jurisdictions other than England, where 'good Samaritan statutes' have been introduced.[277])

Recently, in *ICL Tech Ltd v Johnston Oils Ltd*,[278] the Scottish Outer House confirmed that C did **not** have to prove that the supplier of a hazardous substance or a dangerous product (LPG gas, in that case), D, should only be liable if it had demonstrated gross negligence – a position which reflects English law too. In the context of barristers who provide specialist advice, HH Judge Brown QC noted, in *West Wallasey Car Hire Ltd v Berkson & Berkson*,[279] that previous references (e.g., in *Saif Ali v Sydney Mitchell & Co*[280]) to the need to prove a 'blatant error' on D's part should **not** be read to mean that 'gross negligence' was required.

Hence, the test of gross negligence is extremely rare in English negligence law, insofar as a test of breach is concerned. Indeed, in *West Wallasey*, Judge Brown stated that 'gross negligence' has not been the test of breach in the tort of negligence, 'since at least 1910 upon the case law'.[281] However, there are a couple of exceptions to this general rule.

Exceptions. In the case of amateur referees, the Court of Appeal rejected the submission, in *Smoldon v Whitworth*,[282] that a referee should only be liable for breach if he had shown a deliberate or reckless disregard for the safety of player C. That was framed as a test of gross negligence, and was comprehensively rejected. However, as the discussion of participants and

---

[276] QB, 25 Nov 1988 [no pp available].
[277] See: Mulheron, *Medical Negligence: Non-Patient and Third Party Claims* (Ashgate Publishing, 2010), ch 6.
[278] [2012] CSOH 62, [13].   [279] [2009] EWHC B39 (Merc), [2010] PNLR 14, [30].
[280] [1980] AC 198 (HL) 220–21 (Lord Diplock).
[281] [2009] EWHC B39 (Merc), [2010] PNLR 14, [32], citing: *Ridehalgh v Horsefield* [1944] Ch 205 (CA) 237.
[282] [1997] PIQR 133 (CA) 138–39.

spectators in Chapter 6 demonstrates, the standard of care required of participants is so lowly-set that proof of gross negligence **will** be required in that context.

Furthermore, proof of gross negligence may be required, if the contract between C and D states that D will **only** be liable for that substandard performance. The following clause – as used in *Camerata Property Inc v Credit Suisse Securities (Europe) Ltd*[283] – provides an example:

> we shall not be liable for any losses, liabilities, costs, claims, damages, expenses, demands … incurred or suffered by you … other than Costs arising directly as a consequence of the gross negligence, fraud or wilful default of us or any of our directors, officers, or employees.

Some English judges have clearly been uncomfortable with the use of 'gross negligence' – witness, e.g., the comments in *Tradigrain SA v Internek Testing Services*,[284] that the term, 'although often found in commercial documents, has never been accepted by English civil law as a concept distinct from civil negligence'. However, having cited that case, the Court in *Camerata* preferred the view that, where used in contract to limit D's liability for negligence, the term must mean something different from 'mere' negligence, and that it was capable of meaning that D acted with 'serious disregard of or indifference to an obvious risk'. (Interestingly, the *Camerata* term survived the test of 'reasonableness' in the Unfair Contract Terms Act 1977.)

---

[283] [2011] EWHC 479 (Comm) [161], citing: *Red Sea Tankers Ltd v Papachristidis (The Ardent)* [1997] 2 Lloyd's Rep 547 (HL) 586 (Lord Mance).

[284] [2007] EWCA Civ 154, [23] (Moore-Bick LJ).

8

Causation of damage

INTRODUCTION

§8.1   In his negligence suit against D, C can only recover damages from D where D caused, or materially contributed to, C's harm; or where, exceptionally, some weaker causal link is established between D's breach and C's harm.

In most cases, C will have to prove a causal link between D's breach and his own damage on the balance of probabilities. In rare cases, something less than proof on the balance of probabilities will be sufficient to fix D with liability in negligence for causing C physical, property or economic damage.

A few introductory points will predicate the difficult issues which arise under this element.

Principles, with a splash of 'common sense'

Causation is, arguably, the most doctrinally complex of the elements of negligence. In most cases, the application of causation principles is straightforward. In other cases, however, some judicial statements verge on the despairing, when discussing the area's difficulties. Recently, in *Zurich Ins plc v UK Branch v Intl Energy Group Ltd*, Lord Mance admitted that 'the courts are still working out the implications' of previous appellate rulings on causation,[1] whilst in *Sienk-iewicz v Greif (UK) Ltd*, Lady Hale 'pit[ied] the practitioners, as well as the academics, who have to make sense of our judgments in difficult cases' in this nook of the law.[2]

Indeed, at one end of the spectrum, some senior appellate judges have described causation as a question of mere pragmatism and 'common sense'. In *BAI Run-Off Ltd v Durham (the Trigger Litigation)*,[3] Lord Mance noted that causation '[n]ormally ... reflect[s] a common sense understanding of what is ordinarily understood when we speak of a cause'; in *Stapley v Gypsum Mines*,[4] Lord Reid said that causation 'must be determined by applying common sense to

[1] [2015] UKSC 33, [1] (Lord Mance).
[2] [2011] UKSC 10, [2011] 2 AC 229, [167]. To those categories, students should be added!
[3] [2012] UKSC 14, [2012] 1 WLR 867, [55].   [4] [1953] AC 663 (HL) 681.

the facts of each particular case'; while in *McGhee v National Coal Board*,[5] Lord Wilberforce decried that causation 'is not based on logic or philosophy, [but] on the practical way in which the ordinary man's mind works in the everyday affairs of life'.

At the other end of the spectrum, however, some judges have vigorously disagreed with that notion. In *Six Continents Retail Ltd v Carford Catering Ltd*,[6] Laws LJ said that 'an appeal to common sense is sometimes apt to be little more than an alibi for want of principle', and likened causation to 'metaphysics'. In similar vein, Lord Hope remarked, in *Chester v Afshar*,[7] that 'commonsense on its own, and without more guidance, was no more reliable as a guide to the right answer than an appeal to the views of the traveller on the London Underground'. Lord Nicholls, dissenting, in *Gregg v Scott*,[8] remarked that, if the majority's view were to prevail, it would be to liken the law to the 'proverbial ass'; and Laws LJ (again) compared causation to 'philosophical thickets' (in *Rahman v Arearose Ltd*[9]). Lord Matthews put it succinctly in *Percy v Govan Initiative Ltd*: 'no doubt this is one of the most difficult areas of the law'.[10]

In the midst of the brouhaha is C, who may find great difficulty in linking D's breach (whether admitted or proven) to the damage which C alleges. This has been especially evident in two oft-litigated contexts: medical incidents (which 'often raise particularly difficult questions of causation'[11]) and workplace illnesses. Sometimes, the evidence cannot say whether D's breach had any, or any significant, part to play in C's damage – and the scientific knowledge is not robust or advanced enough to satisfy the traditional causation principles. Alternatively, the facts themselves may not be sufficiently ascertainable, so as to point towards, or away from, a causal link.

The principles in this chapter seek to set out how causation may be established by C (upon whom the burden of proof always rests). However, given the judicial comments above, and more so than in any other chapter in this book, the principles espoused herein seek to represent legal propositions which are defensible by reference to majority judicial viewpoints – whilst acknowledging that, with the courts still feeling their way, some of the principles will be open to debate, particularly under the exceptional theorems of causation.

A note on terminology

The notion of 'factual causation' is used in some contexts, to describe whether D's negligent conduct played a legally sufficient role in bringing about C's harm. That topic is considered in this chapter. It is to be distinguished from the ancillary subject of remoteness of damage (sometimes called 'legal causation'), which deals with whether D *ought* to be held liable to pay damages for that harm (discussed in Chapter 9). It follows that establishing a causal link between D's breach and C's damage does not necessarily mean that liability will follow.

Lord Nicholls explained the diverse, but unified, concepts, in *Kuwait Airways Corp v Iraqi Airways Co*[12] as follows: 'the extent of [D's] liability for [C's] loss calls for a twofold inquiry: whether the wrongful conduct causally contributed to the loss; and, if it did, what is the extent of the loss for which [D] ought to be held liable. The first of these inquiries, widely undertaken as a simple "but for" test, is predominantly a factual inquiry'.

---

[5] [1973] 1 WLR 1 (HL) 5.   [6] [2003] EWCA Civ 1790, [18]–[19].   [7] [2004] UKHL 41, [2005] 1 AC 134, [83]
[8] [2005] UKHL 2, [43].   [9] [2001] QB 351 (CA) [32].   [10] [2011] ScotCS 177 (OH) [16].
[11] *Bank of Credit and Commerce Intl SA (in liq) v Ali (No 2)* [2002] EWCA Civ 82, [70] (Robert Walker LJ).
[12] [2002] 2 AC 883 (HL) [69].

The second enquiry (remoteness) is just as important as the first – as the Supreme Court noted in *R v Hughes*,[13] if factual causation was conclusive or sufficient for liability, it would expand the boundaries of liability far too widely: 'if a woman asked her neighbour to go to the station in his car to collect her husband, [she] would be held to have caused her husband's death if he perished in a fatal road accident on the way home'. In *Chester v Afshar*,[14] Lord Bingham (dissenting, but not on this point) also emphasised that a literal application of factual causation, 'applied simply and mechanically, gives too expansive an answer: "But for your negligent misdelivery of my luggage, I should not have had to defer my passage to New York and embark on *SS Titanic*"'. Holding the wife and the baggage handlers liable in negligence respectively, in these examples, would be a legal nonsense.

Further, where D1, D2 and D3 act as 'joint tortfeasors', as 'several concurrent tortfeasors', or as 'independent tortfeasors', each D did cause *some* injury to C. The question then is how to apportion responsibility among them. That difficult issue – which arises when liability has already been established, and where quantification of the damages per D is at issue – is considered in 'Multiple defendants' (an online chapter).

The role of policy

It should be acknowledged, at the outset, that policy considerations and value judgments infuse the analysis of causation, to an equivalent extent as they find a role in remoteness enquiries. For example, the topic of intervening acts involves considerations of 'reasonableness' – which *always* invokes value judgments, as Ward LJ pointed out in *Corr v IBC Vehicles Ltd*.[15]

This can lead to an impression, at least, of imprecision in legal reasoning – although some call it an exercise in pragmatism. As Laws LJ remarked in *Rahman v Arearose Ltd*,[16] '[t]he common law on the whole achieved just results, but the approach has been heavily pragmatic'. The impression of controversy is also enhanced by the number of bare majority judgments with which the area is afflicted (e.g., 3:2 majorities in both *Gregg v Scott* and *Chester v Afshar*). Clearly, reasonable judicial opinion will differ on the causation enquiry.

This chapter will consider the following 12 topics in turn:

A nutshell of the causation analysis	
Pre-requisite	C suffered compensable damage
The first step	The classic 'but-for' test (that rules out legally irrelevant causes)
Exception #1	The doctrine of material contribution to risk
Exception #2	The doctrine of material contribution to damage
Exception #3	The *Bolitho* causation theorem
Exception #4	The *Chester v Afshar* causation theorem
Severance	Intervening acts in the causal chain

[13] [2013] UKSC 56, [23].   [14] [2004] UKHL 41, [8].
[15] [2006] EWCA Civ 331, [37] (not adversely commented upon on appeal).
[16] [2000] EWCA Civ 190, [2001] QB 351, [31].

A weaker causal link	Causation and 'pure omissions'
Reframing the 'damage'	Loss of a chance claims
Supervening event #1	D damaged an already-damaged C
Supervening event #2	Innocent reasons would have led to the same damage
Evidentiary	The burden of proof

PRE-REQUISITE: PROOF OF COMPENSABLE DAMAGE

§8.2 The tort of negligence is not actionable *per se*. C must have suffered some legally-recognised compensable damage, to found a cause of action.

This is 'trite law', requiring 'no reinforcement by an anxious parade of supporting authority' (per *Clough v First Choice Holidays and Flights Ltd*[17]). In *Gregg v Scott*,[18] Baroness Hale reiterated that, 'damage is the gist of negligence. So it can never be enough to show that [D] has been negligent. The question is still whether his negligence has caused [C's] actionable damage'.

However, proving damage has been problematical in two particular instances in English law.

The *de minimis* threshold of damage

The general principle

§8.3 Per the principle of '*deminimis non curatlex*' – 'the law does not take account of trifles' – it is only damage (physical, psychiatric, property or economic) which meets a minimal threshold of harm which the law will compensate. Both pleural plaques, and 'loss of a chance' personal injury claims, are not compensable injuries in English law.

If C's symptoms, which allegedly flow from D's breach, are 'trifling', then they will lack 'the significance required to turn the non-actionable into the actionable' (per Maurice Kay LJ in *Hussain v CC of West Mercia Constabulary*[19]). In *Cartledge v E Jopling & Sons Ltd*[20] too, the court emphasised that it will always be a question of fact and of degree, but that C's injury had to be 'beyond what can be regarded as negligible', or 'real damage, as distinct from purely minimal damage'.

In the following cases, the physical symptoms suffered by C were **not** sufficient injury to constitute actionable damage, and hence were not worthy of compensation:

> In *Hussain v CC of West Mercia*, Mr Hussain claimed that the police's actions placed him 'under stress', leading to physical symptoms of anxiety, *viz*, discomfort and numbness in his arm and leg (the action was actually brought under misfeasance in public office – which tort is not actionable *per se* either). In *Reilly v Merseyside HA*,[21] Mr Reilly was trapped in a lift, a 'most unpleasant experience', during which he suffered anxiety and fear, and had some physical consequences (vomiting and sweating).

---

[17] [2006] EWCA Civ 15, [30].   [18] [2005] UKHL 2, [217].   [19] [2008] EWCA Civ 1205, [19].
[20] [1963] AC 758 (HL) 771–72.   [21] (1994) 23 BMLR 26 (CA) 29, 30.

Furthermore, where C has only suffered some anxiety-based disorder, then that type of damage does not, on its own, surmount the *de minimis* principle. C must prove some actionable *physical* injury, to graft onto that claim the anxiety disorder which falls short of a recognised psychiatric injury. It will be recalled, from Chapter 5, that the only freestanding mental injury claim which is permitted in English law is where a recognised psychiatric injury was suffered by C. This was at the root of the extraordinary *Pleural Plaques* litigation, otherwise known as *Johnston v NEI Intl Combustion Ltd (sub nom Grieves v FT Everard & Sons*[22]).

Pleural plaques are physiological changes to the lung lining, which are usually asymptomatic. The Scottish Inner House described them in *AXA General Ins Ltd v Scottish Ministers*:[23]

> Pleural plaques are physical changes in the pleurae: two layers of tissue comprising the visceral pleura, the inner layer which covers the lungs, and the parietal pleura, the outer layer which lines the ribs and chest wall … Upon radiological examination, pleural plaques present as areas of fibrous tissue … They are normally bilateral and almost exclusively found on the parietal pleura. Over time, they may increase in size and number and become calcified. They can measure more than 10cm across and up to 1cm in thickness, and may fuse into larger sheets as they become more extensive. They are caused by exposure to asbestos and are therefore associated with the construction, shipbuilding and steel industries. Their precise aetiology is unknown, but may involve prolonged inflammation due to cells reacting to, and attempting to engulf, inhaled asbestos fibres. They have a latency period of 20 years or more. In the vast majority of cases, pleural plaques are asymptomatic, causing no discomfort, impairment of the pulmonary function, or external marks. Nor do they actuate, or contribute to, more serious and potentially fatal conditions such as lung cancer, mesothelioma or asbestosis. Nevertheless, their existence evidences significant previous exposure to asbestos, which of itself represents a greatly increased risk of contracting such diseases.

Interestingly, in 1963, the House of Lords endorsed the view that those who sustained physiological changes from inhaled substances **did** suffer actionable damage.

> In *Cartledge v E Jopling & Sons Ltd*,[24] various employees, C, suffered death or serious injury from lung damage caused by inhaling fragmented silica. (This was a limitation problem, concerning the question of when the cause of action accrued.) Given that the silica fragments would be visible on an X-ray (if taken); would reduce C's lung capacity in a way which would be evident in cases of unusual exertion; made C more susceptible to contracting tuberculosis or bronchitis; and would reduce C's life expectancy because of their presence; all of that was sufficient, in combination, to constitute compensable 'damage'.

Subsequently, some first-instance decisions in the mid-1980s held that pleural plaques constituted actionable injury too (and modest sums, ranging between £1,500 and £31,250, were awarded to the affected Cs in *Church v MOD*,[25] in *Sykes v MOD*[26] and in *Patterson v MOD*[27]). None of these decisions was appealed, and, hence, a practice evolved, among English insurers, of settling pleural plaques claims, brought by employees wrongfully exposed to asbestos, for modest payments. Then, a challenge was brought by some insurers on this key question, as to whether these employees had actually suffered any legally-compensable damage. The House of Lords saw the outcome very differently in 2006.

---

[22] [2006] EWCA Civ 27, aff'd: [2007] UKHL 39, [2008] 1 AC 281, with Lord Hope's quote in Table at [42].
[23] [2011] CSIH 31, [9].   [24] [1963] AC 758 (HL).   [25] (1984) 134 NLJ 623.
[26] (1984) 134 NLJ 783.   [27] CA, 29 Jul 1986.

In *Johnston v NEI Intl Combustion Ltd*, 10 employees, C, were negligently exposed by their employers, D, to asbestos dust in their workplaces. Each C had developed pleural plaques, and alleged that it meant that they were at risk of developing long-term asbestos-related diseases (because the plaques signified exposure to asbestos); plus they had suffered some physiological change to their lungs; plus they had suffered anxiety (although only one C, Mr Grieves, had suffered a genuine psychiatric illness, *viz*, depression, and hence, his case was legally different, per Chapter 5). **Held (CA, 2:1; and HL, 5:0):** all Cs failed. The nine test Cs who had only suffered pleural plaques, and anxiety-based disorders, had suffered no actionable damage.

Of course, had the employees suffered a negligently-caused physical injury in this case, then that may have led to other damages consequences for them. For example, had that injury created the chance that C would suffer some other physical damage (i.e., some disease or illness) in the future, then C's general damages would be increased to reflect the chance of that physical injury manifesting (per *Gregg v Scott*[28]). Additionally, any fear or anxiety about developing a future disease would also be compensated under the 'pain and suffering' or 'loss of amenity' heads of damage, as a 'tag' to the physical injury claim. However, the main point of the *Pleural Plaques* litigation was that 9 out of the 10 test Cs could not prove that they had suffered any physical injury at all (even though pleural plaques certainly amounted to a physiological change in the human body) – and hence, there was nothing to which their anxiety-based disorders could attach. They could not recover.

Given the dissenting judgment of Lady Justice Smith in the Court of Appeal, and the prior case of *Cartledge*, it is useful to set out the contrasting viewpoints from the *Pleural Plaques* litigation:

The contrasting reasoning in the *Pleural Plaques* litigation

Why the plaques did not constitute damage (CA majority, all of HL):	Why the plaques did constitute damage (Smith LJ):
• none of the individual components of the alleged 'damage' constituted damage – the fibre penetration which resulted in the formation of the pleural plaque + the risk that pleural plaques could give rise to disease + C's anxiety generated about this risk – as Lord Hope said, '0 + 0 + 0 = 0'; Looking at the individual components: • a mere physiological change in the body is not sufficient to constitute damage. English law requires a *de minimis* threshold of damage, and something which is symptomless, having no adverse effect on any bodily function, and no effect on appearance, does not meet that threshold;	• the pleural plaques were an *injury*, because they were 'an abnormal tissue change', and were also a *disease*, because 'they were capable of progression'; • symptoms could result from large amounts of plaques (coughing, breathlessness), and it was not the symptoms which were the injury, but the plaques themselves. Symptoms merely showed how serious the injury was;

---

[28] [2005] UKHL 2, [67] (Lord Hoffmann).

Why the plaques did not constitute damage (CA majority, all of HL):	Why the plaques did constitute damage (Smith LJ):
• the pleural plaques did not increase susceptibility to asbestos-related or other diseases or shorten life expectancy (cf. *Cartledge*, where silica dust damage *did* increase susceptibility to TB and bronchitis, and *did* reduce life expectancy); • no claim could be made for the chance of contracting a future disease, unless that risk was based upon some existing physical injury – and none existed here. <u>Policy reasons also dictated against pleural plaques being damage:</u> • it would encourage stressful litigation by employees against employers; • the litigation may be driven by claims managers; • the costs of the litigation would far exceed the damages recovered; • some Cs may accept final awards and therefore preclude themselves from ever claiming for asbestos-related diseases that they might develop in the future.	• it was no different from a skin lesion on the outside skin – both hidden plaques and lesions were a 'tissue change' and, therefore, constituted an injury to the body.

As Lord Hoffmann remarked in *Johnston*, '[b]ecause people do not often go to the trouble of bringing actions to recover damages for trivial injuries, the question of how trivial is trivial has seldom arisen directly'.[29] However, be that as it may, the case was an object lesson in illustrating that, without compensable damage, there is no actionable negligence.

Other perspectives

The appellate decisions which declared pleural plaques not to be physical injury represented a sea-change in English common law – which attracted some vehement media commentary at the time:

Media comments on the *Pleural Plaques* litigation

'*Asbestos Condition not Compensable: UK Court*', *Reuters* (26 Jan 2006):
'The Association of British Insurers and their members are delighted with an outcome which could prevent 100,000 court cases, thereby saving the industry £1–1.4 billion'.
'*A Wrong-Headed Ruling on Asbestos*', *The Independent* (27 Jan 2006):
'The claimants and their representatives are seriously concerned at the implications of the Appeal Court's decision. The General Secretary of *Amicus*, the trade union which brought the case, condemned the judgment as "dreadful": "[it] harms many of our members who have been exposed in their working lives to asbestos. We believe that people with pleural plaques should be compensated, and we will fight on'.

---

[29] [2007] UKHL 39, [2008] 1 AC 281, [8].

Subsequently, the Scottish Parliament enacted legislation specifically to overrule the House of Lords' decision. The Damages (Asbestos-related Conditions) (Scotland) Act 2009 was passed, to provide (per s 1) that asbestos-related pleural plaques, and certain other asbestos-related conditions (pleural thickening and asbestosis), constituted personal injury which was **not** negligible, and which **was** actionable under Scots law. Unsurprisingly, insurance companies who were potentially 'on the hook' to pay out pleural plaque claims under Scottish employers' liability insurance policies, brought a petition for judicial review, seeking a declaration that the 2009 Act was unlawful. That application, in *AXA General Ins Ltd v Scottish Ministers*, failed. The Scottish Inner House noted that: '[i]n deciding that, notwithstanding *Johnston*, in Scotland pleural plaques should be, and have always been, a condition for which compensation should be paid and that, in effect, the insurers of negligent employers would be liable to meet claims for that compensation, the Scottish Parliament was, as a matter of political judgment, entitled to take into account that such insurers had, for a significant period, accepted such liability'.[30]

The 'loss of a chance' claim

Essentially, suppose that C cannot prove that D's breach caused his physical injury, on the balance of probabilities. There was a 25% probability that the breach caused C's harm; but there was a 75% probability that some innocent (non-tortious) reason caused C's injury. The finding that D's breach had a 25% chance of causing C's injury will not satisfy the traditional test of causation (considered in the next section), and C will lose his case.

However, by framing the damage in a different way – not as the physical injury, but as the loss of a chance – C may seek to prove that, because of D's negligence, C lost a 25% chance of a better outcome. Had the 25% chance that breach caused the injury not been 'in play', then C's prospects of avoiding the adverse outcome would have improved.

This type of claim (as discussed later in the chapter[31]) has met with a distinct lack of success in English law in *personal injury* litigation, but has garnered more traction in *economic loss* claims. This is a rare instance in which courts have proven to be more, rather than less, sympathetic towards Cs who have only suffered from economic loss. In any event, it is convenient to analyse traditional causation principles first, for they provide a proper context in which 'loss of chance' claims can be considered as a means of circumventing the traditional means of proving causation.

THE FIRST STEP: THE CLASSIC 'BUT-FOR' TEST

§8.4   The conventional test of causation – the 'but-for' test – states: 'would C's harm have happened, but for (or absent) D's breach? If probably not, then D's breach caused C's harm. However, if C's harm would probably have happened anyway, then D's breach did not cause that harm.'

The 'but-for' test of causation is sometimes referred to as a '*causa sine qua non*' (literally, 'a cause without which not'). The expression, 'but for', means in this context, 'were it not for'. The purpose of the test is to exclude causes of C's injury which the law regards as being legally insignificant, or 'irrelevant' (per *Corr v IBC Vehicles Ltd*[32]).

---

[30] [2011] CSIH 31, [93].   [31] See pp 469–77.
[32] [2006] EWCA Civ 331, [18] (Ward LJ), and not doubted on further appeal.

In general, the key to the test's application is hypothetically to fix D's breach, and then to ask whether the damage would have happened to C in any event – if the answer to that is, 'yes, C's damage would probably have happened anyway', then D's breach did not cause C's damage. In *Allied Maples Group Ltd v Simmons and Simmons*,[33] Stuart-Smith LJ remarked that to ask whether a *positive act* by D caused C's harm is 'a question ... of historical fact' (i.e., take the act away hypothetically, and would the damage still have occurred?), whereas in the case of *omissions*, it depends upon a hypothetical enquiry as to what would have happened if D's omission had been corrected. Lord Browne-Wilkinson described it, in *Bolitho v City and Hackney HA*,[34] as 'the factual inquiry [which] is, by definition, in the realms of hypothesis'. In most cases, no absolute answer is possible – except in unusual cases (discussed below) where certainty, and not probability, rules the day.

The leading English authority for the 'but-for' test is an unusual case of medical negligence.

In *Barnett v Chelsea and Kensington Hosp Management Committee*,[35] William Barnett, C, was employed as a night watchman at the Chelsea College of Sciences and Technology. On the night of 31 Dec 1965, C's colleague was attacked by an intruder at the college with an iron crowbar around 4 am, and taken to St Stephen's Hospital, Chelsea, D, for checking. C and his injured colleague then returned to Chelsea College. Around 5 am, C had a cup of tea with his colleague and the senior watchman on duty. All three men started vomiting immediately afterwards, and for the second time that day, C visited the casualty department of St Stephen's – this time as a patient – shortly after 8 am. The three men asked the duty nurse to fetch a doctor. Delays occurred, partly because the nurse suspected that the men had been excessively drinking. The nurse telephoned a doctor, D, on an upper floor. D's response was: 'Well, I'm vomiting myself, and I have not been drinking. Tell them to go home, and go to bed, and call in their own doctors – except [the injured colleague] who should stay because he is due for an X-ray later this morning'. C left the hospital, went back to the College, lay down on the floor to rest, and died later at 1.30 pm. The medical evidence was that all three men had been poisoned by arsenic, deliberately introduced into the tea. The coronial verdict was 'murder by person or persons unknown'. Mrs Barnett sued D, on behalf of herself and two of her children, as dependants of C. **Held:** negligence failed.

Would Mr Barnett's damage (i.e., death) have occurred, but for D's breach (their failing to admit and to treat him)? Unfortunately yes – death was inevitable from enzyme disturbance induced by arsenical poisoning. Had the breach been fixed, and Mr Barnett examined in the hospital emergency room, he would have been admitted to a ward, a blood and urine specimen taken, and an antidote to arsenic poisoning administered. However, because that antidote had to be given within 75 minutes (maximum) of the ingestion to reverse the disturbance of the enzyme processes, causation had to fail, because the death would have occurred in any event. Mr Barnett had presented to hospital too late.

The importance, and limits, of probability

The usual 'probability' scenario

§8.5 Any cause which is assessed as being, on the balance of probabilities, the source of C's harm, is legally assessed as being the sole, or certain, cause of C's harm. In that regard, at law, 51% = 100%.

[33] [1995] 1 WLR 1602 (CA) 1609–10.   [34] [1998] AC 232 (HL) 239.   [35] [1969] 1 QB 428.

Causation is a balance-of-probabilities assessment, but having been assessed, D is either fully liable or not liable at all – '[i]n determining what did happen in the past, a court decides on the balance of probabilities. Anything that is more probable than not, it treats as certain', according to Lord Diplock in *Mallett v McMonagle*.[36] While the expression, '51% = 100%', is a mathematical nonsense, it is legally rational and defensible. If there is an underlying uncertainty as to what precisely caused C's harm, the law disregards this in the search for pragmatic, and rough-at-times, justice.

In that regard, the 'but-for' test is truly a misnomer, because (as Sir Igor Judge pointed out in *Clough v First Choice Holidays and Flights Ltd*[37]), the words 'can mislead. They may convey the impression that C's claim for damages for personal injuries must fail unless he can prove that D's negligence was the only, or the single, or even chronologically the last cause, of his injuries ... [but] such an impression would be incorrect'. In the majority of negligence cases, there is D's breach, and also an innocent (non-tortious) reason for C's damage, both contributing to the maelstrom of C's factual story. C's task is to prove that, on the balance of probabilities (i.e., >50%), his harm would not have occurred, had D's breach not happened. As remarked in *Various Claimants v Flintshire CC*,[38] usually 'one is not dealing with certainties' as to the cause/s of C's problems.

It is not necessary for a trial judge to attribute percentages to the breach and to the innocent cause – in fact, it is probably easier **not** to descend into percentage discussion, according to Lord Ackner in *Hotson v East Berkshire AHA*:[39] '[u]nless there is some special situation, e.g. joint defendants, where the apportionment of liability between them is required, there is no point or purpose in expressing in percentage terms the certainty, or near certainty, which [C] has achieved in establishing his cause of action'.

There are thousands of cases which could usefully illustrate the 'but-for' test, where both negligent and innocent reasons for the damage were 'in play'. An illustrative example from each of the two most problematical contexts of causation – medical and employment scenarios – will suffice:

In *McWilliams v Sir William Arrol & Co Ltd*,[40] William McWilliams, C, was employed by Sir William Arrol, D, as an experienced steel erector. In the Kingston shipbuilding yard, Port Glasgow, he was working about 70 feet above the ground, on the steel lattice work of a tower crane being constructed, when he fell to his death. A safety belt, which would have prevented the death, had been available until 2–3 days before the accident, but was then transferred to another site. C's widow sued D, alleging that the failure to provide C with a safety belt was in breach of s 26(2) of the Factories Act 1937.

- *the innocent cause*: there was a **strong probability** that C himself would have elected **not** to wear a safety belt on the occasion of the accident, even if provided. His colleagues gave evidence that C did not normally wear a safety belt, even when working at greater heights than 70 feet. Sometimes, when conditions were dangerous (windy), some steel-workers did, but conditions were not windy that day;
- *the negligent cause*: there was a **very slight possibility** that C would have worn a safety belt, if it had been provided.

---

[36] [1970] AC 166 (HL) 176.　[37] [2006] EWCA Civ 15, [44].
[38] (QB, 26 Jul 2000) [25] (Scott Baker J).　[39] [1987] AC 750 (HL) 793.
[40] [1962] 1 WLR 295 (CA) 300 (Viscount Kilmuir LC), 307 (Hodson LJ).

Held: causation failed. (Separately, it was not proven that D should have exhorted or instructed C to use a safety belt. By virtue of the statutory wording, employees could 'elect to use' safety belts.)

In *Hotson v East Berkshire AHA*,[41] Stephen Hotson, C, 13, fell out of a tree at school, and fractured his left femoral epiphysis (hip joint). When he presented at D's hospital, it was not correctly diagnosed and treated, and he was sent home with instructions to take pain-killers. C returned five days later, in great pain, and a correct diagnosis was made. By that time, the hip joint had turned necrotic, due to ruptured blood vessels and a lack of blood supply to the joint. C was left with permanent disability. There were two potential causes of C's harm:

- *the innocent cause*: the original crush and fracture from the fall left insufficient blood vessels intact to keep the epiphysis alive, no matter what the treatment or how promptly it occurred – essentially, the blood vessels running along the back of the femoral neck contained about one-half of the total blood supply to the epiphysis, and if they were ruptured by the fall, that would doom the hip to necrosis, regardless of delay (assessed at 75% probability);
- *the negligent cause*: there were enough intact blood vessels surviving after the fall to keep the epiphysis alive, but these were subsequently (over the 5-day negligently-caused delay) occluded by pressure caused by bruising or bleeding into the joint, leading to necrosis (assessed at 25% probability).

Held: causation failed.

Hence, even if a breach by D occurs, and it has some causative effect on C's sustaining harm, causation will only be proven if the breach *probably* caused that harm. In legal terms, the breach then *definitely* caused that harm. In *Hotson*,[42] that simply could not be proven. The finding that too many blood vessels had been ruptured by the fall 'amounted to a finding of fact that the fall was the *sole* cause of the avascular necrosis' (Lord Bridge); that even 'before admission to hospital and therefore before the duty was imposed upon the doctor properly to diagnose and treat, the epiphysis was doomed' (Lord Ackner); and that 'when Stephen Hotson arrived at the authority's hospital for the first time, he had no chance of avoiding [necrosis]' (Lord Mackay).

The exclusive 'certainty' club

§8.6 Where C's harm would have occurred with absolute certainty because of some innocent (non-tortious) causes, regardless of D's breach of duty, then the breach did not cause the harm. Conversely, proving causation to the standard of certainty is not required in negligence law.

The leading case of *Barnett* (arsenic poisoning) was an example of a causal link being precluded with absolute certainty. Even had D's breach been hypothetically fixed in that case, the death of Mr Barnett would certainly have occurred, regardless. Conversely, if C can prove with 100% certainty that D's breach caused his harm, and that no innocent agent was in play, then causation will inevitably be proven. However, these scenarios are very unusual – and proving causation to a level of absolute certainty is **not** required on C's part.

---

[41] [1987] AC 750 (HL).

[42] *ibid*, with quotes at: 782 (Lord Bridge), 792 (Lord Ackner), 789–90 (Lord Mackay).

In *Bull v Devon AHA*,[43] baby Stuart Bull, C, claimed that a county hospital which was built over two sites failed to have an adequate system in place for summoning the obstetrician, D, which led to a 68-minute delay between delivery of first twin Darryl and C (the latter suffered profound mental disability with spastic quadriplegia). There were two possible causes canvassed for this tragedy:

- *the innocent cause*: where uni-ovular twins share the same placenta during pregnancy, one twin may draw more than its fair share of nutrient at the expense of the other (foeto-foetal transfusion), which may deprive the second twin of oxygen. It was common ground between *all* the medical experts that C had suffered some measure of foeto-foetal transfusion to Darryl;
- *the negligent cause*: hypoxia occurred during the negligent birthing process, depriving C of sufficient oxygen in those 68 minutes.

Held: negligence proven. The innocent cause of foeto-foetal transfusion was entirely discounted by the trial judge as causing C's disabilities, partly because C had grown as fast as Darryl after birth. Hypoxia was the sole cause, held the trial judge.

However, the Court of Appeal noted that the trial judge sought to place the blame for C's harm at D's door to a standard higher than was necessary, noting of hypoxia that, '[i]t would have sufficed for him to make the less unqualified finding that this cause was established on the balance of probabilities ... however, he was entitled to make such a finding'.

Therefore, *Bull* properly belongs, with *Barnett*, in a fairly rare cadre of cases in which the 'but-for' test operated in the realm of certainty.

No fractional damages

§8.7 Where D's breach has a <50% probability of causing C's harm, C cannot recover a fraction of the total damages, on the basis that there was a possible chance that his injury was caused by that breach. In other words, 49% = 0%. However, it is important to distinguish discounting at liability stage (which is not permitted) from discounting at damages assessment stage (which is allowed).

In quantification terms, if C can show a >50% chance that, but for D's breach of duty, he would not have suffered the injury, C recovers **full** damages, and there is no question of fractional damages (say, 75%) being awarded to take account of the fact that there was a 25% chance that negligence did not cause the injury. As Lord Ackner stated in *Hotson*,[44] C's loss is 'not discounted by reducing his claim by the extent to which he has failed to prove his case with 100% certainty'.

Conversely, where there was a <50% chance that D's breach caused C's harm, C cannot recover fractional damages. Stephen Hotson was not entitled to recover 25% of what a fully-compensated-for necrotic hip injury would have been worth. To reiterate, at liability stage, 49% = 0%; and 51% = 100%.

Despite the House of Lords' rulings on the subject, the point has proven somewhat contentious, where judicial attempts have been made to discount damages at liability stage:

[43] (1989) 22 BMLR 79 (CA).   [44] [1987] AC 750 (HL) 792.

In *Bagley v North Herts HA*,[45] the trial court held that it should assess C's claim on the basis that D was negligent, 'and then make the necessary discount' for the 5% risk that her baby would have been stillborn anyway, even absent medical negligence. In *Hotson*, Lord Ackner held this approach to be 'clearly wrong'.[46] C had proven her case with 'near certainty', and she ought to have recovered 100% of the damages assessed. To discount 'would be to propound a wholly new doctrine, which has no support in principle or authority, and would give rise to many complications in the search for mathematical or statistical exactitude'. In *Tahir v Haringey HA*,[47] the trial judge had reduced C's harm (spastic gait and bowel/bladder problems, worth £30,000) to the proportion (13%) of the delay for which D was negligently responsible (2–3 hours, of a total 20–hour period in which a spinal operation on C was not performed – only D's delay of 2–3 hours was negligent). Hence, at trial, C was awarded £4,000 for his injuries (13% of £30,000). The Court of Appeal unanimously overruled this decision: 'this arithmetic or apportionment or proportionate method ... is not a valid method of assessing damages ... in adopting this approach, the learned Deputy Judge fell into error. [C] had failed to prove that any of his loss of amenity was caused by the negligent delay'.

On the other hand, where C actually proves D's liability in negligence and suffers damage, then the assessment of damages may properly involve an evaluation of chances in the future which could affect C's damages. In the *Creutzfeldt-Jakob Disease Litig*,[48] where the Department of Health had committed a breach in not informing treating doctors that they should tell those being treated with human growth hormone about the risk of contracting Creutzfeldt-Jakob disease, liability was proven (via rather unorthodox means, as explained shortly) – but then, the assessment of the damages **could** reflect discounts for possibilities. Take the head of damage, future loss of earnings, which was part of the damages assessment for these claimants. Adjustments for chances 'arise only at the quantification stage; e.g., what were the chances of a [CJD recipient] being promoted [at work], but for the onset of CJD? If he had a 25% chance, that chance will be reflected in the assessment of loss of earnings.' Obversely, if there was a chance of C's ceasing employment for non-CJD-related reasons, a discount would be similarly appropriate. However, those questions arise at quantification – at the liability stage, it is all or nothing.

Legal points about the balance-of-probabilities assessment

Epidemiological and statistical evidence

§8.8   Epidemiological and statistical evidence can be used, in some cases, to prove the causal link between breach and damage. However, neither can be used to reverse the burden of proof, so as to place the burden on D to disprove causation.

Epidemiological evidence. Such evidence seeks to establish causation by comparing a class of persons suffering from condition X, who were exposed to the suspected disease-causing agent, with the general population's contraction of condition X. According to Akenhead J in *Re Corby Group Litig*,[49] 'epidemiology is that branch of medical science which addresses epidemics. In practice, it is a statistical-based discipline which seeks to investigate, collate information, and

[45] (1986) 136 NLJ 1014 (QB) 1015 (Simon Brown J).   [46] [1987] AC 750 (HL) 793.
[47] [1998] Lloyd's Rep Med 104 (CA) (trial judgment on 12 Nov 1993).
[48] (1998) 54 BMLR 104 (QB), quote at 107–8.   [49] [2009] EWHC 1944 (TCC) [706].

analyse whether medical conditions or diseases have occurred in any given country, or part of a country, to an extent which is over and above what might otherwise be expected'. There are two aspects to its use (according to French J in *Reay v British Nuclear Fuels Ltd*[50]), viz, association and cause: '[t]he purpose of epidemiological studies ... is to make an assessment of the probability (a) that there is an association between the [exposure and the disease] and (b) that the association, if any, is causal'. Those two limbs to epidemiology were later confirmed by the Supreme Court in *Sienkiewicz v Greif (UK) Ltd.*[51]

The scenario can arise where, say, it is alleged that a doctor's failure to implement infection controls, or a local authority's dumping of toxic waste near residential areas, caused damage (i.e., disease or infirmities) to a class of persons.

In *Corby Group Litig*,[52] 18 Cs brought a group litigation order, alleging that birth defects (i.e., shortened or missing legs, arms and fingers) occurred in children born 1986–99, near a British Steel site east of Corby, which had been reclaimed by the Corby BC, D. The defects allegedly occurred because the mothers ingested or inhaled cadmium, nickel and other heavy metals whilst pregnant. This came about because, during the reclamation works, D allegedly followed a 'dig and dump' policy of burying slurry, and the method of transporting metals led to airborne contamination. The purpose at trial was to decide the generic issue as to whether any breach of duty by D 'had the ability to cause upper and/or lower limb defects of the type complained of'. **Held:** generic causation proven. Epidemiological evidence showed that there was an unexplained cluster of birth defects to the children of mothers living in Corby during 1986–99; plus evidence pointed to continuing breaches of the duty of care owed to C, which led to the extensive dispersal of contaminated materials from 1985–97.

Notwithstanding the support for epidemiological evidence in *Corby*, two caveats apply:

- in *Reay*,[53] French J noted that an assessment of causation will always depend upon the court's acceptance (or non-acceptance) of the credibility of the epidemiological evidence itself: '[t]he fact that epidemiologists or another scientist would, or would not, find an association and/or a cause to be established to his satisfaction is most helpful to a judge, but only within the limits imposed by their respective disciplines'; and
- it is not legally permissible to argue along the lines that, 'a group of us have this disease, and D's breach was the common factor, and it is all too much of a coincidence to attribute our disease to anything else, so it is up to D to prove that his breach was **not** the cause of our disease'. Such an argument would unacceptably reverse the burden of proof on causation. As discussed later,[54] that burden always rests on C in English law.

Statistical evidence. Convoluted statistical theories can also assist to prove causation in difficult cases, where otherwise it would be impossible to prove whether or not D's breach caused C's harm:

In *Creutzfeldt-Jakob Disease Litig, Group A and C Plaintiffs*,[55] several young children, Cs, who showed signs of stunted growth, were injected with human growth hormone (HGH) in a clinical trial. This type of HGH was capable of infecting injectees with Creutzfeldt-Jakob disease, a brain-wasting and untreatable condition that consigned its sufferers 'to unimaginable suffering and certain death'.

---

[50] (1994) 5 Med LR 1 (QB) 12.   [51] [2011] UKSC 10, [80] (Lord Phillips).   [52] [2009] EWHC 1944 (TCC) [689], [885].
[53] (1994) 5 Med LR 1 (QB) 12.   [54] See pp 483–86.   [55] (1998) 54 BMLR 100 (QB).

Cs were told of the CJD contamination of HGH, and their risk of developing CJD, some years after the trial. Some Cs contracted CJD, whilst others sustained psychiatric injury from the worry that they would do so. For any HGH injections administered after 1 July 1977, and which contained a sufficient titre of the CJD agent to be lethal, they were 'negligent injections', for by that date, the risk of CJD contamination causing brain-wasting was known. For any injections which contained a sufficient titre of the CJD agent to be lethal and which were given prior to that date, those were 'innocent injections'. Some Cs received HGH treatment both before and after 1 July 1977, and contracted CJD. However, it was impossible to say whether C received the 'tainted' injection before or after 1 July 1977. CJD could be caused by a single injection containing a sufficient titre of the CJD agent, and it had no cumulative effect. **Held:** for those Cs who received more doses after 1 July 1977 than prior to that date, causation succeeded.

Notwithstanding the complicated mathematical evidence in the case, ultimately a fairly 'rough and ready' statistical analysis was applied. Morland J treated the lethal dose received by C as a so-called 'an Ace of Spades'. If C received 27 doses after the cut-off date and 25 before that date, then it was slightly more likely that the Ace was in the pile of 27. More than one 'Ace' per C was unlikely, given the rarity of CJD contamination.

The drawing of inferences

§8.9 Where the causal chain of events by which C's damage occurred is not capable of precise proof, the court may rely on an inference to establish a causal connection between D's breach and C's harm.

Where direct proof of what happened to bring about C's harm is impossible, then recourse may be sought to the doctrine of *res ipsa loquitur* (discussed in Chapter 7). Alternatively, the court may be prepared to draw an inference that the causal link was proven – which necessarily requires that the court 'be prepared to take a reasonably robust approach to causation' (per *Roadrunner v Dean*[56]). Inferences are especially useful where the court is not inclined expressly to rely on *res ipsa loquitur*, although some of the reasoning is similar under both.

In *Drake v Harbour*,[57] Toulson LJ explained that two pre-requisites apply for an inference of causation:

i. C's damage must be of a type that would ordinarily follow from the proven breach against D: 'where [C] proves both that [D] was negligent, and that loss ensued which was of a kind likely to have resulted from such negligence, this will ordinarily be enough to enable a court to infer that it was probably so caused, even if [C] is unable to prove positively the precise mechanism';

ii. any other causal explanation was improbable: '[t]he court must consider any alternative theories of causation advanced by [D] before reaching its conclusion about where the probability lies. If it concludes that the only alternative suggestions put forward by [D] are, on balance, improbable ... it is legitimate to infer that the loss was caused by the proven negligence'. However, Toulson LJ noted that there is no reversal of the burden of proof under this requirement; 'rather, it is a matter of applying common sense'.

---

[56] [2003] EWCA Civ 1816, [29].   [57] [2008] EWCA Civ 25, quotes at [28].

In *Drake v Harbour*, D negligently undertook electrical rewiring of C's house whilst C was absent, when installing festoon lights in the loft. Old cabling was used for the festoon lights, and D failed to inspect it properly. The lights were plugged into a light socket, and the house was then destroyed by a fire which was seated in the loft, whilst D's workers were absent overnight. **Held:** how the fire started was not conclusively determined. But it was 'more likely than not', via an inference, that the insulation of the festoon lights' cabling was damaged, causing arcing and overheating.

However, the 'Sherlock Holmes' inferential approach to causation, i.e., that if every other causal link between the breach and the damage has been ruled out as being unlikely, then whatever causal argument left, however implausible, must be the relevant cause of the damage, is not an acceptable route by which to prove causation in English law (per *Rhesa Shipping Co v Edmunds, The Popi M*[58]). As recently confirmed in *Graves v Brouwer*,[59] the upshot of that scenario is that C has not proven its case on causation on the balance of probabilities. The court is not required to choose between two implausible causes, and ignore the option that C simply failed to prove the cause of the damage. This topic is considered further in 'Defective products', an online chapter.

Exceptions to 'but-for' causation

The 'but-for' test is not the exclusive test of causation. The limits of that test have been widely acknowledged. In *Kuwait Airways Corp v Iraqi Airways Co (Nos 4 and 5)*,[60] Lord Hoffmann remarked that 'it would be an irrational system of tort liability which did not insist upon there being some causal connection between the tortious act and the damage. But causal connections can be of widely differing kinds'. In essence, the 'but-for' test cannot (per Sir Igor Judge in *Clough v First Choice Holidays*[61]) be treated 'as a single, invariable test applicable to causation issues'.

In *Fairchild v Glenhaven Funeral Services Ltd*, Lord Nicholls noted that any exception to the 'but-for' test is just that – an *exceptional* scenario:

> In the normal way, in order to recover damages for negligence, [C] must prove that but for [D's] wrongful conduct, he would not have sustained the harm or loss in question. He must establish at least this degree of causal connection between his damage and [D's] conduct before [D] will be held responsible for the damage. Exceptionally this is not so ... [and] a lesser degree of causal connection [is sufficient]'.[62]

There are **four** exceptions to the 'but-for' test, the most important of which is the *McGhee/Fairchild* exception. Its application has arisen particularly in the contexts of employment and medical negligence.

EXCEPTION #1: THE 'MATERIAL CONTRIBUTION TO RISK' EXCEPTION

Suppose that C cannot prove that D's breach caused his harm on the balance of probabilities. There is at least one innocent cause, and the breach itself, swirling around in the factual matrix – but it is beyond the ken of scientific or medical knowledge to say which of these probably caused C's harm. The respective causes may have operated solely, or in combination to an

---

[58] [1985] 1 WLR 948 (HL).   [59] [2015] EWCA Civ 595, [30].

[60] [2002] UKHL 19, [2002] 2 AC 883, [127], citing: *Bonnington Castings Ltd v Wardlaw* [1956] AC 613 (HL) and *McGhee v National Coal Board* [1973] 1 WLR 1 (HL).

[61] [2006] EWCA Civ 15, [43].   [62] [2002] UKHL 22, [2003] 1 AC 32, [37].

unknown degree, or not at all, to bring about C's damage. It is impossible to say – exposing a so-called 'evidential gap'.

An express reference to that 'gap' has arisen in several of the most difficult causation-in-negligence cases in English law, *viz*, *Gregg v Scott*,[63] *Fairchild v Glenhaven Funeral Services Ltd*,[64] *McGhee v National Coal Board*[65] and *Wilsher v Essex AHA*.[66] Into that gap has stepped 'the doctrine of material contribution' in a couple of the aforementioned cases, i.e., a series of legal principles have been developed as a pragmatic solution to the causal conundrum.

Essentially, C can prove causation under this theorem, only where he can align his case with *McGhee/Fairchild* (or with the so-called 'enclave' which developed from that line of authority that includes *Sienkiewicz v Greif (UK) Ltd*[67] and *Barker v Corus UK Ltd*[68]). Causation will fail, however, if C's scenario aligns with the *Wilsher* scenario; while the 'doubling the risk' doctrine has a very limited application. It is also necessary to correctly distinguish *McGhee/Fairchild* scenarios from *Bonnington*-type 'material contribution to damage' scenarios, as the legal ramifications are different for each. These difficult issues are discussed in this and the following sections.

The *McGhee/Fairchild* scenario

§8.10 According to the *McGhee/Fairchild* principle, C can prove a sufficient causal link where D's breach materially contributed to the risk of C's suffering damage. The doctrine applies where the following conditions are satisfied:

i. only one 'candidate' (agent) could have caused C's harm; and C was exposed to that agent, both tortiously (because of D's act or omission), and innocently, for a reason other than D's breach. That innocent exposure could be brought about because of some naturally-occurring environmental exposure to the agent; by C's own conduct by which he exposed himself to the agent; or by some lawful exposure to that agent which was brought about either by D or by some other party;

ii. D failed to take precautions against the risk of the agent causing C harm (i.e., proof of breach);

iii. D's breach preceded C's suffering the precise harm which that agent causes;

iv. C cannot (because of the current limits of scientific knowledge) prove, on the balance of probabilities, that his harm was the result of the particular exposure to the agent which that D's breach brought about; and

v. the highest that C can prove is that D's breach materially increased the risk of harm to him (somewhere between the balance of probabilities and *de minimis*).

In the *McGhee/Fairchild* scenario, the 'but-for' test will fail, because there are tortious and innocent contributors to C's harm, and none of them surmounts the 50% threshold of probability required for the 'but-for' test to apply. Nevertheless, under the exceptional theorem of causation known as 'the material contribution to the risk exception', C can still establish a sufficient causal link.

The abovementioned principle is derived from the leading cases of *McGhee v National Coal Board* and *Fairchild v Glenhaven Funeral Services Ltd*,[69] which, in turn, have been interpreted

[63] [2002] EWCA Civ 1471, [53]   [64] [2002] UKHL 22, [150].
[65] [1973] 1 WLR 1 (HL) 7.   [66] (1984) 135 NLJ 383 (QB).
[67] [2011] UKSC 10, [2011] 2 AC 229, [167].   [68] [2006] UKHL 20, [2006] 2 AC 572.
[69] See especially, *Fairchild* [2003] AC 32 (HL) [2] (Lord Bingham), [61] (Lord Hoffmann), [170] (Lord Rodger).

and clarified by subsequent cases, *viz*, *Sienkiewicz* and *Barker v Corus*. There are **five** conditions for the exception to apply, **all** of which must be satisfied.

Dealing with each pre-requisite in turn:

Pre-requisite (i): Only one 'candidate' (agent) could have caused C's harm; that agent had both 'guilty' and 'innocent' incidents; C was exposed to both

The single agent is absolutely crucial to the *McGhee/Fairchild* principle. Indeed, as the 'Fairchild enclave' of authority (as it was termed recently by the Supreme Court in *Zurich Ins plc UK Branch v Intl Energy Group Ltd*[70]) has developed, it has become increasingly apparent that, if this exceptional theorem is to be contained within reasonable limits, this pre-requisite must apply.

This was emphasised in *Fairchild*[71] itself, where Lord Bingham stated that, '[i]t is one thing to treat an increase of risk as equivalent to the making of a material contribution where a single noxious agent is involved, but quite another where any one of a number of noxious agents may, with equal probability, have caused the damage'. Lord Hutton agreed that *McGhee's* principle could only apply, 'where there is only one causative agent'. Lord Hoffmann dissented on this point in *Fairchild*, but later considered his view to have been wrong, in *Barker v Corus UK Ltd*.[72]

If there are multiple agents in play, then the *Fairchild/McGhee* exception cannot apply (instead, it will be a *Wilsher* scenario, where causation will not be proven, as discussed below). If *Fairchild* were to extend to multi-agent cases as well, then identifying the contribution of each particular agent to C's harm would be 'well nigh impossible and highly artificial' (per Lord Scott in *Barker v Corus*[73]).

In *Fairchild v Glenhaven Funeral Services Ltd*,[74] three test cases were brought by employees (Arthur Fairchild *et al.*, C), who were wrongfully exposed to significant quantities of asbestos dust in their workplaces by their employers, D. Each employee suffered from mesothelioma. For each C as against each D, there were essentially two possible causes of his mesothelioma:

- C's exposure to asbestos which one particular employer, D, did not take adequate precautions to prevent ('*the guilty asbestos*'); or
- C's exposure to asbestos which those other employers who had employed C during his career did not take adequate precautions to prevent ('*the innocent asbestos*').

It was impossible to prove scientifically which employer's asbestos fibre/s had caused C's mesothelioma on the balance of probabilities. It was also not clear whether it was one fibre, or an accumulation of fibres, that caused mesothelioma – all that science could say was that the greater the exposure to asbestos, the greater the risk of contracting the disease; but that, once contracted, further exposure did not worsen the disease. **Held:** causation succeeded against each D. The breach by each D increased the likelihood of mesothelioma being suffered by C.

In *McGhee v National Coal Board*,[75] James McGhee, C, worked in a brick kiln in hot and dusty conditions whereby brick dust adhered to his sweaty skin. His employer, National Coal Board, D, committed no breach of duty in respect of these working conditions. However, D failed to provide adequate washing facilities, thus requiring C to cycle home after work with his body still caked in brick dust.

[70] [2015] UKSC 33, [1] (Lord Mance), [102] (Lord Hodge).
[71] *ibid*, with quotes at: [22] and [115], and see too, [149] (Lord Rodger), and [72] (Lord Hoffmann).
[72] [2006] UKHL 20, [2006] 2 AC 572, [23].   [73] *ibid*, [64].   [74] [2003] 1 AC 32 (HL).   [75] [1973] 1 WLR 1 (HL).

C contracted industrial dermatitis (a condition caused by abrasive brick dust removing the upper skin layer, exposing the tender skin beneath). Brick dust adhering to the skin was a recognised cause of industrial dermatitis; and providing showers to remove it after work was a usual precaution to minimise the risk of the disease. There were two possible causes of C's dermatitis:

- the brick dust which abraded the skin, and which ought to have been washed off before his ride home if shower facilities had been provided ('*the guilty brickdust*'); or
- the brick dust which abraded C's skin during his work in the brick kiln during working hours, and against which D had no duty to provide preventative measures ('*the innocent brickdust*').

It was impossible for C to prove that, had D provided washing facilities, then on the balance of probabilities, the dermatitis would not have occurred. The 'but-for' test failed. Even if the brickdust had been washed off before C's ride home, C's dermatitis may still have been suffered in any event. **Held:** nevertheless, causation succeeded.

This exceptional theorem has some key points, under its first pre-requisite.

One D or multiple Ds. The 'innocent exposure' to the harmful agent needs to be clarified. Of course, *McGhee* and *Fairchild* were entirely different cases. In *McGhee*, there was only one D, but that employer D had exposed C to brickdust, both innocently and tortiously. In *Fairchild*, there were numerous employer Ds, all of whom were in breach by exposing C wrongfully to asbestos dust in each of those employment stints – but insofar *as each particular D* was concerned, C had been exposed to that D's 'tortious asbestos dust', but C had been exposed to asbestos dust by someone else altogether (so that was 'innocent' asbestos dust, as far as that particular D was concerned, as it certainly was not his). Hence, in *McGhee*, there truly was innocent exposure; whereas in *Fairchild*, all of the asbestos dust was tortious when looked at as a whole, but when taking each employer D individually, any other asbestos dust caused by another employer was the innocent dust, as far as that employer D was concerned. For that reason, *Fairchild* shares a close commonality with *McGhee*, and both fit within the five-pronged principle articulated at the commencement of this section.

Additionally, the 'innocent exposure' which C suffered could be caused by something else altogether. The *McGhee/Fairchild* one-agent exception also applies, to enable C to prove a sufficient causal link, where C was exposed to the harmful single agent via (1) his own contributory negligence, or (2) some natural occurrence which is completely out of either C's or D's control (e.g., some environmental exposure to the agent). Post-*Fairchild*, the House of Lords held that the exception applies to those 'one-agent' scenarios too. Dealing with each in turn:

Contributory negligence. The fact that some exposure to the harmful agent was brought about by C's failure to take reasonable care to protect himself against that agent will mean that C's damages will be reduced to the extent of that contributory negligence. However, C's ability to prove causation via the weaker causal link supplied by the *Fairchild/McGhee* exception against some party D who also exposed him to that same harmful agent, is unaffected by any contributory negligence. Once again, the harmful agent in the relevant case was asbestos dust:

In *Barker v Corus (UK) plc*,[76] Mr Barker died of mesothelioma. He had been wrongfully exposed to asbestos dust on three occasions during his working life – for six months when working for Corus, D1; for six weeks when working for another employer, D2 (now insolvent); and for three short periods over

---

[76] [2006] UKHL 20, [2006] 2 AC 572, [48]. Two other appeals, of Mr Patterson and Mr Murray, were conjoined in this appeal, but they did not involve any contributory negligence.

7 years, when working as a self-employed plasterer (when he failed to take reasonable precautions against asbestos for his own safety). Mrs Barker, C, sued D1 and D2 under the FAA. **Held (HL):** C's damages were reduced by 20%, to reflect Mr Barker's contributory negligence. However, Mr Barker's own negligence did not prevent the application of the *Fairchild* theorem. (Additionally, under the *Fairchild* theorem, each employer should only be liable for that proportion of the damages which represented his contribution to the risk that the employee would contract mesothelioma, as discussed in 'Multiple defendants', an online chapter.)

A natural event. Even where C is exposed to the harmful agent innocently, because that agent occurs naturally in the environment, the *McGhee/Fairchild* exception still applies, for C's benefit.

In *Sienkiewicz v Greif (UK) Ltd*,[77] Enid Costello, C, 74, died of mesothelioma. She was an office worker at a factory at Ellesmere Port from 1966–84. Her employer, Greif (UK) Ltd, D, manufactured steel drums, and during that work, asbestos dust was released around the factory, wrongfully exposing employees to that dust. C's duties took her all over the factory, including areas contaminated with asbestos. Whilst C had not been exposed to asbestos during any other employment, she was exposed to a low level of asbestos in the general atmosphere, given that she lived in close proximity to Ellesmere Port (in common with all other residents of that area). It could not be proven when C contracted mesothelioma (i.e., whether it was a fibre to which she was exposed during her employment, or during her exposure to the atmospheric asbestos dust). **Held:** causation proven, as a *Fairchild* scenario.

The application of the *Fairchild* exception, in any circumstances where D materially increased the risk that C would suffer damage, but where some other source of that risk was also present – whatever source that might be – has been affirmed at the highest appellate level. In *Barker v Corus*,[78] Lord Hoffmann (who gave the leading speech) commented that, for the purposes of the *Fairchild* exception, 'it should be irrelevant whether the other exposure was tortious or non-tortious, by natural causes or human agency or by C himself'. Similarly, in *Zurich Ins v Intl Energy Group*, Lord Mance noted that *Fairchild's* 'special rule' applied, wherever C had been exposed to 'asbestos dust originating from different sources over the same or different periods'.[79]

The 'single agent'. What is meant by a 'single agent' – sufficient to invoke the application of this exceptional theorem of causation – has provoked some real uncertainty. In *Sienkiewicz*, for example, Lord Brown doubted whether the distinction was easily recognisable in some cases (and even doubted whether it should continue to base an exception to 'but-for' causation which was any wider than asbestos causing mesothelioma).[80] Obviously, judges have been concerned to ensure that the *McGhee/Fairchild* exception is not applied too widely, so as to circumvent the 'but-for' test.

It seems that it does not matter that there were different mechanisms, or ways, in which the single agent acted to bring about C's harm. However, C's condition must have 'the same distinctive aetiology and prognosis', no matter which innocent or tortious exposure he suffered (as Lord Walker put it in *Barker*[81]). In the same case, Lord Scott said that he would regard different

---

[77] [2011] UKSC 10, [2011] 2 AC 229. In a conjoined appeal, Dianne Willmore alleged tortious exposure to asbestos whilst a pupil at school, together with environmental exposure. Both Cs succeeded on causation.
[78] [2006] UKHL 20, [17].   [79] [2015] UKSC 33, [3].   [80] [2011] UKSC 10, [187].
[81] [2006] UKHL 20, [114] (Lord Walker).

types of asbestos as constituting a single agent, whilst Lord Hoffmann gave an example of what would **not** involve the 'single agent' necessary for the *McGhee/Fairchild* exception to apply, i.e., where C 'suffers lung cancer which may have been caused by exposure to asbestos or some other carcinogenic matter, but may also have been caused by smoking, and it cannot be proved which is more likely to have been the causative agent'.[82] Undoubtedly, this particular aspect of pre-requisite (i) will continue to develop jurisprudentially.

Pre-requisite (ii): D failed to take precautions against the risk of the agent causing C harm

Proving that D was culpable for exposing C to the harmful agent is necessary, in order to establish causation under the *McGhee/Fairchild* principle. As the Court of Appeal pointed out in *Rolls Royce Industrial Power (India) Ltd v Cox*,[83] '[a]lthough *Fairchild* assists [C] in relation to causation, it does not relieve them of the requirement to prove a breach of the duty of care on the part of [D]'. The wrong can be a negligent breach of duty, or a breach of statutory duty – the point is that there must be a wrong (per *Zurich Ins plc v Intl Energy Group*[84]).

In some cases (e.g., in *Fairchild* itself), breach (in failing to provide safety precautions to prevent the inhalation of asbestos) was admitted. In cases where breach cannot be proven though, there is no room whatsoever for the exception to apply.

> In *King v King*,[85] C, 22, had a vaccination course for typhoid and cholera at D's surgery before a trip to Morocco. About six hours after the second vaccination, C suffered a stroke. C alleged that D should not have given him the injection because he had a boil and a temperature, which materially increased the risk of an adverse reaction. (C could not prove that the vaccination caused his stroke on the balance of probabilities.) **Held:** the claim failed, as there was no breach. In *McGhee*, 'the problem ... arose because there had been a breach of duty by [D], and the question to be decided was whether that breach was causative' of C's dermatitis, whereas in this case, 'that prerequisite to such an enquiry is missing'.

Pre-requisite (iii): D's breach preceded C's suffering the precise harm which that agent causes

Brick dust was the **only** explanation for Mr McGhee's dermatitis and (as explained subsequently by the House of Lords in *Wilsher*[86]), the failure 'to take a precaution against brick dust causing dermatitis was followed by dermatitis caused by brick dust ... I can see the common sense, if not the logic, of holding that, in the absence of any other evidence, the failure to take the precaution caused or contributed to the dermatitis'. Similarly, mesothelioma is caused by the inhalation of asbestos particles (per *Fairchild*).

In some medical cases, the application of the *McGhee/Fairchild* exception has been tested on the basis that one agent may have operated tortiously, or innocently, or a mixture of both, to bring about a patient's harm – but the patient cannot prove which applies on the balance of probabilities. If the agent has **never** been known to cause that damage, however, then the exception simply cannot apply.

---

[82] *ibid*, [64] (Lord Scott), [24] (Lord Hoffmann).   [83] [2007] EWCA Civ 1189, [3].

[84] [2015] UKSC 33, [3].   [85] CA, 9 Apr 1987 (Croom-Johnson LJ).

[86] [1988] AC 1074 (HL) 1091–92 (Lord Bridge), approving: [1987] QB 730 (CA) 779 (Browne-Wilkinson V-C, dissenting).

In *Kay v Ayrshire and Arran Health Board*,[87] toddler Andrew Kay, C, was admitted to hospital with pneumococcal meningitis. During treatment, he was negligently given an overdose of penicillin, which was immediately counteracted by remedial treatment. After recovering from the meningitis, C was found to be deaf. There were two possible causes of C's deafness (neither of which could be proven on the balance of probabilities):

- C already was at risk of neurological damage from the meningitis ('*the innocent cause*');
- C was overdosed with penicillin, which increased the risk of suffering some neurological injury ('*the guilty cause*').

Held: there was no evidence that an overdose of penicillin had ever caused, or even contributed to, deafness. Hence, C's deafness had to be regarded as resulting solely from the meningitis: '[t]he principle in *McGhee* would only fall for consideration if it was first proved that it was an accepted medical fact that penicillin in some cases caused or aggravated deafness ... because the necessary factual background cannot be established on the evidence in this case, this difficult question does not arise'.

Just as problematically in *Kay*, there were 'two competing causes of deafness, namely meningitis and penicillin', but these agents (alleged to bring about neurological damage) were quite different. One was a drug, and one was a bacterium. It could not be a *McGhee*-type case in any event, because it failed pre-requisite (i).

Pre-requisite (iv): C cannot (because of the current limits of science) prove, on the balance of probabilities, that his harm was the result of the exposure to the agent which D's breach brought about

As explained earlier, C has an 'evidential gap', in that there is no objective basis upon which science or medicine can determine whether or not C would have developed the harm anyway, even if D's breach had never occurred. The whole point of the exception is to assist C with this dilemma.

Undoubtedly the exception is policy-driven. As Toulson LJ explained in *Intl Energy Group Ltd v Zurich Ins plc*,[88] in the case of employment scenarios, *Fairchild* demonstrates 'the protective approach which the courts have taken towards the health of employees, and the difficulty of knowing the particular moment of exposure which has caused the onset of the disease' – in such cases, a 'broader test' of causation is appropriate.

In any case in which it can be proved that D's breach either did, or did not, cause C's harm on the balance of probabilities, reliance on *McGhee/Fairchild* is inappropriate. Hence, the *CJD* case[89] was 'a different problem of causation' from that arising in *McGhee*, as was *Hotson v East Berkshire AHA*.[90]

Presently, the contracting of mesothelioma from asbestos exposure falls within this 'evidential gap'. Where someone is exposed to asbestos fibres, those fibres may not trigger the malignant mutation necessary to form a mesothelioma tumour, it appears to depend on different fibres interacting to bring about a series of genetic alterations, ending with a malignant cell in the pleura.[91] Further, the point at which a tumour does form, i.e., 'present and assured of growth ... [so] has passed the stage where that mutation may die off' (as described in the *Trigger Litigation*[92]), is not presently capable of being ascertained scientifically, so that it is not

---

[87] 1987 SC 145, 168–69 (Lord Griffiths).   [88] [2013] EWCA Civ 39, [24],
[89] (1998) 54 BMLR 100 (QB), quote at 106.   [90] [1987] AC 750 (HL).
[91] *Zurich Ins v Intl Energy Group Ltd* [2015] UKSC 33, [1] (Lord Mance).   [92] [2011] 1 All ER 605 (CA) [51] (Rix LJ).

possible to tell which particular fibre/s caused the mutation. However, that gap in scientific knowledge may be rectified in time to come, in which case the usual 'but-for' test will apply in that scenario (and 'the problem which gave rise to the *Fairchild* exception will have ceased to exist', per *Sienkiewicz v Greif (UK) Ltd*[93]). That day, however, lies in the future.

Pre-requisite (v): The highest that C can prove is that D's breach materially increased C's risk of harm

Whether D materially increased (i.e., added to) the risk of harm to C is a question of degree. It lies somewhere between the balance of probabilities and *de minimis*.

Courts have been reluctant to be too specific as to what amounts to something more than a *de minimis* contribution. Lord Reid stated, in *Bonnington Castings Ltd v Wardlaw*, that 'any contribution which does not fall within that [*de minimis* scope] must be material. I do not see how there can be something too large to come within the *de minimis* principle, yet too small to be material'.[94] Some sort of quantitative assessment as to whether a contribution to risk was greater than *de minimis* is not a path that the Supreme Court has been willing to go down – rather, in *Sienkiewicz*, Lord Phillips said that it 'must be a question for the judge on the facts of the particular case.'[95] Although, in *Zurich Ins v Intl Energy Group*, Lord Mance referred to a requirement, under the *Fairchild* principle, that D had exposed C to '*significant* quantities of asbestos dust', that is not to impute that the contribution had to be 'significant' in probability terms.[96] Something greater than *de minimis* is all that is required.

In the case of occupational disease cases (such as mesothelioma), the courts have also declined to set a minimum period of employment which C must satisfy, in order to succeed on the *Fairchild* principle – although some patients have found the *de minimis* threshold too difficult to surmount.

> In *Sienkiewicz*, facts previously, **held:** causation proven. Greif, D, wrongfully exposed Mrs Costello, C, to asbestos dust, which increased the environmental exposure to which C was already subject by 18%. That incremental exposure in the workplace materially increased her risk of contracting mesothelioma, over and above the *de minimis* threshold. In *Rolls Royce Industrial Power (India) Ltd v Cox*,[97] C was employed by D as a welder, during which he stripped down large boilers and was exposed to asbestos for 'at least a few months'. C had been exposed to asbestos at other stages of his working career too. C suffered mesothelioma. **Held:** causation proven. Three months was sufficient to fall within the *Fairchild* exception (indeed, D conceded that one week of exposure would be greater than *de minimis*). In *King v King*,[98] facts previously, **held:** causation failed. Any hope of relying on *McGhee* was precluded because there was 'no evidence that the inoculation of an unhealthy patient increased the risk of a neurological reaction'.[99] Hence, administering the vaccination did not contribute to C's risk of stroke in any way that was greater than *de minimis*. In *Brown v Lewisham and North Southwark HA*,[100] Mr Brown, C, was sent from London to Blackpool by train and taxi, following heart by-pass surgery, when he was physically unfit to travel. Ultimately, C suffered from

---

[93] [2011] UKSC 10, [142] (Lord Rodger), and also, [208] (Lord Dyson).

[94] [1956] AC 613 (HL) 621. Also: *Nicholson v Atlas Steel Foundry and Engineering Co Ltd* [1957] WLR 613 (HL) 622.

[95] [2011] UKSC 10, [108].   [96] [2015] UKSC 33, [3] (emphasis added).   [97] [2007] EWCA Civ 1189, [21]–[22].

[98] CA, 9 Apr 1987 (Balcombe LJ).

[99] See also, for similar result: *Murray v Kensington and Chelsea and Westminster AHA* (CA, 11 May 1981), citing the *de minimis* threshold in *Bonnington Castings Ltd v Wardlaw* [1956] AC 613 (HL).

[100] (1999) 48 BMLR 96 (CA) 106. Also: *McDonald v Tees HA* (CA, 21 Oct 1996) (Brooke LJ; with Aldous LJ and Lord Woolf MR agreeing, and upholding the trial judge's view that causation failed).

serious blood-clotting, which occluded the common iliac vein, compromising blood supply to his left leg, and led to his left leg being amputated after it turned gangrenous. There were three possible causes of the blood-clotting (none of which could be proven on the balance of probabilities):

- C's journey to Blackpool had contributed to enlarge or extend deep vein thrombosis which was already in his left leg when he left the hospital by train and taxi, and the presence of which should have ruled out his travelling (*guilty blood-clotting circumstances*);
- a blood clot may have formed in C's leg, sometime before his transfer, but where doctors at London were not negligent in failing to diagnose that before agreeing that C could return to Blackpool (*innocent blood-clotting circumstances*);
- blood clotting may have been caused by administering heparin after the transfer, because heparin given after by-pass surgery could cause the onset of heparin-induced thrombocytopena thrombosis (*innocent blood-clotting circumstances*).

Held: causation failed. There was one agent for the damage, *viz*, blood clotting, and occlusions which led to the amputation were the precise damage which blood-clotting could cause. However, when C arrived at Blackpool hospital, there were no objective symptoms that the journey had, in fact, caused an extension or aggravation of the deep vein thrombosis which C was found to be suffering. Any impact from the journey was very insignificant, and did not overcome a *de minimis* contribution to C's injury.

The *Wilsher* scenario

§8.11 According to the *Wilsher* principle, where C was exposed to multiple causal agents which could give rise to the risk of harm to C, but which of those agents caused C's harm cannot be proven on the balance of probabilities, then the *McGhee/Fairchild* 'material contribution to risk' test cannot apply, and causation must fail.

The *Wilsher* scenario differs from *McGhee/Fairchild* because there is no 'one agent' in play which may have had an innocent or a guilty contribution to C's harm. Rather, there are several different agents in play, any of which may have caused C's harm, and none of which surmounts the balance-of-probabilities threshold. Causation must fail, in the *Wilsher* scenario.

In *Wilsher v Essex AHA*,[101] Martin Wilsher, C, was a very premature baby, who was cared for in a special care baby unit by a team of doctors and nurses. C required oxygen, and during the first 36 hours of his life, a mistake occurred. Instead of inserting the catheter in C's umbilical artery to read his arterial blood oxygen levels, a junior doctor inserted the catheter into his umbilical vein, which read venous blood. Due to the lower-than-expected readings of blood oxygen levels, more oxygen was mistakenly administered. C was 'supersaturated' with oxygen for up to 8–12 hours. After inserting the catheter, the junior doctor asked a senior registrar to check what he had done. The registrar inspected the X-ray with the junior doctor, but failed to detect that the catheter was misplaced, and subsequently, when replacing the catheter, did exactly the same thing himself. It was not the insertion of the catheter into a vein instead of an artery which was negligent (it was a difficult task), but rather, the failure to detect, from the X-ray, that the catheter was wrongly placed. C ultimately developed the incurable eye condition, retrolental fibroplasia (RLF), which resulted in blindness. There were five possible causes of C's RLF (none of which could be proven on the balance of probabilities):

[101] [1988] AC 1074 (HL).

- super-saturation of oxygen within the first 30 hours of C's life, via the doctors' mistake – excess oxygen could have a toxic effect on the immature blood vessels in C's retina, leading to RLF (*the guilty cause*);
- hypercarbia (hypercapnia) – the presence in C's blood of an abnormally high concentration of carbon dioxide (*an innocent cause*);
- intra-ventricular haemorrhage – ruptured blood vessels within the ventricle of C's heart (*an innocent cause*);
- apnoea – a temporary cessation of breathing, from a reduction in nasal airflow, a common occurrence in newborn babies (*an innocent cause*);
- patent ductus arteriosus – the ductus is a blood vessel connecting the pulmonary artery directly to the aorta, and where it fails to close, that produces a murmur, affecting pulmonary circulation (*an innocent cause*).

C suffered from *all five* conditions in the first two months of his life. **Held:** causation failed. Due to factual disputes, a re-trial was ordered (and the case settled before that re-trial). Similarly, in *Kay v Ayrshire and Arran Health Board*,[102] facts previously, there were two possible causes of C's deafness: meningitis and penicillin. **Held:** causation failed. Even if penicillin was proven to have been a possible cause of deafness (which it was not), C would have failed, because it was a multi-agent *Wilsher* case.

In *Barker v Corus*,[103] the House of Lords reiterated that *Wilsher* did not fall within the *McGhee/Fairchild* scenario. There, C's dermatitis could only have been caused by brick dust. In *Wilsher*, by contrast, 'a failure to take preventative measures against one out of five possible causes is no evidence as to which of those five caused the injury'.[104]

Of course, the *McGhee/Fairchild* exception would be capable of far wider application – and would assist far more Cs over the causal threshold – if multi-agent causes that did not satisfy the balance-of-probabilities test were nevertheless sufficient to establish a causal link, merely because each agent materially contributed to the risk of injury to C. However, English negligence law is not that liberal. It is not enough that D contributed to the overall risk that C suffered damage (per *Clough v First Choice Holidays and Flights Ltd*[105]). Were that to be the law, then it would constitute (in the words of Nourse LJ in *Fitzgerald v Lane*[106]) 'a benevolent principle [which] smiles on these factual uncertainties and melts them all away', and would entail (per Lord Rodger in *Fairchild*[107]) 'an obvious injustice to the defendants'.

Finally, it is useful to contrast *Wilsher* with the earlier (1981) case of *Murray v Kensington and Chelsea and Westminster AHA*.[108]

In *Murray*, C was a very premature baby who sustained RLF and blindness during his hospital treatment, due to the over-administration of oxygen during the first dire days of his existence. The baby's treatment could be divided into two periods: the first 36 hours, and the next 3–4 weeks. During both periods, the oxygen levels administered to the baby were elevated, but the trial judge held that it was only the first period that was negligent (which was doubted on appeal). In any event, the medical evidence was that '[w]e cannot say what was the cause of the blindness – whether it was

---

[102] [1987] 2 All ER 417, 1987 SC 145 (HL).

[103] [2006] UKHL 20, [18]–[24] (Lord Hoffmann), [64] (Lord Scott), [114] (Lord Walker).

[104] [1988] AC 1074 (HL) 1091.   [105] [2006] EWCA Civ 15, [38] (Sir Igor Judge).

[106] [1987] QB 781 (CA) 800 (Nourse LJ) (*Fitzgerald* was delivered before *Wilsher* (HL), but pre-empted the outcome).

[107] [2002] UKHL 22, [149] (Lord Rodger).   [108] CA, 11 May 1981.

caused by a mistake in the first 36 hours, or whether it occurred during the next 3–4 weeks (when there was no negligence). We simply cannot say'. Hence, there were two possible causes of C's RLF:

- super-saturation of oxygen in hours 1–36 of C's life (*'the guilty oxygen'*);
- super-saturation of oxygen in weeks 1–4 (*'the innocent oxygen'*).

Held: the excess ambient oxygen for the first 36 hours of C's life played only a minimal, if any, part in the onset of RLF and the consequential blindness, i.e., it did not meet the *de minimis* threshold, and made no material contribution to the risk of blindness.

Although, at first glance, the facts in *Murray* and *Wilsher* bear passing resemblance to each other, they are, in fact, entirely different cases. Were the *de minimis* threshold to have been crossed, then *Murray* would have been a *McGhee/Fairchild*, rather than a *Wilsher*, scenario, and C would have been entitled to recover in full for his blindness. As it was, he had been abandoned by his parents at birth, and this action was brought by his foster parents – unsuccessfully, as it turned out.

Limiting the scope of the *McGhee/Fairchild* exceptional theorem

The impact of *Sienkiewicz*

§8.12 English law remains currently unsettled as to the extent to which the *Fairchild* exception can be applied beyond the scope of its precise facts (i.e., where D is one of a number of employers who committed a breach by tortiously exposing C to asbestos, and where C later suffers mesothelioma), to where C suffers harm from other occupational illnesses/injuries, from medical negligence, or from pharmaceutical products, where C was exposed to one harmful agent, both tortiously and innocently.

As has been evident from preceding discussion, the *McGhee/Fairchild* exception has been considered in medical negligence cases (e.g., *Brown*, *King v King*) – wherein, as in *McGhee* itself, there was one D, and it was claimed that D had exposed C to the risk of harm via one agent, both tortiously and innocently.

However, where D has exposed C to a harmful agent, but so too have other parties exposed C to that same agent by committing breaches of duty similar to those of D, then some judicial statements in *Sienkiewicz v Greif (UK) Ltd*,[109] seem to suggest that the application of the *Fairchild* exception **only** occurs where C suffers mesothelioma as a result of the wrongful exposure to asbestos, and that it should not be extended more widely than that. For example, Lord Brown considered that 'mesothelioma cases are in a category all their own', and that other types of Cs should expect to have to adhere to the traditional causation principles, whilst Lord Rodger referred to the *Fairchild* exception as a 'special rule' applying to mesothelioma.

Since *Sienkiewicz*, some judges have also considered the *Fairchild* exception to be a narrow one. In *Zurich Ins plc UK Branch v Intl Energy Group*,[110] Lord Mance (writing for the majority) referred to *Fairchild*, *Barker v Corus*, and *Sienkiewicz* as 'operating within what might be called the *Fairchild* enclave, to govern liability between victims and those who, in breach of duty, had exposed them to asbestos dust'. In *Re J (children)*,[111] Lady Hale remarked that the

---

[109] [2011] UKSC 10, [174], [186] (Lord Brown), [113] (Lord Rodger).
[110] [2015] UKSC 33, [1] (Lords Hodge, Clarke and Carnwath agreeing).
[111] [2013] UKSC 9, [2013] 2 WLR 649, [41].

Fairchild exceptional theorem 'applies only where [C] has contracted mesothelioma, has been exposed to asbestos from more than one source, and it cannot be shown which source was responsible for the disease ... in *Sienkiewicz*, the Supreme Court made it clear that this is a special rule, created only because of the special difficulty of proving causation in mesothelioma cases'. Furthermore, in *Jones v Sec of State for Energy and Climate Change*,[112] Swift J considered the effect of *Sienkiewicz*, and stated that, '[i]t does not appear that there is any appetite in the appellate courts for extending the *Fairchild* exception to cases involving diseases other than mesothelioma'.

However, in *Zurich*, Lord Hodge (also writing for the majority in a separate judgment) remarked that the *Fairchild* exception 'is not confined to mesothelioma', and that 'the boundaries of the *Fairchild* enclave ... are not coterminous with liability for mesothelioma, and that the precise boundaries of the *Fairchild* principle, like those of *McGhee*, may have to be worked out in other cases'.[113] Furthermore, there was nothing in *Fairchild* itself that indicated that it should be solely restricted to its own facts. *McGhee* did not involve mesothelioma, but dermatitis – and the House of Lords expressly based *Fairchild* on *McGhee's* reasoning. Indeed, Lord Bingham contemplated that the *Fairchild* principle would become 'the subject of incremental and analogical development', whilst Lord Hoffmann noted that, whilst the actual rule in *Fairchild* should be limited to cases where an employee was wrongfully exposed to asbestos, '[t]hat does not mean that the principle is not capable of development and application in new situations'.[114] Furthermore, the abovementioned suggestions, in and since *Sienkiewicz*, that the scope of the *McGhee/Fairchild* exception should be restricted to asbestos/mesothelioma, in the case of multiple Ds against none of whom can 'but-for' causation be established, were dicta only, as those cases were not directly concerned with, say, medical or pharmaceutical contexts.

Certainly, at *quantification-of-damages* stage, the apportionment of damages among various defendants, stipulated in s 3 of the Compensation Act 2006, only applies to mesothelioma cases (discussed shortly). However, on the current state of authority, whether the *Fairchild* principle (in establishing a causal link *at liability stage*) is restricted only to cases of mesothelioma where multiple Ds are involved, remains unsatisfactorily unsettled.

The employer versus the insurer: what was the insured event?

§8.13   Notwithstanding a line of authority which states that the *Fairchild* exception renders employer D liable for contributing to *the risk of the employee contracting mesothelioma* by wrongfully exposing that employee to asbestos, more recent authority has endorsed the view that the employer contributed to *the disease suffered by the employee*, thus enabling the employer to 'lay off' its liability for damages to a third party insurer.

It is perhaps of limited comfort, when examining this difficult legal area, to realise that Roman jurists apparently had the same difficulty in the first century BC, when deciding who was responsible in law for the death of a slave, where a number of people struck the slave, but it was impossible to say who struck the fatal blow.[115] Centuries later, and in the interval between *McGhee* (1973) and *Fairchild* (2003), there was much judicial debate, at the highest appellate

---

[112] [2012] EWHC 2936 (QB) [543].

[113] [2015] UKSC 33, quotes at [98] and [109], respectively, and also [127] (Lord Sumption).

[114] [2003] AC 32 (HL), with quotes at [34] and [74] respectively.

[115] Noted by Lord Rodger in *Fairchild, ibid*, [158]–[160] – the remedy accruing to the owner of that slave.

level in England, as to precisely what damage D was liable for. That debate continues to this day – and assumed particular importance in 2012, in a dispute between insured employers and their insurers.

McGhee was interpreted by the House of Lords in *Wilsher v Essex AHA* (1987) to mean that the 'guilty' brick dust contributed to Mr McGhee's actual *injury*, the dermatitis. In *Wilsher*,[116] Lord Bridge stated that '*McGhee* laid down no new principle of law whatever'. Rather, the inference could be drawn, in *McGhee*, that 'the consecutive periods when the brick dust remained on the body probably *contributed cumulatively to the causation of the dermatitis*'. However, that was definitely **not** what *McGhee* stood for. The medical evidence was that C's dermatitis may well have occurred, even if only the brick dust from the brick kiln had been on C's skin and had been immediately showered off after work ended for the day. D's failure to provide the showers (i.e., the breach) merely increased the risk of C's contracting dermatitis, it did not contribute to C's actual injury (at least, the evidence could not establish that).

Three decades later, in *Fairchild*, the House of Lords admitted that a new principle of causation – a 'material contribution to *the risk* of injury' – is precisely what *McGhee* **did** create, and that Lord Bridge's interpretation of *McGhee* was incorrect.[117] The result of this exceptional theorem was that D may be liable to pay damages to C for an injury for which D was entirely fault-free, in the sense that it was possible that Mr McGhee's dermatitis was caused solely by particles of 'innocent brickdust'. D was liable in negligence merely for materially increasing the risk of harm to C – and that was an entirely new method of proving the causal link, despite Lord Bridge's assertion to the contrary. Lord Hoffmann summarised the principle of what D was liable for, in the *McGhee/Fairchild* scenario, in this way: 'a breach of duty which materially increased the risk should be treated *as if* it had materially contributed to the disease ... the House [in *McGhee*] treated a material increase in risk as sufficient in the circumstances to satisfy the causal requirements for liability. That this was the effect of the decision seems to me inescapable'.[118] Lord Nicholls described it as a 'less stringent causal connection'.[119] In *Barker v Corus*,[120] Lord Hoffmann (who gave the leading speech) again reiterated the view that '[t]he purpose of the *Fairchild* exception is to provide a cause of action against D who has *materially increased the risk that C will suffer damage* and may have caused that damage, but cannot be proved to have done so because it is impossible to show, on a balance of probability, that some other exposure to the same risk may not have caused it instead'.

These two contrasting schools of thought – that D contributed to the risk of C's injury, versus that D contributed to C's actual injury – came to the fore in *Durham v BAI (Run-Off) Ltd (the Trigger Litigation)*.[121] This litigation essentially concerned a dispute between those employers rendered liable under the *Fairchild* exception for their employees' mesothelioma, and the employers' third party insurers. It was crucial to the case – because of the contractual wording of the insurance policies – that each insured employer's conduct contributed to employee C's actual disease, and that it did not merely contribute to the risk of C's suffering the disease. That is because the insurance policies were triggered, only where each employer's conduct

---

[116] [1988] AC 1074 (HL) 1087, quote at 1090 (Lord Bridge, with whom the rest of the court agreed).

[117] [2003] 1 AC 32 (HL) [22], [34] (Lord Bingham), [44]–[45] (Lord Nicholls), [70] (Lord Hoffmann), [150] (Lord Rodger).

[118] *ibid*, [65] (original emphasis). Only Lord Hutton preferred the view that materially increasing the risk of the onset of mesothelioma 'involved a substantial contribution to the disease suffered by [Mr Fairchild]': [109], [116].

[119] *ibid*, [44]. [120] [2006] UKHL 20, [17] (emphasis added). [121] [2012] UKSC 14, [2012] 1 WLR 867.

contributed to C's suffering '*personal injury by accident or disease*', or '*bodily injury or disease*' arising from that employment. Merely contributing to *the risk of C's suffering disease* was not an insured event for which the insurer had agreed to provide cover to the employers under the various policies.[122]

Ultimately, the Supreme Court divided on the issue. The majority (for whom Lord Mance delivered the leading judgment[123]) held that the insurance policies **were** triggered, because each employer's conduct had, on a 'weak or broad causal link', caused C's mesothelioma where it was proved that the employer had in fact exposed C to asbestos dust. As Lord Mance subsequently explained his view, the *Fairchild* exception meant that 'the ordinary requirements of causation (proof on a balance of probability) were modified as between the [employee C] and the responsible [employer D], so as to make the latter liable for the mesothelioma because of the risk of sustaining mesothelioma to which the victim had been exposed during the relevant period' – and that the same sort of 'weak' or 'broad' meaning of causation should be carried through to the insurance policies which covered the insured employer (per *Zurich Ins plc UK Branch v Intl Energy Group Ltd*[124]). This viewpoint may have rendered the insurers liable under the policies, but it also tended to veer the law back to the views of Lord Wilberforce in *McGhee* and Lord Bridge in *Wilsher*, that the dust contributed to C's actual injury – which view was so roundly rejected by the majority in *Fairchild* itself. Lord Hoffmann considered it 'inescapable' in *Fairchild* that it was the 'creating of a material risk of contracting mesothelioma' for which D was liable to C, and nothing more than that (as nothing more than that could be proven, scientifically – D's particular dust may not have caused, or contributed to, C's disease at all). In any event, the majority's decision in the *Trigger Litigation* meant that the necessary causal requirement was met, in the case of mesothelioma, where the employer negligently exposed C to asbestos during the insurance period, so that the insurer had to indemnify the employer against that insured liability.

Lord Phillips vehemently dissented in the *Trigger Litigation*,[125] holding that an employer's liability under the *McGhee/Fairchild* exceptional theorem did **not** mean that D had, in any sense, caused C's mesothelioma, but only meant that D had created the risk of causing the disease. On that basis, the insurance policies were not available to cover the employers' liability, because the trigger point – D's causation of a disease – had not been met. In other words, merely contributing to the risk of their employees contracting mesothelioma was not an insured event. Lord Phillips' reasoning of what, precisely, D was liable for under the exceptional theorem adheres closely to the views of the majority in *Fairchild*. Clearly, Lord Phillips regarded the majority's view in the *Trigger Litigation* as entirely policy-driven, to enable the employers to lay off their liability to their third party insurers, and not in accordance with strict precedent.

As the *Trigger Litigation* aptly demonstrates, these are not merely semantic matters of terminology. Millions of pounds of insurance exposure turns upon their outcome. This author considers that the views of Lord Phillips in the *Trigger Litigation* and of Lord Hoffmann in *Fairchild* are far preferable to the strained interpretation that Lord Bridge adopted in *Wilsher*, and which the majority preferred in the *Trigger Litigation*. Even given the developing scientific knowledge of how mesothelioma is caused, the fact presently remains that any D rendered liable under the *McGhee/Fairchild* exception may be paying damages for C's harm to which his particular asbestos dust contributed nothing. All that can be established is that D's wrongful conduct exposed his employee C to *a risk* of contracting mesothelioma. For now, that is as

---

[122] The various wordings were slightly different, set out in *ibid*, [7]–[9], but the nub of the issue remained the same.
[123] See, especially, *ibid*, [59], [71]–[74].   [124] [2015] UKSC 33, [21].   [125] [2012] UKSC 14, [131]–[134].

much as the scientific evidence will permit. While the *Trigger Litigation* may ultimately have been a policy decision to ensure that employers subjected to a weaker causal theorem were able to recoup their liability from their insurers, the majority decision obscures the doctrinal basis which underpins this exceptional theorem of causation.

Defective products

§8.14 Whether the *Fairchild* exception applies to render a producer liable for contributing to the risk of a consumer suffering harm from a defective product remains somewhat unsettled in English law. On a differential scenario, however, the 'market share' theorem of liability has not been imported into English law to date.

The actions available to C where he is injured by a defective product – *viz*, in negligence, and under the Consumer Protection Act 1987 – are discussed in 'Defective products', an online chapter, where causation is covered in some detail. As noted previously, given that, in *Sienkiewicz*, some members of the House of Lords seemed to suggest that the 'material contribution to risk' exceptional theorem should be restricted to mesothelioma claims when multiple Ds are in play, the *Fairchild* principle may not be transposed to defective product claims more generally – although (so far as the author's searches can ascertain) a determinative case is yet to arise on that point.

The issue is potentially significant, however, where: C consumes a drug over a time period; that drug is manufactured by multiple producers D; C consumes the drug from each manufacturer; one or more capsules of the drug were contaminated; C suffers damage from that consumption; but it is impossible to ascertain which manufacturer made the defective capsule which C consumed. This is a 'material contribution to risk' scenario, to which the *Fairchild* theorem could potentially apply.

Twisting that scenario somewhat: suppose that a drug is defective in that each and every capsule of it does not meet the public's legitimate expectations as to safety; the drug is manufactured by numerous producers who supply the entire market with the drug under a generic name; it is not possible to ascertain which particular manufacturer produced the drug capsules which were consumed at any given time by C; but each capsule was harmful to C. As Lord Hoffmann pointed out in *Fairchild*,[126] that is not a 'material contribution to risk' scenario of the type which arose in *Fairchild*. At any given employer's premises, there could have been many innocent asbestos fibres which did not trigger mesothelioma for Mr Fairchild; his exposure to those asbestos fibres at the hands of many employers merely increased the risk of his injury, i.e., contracting mesothelioma. However, there are no innocent capsules of this defective drug; so consuming those capsules at the hands of many manufacturers does not increase the risk of C's consuming a tainted capsule.

In the abovementioned scenario, the Californian Supreme Court developed a 'market share' theorem of liability in *Sindell v Abbott Laboratories*,[127] which concerned the anti-miscarriage drug diethylstilbestrol, or DES. The theory applies in the case of a interchangeable substance such as a generic drug, where the specific manufacturer of the substance used by each consumer is unknown, but the product manufactured by different manufacturers is the same. According to the theory, each manufacturer is liable only to the extent of its own market-share. However, no case to date has imported the 'market share' doctrine into English law.

---

[126] [2002] UKHL 22, [2003] AC 32, [74].   [127] 607 P 2d 924 (SC Cal, 1980).

Apportionment of damages

The common law reversed

The principles governing apportionment as between Ds under the *Fairchild* principle are considered in detail in 'Multiple defendants' (an online chapter). The section below provides a brief summary for present purposes.

In *Fairchild*, the House of Lords did not need to answer the question as to whether the liability of C's various employers, D1, D2, D3, etc, whose tortious conduct each materially increased the risk of mesothelioma to C during his various employments with them, was joint and several; or whether each of D1, D2, D3, etc, was severally liable only for the proportionate contribution which his asbestos had made to C's risk of developing the disease.

In 2006 in *Barker v Corus UK Ltd*,[128] a majority of the House of Lords favoured the proportionate (or 'aliquot') liability solution, i.e., that the liability of each of D1, D2, D3, etc, should be attributed according to each D's relative degree of contribution to the risk, measured by reference to factors such as the duration and intensity of C's asbestos exposure during his employment with each D. Under this solution, no one D would be liable for the whole of C's damage; each would have its exposure to damages capped by the proportion which it bore for the overall damage C suffered. Indeed, this common law solution still receives support to this day. In *Zurich Ins plc v Intl Energy Group*,[129] Lord Mance (for the majority) considered that it was both 'coherent and understandable' as to why joint and several liability was not adopted in *Barker*, as a *quid pro quo* for the weaker causal theorem which D had to endure, courtesy of *Fairchild's* theorem. Indeed, in *Zurich*, it was held (unanimously) that *Barker v Corus* remains part of the common law of England and Wales.[130]

However, the effect of *Barker v Corus* was subsequently (indeed, almost immediately) reversed by s 3 of the Compensation Act 2006, but **only** in respect of mesothelioma cases. Hence, where the *Fairchild* exception applies, D1, D2, D3, etc's liability is joint and several. That has the (beneficial-to-C) effect of enabling C to recover full compensation from **any** of D1, D2, D3, etc, who is found liable under the *Fairchild* exception and who is solvent, as each of them is severally liable.

Further, for the *Sienkiewicz*-type scenario too, where there is environmental exposure to asbestos swirling in the factual matrix, and where C ultimately suffers mesothelioma, the Supreme Court confirmed in that case that s 3 of the Compensation Act applies – just as it does in the *Barker v Corus* scenario – as to render employer D fully liable for any damages, on a joint and several basis.

No insured employer

Where employee C, who has suffered from mesothelioma from wrongful workplace asbestos, is unable to trace any solvent employer with an attached viable insurer, that would leave C without any practical hope of obtaining damages, even where the *McGhee/Fairchild* exception theoretically applied.

Parliament saw fit to remedy this gap in redress, by enacting the Mesothelioma Act 2014.[131] Under that Act, an insurance fund was created (via the contribution of insurers), by which any

---

[128] [2006] UKHL 20, [2006] 2 AC 572.   [129] [2015] UKSC 33, [27].

[130] *ibid*, [28], [31], The point was important, because the law of Guernsey governed the contracts of insurance in the case; Guernsey had not enacted the equivalent of s 3 of the Compensation Act 2006; and the common law of Guernsey was identical to English common law on this point.

[131] Received Royal Assent on 30 Jan 2014.

eligible employee will recover damages according to a schedule, based in part upon C's age. It is estimated that approximately 300 eligible employees will claim per year (which will reduce year upon year), and that the average compensation package will be about £123,000 (plus £7,000 towards legal expenses[132]).

An insurer for only 'part of the period'

Where an employer has exposed an employee to asbestos, and insurer D has covered the insured employer for only **some** of the period for which that employer had negligently exposed C, the question arises as to whether insurer D is liable for the employee's full loss or for only a proportionate part of it. That was the issue in *Zurich Ins plc v Intl Energy Group Ltd.*[133]

Where the 2006 Act does **not** apply, then under *Barker v Corus*, the employer is only liable proportionately for the extent of exposure for which that employer was responsible. It follows consistently, therefore, that the insurer's obligation to indemnify that insured employer should be limited to proportionate liability too.

> In *Zurich Insurance*, IEG, formerly Guernsey Gas, the employer, employed Mr Carre, C, for 27 years, from 1961–88, exposing him to asbestos wrongfully throughout that period. Mr Carre died of mesothelioma. During those years of exposure, IEG had insurance cover for only 6 years with Zurich Insurance (1982–88). **Held:** Zurich Insurance should only cover employer IEG for 6/27ths of the period of C's exposure to asbestos (22% of that period), and hence, was only liable to insure IEG for 22% of the damages to which C was entitled (22% of £278,500), consistent with the proportionate liability established by the common law in *Barker v Corus*. Guernsey law, which governed this dispute, had not enacted any equivalent to s 3 of the Compensation Act 2006.

However, in jurisdictions where the 2006 Act **does** apply (as in England), then the employer is jointly and severally liable for the entirety of C's damage (overturning the proportionate liability favoured in *Barker v Corus*). Further, under the *Trigger Litigation*, the outcome for insurers was that employee C's mesothelioma was caused 'in, a broad sense, in each and every period of any overall period of exposure', rendering the insurer fully liable under the employer's insurance policy. Consistent with this view of transporting a 'weak' or 'broad' concept of causation into the insurance context between employer and insurer, a majority of the Supreme Court in *Zurich Insurance* held that an insurer which provided insurance for a limited period of C's total exposure will be exposed to the **whole** of the C's damages claim, if employer D wrongfully exposed employee C to asbestos during that period of insurance. This rather onerous view, however, is subject to an important caveat.

The *quid pro quo* was that the insurer should be able to seek contribution from any successive co-insurers, or from the employer itself, in respect of any periods of exposure to which the employer exposed C, and for which the insurer had not covered that insured employer, under the Civil Liability (Contribution) Act 1978. In that regard, the

---

[132] See Dept of Work and Pensions, *News Article* (dated 6 Mar 2014), available at: <https://www.gov.uk/government/news/asbestos-victims-to-get-123000-in-compensation>.

[133] [2015] UKSC 33, [51]–[52], [54] (Lord Mance, for the majority), and [104] (Lord Hodge, also for the majority). Lords Sumption, Reed and Neuberger dissented.

Supreme Court sought to relieve the heavy burden which would otherwise be placed upon an insurer (via a combination of the 2006 Act and the *Trigger Litigation*), by creating a new equitable right of recoupment for insurers in *Fairchild*-type cases. Hence, an insurer who insured an employer for only part of the exposure period to asbestos giving rise to employee C's mesothelioma should indemnify the employer in full – but with a right to recover contributions on a pro rata basis from successive insurers of the employer and from the employer itself. Lord Mance (for the majority) acknowledged that this was a policy-driven response to the weaker causal theorem created by *Fairchild*, in yet another conundrum thrown up by asbestos litigation: 'by introducing into tort and liability insurance law an entirely novel form of causation in *Trigger*, the courts have made it incumbent on themselves to reach a solution representing a fair balance of the interests of victims, insureds and insurers.'[134] Lord Hodge (also for the majority) approved of this solution too, being one that 'the London insurance market is prepared to live with' – and it also permitted an employee to recover his damages from one employer/one insurer, 'in a straightforward way' (rather than having to pursue several parties to obtain the totality of his damages), thereby leaving any dispute over contribution to be dealt with between employers and their insurers.[135]

The preceding discussion under this section, 'Exception #1', starkly demonstrates the evolving, complex and divisive landscape to which the *McGhee/Fairchild* exception has given rise. Piecemeal judicial responses to each new problem associated with asbestos exposure has fragmented the law to the point where consistency and certainty of reasoning seem to be something of a mirage. However, any further legislative clarification or codification in the area appears very unlikely.

The 'doubling the risk' theorem

§8.15   According to the 'doubling the risk' causal theorem, where:

i. D's breach exposed C to a harmful agent;
ii. C was also exposed to that same agent, or to some other agent, for innocent reasons (i.e., for reasons other than D's breach) (the innocent agent);
iii. D's breach preceded C's suffering the precise harm which the harmful agent causes; and
iv. the risk of injury created by D's breach was more than double the risk of injury which C faced from the innocent agent, then D's breach caused C's harm. The test has only been applied intermittently. However, where C suffers from mesothelioma because D wrongfully exposed C to asbestos in the workplace, the 'doubling the risk' test does not apply.

The 'doubling the risk' theorem is another means of proving a 'material contribution to risk', where C cannot prove that D's breach caused C's harm, on the balance of probabilities. Under the theorem, C must seek to prove that the risk of injury from innocent exposure to a harmful agent was Y%, and that the risk of that same injury from D's breach was 2.1 x Y% – in that event, then D's breach materially contributed to the risk of C's injury. The theorem has been applied from time to time in a variety of contexts, as the following sample of cases shows:

---

[134] *ibid*, [51].   [135] *ibid*, [105]–[106].

Emergence of the 'doubling the risk' theorem

Year of case	C's harm	The facts
2002	DVT	In *XYZ v Schering Healthcare Ltd (the Oral Contraceptive litigation),*[a] the case concerned the risk of developing deep vein thrombosis from two different types of oral contraceptive. The parties, and Mackay J, agreed that C could succeed only if the epidemiology showed that the risk of harm arising from contraceptive A (for which no warning had been given) was at least twice that arising from contraceptive B (for which appropriate warning had been given).
2007	Bladder cancer	In *Novartis Grimsby Ltd v Cookson,*[b] C suffered bladder cancer. He had been tortiously exposed to carcinogens during his employment at a dye works, and non-tortiously exposed to cigarette smoke as a regular smoker. Both were potent causes of bladder cancer. If the risk of bladder cancer from carcinogenic exposure was more than double the risk of bladder cancer from smoking, C could succeed. This was proven, and hence, C succeeded.
2007	Mesothelioma	In *Jones v Metal Box Ltd,*[c] C was held to be entitled to succeed, if he could show that the risk of mesothelioma arising from asbestos exposure at work had more than doubled the risk arising from environmental asbestos exposure. The judge found that the risk had been more than doubled, and C succeeded.
2008	Lung cancer	In *Shortell v BICAL Construction Ltd,*[d] C died of lung cancer. He had been exposed to asbestos by his employer, D, and had no other asbestos exposure, but had been a fairly heavy smoker. Both asbestos and cigarette smoking are common causes of lung cancer. D conceded that if C could prove that the risk of contracting lung cancer from asbestos exposure at work had more than doubled C's risk of contracting lung cancer from smoking, C would succeed. This was proven.

[a] [2002] EWHC 1420 (QB).
[b] [2007] EWCA Civ 1261.
[c] Cardiff CC, 11 Jan 2007 (HHJ Hickinbottom).
[d] QB, 16 May 2008 (Liverpool District Registry).

The 'doubling the risk' theorem has the **disadvantage** to C that it is potentially more onerous than the *McGhee/Fairchild* test, because an exposure which materially increased the risk under the *Fairchild* exception (in a sense that it made a greater than *de minimis* contribution to C's harm) may not, in fact, have doubled the risk of disease caused by the innocent exposure. Also, the theorem can only be applied where there is a sufficiently-good quality of epidemiological evidence to support the assessment of relative risks. However, the **benefit** to C of the 'doubling the risk' test is that it can equally apply to multi-agent scenarios (where cause A is one agent, and cause B is a different agent) as to single agent cases, thereby avoiding the *Wilsher* problem of multi-agent causes.

Whether the 'doubling the risk' theorem could be correctly applied was very much at issue in *Sienkiewicz v Greif (UK) Ltd*. C argued that the theorem did not follow the *Fairchild*
line of authority, whereas D relied upon the theorem and submitted that it was not met. At
first instance[136] (affirmed by the Court of Appeal), Judge Main accepted the application of
the 'doubling the risk' theorem to C's mesothelioma case. However, C failed, because the risk
of mesothelioma from D's exposing her to asbestos in the factory did not double the risk of
contracting mesothelioma from environmental exposure which she already faced because she
lived in Port Ellesmere:

In *Sienkiewicz v Greif (UK) Ltd*, facts previously, the figures were:

- the environmental exposure created a risk of mesothelioma of 24 cases per million;
- the occupational exposure created a risk of an extra 4.39 cases per million;
- thus, the occupational exposure was modest, and increased the already-existing risk of mesothelioma due to the environmental exposure by only 18%;
- hence, C had not shown that the (negligent) occupational risk had more than doubled the risk
  from (innocent) environmental exposure.

However, ultimately, the Supreme Court rejected the 'doubling the risk' theorem as a means of
establishing a causal link in cases where C contracted mesothelioma after being wrongfully exposed to asbestos in the workplace.[137] According to Lord Phillips, special features about mesothelioma, the gaps in knowledge about the disease, the potential unreliability of the epidemiological data and the importance of C's own characteristics and behaviour, all combined to make
it inappropriate to decide causation on epidemiological data. Essentially, a test of 'doubling the
risk' was a 'tenuous basis' for deciding that 'the statistically probable cause of a disease is also
the probable biological cause'. In such cases, C could rely on the ordinary 'material contribution
to risk' test in *McGhee/Fairchild*. The Supreme Court did not rule out the 'doubling the risk' test
as being potentially applicable in other contexts though (e.g., for medically-caused injuries) –
although Lady Hale considered that there were considerable problems in adopting the test in
any context. Notwithstanding, anything said about using the 'doubling the risk' test, in **any**
context other than mesothelioma, was only dicta in *Sienkiewicz*.

As a result of *Sienkiewicz*, the current position is that the 'doubling the risk' test survives as a
causal theorem which is exceptional to the 'but-for' test, but that it is inappropriate for mesothelioma cases. As Swift J noted in *Jones v Sec of State for Energy and Climate Change*,[138] '[i]t is plain
that the majority in *Sienkiewicz* considered that the test can be used in appropriate circumstances,
although there was obvious concern about over-reliance on epidemiological evidence alone'.

> In *Jones v Sec of State for Energy and Climate Change*, three lead Cs suffered from lung cancer, hav-
> ing been exposed to carcinogens, from dust and fumes, at the Phurnacite Plant. Each C was also a
> regular smoker, and exposed to carcinogens from that source, plus the scientific evidence was that
> each C would have been subject to environmental exposure to carcinogens too (albeit usually at a
> low level). 'All these factors are likely to have played some part in the carcinogenic processes going
> on in [Cs'] bodies, processes which are, by their nature, wholly random.' **Held:** causation failed. The
> 'doubling of risk' theorem was appropriate to consider here, but no C could satisfy it.

---

[136] Liverpool CC, HHJ Main, 15 Dec 2008.

[137] [2011] UKSC 10, [83] (Lord Phillips), [160]–[161] (Lord Rodger), [169]–[170] (Lady Hale), [189]–[191] (Lord
Mance).

[138] [2012] EWHC 2936 (QB) [8.62].

The 'hunting cases'

§8.16   Where there is an evenly-split probability that each D caused C's harm, but it cannot be proven which D was culpable, the 'but-for' test cannot be met (as no cause will be >50%). However, an exception to the 'but-for' test is permitted in order to establish a causal link.

The 'but-for' test does not handle a *Cook v Lewis*-type scenario, one of the so-called 'hunting cases' emanating from Canada, where there was precisely a 50% probability that each one of two hunters caused C's harm – but which hunter caused C's harm could not be proven.

> In *Cook v Lewis*,[139] Mr Cook, D1, and Mr Akenhead, D2, hunting for blue grouse during the hunting season, fired almost simultaneously at a covey of grouse in a clump of trees, where Mr Lewis, C, was crouched. C received several shots in the face, and lost his eye. C sued D1 and D2, but could not prove from which gun the offending shot which damaged his eye was fired. If C had asked, 'would my lost eye have happened, but for D1's breach?', the answer would be, 'yes, it may have happened anyway, due to the negligence of my co-hunter, D2'. **Held:** both D1 and D2 could be liable (a new trial was ordered).

In *Fairchild v Glenhaven Funeral Services Ltd*,[140] Lord Nicholls expressly approved of *Cook v Lewis* as a valid exception to the 'but-for' test, because the scenario involved an 'evidential difficulty ... [which] justifies a relaxation in the standard of causation required. Insistence on the normal standard of causation would work an injustice'. If D1 and D2 did not share culpability in this type of case, then the 'unattractive consequence' would be that C would go uncompensated, even though one of the two hunters negligently injured him. Indeed, in *Dickie v Flexcon Glenrothes Ltd*, the court remarked that it would be 'repugnant to any legal system that both hunters should escape liability',[141] while in *Fairchild*, Lord Nicholls called the outcome in *Cook v Lewis* a 'value judgment'.[142] Indeed, the analogy with *Fairchild* is close. One (or more) of the shots from the hunters' guns caused C to lose his eye, just as one (or more) of the asbestos fibres at the employers' premises caused C's mesothelioma. The asbestos fibre is akin to the bullet – it is impossible to say which employer/gun it came from, but each D created the risk that his fibre/bullet was the 'guilty' agent of C's injury. Hence, the hunting cases and the scenario in *Fairchild* both represent acknowledged exceptions to 'but-for' causation.

EXCEPTION #2: THE 'MATERIAL CONTRIBUTION TO DAMAGE' EXCEPTION

The *Bonnington* principle

§8.17   According to the *Bonnington* principle, C can prove causation if D's breach materially contributed to C's actual harm, in circumstances where D's breach exposed C to a harmful agent, and where C was also exposed to that agent innocently – but where the tortious exposure had a cumulative effect upon the severity of the injury which C suffered. Under this principle, D is liable where his breach exposed C to an agent which increased *the severity of C's injury* (whereas the *McGhee/Fairchild* principle applies where D's breach exposed C to an agent which only increased *the risk of injury* to C).

---

[139] [1952] 1DLR 1 (SCC, Locke J dissenting). See too: *Summers v Tice*, 199 P 2d 1 (1948).
[140] [2002] UKHL 22, [39]–[40].   [141] [2009] ScotSC 143 (Kirkcaldy, Sheriff Peter J Braid) [136].
[142] [2002] UKHL 22, [40].

The *Bonnington* principle provides a further exception to the classic 'but-for' test, because C cannot prove that D's wrongful act in exposing C to a harmful agent caused C's injury on the balance of probabilities – and, yet, D can be rendered liable in negligence. *Bonnington* applies where (unlike under the *McGhee/Fairchild* principle) the harmful agent did undoubtedly contribute to C's *damage* (and not just to the *risk* of that damage). Yet, C may have suffered an equal degree of damage from the innocent exposure to the harmful agent, without D's wrongful exposure – medical evidence cannot say. Therein lies the causal conundrum which *Bonnington* addresses.

Bonnington itself arose out of occupational exposure to harmful agents in the workplace. However, it has notably been applied in medical cases too.

> In *Bonnington Castings Ltd v Wardlaw*,[143] Mr Wardlaw, C, developed pneumoconiosis as a result of inhaling silica dust whilst working at his employer's, D's, factory. C worked in the 'dressing shop', where minute particles of sand swirled around constantly in the atmosphere when C was operating the pneumatic hammers. This was 'innocent silica dust', because there was no means of collecting and neutralising it. However, a considerable amount of silica dust also emanated from the swing grinders, which was 'negligent dust', because D allowed the dust extraction plant for those grinders to become clogged and ineffective, which was a breach of statutory duty. The exposure to the 'negligent silica dust' had materially aggravated (to an unknown degree) C's pneumoconiosis, but C might have developed that disease in any event, from his exposure to the 'innocent silica dust' from the pneumatic hammers. It was impossible to say. **Held:** causation proven. D's breach made a material contribution to C's disease. In *Bailey v MOD*,[144] C was operated on for a gallstone problem, which was competently performed, but there was a negligent lack of aftercare by D, which weakened her condition. C then developed acute pancreatitis, a naturally-occurring illness, which was not a consequence of D's negligence, but which weakened her still further. A few days after her operation, and without knowing how great a contribution each (negligent aftercare and pancreatitis) had made to C's overall weakness, save that each was material, C was too weak to protect her airway when she vomited, leading her to choke on her vomit. This resulted in cardiac arrest which, in turn, led to hypoxic brain damage. **Held:** causation proven. D's breach, the post-operative care, made a material contribution to the injury, per the *Bonnington* principle.

The fact that a *Bonnington* scenario is an exception to the 'but-for' test was explicitly acknowledged by the Court of Appeal in *Bailey v MOD*. In any case of 'cumulative causes', the 'but-for' test has to be modified. Waller LJ explained the point this way: '[i]f the evidence demonstrates, on a balance of probabilities, that the injury would have occurred as a result of the non-tortious cause in any event, [C] will have failed to establish that the tortious cause contributed ... [but] in a case where medical science cannot establish the probability, but can establish that the contribution of the negligent cause was more than negligible, the 'but for' test is modified, and [C] will succeed'.

A comparison with the *McGhee/Fairchild* principle

In several respects, for the *Bonnington* principle to apply, the same conditions must be met as were required for the *McGhee/Fairchild* exception – but with one key difference. Referring to those pre-requisites, whether overlapping or different:

---

[143] [1956] AC 613 (HL).   [144] [2008] EWCA Civ 883, [2009] 1 WLR 1052, [46].

i. **Same agent.** As an overlapping condition, the *Bonnington* principle applies where C has been exposed to one agent, both tortiously and innocently.

> In *Bonnington* itself, the sole agent was silica dust to which C was exposed (negligently from the swing grinders, and innocently from the pneumatic hammers), whereas in *Bailey*, it was C's generally weakened state (negligently from D's lack of medical care, and innocently from pancreatitis) which contributed to C's injury.

ii. **Proof of breach.** As an overlapping condition, a wrongful exposure to the harmful agent must be proven against, or conceded by, D.

iii. **A *de minimis* contribution.** As an overlapping condition, a material contribution to C's injury from D's breach is any contribution greater than *de minimis*, but smaller than balance of probabilities (51%).

However, the big difference between the principles is that, in *Bonnington*, it was medically possible to prove that the inhalation of the 'negligent silica dust' actually contributed to C's injury. D's breach in wrongfully exposing C to silica dust did not increase *the risk of harm*; it increased *the actual harm* to C. Neither the innocent nor the guilty agent got over the balance of probabilities threshold, and it was impossible to say how great a contribution each actually made to C's injury. By removing the negligent exposure to the harmful agent which D brought about, C **may** have suffered the harm anyway.

By contrast, in *McGhee*, it was not possible to say whether or not the lack of a shower had in fact contributed to C's dermatitis; it had only increased the risk of contracting that dermatitis; and in *Fairchild*, it was not possible to say at which employer's premises the employee had inhaled the relevant asbestos fibre which led to the fatal mesothelioma condition, but all of the employers had exposed that employee to the risk of contracting mesothelioma. Hence, in *McGhee/Fairchild* scenarios, D's breach exposed C to the **risk** of injury only, and the duration of D's exposing C to the harmful agent did not increase the severity of C's injury in any way (because one single exposure was sufficient). All that the duration of exposure dictated was that the risk of C's suffering the injury increased correspondingly. That is the major difference between the principles.

> In *AB v MOD (the Atomic Veterans case)*,[145] 10 former servicemen, Cs, alleged that they had suffered various types of cancer from exposure by D to ionising radiation during thermonuclear tests in the Pacific Ocean region in the 1950s. The case turned on limitation periods, but causation was also relevant. There were many potential causes of Cs' cancers, other than ionising radiation. 'But-for' causation could not be proven, because even if Cs' exposure to the ionising radiation had not occurred, their cancers may have developed in any event. However, Cs argued that expert evidence showed that their exposure to radiation had materially increased their risk of developing cancers. **Held:** causation failed per the *McGhee/Fairchild* exception, because it could not be said that there was *one agent* in play that was responsible for Cs' cancers. Ionising radiation was one possible agent; but two Cs had smoked 20 cigarettes a day for >20 years, introducing the multi-agent *Wilsher* problem. There were 'multiple potential causes [of Cs' cancers], some of which had not even been identified'. The *Bonnington* principle could not apply either. The exposure to ionising radiation did not increase the actual harm to C, but only increased the risk of harm. Cs could not prove that their exposure to radiation had made a material contribution to their cancers. The case fell outside the *Bonnington* principle for that reason.

---

[145] [2012] UKSC 9, [2013] 1 AC 78.

Damages under the *Bonnington* principle

§8.18 Under the *Bonnington* principle, D is liable to compensate C for the proportion of C's divisible injury which is attributable to D's breach.

Typically, the *Bonnington* principle can only apply if the injury is divisible, i.e., where the injury which C suffers is termed, by law, a 'divisible injury', because it is 'dose-related' or 'time-related'. For divisible injuries, each dose of exposure contributes to the extent of injury that C suffers. The tortious component of the exposure (caused by D's breach) makes a material contribution to the disease (for further discussion of 'divisible' versus 'indivisible' injuries, see 'Multiple defendants', an online chapter).

> In *Bonnington* itself, pneumoconiosis was a divisible disease, in that the severity of the disease was entirely dependent upon the quantity of dust inhaled. In *Bailey* too, C's weakened condition was treated as a divisible injury. In both, causation succeeded. By contrast, in the *Atomic Veterans* case, Cs' cancers were an indivisible injury, and the *Bonnington* principle did not apply, hence causation failed. As Swift J put it in *Jones v Sec of State for Energy and Climate Change*, '[c]ancer is an indivisible condition; one either gets it or one does not. The condition is not worse because one has been exposed to a greater or smaller amount of the causative agent'.[146]

In *Bonnington* itself, no apportionment as between tortious and non-tortious exposure to the silica dust was assessed, and C was awarded damages against his employer D on a 100% basis. D had not argued otherwise. However, that particular aspect of *Bonnington* no longer applies.

In *Jones v Sec of State for Energy and Climate Change*,[147] Toulson LJ noted that, since *Bonnington* was decided, 'there have been a number of decisions involving divisible conditions (such as industrial deafness, vibration white finger, and types of lung disease) in which liability had been apportioned as between different defendants and/or as between tortious and non-tortious exposures to the causative agent'. Apportionment of damages, as between D's breach and the non-negligent causes that contributed to C's injury, is judicially mandated now. D will be liable in respect of the precise share of the disease for which he was responsible – albeit that, in *Sienkiewicz*, Lord Phillips remarked that the apportionment 'may necessarily be a rough and ready exercise'.[148]

Conclusion

Principally, C will seek to prove that, had D's breach been hypothetically fixed, C's damage probably would not have happened (per the classic 'but-for' test, per *Barnett v Chelsea and Kensington Hosp*[149]). If C cannot do so, these are his exceptional options:

- D's breach materially contributed to the risk of C's suffering harm, injury or disease, where that risk was created both tortiously, and innocently, via C's exposure to a sole harmful agent;
- C's risk of contracting injury or disease from D's breach, in exposing C to a harmful agent, at least doubled the risk of C's contracting that injury or disease from an innocent exposure to that same or another agent – although that causal principle is inappropriate where C suffers mesothelioma from asbestos exposure; or

---

[146] [2012] EWHC 2936 (QB) [554].   [147] [2012] EWHC 2936 (QB) [531].
[148] [2011] UKSC 10, [2011] 2 AC 229, [17].   [149] [1969] 1 QB 428.

- D's breach, in exposing C to a harmful agent, materially contributed to C's actual injury or disease – but where C's harm may have happened anyway, due to an innocent exposure to that same agent.

In each scenario, there has been a 'material contribution' by D to either C's risk of harm, or to C's actual harm. Causation is, exceptionally, proven – even though C cannot prove, on the balance of probabilities, that D caused his harm.

EXCEPTION #3: THE *BOLITHO* CAUSATION THEOREM

The causal theorem adopted by the House of Lords in *Bolitho v City and Hackney HA*[150] permits a causal link, where an omission by D does not meet the 'but-for' test.

The leading case and theorem explained

§8.19   Where D (1) commits a breach by omission; and (2) alleges that, even had he hypothetically fixed that breach by some positive act, C's damage would still have occurred (thus defeating the 'but-for' test), C may establish a causal link between D's original omission to act and C's ultimate damage (per the *Bolitho* causal theorem) by proving that *either:*

i. on the balance of probabilities, D would have done a further act, X, in order to prevent C's harm (although there was no legal duty on D to do X); *or*

ii. D would not have done the further act X to prevent C's harm, and it would have been negligent of D not to have done X (because the continuing proper discharge of D's duty towards C required that he do X).

The *Bolitho* causation theorem arose out of a medical negligence (failure-to-attend) case, but it has been applied or considered beyond that context – e.g., in cases of alleged legal negligence (*D Morgan plc v Mace & Jones (a firm)*[151]), and allegedly negligent pensions annuity advice (*Beary v Pall Mall Investments (a firm)*[152]).

It potentially arises where D's negligence is an omission. When the court asks, 'would C's harm have occurred, but for that omission?', the answer may well be: yes, C's harm would have occurred anyway, because hypothetically fixing that breach (by D's acting positively to fix it) would not have prevented C's damage. That is because D would not have done a further positive act, X, to prevent C's harm. If that version of hypothetical events is accepted by the court, then 'but-for' causation should fail (as C's harm would have happened anyway). However, an exception to the 'but-for' test has been judicially-crafted, per the principle above, so as to create a causal link between D's breach (the omission) and C's damage, and to render D liable, in these limited circumstances.

Limb #1: Under the first limb of the *Bolitho* causal theorem, the court does not make any finding of fact as to what D actually did after his omission – rather, the court must assess what D *would* have done in a hypothetical situation, had he fixed that omission. The credibility of D's evidence will be crucial under this limb. D undoubtedly will say that he would not hypothetically have done anything further, having fixed the original breach – and if the court believes that, then the first limb of *Bolitho* must fail (unless some TP might have intervened to prevent

---

[150] [1998] AC 232 (HL).   [151] [2010] EWHC 3375 (TCC).   [152] [2005] EWCA Civ 415, [31].

C's harm, which is sufficient to prove the causal link, as discussed below). To reiterate, D was under no legal duty to do that further act X, but it is a matter of credibility as to whether, having fixed the breach, he would have done so (as C will allege).

Given that the first limb of *Bolitho*'s test is in the realm of the hypothetical, as to what D would have done, had the omission been hypothetically fixed, then if D fails to give evidence in the trial, the court may draw inferences damaging to D, as to what D would have done. The Court of Appeal noted, in *Wisniewski v Central Manchester HA*,[153] that if D chooses not to turn up to the trial to attest what he would have done (D, in that case, had moved to Australia and refused to return to England for the trial, or to have his evidence taken in Australia by an appropriate official), 'it may be easier for [C] to set up an affirmative case on that issue, which is liable to be strengthened if, for no good reason, [D] is unwilling to submit himself to questioning before the judge as to what he would probably have done'. The *Bolitho* causal theorem succeeded in *Wisniewski*.

There is, however, an **alternative** method of proving the causal link, even if limb #1 fails.

Limb #2: Under *Bolitho*'s second limb, C must prove that D would not have done that further positive act X, and it would have been negligent for D not to have done that act X. In other words, D cannot escape liability by saying that C's damage would have occurred in any event, because he would have committed some other breach (breach #2) after the original omission (breach #1).

The second limb depends upon *Bolam* evidence, i.e., what a body of peer professional opinion would have regarded as reasonable conduct, upon redressing the breach-by-omission. In *Bolitho*, Lord Browne-Wilkinson noted that a *Bolam* assessment did **not** have any relevance to the first limb of the *Bolitho* test, but that it 'is central to the second [limb]'.[154] In no other aspect of causation is *Bolam* relevant, except under this second limb of *Bolitho's* causal theorem.

In *D Morgan plc v Mace & Jones (a firm)*,[155] Coulson J described the two *Bolitho* limbs as the 'would' and the 'should' limbs, respectively, and that they were entirely alternative routes for C to pursue. The 'should' limb was to counter any possibility that D could escape liability by saying that he would have failed to do something that a reasonably careful doctor would have done.

In *Bolitho v City and Hackney HA*,[156] Patrick Bolitho, C, 2, suffering from croup, was treated in hospital under the care of a pacdiatrician, D. D saw C in the morning looking a little better, and C ate a large lunch. However, after lunch, C's health (and especially his breathing) deteriorated. Two urgent calls were put through to the senior registrar and to D, but no doctor responded. C suffered cardiac arrest and brain damage, being without oxygen for 10 minutes until he was resuscitated. D gave evidence that, had she attended C when the crash call was put through, she would not have intubated C to clear his airways, because she had been satisfied at C's earlier presentation, so she would not have believed that C had blocked airways. So (submitted D), the outcome would have been the same for C, because if the breach (failing to attend after the crash call) was fixed, C's harm would have happened anyway, as she would not have done further act X (i.e., intubated). Applying the causal theorem, **held:** causation failed:

- limb #1: C argued that, having fixed the alleged omission and turned up to Patrick's bedside, D would have intubated Patrick – but D's evidence was that she would not have, and that was believed by the court. Hence, the first avenue by which to prove the causal theorem failed;

---

[153] [1998] PIQR P324 (CA) P343 (in some reported versions of this case, its name is *Wiszniewski*).
[154] [1998] AC 232 (HL) 240.   [155] [2010] EWHC 3375 (TCC) [392].   [156] [1998] AC 232 (HL).

- **limb #2:** C argued that, if D had not intubated Patrick, that further omission would amount to negligence – but a reasonable body of medical opinion considered that it was reasonable not to intubate C, given his earlier presentation that morning. Hence, the second avenue by which to prove causation also failed.

Although the theorem was developed in *Bolitho* itself, it did not obtain for C, in that case, any positive outcome in establishing causation. Ironically, though, later claimants – especially in the medical context – have had better success in using the theorem to establish causation in cases of breach-by-omission.[157] For example:

In *Wisniewski v Central Manchester HA*,[158] Philip Wisniewski, C, suffered irreversible brain damage in the 13 minutes immediately prior to his birth because, as he moved down the birth canal, the umbilical cord was wrapped round his neck and had a knot in it (a very rare occurrence), so that he was effectively being strangled during delivery. The alleged omission on the part of the gynaecologist, D, was that he did not perform an artificial rupture of the birth membranes. Had that occurred, then C alleged that the presence of a substance, meconium, would have been revealed, which would have led to birth by caesarian section, rather than via birth canal delivery. Ultimately, that would have avoided the hazards of a natural birth. Applying the *Bolitho* exception, **held:** causation proven:

- **limb #1:** if D had fixed the omission hypothetically (i.e., ruptured the membranes), the court was satisfied that D would have done further act X, *viz*, performed a caesarian section (D did not attend trial – and an adverse inference was drawn against him, that he would have proceeded to perform a caesarian). Hence, causation was proven under this avenue;
- **limb #2:** if D had not done X (performed a caesarian), the court was satisfied that it would have been negligent for him not to have done so, as a decision to delay rupturing the membrane, and to continue observation, was not consistent with a responsible body of medical opinion. Hence, this limb of the theorem succeeded for C too.

In *Wright v Cambridge Medical Group*,[159] Lord Neuberger MR justified *Bolitho's* causal theorem on two policy grounds. Limb #2 was essential, as it would be an 'affront to justice if D could escape liability by contending that, if he had not been negligent as alleged, the same damage would have occurred because he would have subsequently committed a different act of negligence'. Furthermore, wherever D commits a breach of duty by omission, D has deprived C of the opportunity of being treated appropriately. If C had been given that opportunity, he should have a claim for damage for the first breach – no matter what happens afterwards.

Extending the *Bolitho* causal theorem to 'out-of-house' scenarios

§8.20   As an extension of the original *Bolitho* causal theorem, C may establish a causal link by proving that, once D had hypothetically corrected his breach-by-omission, then *either:*

i. on the balance of probabilities, a third party (TP) would have done a further act, X, in order to prevent C's harm (although there was no legal duty on TP to do X); *or*
ii. neither D nor TP would have done further act X to prevent C's harm, and it would have been negligent of D and of TP not to have done X.

---

[157] See also, for mixed results, e.g.: *Holt v Edge* [2006] EWHC 1932 (QB) [57], [61], [75], aff'd: [2007] EWCA Civ 602; *Jones v South Tyneside HA* [2001] EWCA Civ 1701, [22]–[27]; *Zarb v Odetoyinbo* [2006] EWHC 2880, [17].

[158] [1998] Lloyd's Rep Med 223 (CA).   [159] [2011] EWCA Civ 669, [2013] QB 312, [57].

Notably, in *Bolitho*, all the factors making up the causal theorem – the original breach-by-omission, and then the hypothetical enquiry as to what D would, or should, have done if that breach had been fixed – were 'in-house'. However, in *Gouldsmith v Mid Staffordshire General Hospitals NHS Trust*,[160] the *Bolitho* analysis was applied when the original omission was by D, a GP, for a failure-to-refer, and thereafter the court had to assess what *another* party – a surgeon in a specialist tertiary hospital – would have done, had the referral occurred. It was held, by majority, that the *Bolitho* causal theorem could nevertheless apply.

> In *Gouldsmith v Mid Staffordshire*, Irene Gouldsmith, C, entered hospital with blood circulation and ulceration problems. She was treated with anti-coagulation drugs. C claimed that her treating physician, D, failed to refer her to a specialist tertiary hospital, when problems with her left hand were encountered; and that had she been referred, some more radical treatment than anti-coagulation would have been considered urgent and necessary while the limb was still viable; that a vascular specialist surgeon would have operated on a lesion on her left subclavian artery; and that her left hand thumb and fingers would have been saved (ultimately, they were all amputated). **Held (trial):** causation failed. **Held (CA, 2:1):** causation proven, and the case was remitted back to trial for an assessment of damages. Applying the *Bolitho* exception:
>
> - limb #1: if D had hypothetically fixed the omission (i.e., referred C on to a specialist tertiary hospital), another surgeon would have done a further act X (i.e., performed surgery) – a medical expert from the tertiary hospital gave evidence that, had C been referred, a digit-saving operation would have been conducted. Hence, this first avenue of proving causation succeeded for C;
> - limb #2: did not arise, given that limb 1 was answered in C's favour.

Of the majority, Wilson LJ held that there was 'no relevant difference' between the *Gouldsmith* and *Bolitho* situations, and Pill LJ was also content to adopt *Bolitho* as the correct approach.[161]

However, potential problems in extending the *Bolitho* theorem in this way were noted by the dissenter, Sir Maurice Kay:

> factual circumstances involving hypothetical reference elsewhere put different obstacles in the way of [C], when compared with the entirely 'in-house' circumstances of *Bolitho* ... It seems to me that it was such difficulty that led Lord Hoffmann in *Gregg v Scott* to opine that, where it is the hypothetical response of a *non-party*, rather than the act of [C], [D], or someone for whom [D] is responsible, that is in issue, the question should be approached on the basis of loss of a chance rather than proof on a balance of probability. However, that is a road down which neither counsel in the present appeal, and neither of the other members of the court, wish to travel on this occasion.[162]

A similar third-party '*Gouldsmith*-type' could have arisen in the *Creutzfeldt-Jakob Disease Litigation*, which was decided around the same time as the *Bolitho* case – but the *Bolitho* theorem was not referred to:

> In *CJD Groups A and C v Sec of State for Health*,[163] the patients, C, received human growth hormone (HGH) treatment, and their treating doctors (endocrinological paediatric clinicians) were not informed of the remote risks of Creutzfeldt-Jakob Disease (CJD) arising out of the injections of HGH.

---

[160] [2007] EWCA Civ 397.   [161] Respectively, *ibid*, [53]–[60] and [26], [37].
[162] *ibid*, [49]–[50].   [163] (1998) 54 BMLR 104 (QB) 110.

It was the Dept of Health which committed the breach, by failing to send out letters to the treating doctors, informing them of the risk. **Held:** causation proven. As part of the causal chain, C had to prove, on the balance of probabilities, that their treatment would have been stopped by their treating doctors, had the doctors been properly informed by the Dept. The court held that, because '[t]he endocrinological paediatric clinicians being so small in number and a close-knit group, ... peer pressure would have been such that no clinician would have stood out alone and continued treatment'.

Hence, it was a *Gouldsmith*-type scenario, although *Bolitho* was not referred to. Further causal difficulties, to which a robust 'statistical approach' was adopted (discussed previously in the chapter[164]), were also resolved in C's favour.

EXCEPTION #4: THE *CHESTER v AFSHAR* CAUSAL THEOREM IN 'FAILURE-TO-WARN' CASES

The causation principle in *Chester v Afshar*[165] arises exclusively in failure-to-warn medico-legal jurisprudence – where patient C concedes that, had a warning of material risks been given prior to a medical procedure or treatment as required by law (discussed in Chapter 3), C would have proceeded with the procedure or treatment in any event. Exceptionally, however, the failure-to-warn can be causally responsible for C's harm when the risk manifests, under a principle which the majority called, in *Chester v Afshar*, a 'narrow modification' to the 'but-for' test. Subsequently, the case has been widely considered to be an example of where English courts departed from conventional causation 'for policy reasons', to permit C to recover damages.

However, for the most part, causation in failure-to-warn cases follows the general 'but-for' test, which will be considered first in this section.

The general rule

§8.21   As a general rule, the 'but-for' test applies to the failure-to-warn scenario – would C's damage (caused by the manifestation of a material inherent risk) have occurred, but for D's failure-to-warn of that risk? If the harm which befell C would not have happened, because C would have declined the treatment, causation is proven. If the harm would have happened anyway, because even armed with information about material risk, C would have proceeded with the treatment, causation fails. The better view is that determining what C would have done is assessed, in English law, according to a 'hybrid objective/subjective' test (i.e., by reference to what a reasonable person in that patient's position, and with his particular hopes and concerns, would have chosen to do, had the warning about material risks been properly given by D).

Different approaches

A central debate in failure-to-warn scenarios is whether the causal link should be assessed *subjectively* (by seeking evidence from *that particular patient* as to what he would have chosen to do); *objectively* (by reference to what a reasonable patient would have done); or by a *hybrid* objective/subjective analysis (according to the principle above).

There have been judicial indications in English law that the test certainly has a subjective component. In *Chatterton v Gerson*, it was said that patient C 'must prove ... that, had the duty not been broken, she would not have chosen to have the operation'.[166] In *Smith v Barking*,

---

[164] See pp 416–18.   [165] [2005] 1 AC 134 (HL).   [166]   [1981] QB 432, 442.

Havering & Brentwood HA too, the court said that, '[b]oth counsel invited me to accept that, in the end, the matter must be one for decision on a subjective basis. As a matter of principle, this must plainly be right, because the question must be: if this plaintiff had been given the advice that she would have been given, would she have decided to undergo the operation or not?'.[167]

However, a purely subjective test has two considerable difficulties:[168]

- having suffered harm from the medical treatment, the patient invariably will say that, in hindsight, he would not have had the treatment. Such a response is understandable, but not necessarily credible: '[t]hat is not to impugn [C's] honesty as a witness. It is simply that … in the light of the terrible results of his operation, hindsight is almost bound to rule' (per *Smith v Salford HA*[169]); and 'one would need almost to be a saint to answer such questions objectively – i.e., without allowing one's reaction to be influenced by the knowledge of what had, in fact, happened and appreciation of the vital significance of the question' (per *Smith v Barking, Havering and Brentwood HA*[170]). Indeed, even commencing proceedings against doctor D surely indicates C's subjective belief that he would not have proceeded with the treatment if due warning had been given (a point made by the Supreme Court of Canada in *Reibl v Hughes*[171]).
- moreover, C's credibility – in seeking to convince the court that he would not have had the operation – is all-important under a purely subjective test. Any adverse findings which the trial judge makes about C's credibility may influence the finding on causation, and be difficult to reconsider on appeal (a point explicitly made in the Australian case of *Percival v Rosenberg*[172]).

A purely objective test in failure-to-warn litigation is not without problems either. As the Ipp Committee pointed out,[173] when reviewing Australian negligence law, an objective test could ignore what that particular patient would have done; it may not sit well with a patient for whom certain risks are subjectively-significant and who is not necessarily acting rationally; and the test answers, 'what should have happened' rather than 'what would have happened', had the warning been given.

According to English case law, however, it is plain that a hybrid test is favoured. Most recently, in *Montgomery v Lanarkshire Health Board*,[174] the Supreme Court referred to the prospect of the patient's evidence being affected by hindsight, but referred to other evidence by which to assess whether that patient would have proceeded with a vaginal birth (and concluded that she would not have done so, but would have opted for a caesarean section). In other words, a patient's answers have been judicially tempered and tested against a consideration of various objective factors as to what a reasonable person in that patient's position would have done.

Relevant factors under the hybrid test

The following factors have figured as relevant, in failure-to-warn causation.[175] However, none of them is conclusive, and more than one may have to be balanced in the scales, before coming to a conclusion on the crucial question: would the patient have proceeded anyway?

---

[167] QB, 29 Jul 1989.

[168] Both noted, e.g., in: *Review of the Law of Negligence: Final Report* (Sep 2002) ('*Ipp Report*') [7.40].

[169] (1994) 23 BMLR 137 (QB) 149.   [170] [1994] Med LR 285 (QB) 289 (Hutchinson J).   [171] [1980] 2 SCR 880, 898.

[172] (WAFC, 25 May 1999) 3, 19.   [173] *Ipp Report*, [7.38].   [174] [2015] UKSC 11, [104].

[175] See, for these factors in an Australian context, R Mulheron, 'Observations upon Causation in Recent "Failure to Warn" Cases' (2000) *National Law Rev* 2. Further factors mentioned therein, but which have no illustrative counterpart in English law to date, include: whether patient C nominated the form of treatment, not the doctor D; whether C feared medical disease and strongly desired an investigative procedure; whether C had an immutable image of the procedure's outcome; and whether C was unwilling to undergo any other alternative procedures to address the medical problem.

i. Was the procedure advisable or necessary for medical or therapeutic reasons? If patient C was in such chronic pain or suffering that an operation or some treatment was needed from a therapeutic point of view, then that indicates that, no matter whether or not D gave the risks information, C would have persisted with it.

> In *Chatterton v Gerson*,[176] surgeon D performed an operation on patient C to block the sensory nerve between a painful post-operative scar in the right groin and her brain, in order to relieve pain. C alleged that D failed to warn her that permanent numbness to her right leg could result. C gave evidence that she would have chosen not to have the procedure, and that she was learning to put up with her condition. **Held:** no breach proven; and causation failed too: '[t]he whole picture ... is of a lady desperate for pain relief'. In *Hills v Potter*,[177] patient C underwent an operation at the Radcliffe Infirmary, Oxford, to alleviate spasmodic torticollis, a deformity of the neck. From the operation, C was paralysed from the neck down. **Held:** no breach proven; and causation failed too: 'having regard to the evidence as to the gravity of her condition, I think it is more likely than not that she would have agreed to go ahead with the operation, notwithstanding'.

ii. Did the patient have prior positive experiences of medical treatment which pointed in favour of the treatment? If patient C had tried the operation or treatment previously, with no adverse consequences, then that can be one factor suggesting that the patient would have proceeded with the treatment. Similarly, if C's previous experiences with alternative treatments/ procedures were unhappy ones, that may indicate that C would have been prepared to have the new treatment in any event, even if the risks had been duly warned about.

> In *Chatterton v Gerson*, facts previously, patient, C, had undergone the blocking operation on a previous occasion, and whilst not successful, it did not produce the level of numbness in the right leg that C suffered the second time around. **Held:** causation failed. In *Sem v Mid Yorkshire Hosp NHS Trust*,[178] Miss Fishwick, C, underwent a hysterectomy and other gynaelogical procedures. They were not successful, and left C an invalid, largely confined to her room and her bed. C alleged that, had she been warned of the risks, she would have undertaken less interventionist methods, such as pelvic floor exercises, physiotherapy, change of diet and a bladder drill programme. **Held:** causation failed. Non-surgical procedures had been tried previously for C, to alleviate her symptoms, but none proved satisfactory. It was likely that, even if offered warning of the surgical treatment actually undertaken, C would still have elected it. Also, C had been prepared, in the past, to undertake repeated investigations and surgical procedures, even when given very full warnings about the risks involved, e.g., when given the choice between a laparoscopy and a laparotomy, C decided to undergo the more invasive procedure. All of this indicated that C would have proceeded in any event.

However, even C's prior bad experiences with a procedure may not clinch causation in C's favour, where warnings were not given. The court may still consider that C would have proceeded, regardless.

> In *Jones v North West Strategic HA*,[179] Jack Jones, C, suffered from cerebral palsy and brain impairment, because of oxygen starvation for about 15 minutes during his natural birth. His shoulder was lodged behind his mother's pelvic bone, in a condition of shoulder dystocia (an obstetric emergency). Babies can tolerate asphyxia for about 7–8 minutes without permanent damage, but after 9–10 minutes, some brain damage is likely. C alleged that his mother should have been

---

[176] [1981] QB 432, 445.   [177] [1984] 1 WLR 641 (QB) 653.
[178] [2005] EWHC 3469 (QB).   [179] [2010] EWHC 178 (QB).

advised, as part of her antenatal care, of the risk of shoulder dystocia, and told of the possibility of having a caesarean section as an alternative to natural birth. If C's mother had been warned of that risk, she would have opted for a caesarean, and Jack would have been born without damage. During the birth of Jack's elder sister, Rebecca, there was some slight shoulder dystocia, and C's mother said that she found that to be very dramatic, scary and traumatic. She claimed that she did not want that repeated, and would have opted for a caesarean. D's evidence was that a natural birth was far preferable for Mrs Jones and C. **Held:** causation failed. The evidence given by Mrs Jones was important, but other objective factors (below) suggested that she would have proceeded with natural birth in any event.

iii. Was the patient strongly motivated either to undergo, or forego, the treatment because of employment or family reasons? If patient C desperately needed the surgery to be profitably employed in his chosen field of work, then that may be a factor precluding a causal link, because C would have proceeded with the surgery, even if the risks information had been given.

> In *McAllister v Lewisham and North Southwark HA*,[180] Ms McAllister, C, had brain surgery to rectify a neurological defect in her left leg. C was warned of the risk that the surgery could make her leg worse, but not of the risk of haemiplegia which, in fact, manifested. **Held:** causation proven. Rougier J was satisfied that C would not have had the operation, had the risk of haemiplegia been disclosed, because she would have wished to first seek security in her job, and could not afford any lengthy period of sick leave. In *Smith v Salford HA*,[181] Mr Smith, C, had been off work as a window cleaner for several months, with a back complaint. C claimed that he was not warned of the risks of damage to the spinal cord during surgery to fix a congenital spinal fusion. **Held:** causation failed. The court was satisfied that C would have proceeded with the operation, even if the warning had been given, given his need to return to work. (However, C succeeded in negligence on the separate ground of failure to treat with adequate care by the use of an inappropriate instrument.)

Furthermore, if the well-being and/or health of C's spouse or family was uppermost in C's mind in wishing to proceed with the operation, then that is a factor that will likely disprove causation.

> In *Winston v O'Leary*[182] (an Irish case), John Winston, C, underwent a vasectomy operation after the birth of his 7th child. His wife had recently given birth to their youngest child. The couple managed a family-run news agency which was stressful and time-consuming, and a full-time undertaking. The birth of the couple's 2nd-last child had been difficult, and hence, the Winstons considered their family was complete. Unfortunately, the vasectomy left C with very considerable long-term pain and disability. He alleged that his surgeon, C, did not warn of him the risk of long-term pain. **Held:** causation failed. C's evidence was that the procedure was simple, he was 'anxious' to undergo it, and his wife's continued ill-health was an issue uppermost in his mind. Furthermore, there was nothing to indicate that C was unusually cautious, or the kind of patient who would have backed away at the mention of a remote risk.

iv. Was the patient strongly motivated by personal reasons? Patient C's psychiatric condition or religious convictions may point in favour of proceeding with, or alternatively declining, the treatment. Psychiatric evidence can prove crucial in this regard.

---

[180] [1994] 5 Med LR 343 (QB).   [181] (1994) 23 BMLR 137 (QB).   [182] [2006] IEHC 440 (MacMenamin J).

In *Sem v Mid Yorkshire Hosp NHS Trust*,[183] facts previously, **held:** causation failed. A joint psychiatric report indicated that C 'would have been highly dissatisfied with any treatment intervention other than surgery, on the basis that individuals with the tendencies towards illness behaviour exhibited by [C] tend to seek out more dramatic interventions rather than more conservative ones. Given that her symptoms were at least partly psychogenic in origin, conservative intervention was most unlikely to mollify them in any way. Thus, if the surgery had not taken place in July, it would have occurred a few month[s] later, after a more prolonged period of continuing complaint [by C]'. In *Jones v North West Strategic HA*,[184] facts previously, **held:** causation failed. Mrs Jones had an antipathy to blood transfusions, as she was brought up as a Jehovah's Witness. She also had a medically-acknowledged phobia of blood transfusions. It was not accepted that C's mother would have still been willing to have a caesarean, with its added risk of bleeding, and the possible need for a transfusion.

v. **Did comparative treatments or procedures objectively carry far less risk?** If the procedure which C underwent carried a risk about which C was properly warned – but another procedure carried a much-lower-to-nil risk, and C was not informed about that at all, then that objective risk is relevant when determining whether C would have undergone the higher-risk treatment anyway.

In *Montgomery v Lanarkshire Health Board*,[185] Mrs Montgomery, C, was concerned about the prospect of a natural birth, given her small size, and because she had been advised that it was a large baby (this was common for diabetic mothers, such as C). C was not advised of the risk of shoulder dystocia with a large baby, and that an elective caesarean would reduce the risk of injury to her and to the baby to almost nil. **Held:** had C been duly advised of the risk of shoulder dystocia and of the alternative, C would probably have elected to have her baby by caesarean section, in which case the baby would have been born unharmed. In *Birch v UCL Hosp NHS Foundation Trust*,[186] Mrs Birch, C, underwent an angiogram to exclude the possibility of an artery aneurysm. This required that a catheter be inserted from the groin to the brain. C was properly warned that undergoing the procedure of cerebral angiogram carried with it a 1% risk of a stroke. This risk materialised. However, C was not told that an MRI scan was an alternative diagnostic procedure which, although not as good a diagnostic procedure as the cerebral angiogram, carried no risk of stroke at all. **Held:** failure-to-warn of the comparative risks amounted to a breach. Further, causation was proven, because if C had been properly informed, she would not have consented to the angiogram. C's evidence was that she would have chosen the MRI scan, and objective factors supported this – she had had poorly-controlled diabetes for many years, and had previous ischaemic lesions in the immediate past which had resolved spontaneously without the need for risk-carrying tests. All this would have persuaded C to adopt the low-risk alternative which could not lead to a stroke.

vi. **The patient trusted his medical advisers, and was strongly influenced by their recommendations.** If patient C was accustomed to trusting the advice of his medical advisers, then the inference may be drawn that he was likely to proceed with the recommended operation (about which proper risk warnings were not given), thus precluding a causal link – as occurred in both of the following cases:

---

[183] [2005] EWHC 3469 (QB), quote at [55].   [184] [2010] EWHC 178 (QB).
[185] [2015] UKSC 11, [104].   [186] [2008] EWHC 2237, [81].

In *Chatterton v Gerson*,[187] facts previously, a respected neurosurgeon who was also treating patient C recommended that she give the procedure another try, which advice she trusted. In *Jones v North West Strategic HA*,[188] facts previously, C's doctor recommended that a natural birth was the safest course for her and for her baby Jack. During evidence, C said that she 'put her trust in the doctor'. That put C 'in the mainstream of patients in 1992, rather than in the category of the unusual patient who would take a course contrary to the doctor's advice (at least where it did not conflict with her attitude to transfusions)'.

This factor tends to be cited by judges, where other factors also point against a causal link, so as to emphasise that C would have had the operation anyway. For example, in *Sem v Mid Yorkshire Hosp NHS Trust*,[189] the court made the broad generalisation that C 'acting as a reasonable patient ... would have been likely to follow the surgeon's advice. Patients do normally follow the advice of a consultant, and I cannot see in this case any factors which lead me to suppose that [C] would have done otherwise'.

The factor is very 'light-weight', however, because even if the patient shows some tendency to follow the 'doctor knows best' philosophy, other factors may nevertheless show that C would have decided against the treatment/operation, thus proving causation.

In *Birch v UCL Hosp NHS Foundation Trust*,[190] facts previously, **held:** causation proven. Cranston J was not satisfied that Mrs Birch, C, would have agreed to a catheter angiogram, had that been explained to her as being a necessary tool by which to eliminate an aneurysm – even though she took the view of 'doctor knows best' – given her history of poor health, and previous positive experience with low-risk tests.

The *Chester v Afshar* exception

The principle and reasoning

§8.22 Under the *Chester v Afshar* theorem, causation is established where patient C proves that, whilst he would or might have needed to proceed with the operation/treatment (for therapeutic or other reasons), he would have deferred that operation/treatment until a later occasion, had D provided proper warning of material risks. However, since it was delivered, *Chester* has been narrowly construed and infrequently applied.

The controversial decision of *Chester v Afshar*[191] provides an avenue in which a patient, C, may concede that, had the risks information been given, he still would or might have needed an operation or treatment – which supposedly should preclude a causal link – but C would have chosen to have the operation at a later time, at another venue, and with another doctor.

In *Chester v Afshar*, Dr Afshar, D, failed to warn Miss Chester, C, of a 1–2% risk of serious neurological damage resulting from a lumbar surgical procedure. C had suffered episodes of lower back pain for six years, and towards the end of that period, she could 'hardly walk' for the pain. The operation was undertaken, and C developed cauda equina syndrome. The operation was performed carefully and competently, but it was common ground at the trial that the risk ought to have been

---

[187] [1981] QB 432, 445.   [188] [2010] EWHC 178 (QB), quote at [66].
[189] [2005] EWHC 3469 (QB) [54].   [190] [2008] EWHC 2237 (QB).   [191] [2004] UKHL 41, [2005] 1 AC 134.

disclosed.[192] The appeal turned on the issue of causation. The surgery was elective. C argued that, had she been informed of the small risk of cauda equina syndrome, she would have sought advice on alternative treatments, surgeons and risks, and the operation would not have occurred when it did. C accepted that it was likely that she would have required the procedure at some future stage because of the pain that she had long endured, and that, at any later time, the same small risk of cauda equina syndrome would have been present. **Held:** causation proven.

If C would have undergone the operation in any event, even if the warning of cauda equina syndrome had been given, then the 'but-for' test of causation should have failed. However, according to the House of Lords' majority, justice required a 'narrow and modest' modification of the traditional 'but-for' test.[193] Notably, the two most senior Law Lords strongly dissented, and rejected that any exception to the 'but-for' test should have been created in this scenario. Contrasting the judicial points of view:[194]

The disparate points of view in *Chester v Afshar*	
The majority (Lords Steyn, Walker and Hope) – to find causation would ...	The dissenters (Lords Bingham and Hoffmann) – no causal link should have been found, because ...
• vindicate the right of patient C to make an informed choice as to whether, and if so when and by whom, to be operated on – it can be a more complex decision than simply whether or not to undergo the operation. To find against C would be to 'strip [the duty to warn] of all practical force and devoid of all content. It will have lost its ability to protect the patient' (Lord Hope); • reiterate the importance which the medical profession itself places upon risks disclosure (Lord Hope); • reward the honest patient who cannot say that he would have declined the operation, if he had been warned (Lord Hope);	• the fact that patient C would have needed the operation at some point in the future meant that the 'but-for' test of causation was not met; • the fact that C would have had the operation at a different date/time from when she did have it is irrelevant, because changing the timing of the operation was 'irrelevant to the injury she suffered ... [t]hat injury would have been as liable to occur, whenever the surgery was performed and whoever performed it' (Lord Bingham), and 'the risk could have been precisely the same, if she had had it at another time or by another surgeon' (Lord Hoffmann); • to allow C to succeed would be as logical as telling C that the odds on No 7 coming up on the roulette wheel are 1 in 37 on Monday, so C goes away and comes back on Tuesday. 'The question is whether one would have taken the opportunity to avoid or reduce the risk, not whether one would have changed the scenario in some irrelevant detail ... the risk [to C] would have been precisely the same, whether it was done then or later, or by that competent surgeon or by another' (Lord Hoffmann);

---

[192] Noted in: *Chester v Afshar* [2002] EWCA Civ 724, [15].

[193] [2004] UKHL 41, [24] (Lord Steyn).

[194] The quotes in the Table are locatable at: [87] (Lord Hope), [8]–[9] (Lord Bingham), [31] (Lord Hoffmann), [94] (Lord Walker).

The majority (Lords Steyn, Walker and Hope) – to find causation would ...	The dissenters (Lords Bingham and Hoffmann) – no causal link should have been found, because ...
• be fair, because the injury suffered by C was not some coincidental injury (such as an interruption in anaesthesia) which occurred in the operation, but was the precise injury that D should have warned C against (Lord Walker); • reflect the reasonable expectations of the public in contemporary society, in reinforcing patient autonomy and control in their own decision-making (all majority Lords).	• if a failure-to-warn of a breach + the occurrence of the very injury which should have been warned about are enough to prove negligence, then other claims where C probably would have consented to the operation even if properly advised (because C was in pain, or it was required for therapeutic reasons) should succeed too (Lord Bingham); • the law did not have to reinforce the duty to warn, which 'few doctors in the current legal and social climate would consciously or deliberately violate', by requiring the payment of 'potentially very large damages' by D (or his insurer) (Lord Bingham); • there was no justification for creating a special causation rule for doctors – doctors should not be made insurers, especially where the operation was carefully and competently performed (Lord Hoffmann).

The limitations of *Chester v Afshar*

The causal theorem in *Chester v Afshar* has not been much applied in English law, so far as can be ascertained – which is an odd outcome, given the amount of ink which has been devoted to it.

Indeed, in *Chester* itself,[195] Lord Hope remarked that the modification was required 'in the unusual circumstances of this case', suggesting that the approach was not intended to have a general or wide application. Later cases have noted *Chester's* 'policy' nature – that it, e.g., was 'a policy decision with no application to cases like this' (per *Clough v First Choice Holidays and Flights Ltd*[196]); was an unusual decision where, 'for policy reasons, the courts have departed from conventional causation principles' (per *Reynard v Exquisite Cuisine Ltd*[197]); and 'depended peculiarly on the facts of that case' (per *Stephen v Peter*[198]). In *Wright v Cambridge Medical Group*,[199] Elias J remarked that this causal exception was due to the fact that there was a duty to warn, a breach of it and an infringement of C's personal autonomy – it was certainly not because surgeon D had increased the risk of an adverse outcome in the operation: '[t]he basis of liability was that the obligation to warn was an important protection of patient autonomy which should not be undermined, even if it is clear that the patient would have taken the risk of having the operation in any event ... It was quite arbitrary when that risk would materialise; the risk was the same whenever the operation occurred. The majority only imposed liability in order to give an effective remedy for breach of the right to warn'.

To emphasise *Chester v Afshar's* limitations/non-applications, as evident from case law since:

[195] *ibid*, [85].   [196] [2006] EWCA Civ 15, [42].   [197] [2005] CSOH 146, [51].
[198] [2005] CSOH 38, [26].   [199] [2011] EWCA Civ 669, [107].

i. **Where C is clear: he would have opted for a different course of conduct.** C's position may be that he would have proceeded with treatment #2, had the material risks associated with treatment #1 been provided. If this scenario applies, then the causal theorem in *Chester v Afshar* does not apply. The narrow facts of *Chester v Afshar* were that C was not informed of the material risks for treatment #1, and then proceeded with treatment #1 in an uninformed way. If C argues that, had he been warned about treatment #1, he would have undergone another form of medical treatment altogether, which did not carry the same risk at all, then that is a straightforward application of the 'but-for' test. The ratio of *Chester v Afshar* does not apply in that type of case. Two remarkably similar, and tragic, cases, from Scotland and England, illustrate the point:

> In *Khalid v Barnet & Chase Farm Hosp NHS Trust*,[200] Fahima Khalid, C, was born with severe brain damage as a result of oxygen starvation (hypoxia) during labour. Had C been born by caesarean section 20 minutes earlier, she would not have sustained any damage. The labour involved a 'trial of scar' or 'trial of labour', because C's mother had a scar in her uterus from the caesarean birth of her first child. This scar carried a known, but small (about 2%), risk of rupture during the subsequent labour. C's mother had 'plainly set her heart on a normal delivery for her second child'. According to the evidence, in 30% of trial of scar pregnancies, natural delivery is abandoned in favour of a caesarean, as such pregnancies are high risk. C alleged that her parents should have been told of the risk of rupture if proceeding with a natural birth, and of the caesarean alternative. **Held:** causation succeeded. *Chester v Afshar* was raised in argument, but discounted as being 'irrelevant'. A natural labour undoubtedly led directly to the delay in C's delivery, whereas terminating the labour would have led to an earlier caesarean. Causation was proven on 'but-for' principles, and '[t]he problem that arose in *Chester* does not arise'. In *Montgomery v Lanarkshire Health Board*,[201] facts previously, the Scottish Inner House noted that *Chester v Afshar* did not apply: 'the situation in which the majority in *Chester v Afshar* considered that liability should exist was one where (1) a warning of risk would have resulted in the patient seeking further advice elsewhere, and (2) with resultant uncertainty as to whether the patient would have undergone at a future date *an identical procedure in which the same risk might or might not have materialised*.'

ii. **Where no credible evidence is given by C.** As noted in *REM v Mid Yorkshire Hosp NHS Trust*,[202] the *Chester v Afshar* causation exception will only arise where C gives credible evidence, accepted by the court, that if the warning had been given, C would not have had surgery then, but would or might have had surgery at some later time. It is only then that C 'could possibly rely on the loosening of the conventional approach to the problem of causation which underpinned the decision in *Chester v Afshar*.' In that case, the court was satisfied that if C had been warned of the risk, C 'would have elected for precisely the surgery which was, in fact, performed some weeks later' – thus rendering *Chester* inapplicable on the facts.

More recently, in *Meiklejohn v St George's Healthcare NHS Trust*,[203] Robinson J reiterated that, even if it is argued, along *Chester* lines, that C would have postponed the treatment or operation to another occasion when the risk probably would not have developed, if 'there is simply no evidence in support of such a proposition', then the argument cannot possibly succeed. On appeal,[204] the Court of Appeal confirmed that *Chester's* theorem, 'based on narrow facts far from analogous to those we are considering', did not apply, because C trusted his medical adviser and would have accepted her advice.

---

[200] [2007] EWHC 644 (QB) [3], [68].

[201] [2013] CSIH 3, [51] (emphasis added). The Supreme Court similarly disapplied *Chester's* theorem: [2015] UKSC 11, [105].

[202] [2005] EWHC B3 (QB) [37].   [203] [2013] EWHC 469 (QB) [163].   [204] [2014] EWCA Civ 120, [34]–[36].

iii. Limited to medical negligence. In *Beary v Pall Mall Investments (a firm),*[205] the Court of Appeal indicated that *Chester v Afshar* should not extend beyond the realms of medical failure-to-warn, to claims for negligent financial advice.

Several reasons were given for this: (1) the *Chester* majority clearly provided that this narrow modification of 'but-for' causation was exceptional; (2) it was justified by the particular policy considerations that applied to a breach of the doctor's duty to advise a patient of the disadvantages and dangers of proposed treatment – but the policy considerations applicable to the duty to give proper financial advice 'are quite different'; and (3) to extend *Chester* to all cases of negligent financial advice was 'breathtakingly ambitious, contrary to authority and ... wrong.' The view had been expressed earlier, in *White v Paul Davidson & Taylor,*[206] that the principle in *Chester v Afshar* did not apply to legal negligence either – the 'special importance' of fully disclosing material risks to patients was the policy reason underpinning *Chester* (said Lady Justice Arden), but that was not translatable to the context of professional negligence generally.

Hence, in combination, these factors demonstrate why *Chester v Afshar's* causal theorem has had a very limited application, since it was handed down. It was stated to be an 'exceptional case', and case law in the decade since confirms that.

Notably, in *Chester v Afhsar*, there were several references to the similar Australian decision of *Chappel v Hart* – which coincidentally achieved a positive result for C, and also by a bare majority.

The comparative corner: An Australian vignette

In *Chappel v Hart,*[207] Mrs Hart, C, was a principal education officer, and a singing teacher. Due to ongoing throat infections, she was advised that the best treatment would be the removal of the pharyngeal pouch in the oesophagus. There was a risk of a loss of function of C's vocal cords, but it was so remote that it was 'not even mentioned in some clinical textbooks'. The surgery was elective, although the evidence was that C would have had to have surgery sooner or later. During the procedure, C's oesophagus was perforated, an infection called mediastinitis followed, which damaged C's laryngeal nerve, and led to paralysis of her right vocal cord. C's surgeon, Dr Chappel, D, an ENT specialist, advised C of the risk of perforation, but not of the risk of loss of her voice. C had to retire from her employment, following paralysis of her vocal cord. The risk of voice loss was material for C's employment, and should have been disclosed. **Held (3:2):** causation proven, even though C probably would have required the operation in the future in any event. To find causation was 'conducive to better health care' (Kirby J).

INTERVENING ACTS IN THE CAUSAL CHAIN

Even where the 'but-for' test is satisfied, the requisite causal link may still fail. The law imposes a number of 'exclusionary devices', which circumscribe D's liability where his acts or omissions are considered too 'remote' in law. The doctrine of intervening acts (or *novus actus interveniens*[208]) is one such legal device.

---

[205] [2005] EWCA Civ 415, [38].   [206] [2003] EWCA Civ 1511, [40]–[42].

[207] [1998] HCA 55, 195 CLR 232 (Gaudron, Gummow and Kirby JJ; with McHugh and Hayne JJ dissenting).

[208] Latin for 'a new intervening act': E Martin and J Law, *Oxford Dictionary of Law* (6th edn, Oxford University Press, 2006) 361.

These occur where D1 is the party who commits a breach; but the most direct agent of C's harm is something other than D1's conduct – something that constitutes a separate and independent cause of C's injury, intervening between D1's breach and C's damage. The intervening act is connected factually with D1's breach, however, in that the breach created the opportunity for that 'something else' to occur (i.e., the intervening act would not have occurred, had the breach not occurred) – if there is no factual connection between D1's breach and the intervening act, then that act is truly a supervening event (another legal conundrum which is dealt with in a later section of this chapter[209]).

Whilst most judges seem to consider that intervening acts are best dealt with as an issue of causation, others have favoured the view that the topic fits better within remoteness of damage. In *Chubb Fire Ltd v Vicar of Spalding*,[210] the Court of Appeal considered that it was a distinction without importance – and that it is a doctrine used to determine whether a wrongdoing D 'will be responsible for certain consequences of that negligence and the damages that are claimed to flow from those consequences'.

The characteristics of an intervening act

§8.23   Where D1 has committed a breach of duty against C, an intervening act can be due to any of the following: (1) unreasonable or deliberate behaviour of D2, which occurs after D1's breach; (2) criminal or negligent conduct committed by either an identified or an unknown third party (TP); (3) conduct on TP's part which was neither negligent nor criminal; (4) careless conduct by C himself, which exacerbates or brings about his own injury; or (5) some naturally-occurring event. An intervening act will only be upheld where it would be fair and just to relieve D1 of all liability for C's damage, because D1's breach lost its causative potency in light of the 'new cause'. Whilst it will assist proof of an intervening act if the act was (1) unreasonable, (2) reckless, (3) deliberate, or (4) unforeseeable, none of these is a pre-requisite for proving an intervening act.

The principle underlying the law's willingness to recognise intervening acts is one of fairness, as Lord Bingham made plain in *Corr v IBC Vehicles Ltd*: '[i]t is not fair to hold [D] liable, however gross his breach of duty may be, for damage caused to [C] not by [D's] breach of duty but by some independent, supervening cause (which may or may not be tortious) for which [D] is not responsible'.[211] Hence, a value judgment inevitably enters an assessment of what constitutes a break in the causal chain. Essentially, it comes down to the question: what **should** D be liable for, damages-wise? Whether the intervening act has the effect of relieving D1 from liability for his earlier negligent conduct 'depends on whether it is just that this should be so ... considerations of policy loom large in the analysis ... although they are generally concealed beneath the legal concepts used to justify the result' (per *Wright v Cambridge Medical Group*[212]). This infusion of policy can make the operation of the doctrine of intervening acts difficult to predict with any confidence.

As the aforementioned principle shows, an intervening act can be any one of several possibilities – C's own conduct, D2's later act, the act of an entirely unknown TP, or a natural event. However, defining the essential characteristics of that *novus actus interveniens* may well be a fruitless exercise. Judges have rarely agreed on them: indeed, in *Horton v Evans*,[213] Keith J remarked that, '[t]he guiding principle is that there is no guiding principle'.

---

[209] See pp 477–83.   [210] [2010] EWCA Civ 981, [63] (Aikens LJ).
[211] [2008] UKHL 13, [2008] 1 AC 884, [15].   [212] [2011] EWCA Civ 669, [2013] QB 312, [110].
[213] [2006] EWHC 2808 (QB) [53].

The characteristics noted in the abovementioned principle are derived from the judgment of Evans-Lombe J in *Barings plc v Coopers & Lybrand (a firm)*.[214] In fact, intervening acts have been judicially described in various terms: an act that was 'so unforeseeable as not to be something likely to flow from the original negligence [of D1]' (per *Knightley v Johns*[215]); 'a new cause which ... can be described as either unreasonable or extraneous or extrinsic' (per *The Oropesa*[216]); an act that was 'reckless ... shutting his eyes to the obvious risks that existed [for C]' (per *Wright v Lodge*[216a]); and 'an independent, supervening event' (per *Humber Oil Terminal Trustee Ltd v Sivand, Owners*[217]). Clearly, it will be a fact-sensitive enquiry, in which a range of conduct may constitute a 'new cause'.

There are two oft-repeated *common* elements emerging from the abovementioned judgments, however, as to what will constitute an intervening act. First, D1's breach must be so 'obliterated' or 'eclipsed' by the intervening act that it deprives D's breach of its causative potency. Secondly, it would not be fair or just to hold D1 responsible for C's damage.

The effect of an intervening act

§8.24   Where an intervening act occurs, D1's breach is not considered to have been legally responsible for C's damage, and D1 will avoid liability altogether, for any damage on, and from, the occurrence of that intervening act. It is a mixed question of fact and of law, as to whether an intervening act breaks the 'chain of causation' between D's breach and C's damage.

An intervening act is considered by law to be a new cause of C's injury. It severs the causal link between D's breach (negligent though it was) and C's harm. It is true that C's injury would not have occurred, but for D's negligence – but the intervening act severs the **legal** effect of D's breach. D's breach is no longer the legally operative cause of C's harm.

Hence, an intervening act represents an all-or-nothing outcome for C. Where an intervening act is found, then D1 'walks way' without incurring any liability in negligence at all. This is especially important, when the intervening party may be unidentified, or lacking any assets with which to satisfy a judgment. D1 may well have represented the only feasible option for C to recover compensation for his injury. For this reason – and similarly to the court's reluctance to find in favour of D1 on the 'all-or-nothing' defence of *volenti* (see Chapter 10) – intervening acts are a fairly rare creature in English negligence law.

The lack of judicial enthusiasm for the device of the *novus actus interveniens* is also due to two pieces of legislation.

First, where C's own conduct is alleged to have constituted an intervening act, the alternative is to hold that C carelessly contributed to his own injury and was contributorily negligent (pursuant to the Law Reform (Contributory Negligence) Act 1945). That statute entails apportionment, and not an all-or-nothing outcome (as per Chapter 10). It means that D1 is liable for some damages, notwithstanding C's careless conduct (e.g., in *Dalling v JR Heale & Co Ltd*,[218] there was no intervening act, but contributory negligence of 33% was assessed against C, for the damages relating to the incident to which C contributed).

Secondly, where D2's conduct is alleged to have broken the causal chain, the court may instead find that D1 and D2 both contributed to C's harm – which will invoke an apportionment between the defendants, pursuant to the Civil Liability (Contribution) Act 1978. Again, that outcome will prevent D1 from 'walking away' from any liability 'scot-free'.

---

[214] [2003] EWHC 1319 (Ch) [838].   [215] [1982] 1 WLR 349 (CA) 366.   [216] [1943] 1 All ER 211 (CA) 215.
[216a] [1993] PIQR P31 (CA) P37.   [217] [1998] EWCA Civ 100 (Evans LJ).   [218] [2011] EWCA Civ 365.

Where an intervening act occurred, then in some cases, D1 will not be liable for any damages whatsoever, as C suffered no harm prior to that point. However, in other cases, D1 will be liable for the immediate effects of D1's breach, but not for the damage caused by the intervening act. In other words, the intervening act stops the extent of the D1's liability for damages.

This principle of intervening acts involves a mixed question of fact and of law. This was confirmed in *Roberts v Bettany*, where Buxton LJ remarked that, although the doctrine of *novus actus interveniens* is 'sometimes talked of as, and presented as, simply a question of causation, which at first sight might appear to be an issue of fact, it is well recognised that the matter is more complex than that. The issue is one of law, whereby the court has to be satisfied that the acts of the third party were sufficient as a matter of law to exculpate [D1] from liability for the particular result, proximate or distant though it might have been, of his negligent act'.[219] Whether something constituted an intervening act will always involve *some* degree of value judgment, thus rendering it a policy question too, and divorcing it from a purely factual assessment (per Lord Nicholls in *Kuwait Airway Corp v Iraqi Airway Co (Nos 4 and 5)*[220]).

Particular contexts

Of the multitude of cases which have turned on the question of whether or not an intervening act was committed, it is useful to give some contrasting examples in different contexts. Diagrammatically, the various leading cases in this section are illustrated below:

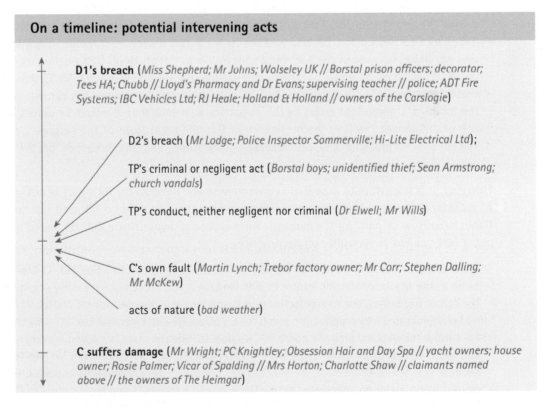

On a timeline: potential intervening acts

D1's breach (*Miss Shepherd; Mr Johns; Wolseley UK // Borstal prison officers; decorator; Tees HA; Chubb // Lloyd's Pharmacy and Dr Evans; supervising teacher // police; ADT Fire Systems; IBC Vehicles Ltd; RJ Heale; Holland & Holland // owners of the Carslogie*)

D2's breach (*Mr Lodge; Police Inspector Sommerville; Hi-Lite Electrical Ltd*);

TP's criminal or negligent act (*Borstal boys; unidentified thief; Sean Armstrong; church vandals*)

TP's conduct, neither negligent nor criminal (*Dr Elwell; Mr Wills*)

C's own fault (*Martin Lynch; Trebor factory owner; Mr Corr; Stephen Dalling; Mr McKew*)

acts of nature (*bad weather*)

C suffers damage (*Mr Wright; PC Knightley; Obsession Hair and Day Spa // yacht owners; house owner; Rosie Palmer; Vicar of Spalding // Mrs Horton; Charlotte Shaw // claimants named above // the owners of The Heimgar*)

Dealing with each in turn:

[219] [2001] EWCA Civ 109, [12].   [220] [2002] UKHL 19, [2002] 2 AC 883, [70].

D2's acts or omissions

Reckless behaviour on D2's part, amounting to a disregard for the consequences of his conduct, may be sufficient to break the causal chain between D1's breach and C's harm. Alternatively, D2's conduct may have been unforeseeable, rather than reckless. That can also constitute an intervening act for which it would not be fair to hold D1 liable to C:

> In *Wright v Lodge*,[221] Miss Shepherd, D1, was driving along a busy roadway when her Mini car petered out and came to a stop on the eastbound carriageway. Conditions were very foggy, with visibility down to 60 yards. D1 was negligent in not getting her passenger to help push the car off the carriageway onto the verge, which would have been an easy task. Mr Lodge, D2, was driving his articulated lorry at about 60 mph (in a 50 mph speed zone), and had to swerve and brake to avoid D1's Mini. His lorry overturned, and crossed over into the westbound carriageway, colliding with Mr Wright's, C's, vehicle. **Held:** D2's conduct amounted to a *novus actus interveniens* between D1's negligence and C's harm. D2 was driving recklessly, at a speed which was obviously unsafe for his vehicle and contrary to the law, and in thick fog. Although D2 would not have had to swerve and brake if D1's car had not been negligently left where it was, the accident was wholly attributable to D2's reckless driving. 'It was unwarranted and unreasonable', and D1's conduct was excluded as being causative of the accident. In *Knightley v Johns*,[222] due to his negligent driving, Mr Johns, D1, overturned his car at the end of a one-way tunnel in Birmingham. Police Inspector Sommerville, D2, was called to the scene, but forgot to close the tunnel in the chaos. He then instructed PC Knightley, C, and a colleague, to ride the wrong way down the tunnel to close it. In doing so, C was hit by an oncoming car driven by Geoffrey Cotton, D3, and was seriously injured. C sued all three Ds in negligence. D3 was not liable, because of the doctrine of 'inevitable accident'. **Held:** D2's negligence broke the chain of causation between D1's negligent driving and C's collision with Mr Cotton. None of these events would have happened, had D1 not negligently overturned his car, but thereafter, the long list of important errors by D2, in particular, meant that it would be unjust to attribute what happened to C to the negligence of D1: 'the breakdown of the system ... provid[ed] evidence of improbable and unforeseeable ineptitude, and the breaches of the standing orders'.

However, it is important to note that even unreasonable conduct on D2's part is not conclusive of an intervening act. The court may still determine that it would be fair and just to hold D1 liable (wholly or in part) for C's damage. Such decisions demonstrate that the proof of a *novus actus interveniens* is very difficult, in practice.

> In *Hi-Lite Electrical Led v Wolseley UK Ltd*,[223] Obsession Hair and Day Spa Ltd, C, owned a hair salon in the Mailbox shopping centre in Birmingham. A fire broke out very early one morning, in the colour dispensary, due to a defective pump, and the salon was destroyed. Wolseley UK Ltd, D1, had manufactured and supplied the pump for C's salon. Hi-Lite Electrical Ltd, D2, was the electrical contractor who installed the pump in C's salon. D2 alleged that D1's pump was manufactured with an electrical fault which caused the fire. D1 alleged that D2 committed an intervening act, because it failed to fit a device, an RCD (a circuit-breaker), which would have prevented the fire from starting. **Held:** no intervening act by D2. It was true that D2's negligent failure to fit the RCD

---

[221] [1993] RTR 123 (CA) 129–30 (Parker LJ).   [222] [1982] RTR 182 (CA) 189–90 (Stephenson LJ).
[223] [2011] EWHC 2153 (TCC) [182]–[208], [239] (Ramsey J).

failed to prevent the fire, and this was 'essentially unreasonable conduct'. However, the cause of the fire was the defective pump, and D2's failure to fit the RCD did not deprive D1's defective pump 'of its causative potency'.

Where D1 breached its duty of care to C in failing to take reasonable steps to prevent harm from occurring to C, D1 cannot argue that D2 failed to detect the same problem which D1's own breaches of duty failed to detect, and that D2's failure to fix the problem constituted a break in the causal chain. To find that D1 could escape liability in such a scenario would be unfair, and as a matter of 'simple and common sense', cannot be sustained (per *Carillion JM Ltd v Phi Group Ltd*[224]).

> In *Carillion JM Ltd v Phi Group Ltd*, the Chiltern Railways train servicing depot near Wembley Football Stadium was designed and built in 2004–6, whilst the new stadium was being constructed. Carillion, C, was the contractor engaged to build the depot. Robert West Constructing, D1, was the engineering firm which undertook the soil excavations, and Phi Group, D2, was engaged to perform 'soil nailing work'. To create space for the depot, substantial excavations had to be made into the clay ground, leaving 70°–80° slopes each side. Those slopes became unstable in 2005, due to instability in the shear face and upper layers of the London Clay. Remedial work was done. However, later on, the deep-lying layers also became unstable. Apparently, London Clay is well-known for giving rise to different types of instability. C sued D1 for failing to redesign the works following the slip in 2005, which would have revealed the extent of the deep-lying instability that occurred later. D1 argued that C's reliance on D2, when the 2005 slippage happened, broke the chain of causation between D1's failure to redesign the works and the ultimate damage caused by the later slippages of the clay slopes. **Held:** D2 did not break the chain of causation. If D1 had acted carefully and competently *at the various stages of the project*, then the deep-seated instability would have been picked up and addressed. The causal chain was not broken, simply because D2, C or anyone else, might or should have realised the existence of the deep-lying instability.

The criminal or negligent acts of TP

A TP's criminal or negligent acts may conceivably break the chain of causation, where TP enters the scenario unheralded, neither known nor reasonably foreseeable by D1, and then creates havoc. In this scenario, English law supports the proposition that TP's acts may constitute a *novus actus interveniens*, severing the chain between D1's breach and C's damage.

> In *Chubb Fire Ltd v Vicar of Spalding*,[225] three teenage boys (TP) entered the medieval parish church of St Mary and St Nicholas, at Spalding, whilst it was briefly unlocked and unattended. They took two dry powder fire extinguishers from the kitchenette next to the vestry, and discharged them around the church, including onto the organ. The cleaning-up operation was complex, laborious and expensive (costing about £250,000). The Vicar of Spalding, C, sued Chubb Fire Ltd, D1, who had supplied the dry powder extinguisher to the church in 1999, alleging that D1, when supplying the extinguisher, owed a duty to warn the church that any discharge of the extinguisher was likely to cause a mess. Had that warning been given, C said that he would not have had a dry powder extinguisher in the church. D1 argued that the vandals' acts were a *novus actus interveniens*.

---

[224] [2011] EWHC 1379 (TCC) [146].

[225] [2010] EWCA Civ 981. See too: *Lamb v Camden LBC* [1985] QB 625 (CA) (damage by squatters an intervening act).

Held: there was an intervening act by the vandals TP, and D1 was not liable for the damage caused by their independent acts. It would not be fair to hold D1 liable for that damage, some seven years after the extinguishers were provided. Also, TP's acts were deliberate and criminal, by persons for whom D1 had no responsibility and over which D1 had no control. Although vandals entering an unlocked church was foreseeable, the precise combination of events that led to such damage to the church was not reasonably foreseeable in 1999.

On the other hand, where D1's alleged wrongdoing is a failure to supervise or control the actions of that TP, who then ends up either injuring or killing C (these cases were discussed in Chapter 3), arguably the direct cause of C's injury was TP's wrongful or criminal act. Yet, that TP's conduct will **not** constitute an intervening act, according to English case law. The intervention is certainly foreseeable, given the violent or dangerous characteristics of TP – but even foreseeable events can constitute intervening acts. The more significant problem is that to hold that TP's act broke the chain of causation would permit D1 to evade liability, when the very duty cast upon D1 was to supervise or control TP. In *Dorset Yacht Co Ltd v Home Office*,[226] Lord Reid noted that, if what was relied on as a *novus actus interveniens* is the very thing which is likely to happen if D1 commits a breach of the duty which he owed, then D1 cannot rely on the intervening act.

> In *Dorset Yacht Co Ltd v Home Office*, Borstal officers, D1, owed a duty to take reasonable care to prevent seven Borstal boys under their control, TP, from escaping from custody on Brownsea Island and causing damage to C's yacht moored nearby in Poole Harbour. **Held:** TP's criminal behaviour did not sever the chain of causation between the Borstal officers' lack of supervision of TP and the property damage which ultimately occurred to C's yacht. In *Stansbie v Troman*,[227] a decorator, D1, was working alone in C's house, and went out to buy wallpaper. He left the front door unlocked, despite being warned not to. Whilst he was away, an unidentified thief, TP, entered the house and stole items. **Held:** TP's deliberate act was not an intervening act, and D1 was liable for the lost items. D1's duty, in decorating the house, was to take reasonable care to guard the house against thieves.

Of course, if a mentally-ill person, TP, injured C for some other reason – e.g., attacking someone in a pub whilst drunk – then that may be an intervening act, given that the mental illness is **not** the provocation for TP's behaviour, it is some new and quite independent cause. That case has yet to arise in English law.

In any event, *Chubb* was distinguished from *Dorset Yacht*, because in *Dorset Yacht*, D1 was under a duty to take reasonable steps to supervise the Borstal boys, whereas in *Chubb*, D1 had no duty to protect the church from the violence of vandals; it had no control over the vandals, nor any responsibility for them.

TP's conduct which is neither negligent nor criminal

In some cases, TP gets involved in the 'story', and is neither negligent nor criminal, and yet, it is that TP's acts that are the most direct cause of C's suffering harm. For such an act by TP to be an intervening act, it must be unreasonable or unforeseeable. Further, if TP's intervention (or the effects of that intervention) were foreseeable to D1, then to uphold it as an intervening act is very unlikely.

---

[226] [1970] AC 1004 (HL) 1030.   [227] [1948] 2 KB 48.

In *Horton v Evans*,[228] Cathy Horton, C, a high-earning lawyer, businesswoman, athlete and priest, was mis-prescribed some medication (dexamethasone) for a minor ailment (4 mg per day, instead of 0.5 mg per day), and her health deteriorated very markedly. C sued the GP who prescribed the wrong dose, and settled on confidential terms. C also sued pharmacist, Lloyds Pharmacy, D1, who dispensed the script, on the basis that they were negligent in not questioning the prescription and in proceeding to dispense the medication as prescribed. The medication was also mis-prescribed by another GP, Dr Elwell, TP, a few weeks later, whilst C was holidaying with her mother in New York State. C asked TP for a repeat prescription, of 4 mg a day, based upon C's showing TP the bottle of the previous prescription. TP based his prescription on viewing that label, which act D1 argued had the effect of breaking the chain of causation between any breach by D1 and C's deterioration in health. **Held:** TP's act was not an intervening act. TP was not negligent in prescribing C with the prescription which he did. Furthermore, it could not be said that D1's failure to question the GP's prescription was so eclipsed by TP's intervention that D1's conduct could properly be relegated to no more than a mere occurrence in the history of events. D1 should reasonably have foreseen the reliance which might be placed by a physician on the label on the bottle, and bore a 'real responsibility' for why TP thought that C had been prescribed 4 mg a day. In *Wilkin-Shaw v Fuller*,[229] Charlotte Shaw, C, 14, fell into a fast-flowing stream while on a training exercise on Dartmoor, was swept away by the strong current, and drowned. She had been on the Moor with 10 other children from the Kingsley School, North Devon, training for a Ten Tors expedition. C's mother sued the supervising teacher and school, D1, in negligence, on behalf of C's estate. The trip was undertaken in bad weather. Trevor Wills, TP, a scoutmaster, encountered the group at Watern Tor, when they were cold, distressed and wet, and advised them to cross at Walla Brook, where the accident occurred. (TP died prior to trial, and his police witness statement was relied upon.) **Held:** D1 were not negligent (although, on appeal, another D was found in breach, but 'but-for' causation failed). In any event, TP's conduct **would** have been an intervening act in advising the group that it was possible to cross the Walla Brook, and in guiding them to the crossing point where he oversaw the crossing. The effect of TP's intervention was to countermand D1's instructions: 'the intervention of a third party, anxious to help and apparently authoritative, would have broken the chain of causation. It could not have been foreseen that [the children] would have disobeyed instructions' given by the project leader and other responsible adults about the risks of water crossings (note that, on appeal, it was doubted whether TP's advice was indeed negligent).

C's own conduct

C's own conduct may break the causal chain if it amounts to 'unreasonable conduct' – but even then, it may not be sufficient to allow D1 to escape liability, for D1's breach may still remain the effective cause of C's damage (per Gross LJ in *Borealis AB v Geogas Trading SA*[230]). In *Mueller Europe Ltd v Central Roofing (South Wales) Ltd*, Stuart-Smith J noted, too, that even where C's conduct was reckless, it does not necessarily follow that C committed a *novus actus interveniens*.[231] (Both of these statements were made in the context of breach of contract, but the test for an intervening act is the same for both negligence and breach of contract.)

Hence, it comes as no surprise that it can be very difficult to establish that C's own conduct amounted to a break in the causal chain. It may well trigger a finding of contributory

[228] [2006] EWHC 2808 (QB).
[229] [2013] EWCA Civ 410, [53], affirming: [2012] EWHC 1777 (QB) [136]–[137].
[230] [2011] 1 Lloyds LR 482, [45].   [231] [2013] EWHC 237 (TCC) [122].

negligence against C (and hence reduce D1's liability for damages), but it will not sever the chain and exculpate D1 altogether. There are several reasons for the judicial unwillingness to hold C accountable as having committed an intervening act:

- if D1's duty of care towards C was to guard C against the very misfortune which befell C by virtue of C's own conduct, then it will be virtually impossible for C's conduct to break the chain of causation:

    In *Reeves v Commr of Police*,[232] Martin Lynch was put in a police cell whilst on remand for credit card fraud. He was on a suicide observation watch by the police, D1. Between observations, he hanged himself in his cell. **Held:** his act of suicide did not sever the chain of causation between D1's breach and the death of C. The very duty which D1 owed to C was to exercise reasonable care to prevent his taking his own life.

- if C's conduct was a panic or reflex reaction, in light of an emergency which D1's negligence created, then it will not amount to an intervening act – that would 'be wrong as a matter of principle'. As Lord Hoffmann stated in *SAAMCO's* case,[233] where D's breach lands C in a predicament, then C's 'reasonable attempt to cope with the consequences of D's breach of duty does not negative the causal connection between that breach of duty and the ultimate loss':

    In *Trebor Bassett Holdings Ltd v ADT Fire and Security plc*,[234] a large confectionery factory in Pontefract, owned by Trebor Bassett Holdings, C, was destroyed by fire in 2005, causing damage estimated at over £100m. The fire originally started in the popcorn production area where popcorn caught fire. Employees thought that the fire had been put out satisfactorily, but that was wrong, and a catastrophic fire followed. ADT Fire and Security, D1, provided a CO_2 fire suppression system for the popcorn machinery. D1 argued that C's own negligence broke the chain of causation between any defects in that suppression system and the destruction of the factory, because hardly any of C's employees were aware that the suppression system could be manually activated, and even fewer knew how to trigger it. **Held:** C's lack of staff training was negligent, but was not an intervening act. C's employees were striving to deal with the emergency which had been created by the lack of effectiveness of D1's CO_2 suppression system. Also, by the time that the fire was visible, when staff could manually activate the system, that would have come too late to have any causal effect. In *The Oropesa*,[235] *The Oropesa* steam ship was hit by D1's steam ship, the *Manchester Regiment*. The Master of *The Oropesa* decided to embark in a lifeboat, in rough and stormy weather, to get to the other ship and confer with her Master on what should be done to save the crews. Before the lifeboat could reach *Manchester Regiment*, it capsized and sank, drowning nine occupants, including the sixth engineer, C. **Held:** C's getting into the lifeboat with the Master was not an intervening act between D1's negligence in causing the collision, and C's ultimate drowning. C and his Master had not 'done something which was outside the exigencies of the emergency'. They were placed in this awful predicament by D1's negligence.

- if D1's original tort affected C physically or psychiatrically (or both), and put C in a position of vulnerability, whereby C was prone to act to the detriment of his own physical well-being, then it is very unlikely that C's conduct will be legally treated as breaking the chain of causation.

---

[232] [2000] 1 AC 360 (HL).   [233] [1997] AC 191 (HL) 218.
[234] [2011] EWHC 1936 (TCC), quote and points from section M4.
[235] [1943] P 32 (CA), quote at 39 (Lord Wright).

In *Corr v IBC Vehicles Ltd*,[236] Mr Corr, C, suffered a very serious and disfiguring head injury at a car factory in Coventry, for which his employers, D1, were liable. As a result of that head injury, C became depressed. Six years later, he committed suicide by jumping off a multi-storey carpark. C's estate brought an action against D1 for the consequences of the suicide. **Held:** C's suicide was not an intervening act. Although the suicide had been a deliberate conscious act, it had been the result of a depressive illness which was caused by D1's tort. In *Dalling v RJ Heale & Co Ltd*,[237] Stephen Dalling, C, was injured at work in 2005 when he fell about 5 metres whilst working as a ceiling fitter. His employer, RJ Heale, D1, admitted breach for the fall. However, three years later, C had a second accident, when he fell over backwards in a pub, having had too much to drink, and suffered a further head injury. **Held:** C's pub accident was not a *novus actus interveniens*. The first head injury played some part in the second accident, and the second accident could not sever the chain of causation between D1's original breach and C's ultimate damage. The original head injury had impaired C's judgment and ability to control his drinking. Both C and D1 had made substantial contributions to the happening of the second accident (33% CN was attributed to C). In *Wieland v Cyril Lord Carpets Ltd*,[238] Mrs Wieland, C, was injured in a bus accident, due to driver D1's negligence. She had to wear a neck collar and a brace afterwards, which affected her ability to use her bi-focals. C fell down some steps at her office, whilst in the company of her son. **Held:** the fall was not an intervening act, and hence, D1 was liable for the additional damage caused by that fall.

Notwithstanding the causal difficulties associated with C's conduct, C's own carelessness and unreasonable behaviour **can** constitute a *novus actus interveniens* at law (even if it was reasonably foreseeable to D). As Lord Reid stated in *McKew v Holland & Hannen & Cubitts (Scotland) Ltd*,[239] C's unreasonable conduct may have been entirely foreseeable, 'but that does not mean that [D] must pay for damage caused by the *novus actus*.'

In *McKew v Holland*, Mr McKew, C, was injured at work, caused by the breach of his employer, D. His back and hips were badly strained, he could not bend, and on several occasions his left leg suddenly 'went away from' him. A couple of weeks later, C was offered a tenancy of a flat in Glasgow, and went to inspect it. The flat was reached by a steep staircase with no handrail. When coming down the steps, C was carrying his young child, and his left leg 'vanished under him'. He threw his daughter back, and then, 'instead of toppling down head first, I threw myself and I landed on my feet'. C jumped about 12 feet from the top of the stair to the next landing, badly breaking his ankle. C claimed that the effect of the original breach was to weaken his leg and make him more prone to fall. D argued that C undertook a very hazardous exercise for which he, alone, was solely responsible. (If D was liable for the damage caused by the second accident, damages were agreed at £4,915, while if D was not, they were agreed at £200.) **Held:** the second accident was an intervening act. The second injury was caused by C's disability, which in turn was caused by D's breach, but C 'did something which a moment's reflection would have shown him was an unreasonable thing to do ... he chose to descend in such a way that, when his leg gave way, he could not stop himself'.

Acts of nature

An intervening act may be some 'exceptional natural event' (per dicta in *Kuwait Airways Corp v Iraqi Airways Co*[240]). In *Humber Oil Terminal Trustee Ltd v Sivand, Owners*,[241] the hypothetical

[236] [2008] AC 884.   [237] [2011] EWCA Civ 365.   [238] [1969] 3 All ER 1006 (QB) 1009–1111.
[239] 1970 SC (HL) 20, 25.   [240] [2002] UKHL 19, [2002] 2 AC 883, [127].   [241] [1998] EWCA Civ 100.

example was given of an earthquake which disrupts repair work to C's vessel which D1 had negligently performed; and the actual example of *Carslogie Steamship Co Ltd v Royal Norwegian Govt*[242] was cited, where an intervening act occurred due to bad weather.

> In *Carslogie*, C's ship, *The Heimgar*, collided with D's ship, *The Carslogie*, due to D's negligence. Temporary repairs were carried out to *The Heimgar* at Port Glasgow to make her seaworthy, but she had to make her way to New York where permanent repairs were to be carried out. She met heavy weather, and suffered damage which rendered her unseaworthy. That damage required 30 days of repairs; whereas the collision's effects required 10 days of repair. The repairs were done concurrently. **Held:** C was not able to recover the costs of the 10 days of repairs. The bad weather intervened to overtake the original tortious conduct of D; 'I cannot see that [C] sustained any damages in the nature of [tortious recovery against D] by reason of the fact that for I0 days out of the 30, she was also undergoing repairs in respect of the collision'.

Subsequent medical treatment

§8.25   Where C is injured by D1's breach and requires medical treatment as a result, and that treatment is negligently peformed by healthcare practitioner D2, that negligent medical treatment will not constitute an intervening act – unless the medical negligence is so gross and egregious as to be unforeseeable.

In *Wright v Cambridge Medical Group*, Elias LJ was of the view that intervening acts only apply where the new act is unforeseeable (which is not a view uniformly held among all judges, as discussed previously). In any event, it is (said Elias LJ) entirely foreseeable that hospital doctors and other medical professionals 'will be negligent from time to time', and that only medical negligence that was 'gross or egregious' could break the chain of causation, albeit that such a degree of negligence will be very difficult to prove.[243]

Even medical negligence with very serious outcomes for C will not break the chain of causation, where such negligence is foreseeable; and not grossly negligent. Hence, where C is injured at work or in a road accident, and there is subsequent negligence by a doctor brought in to treat the original injury, but who in fact made it worse, that medical treatment is very unlikely to constitute a *novus actus interveniens*.

> In *Webb v Barclays Bank plc and Portsmouth Hospitals*,[244] Elizabeth Webb, C, contracted polio when 2 years old, and her left knee was left with a disability. While employed at Barclays Bank, D1, C stumbled over a protruding flagstone in their forecourt, C hyper-extended that knee, and was left with a grossly unstable knee. A long-term calliper was recommended, but C initially refused because of childhood experiences with callipers, but after terrible pain developed, she tried a calliper, without success. Her surgeon, Dr Jeffrey, D2, suggested an above-knee amputation of the left leg, which C accepted. After it was performed, it became apparent that an amputation had not been necessary to treat the condition. C sued D1 in negligence for failing to properly maintain the forecourt, and also sued D2 for negligent medical advice. **Held:** D2's medical negligence did **not** constitute a *novus actus interveniens*. D1's original wrongdoing remained a causative force of the amputation, as it had increased C's vulnerability and reduced her mobility. The medical intervention

---

[242] [1952] AC 292 (HL).   [243] [2011] EWCA Civ 669, [2013] QB 312, [111].
[244] [2001] EWCA Civ 1141.

was plainly foreseeable, and given D2's conduct was negligent, but not grossly negligent, it would not be just and equitable to relieve D1 of all liability for the amputation. 'In short, the negligence in advising amputation did not eclipse the original wrongdoing. The Bank remained responsible for their share of the amputation damages. The negligence of Dr Jeffrey was not an intervening act breaking the chain of causation'. D1's responsibility was assessed at 25% and the doctor's (D2's) at 75%. In *Wright v Cambridge Medical Group*, Clarice Wright, C, 11 months, contracted chickenpox. She developed a high temperature and tachycardia, and was admitted to hospital on 9 April. Within a couple of days, C developed a very serious infection which went undiagnosed at the point of her discharge on 12 April. The bacteria seeded into part of C's hip-bone, infecting the bone on 13 or 14 April. C was taken by her mother to see her GP, D1, on 15 April, but the GP failed to arrange for C to be seen (this was a conceded breach). C was admitted to hospital again on 17 April, and eventually seen by a specialist paediatrician on 20 April, but a proper diagnosis of septic arthritis was not made until 21 April. C was left with a permanently unstable hip, and a discrepancy in leg length. Had D1 referred her to hospital on 15 April, as he should have done, and had C then been prescribed the right type of antibiotic in hospital, she would have fully recovered. No claim against the hospital was brought by C (which was 'highly unfortunate', said the court). **Held (2:1):** the negligent treatment which C received in hospital was not an intervening act. D1's delay retained its causative potency, because the less time that C was in hospital before the critical point of no return was reached re the infection, the more chance there was of not being able to give appropriate treatment. The GP's negligent delay did indirectly increase the risk of C's injury and was to that extent causally related to the injury.

Turning to a different scenario, that of 'wrongful conception' claims (discussed in Chapter 2), the leading case of *MacFarlane v Tayside Health Board*[245] confirmed that the parents' failure to either place an unplanned child for adoption, or to abort the child once the unplanned pregnancy was confirmed, will not constitute an intervening act, limiting the doctor D's liability for damages arising from the negligently-performed sterilisation operation. As Lord Slynn remarked, '[t]here was no legal or moral duty to arrange an abortion or an adoption of an unplanned child'.

CAUSATION AND 'PURE OMISSIONS'

Where it is alleged that D did not control or supervise TP with adequate care, or did not warn C of TP's propensities for violence – and then TP harms C – TP's acts are **not** an intervening act. As discussed in the previous section, it would not be legally logical for D to escape liability on the basis of an intervening act, when the very wrong alleged against D is that he should have taken steps to prevent TP from harming C.

However, a separate legal issue is how the causal link is proven in the case of 'pure omissions'.

§8.26   Where D's breach amounts to a 'pure omission' – including an omission to supervise or monitor a third party (TP), thereby providing TP with an opportunity to negligently or intentionally harm C's person or property – D's omission can cause C's harm, on the basis that D *created the opportunity* for that harm to occur. It is an indirect means of establishing causation, albeit that the 'but-for' test will be met in such cases.

[245] [2000] 2 AC 59 (HL), quote at 68 (Lord Slynn).

Pure omissions or non-feasances can undoubtedly constitute a 'cause' of harm in English law, based upon the more elliptical method of proving that D *created the opportunity for harm to occur*. Some classic 'omissions' cases (discussed earlier in Chapter 3) demonstrate this.

In *Haynes v Harwood*,[246] a carter, D, left a horse-drawn van unattended in a crowded street, and the horses bolted when a boy threw a stone at them. C, a police officer, suffered injury in stopping the horses before they injured a woman and children who were in the path of the bolting animals. The most directly responsible causes of the damage were:

- the actions of the mischievous boy; and
- the inherent nature of the animals, susceptible to sudden noise and movement.

The carter merely created a source of danger by leaving his horses unattended in a busy street, but that was sufficient for causation.

In *Goldman v Hargrave*,[247] an occupier of a West Australian station property, D, failed to douse a burning tree which had been struck by lightning. He felled the tree, preparatory to its being removed by a contractor. Unfortunately, the fire spread to adjoining land when gusty hot winds blew up. The direct and immediate causes of the disaster were:

- the naturally windy conditions and tinder-dry land; and
- the actions of the contractor in not removing the tree sooner.

The occupier was liable to the adjoining landowners in negligence.

Hence, pure omissions on D's part have not precluded causation in English law, quite the reverse.

Similarly, where D fails to prevent damage to C, brought about by the deliberate or criminal acts of TP who was under the control or supervision of D, causation can be established against D on the same basis. D committed no positive act against C, of course – TP did that – but D may still be liable in negligence, on the basis of this weaker causal link of creating an opportunity for harm to occur.

In *Dorset Yacht Co Ltd v Home Office*,[248] facts previously, **held:** causation proven: 'the injurious interference with the boats was caused by the acts and omissions of [D's] officers in bringing the Borstal boys to Brownsea Island and keeping them there under detention for compulsory training and yet taking no care for the safety of [Cs'] boat and the other boat or boats in the immediate vicinity of the place where the boys were being kept'. In *Carmarthenshire CC v Lewis*,[249] a kindergarten, D, was liable for failing to keep its premises secure, allowing toddler David to escape onto the main road into the path of Mr Lewis's lorry. Mr Lewis, C, was killed in trying to avoid David. **Held:** causation proven. The kindergarten created an opportunity for harm to occur to C.

It should be reiterated that, in these scenarios, the 'but-for' test is actually met. If D's breach had been hypothetically fixed (i.e., if the Borstal boys had been properly supervised, and if David had not been allowed to go wandering off), then the damage to C would not have occurred.

---

[246] [1935] 1 KB 146 (CA) (also known as *Hynes v Harwood*).   [247] [1967] 1 AC 645 (PC).
[248] [1970] AC 1004 (HL) 1053 (Lord Pearson).   [249] [1955] AC 549 (HL) 571.

Hence, these scenarios are not exceptions to the 'but-for' test. They are truly applications of it, but in a particular circumstance.

Similarly, were a duty of care to be owed by a 'Bad Samaritan' to C, whom that bystander did not rescue or assist (which is not presently the case, as discussed in Chapter 2), the causal link would be capable of being proven on the basis that D's failure to rescue/assist created the opportunity for C's harm to occur. The dilemma can be demonstrated by means of Lord Keith's example of the blind man (from *Yuen Kun Yeu v A-G of Hong Kong*[250]), who is observed to walk over the edge of a cliff, and the bystander, D, shouts no warning at all. There are two innocent potential causes of the blind man's death or injury – his own disability, and the natural topography of the land – together with the breach, i.e., D's failure to shout the warning. D did not create the terrain or the disability, but his failure to shout created the opportunity for the harm to happen to the blind man. Hence, despite Lord Rodger's assertion in *Mitchell v Glasgow CC*, that, in the case of a person watching a child drown in a pool or a blind man walking out into traffic, that observer 'plays no part in the events',[251] a successful causal link would nevertheless be likely in 'Bad Samaritan' cases.

'LOSS OF A CHANCE' CLAIMS

What 'loss of a chance' means

§8.27   'Loss of a chance' claims arise when C frames his damage (resulting from D's breach) as the loss of a chance either to avoid a worse outcome or to gain a better outcome – and not as personal injury, property damage, psychiatric injury, or economic loss.

'Loss of chance claims' arise where C is having difficulty in proving a causal link between D's breach and the traditional forms of damage (physical, property, psychiatric or economic). This is to be distinguished from scenarios where C has already proven D's liability in negligence (including causation) – then lost chances, or the prospect that the outcome for C may get much worse, can be recovered as heads of damage. That is a **quantification** issue. In *Grieves v FT Everard & Sons Ltd*,[252] Lord Scott confirmed that, if D's breach caused C some physical injury, so that a tortious cause of action has accrued to C, then C 'can recover damages not simply for his injury in its present state, but also for the risk that the injury may worsen in the future, and for his present and ongoing anxiety that that may happen'. However, those matters that may occur in the future, which could diminish C's damages, 'have nothing to do with C's inability to prove causation to a balance of probabilities or the doctrine of loss of a chance; by the time this stage of the argument is reached, [C] will already have succeeded on the issue of causation' (per *Aercap Partners 1 Ltd v Avia Asset Management AB*[253]).

However, it is quite another matter, where C cannot prove that D's breach caused any actionable physical injury on the balance of probabilities – and so, in order to found a claim for damage which the tort of negligence requires, lost chances have been framed *as damage themselves*. This is a far more controversial proposition than merely claiming lost chances as heads of damage consequent upon already-proven injury. As Baroness Hale put it in *Gregg v Scott*, using loss of a chance is a 'radical way of defining [C's] damage'.[254]

---

[250] [1988] AC 175 (PC) 192.   [251] [2009] UKHL 11, [2009] 1 AC 874, [55].

[252] [2007] UKHL 39, [2008] 1 AC 281, [67] (emphasis added).

[253] [2010] EWHC 2431 (Comm) [76] (Gross LJ).   [254] [2005] UKHL 2, [2005] 2 AC 176, [209].

In some contexts (notably, in economic loss cases), the law **may** compensate that 'lost chance' as a type of damage. However, English law has set its face against awarding C compensation for a reduced chance of a more favourable outcome in personal injury claims (at the widest), and in medical negligence claims (at the narrowest). The basis for the distinctions can be finely-drawn and policy-driven, and the reasons for rejecting loss of a chance claims (especially in medical negligence) can be multifarious (and differ across judgments in the one case) – all of which adds considerably to the complexity of this area of causation.

Each context is considered in turn.

In the medical negligence context

§8.28   Where a breach by a healthcare practitioner, D, has not caused patient C's physical injury on the balance of probabilities, C may yet have lost a chance of a better outcome which can be measured in percentage terms. However, to date, English law does <u>not</u> uphold a compensable claim, where C has lost a chance of better outcome of <50%. However, the prospect of a successful 'loss of a chance' claim has not been entirely ruled out, judicially.

Leading cases, and outcomes

In the two leading House of Lords' decisions on this point – principally, in *Gregg v Scott*, and much earlier in *Hotson v East Berkshire HA* – neither C had any success. The reasons were wide-ranging. The area has been complicated somewhat by the fact that, in *Gregg v Scott*, the dissenters, Lords Hope and Nicholls, vehemently disagreed with the proposition that a loss of a chance claim should not be recognised for physical injury claims – and Lord Phillips, of the majority, did not entirely rule out the prospect of a future successful claim. Nor was it entirely ruled out in *Hotson* either.

> In *Gregg v Scott*,[255] Malcolm Gregg, C, consulted Dr Scott, his GP, D, about a lump under his arm. D diagnosed it as a benign lump of fatty tissue, without further investigation. Nine months later, non-Hodgkin's lymphoma was diagnosed. During that period of delay in achieving the correct diagnosis, C's chance of cure (i.e., survival disease-free for 10 years) dropped from 42% to 25%. C could not prove, on the balance of probabilities, that the delay caused the non-Hodgkin's lymphoma. C sued D for the loss of a chance of a cure over the 9-month period of delay. **Held:** the lost chance of better survival prospects was not a compensable harm. In *Hotson v East Berkshire HA*,[256] the trial judge held that, when Stephen Hotson, C, 13, first presented at the hospital following a fall from a tree, he had a 25% chance of avoiding necrosis of his hip joint. However, 5 days later, after the hospital, D's, negligently-delayed diagnosis and treatment of his hip, the hip joint was doomed to necrosis, and whatever 25% chance existed, of saving the hip joint, when he first turned up to hospital, was lost. **Held:** the lost 25% chance was not a compensable harm.

Later, in *Barker v Corus UK Ltd*,[257] the House of Lords confirmed that *Fairchild's* exceptional theorem of causation did not permit the *Gregg v Scott*-type lost chance to be compensated for.

---

[255] [2005] 2 AC 176 (HL).   [256] [1987] AC 750 (HL).
[257] [2006] UKHL 20, [2006] 2 AC 572, [5] (Lord Hoffmann), also, [57] (Lord Scott).

The contrasting viewpoints in *Gregg v Scott* are noted in the following Table:[258]

The contrasting viewpoints in *Gregg v Scott*	
The majority (Lords Hoffmann and Phillips and Baroness Hale) held that the claim for a lost chance was not compensable because ...	The dissenters held that the claim was compensable because ...
• this was analogous to *Wilsher's* case, because it was a multi-agent case, in which no one cause achieved the balance of probabilities threshold. The problem in both *Wilsher* and *Gregg* was that, whilst the doctors', Ds', breaches undoubtedly increased the risk of harm to their patients, Martin Wilsher and Malcolm Gregg, a mere increase in risk is not enough in multi-agent cases to render Ds liable. In *Gregg*, there were three possible causes of C's lost chance of survival in the 9 months: the missed diagnosis (the breach); C's lifestyle; and C's genetic make-up. To hold that the breach merely increased the chance of a bad outcome for Mr Gregg (an early death) was not sufficient. Otherwise, D would have been liable in *Wilsher* for increasing the chances of the baby sustaining RLF. Hence, *Gregg* was a *Wilsher*-type case – the articulation of the damages was different (the former articulated it as a lost chance, and the latter articulated it as blindness), but both were multi-agent cases. Hence, the *McGhee/Fairchild* 'single agent' exception could not apply to either of them (Lord Hoffmann); • neither *Hotson* (who lost a 25% chance of a good outcome) nor *Gregg* (whose chance of a good outcome reduced from 42% to 25%) was a true 'loss of a chance' case at all – what chance had each C lost? On the balance of probabilities, they were both always doomed to an adverse outcome at the point of breach, because Stephen Hotson had a 75% chance that his hip joint would turn necrotic from the minute he fell from the tree, and Malcolm Gregg had a 58% chance of not surviving the cancer at the point of the missed diagnosis (Baroness Hale, Lord Phillips);	• before the negligence, Mr Gregg had a less-than-evens chance (45%) of avoiding the deterioration in his condition which ultimately occurred, and the delay did not extinguish this chance, but reduced it by roughly half – what has to be valued is what the patient has lost, and this patient lost *some* chance of survival (from 45% down to 25%). That 'lost chance' was calculable, whether the prospects of survival were better or less than 50% at the time that the negligent diagnosis occurred (Lord Hope);

258 The points are at: [2005] 2 AC 176 (HL) [90], [114], [172], [189]–[190] (majority); [43], [121] (dissenters).

The majority (Lords Hoffmann and Phillips and Baroness Hale) held that the claim for a lost chance was not compensable because …	The dissenters held that the claim was compensable because …
• if causation was upheld in *Gregg*, then it would have to be on a 'piecemeal' basis to remedy a perceived injustice, and 'the coherence of our common law would be destroyed' (Lord Phillips), plus it would lead to much uncertainty in many medical negligence cases (Lord Hoffman); • as a policy reason, if C succeeded in *Gregg*, then 'possible rather than probable causation' would be the basis for liability, and that 'would be so radical a change in our law as to amount to a legislative act. It would have enormous consequences for insurance companies and the NHS … any such change should be left to Parliament' (Lord Hoffmann); • Mr Gregg's 'lost chance' was not borne out in reality, because he was very much alive at trial, and with good prospects of survival. A loss of a chance claim would be difficult to prove where C had >50% prospects of a good outcome at trial. *Gregg* was a much weaker case than *Hotson*, because Stephen Hotson was doomed to endure a necrotic hip joint at the point of breach (according to the trial judge), and he had lost whatever chance he had of avoiding that outcome – whereas, at the point of breach, Mr Gregg's chances of survival lay in the future, and happily, the chance of an adverse outcome had not materialised (Baroness Hale).	• 'it cannot be right to adopt a procedure having the effect that, in law, a patient's prospects of recovery are treated as non-existent whenever they exist, but fall short of 50%. If the law were to proceed in this way, it would deserve to be likened to the proverbial ass' (Lord Nicholls).

The principle of *Gregg v Scott* has been followed since, in a variety of medical negligence cases involving missed diagnoses, where the breach did not cause C's eventual damage on the balance of probabilities. To mention a couple:[259]

In *Beech v Timney*,[260] Joseph Beech, C, 35, suffered from recurring headaches and consulted his GP, Dr Timney, D, in Mar 2003. His blood pressure was recorded to be 110/80, but C claimed that it was recorded inaccurately, and was actually 180/100. D attributed C's headaches to ergonomic factors, and recommended postural exercises, and C also had his wisdom teeth removed. C consulted D again in May 2003, complaining of facial pain and 'bad heads'. In Nov 2003, C had a catastrophic stroke, which caused severe and permanent disability. C claimed that, had D measured and correctly recorded his high blood pressure, C would have embarked on a pharmaceutical treatment regime

---

[259] *JD v Mather* [2012] EWHC 3063 (QB) (missed cancerous growth); *Oliver v Williams* [2013] EWHC 600 (QB) (missed ovarian cancer).
[260] [2013] EWHC 2226 (Admin) [82].

which would probably have prevented the stroke. However, the medical evidence was that C would probably have suffered the stroke, even if D had started that treatment in Mar 2003, because such a programme had to be in place for 3–5 years before a 50% reduction in stroke risk occurred. By Nov 2003, the treatment would have had 'negligible' effect. **Held:** causation failed. Whatever chance of a better outcome that C may have lost, because the treatment was not started in Mar 2003, could not be claimed: 'the case falls squarely within the parameters of [*Gregg v Scott*]'. In *Carter v MOJ*,[261] Cheryl Carter, C, 34, was an inmate of D's prison, Cookham Wood, and claimed that, on three separate occasions, she consulted a medical officer as to the significance of a lump in her right breast, but it remained untreated. Eventually, after C's release, a large 10cm x 8cm tumour was diagnosed, for which C required chemotherapy and a mastectomy. C argued that, had she been referred for specialist treatment when she first alerted the medical officer with her concerns about the lump, the breast cancer prognosis would have been 'materially better than the one resulting from the eventual referral in November 2005 at the behest of her then GP'. **Held:** breach proven, but 'taking into account potential difficulties in distinguishing her case from that of [*Gregg v Scott*], the quantum of her claim may, at best, be moderate.'

Could a 'loss of chance' claim succeed in the future?

Despite their outcomes which rejected loss of a chance claims where C has suffered personal injury, neither *Hotson* nor *Gregg v Scott* entirely ruled out 'loss of chance' claims, according to senior English judiciary. Although Lord Bridge, in *Hotson*, perceived formidable difficulties in the concept of 'the lost chance of a better medical result which might have been achieved by prompt diagnosis and correct treatment', Lord Mackay remarked that it would be unwise to lay down a rule that a patient could never succeed by proving loss of a chance in a medical negligence case.[262]

The Court of Appeal has since indicated the same. In *Wright v Cambridge Medical Group*,[263] Lord Neuberger MR said that *Gregg v Scott* 'does not conclusively shut out, as a matter of strict logic', loss of a chance claims, and that, in this 'difficult area', 'the question would be appropriate for reconsideration by the Supreme Court'. However, no recovery for loss of a chance was countenanced in *Wright*, because, 'at this level, we should probably not expand the loss of a chance doctrine into the realm of clinical negligence'. Elias LJ agreed that *Gregg v Scott* 'effectively precludes this court from applying those principles to personal injury – and particularly clinical negligence – cases'.

For example, proving that C lost a 'chance of a better outcome' would appear to be crucial to the prospects of distinguishing *Gregg v Scott*. In *Hotson*, on the balance of probabilities (in fact, with a 75% probability), too many blood vessels were ruptured by the fall from the tree, and the hip joint was doomed to turn necrotic. Even prior to the occurrence of D's breach, a certain outcome was 'ordained', regardless of the delayed diagnosis and treatment. According to Lord Bridge in *Hotson*, '[t]he debate on the loss of a chance cannot arise where there has been a positive finding that ... the damage complained of had already been sustained or had become inevitable'.[264] That was sufficient to rule out any 'loss of chance' claim in that case. Similarly,

---

[261] [2010] EWHC 60 (QB), [30].

[262] [1987] AC 750 (HL), with quotes at 782 and 786, respectively. See too: *Bank of Credit and Commerce Intl SA (in liq) v Ali (No 2)* [2002] EWCA Civ 82, [71] (Robert Walker LJ).

[263] [2011] EWCA Civ 669, [2013] QB 312, with quotes at [84] and [93], respectively.

[264] [1987] AC 750 (HL) 782, 792. Lord Ackner agreed, at 793.

Mr Gregg's chances of survival were already less than the balance of probabilities (around 42%) when he first presented with the lump under his arm. Hence, whilst the delay reduced his chances of survival by about 20%, at the point of breach, Mr Gregg probably would not have survived anyway. Ostensibly, neither had lost a 'chance of a better outcome'.

Clearly, there has been a great deal of disquiet about that proposition, at senior judicial levels. It will be recalled that the dissenters in *Gregg* considered that a dropped chance of survival from 42% to 25% was something of value that C had lost. Other appellate judges have agreed, with Laws LJ commenting, in *Coudert Bros v Normans Bay Ltd (t/a Illingworth, Morris Ltd)*, that surely it should not be necessary for Mr Gregg to prove that he had >50% of a cure, in order to recover any damages for loss of a chance, because if it was, then 'I am driven to an unhappy sense that the common law has lost its way'.[265] In other contexts of professional negligence (e.g., solicitors who did not issue writs in time, such as in *Kitchen v RAF Assn*,[266] or in breach of contract cases, such as *Chaplin v Hicks*[267]), general damages have been awarded for loss of a chance, even though the chance lost was < 50%.[268]

In any event, if C **did** lose something which was assessed as a >50% prospect of a better outcome for C at the time of D's breach, then it would clearly be a distinguishable scenario from *Gregg v Scott*. This has been suggested, in dicta, by the Court of Appeal since.

> In *Yearworth v North Bristol NHS Trust*,[269] C and another five men were diagnosed with cancer, and were treated with a course of chemotherapy. The treating hospital, D, advised C that the treatment might damage their fertility. C agreed to produce samples of semen prior to the start of the treatment, so that it could be stored at D's fertility unit. The sperm was to be stored in liquid nitrogen (at minus 196°C) at D's facility, free of charge. Unfortunately, the amount of liquid nitrogen in the tanks in which it was stored fell below the requisite level, and the automatic topping-up of the levels did not work. The sperm perished irretrievably. **Held:** no damage occurred, as loss of the sperm did not constitute 'personal injury': 'it would be a fiction to hold that damage to a substance generated by a person's body, inflicted after its removal for storage purposes, constituted a bodily or "personal injury" to him ... We must deal in realities'. Also, no loss of a chance was compensable either.

The *Yearworth* court held that *Gregg v Scott* 'compelled a conclusion that, unless [C] were to demonstrate a greater than even chance that the lost sperm could have been used in order to achieve conception, then ... they could not claim in respect of such physical damage to their overall ability to become fathers'. This indicates the sort of distinguishable case that may succeed in the future.

An alternative claim

Although proving that C lost a compensable chance of a better outcome may not be legally possible, nevertheless, Baroness Hale pointed out, in *Gregg v Scott*,[270] that someone in Mr Gregg's position would have been entitled to a smaller type of damages claim 'on conventional [but-for causation] principles', had the claim been framed differently at trial – *viz*, damages for the following, as caused by the delayed diagnosis:

---

[265] [2004] EWCA Civ 215, [68]. In the same case, Waller LJ also expressed 'disquiet' about the trial judge's conclusions and the CA's dismissal of the appeal in *Gregg*.

[266] [1958] 1 WLR 563 (HL) 576–77. Also: *Cook v Swinfen* [1967] 1 WLR 457 (HL) 460.

[267] [1911] 2 KB 786.

[268] Noted, e.g., in: *Dyne, Hughes & Archer (a firm) v Cross* (CA, 11 Apr 1990).

[269] [2009] EWCA Civ 37, [2010] 1 QB 1, [23]–[24].   [270] [2005] UKHL 2, [2005] 2 AC 176, [205]–[207].

- any extra pain and suffering and loss of amenity resulting from the delay of diagnosis of 9 months. If the misdiagnosis had not happened and the cancer been detected straightaway, C would likely have enjoyed a longer period before more radical chemotherapy, and C would be entitled to damages for that ('to reflect the acceleration in his suffering'); and if the pain and suffering was greater because of 'the anguish of knowing that his disease could have been detected earlier', then that too would be compensable;
- any financial losses that C suffered during that delay of 9 months would also be recoverable;
- finally, any loss of expectation of life caused by the delay would be compensable – had C been treated when he should have been treated, 'his median life expectancy then would have been x years, whereas given the delay in treatment, his median life expectancy from then is x minus y ... There might therefore be a modest claim in respect of the "lost years".'

This alternative type of claim was taken up subsequently:

> In *JD v Mather*,[271] JD, C, consulted his GP, D, on 8 Mar 2006, being concerned about a growth in his right groin. C complained that the growth was growing, itching and bled when he had scratched it. D diagnosed it as a seborrhoeic wart, and nothing to worry about. The groin lesion turned out to be cancerous. It was diagnosed correctly in Oct 2006. The evidence was that, as at Mar 2006, C's chances of a cure (i.e., survival for >10 years), with an ulcerated primary tumour with at least one regional nodal micrometastasis, was <50%. **Held:** C's principal claim was unsustainable, per *Gregg v Scott*. However, the failure to diagnose the tumour reduced C's life expectancy by three years, which was compensable (damages to be agreed, or tried).

In the economic context

In comparison with the less-than-sympathetic view which English law adopts towards loss of chance claims in medical negligence, the loss of an economic chance has been permitted in two situations, *viz*, where (1) the loss is of a chance to secure a legal right (where rights are treated as equivalent to the loss of a property right), and (2) the loss is of a chance to follow up an economic opportunity. Recently, in *McCrindle Group Ltd v MaClay Murray & Spens*, the Scottish Outer House reiterated that 'it is important ... to distinguish those cases which involved the loss of a right, and those which did not.'[272]

Loss of legal rights

§8.29 Where D's breach causes C to lose a legal right, then even if the prospects of successfully pursuing that legal right fall short of the balance of probabilities, C may prove that the lost chance is compensable. It is sufficient that C had reasonable prospects of converting that legal right into an economic benefit.

The types of legal rights that the law has compensated for under loss of a chance, include the following:

> In *Chaplin v Hicks*,[273] C lost a contractual entitlement to compete for a prize. In *Kitchin v RAF Assn*,[274] C lost the chance of pursuing his legal claim (a right to sue) because his solicitors, D, failed to file the claim within the limitation period, such that D's negligence deprived C of a right of action.

---

[271] [2012] EWHC 3063 (QB) [43]–[48].   [272] [2013] ScotCS 72 (OH) [123] (Lord Hodge).
[273] [1911] 2 KB 786.   [274] [1958] 1 WLR 563 (CA).

In these 'loss of right'-type cases, the court has to quantify that lost right, which (according to the Court of Appeal in *Parabola Investments Ltd v Browallia Cal Ltd*[275]) is a case of assessing the prospects, in percentage terms, of C's obtaining a positive outcome from the exercise of that right. C does not have to prove that he would have obtained an economic benefit, via that right, on the balance of probabilities: '[r]ather, it estimates the loss by making the best attempt it can to evaluate the chances great or small (unless those chances amount to no more than remote speculation), taking all significant factors into account'. More recently, the Court of Appeal suggested, in *Lillington v MOD*,[276] that C's lost right to seek a promotion due to negligently-caused injury could also fall within the *Gregg v Scott*-type loss of a chance cases (albeit that the suggestion was not taken up by counsel in that case).

Loss of economic opportunity

§8.30   Where D's breach causes C to lose the chance to pursue economic opportunities, then C has not lost a legal right, but rather, an opportunity to pursue an economic benefit. C must prove the so-called '*Allied Maples* conditions' in order to prove that causal link.

This type of claim is 'more in the realm of cases concerned with negligent failure to advise, where the client is deprived of information which he might have used to his economic benefit, rather than the loss of an item of property such as a right' (as explained in *McCrindle*[277]). In order to recover damages for the lost chance, C must prove three steps ('the *Allied Maples* conditions'):

i.   on the balance of probabilities, C would have taken action to obtain the financial opportunity (either on his own account, or by approaching a third party);

ii. if acquiring the financial benefit depends on the hypothetical action of a third party (TP), then C must also prove that there was a real or substantial chance that the third party would have conferred the benefit on C; and

iii. C must prove, on the balance of probabilities, that he would have accepted that benefit.

This is an application of the principle in *Mallett v McMonagle*,[278] in that the court applies a balance of probabilities approach to proof of past facts and events.

> In *Allied Maples Group Ltd v Simmons & Simmons*,[279] Allied Maples, C, lost the chance to negotiate a warranty or other protection in a share purchase agreement, as a result of their solicitor's, D's, negligent failure to advise. **Held:** causation failed. C had to prove on balance of probabilities that he would have negotiated with the seller to obtain the benefit of the warranty, and C also had to prove that there was a real and substantial chance that the seller would have conferred the warranty. These could not be proven.

The *Allied Maples* scenario is distinguishable from the 'loss of right' case, because, in *Allied Maples*, D's negligent failure to advise did not cause C to lose a legal right. It merely deprived C of information which he might have used positively in negotiating further benefit. As the court in *McCrindle* put it, the *Allied Maples* court 'was not valuing a lost right, but was dealing

[275] [2010] EWCA Civ 486, [25] (Toulson LJ).
[276] [2015] EWCA Civ 775, [4] (Vos LJ) (lost chance to pass an exam and become a corporal).
[277] [2013] ScotCS 72 (OH) [125].   [278] [1970] AC 166 (HL).   [279] [1995] 1 WLR 1602 (HL).

with the prior question of causation'.[280] The *Allied Maples* approach is difficult to apply, however, because the court must assess what TP would have done, and whether C would have accepted the benefit. Judging what one party hypothetically may have done is difficult enough – but judging what C would have done, where his interests were not necessarily aligned with TP's, can be even more so. It is an exercise in reconstruction and hypothesis, which is highly dependent upon the evidence given by the parties, well after D's breach occurred, as to what they would have done, had the breach not happened.

> In *Dayman v Lawrence Graham*,[281] Mrs Fielding, C, sold her house and bought another. She was subsequently declared bankrupt, due to her indebtedness to Royal Bank of Scotland. C's solicitors, D, handled the sale and purchase, but did not recommend to C to negotiate her release from debts to RBS in return for payment of the sale proceeds. **Held:** causation proven. Applying the *Allied Maples* approach: (1) C proved, on the balance of probabilities, that she would have approached RBS; (2) there was a real or substantial chance that RBS would have responded to such an approach by proposing a deal to C; and (3) on the balance of probabilities, C would have accepted that deal.

In any event, the support for 'loss of a chance' claims in the economic context cannot be translated to the personal injury context, where English law has set its face against the loss of a better physical outcome as a compensable damage. It is one of the rare instances in which C's claim for economic loss is treated more favourably than where C suffers from some physical detriment allegedly arising from D's breach.

SUPERVENING EVENT #1: D2'S SUPERVENING TORT DAMAGED AN ALREADY-DAMAGED CLAIMANT

§8.31   Intervening acts have some factual linkage to D1's original breach, in that the breach created the opportunity for the intervening act to occur (i.e., the intervening act would not have occurred, had the original breach not occurred). By contrast, supervening acts are unrelated to the original tort, and are coincidental in occurrence.

This section concerns the unusual, but problematical, scenario of where D1 and D2, via separate and consecutive acts, injure C, such that D1 caused C a particular injury – but that same injury would have happened anyway at a later date (but prior to trial), courtesy of D2's unrelated act. These scenarios are treated as supervening events. According to the Court of Appeal in *Rahman v Arearose Ltd*, they arise where 'the effects of the first tort, which caused injuries to [C], were obliterated by the second [tort]', i.e., different and unrelated torts committed at entirely different times against the same C.[282] Supervening events may also occur where D caused C's harm – but naturally-occurring events in C's life would have led to the same injury.

The scenario causes legal difficulties. A number of English judges have acknowledged the conundrum: '[t]he law's approach to causation is pragmatic, where there are several concurrent or successive factors operating to cause injury' (per *Reynard v Exquisite Cuisine Ltd*[283]); the task of allocating liability involves 'swings and roundabouts', and some 'inevitable imprecision' (per Moore-Bick LJ in *Smithurst v Sealant Construction Services Ltd*[284]); and cases which

---

[280] [2013] ScotCS 72 (OH) [131] (Lord Hodge).   [281] [2008] EWHC 2036 (Ch) (Judge Hodge QC).
[282] [2000] EWCA Civ 190, [2001] QB 351, [31].   [283] [2005] CSOH 146, [51].
[284] [2011] EWCA Civ 1277, [43].

involve supervening events 'all raise, in one form or another, the question: on what disabling supervening events is [D1] entitled to rely to reduce or extinguish the consequences of his tort? Put another way: from what further misfortunes of [C] should [D1] be held entitled to benefit?' (per *Gray v Thames Trains Ltd*[285]).

Notably, there is **no** question of these successive tortfeasors being ***concurrent*** tortfeasors (see 'Multiple defendants', an online chapter), as the supervening acts arose from respective torts committed by separate Ds which were quite unrelated, and which did not concurrently cause a single indivisible injury. Hence, the Civil Liability (Contribution) Act 1978, whereby responsibility for damages can be apportioned between D1 and D2, does **not** apply. It will be the court's responsibility to arrive at a just conclusion, on the evidence, as to the respective damage caused by each D, 'even if it can only do it on a broad-brush basis which then has to be translated into percentages' (as Laws LJ noted in *Rahman*[286]). Wherever the original and supervening torts are concurrent torts, the discussion in this section is irrelevant. In the case of concurrent torts, the 1978 Act must be applied to apportion liability between the concurrent tortfeasors, unless the second tort constitutes an intervening act.

In *Webb v Barclays Bank plc*,[287] facts previously, **held:** Mrs Webb's employer, and the negligent doctor, were concurrent tortfeasors, and hence, apportionment under the 1978 Act applied. Once the Bank's liability for the period up to the amputation was assessed (£53,000), then the liability for the effects of the amputation were apportioned between bank and doctor, in the proportions of 25% and 75%, to reflect that the doctor's negligence 'was much more responsible for the amputation and all that went with it'.

Successive tortfeasors

§8.32 According to the *Baker v Willoughby* principle, where D1 causes C a tortious injury, but that same injury would have occurred later, via a separate, successive and unrelated act committed by D2, D1's liability for damages does not cease at the point at which D2's tort occurs. The 'causation principle' provides that D2 should only be liable for the damage which he inflicted upon C, and no more, i.e., D2 has damaged an already-damaged C.

Baker v Willoughby's principle arises where there are two successive tortfeasors, and two separate acts, which meant that the damages arising from C's injury, caused by D1's act, would have occurred via D2's tort in any event. Under the principle, D1 cannot 'benefit' from D2's tort, and use D2's tort to reduce the extent of damages for which D1 is liable. Specifically, D1's liability for damages does not cease, or cut off, at the point at which D2's tort occurs; D1's liability extends beyond D2's tort. D2 can only be liable for the additional damage which his tort causes, bearing in mind that he has damaged an already-damaged C. Hence, D2 appears to get off relatively lightly from the effects of his negligence against C.

In *Baker v Willoughby*,[288] Mr Baker, C, was injured by the negligent driving of Mr Willoughby, D1, in a car accident in 1964. C's left leg and ankle were left permanently stiff. In 1967, and just before his trial against D1, C was working in a scrap metal yard alone, and was shot in the left leg by two robbers, D2, in an armed robbery. His left leg had to be amputated. D2 (committing the tort of assault)

---

[285] [2009] UKHL 33, [2009] AC 1339, [97] (Lord Brown).   [286] [2001] QB 351 (CA) [23].
[287] [2001] EWCA Civ 1141, [51], citing trial judge Rougier J.   [288] [1970] AC 467.

were never located, and hence, were never sued. The events were entirely unrelated, there was no question of C's being unable to evade the robbers because of his 'gammy leg', which ruled out an intervening act. The question arose as to what damages D1 was liable for. **Held:** D2's tort could not reduce the amount of the damages which D1 had to pay for the particular disabilities caused by D1's breach. Hence, D1 had to pay damages for C's stiff leg (even though it had actually been amputated as a result of the second tort), to the extent that the heads of damage for the stiff leg were still applicable to C, i.e., damages for loss of mobility, damages for loss of amenity and enjoyment of life, and damages for loss of earnings.

There were two key points in *Baker v Willoughby*, re D2's liability for damages:[289]

i. if the robbers, D2, had been capable of being sued, then D2 would have damaged an already-damaged man, and would only have been liable for the very limited damages of the costs of the artificial limb used by C, and damages for pain in the stump of the leg (for those were 'extra damages' incurred by the second tort, the assault of shooting). Additionally, had the robbers D2 been sued, then they would have been liable to Mr Baker, C, for any *additional* loss of earnings brought about by the amputated leg, which were over and above the lost earning capacity which he already suffered by virtue of the stiff leg. D2 has to 'take his victim as he finds him'. By virtue of the causation principle, where D2 has injured an already-injured C (where that injury was inflicted by D1), then D2 is only liable for the 'extra' damage which his negligence caused. If no extra damage was caused (because the injury caused by D1 merged into the injury inflicted by D2), then C is not entitled to recover anything from D2. In *Baker*, however, there was additional damage;

ii. if D1 was only liable for the damages for which he was responsible (i.e., loss of mobility, loss of amenity and enjoyment of life) up to the second tort (the shooting) but not beyond, then that would create an injustice. D2 would still only be liable for the additional damages caused by the shooting. That would then leave a 'gap in the damages' after the shooting, in that C would be left without any damages for the continuing loss of amenity and loss of mobility which the car accident caused him. That is why D1's liability for damages must continue beyond the second tort.

It is a controversial principle which has drawn considerable judicial criticism since. Courts have shown no inclination to extend the principle beyond its strict facts (i.e., successive torts against C by D1, and then D2). Where the subsequent event was a naturally-occurring infirmity (per *Jobling v Associated Dairies Ltd*[290]), or C's own action (per *Gray v Thames Trains Ltd*[291]), the principle does not apply (discussed below).

The principle in *Baker v Willoughby* was, in truth, earlier espoused in the Court of Appeal in 1962 – and has been applied since, with similar controversial results:

In *Performance Cars Ltd v Abraham*,[292] C's car was involved in a collision with D1's car, which damaged the rear wing of C's car. It was not repaired, by the time that C's car was involved in a second accident with D2's car, due to D2's negligent driving. The front wing of C's car was damaged, and to fix the damage, the whole of the lower part of the car would have to be repainted (costing £75).

---

[289] [1970] AC 467 (HL) 493 (Lord Reid).
[290] [1982] AC 794 (HL) 809 (Lord Edmund-Davies), 815 (Lord Russell).
[291] [2009] UKHL 33, [2009] 1 AC 1339, [76], [96] (Sir Anthony Clarke MR).
[292] [1962] 1 QB 33, quote at 40 (Lord Evershed MR).

The same respray would have been required to make good the damage from the first and the second accidents. C sued D1 and recovered judgment for the cost of the respray (£75), but D1 did not satisfy the judgment. C then sued D2 to recover the cost of the respray. **Held:** C could not recover any sum for the respray from D2. D2 had damaged an already-damaged car, and was only liable for the 'extra' damage which his tort caused. There was no *extra* damage, and hence, C could recover nothing from D2: 'the necessity for respraying was not the result of [D2's] wrongdoing, because that necessity already existed'. Given that D2 had injured an already-injured car, 'the damage claimed did not flow from [D2's] wrongdoing. It may no doubt be unfortunate for [C] that the collisions took place in the order in which they did'. In *Rahman v Arearose Ltd*,[293] Mr Rahman, C, branch manager of the Burger King chain at King's Cross, London, was assaulted one night by two gang members. C suffered a fractured orbital wall of his right eye. That assault was due to the negligent system of work established by his employer, D1. The eye injury was medically treated by D2, and a bone graft attempted, but due to D2's negligence, C was blinded, because his optic nerve was severed during the operation. C suffered serious PTSD and depression, with severe impact upon his earning capacity. **Held:** D1, the employer, was liable for the psychiatric injuries (and economic consequences) sustained by C throughout the ordeal of both torts, and for a period of three years beyond the second tort. D2 was liable for the remainder of the future economic loss.

On a timeline: supervening events

point A — a breach by D1, causing C injury (*accident to car's left rear wing in* Performance Cars; *a stiff left leg in* Baker v Willoughby; *injured right eye and psychiatric injuries in* Rahman)

point B — a breach by D2, causing C's injury that merged into the first injury caused by D1 (*accident to car's front left wing; an amputated left leg; blindness to right eye and psychiatric injuries*)

trial — where C's damages, past and future, must be assessed: no cut-off point applies for D1 — liability for damages continues beyond point B

Judicial reaction to the *Baker v Willoughby* principle

It is fair to say that judicial reaction to the correctness of the *Baker v Willoughby* principle – by imposing on D1 liability for damages, for that period after the actions of D2 which 'obliterated' the effects of D1's tort – remains divided.

In favour of the outcome, the Court of Appeal remarked, in *Halsey v Milton Keynes General NHS Trust*,[294] that the decision produced a just and fair result for D1 and D2, albeit that it could cause inconvenience to C if D1 could not be found, or was insolvent. The court reasoned that, as 'a matter of logic and common sense, [*Performance Cars*] is clearly correct', because C was entitled to recover damages from D1 for the losses inflicted by him, and from D2 for any *additional* losses inflicted by him. If D1 was unlocatable or insolvent, then C would not be fully compensated for all the losses that he had suffered from the two accidents, but 'that is not a reason for making each defendant liable for the total loss'. But by corollary, D2 cannot

---

293 [2001] QB 351.   294 [2004] EWCA Civ 576, [2004] 1 WLR 3002, [66]–[70].

be responsible for the consequences of the injury caused by D1, because D2 did not cause C's damage, it had already occurred.

On the other hand, the outcome in *Baker v Willoughby* has been doused in, not cold, but frozen water, by some subsequent judicial statements. For example:

- in *Jobling*,[295] Lord Edmund-Davies could discern 'no convincing juristic or logical principles supportive of the decision in *Baker v Willoughby*, and none were there propounded', and that the result was 'unrealistic'; whilst Lord Keith noted that *Baker* was 'mistaken in approaching the problems common to the case of a supervening tortious act and to that of supervening illness wholly from the point of view of causation', that the result in *Baker* was 'not acceptable'; and Lord Bridge doubted that the ratio of *Baker* 'could be sustained', but may be best regarded as 'a decision on its own facts';
- in *Heil v Rankin*,[296] Otton LJ agreed with Lord Keith in *Jobling* that the principle in *Baker*, of 'ignoring the occurrence of a second tort when awarding damages against [D1], could not be justified on any identifiable juristic basis, but rather was a just and practical solution to avoid the barrier to full compensation that would arise if the normal rules were applied to their full extent';
- in *Gray v Thames Trains*,[297] Lord Rodger labelled *Baker v Willoughby* as 'uncomfortable company';
- in *L(R) v Minister for Health and Children*,[298] the Irish High Court noted that the problem of supervening events occurring before the date of assessment of damages was a 'vexed question', for which neither *Jobling* nor *Baker* had provided a 'clear or persuasive solution'. In fact, the Irish Court was quite damning of the House of Lords' consideration of supervening events, noting that 'the outcome of their extensive consideration of the subject was defeat, in the sense that they were unable, individually or collectively, to convincedly adopt a set of principles to apply, both in circumstance of the supervening event being tortious and non-tortious'.

However, despite these numerous reservations, *Baker v Willoughby* retains its standing as authoritative law in England.

SUPERVENING EVENT #2: NON-TORTIOUS REASONS WOULD HAVE LED TO THE SAME DAMAGE

§8.33   According to the *Jobling* principle, where D has caused some injury to C – and then, after the initial tort but prior to trial, C suffers from an infirmity or illness which would have caused the same injury in any event – D cannot be liable for damages beyond the point at which the naturally-occurring physical infirmity arose.

Where D's breach causes C injury – but a subsequent non-tortious event would, on the balance of probabilities, have caused C the same type of injury in any event – D must not be liable for more damages than is fair and just.

According to the principle derived from *Jobling v Associated Dairies*,[299] D is not liable to C for the effects of the breach, after the point at which C would have suffered the same damage

---

[295] [1982] AC 794 (HL) 808–9 (Lord Edmund-Davies), 815 (Lord Keith), 821 (Lord Bridge).
[296] [2001] PIQR Q3, [17].   [297] [2009] UKHL 33, [2009] 1 AC 1339, [76].
[298] [2001] IEHC 64, [2001] 1 IR 744, [16].   [299] [1982] AC 794 (HL).

through supervening illness – even though C would have (hypothetically) continued to suffer that very disability from D's breach, if the supervening infirmity had not arisen. There is a limit, or cut-off, to D's responsibility for the damage to C:

> In *Jobling v Associated Dairies Ltd*, Mr Jobling, C, suffered a back injury which was caused by the breach of statutory duty by his employer, Associated Dairies Ltd, D. This impairment reduced his earning capacity, because he could only be given light duties. Three years later (and before trial), C was found to be suffering from a spinal disease, myelopathy, an unrelated illness, which would have precluded his continuing to work in any event. The question arose as to what damages D should be liable for. **Held:** D could only be liable to C for damages up to the point at which the naturally-occurring infirmity arose, but not beyond that. D's liability ceased at that point.

If Mr Jobling's condition had arisen post-trial, such that he had already obtained damages for D's breach, but then it turned out that he was unable to work because of his naturally-occurring infirmity, his damages payout would never be reassessed, to take account of the fact that C would have been disabled from work, even had D's negligence not occurred. In that respect, Mr Jobling is perceived to be at a disadvantage – even though courts typically reduce damages assessments for any C, to take account of the 'vicissitudes of life' (i.e., future contingencies affecting earning capacity, as discussed in Chapter 11).

As Lord Diplock noted in *Mallett v McMonagle*,[300] whatever discounting of the damages must occur in this scenario is solely a question of assessment of damages, and not strictly of causation *per se*. Lord Keith agreed with this view in *Jobling*: 'when an event ... has actually happened prior to the trial date, that event will fall to be taken into account in the assessment of damages'.[301]

The *Jobling* principle is also applied where C would have suffered the same damage via *his own conduct*, and not via illness or infirmity. The important point is that, where it is not a case of two successive tortfeasors D1 and D2, the *Jobling* principle continues to apply.

> In *Gray v Thames Trains Ltd*,[302] Mr Gray, C, was a passenger on a train which was involved in the Ladbroke Grove rail crash near Paddington. The crash was caused by the negligence of Thames Trains, D. In the accident, C suffered only minor injuries, but later suffered from PTSD. While being treated for that, C became enraged at a drunken pedestrian, Mr Boultwood, who had stepped in front of his car. He went to the house of his girlfriend's parents, took a knife, located the pedestrian, and stabbed him to death. C gave himself up to the police, pleaded guilty to manslaughter, and thereafter was detained indefinitely in a mental prison facility. C sued D for damages relating to his conviction, detention, feelings of remorse, and guilt, and damage to his reputation. It was accepted that he would not have committed the killing, but for the PTSD. **Held:** C could not claim damages for any lost earnings for the period after his arrest and detention for manslaughter, as that would have meant that his earning capacity ceased in any event. D was not liable to compensate C for his losses after the arrest, following *Jobling*.

Notably, *Gray* was a different case from *Jobling*, though. In *Jobling*, C was 'overtaken before trial by a wholly unconnected and disabling illness', i.e., that of myelopathy, but that event had nothing to do with D's conduct. By contrast, in *Gray*, C was 'overtaken before trial' by arrest and detention which prevented him from working because of the manslaughter, but C would

---

[300] [1970] AC 166 (HL) 178. [301] [1982] AC 794 (HL) 813.
[302] [2009] UKHL 33, [2009] AC 1339, quote at [49].

not have committed that manslaughter, if he had not been suffering from the PTSD which was a direct consequence of D's negligently-caused train crash. Nevertheless, despite this difference, the *Jobling* principle applied. Various judges in *Gray* justified the application of *Jobling* as follows:[303]

- C was 'wholly blameless' for the back condition that stopped D's liability for damages in *Jobling*, so it would be a 'strange conclusion' if, in *Gray*, C could 'ignore a vicissitude for which he has been held responsible (if only to a diminished extent)';
- the outcome was consistent, because Mr Gray had been lawfully detained, first in prison and then in a psychiatric prison hospital, for the public's protection. Hence, it would inconsistent with the policy underlying these orders by a criminal court, for a civil court to award Mr Gray damages for loss of earnings relating to the period when he was subject to those orders.

Summarising the two leading cases in diagrammatic form:

On a timeline: supervening events	
point A	a breach by D, causing C injury (*Associated Dairy's breach of statutory duty at work; Thames Trains' negligence in train safety*)
point B	some physical infirmity or other non-tortiously-caused detriment happened to C, prior to trial, which produced the same outcome for C as the breach did (*Mr Jobling's myelopathy; Mr Gray's arrest for manslaughter*)
trial	C's damages, past and future, must be assessed: D's liability for damages cuts off at point B

Hence, the *Jobling* principle cannot be applied – to limit the damages payable by D1 – where there are successive tortfeasors (D1, and then D2) who have both committed breaches against C and which have caused the same injury to C. That scenario is governed by the *Baker v Willoughby* principle. As Lord Rodger put it in *Gray v Thames Trains*,[304] it would not be right to put *Gray*, *Jobling*, and like cases, in the 'uncomfortable company' of *Baker v Willoughby*.

THE BURDEN OF PROOF

§8.34   The burden of proving that D's breach caused C's damage always rests with C. English law has refused to reverse the burden of proof, where C has confronted an 'evidential' gap in proving a causal link between D's breach and C's damage, whether due to factual uncertainty or the obfuscatory effects of D's breach.

The general position
The burden of proving causation must be discharged by C on the balance of probabilities. It is a basic tenet of English law. Judicially: '[C] must prove not only negligence or breach of duty, but also that such fault caused or materially contributed to his injury' (per *Bonnington Castings*

---

[303] [2009] UKHL 33, with quotes at [202] (Lord Brown), [75] (Lord Rodger), respectively.
[304] *ibid*, [76].

Ltd v Wardlaw[305]); and '[i]t is established on high authority (*Bolitho, Wilsher*) that the burden of proof on causation lies, and remains, on [C]' (per *Shawe-Lincoln v Neelakandan*[306]).

It has been judicially acknowledged that this burden can be extremely onerous – even impossible – in some cases in which evidential gaps confront C. For one thing, the origin of some conditions can be medically and factually impossible to ascertain. In *Bull v Devon AHA*,[307] in an action against doctors for negligent delivery of C as a baby, the Court of Appeal noted that, 'in very many cases of cerebral palsy ... or brain damage, the cause is never discovered' (albeit that causation was proven in *Bull* itself: '[t]he onus was on [C] Stuart ... the hypoxia which occurred at birth was of such a degree that it did cause [C's] disability, and [the trial judge] found that [C] had excluded the possibility that there was another cause').

If a judge is faced with two theories for C's damage – 'one of which he regard[s] as extremely improbable, and the other of which he regard[s] as virtually impossible' – it is not a matter of choosing one over the other. The correct approach is to hold that C has failed to discharge the burden of proof (per *Skelton v Lewisham and North Southwark HA*[308]).

In failure-to-warn actions too, the burden of proof resting on C has occasionally drawn controversy. In *Smith v Barking, Havering & Brentwood HA*,[309] however, Hutchinson J categorically rejected an earlier suggestion (in *Heywood v Wellers*[310]) that, where adequate disclosure of risks had not been made to C, and C alleged that she would have refused the operation, the burden is on D to prove that C would not have refused the operation.

Any uncertainty about probability may be solely due to D's breach. Nevertheless, English law will still not permit a reversal of the burden of proof. The fact that, in *Hotson*, Stephen Hotson could not establish with certainty which of the two causes was operative – either too many already-ruptured blood vessels to save the epiphysis (innocently caused, after his fall from the tree), or bleeding into the hip joint over the (negligently-caused) 5-day delay that killed off the rest of the intact blood vessels – rested entirely with the hospital doctors, D. After five days of bleeding and haematoma, it was impossible to say how many intact blood vessels existed when C was first seen at the hospital. As Lord Hoffmann remarked in *Gregg v Scott*, 'the need to prove causation was more unfair on Hotson, since the reason why he could not prove whether he had enough blood vessels after the fall was that the hospital had negligently failed to examine him'.[311] Hence, however unfair it may seem, if C cannot prove causation on the balance of probabilities because of D's own omissions and breach, that will not reverse the burden of proof – *Hotson* bears testament to that.

Twists and turns

There have been some twists in English law, which appellate courts have been at pains to correct.

For example, in *Keefe v Isle of Man Steam Packet Co Ltd*[312] (an employment case), the Court of Appeal was sympathetic towards C, where her lack of ability to prove causation was attributable to D:

> In *Keefe*, Mr Keefe's widow brought a deafness claim on her husband's, C's, behalf, against his former employer, D. The Dept of Employment's Code of Practice required D to measure noise in its

---

[305] [1956] AC 613 (HL) 620 (Lord Reid).   [306] [2012] EWHC 1150 (QB) [80] (Lloyd Jones J).

[307] (1989) 22 BMLR 79 (CA) 110.   [308] [1998] Lloyd's Rep Med 324 (QB).

[309] QB, 29 Jul 1989.   [310] [1976] 1 QB 446, 459.   [311] [2005] UKHL 2, [2005] 2 AC 176, [88].

[312] [2010] EWCA Civ 683.

premises and, if exceeding a certain level, to reduce the noise or to provide ear protectors. However, D never measured the noise levels (a breach of duty), and there was engineering evidence of excessive noise levels in the ships in which C had served. **Held (trial):** C failed; C could not prove exposure to excessive levels for periods in excess of 8 hours with any regularity. **Held (CA):** negligence proven; C's loss of hearing was caused by excessive noise on D's vessels.

The Court of Appeal in *Keefe* made several observations which, had they applied in *Hotson*, may have assisted Stephen Hotson to prove his claim. For one thing, Longmore LJ noted C's difficulty in proving D's breach of duty in not taking noise measurements, and that 'it hardly lies in [D's] mouth to assert that the noise levels were not, in fact, excessive. In such circumstances the court should judge [C's] evidence benevolently and [D's] evidence critically ... [D] who has, in breach of duty, made it difficult or impossible for [C] to adduce relevant evidence must run the risk of adverse factual findings. To my mind this is just such a case'.[313] The case is starkly similar to Stephen Hotson's difficulties.

Nevertheless, *Keefe* does **not** authorise a reversal of the burden of proof. In *Shawe-Lincoln v Neelakandan*[314] (a medical case), C argued that *Keefe* warranted a 'benevolent' treatment of C's case there too, given that the effect of D's negligence (no hourly neurological observations) had been to deprive C of evidence about the deterioration of his neurological condition. However, Lloyd-Jones J concluded that there could be no reversal of the burden (on the authority of *Bolitho, Bonnington*, etc): '[r]ather, *Keefe* is concerned with the weight which is to be attached to evidence and the circumstances in which the court may draw inferences'. In *Shawe-Lincoln*, it was not appropriate to draw an inference in favour of C either.

A rare House of Lords' indication that the burden of proof should shift to D occurred in the judgment of Lord Wilberforce who, in *McGhee v National Coal Board*, remarked: 'it is a sound principle that where [D] has, by breach of a duty of care, created a risk, and injury occurs within the area of that risk, the loss should be borne by [D], unless he shows that it had some other cause'.[315]

However, the House of Lords has since strongly reiterated that there can be **no** shift of the burden of proof in causation. Lord Wilberforce's opinion in *McGhee* was categorically overruled by *Wilsher*,[316] with Lord Bridge calling it a 'minority opinion'. In *Fairchild*,[317] Lord Bingham confirmed that Lord Bridge's dismissal of Lord Wilberforce's sentiments was entirely correct, while Lord Hutton remarked that, whatever the differing position in other jurisdictions may be, English precedent did not support the reversal of the burden of proof, as a matter of law. Further, in *Fairchild*, Lord Nicholls stated that any exceptions to the 'but-for' test are just that, true exceptions, and that the *Fairchild* exception itself 'is emphatically not intended to lead to such a relaxation whenever [C] has difficulty, perhaps understandable difficulty, in discharging the burden of proof resting on him'.[318] In *Bonnington Castings Ltd v Wardlaw*,[319] the House of Lords had already overruled an earlier decision which **did** shift the burden to D, viz, *Vyner v Waldenberg Bros Ltd*,[320] where it was held that the burden was on an employer to show that the breach of safety regulation was not the cause of an accident to the employee.

---

[313] *ibid*, [18]–[19].   [314] [2012] EWHC 1150 (QB) [80]–[81].   [315] [1973] 1 WLR 1 (HL) 6.

[316] [1988] AC 1074 (HL) 1087, and confirmed in: *Graham v Re-Chem Intl Ltd* (QB, Forbes J, 16 Jun 1995).

[317] [2002] UKHL 22, [22] (Lord Bingham), [10] (Lord Hutton); and also: [131], [144] (Lord Rodger).

[318] *ibid*, [43]. Also: *Barker v Corus UK Ltd* [2006] UKHL 20, [104] (Lord Walker).

[319] [1956] AC 613 (HL) 620.   [320] [1946] KB 50 (CA).

The comparative corner: **Reversing the burden of proof**

Given the difficulties caused by the burden always resting on C, a couple of examples from other jurisdictions – of how the burden could feasibly be shifted – may be of interest.

i 'once [C] demonstrates that a breach of duty has occurred which is closely followed by damage, a *prima facie* causal connection will have been established. It is then for [D] to show, by evidence and argument, that [C] should not recover damages' (per the Australian decision of *Chappel v Hart*,[321] where the burden was ultimately not shifted, but where Kirby J described this formulation as 'compelling');

ii C must prove that D, by his breach, created a risk that the injury which actually occurred would occur. Once the court is 'convinced' that D had a 'substantial connection to the injury', then D has the burden of disproving causation, because an 'inference' of causation has arisen (per the Canadian decision of *Snell v Farrell*,[322] where Sopinka J described that formulation as explaining the outcome of *McGhee v National Coal Board*).

Were these formulations to be the English law, then that would have a marked impact in the two areas in which causation has had the most difficulty to date, *viz*, in medical and in employment negligence – e.g., having proved that oxygen was over-administered in *Wilsher v Essex AHA*, the doctors would have had to establish that one of the other four possible reasons was responsible for baby Martin's RLF, and not the excess oxygen; and having proved that the employer in *Fairchild* owed a duty to protect the employee from the risk associated with a single noxious agent like asbestos, and that the employer breached that duty by exposing the employee to that very risk, the employer would have to prove that it was not *his* period of employment that caused that employee to contract the disease of mesothelioma.

From the law reform perspective, however, the Australian Ipp Committee strongly opposed the notion that the burden of proof of causation should shift to D, under any circumstances. The Committee gave three reasons:[323]

- the evidentiary gap confronting C exists just the same for D, who may also find it impossible to discharge the burden of proof too;
- the reversal (if it were permitted) could feasibly apply, regardless of whether there was an evidentiary gap at all, but simply to cast on D the task of proving that C's damage was due to something other than his breach; and
- there was a consequent risk that courts would find in favour of C too readily by defining too widely the scenarios in which the 'but-for' test of causation should be departed from.

[321] (1998) 72 ALJR 1344 (HCA).
[322] [1990] 2 SCR 311 (SCC) 326–27.
[323] *Ipp Report*, [7.33]–[7.36].

9

Remoteness of damage

INTRODUCTION

Remoteness is the fourth limb of the negligence action, and represents the final opportunity for the court to circumscribe D's liability. This element asks whether the damage complained of, although factually caused by D's act or omission, was legally too remote. This principally (but not solely) involves an enquiry as to whether the kind or type of damage was reasonably foreseeable by D at the relevant time. As a general rule, D cannot be liable in law for damage that was not reasonably foreseeable.

The remoteness enquiry serves two limiting purposes, as a 'control mechanism' in ring-fencing D's liability: (1) it is the final element which C must prove, in order to make the cause of action complete; and (2) it provides the basis upon which the quantum of C's damages will ultimately be assessed, and ensures that D is not necessarily liable for **all** of the damage which his breach has caused – for C cannot recover from D any part of his damage which is adjudged to be too remote.

What the remoteness enquiry addresses

Remoteness is directed towards the *kind or type of damage* suffered by C. Is the damage, which is causally linked to D's breach, of the type for which the law regards D as properly being liable? Or is the damage too remote – too distant or unrelated – from the breach, to be fairly laid at D's door?

As a matter of terminology, the remoteness limb is sometimes referred to in modern jurisprudence as 'causation-in-law' or 'legal causation'. This distinguishes it from the factual enquiry as to whether D's breach caused the damage in fact, which is the function of the 'but-for' and other causation tests (per Chapter 8). In most remoteness problems, the damage would not have occurred, but for D's breach – but the purpose of remoteness is to ring-fence the 'but-for' consequences of a negligent act or omission. However, the label, 'legal causation', is something of a misnomer. As the Court of Appeal noted in *Robb v FT Everard & Sons Ltd*,[1] whilst remoteness is essentially an issue of law, the test of reasonable foreseeability (which applies at the remoteness stage) certainly requires findings of fact. Moreover, in *Jolley v Sutton LBC*,[2] Lord

---

[1] [1999] EWCA Civ 1022.   [2] [2000] 3 All ER 409 (HL) 416.

Steyn instructed that remoteness is a fact-specific enquiry, requiring an 'intense focus on the circumstances of each case'.

Indeed, remoteness is a notoriously unpredictable area within the negligence action – driven, as it is, by 'common sense' (per *Barings plc v Coopers & Lybrand (a firm)*[3]), 'an immediately intuitive response' (per *Kuwait Airways Corp v Iraqi Airways Co*[4]), and by 'current ideas of justice and morality' (per *Overseas Tankship (UK) Ltd v Morts Dock & Engineering Co Ltd (The Wagon Mound)*[5]). When judges speak in such terms, then ascertaining the line between damages which D should lawfully bear, and those which should not fairly be transferred to D in the law's eyes, can be problematic ('riddled with indeterminacy', as one judge aptly put it[6]).

A few decades ago, Lord Denning optimistically remarked, in *SCM Ltd v WJ Whittall*,[7] that whereas 'lawyers are continually asking the question' whether or not damage is too remote, 'judges are never defeated by it. We may not be able to draw the line with precision, but we can always say on which side of it any particular case falls'. However, the number of successful appellate decisions discussed in this chapter would appear to indicate that not all judges share such a robust view! For example, in *Jolley v Sutton LBC*,[8] in a typically difficult remoteness scenario, the Court of Appeal unanimously disagreed with the trial judge, and the House of Lords unanimously overruled the Court of Appeal and reinstated the trial judge's view that Justin Jolley's damage was not too remote – hardly a model of predictability!

Finally, in addition to the arbitrary and fact-specific enquiry which remoteness inevitably entails, it is also invested with a decent 'dollop' of pragmatism. This is especially evident in economic loss cases, where D's exposure can be quite exacting. In the case of negligent audits/accountancy oversights, one court commented that 'an auditor is watchdog, not a bloodhound' (per *Re Kingston Cotton Mill Co (No 2)*[9]), while another acknowledged that the advisee company and directors 'have generally left the scene, headed in most cases for government-supervised liquidation or the bankruptcy court. The auditor has now assumed centre stage as the remaining solvent [D], and is faced with a claim for all sums of money ever loaned to or invested in the client' (per *Bily v Arthur Young & Co*[10]). Hence, judicial pragmatism under this element provides a valuable, if somewhat unpredictable, ring-fence around the quantum of damage for which D is liable.

Framework for analysis

A convenient framework for the remoteness enquiry is encapsulated in the Table below:

Nutshell analysis: Remoteness of damage

Checklist of issues to consider:

1 Whether the kind or type of C's damage was reasonably foreseeable (subject to the *Page v Smith* exception)
2 Whether C had any pre-existing vulnerability to that type of damage (and its legal effect)

---

[3] [2003] EWHC 1319 (Ch) [819]. [4] [2002] UKHL 19, [2002] 2 WLR 1353, [71].
[5] [1961] AC 388 (PC) 422. [6] *Perre v Apand Pty Ltd* [1999] HCA 36, 198 CLR 180, [82] (McHugh J).
[7] [1971] 1 QB 337 (CA) 346. [8] [2000] 3 All ER 409 (HL). [9] [1896] 2 Ch 279 (CA) 288 (Lopes LJ).
[10] P 2d 745, 763 (Cal Sup Ct 1992), both cited in *Barings plc v Coopers & Lybrand* [2003] EWHC 1319 (Ch) [822].

> 3 Whether the type of damage (even reasonably foreseeable damage) should be irrecoverable because:
>   • the type of damage fell outside the scope of D's duty to avoid causing C damage;
>   • there were too many causal links between D's breach and C's damage; or
>   • reasons of public policy precluded recovery of C's damage.
>
> Miscellaneous issues:
>
> • The ongoing relevance of *Polemis*
> • The difference between contract and tort

The issues in this framework will be considered in turn.

THE KIND OR TYPE OF DAMAGE

From *Re Polemis* to *Wagon Mound*

§9.1   The kind or type of damage suffered by C, as a result of D's act or omission, must have been reasonably foreseeable (per *Wagon Mound No 1*, which overruled the 'direct consequences' test, i.e., that D should be liable for any injuries which were 'directly caused' to C by D's negligent act, whether or not that injury was reasonably foreseeable).

According to the Privy Council in *Overseas Tankship (UK) Ltd v Morts Dock & Engineering Co (Wagon Mound No 1)* in 1961,[11] 'it is the foresight of the reasonable man which alone can determine responsibility'. Two years later, Lord Pearce reiterated, in *Hughes v Lord Advocate*,[12] that D are 'liable for all the foreseeable consequences of their neglect. When an accident is of a different type and kind from anything that [D] could have foreseen, he is not liable for it'. Reasonably foreseeable damage can be unlikely, but not so unlikely as to be 'brushed aside as far-fetched' (per *Wagon Mound*). This principle of remoteness in English law had its genesis in Sydney Harbour, of all places:

> In *Wagon Mound (No 1)*,[13] Morts Dock, C, owned the timber Sheerlegs Wharf at Morts Bay, Balmain, in Sydney Harbour, and conducted ship-building, ship-repairing and general engineering at the wharf. The wharf itself, plus the vessel, *The Corrimal*, which C was refitting at the wharf, were severely damaged by fire on 1 Nov 1951, which happened in a most unusual way. C's employees were working on *The Corrimal* with welding equipment, whilst a vessel, the *Wagon Mound*, was moored at Caltex Wharf on the north shore of Sydney Harbour. Overseas Tankship, D, chartered the *Wagon Mound*, and whilst filling it with bunkering oil, D's chief engineer negligently allowed a large quantity of oil to spill into Sydney Harbour, which D did not attempt to clean up. Meanwhile, C instructed its workmen not to undertake any welding work until it asked Caltex Oil whether C's workmen could safely continue their work on *The Corrimal*. C were told 'yes', that the oil was inflammable. C's management also believed that bunkering oil in the open, and floating on water, was inflammable. Unfortunately, two days later, the oil near Sheerlegs Wharf was ignited, and a fierce fire burnt the wharf and *The Corrimal*. The fire ignited because a cotton rag was floating on some debris in the oil;

---

[11] [1961] AC 388 (PC, on appeal from NSWSC) 424.   [12] [1963] AC 837 (HL) 857.
[13] [1961] AC 388 (PC) 422–23, 425–26.

the cotton was set on fire by molten metal falling from Sheerlegs Wharf during welding; the cotton rag caught fire; those flames set the floating oil alight; and the flames then spread over the surface of the water in Sydney Harbour, reaching Sheerlegs Wharf itself. **Held:** fire damage to C's wharf was too remote to be compensable at law. That fire damage was the direct consequence of the oil's escape, but D could not reasonably be expected to have known that the oil would catch fire. Property damage from pollution was foreseeable; but damage by fire was unforeseeable.

The Privy Council overruled the then-current test of remoteness – *viz*, the *Polemis* 'direct consequences' test, which had been in force since 1921 – which was unfortunate for Morts Dock, C, given that the direct link between D's breach and their damage was, in fact, upheld:

> In *Re Polemis and Furness, Withy & Co Ltd (Re Polemis)*,[14] Mr Polemis, C, owned the Greek steamship, *Thrasyvoulos*, which was chartered to Furness, Withy & Co, D, in 1917, for trading purposes, for the duration of the war. The vessel was loaded with cargo at Lisbon (*viz*, cases of benzine and/ or petrol and iron), and whilst being unloaded at Casablanca, it was discovered that some of the benzine/petrol had leaked *en voyage* in rough weather, and a lot of petrol vapour had accumulated in the hold, due to that leakage. Cases of benzine had to be transferred to another part of the ship, and D's stevedores placed heavy planks across the hatchway, to use as a platform for transferring the cases. However, with the ship's heaving, and due to D's stevedores' negligence, several cases hit a plank, causing it to fall into the hold. A rush of flames immediately occurred in the hold, and the ship was destroyed by fire. The fire arose from a spark igniting petrol vapour in the hold, which was caused by the falling board creating a spark. **Held:** the loss of the ship was not too remote. D (via their employed stevedores) were liable for all the direct consequences of the negligence, even though those consequences (i.e., the spark, the falling board) and the type of damage (damage by fire) could not reasonably have been foreseen.

The *Polemis* 'direct consequences' test is generally viewed to have been a **wider** test of remoteness, embracing more damage within its net, than the test of reasonable foreseeability. Certainly, the *Wagon Mound* approach is a more favourable test for D than was the *Polemis* test (as Morts Dock discovered, to its cost). As noted in *Essa v Laing*,[15] the test of reasonable foreseeability acts as a real control mechanism upon the ambit of claims for which D ought to be liable.

The meaning of 'reasonable foreseeability'

Test of foreseeability at other stages

§9.2

The test of reasonable foreseeability, for the purposes of remoteness, differs from that test at duty of care and breach stages, because it is focused on the kind or type of damage which resulted *from the accident or event which occurred*.

Some courts have suggested that there is **no** difference in the foreseeability analyses across the tort of negligence – whether considered at duty of care, breach, or remoteness stages. In *Jolley v Sutton LBC*,[16] Lord Hoffmann suggested that the test of foreseeability in *Wagon Mound* was relevant to the establishment of a duty of care, or remoteness, 'according to taste'. In *Corr v IBC Vehicles*,[17] Ward LJ noted that, 'there are considerable overlaps between the elements

---

[14] [1921] 3 KB 560 (CA).   [15] [2004] EWCA Civ 2, [2004] IRLR 313, [37]–[38].
[16] [2000] 1 WLR 1082 (HL) 1091.   [17] [2006] EWCA Civ 331, [2007] QB 46, [9].

of the scope of the duty of care, any break in the causal chain and remoteness of damage. Questions of foreseeability are the common thread, but into which compartment one places it, and even whether it matters where one places it, are not matters which are always abundantly clear'. In *Foster (nee Billington) v Maguire*[18] too, the Court of Appeal said that the question of whether C's damage was of the kind or type that was reasonably foreseeable was a question which overlapped between duty of care and remoteness, and which could be 'telescoped into one issue of fact'.

However, not all judges have treated the test of foreseeability as a seamless continuum. In *Corr v IBC Vehicles Ltd*,[19] Lord Bingham indicated that the query at remoteness stage is extremely focused – 'foreseeability is to be judged ... with reference to the *very accident which occurred*' – to be contrasted with the test at duty stage, which Lord Hoffmann described in *Jolley v Sutton LBC* as extremely general: 'whether injury *of some kind* was foreseeable'.[20]

In light of these comments, it is suggested that there is a distinct difference in the test of foreseeability at duty and remoteness stages. At remoteness stage, while it is not necessary that all the causal steps leading from breach to damage are foreseeable, the court will pay close attention to *precisely what damage* C sustained *as a result of the accident which occurred*. By contrast, at duty stage, the task is more general (as discussed in Chapter 2) – i.e., was it reasonably foreseeable that *some* damage could likely result from D's act or omission?

Furthermore, the remoteness enquiry depends upon what could reasonably have been foreseen at the time of D's breach, and not later (per *C Czarnikow Ltd v Koufos (The Heron II)*[21]).

General principles

§9.3   The kind or type of damage may be construed quite widely, so as to encompass the reasonable foreseeability of 'some personal injury' arising from D's breach. The specific kind or type of personal injury (e.g., damage by disease, damage by burns) is not required in that context. However, although the legal position remains unsettled, the better view is that reasonable foreseeability of a more specific kind of damage may still be required for property damage.

This principle has undergone some significant change over the past 50 years or so, at least in the context of personal injury. Under older cases, the kind or type of injury which had to be reasonably foreseeable was defined quite narrowly, e.g.:

- injury by burns:

> In *Hughes v Lord Advocate*,[22] Post Office employees, D, were working on telephone cables below a street in Edinburgh. They removed the manhole cover, put a canvas shelter tent over it, and put four red warning paraffin lamps around the hole, per normal procedure. Soon after 5 pm, when it was dark, D left the site for their 15-minute tea break, removing a ladder from the manhole and pulling a tarpaulin cover over the entrance to the shelter. Russell Hughes, 8, C, and his 10-year-old uncle, decided to enter the shelter, taking one of the paraffin lamps with them to explore the manhole. The lamp was either knocked or dropped into the manhole, and a violent explosion occurred, sending flames 30 ft into the air. C fell into the manhole from the force of the explosion, and was badly burnt. The accident occurred because, when the lamp fell down the hole and broke, some paraffin escaped, and enough vaporised to create an explosive mixture which was detonated by the naked

---

[18] [2001] EWCA Civ 273, [21].   [19] [2008] UKHL 13, [2008] 1 AC 884, [11] (emphasis added).
[20] [2000] 1 WLR 1082 (HL) 1091 (emphasis added).   [21] [1969] 2 AC 350 (HL).   [22] [1963] AC 837 (HL).

light of the lamp. **Held:** C's burn injuries were not too remote. Damage from burns was foreseeable, whether those burns were caused by explosion of vapour or the (more likely) ignition of liquid paraffin. The cause of the accident was a known source of danger, the lamp, but the risk of burns had happened unpredictably. The explosion of vaporised paraffin was an unforeseeable way for this accident to happen. But the end result – injury by burns – was not unforeseeable. If the lamp had simply fallen over and broken, C likely still would have been burned, possibly seriously.

- injury by disease:

    In *Tremain v Pike*,[23] William Tremain, C, was employed as a herdsman by farmer, Mr Pike, D. C contracted Weil's disease (leptospirosis) through contact with rats' urine. C alleged that he was infected by using or washing in contaminated water, or handling bales of hay, which contained the urine, because of an infestation of rats around the farm buildings. **Held:** C's damage (injury by disease) was too remote. Reasonably foreseeable damage caused by rat-associated disease was disease associated either with rat bites or food contamination, but contamination through exposure to rats' urine was very rare, and there was no evidence that the farming community knew, or ought reasonably to have foreseen, that a disease could be contracted by merely handling matter contaminated by rats. The possibility of contracting Weil's disease was a remote one which could not reasonably be foreseen, and the damage was irrecoverable.

- injury/damage by explosion:

    In *Vacwell Engineering Co Ltd v BDH Chemicals Ltd*,[24] Vacwell Engineering, C, had a laboratory in Surrey, and purchased a chemical, boron tribromide, from BDH Chemicals, D, in glass ampoules. A Russian physicist, Mr Strouzhinski, was working in the lab, removing the labels from these glass ampoules by immersing the ampoules in sinks of water, when an explosion occurred, killing Mr Strouzhinski, and seriously damaging the lab. The probable cause of the explosion was that Mr Strouzhinski had put or dropped these ampoules into the sink, the ampoules broke releasing the chemical, it reacted violently with water in the sink shattering other ampoules in the sink, and it all caused a violent explosion. **Held:** C's damage was not too remote. D committed a breach in failing to warn C of the risk of explosion of the chemical if it came into contact with water. It was foreseeable that, in the ordinary course of industrial use, D's chemical could come into contact with water and cause a violent reaction and an explosion, and that some damage to persons and property could result.

- damage by fire:

    In *Overseas Tankship (UK) Ltd v Miller Steamship Co Pty (Wagon Mound (No 2))*,[25] the case arose out of the same facts as in *Wagon Mound I*, but this time, the owners of the two ships damaged by fire, *The Corrimal* and the *Audrey D*, sued the charterers of the *Wagon Mound*, D, for negligently discharging the bunkering oil into Sydney Harbour. It will be recalled that, in *Wagon Mound (No 1)*, it was held that D did not know, nor could it have reasonably foreseen, that bunkering oil was capable of being set alight when spread on water. That was how the evidence was led, because the wharf owners, Morts Dock, C, would have been compromised, had it been proven that damage by fire was reasonably foreseeable, because their own actions in resuming welding would have given rise to a potential finding of contributory negligence, which was, at that time, a complete defence in New South Wales. Hence, Morts Dock had sought to rely on the *Polemis* 'direct consequences' test

[23] [1969] 1 WLR 1556 (Exeter Assizes) 1560.   [24] [1971] 1 QB 88 (Rees J).
[25] [1967] AC 26 (PC, on appeal from NSWSC).

of remoteness, and failed with that argument. In *Wagon Mound (No 2)*, C led different evidence to show that damage to their ships by fire **was** reasonably foreseeable. **Held:** Cs' damage was not too remote. The discharge of so much bunkering oil must have taken a good while, and a vigilant ship's engineer would have noticed that discharge, and ought to have known that it was possible to ignite this kind of oil on water (and that this had actually happened previously). Hence, damage by fire, whilst unlikely, was reasonably foreseeable.

These are the principal older cases.

However, in the context of personal injury, more recent case law has held that the kind or type of injury should be defined much more broadly to amount to 'some physical injury' to C (per *Jolley v Sutton LBC*[26]). This is a far more sympathetic-to-C principle than was evident in *Tremain v Pike* – for the wider the type of damage, the more likely that C's damage will fall within the requisite description.

In *Jolley v Sutton LBC*, the council, D, owned a block of council flats in Surrey, where an abandoned and derelict boat was left by some unknown person on a grassed area where children played. Flat residents complained to D about the boat, and D put a warning sign on it, but the boat was not removed for two years (until after the accident). Justin Jolley, C, 14, and his friend, rather poignantly planned to repair the boat and take it to Cornwall to sail it. C had the strength and ability to jack up the boat onto a car jack and some wooden blocks, to repair and paint underneath it. One day, while C was under the boat, it rocked (for some unexplained reason), and before he could get out from underneath, it fell onto him, broke his back, and rendered him a paraplegic. **Held:** C's type of damage was not too remote – 'some physical injury', as a result of meddling with the boat, was reasonably foreseeable. It would have been much more likely for C to have been injured by climbing onto the boat, and falling through its rotten deck, than the boat falling on top of him. However, it was reasonably foreseeable that young boys could try to mimic adult behaviour by repairing a boat, and that in doing so, a propped-up boat could collapse, causing C injury.

This case essentially reduced to **two** competing arguments: whether the trial judge was correct to define the type of damage along the lines that, 'children would meddle with the boat at the risk of some physical injury' – or whether the Court of Appeal was correct in defining the type of damage more narrowly, that 'children would be drawn to the boat, climbing upon it, and being injured by the rotten planking giving way beneath them'. The former (wider) view prevailed, as being the type of damage which should be reasonably foreseeable – and clearly, C's injury (caused by the boat falling on top of him, having jacked it up) fell within that description of the requisite type of damage. Curiously, the narrower views of the relevant type or kind of injury which were adopted in *Tremain v Pike* and *Vacwell Engineering* were not even referred to in *Jolley*. In any event, the wider view has been recently applied, again to C's benefit:

In *Hicks v Young*,[27] Kristopher Hicks, C, 23, caught Michael Young's, D's, taxi late at night in Bath to go home. After arriving at the intended address and letting C's companion out, D then drove off with C still in the taxi. The reason for this is that D believed that C and his companion were going to 'do a runner' without paying for the fare, and D intended to return with C to the taxi rank to sort out the matter. On that journey, C jumped out of the taxi when it was travelling at 20 mph, hit

---

[26] [2000] 1 WLR 1082 (HL) 1091.

[27] [2015] EWHC 1144 (QB), quote at [33]. See too, for further application: *ST v Maidstone and Tunbridge Wells NHS Trust* [2015] EWHC 51 (QB) (dicta only; causation ultimately failed).

his head hard, and suffered serious brain injury. **Held:** D was negligent (subject to C's contributory negligence). It may not have been foreseeable that C would jump out at that speed, but that was irrelevant. It was foreseeable that C would try to leave the taxi when it was moving, and that he may have suffered a bruised knee, broken wrist, etc. Catastrophic injury was less foreseeable, but it was the kind of damage which occurred, 'namely personal injury, which is required and not of the precise mechanism by which it occurred'.

However, an equivalent widening of the kind or type of damage, to equate to 'some property damage', has not been evident. Those types of Cs cannot take advantage of the benevolently-wide view of what amounts to a 'type of damage'. The aforementioned cases of *Wagon Mound (No 1)*, *Wagon Mound (No 2)* and *Vacwell* demonstrate a fairly narrow interpretation of the kind of property damage suffered (and *Vacwell's* description of the type of damage was approved in *Free Grammar School of John Lyon v Westminster CC*[28]).

§9.4   C's damage is not too remote, merely because the extent of C's damage is greater than was foreseen, or which could have been reasonably foreseeable, by D. D cannot limit his liability by contending that the *extent* of C's injuries could not have been reasonably foreseeable.

> In *Hughes v Lord Advocate*, Lord Reid stated that D 'is liable, although the damage be a good deal greater in extent than was foreseeable'. In *Jolley v Sutton LBC*, Justin Jolley's paraplegia was a type of damage which was reasonably foreseeable, notwithstanding the severity of those injuries. In *Vacwell Engineering Co Ltd v BDH Chemicals Ltd*, it was also irrelevant that the magnitude of the explosion and the extent of the damage (i.e., the death of the Russian scientist, and the severe damage to the lab) was not foreseeable.

While this principle is often evident in the case of the 'egg-shell skull claimant' (who has a particular vulnerability to the damage which befell him), the rule has **general** application, applying equally to persons of normal fortitude (as with Russell Hughes, Justin Jolley and the Russian scientist working in Vacwell's lab).

Albeit that the abovementioned cases involved personal injury sustained by C, the principle is just as applicable to both greater-than-foreseen property damage (per *Vacwell Engineering*) and economic losses too:

> In *Barings plc (in liq) v Coopers & Lybrand*,[29] the Barings group collapsed in February 1995, caused by the unauthorised trading on the Singapore International Monetary Exchange (SIMEX) by Nicholas Leeson (NL), the general manager of Barings Futures (Singapore) Ltd, C, who incurred losses for the group of about £791m. Those losses had been funded by other members of the Barings group, in ignorance of the trading activities for which the funds were being used. C sued Deloitte & Touche (Singapore), D, who were its auditors in 1992–93, claiming negligence because the auditors did not detect the unauthorised trading of NL. **Held:** D's audits were negligent, in failing to pick up NL's efforts to conceal significant losses in C's accounts. The damage flowing from losses, made by unauthorised trading in the course of a securities trading business of the type being operated by C, was foreseeable and not too remote. That the scale of those losses turned out to have been much greater than a reasonable auditor could have foreseen did not legally matter.

---

[28] [2012] UKUT 117 (Upper Tribunal, Lands Chamber) [78]–[79].   [29] [2003] EWHC 1319, [2003] PNLR 34 (Ch).

Hence, if C suffers a particularly severe case of injury, then C must prove that his damage was not unforeseeable damage of a different kind from that which was foreseeable, but simply more extensive damage of the same kind.

§9.5   C's damage is not too remote, merely because the precise manner or sequence of events giving rise to that damage was not foreseen, nor reasonably foreseeable, by D (i.e., it is the type of damage which must be reasonably foreseeable). Nevertheless, whilst that precise chain of events need not be foreseeable, there must be a *causal* link between D's breach and C's damage. As a further principle in C's favour, the precise chain of events between D's wrongdoing, and the ultimate damage that befell C, does not have to be reasonably foreseeable.

The abovementioned authorities of *Hughes v Lord Advocate* and *Jolley v Sutton LBC* provide ample authority for that in the context of C's physical injury. Provided that no 'new and unexpected factor' occurred that could be regarded as a *novus actus interveniens*, the fact that D could not have reasonably foreseen *the precise mechanics of just how the accident occurred* is no escape for D. The important point is whether C was 'injured as a result of the type or kind of accident or occurrence that could reasonably have been foreseen' (per Lord Reid in *Hughes v Lord Advocate*[30]); whether 'the accident is of a class that might well be anticipated as one of the reasonable and probable results of the wrongful act' (per Greer LJ in *Haynes v Harwood*[31]); and whether C can prove 'foreseeability, not as to the particulars, but the genus' (per Lord Hoffmann in *Jolley v Sutton*[32]). To the extent that decisions such as *Doughty v Turner Manufacturing*[33] held that an unforeseeable sequence of events rendered C's damage too remote, those have not been followed (and given the precedential hierarchy, courts since have expressly followed the reasoning in *Hughes* rather than in *Doughty*, as in, e.g., *Hadlow v Peterborough CC*[34]).

Remoteness arguments arise, in practice, when the 'precise form' by which C suffers his injuries was unlikely, but C argues that the class of accident was entirely foreseeable, and thereby produced a kind or type of damage which was foreseeable. The sequence of events in *Jolley* and *Hughes* were most unlikely, even fanciful – involving, as they did, the unpredictable activities of children – but in both, the damage was compensable. Other cases of physical injury have demonstrated the same principle – in both a medical and an employment context. For example:

In *Wisniewski v Central Manchester HA*,[35] Philip Wisniewski, C, suffered severe and irreversible brain damage during the 13 minutes immediately prior to his birth, because as he moved down the birth canal, the umbilical cord was wrapped round his neck and had a knot in it, effectively strangling him. His mother had been admitted to D's hospital three hours earlier. Had her care not been negligently mismanaged, a doctor would have carried out an artificial rupture of the membranes, which would have led to C's being born by caesarean, thus obviating the hazards of a natural birth. The strangling of C by the umbilical cord was very rare (1–2 a year, in a busy teaching hospital), and D argued that the damage was too remote to be compensable (a far more likely harm was the risk of damage by oxygen starvation whilst C was in the womb). **Held:** C's damage was not too remote. The foreseeable kind or type of damage was hypoxia (oxygen deprivation to the brain), and it made no

---

[30] [1963] AC 837 (HL) 852.   [31] [1935] 1 KB 146 (CA) 156.   [32] [2000] 1 WLR 1082 (HL) 1091.
[33] [1964] 1 QB 518 (CA).   [34] [2011] EWCA Civ 1329, [15]–[22].
[35] [1998] EWCA Civ 596, [1998] Lloyd's Rep Med 223. See similarly, in the medical context: *Loraine v Wirral Univ Teaching Hosp NHS Foundation Trust* [2008] EWHC (QB), and approved in: *ST v Maidstone and Tunbridge Wells NHS Trust* [2015] EWHC 51 (QB) [193].

difference that the precise mechanism by which the hypoxia arose was not foreseeable. In *Hadlow v Peterborough CC*,[36] Jean Hadlow, C, 63, was employed as a teacher at a secure unit for young women operated by Council D. She was due to teach a class of three women. The unit's policy was that no member of staff would be alone with a group of more than two young women. C's teaching assistant (TA) would normally have been present. The foreseeable source of danger here was a risk of attack on C. On this day, however, C was about to be left alone (her TA was due to arrive late), and C hurried to the door of the classroom to attract the attention of a carer to stay behind. In doing so, C tripped on a chair in her rush and badly injured herself. **Held:** C's damage was not too remote. The accident did not happen in the most likely way (i.e., an attack), but the risk of physical injury was foreseeable. It was unnecessary to show foreseeability of the precise chain of events leading up to the accident.

The precise sequence of events leading to C's consequential psychiatric injury does not need to be foreseeable either:

In *Corr v IBC Vehicles Ltd*,[37] Mr Corr, C, was a maintenance engineer employed by IBC Vehicles Ltd, D, at its Coventry factory. In 1996, C was badly injured whilst trying to remedy a fault on the automated presses which produced panels for Vauxhall vehicles. The automated arm threw a panel in C's direction without warning. C would have been decapitated, had he not ducked. His right ear was severed. Thereafter, C suffered disfigurement, bad headaches, PTSD and severe depression. He was treated by electro-convulsive therapy, was frequently hospitalised, and assessed as a high suicide risk. Six years after the accident, C committed suicide by jumping from the top of a multi-storey carpark. D admitted breach, but argued that C's suicide was too remote to be compensable, and because C was not technically insane at the time of his death, and could invoke personal autonomy, such that D was not 'his keeper'. **Held:** C's suicide was not too remote. Lord Bingham noted that suicide as a result of a severe depression was 'not uncommon', and that '[i]t was well known that between 1 in 6 and 1 in 10 sufferers from severe depression kill themselves'. Although some behaviour of severely depressed people could be 'so unusual and unpredictable as to be outside the bounds of what is reasonably foreseeable, suicide cannot be so regarded'. Also, given the extent and severity of C's physical injuries, some psychological harm, as a concomitant of physical harm suffered by C, was reasonably foreseeable. (By contrast, Lord Scott held that the risk of C's suicide was between 2–4%, which was 'possibly foreseeable', but not 'reasonably foreseeable'. However, Lord Scott too found for C, on the basis that depression was definitely foreseeable, such that the extent of the damage (suicide) did not need to be so.)

The treatment of *pure* psychiatric injury, and the remoteness rules applicable thereto, are considered shortly, under the next principle.

The principle that the sequence of events giving rise to C's consequential economic loss does not have to be foreseeable is also well established. In a complex business world, D may have no idea of the complicated financial arrangements into which C, the victim of his negligence, has entered, and the chain of events leading to C's losses may be very unlikely – and yet, C's economic losses will not be too remote on that score.

---

[36] [2011] EWCA Civ 1329.

[37] [2008] UKHL 13, [2008] 1 AC 884, with quotes at [5], [13] (Lord Bingham), [28] (Lord Scott), respectively. The other members of the House concurred with Lord Bingham on this point.

In *Conarken Group Ltd v Network Rail Infrastructure Ltd (Rev 1)*,[38] Network Rail, C, was responsible for the rail track system, and awarded train-operating companies franchises to operate on different parts of the system. C entered into 'track access agreements' to pay those train companies damages, should the rail network be unusable. In fact, Conarken's, D's, driver negligently caused damage to the parapet walls of a railway bridge, causing rubble to be strewn on railway tracks in Yorkshire. The line was closed for five days while repairs were carried out. **Held:** the contractual payments required from C to the train companies was not too remote. A revenue-earning asset was affected, and the complicated business arrangements entered into by C did not render that particular loss uncompensable. It was part and parcel of foreseeable economic loss arising from an accident such as this.

However, it is one thing to hold that D may be liable, even though the precise chain of events leading to C's accident was not a reasonably foreseeable chain of events. Nevertheless, C must still prove the requisite causal link between D's breach and his damage. If D's breach played no causal part at all in the accident which befell C, then it does not matter whether or not the chain of events is foreseeable – causation, and the negligence action as a whole, will fail. As the Court of Appeal stated in *Green v Sunset & Vine Productions Ltd*,[39] the principle in *Jolley* has 'no relevance at all to a case in which D's negligent act has not in fact played any causative role in the loss and damage suffered by C'.

In *Green v Sunset & Vine Productions*, Willie Green, C, an experienced driver of historic racing cars, was driving a Maserati in a Goodwood Revival race meeting, when he lost control of the car, was flung out, and the car ran over his legs, causing severe injury. C alleged that the car had hit a kerb cam set up by D, and that this impact caused the car to veer off the track. **Held:** C's damage was not caused by the kerb cam. The presence and installation of the camera did not materially cause the accident; the accident would probably have happened, even had it had not been there. Without causation, then the fact that it was reasonably foreseeable that a car passing over the kerb cam might lead to injury to a driver, even if the precise chain of events leading to C's accident was not a reasonably foreseeable chain of events, was irrelevant.

Exception to the requirement of reasonable foreseeability

There is **one** exception in English law – where an unforeseeable type of damage (i.e., psychiatric injury) **can** properly be recovered at law.

§9.6 Where D's breach puts C in a 'zone of physical danger' but where C suffers from psychiatric injury, then foreseeability of the risk of physical injury is sufficient, whether or not that psychiatric injury was reasonably foreseeable. If that psychiatric injury was indeed unforeseeable (as being remote and fanciful), then some physical injury will be reasonably foreseeable, precisely because C was put in that zone of physical danger ('the *Page v Smith* principle'). Otherwise, where C suffers pure psychiatric injury for reasons unconnected with being put in any 'zone of physical danger', C must prove that his psychiatric injury was reasonably foreseeable, in accordance with the usual *Wagon Mound* principle.

---

[38] [2011] EWCA Civ 644, [2011] BLR 462, [148]–[155].   [39] [2010] EWCA Civ 1441, [44].

Set down in the controversial decision of *Page v Smith*,[40] this is the **only** circumstance in English law where a type of damage that was unforeseeable is, nevertheless, compensable (as discussed in Chapter 5).

> In *Page v Smith*, Mr Page, C, was involved in a minor car accident with a car being driven by Mr Smith, D, when D turned in front of C carelessly. C suffered no physical injury, but three hours after the accident he began to feel exhausted. That exhaustion manifested as ME, or chronic fatigue syndrome, which C had suffered in mild form previously, and which he now suffered in a chronic and intense form. **Held (trial):** C won. **Held (CA):** C lost. Psychiatric reaction of this sort was not foreseeable in a person of ordinary fortitude as a result of what happened to C in that car accident. **Held (HL, by majority):** C could recover; his psychiatric condition was not too remote: 'it was enough to ask whether [D] should have reasonably foreseen that [C] might suffer physical injury as a result of [D's] negligence, so as to bring him within the range of [D's] duty of care. It was unnecessary to ask, as a separate question, whether [D] should reasonably have foreseen injury by shock; and it is irrelevant that [C] did not, in fact, suffer any external physical injury'.

Strictly speaking, however, this is **not** an exception at all, because Lord Lloyd (delivering the majority judgment) attributed this generous-to-C legal principle to the lack of distinction between the two types of personal injury (physical and psychiatric), insofar as medical science is concerned:

> The test ought to be whether [D] can reasonably foresee that his conduct will expose [C] to risk of personal injury ... There is no justification for regarding physical and psychiatric injury as different 'kinds' of injury. Once it is established that [D] is under a duty of care to avoid causing personal injury to [C], it matters not whether the injury in fact sustained is physical, psychiatric or both ... In an age when medical knowledge is expanding fast, and psychiatric knowledge with it, it would not be sensible to commit the law to a distinction between physical and psychiatric injury, which may already seem somewhat artificial, and may soon be altogether outmoded. Nothing will be gained by treating them as different 'kinds' of personal injury, so as to require the application of different tests in law.[41]

The *Page v Smith* principle applies, whether the psychiatric injury was 'pure' in nature, or consequential upon physical injury. It renders unforeseeable consequential psychiatric injury recoverable at law:

> In *Simmons v British Steel plc*,[42] Mr Simmons, C, was employed as a burner by British Steel, D, at Clydebridge Steel Works. He tripped and fell off the burning table and hit his head on a metal stanchion. Headgear protected him from a very serious head injury, but he suffered a bump, eye disturbances and discharge from his ear. C had complained to D about what he saw as an unsafe system of work, but nothing had been done. The physical injuries were not particularly onerous (£3,573), but C also suffered: (1) exacerbation of a pre-existing skin complaint, psoriasis, and (2) depression, brought on by extreme anger because the accident had occurred despite his attempts to avert it, and without apology from D. Also, D's medical officer refused to allow C to return to work, and D's HR officers failed to visit or take any interest in C, which angered C and caused him to become preoccupied with the accident. **Held:** both further consequences were not too remote at

---

[40] [1996] AC 155 (HL) 190 (Lord Lloyd, with whom Lords Ackner and Browne-Wilkinson concurred; Lords Keith and Jauncey dissented).

[41] [1996] AC 155 (HL) 188.   [42] [2004] SC (HL) 94, [2004] PIQR P33.

law. Personal injury was a reasonably foreseeable result of D's breach, even if the exacerbation of the skin complaint and the depressive illness were not reasonably foreseeable. C was put in the zone of physical danger by D's breach, and hence, there was no reason to distinguish between physical and psychiatric forms of personal injury.

Of course, if the psychiatric injury itself was reasonably foreseeable, then compensation for it does not fall within this exceptional rule – because *Wagon Mound (No 1)* states that any kind of damage that is foreseeable is recoverable, and not too remote (as illustrated by *Corr v IBC Vehicles*, where Mr Corr's depression and suicide *were* held to be foreseeable). It is only for *unforeseeable* psychiatric damage that the exceptional rule in *Page v Smith* has room to apply.

Even then, *Page v Smith* applies in only very limited circumstances. In *Pratley v Surrey CC*,[43] the Court of Appeal pointed out that *Page v Smith's* view that there is 'no stark divide between physical and mental injury' arose specifically in circumstances where C was in the zone of danger, at risk of physical injury, but suffered psychiatric injury instead. As discussed in more detail in Chapter 5, for other types of pure psychiatric injury claims, *viz*, for secondary victims, for stress-at-work claims (of which Ms Pratley's case was an example), for elevated primary victims, and for the residuary type of claimant, C must prove that his *psychiatric* injury was foreseeable (i.e., in compliance with the usual *Wagon Mound* principle).

Some judges have commented, from time to time, that *Page v Smith* may require reconsideration. For example, in the *Pleural Plaques* litigation,[44] both Lord Scott and Lord Rodger indicated that the principle may be revisited in the future. To date, however, the House of Lords/ Supreme Court has not seen fit (nor perhaps had the opportunity) to revise the principle – and until it does, unforeseeable psychiatric injury will be compensable if suffered by C who was at the risk of foreseeable physical injury created by D's negligence.

Nevertheless, even if C's damage was reasonably foreseeable, it may **not** be recoverable. Three reasons, pertinent to remoteness, may preclude C's recovery of compensation for such damage – the damage fell outside the scope of D's duty to prevent; too many causal chains; and public policy. Before dealing with those, however, it is necessary to consider the position, at law, of the fragile, vulnerable, 'egg-shell skull' C.

THE POSITION OF 'EGG-SHELL' CLAIMANTS WITH PRE-EXISTING VULNERABILITIES

§9.7 Provided that it was reasonably foreseeable that a person of normal physical fortitude would suffer *some* damage of the type that was suffered by C ('the normal fortitude' rule), then an 'egg-shell skull' C, who suffers from some unforeseeable manifestation of injury because of his abnormal physical susceptibility, is able to recover compensation for the *full* extent of his damage, even where the manifestation of that abnormal susceptibility was not reasonably foreseeable. D must 'take his victim as he finds him' (the 'egg-shell skull' rule). The same applies to those who suffer from abnormal psychiatric susceptibility (with the exception of the *Page v Smith*-type victim of psychiatric injury noted in §9.6 above, who is not subject to the normal fortitude rule).

---

[43] [2003] EWCA Civ 1067, [2004] PIQR P17, [42]–[43].
[44] *Johnston v NEI Intl Combustion Ltd* [2007] UKHL 39, [77] (Lord Scott), [95]–[97] (Lord Rodger).

The 'normal fortitude' rule

The 'egg-shell skull' C is treated rather beneficently by English law. In the absence of any special knowledge about C's vulnerability, it must be reasonably foreseeable that the kind of damage suffered by C would be suffered by a person of normal fortitude or robustness as a result of D's breach (the so-called 'the normal fortitude rule'). That is, it must be reasonably foreseeable, to a person in D's position, that a person of 'customary phlegm' or 'with a normal standard of susceptibility'[45] would suffer *some* damage of the type that was suffered. As Lord Bingham stated in *Corr v IBC Vehicles Ltd*, under the remoteness enquiry, 'foreseeability is to be judged ... with reference, not to the actual victim, but to a hypothetical [victim]'.[46]

If, however, it is unforeseeable that an ordinarily-robust C would suffer any damage of the type that was suffered, then the damage suffered by C will be too remote at law. In other words, where C is so vulnerable that he – alone, exceptionally and extraordinarily – suffers some damage from D's breach, where a person of normal fortitude would not suffer any such damage, that damage is not reasonably foreseeable.

The normal fortitude rule applies, whether C has suffered from physical or psychiatric damage:

Physical injury: In *Bourhill (or Hay) v Young*, Lord Wright provided a hypothetical example of an egg-shell skull C of the physical variety: '[o]ne who suffers from a terrible tendency to bleed on slight contact, which is denoted by the term, "a bleeder", cannot complain if he mixes with the crowd and suffers severely, perhaps fatally, from being merely brushed against'.[47]

Psychiatric injury: the rule of normal fortitude applies to all Cs, with the exception of the so-called *Page v Smith*-type 'primary victim', who constitutes an exception to the normal fortitude rule, given that Mr Page suffered a recurrence of CFS (as discussed in Chapter 5). This was reiterated in *White v CC of South Yorkshire Police* ('[t]he law expects reasonable fortitude and robustness of its citizens, and will not impose liability for the exceptional frailty of certain individuals'[48]).

The 'egg–shell skull' rule

This is sometimes referred to by the maxim that the wrongdoer must take his victim *talem qualem* (as he finds him). It seems to originate from the judgment of Kennedy J in *Dulieu v White & Sons*:

If a man is negligently run over [by D], or otherwise negligently injured in his body, it is no answer to the sufferer's claim for damages that he would have suffered less injury, or no injury at all, if he had not had an unusually thin skull or an unusually weak heart.[49]

Any person run over by D would have suffered from *some* physical injury from that accident, thus satisfying the rule of normal fortitude. Then, if C happens to be an 'egg-shell skull' C, the full extent of C's injury is compensable.

Hence, it is important to keep the 'rule of normal fortitude' distinct from the 'egg-shell skull' rule. They are different rules, and operate for different purposes. As the House of Lords explained in *White*, the 'rule of normal fortitude' is a rule of liability, because it is an essential component under the remoteness limb.[50] On the other hand, the 'egg-shell skull' rule is a rule of

[45] *Bourhill (or Hay) v Young* [1943] AC 92 (HL) 110 (Lord Wright), 117 (Lord Porter).
[46] [2008] UKHL 13, [2008] 1 AC 884, [11].   [47] [1943] AC 92 (HL) 109, [1942] SC 78, 92.
[48] [1999] 2 AC 455 (HL) 463.   [49] [1901] 2 KB 669, 679.   [50] [1999] 2 AC 455 (HL) 474.

quantum whereby, as a result of a breach of duty, the damage inflicted by D proves to be more serious than expected because of C's abnormal physical susceptibility, and that can properly be taken into account in assessing the quantum of C's damages. Where an exceptionally frail C *can* satisfy the rule of normal fortitude, this principle of remoteness applies in C's favour, by permitting C (or his estate, if he dies) to recover compensation for the full extent of C's damage, however extraordinary or abnormal that damage may be. As Laws LJ explained in *Rahman v Arearose Ltd*,[51] the egg-shell skull principle:

> is a principle designed to protect vulnerable claimants ... It is a modification of the usual rule that a negligent D is liable for damage which he should reasonably foresee. Its justification is that it promotes the basic rule in this area, which ... is that every tortfeasor should compensate the injured C in respect of that loss and damage for which he should justly be held responsible.

As a practical caveat, however, the quantum of the egg-shell skull C's damage may be reduced or discounted, to take into account that C would have been susceptible in the future to the type of damage that befell him. This discount would reflect the 'ordinary vicissitudes of life' which C was likely to endure, given his 'egg-shell' state (e.g., in *Page v Smith*,[52] Mr Page's damages for his psychiatric condition were discounted by 40%, under this caveat).

§9.8 The 'egg-shell skull' rule applies, whether C has suffered from physical or psychiatric damage. Despite some judicial uncertainty, the better view is that the egg-shell skull rule also applies where C suffers economic damage.

The physically-injured C. Least controversially, the 'egg-shell' rule applies to the physically-injured C:

> In *Smith v Leech Brain & Co Ltd*,[53] a small amount of molten metal was splattered in a factory, due to unsafe work practices employed by the factory owners, Leech Brain, D. Some molten metal splashed onto Mr Smith's, C's, face and lip. Due to a predisposition to cancer, the burn injury to C's lip developed into a cancerous state, and three years after the accident, C died of cancer. **Held:** C's death was not too remote. It was not necessary for a reasonable employer in D's position to have foreseen that a burn would cause cancer, and that C would die. It was only necessary that D could reasonably foresee the type of injury C suffered, *viz*, injury by burn (which was proven). The amount of C's damage depended upon his constitution and characteristics, but D was liable for the full consequences. In *Robinson v Post Office*,[54] Keith Robinson, C, slipped on some oil on a ladder whilst engaged as a technician at the Post Office, D, and grazed his shin. He was given an anti-tetanus serum injection eight hours later, and nine days later, developed encephalitis which resulted in brain damage and paralysis. This was a rare reaction, but more likely where the patient had had a previous dose of the serum (as in C's case). **Held:** D was liable for the full extent of D's injuries, including the brain damage and paralysis. Provided that some physical injury caused by slipping was foreseeable (as was the medical treatment which followed it), D had to take this victim as it found him, even where the amount of injury C suffered depended entirely upon C's allergy to the second serum injection.

Similarly, if C, a haemophiliac, suffers some accidentally-inflicted wound caused by D's negligence, then D will be liable to C, because a non-haemaphiliac would have suffered *some*

---

[51] [2001] QB 351 (CA) [30].   [52] *Page v Smith* [1993] PIQR Q55 (QB) 76–77 (Otton J).
[53] [1962] 2 QB 405, 415.   [54] [1974] 1 WLR 1176 (CA).

damage from that wound. The fact that C may **die**, as a result of blood loss, invokes the 'egg-shell skull' rule.

The psychiatrically-injured C. Where C has an 'egg-shell skull' personality or mental state, and suffers psychiatric injury as a result of D's breach, then in *Page v Smith*, Lord Lloyd stated that, '[t]he negligent [D] ... takes his victim as he finds him. The same should apply in the case of psychiatric injury. There is no difference in principle ... between an eggshell skull and an eggshell personality.'[55] Hence, even though the normal fortitude rule does not apply to *Page v Smith*-type victims (see above), the egg-shell rule certainly does.

> In *Page v Smith*,[56] the negligent car-driver Mr Smith, D, could not have reasonably foreseen that Mr Page, C, would suffer extreme chronic fatigue syndrome after the car accident, but C was an egg-shell skull personality, due to his previous condition of myalgic encephalomyelitis. **Held:** C's damage was not too remote. Lord Browne-Wilkinson stated that D 'did owe a duty of care to prevent foreseeable damage, including psychiatric damage. Once such a duty of care is established, D must take C as he finds him'. In *Simmons v British Steel plc*[57] Mr Simmons, C, suffered a knock to the head after a fall due to D's negligence, and suffered from exacerbation of a pre-existing skin complaint, psoriasis, and also depression. **Held:** both consequences were not too remote. D had to take its victim as it found him, including the possibility of exacerbation of pre-existing conditions and anger leading to depression. 'It does not matter whether a psychologically more robust individual would have recovered from the accident without displaying either condition'.

The economically-injured C. C may be an egg-shell skull victim, economically speaking, in various ways. C may be highly-paid, say, a famous actor – and if he is injured via some act of negligence by D, then D must take that victim as he finds him, when it comes to an assessment of the heads of damage pertaining to past and future economic loss (albeit that this example may also be considered pertinent under principle §9.4 above, to do with the unforeseeable extent of C's economic losses). Alternatively, as a result of D's negligence, impecunious C may have to incur expenditure to mitigate his losses, and that expenditure is more expensive than it would have been, had C been financially better-off. C cannot take advantage of a cheaper option X; instead, he must pursue the more expensive option Y. Alternatively, C may be liable, contractually, to pay financial penalties to third parties, if D damages C's property. In that context, C is an economically-vulnerable egg-shell victim, who had incurred additional expenses. Are those further expenses recoverable from D, or are they too remote?

The current legal position is that the law aligns the economically-vulnerable C with his other egg-shell counterparts. According to *Lagden v O'Connor*,[58] where C's expenditure was increased, due to his impecuniosity, D had to take his victim as he found him, so that if it was reasonably foreseeable that C would have to borrow money or incur some other kind of expenditure to mitigate his damages, then that expenditure was compensable and not too remote.

> In *Lagden v O'Connor*, Mr Lagden, C, was involved in a car accident with Mrs O'Connor, D, in Oxford. C was unemployed at the time. While his car was being repaired, C required another car, and had to hire one at a cost of £659. Due to C's straitened financial circumstances, C could not afford to pay for the hire of a replacement car from his own pocket, and so signed an agreement with a

[55] [1996] AC 155 (HL) 189. See too: *MacDonald (or Cross) v Highlands and Islands Enterprise*, 2001 SCLR 547, 2001 SLT 1060 (SCOH) (stress at work; collapse and breakdown; suicide followed; not too remote).
[56] *ibid*, 182.   [57] [2004] UKHL 20, 2004 SC (HL) 94, [56] (Lord Rodger).
[58] [2003] UKHL 64, [2004] 1 AC 1067.

credit-hire company, whereby it provided a hire car by way of the provision of a 26-week credit facility. The fees charged by the credit-hire company were reflected in a higher rate for the car hire than the equivalent 'spot hire rate' charged by traditional car hire firms. D disputed the claim for £659 car hire as being too remote. **Held (3:2):** C's damages were not too remote. An impecunious C who could not afford to hire a replacement car at commercial rates, or to obtain a loan, had no option but to obtain a credit hire package, and was entitled to recover the whole costs from D. It was reasonably foreseeable that there would be some car owners who would be unable to obtain a replacement car other than by use of a credit hire company.

Previously, the law was not nearly as kind to the impecunious egg-shell C. According to *The Liesbosch Dredger v SS Edison (Owners)*,[59] the financial circumstances of the injured C, and whatever additional expenses he was put to because of his 'financial embarrassment', were too remote. Lord Wright (with whom the other members of the House of Lords agreed) explained this principle as one of policy – that C's additional expenses, if arising from his own impecuniosity, arose from some cause 'extraneous to and distinct in character from the tort'.[60] If the impecuniosity was not traceable to D's tort, then the expenses incurred by reason of that impecuniosity were too remote ('[i]n the varied web of affairs, the law must abstract some consequences as relevant, not perhaps on grounds of pure logic, but simply for practical reasons'[61]).

In *The Liesbosch*, the dredge *Liesbosch* was used in the Greek port harbour of Patras. The dredge sank due to the fouling of its moorings by D's vessel, *The Edison*. The *Liesbosch* owners, C, had all their resources invested in the dredging contract, and their deposit under that contract would be forfeited if the dredging work was delayed. C could not afford to buy another dredge, so hired one, *The Adria*, from Italy. It involved high hiring costs, and was more expensive to run than if C had been able to purchase a dredge. C claimed from D all the costs and expenses caused by their hiring *The Adria*. **Held:** C was only able to recover the market price of a comparable dredger at the time of the loss, and the costs of transporting it to Patras and insuring it – but not the additional costs incurred by hiring *The Adria*. Those hiring costs were incurred because C were impeded in the performance of the dredging contract by its own impecuniosity, and were too remote.

Three reasons were given by the House of Lords in *Lagden*,[62] for the change of view from its decision in *The Liesbosch*:

i. First, 'the law has moved on' since *The Liesbosch* decision, so that the overriding and correct test of remoteness today is whether C's economic loss was reasonably foreseeable. The principle that D must take his victim as he finds him applies equally to the economic state of his victim, in the same way as it applies to his physical and mental vulnerability. Hence, D had to take C as he found him, if C would have to borrow money or incur some kind of expenditure to mitigate his damages;[63]

ii. In the 70 years since *The Liesbosch* was decided, the general classification of C's impecuniosity as 'extraneous' or 'extrinsic' was not defensible. It could still be that some loss attributable to C's impecuniosity could be too remote in some cases, but it was no longer correct at law to say that the consequences that flowed from impecuniosity were simply too remote;[64]

iii. The rule in *The Liesbosch* has been distinguished so often that its authority has been greatly reduced (e.g., in *Alcoa Minerals of Jamaica Inc v Broderick*,[65] the Privy Council noted that

---

[59] [1933] AC 449 (HL).   [60] *ibid*, 461.   [61] *ibid*, 460.   [62] [2003] UKHL 64, [2004] 1 AC 1067.
[63] *ibid*, [61] (Lord Hope).   [64] *ibid*, [102] (Lord Walker).   [65] [2002] 1 AC 371 (PC) [36] (Lord Slynn).

'courts have, from time to time, distinguished it or sought to set limits to its scope'), so that the time had come to refute the rule altogether.

Accordingly, the Court of Appeal recently, in *Haxton v Philips Electronics UK Ltd*,[66] expressly followed the view of *Lagden*, holding that the claimed head of economic damage which was consequential upon the death of C's husband (i.e., the diminution in the value of a litigation claim) was not too remote. In the context of property damage to Network Rail's, C's, track which produced some consequential economic loss for C (i.e., an obligation to pay sums to the rail companies under track access agreements, for every hour that the railtracks were unusable), the Court of Appeal also permitted that consequential economic loss in *Conarken Group Ltd v Network Rail*,[67] relying on *Lagden*.

THE 'SCOPE OF DUTY' ENQUIRY

A further control mechanism

§9.9   Notwithstanding that C's damage was reasonably foreseeable, it must fall within the scope of the duty which D owed C, to protect C by the exercise of reasonable care. Otherwise, C's damage will be regarded as being too remote to be compensable.

This particular principle provides a further 'escape route' for D, even where C's damage was reasonably foreseeable in *Wagon Mound* terms. It arises where a duty to avoid that damage did not fall within the *scope of D's duty* to prevent harm befalling C. This scope-of-duty enquiry is another control mechanism, in addition to the ring-fence already provided by the test of reasonable foreseeability. It requires that even foreseeable damage has to be fairly regarded as being within the scope of D's duty towards C.

As remarked by Evans-Lombe J in *Barings plc (in liq) v Coopers & Lybrand*,[68] the use of the 'scope of duty' argument by a negligent D, as a means of imposing a 'control mechanism' to ring-fence the bounds of foreseeable damage, is a rather 'modern development'. Its lineage appears to have commenced in the 1990 decision of the House of Lords in *Caparo Industries plc v Dickman*,[69] in which Lord Bridge stated that '[i]t is never sufficient to ask simply whether A owes B a duty of care. It is always necessary to determine the scope of the duty by reference to the kind of damage from which A must take care to save B harmless'. Since then, in *D Pride & Partners v Institute for Animal Health*,[70] Tugendhat J referred to the remoteness enquiry as one directed to 'the scope of the duty of care'; and in *Corr v IBC Vehicles Ltd*,[71] Lord Bingham explicitly considered, under the remoteness enquiry, that Mr Corr's, C's, damage (suicide) did not fall outside the scope of the duty of care owed to him by his employer.

In contrast, some judges appear to regard the scope-of-duty argument as fitting into **either** duty or remoteness elements. It will be recalled, from Chapter 2, that the establishment of any novel duty of care category requires that three elements are satisfied, per the 'necessary ingredients' of a duty of care laid down by Lord Bridge in *Caparo v Dickman*[72] – the first of which is that there is reasonable foreseeability of some kind of harm or damage arising from

---

[66] [2014] EWCA Civ 4, [2014] WLR 2721, [22]–[23].   [67] [2011] EWCA Civ 644, [2011] BLR 462, [150].
[68] [2003] EWHC 1319 (Ch) [807].   [69] [1990] 2 AC 605 (HL) 627.   [70] [2009] EWHC 685 (QB) [102].
[71] [2008] UKHL 13, [2008] 1 AC 884, 893.   [72] [1990] 2 AC 605 (HL) 609.

D's breach, and the third of which is that it must be 'fair, just and reasonable' for a duty of care to be imposed. In *Jolley v Sutton LBC*,[73] Lord Hoffmann considered that whether one discussed the foreseeability of C's injury as 'outside the scope of the duty' or 'too remote' was 'according to taste'; and in *Union Camp Chemicals Ltd v CRL TCL Ltd*,[74] Judge Thornton QC regarded the concepts as synonymous: 'in ascertaining whether the damage complained of falls within the scope of that duty ... the court may disallow recovery by use of the twin threshold tests for liability in negligence: the relevant damage is too remote, and it is neither fair and reasonable to allow recovery'.

Hence, it is clear that there is a great deal of overlap between the concept of a duty of care, and the 'scope of the duty' enquiry at remoteness stage. To exclude C's reasonably foreseeable damage on the basis that it is not within the scope of D's duty to prevent is driven by policy considerations which seek to protect D from paying for certain types of harm, notwithstanding that the harm was causally linked to D's breach – and whether these policy reasons are dealt with under duty of care, or remoteness, and whether they are attributed the label of 'not fair, just and reasonable', or 'beyond the scope of duty', seems to depend upon judicial preference rather than upon any clear analytical approach.

An excellent illustration of the conundrum is contained in the hypothetical mountaineering example provided by Lord Hoffmann in *South Australia Asset Management Corp v York Montague Ltd*[75] (the *SAAMCO case*). There was no doubt that D, the doctor, owed a duty to C, the mountaineer, as his patient. However, the question was whether the damage suffered by the mountaineer was within the scope of the doctor's duty to prevent – an issue which pertained to remoteness of damage.

> To paraphrase the *mountaineering example in SAAMCO*, suppose a mountaineer, C, is due to undertake a difficult climbing expedition, and is concerned about the fitness of his knee. He goes to a doctor, D, who negligently makes a superficial examination, and pronounces the knee fit. C goes on the expedition, which he would not have undertaken if D had told him the true state of his knee. C suffers a head injury when caught in an avalanche, which is an entirely foreseeable consequence of mountaineering, but has nothing to do with his knee. **Hypothetically, held**: C's injury was entirely and reasonably foreseeable (per *Wagon Mound*). However, the damage resulting from the head injuries are too remote. To hold D liable for the head injuries 'offends common sense because it makes the doctor responsible for consequences which, though in general terms foreseeable, do not appear to have a sufficient causal connection with the subject matter of the duty. The doctor was asked for information on only one of the considerations which might affect the safety of the mountaineer on the expedition. There seems no reason of policy which requires that the negligence of the doctor should require the transfer to him of all the foreseeable risks of the expedition'. In other words, injury to mountaineer C, if the knee gave way, was foreseeable and not too remote, because the scope of the doctor's duty was to advise on the fitness of the knee. On the other hand, head injuries caused by an avalanche were foreseeable, but too remote, because the duty was not so wide as to prevent all injuries occurring to C.

A number of real-life cases illustrate D's attempt to argue that C's damage fell outside the scope of D's duty of care to C, rendering the damage too remote. Selecting some contrasting cases by way of example, where the injuries were not too remote:

---

[73] [2000] 1 WLR 1082 (HL) 1091.   [74] [2001] All ER (D) 95 (TCC) [98].   [75] [1997] AC 191 (HL) 213.

In *Corr v IBC Vehicles Ltd*[76] facts previously, Mr Corr, C, committed suicide several years after his ear was severed in a workplace accident. IBC Vehicles, D, argued that suicide was too remote, and that while an employer owes a duty of care to an employee to provide a safe system of work, C's suicide fell outside the scope of the duty of care owed by D as his employer, because there was no duty on the employer to protect employee C *from self-harm*. C was not technically insane at the time of his death, and could invoke personal autonomy and self-determination, such that the employer was not 'his keeper'. **Held:** the suicide was not too remote. D owed C a duty, as its employee, to take reasonable care to avoid causing him physical injury. C's conduct in taking his own life stemmed from that breach, and did not fall outside the scope of the duty which his employer owed him. In *Jolley v Sutton LBC*[77] facts previously, it was conceded by Council D that it ought to have removed the boat, as it represented a danger and an allurement for children who may have been tempted to play on it. There was a risk that children would have suffered minor injuries if the rotten planking gave way beneath them. However, it was argued that any injury caused by the propped-up boat collapsing fell outside the scope of D's duty to prevent. **Held:** the injuries were not too remote. D would have incurred no extra expense to eliminate that risk of the boat collapsing – if it had removed the boat (as it conceded that it ought to have done, and which it did after the accident happened), then the more unlikely sequence of injury would not have happened. Hence, the injuries suffered (paraplegia) were within the scope of D's duty to prevent.

– and where C's injuries lay outside the scope of D's duty to C:

In *R v Croydon HA*,[78] Mrs R, C, a nurse trained to work with the mentally disabled, applied for a job at the Croydon HA, D, as a community nurse. To be considered for this work, C had to undergo a medical examination, including a chest X-ray. Dr Manners, D, a radiologist, negligently failed to report a significant abnormality on C's X-ray which would have required C to be referred to a cardiologist, who would have diagnosed primary pulmonary hypertension (PPH). PPH, an untreatable condition, diminished limited life expectancy, and was exacerbated if the sufferer became pregnant. D accepted that C would not have become pregnant had she been diagnosed with PPH. C became pregnant four months after commencing her employment, became ill, and was diagnosed with PPH. After the birth of her child, C was unable to return to employment which involved dealing with difficult and potentially violent mental patients. C developed reactive depression and was retired on the grounds of ill health. C claimed the pregnancy and the costs of raising her child as damages resulting from the negligent reading of the chest X-ray. **Held:** the pregnancy and all the losses flowing from it were too remote. The pregnancy itself, and the costs of raising the child, etc, were foreseeable consequences of the failure to diagnose PPH. D's duty as a radiologist was to observe and report on abnormalities which could have affected her fitness for work as an employee of the health authority. However, it was not within the scope of the radiologist's duty to advise C on abnormalities which might render some activities wholly unconnected with employment problematical. Briefly put, C's 'domestic circumstances were not D's affair'. In *Pritchard v JH Cobden Ltd (No 1)*,[79] Mr Pritchard, C, was involved in a car accident with Mr Parrott, D, an employee of JH Cobden, who was driving an articulated lorry. C suffered brain damage resulting in left-sided hemiplegia, blindness in right eye, defective intelligence, concentration and memory and a severe personality change. This led to a breakdown of his marriage and eventual divorce. He sought (and recovered at trial) damages in respect of the additional cost of maintaining two households as a result of his divorce. **Held:**

[76] [2008] UKHL 13, [2008] 1 AC 884.   [77] [2000] 1 WLR 1082 (HL).
[78] [1998] 2 Lloyd's Rep Med 44 (CA).   [79] [1987] 2 WLR 627 (CA).

the damages for maintaining his wife were too remote, such that C was not entitled to damages to compensate him for the break-up of his marriage.

Hence, where domestic consequences for C are wrought by virtue of D's breach, those consequences may very well be outside the scope of D's duty.

The *SAAMCO* principle

The basic principle

§9.10   The *SAAMCO* principle applies in the particular scenario of negligent valuations, i.e., the provision of information on which C relies. The valuer, D, owes a duty to a lender, C, to protect C against losses which C might suffer, if the valued security is worth less than the sum at which D valued the security. However, the scope of D's duty is not to protect C against losses incurred because of a fall in the property market – even where (1) that property downturn was foreseeable, and (2) C would not have lent the money at all, had the valuation been carefully undertaken.

The *SAAMCO* principle, named after the case (a series of three appeals) in which it was espoused – *South Australia Asset Management Corp v York Montague Ltd*[80] – is a particular application of the scope-of-duty test. Again, foreseeably-occurring damage is excluded under this principle, because the duty owed by D can be regarded as limited to one kind of damage, and not to another. Essentially, C's losses, attributable to the fall in the property market, lie outside the scope of D's duty.

> In *the SAAMCO case*, various banks, C, loaned money to developers of the London Docklands project, on the basis of valuations provided by various valuers, D. The valued properties were used as security for the mortgages, but were negligently over-valued. They proved to be inadequate security, when the borrowers defaulted on their loans and the security was called in (i.e., realised) by C. As a result, C suffered loss. While that loss was caused, in part, by the negligent over-valuations of the security (without which C would never have lent the money at all), the loss was also caused, in part, by a substantial fall in the value of property generally over the loan period. The question arose as to what amount of loss D were properly responsible for. **Held (CA[81]):** D were liable for *all the loss suffered* by C, including that referable to the fall in property prices. C would not have entered into the loans, but for the representations they had received from valuer D, and it was fair and reasonable that all the foreseeable losses flowing from that negligent advice should be recoverable from D. **Held (HL):** C was entitled to recover damages, measured by the difference between the true value of the security, and those shown on the negligent valuations, at the date that the loans were made. Whatever losses occurred in the property market after that date were too remote from the negligent valuations, and were not recoverable.

The reasoning of the House of Lords was that the valuer D's duty is **not** so wide as to protect lender C against **all** losses that it suffered because it entered into transactions on the strength of that valuation (even if C proves that it would not have lent the money at all). The scope of D's duty is not to protect C against all the consequences of entering transactions, thinking that the property was worth what valuer D said. Hence, the fall in the property market which adversely affected C's ability to use the security to meet a defaulting borrower's obligations was not to be

[80] [1997] AC 191 (HL).   [81] [1995] QB 375 (CA).

laid at valuer D's door. It was also legally irrelevant that a drop in the property market which affected the property values was foreseeable.

Diagrammatically, the difference between the Court of Appeal and the House of Lords can be illustrated below, with reference to the transaction in *SAAMCO v York Montague* itself:

SAAMCO: The Court of Appeal and the House of Lords contrasted

–£15m—the negligent valuation of the property by the valuer D

–£11m—the amount the lender C loaned to the developer by way of mortgage over that property, on 3 Aug 1990

–£5m—what the property was actually worth, at the date of D's valuation

– £2.5m — following the fall in the property market, this is what the property sold for on 5 Aug 1994, when the borrower defaulted on the loan, and lender C redeemed the security

What the **Court of Appeal** held to be the compensable damage (the lender would not have lent at all if the valuation had been accurate; all foreseeable losses were recoverable):

	£11m (the amount loaned)
Less:	£2.5m
	£8.5m

What the **House of Lords** held to be the correct compensable damage (given that the lender did not have security over a property of the value which it thought it had):

	£15m
Less:	£5m
	£10m

Hence, on a time-line, the much later event, i.e., the date at which the security was redeemed in 1994, could be ignored. Lender C could not recover for this fall in the property market, that was too remote, and hence, the £8.5m was not the appropriate measure. Rather, the consequence of D's valuation being wrong was that lender C had £10m less security than it thought it had. If lender C had held that amount of security when it extended the loan, C would have suffered no loss, when it came time for the property to be redeemed. The HL reasoning ignored any fluctuations in the market, and what lender C actually redeemed the property for.

Limitations

The *SAAMCO* principle has its limits, however. To mention a couple:

i. It seems that there is an important distinction to be drawn, between (a) where D provides information to C on which C relies, but where D does not advise C to follow a course of action (whereupon D will not be liable for all of the consequences arising from C's reliance on the information, per *SAAMCO*); and (b) where D actually advises C to pursue a certain course of action (and C does, and where D will be liable for the reasonably foreseeable consequences of C's acting in reliance on that advice).

For example, in Lord Hoffmann's mountaineering example, doctor D did not advise or recommend his patient to go mountaineering; all he did was to say that the patient's knee was robust, and it was up to the patient as to whether to proceed with the expedition. On the other hand, investment advice is often more directive, in that C is advised to undertake the investment. In

Rubenstein v HSBC Bank plc,[82] Rix LJ noted that an investment adviser, D, 'with his statutory duties of various kinds', owes C a wider duty of care, to avoid **all** foreseeable losses, if D recommends a particular investment, and then some flaw in the investment turns out materially to contribute to a loss of that investment. In this case, the investment adviser, D, 'so to speak, put him in it'. In that scenario, the scope of D's duty will not reduce the foreseeable and compensable damages.

> In *Aneco Reinsurance Underwriting Ltd (in liq) v Johnson & Higgins Ltd*,[83] Aneco, C, sought reinsurance for part of the liabilities which it undertook for Lloyds syndicates. C engaged Johnson & Higgins, D, reinsurance brokers, to obtain that reinsurance. The reinsurance was obtained, but ultimately, most of the policies were avoided by the relevant underwriters, because of non-disclosure of material facts concerning the true nature of the underlying insurance which C was undertaking. C sued D for failing to exercise reasonable care and skill in obtaining the reinsurance on its behalf. D claimed that the correct measure of damages was the value of the reinsurance cover which C lost when the cover was avoided (worth about £10m). C claimed that, had D made full disclosure of the material facts to the underwriters, then reinsurance cover of the kind which C required would not have been available in the London market on commercial terms, C would not have entered into the Lloyds syndicate at all, and hence, the full losses it suffered, of around £30m, would not have been suffered. **Held (2:1):** C's full damage of £30m was not too remote. The scope of D's duty was to obtain satisfactory reinsurance, or if unprocurable, to tell C that no such reinsurance was available or that none was available on acceptable terms. D knew that C would not accept the risk otherwise, and would not have entered the Lloyds syndicate. D was advising C here, as to what course to take. Hence, whatever loss C suffered from entering that transaction was recoverable.

Nevertheless, drawing the appropriate distinction between an 'information' case (which invokes *SAAMCO*) and an 'advice' case (which exposes D to a potentially wider scope of duty) is not easy to do in some cases (as exemplified by the discussion of Richards LJ in *Andrews v Waddingham*,[84] which was held to be an 'information' case; and in *Baillie v Bromhead & Co (a firm)*,[85] where the court frankly admitted that neither counsel was able to 'characterise what quality it was which placed a case in one category or the other').

ii. It is always necessary to establish a causal link between D's breach and C's economic loss, on the 'but-for' test – even where the economic loss suffered by C was reasonably foreseeable. If the 'but-for' cause of C's loss was C's own financial difficulties (unrelated to D's investment advice), together with the effects of a property crash, then that will bring about the failure of C's claim, regardless of whether or not the damage was within the scope of D's duty to avoid (per *Bateson v Savills Private Finance Ltd*[86]).

Failure-to-warn scenarios

§9.11   Where healthcare professional D fails to warn patient C of a material or significant risk which ought to have been warned about; C opts to have the surgical treatment or procedure; and *another* risk (which was not material or significant, and which did not need to be warned about) manifests, it is presently uncertain as to whether the injury arising from that different risk was too remote to be compensable.

---

[82] [2012] EWCA Civ 1184, [103].   [83] [2001] UKHL 51, [2002] PNLR 8, [16]–[17].
[84] [2006] EWCA Civ 93, [46]–[47].   [85] [2014] EWHC 2149 (Ch) [22].   [86] [2013] EWHC 719 (QB) [33].

The 'scope of duty' test suggests that the healthcare practitioner's, D's, liability should be limited to those particular risks of which mention ought to have been made, and which have actually manifested or eventuated. This scenario arguably fits within the previously-mentioned 'information' scenario of *SAAMCO's* mountaineering example provided by Lord Hoffmann – i.e., the warning as to risks is not a recommendation to the patient, C, to follow a course of action (i.e., it is not an advice scenario), but rather, information upon which C can base a decision as to whether or not to proceed with the medical treatment or procedure. That invokes a narrower 'scope of duty' enquiry, according to *SAAMCO*.

Undoubtedly, the fact that C suffered the remote risk satisfies the 'but-for' test of causation, in that C would not have undertaken the treatment or procedure, had warning of the material risk been given as it legally should have been. If patient C undergoes an operation which he would not have undergone, but for the negligent failure-to-warn, then any detriment resulting from the operation should be regarded as caused by the negligent failure-to-warn, in a strict 'but-for' analysis.

However, as the discussion in this chapter demonstrates, remoteness is quite a separate enquiry. On the grounds of fairness and policy, it is highly arguable that the **only** detriment for which damages should be awarded in C's favour are those against the risk of which D should have warned.[87]

Thus far, this conundrum has not been directly answered in English law, so far as the author's searches can ascertain. It is significant, however, that in the leading failure-to-warn case of *Chester v Afshar*,[88] the particular risk which manifested for patient C – paralysis caused by nerve damage – was said to be the precise risk against which warning ought to have been given. The majority noted that it was **not** a coincidental risk which damaged C: '[i]f a patient in the position of Miss Chester had been injured by some wholly unforeseeable accident of anaesthesia ... or because the operating theatre was struck by lightning ... the injury could have been described as coincidental ... [However] the misfortune which befell C was the very misfortune which was the focus of the surgeon's duty to warn'. This suggests that any coincidental damage could have been regarded as being too remote to be compensable.

The comparative corner: An Australian vignette

In *Hribar v Wells*,[89] King CJ gave this example (with a hypothetical scenario in brackets):

'There may be operations (*say, a dental operation*) which result in detriments which are quite unrelated to the risk against which it was the surgeon's duty to warn ... It may be, in some cases, that the detriment against which the surgeon should have warned (*say, the risk of permanent numbness of tongue and lips, following the administering of a particular anaesthetic*) does not materialise at all, but other detriments against the risk of which warning was ... not required (*say, the risk of unclean instruments being used during the procedure*) do ensue.'

King CJ did not have to answer the conundrum, but it was suggested that the other detriment might be too remote.

---

[87] See: Mulheron, 'Observations upon Causation in Recent "Failure to warn" Cases' (2000) *National L Rev* 2, [36]–[39].

[88] [2005] 1 AC 134, [94] (Lord Walker).   [89] (1995) 64 SASR 129 (FC) 130, and also 146–47 (Duggan J).

TOO MANY CAUSAL LINKS

§9.12   Where there are numerous links between D's breach and C's damage, then even reasonably foreseeable damage may be too remote to be recoverable.

Although this principle may seem to be more appropriately dealt with under the causal element, the language of some cases suggest that it is a remoteness issue.

In *Hyde v Tameside AHA*,[90] Lord Denning MR cited the well-known sequence of Benjamin Franklin: 'For want of a nail, the shoe was lost; for want of a shoe, the horse was lost; and for want of a horse, the rider was lost: and for want of a rider, the battle was lost'. In other words, if D negligently failed to nail soldier C's horseshoe directly, then the harm arising to C (and others) from the lost battle would be too remote from D's breach to be recoverable. Those long causal chains have been pointed to in some cases, in order to render the damage too remote. Two cases are worth contrasting:

In *Hyde v Tameside AHA*, Eric Hyde, C, was admitted to hospital for the treatment of a suspected disc lesion. By the 12th night of his admission, C convinced himself (wrongly) that he was dying of cancer, and was going to die in the next hour or so, and he tried to kill himself. In the middle of the night, he got out of his bed on the third floor, smashed the window, jumped out, landed on a parapet and flung himself from there on to the roadway outside. The attempted suicide failed, and C suffered quadriplegia. He sued the hospital, D, in negligence. **Held (at trial):** C recovered £200,000. **Held (CA):** C's damage was too remote. 'If the nurses had reported [C's] depression to the doctors, then the doctors might have called in a consultant psychiatrist. If a consultant psychiatrist had been called in, he might have ordered some treatment which might have had some effect on the depression. If it did have some effect on [C's] depression, it might have prevented him from attempting to commit suicide. All these consequences might have followed. But I think it wrong that the law should chase consequence upon consequence – possibility upon possibility – right down on a hypothetical line – so as to award damages to a man who attempted to commit suicide ... the damages are far too remote' (Lord Denning). In the alternative, no reasonable D would have reasonably foreseen that this C would try to commit suicide (per Watkins LJ).

In *McFarlane v Tayside Health Board*,[91] a sterilisation (vasectomy) operation was performed for Mr McFarlane, which was unsuccessful. However, this was not detected, and the parents were advised that they could dispense with other forms of contraception. A healthy child, Catherine, was subsequently conceived, and Mr and Mrs McFarlane, C, sought to recover, inter alia, the costs of maintenance of Catherine's upbringing. **Held:** that head of damages were rebutted, with a suggestion that the damage was almost too causally remote: 'there are several successive stages from the allegedly negligent advice [that Mr McFarlane was sterile] before one reaches the incurring of the maintenance costs; the intercourse without protection, the conception of the child, the carrying of the child to her birth, and the acceptance of the baby as a further member of the family with all the obligations towards her which parenthood involves. The cost of the maintenance of the child seems to me to be a loss near the limits of the causal chain' (per Lord Clyde). Nevertheless, causation was proven, and the costs of Catherine's upbringing were not rejected on this ground, but for policy reasons (per Chapter 2).

[90] QB, 13 Apr 1981.   [91] [2000] 2 AC 59 (HL) 104.

It follows that, if there are 'several successive stages' between breach and damage, then not only may one of those interim events constitute a *novus actus interveniens*, but the damage itself may be too remote to be compensable in law.

POLICY: A 'FINAL ARBITER'

§9.13   Even if C's damage was reasonably foreseeable, reasons of public policy may render C's damage too remote.

It is perhaps unsurprising that the unruly horse, otherwise known as policy, infuses this last element of negligence as it has elsewhere in the tort – allowing the court to determine for what damages D *ought* to be liable. The Singapore Court of Appeal expressed the position perfectly in *Sunny Metal and Engineering Pte Ltd v Ng Khim Ming Eric*,[92] when it said that the remoteness enquiry:

> unlike that of causation, presents a much larger area of choice in which legal policy and accepted value judgment must be the final arbiter of what balance to strike between the claim to full reparation for the loss suffered by an innocent victim of another's culpable conduct and the excessive burden that would be imposed on human activity if a wrongdoer were to be held to answer for *all* consequences of his default.

Hence, reasonable foreseeability of damage is not determinative, if public policy precludes recovery of damage which was causally connected to D's breach. This factor has largely, perhaps, been subsumed under the 'scope of duty' enquiry – albeit that some cases have discussed the preclusion of recovery in policy terms.

> In *Pritchard v JH Cobden Ltd (No 1)*,[93] facts previously, **held:** the damages for maintaining C's wife were too remote, as it would be against public policy, and open to abuse, to bring into personal injury litigation considerations relevant to matrimonial proceedings.

On the other hand, suicide is a form of personal injury that is 'not beyond the pale' nor too remote on policy grounds. The law does not 'draw up its skirts and refuse all assistance to [a suiciding C]' (per Bingham LJ in *Saunders v Edwards*[94]), notwithstanding that the act might prompt religious condemnation, and was previously-criminalised. Provided that the suicide arises out of depression, and that the depression is causally linked to the breach, the law will not consider it to be uncompensable (per *Corr v IBC Vehicles*).

---

[92] [2007] SGCA 36, (2007) 113 Con LR 112, [56].   [93] [1987] 2 WLR 627 (CA).
[94] [1987] 1 WLR 1116 (CA) 1134.

10

Defences

INTRODUCTION

§10.1 There are six defences to the tort of negligence. The burden of proof rests with D, when seeking to prove any of these defences.

The defences available in negligence comprise the following: (1) contributory negligence, i.e., that C carelessly contributed to his own injury; (2) *volenti*, i.e., that C fully and freely assumed the risk of injury created by D's breach; (3) illegality, i.e., that C was engaged in an illegal purpose when harmed by D; (4) exclusion clauses, i.e., that D can take advantage of a limitation of liability clause in his agreement/contract with C; (5) therapeutic privilege, i.e., that D withheld information about material risks from C, because disclosure might harm C's health and wellbeing; and (6) necessity, i.e., that D's negligence was committed because it was necessary to save life, limb or property.

The burden of proof rests with D (e.g., for necessity, see *Southport Corp v Esso Petroleum Co Ltd*[1]). It is not for C to prove that no defence applies; D bears the persuasive burden to convince the court that it does.

All but one – contributory negligence – is a complete defence. Contributory negligence is a partial defence, and (probably) cannot serve as a complete defence.

This chapter does not traverse other 'defences', such as the doctrines of 'inevitable accident' and *res ipsa loquitur*, which are relevant to the proof of breach (as discussed in Chapter 7). These doctrines arguably do not shift the burden of proof from C, but are ways in which breach may be (dis)proven. Nor does the chapter re-examine the doctrine of 'common employment', which did provide an effective defence for an employer until its abolition, when the Law Reform (Personal Injuries) Act 1948 was passed (see 'Employers' liability', an online chapter).

CONTRIBUTORY NEGLIGENCE

Preliminary matters

§10.2 Contributory negligence means that, notwithstanding D's breach of duty, C was at fault for contributing towards his own damage. The defence is a statutory, not a common law, defence, prescribed by the Law Reform (Contributory Negligence) Act 1945.

[1] [1954] 2 QB 182 (CA).

The defence of contributory negligence has operated in its present statutory form in England from the mid-20th century. The Law Reform (Contributory Negligence) Act 1945 ('the 1945 Act') provides:

> **s 1(1)** Where any person suffers damage as the result partly of his own fault and partly of the fault of any other person or persons, a claim in respect of that damage shall not be defeated by reason of the fault of the person suffering the damage, but the damages recoverable in respect thereof shall be reduced to such extent as the court thinks just and equitable having regard to the claimant's share in the responsibility for the damage.

Two practical matters are worth mentioning at the outset. First, any assessment of contributory negligence by the trial judge is a decision which will not be interfered with on appeal unless the trial judge 'has gone fundamentally wrong' (per *Dixon v Clement Jones Solicitors (a firm)*[2]) or where 'some error in the judge's approach is clearly discernible' (per *Smith v Nottinghamshire Police*[3]). The types of 'identifiable error' necessary, for appellate intervention, include: where the trial court omitted to mention a material fact about C's behaviour (as in *Stapley v Gypsum Mines Ltd*[4]); or recklessness was attributed to C where none existed (as in *Jackson v Murray*[5]); or the appellate court disagreed as to which party should bear the greater share of responsibility (another reason for overturning the apportionment in *Jackson*). Otherwise, if the appellate court disagrees with the (albeit wide) range of appropriate apportionment in which reasonable opinion may fix contributory negligence, then that can also justify appellate overrule (as in *Stapley*, where contributory negligence was varied from 50% up to 80%) – but if the trial judge's assessment of contributory negligence is within that range, albeit that it was 'about as favourable to [C] as it could be, having regard to his behaviour', that will be non-appealable (per *Silverlink Trains Ltd v Collins-Williamson*[6]).

Secondly, C cannot obtain insurance for his own wrongdoing. Hence, as one leading Torts commentator has remarked, 'the only significant group of people who are called upon to pay for the consequences of their negligence are accident victims themselves'.[7]

The defence of contributory negligence entails four elements (per *Badger v MOD*):[8]

> **The framework for contributory negligence**
>
> 1 C was partly at fault in bringing about his own injury or harm
> 2 There must be a causal link between C's contributory negligence and his injury
> 3 The apportionment of contributory negligence must take into account the relative blameworthiness of C's and D's conduct, *and* the extent of their fault in causing C's damage
> 4 C's damages must be reduced by an amount which is just and equitable

Alternative allegations
Wherever contributory negligence arises as a potential allegation, the acts or omissions which raise that defence may give rise to other legal arguments too – although their legal bases and

[2] [2004] EWCA Civ 1005, [51].   [3] [2012] EWCA Civ 161, [36].   [4] [1953] AC 663 (HL) 682–83.
[5] [2015] UKSC 5, [36]–[37].   [6] [2009] EWCA Civ 850, [61].
[7] P Cane, *Atiyah's Accidents, Compensation and the Law* (7th edn, Cambridge University Press, 2006) 56.
[8] [2005] EWHC 2941 (QB) [6] (Stanley Burnton J).

ramifications are quite distinct (per *Gregory v Shepherds (a firm)*[9]). For example, C's acts or omissions may amount to:

- an intervening act, brought about by C's own carelessness, as both of the following held:

  In the Scottish case of *Sabri-Tabrizi v Lothian Health Board*,[10] Ms Sabri-Tabrizi, C, alleged that, due to surgeon D's negligence in performing a surgical sterilisation, she remained fertile. C became pregnant, had this pregnancy terminated, fell pregnant again, and gave birth to a stillborn child. She claimed damages for both pregnancies, but failed. Re the second pregnancy, C's decision to have unprotected intercourse after the first pregnancy was a *novus actus interveniens*. In *McKew v Holland & Hannen & Cubitts (Scotland) Ltd*, Mr McKew, C, was injured at work, caused by his employer's, D's, breach. His back and hips were badly strained, and on several occasions his left leg suddenly 'went away from' him. Despite that, after inspecting a flat in Glasgow, C decided to descend a steep staircase with no handrail, carrying his young child. His left leg 'vanished under him', and he jumped about 12 feet to the landing below. C's conduct was unreasonable, and a *novus actus interveniens*. C 'must have realised ... that he could only safely descend the stair if he either went extremely slowly and carefully, so that he could sit down if his leg gave way, or waited for the assistance of his wife and brother in-law. But he chose to descend in such a way that, when his leg gave way, he could not stop himself'.

- an ability on C's part to prove any breach on D's part, given C's acts or omissions:

  In *Venner v North East Essex AHA*,[11] C was advised to cease taking the contraceptive pill before a sterilisation operation, and to take other contraceptive precautions. C ignored that advice, and was pregnant when the operation took place. In answer to a question as to whether there was any chance that she could be pregnant, C answered 'no', and no further questioning or investigations were done before the operation. C sued D in negligence, for failing to ascertain that she might be pregnant. **Held:** no negligence by D. There was no breach by D, in not 'prying further into the intimate details' of C's life: '[w]here a mature and sensible woman is asked a question to which only she knows the answer, then she bears a real responsibility to give an accurate and truthful answer ... if a woman conducts herself in that way contrary to advice, and then gives an answer which is less than frank, it can scarcely be said that the operating gynaecologist is responsible for the continuing pregnancy'.

However, these are all-or-nothing outcomes. In modern times, courts prefer to apportion fault (if, indeed, there is fault on both sides) under the 1945 Act.

A partial, or a total, defence?

§10.3   The predominant view in English law is that contributory negligence *cannot* operate as a complete defence.

Can C be the sole author of his own misfortune, even though D was negligent towards him? In other words, can contributory negligence of 100% be awarded against C? Prior to the enactment of the 1945 Act, contributory negligence operated as a complete defence at common law.[12] However, under the 1945 Act, dicta are divided.

The 'no' case. The weight of Court of Appeal authority is that a 100% deduction for contributory negligence is not correct in law (per *Pitts v Hunt*,[13] and *Anderson v Newham College*

---

[9] (Ch, 8 Feb 1999) [4.3].   [10] [1998] SC 373 (OH) 377.   [11] QB, 19 Feb 1987.
[12] *Commr of Police v Reeves* [2000] AC 360 (HL) 364 (Lord Hoffmann).   [13] [1991] 1 QB 24 (CA) 48.

of Higher Education[14]). As these cases pointed out, a 100% attribution of negligence to C is seemingly at odds with a finding that D was, in some way, at fault too. After all, the reduction of damages permitted under the 1945 Act is not triggered, unless C's damage is 'partly the fault of any other person' (per s 1(1)). Further, the fact that the statute refers to C's damages 'being reduced' and that the court must assess C's 'share in the responsibility for the damage' means that C should recover some damages and that D must also share in that responsibility. As Sedley LJ stated in *Anderson*, '[i]f there is liability, contributory negligence can reduce its monetary quantification, but it cannot legally or logically nullify it'.[15] Moreover, 100% contributory negligence sits very uneasily with the inherent trust and confidence, or imbalance of power and bargaining position, which the relationship between C and D may entail (note, e.g., the police–prisoner relationship in *Reeves v Commr of Police*,[16] where the trial judge had held 100% contributory negligence against C who hanged himself in custody, but where 50% was eventually held on appeal, given the responsibility of the police in preventing suicides in custody).

In *Pitts v Hunt*, Andrew Pitts, C, 18, sued Mark Hunt, 16, D, for damages for personal injuries received when he was travelling as a pillion passenger on a motor cycle driven by D. The two friends regularly used the bike to go trail bike-riding together. On this occasion, they attended a disco, drank a great deal and then set off home. Their motorcycle collided with another car, and D was killed, while C was severely injured. During the journey, they had behaved in a reckless, irresponsible and idiotic way, shouting, blowing the horn and driving at pedestrians on the verge of the road. D's estate claimed that, by C's getting on the motorcycle as a pillion passenger, knowing D to be drunk, unlicensed and uninsured, C had voluntarily assumed the risk. **Held (trial):** 100% CN. **Held (CA):** at the most, 50% CN, dicta (separately, illegality applied, defeating the claim).

The 'yes' case. The proposition that contributory negligence can be a complete defence does have some support in dicta at House of Lords' level, with Lord Reid stating, in *Imperial Chemical Industries Ltd v Shatwell*, that 'it does not matter in the result whether one says 100% contributory negligence or *volenti*'.[16a] There have been occasional dicta in lower courts too, supporting the notion that contributory negligence can be a complete defence (per *Mitchell v W S Westin Ltd*,[17] *Jayes v IMI (Kynoch) Ltd*,[18] and *Pratt v Intermet Refractories Ltd*[19]) – although these were all disapproved in *Anderson*. In favour of the 'yes' case is that, conceivably, D's negligence may have brought about the *accident* in which C was involved; but C's own negligence was 100% responsible for C's *damage* (as s 1(1)'s language actually requires). Further, if the degree of fault is so great on C's part, then fine assessments of negligence on D's part (say, <5%) are virtually meaningless according to *Jayes*, and equate to a finding of 100% contributory negligence.

The comparative corner: A complete defence

Australian law reform opinion favoured permitting 100% CN against C (i.e., that it become an absolute, rather than just a partial, defence – a change to Australian substantive

[14] [2002] EWCA Civ 505, [10]–[18].   [15] [2002] EWCA Civ 505, [18].

[16] [2000] AC 360 (HL). See also: *Barings plc v Coopers & Lybrand* [2003] EWHC 1319 (Ch) [837] (100% CN was 'a contradiction in terms', per Evans-Lombe J).

[16a] [1965] AC 656 (HL) 672.   [17] [1965] 1 WLR 297 (CA) 305 (Sellers LJ), 308–9 (Pearson LJ).

[18] [1985] ICR 155 (Goff LJ) 158–59.   [19] (CA, May LJ, 21 Jan 2000).

law[20]). The Ipp Committee justified its view thus: 'denying C any damages need not be viewed as inconsistent with a finding that D was negligent ... there may be cases in which C's relative responsibility for the injuries suffered is so great that it seems fair to deny C any damages at all ... apportionment of damages is concerned with the issue of appropriate remedy, not with liability. It does not follow from a decision that C should be denied any damages at all, that D was not at fault. Such a decision only means that, as between the two parties at fault, C should bear full legal responsibility for the harm suffered'.[21] Not all Australian commentators agreed: 'it is difficult to justify a conclusion that [D's] conduct was negligent and caused [C] injury, yet at the same time finding that [C] is not "worthy" of any compensation whatsoever').[22]

The 'last opportunity' rule

§10.4 The 'last opportunity' rule was overruled by the 1945 Act.

The 'last opportunity' rule[23] was ascribed to *Davies v Mann*,[24] where C's donkey was hit by D's cart, but the donkey had been let loose by C's carelessness; D's negligence was the last opportunity to avoid the damage to the donkey, and C recovered in full. Hence, the rule provided that if, in the chain of events, the last opportunity to prevent C's harm rested with D, then the sole cause of C's harm was D's own fault – even where C had committed some prior wrongdoing himself. In effect, D's act or omission was the whole cause of C's loss, and C would be able to recover damages, notwithstanding that contributory negligence.

The rule was implemented in response to the common law position that, otherwise, any contributory negligence on C's part afforded D a complete defence. In those pre-1945 Act days, an all-or-nothing outcome had the potential to wreak real injustice as between the parties. Indeed, one of the purposes of the 1945 Act was to 'do away with the injustices' of the 'last opportunity' rule, and enable the apportionment of damages as between C and D, both of whom were at 'fault' (per *Sahib Foods Ltd v Paskin Kyriakides Sands (a firm)*[25]).

Transferred contributory negligence

§10.5 If D is vicariously liable for an employee's wrongdoing, or if C is claiming under certain statutes, then D can take advantage of any contributory negligence finding which was made against a wrongdoing party.

Vicarious liability against D for an employee's negligence will be reduced by the percentage of contributory negligence found against the wrongdoer C.

> In *Silverlink Trains Ltd v Collins-Williamson*,[26] Silverlink, D, was vicariously liable for its train guard who, having seen passenger Mr Collins-Williamson, C, being 'idiotic' and 'playing the fool' while the train was stationary, gave a signal for the driver to start. **Held:** 50% CN awarded, which could thereby reduce D's damages liability.

[20] Cf: *Wynbergen v Hoyts Corp Pty Ltd* (1998) 72 ALJR 65 (HCA) (CN could not be a 100% defence).
[21] *Ipp Report*, [8.22], [8.24].   [22] M Shircore, 'Drinking, Driving and Causing Injury' [2007] *QUTLJJ* 22.
[23] Also called the 'last clear chance rule'.   [24] (1842) 10 M&W 546.
[25] [2003] EWHC 142 (TCC) [72].   [26] [2009] EWCA Civ 850.

Additionally, under some statutes, contributory negligence on the part of another party also will reduce C's damages. For example, the damages recoverable by a Dependant will be reduced by the amount of the contributory negligence of the Deceased (pursuant to s 5 of the Fatal Accidents Act 1976 (as discussed in Chapter 11); and a child's damages against a health-care practitioner under the Congenital Disabilities (Civil Liability) Act 1976 will be reduced by the extent of his parent's contributory negligence in causing that child be to be born disabled (per s 1(7)).

The elements

When seeking to prove the defence of contributory negligence, the framework for the defence necessarily involves that D prove some fault on C's part, a causal link, and it may even involve some aspects of remoteness, according to judicially-developed principles. In that respect, it somewhat resembles the analysis which C himself must follow, if suing D in negligence. However, when it comes to contributory negligence, it is a nonsense to talk of C's owing any duty of care to D (per Lord Denning MR in *Froom v Butcher*[27]). Rather, the correct question to ask is whether C took reasonable care of himself and/or of his affairs in the circumstances.

Dealing with the four elements of the defence in turn:

Element #1: Fault

§10.6 C must have been partly at fault in bringing about his own injury or loss. D must prove that C should reasonably have foreseen that, if C did not conduct his affairs in accordance with the standard of reasonable care, C might contribute toward his own injuries. C's conduct must be judged against that reasonable standard, although the law takes into account *that particular* C's characteristics and background, or any emergency circumstances in which D's breach placed C, when assessing C's conduct.

Reasonable foreseeability. As with any analysis of breach (per Chapter 7), it is necessary to apply the test of reasonable foreseeability (per *Jones v Livox Quarries*[28]), i.e., whether a reasonable person in C's position ought reasonably to have foreseen that C's acts or omissions might contribute to his own injury or harm. It is an objective test which applies. As Stanley Burnton J stated in *Badger v MOD*, in an employee–employer context, 'it is not necessary to show that [C] *personally* foresaw harm ... [and] the foreseeability need not be of the *precise way* that the damage or injury is caused'.[29] This is important – it may be perfectly obvious to a passenger who gets into a car with a drunk driver of the risks of doing so, but the risks of C's conduct may be less foreseeable to C where there is a knowledge imbalance in the parties' relationship.

Meaning of 'fault'. The trigger for the defence is worth recalling: 'Where any person suffers damage as the result partly of *his own fault* and partly of the fault of any other person ...' (per s 1(1) of the 1945 Act). Under the wide definition of 'fault' in s 4 of that Act, that fault may be negligence, but it may equally be some other tort such as breach of statutory duty, battery or assault. Given that the definition encompasses an 'act or omission which gives rise to liability

---

[27] [1976] QB 286 (CA) 291 (original emphasis). See too: *Badger v MOD* [2005] EWHC 2941 (QB) [7]; *Sahib Foods Ltd v Paskin Kyriakides Sands (a firm)* [2003] EWCA Civ 1832, [62].

[28] [1952] 2 QB 608 (CA) 615–16 (Denning LJ).   [29] [2005] EWHC 2941 (QB) [11]–[12] (emphasis added).

in tort', C's fault has encompassed both a lack of reasonable care on C's part, as well as C's intentional act.

> In *Murphy v Culhane*,[30] Timothy Murphy, C, 29, a self-employed builder, went with some other men to beat up John Culhane, D, at his house. There was a fracas, and during the struggle, D struck C on the head with a plank, and killed him. D was convicted of manslaughter. C's widow brought an action against D for damages under the FAA 1976. **Held:** even if C's widow were entitled to damages under the FAA (which she was not), they would fall to be reduced under the LR(CN)Act 1945, because the death of C was the result partly of his own fault (i.e., going to D's house with the intention of beating him up), and partly of the fault of D. In *Reeves v Commr of Police*,[31] Mr Lynch, C, tried to hang himself in the Kentish Town police station, whilst on remand for credit card fraud, and died shortly thereafter. The police, D, knew that C was a suicide risk, because of earlier self-harming incidents when he had been in police custody. The police surgeon advised that C should be kept under regular observation. C tied his shirt through the flap in the cell door, which had been left down. At the time of his suicide, C was found to be of sound mind. **Held:** 50% CN found. Since C's intentional act was whilst of sound mind, CN could succeed. Responsibility was apportioned equally between C and D.

Notably, C's religious beliefs which contribute to C's harm are not 'fault', and cannot trigger the defence. In the absence of any directly-relevant English authority, a British Columbia case illustrates the point.

> In *Hobbs v Robertson*,[32] Mrs Hobbs, C, a Jehovah's Witness, 35, died because of massive blood loss during a hysterectomy. Prior to surgery, C signed a document, 'Refusal to Permit Blood Transfusion', the legal effect of which was to deny her doctors, D, the opportunity to transfuse C with blood or blood products that would have saved her life. Contributory negligence was not pleaded by D, 'undoubtedly because it cannot be said that adherence to a sincerely held religious belief amounts to fault for purposes of apportioning liability'. **Held:** C's claim failed because the Refusal was a term of the doctor–patient contract, and it constituted an express agreement by C to assume the risk of harm (even death) if the surgeon could not transfuse. C was not at fault in this scenario.

Proving breach. The test of contributory negligence is whether a reasonable person in C's position would have acted in the same manner as C did. The relevant enquiry 'is not whether [C's] conduct fell below the standard reasonably to be expected *of him*, but whether it fell below the standard reasonably to be expected of a person in his position: did his conduct fall below the standard to be expected of a person of ordinary prudence?' (per *Badger v MOD*[33]). Hence, in the usual course, C's conduct must be judged against the standard of a reasonable person. However, that is subject to two caveats:

i. Occasionally, the characteristics of *the particular* C have been taken into account to decide whether C attained the standard of reasonable self-care. These broadly reflect the matters which could affect the standard of care applicable to D too (discussed in Chapter 6). For example, the more sophisticated and knowledgeable C is – the fact that C 'should have known better' – the more likely contributory negligence is to be held. By contrast, if C is: naive and unknowledgeable; a child; or mentally-incapacitated, then it is less likely that the defence will be triggered – or, at least, any contributory negligence will be much reduced.

[30] [1977] QB 94 (CA).   [31] [2000] AC 360 (HL).   [32] [2004] BCSC 1088, [78], [91]–[92] (Pitfield J).
[33] [2005] EWHC 2941 (QB) [7], citing: *Froom v Butcher* [1976] QB 286 (CA) 291.

In *Gibson v Grampian Health Board*,[34] Mr Gibson, C, underwent a bowel examination under general anaesthetic at D's hospital, and for that purpose, an intravenous cannula was inserted in the back of his hand. Unfortunately, when C left hospital later that day, so too did the cannula in his hand. It was removed by his GP later that evening, after a period of severe pain. **Held:** no negligence was proven; but had it been, contributory negligence of 20% would have been held because had C 'been simply a rather naive patient with no previous experience of hospital, I should have been inclined to exclude contributory negligence altogether. [C], however, has unfortunately had a long experience of hospital treatment of one kind or another, and I find it hard to believe that he was in fact as naive as he sought to appear'. In *Jackson v Murray*,[35] Miss Jackson, C, 13, was let off on a winter's evening by the school bus, just opposite her parents' farm, and she ran from behind the bus directly into the path of Mr Murray's, D's, car, and was severely injured in the collision. D was driving negligently, in that he did not reduce his speed from 50 mph, even when seeing the stationary school bus ahead. **Held:** 50% CN, given C's youth. A 13-year-old 'will not necessarily have the same level of judgment and self-control as an adult ... she had to take account of D's car approaching at speed, in very poor light conditions, with its headlights on ... the assessment of speed in those circumstances is far from easy, even for an adult, and even more so for a 13-year-old.' In *Dalling v RJ Heale & Co Ltd*[35a], Stephen Dalling, C, was injured at work in 2005, and recovered damages for that injury, against his employer, D. In 2008, C then suffered a second accident, where he fell backwards in a pub and suffered a further head injury, having had too much to drink. C alleged that the additional injuries in 2008 were causally related to his first head injury, because that head injury had impaired his judgment and his ability to control his drinking. **Held:** D liable for negligence, because the first head injury had a causative effect in relation to the second accident. However, 33% CN awarded against C.

Where D's breach has caused C to suffer from mental instability, and then C contributes to his own injury or death (via suicide or other acts of self-harm), English law countenances that some finding of contributory negligence will nevertheless be possible against C as a matter of law:

In *Reeves v Commr of Police*, facts previously, Mr Lynch, C, was of sound mind, but mentally-disturbed, when he hanged himself whilst on remand. 50% CN was awarded against C. In *Corr v IBC Vehicles Ltd*,[36] Mr Corr, C, worked on the assembly line of a Vauxhall vehicle factory in Coventry. Whilst he was fixing an automated machine, the machine suddenly picked up a steel plate and threw it. If C had not ducked, he would have been decapitated. As it was, he lost his right ear and suffered serious facial injuries, plus severe depression. Six years later, C committed suicide by jumping from a multi-storey carpark. **Held:** no CN found against C, given that evidence on the point was not given at trial. However, the majority (Lords Scott, Mance and Neuberger) held that 20% CN would have been appropriate, given that C was not insane, retained personal autonomy, was not an automaton, and made the decision to end his life. (Lords Bingham and Walker, dissenting, held that C's mental instability was the doing of his employer, and that CN against C was not appropriate.)

ii. Where D's breach places C in a situation of peril or danger, then the standard of care expected of C will likely be reduced, such that contributory negligence is less likely to be found. This is particularly evident where rescuer C suffers some injury during the rescue, sues D whose negligence put him in that boat, and D argues that the rescuer was contributorily negligent during the rescue.

---

[34] (1985) OH Cases (15 Mar 1985) (Lord Murray).   [35] [2015] UKSC 5, [41].
[35a] [2011] EWCA Civ 365, [26]–[27].   [36] [2008] AC 884 (HL) [18].

In *Baker v TE Hopkins & Son Ltd*,[37] Dr Baker, C, went down into a well filled with carbon monoxide gases, on D's premises, to try to save two workers who had entered the well, and died in the rescue attempt. C had asked to be lowered down with a rope tied to him, despite warnings against it, but all three men died. C's estate sued D; and CN was alleged against C. **Held:** no CN found: 'the court should not be quick to accept criticism of the rescuer's conduct from the wrongdoer who created the danger'.

Hence, predicting the outcome of contributory negligence pleas may be very difficult without knowing the characteristics of *that particular C*. It is not always a case of how the law should have expected a reasonable C to have conducted himself.

Element #2: Causation

§10.7   C's lack of reasonable care for his own safety and well-being must, in part, have caused or contributed to his *injury or harm*. However, it is not necessary to prove that C's lack of reasonable care caused or contributed to *the accident*.

It is not enough that C failed to act prudently in looking out for his own health or well-being. A causal link must be proven between that lack of prudence and C's injury or harm – notwithstanding that establishing that 'causal link' is **not** referred to in s 1(1) of the 1945 Act. The burden of proving that causal link (as with all elements of the defence) rests with D (per *King v Medical Services Intl Ltd*[38]).

In order to rely on the defence, D does **not** need to prove either of the following:

- that C partly caused *the accident* to occur. This distinction was reiterated recently by the Supreme Court in *Jackson v Murray*.[39] For example, by failing to wear a seatbelt, passenger C will have partly caused his own *injuries*, but he will not have caused the accident itself, if driver D ran a red light and collided with another vehicle – nevertheless, the defence can be proven against C (per *Froom v Butcher*,[40] where contributory negligence of 20% was held against C, for failing to wear a seatbelt).
- that C caused his own injuries, *on the balance of probabilities*. All that D needs to show is that some act or omission on C's part *contributed to* identifiable injury or harm to C. On that basis, as judicially acknowledged in *Badger v MOD*,[41] establishing a causal link between C's own wrongdoing and his damage may be 'impossible, and a broader and less defined approach is necessary'. What it may come down to is for D to prove that C's unreasonable behaviour caused, in part, his own injury, rather than (as Denning LJ memorably put it in *Jones v Livox Quarries Ltd*[42]) merely being part of C's 'history'. A hypothetical scenario was provided by the British Columbia Supreme Court in *Bevilacqua v Altenkirk*[43] – suppose that C takes the wrong bus due a careless lack of attention, and is then a victim of the bus driver's negligent driving. Had the passenger not made his own mistake, his injury would not have happened, causally-speaking; but there was only a 'fortuitous connection', an accidental link, between C's fault and his injury, and hence, C could not be contributorily negligent. This invokes a remoteness-type enquiry (as discussed in Chapter 9).

---

[37] [1959] 1 WLR 966 (CA).   [38] [2012] EWHC 970 (QB [282]).   [39] [2015] UKSC 5, [20].   [40] [1976] QB 286 (CA).
[41] [2005] EWHC 2941 (QB) [14] (the employee's smoking was accepted to be a substantial cause of his death).
[42] [1952] 2 QB 608 (CA) 616.   [43] [2004] BCSC 945 (Groberman J) [39].

In *Beasley v Alexander*,[44] a car accident occurred, where Paul Alexander, D, turned across the path of Marcel Beasley's, C's, motorcycle. C suffered severe brain damage in the accident. **Held:** D was negligent; and no CN applied. C was travelling too fast; but even if he had been travelling at a 'top safe speed', there would nonetheless have been an accident in which he would have sustained serious injury. C's injury would have happened anyway, regardless of his negligence; and hence, C's negligence did not cause his damage.

Causation dilemmas can arise whenever it is alleged that C **failed** to do something, and that omission contributed to his own downfall – the court must then operate in the realms of the hypothetical, and that 'less defined approach' cited in *Badger* may be necessary. A couple of examples, in the medical context, illustrate the conundrum:

i. Where it is alleged that patient C failed to give sufficient information about his symptoms to doctor D, then D has to prove the requisite causal link as follows – that, on the balance of probabilities: D's diagnosis would have been different if he had received the information; that C would have taken whatever steps that the treatment had required; and D's treatment (had he given it) would have forestalled or prevented C's injury or harm. If, however, D's diagnosis would probably *not* have been different, had the information been disclosed by C, then it cannot be said that C contributed to his downfall, because the information held back would have made no difference. Then, the defence of contributory negligence will fail.

> In the **Ontario** case of *Taylor v Morrison*,[45] Mr Taylor, C, was a reticent patient, and did not disclose his symptoms at two appointments with his GP, D. He was not diagnosed with severe coronary heart disease; heartburn was initially diagnosed. **Held:** D was liable in negligence; and no CN found. C 'would have taken *some steps* to manage his risk factors if he had been diagnosed with coronary heart disease and advised of the life threatening consequences of a failure to do so'. That part of the causal link was made out. However, D also had to establish that, had C disclosed his symptoms at two appointments, he would have diagnosed and investigated a cardiac cause for his presentations, and C's life would then have been extended. However, D could not prove that he would have diagnosed a cardiac cause – 'Nor am I satisfied that, had [C] made disclosure, [D's] diagnosis would have been different'. Hence, no CN found.

ii. Where it is alleged that C failed to attend an appointment with D, and thereby lost the opportunity to receive further information or assistance that would have probably prevented C's injury, the court must be satisfied, on the balance of probabilities that, if C had attended as he ought to have done, then that would have produced a better outcome for C. That establishes the causal link between C's omission, and C's injury. Only then can contributory negligence be made out. If, however, C's turning up would not have produced a better outcome for C, then there is no causal link, and no contributory negligence will arise. Particularly difficult causal problems arise, if C's turning up to the appointment would have produced a better outcome, but only coincidentally and incidentally.

> In the **Ontario** case of *Rupert v Toth*,[46] patient C died of inverting papilloma, which was not diagnosed and treated properly by D before turning malignant and invading C's cranial cavity. C had missed a follow-up appointment, and D argued that, had C turned up, D was intending to tell C

---

[44] [2012] EWHC 2197 (QB).   [45] (Ont SCJ, 19 Jul 2006) [133], [153].
[46] (2006), 38 CCLT (3d) 261 (SCJ) [140]–[141].

certain information at the follow-up appointment, and C would have undergone further surgery to have an inverting papilloma removed, thereby increasing his life expectancy. **Held**: D negligent; but CN of 50% held. In the **British Columbia** case of *Bevilacqua v Altenkirk*,[47] patient C underwent a vasectomy operation, but it failed, and a third child was born to C and his wife. Surgeon D admitted negligence, for misreading the post-operative laboratory report and telling C (incorrectly) that his sperm count was zero and that it was safe to cease other forms of contraception. However, C failed to return to his urologist for a post-operative examination three months later. Had he done so, the urologist would have re-read the laboratory report and discovered D's mistake in time to prevent subsequent conception of the third child (albeit that the post-operative examination was to physically check for any early signs of the vas recanalising, and not for the purposes of checking a post-operative sperm count). Hence, C's failure to turn up was a cause of his damage (the birth of the third child) – but was it an *effective cause* of C's damage? **Held:** no CN. There was no causal link between C's non-attendance and the birth of the third child, because the return to the urologist did not deal with the risk that the laboratory report had been misread; it was to deal with 'a separate risk – that of the *vas* being in the early stages of recanalisation. In failing to go for an examination by Dr Chartrand, Mr Bevilacqua assumed the risk that early-stage recanalisation might go undetected. He did not assume a risk that the operation failed from the outset to render him sterile. While Dr Chartrand would undoubtedly have corrected Dr Altenkirk's error had Mr Bevilacqua attended for a re-examination, that would have occurred only incidentally – it was not the purpose for which a re-examination was required'.

It is suggested that these cases would be decided in the same way in English law.

Element #3: Comparative responsibility

§10.8 Under the 1945 Act, the apportionment of contributory negligence must take into account the relative blameworthiness of C's and D's conduct, and the extent to which that fault caused the damage (i.e., the causative potency of their acts).

The assessment of contributory negligence against C must entail a comparative assessment of culpability or fault of C and D (i.e. of their degrees of departure from the reasonable standard of care), **and** of the relative importance of the acts of C and D in causing C's damage (i.e., the causative potency of their acts), when assessing the apportionment of damages which C and D must each bear (per *Stapley v Gypsum Mines Ltd*[48]).

This is not an easy, nor precise, evaluative step, however. As the Supreme Court pointed out in *Jackson v Murray*, the court is not comparing 'like with like' – it is comparing D's breach of a duty which the law required of him, with C's lack of reasonable care for his own interests.[49] Moreover, translating the facts of one accident to those of another is not a good general guide to apportionment (per *Groves v Studley*[50]).

It follows that, if D should bear 'the lion's share of responsibility', C's contributory negligence is likely to be assessed at well below 50%. In the employment context, this comparison is particularly important, in that while the injured employee may have failed to take due care in what he was doing, that lack of care may be modest and 'far outweighed by the breaches of

---

[47] [2004] BCSC 945, [39]–[47], with quote at [44].
[48] [1953] AC 663 (HL) 682. Also: *Badger v MOD* [2005] EWHC 2941 (QB) [16]; *O'Connell v Jackson* [1972] 1 QB 270 (CA) 277–78.
[49] [2015] UKSC 5, [27].   [50] [2014] EWHC 1522 (QB) [44].

duty [by the employer] which had placed him in the position in which he found himself' (per *Milroy v BT plc*,[51] where 30% contributory negligence was found). However, if C was significantly more at fault than was D, contributory negligence is likely to be 50% or greater.

In *Stoddart v Perucca*,[52] Sally Stoddart, C, 14, was riding her horse, Trigger, along a bridleway near Sunderland, when she emerged into a road, colliding with D's campervan and trailer. D was driving at approximately 35 mph, and the speed limit was 60 mph. The horse reared and fell on C, causing serious injury. C was an experienced rider, riding since she was seven, and Trigger was a dependable horse. **Held:** 50% CN. C was 'significantly more at fault in terms of simple blameworthiness than [D]', especially given that D was well within the speed limit and keeping a good lookout. C 'was an experienced rider who knew this road well and was doing something foolish when she rode out without looking'. However, that was balanced against the greater 'causative potency' that D's driving a car (a 'potentially dangerous weapon'), posed to C. In *Badger v MOD*,[53] Mr Badger, C, died of lung cancer as a result of being exposed wrongfully to asbestos whilst working as a boiler maker for the MOD, D. C also smoked, which was causative of his cancer. **Held:** 20% CN. Significantly greater blame was to be attributed to employer D, than to C, as D was guilty of statutory breaches at a time when the dangers of asbestos were well-known. Further, not all of C's smoking was blameworthy. In *Stapley v Gypsum Mines Ltd*,[54] Mr Stapley, C, and his colleague, Mr Dale, were told by their employer, D, to bring down a dangerous roof (an underground stope), and not to work beneath it, in the meantime. Their efforts to bring down the roof failed, so C then proceeded to work beneath the roof in breaking up gypsum. The roof collapsed and killed him. **Held:** 80% CN, as C's conduct in entering the stope contributed more immediately to the accident created by the dangerous roof.

It will be rare for a pedestrian to bear a greater share of responsibility than the driver, given the causative potency of a car being driven by D ('a car is potentially a dangerous weapon, and accordingly, the attribution of causative potency to the driver must be greater than that to the pedestrian'[55]).

In *Jackson v Murray*,[56] facts previously, **held:** 50% CN held (reduced from 90% at trial and 70% on appeal). D's conduct 'played at least an equal role to that of [C] in causing the damage, and was at least as blameworthy'. The dangerous nature of a car being driven at speed and D's failure to modify his driving, plus that C was only 13 at the time, was to be balanced against C's knowledge of the road, the risks of traffic, and the need to exercise care when crossing the road. In *Ayres v Odedra*,[57] C stood in front of D's car at a traffic light in a traffic-calming area of Leicester, drunk and having dropped his trousers, and D moved forward in his car and ran over C, severely injuring him. **Held:** 20% CN. C deliberately placed himself in the road in front of D's car, remained there when he should have known that the traffic lights were likely to change and D would want to move forward, and where his drunken state and dropped trousers hampered his ability to move freely and out of the way of D's car.

Element #4: Reduction

§10.9 The damages recoverable by C will be reduced to the extent that the court thinks just and equitable, having regard to C's share in the responsibility for C's damage (where that 'damage' may constitute C's death, personal injury, property damage, or economic damage).

---

[51] [2015] EWHC 532 (QB) [37].   [52] [2011] EWCA Civ 290, [18].
[53] [2005] EWHC 2941 (QB) [55].   [54] [1953] AC 663 (HL) 682 (Lord Reid).
[55] The Supreme Court quoted the Extra Division, Inner House, Court of Session with approval on this point, *ibid*, [15], although the ultimate percentage was varied.
[56] [2015] UKSC 5, [39]–[44].   [57] [2013] EWHC 40 (QB) [153].

There is no *de minimis* principle applying to contributory negligence in English law – 'the words of s 1(1) … do not seem to leave much room for an application of the *de minimis* principle … [but] I very much doubt if they permit … no reduction at all because the court thinks it just and equitable that there should be no reduction' (per *Boothman v British Northrop Ltd*[58]). Therefore, it is not possible for C to argue that his own contribution to his injury was so negligible that it can be disregarded – once C is found to have been at fault within the language of s 1(1), *some* reduction in his damages is obligatory.

In some scenarios, the range of percentage of contributory negligence is reasonably fixed by case law. For example, where passenger C fails to wear a seatbelt and suffers injury in a car accident, the Court of Appeal noted, in *Froom v Butcher*,[59] that the range of contributory negligence will appropriately fall between 15–25%. That extent of any reduction of a passenger's damages by reason of contributory negligence must be proportionate, given that domestic rules governing contributory negligence must be compatible with the principles underpinning the EU Directives governing motor insurance (per *Candolin v Pohjola*[60]). The range identified in *Froom* has been confirmed by the English Court of Appeal as being appropriate for domestic law in *J (a child) v Wilkins*.[61]

The 'damage' suffered by C, recovery for which is reduced under the 1945 Act, is defined to include 'loss of life and personal injury' (per s 4). However, contributory negligence may also be found in the context of both property damage (per *Wessanen Foods Ltd v Jofson Ltd*,[62] in dicta) and economic loss (per *Playboy Club London Ltd v Banca Nazionale Del Lavoro Spa*,[63] where 15% was held).

The doctor–patient context: a policy and a comparative vignette

§10.10 Notwithstanding that the doctor–patient relationship exhibits two characteristics, *viz*: (1) trust, confidence and reliance by the patient on the doctor's knowledge, skill and care, and (2) vulnerability on the patient's part, given his illness/injury and the information imbalance, a patient can nevertheless be found to have contributed to his own damage.

Any professional relationship, and the defence of contributory negligence, are not necessarily comfortable bed-fellows. It is **not** the same scenario as in the other more common applications of contributory negligence – say, a passenger not wearing a seatbelt who sues the negligent driver, an employee who fails to exercise due care for his own safety in circumstances where his employer has provided an unsafe system of work, or where a lawful entrant is drunk and falls over some hazard left on the land by the negligent occupier – where the litigants are in a relatively equal position with respect to the ability to control their own welfare.

In the context of medical negligence, English courts have been quite resistant to the notion of contributory negligence, but not necessarily averse to it altogether.

In *Pidgeon v Doncaster HA*,[64] C sued for a 'false negative' cervical smear test, and which showed a pre-cancerous condition that should have warranted further investigation and treatment. Invasive

---

[58] (1972) 13 KIR 112 (CA, Stephenson LJ), and reiterated by: *Badger v MOD* [2005] EWHC 2941 (QB) [15].
[59] [1976] QB 286 (CA).   [60] [2005] ECHR I-5745 (ECJ, Case C-537/03).   [61] [2001] PIQR 179 (CA) [21].
[62] [2006] EWHC 1325 (TCC) [209].   [63] [2014] EWHC 2613 (QB) [63]–[64].
[64] [2002] Lloyd's Rep Med 130 (CC Sheffield, 23 Nov 2001).

cervical cancer, in fact, developed. **Held:** C's damages were reduced by two-thirds (from £55,000 to £18,500), because of C's refusal to follow medical advice and to undergo further smear tests in the intervening period between the false negative and the correct diagnosis. In *Hardaker v Newcastle HA*,[65] a diver decided to re-immerse himself in water, and then delayed making the emergency call, once he recognised the symptoms of decompression illness. His claim against D, which operated the decompression chamber, for systemic negligence, failed. Contributory negligence was raised, but was not necessary to deal with. In *Gouldsmith v Mid-Staffordshire General Hosp NHS Trust*,[66] a patient with ulceration and circulatory problems in her left hand had 'not fully co-operate[d] with treatment' prescribed for her – but there was no allegation of contributory negligence there. In a somewhat similar Irish case, *Byrne v Ryan*,[67] a patient suffered a failed sterilisation and then failed to attend hospital for her six-week check-up as advised. She had acted 'imprudently' and 'negligently', but 'no case of contributory negligence was pleaded against C, nor was it urged on me that her failure to take the advice offered to her on her discharge from the hospital amounted to such', so the court did not consider the issue further.

The area is ripe with judicial differences of opinion, however. A comparative analysis of Australian and Canadian jurisprudence reveals a surprising disparity in the application of contributory negligence to cases of medical negligence. There have been four scenarios, in particular, in which patients have failed to take reasonable measures of 'self-care'.

A comparative corner: Commonwealth examples

Failing to provide full information. As the Ontario court put it in *Lurtz v Duchesne*,[a] the law cannot expect a doctor to 'act as a clairvoyant', whilst the Alberta court pointed out, in *Rose v Dujon*,[b] that '[b]oth parties in the doctor-patient relationship have obligations – the doctor to the patient, and the patient to himself – and inherent in the discharge of such obligations is the need to communicate fully with each other. To be effective, communication must be bilateral. Doctors are not mind readers'. In the Queensland case of *Locher v Turner*,[c] C was diagnosed with and treated for colon cancer. That diagnosis by her GP was negligently-delayed (attributing the symptoms to irritable bowel syndrome to begin with). **Held:** 20% CN. The evidence suggested that C had been suffering from bowel troubles which were much more frequent and indeed serious than she had disclosed to D.

Failing to attend follow-up/recommended appointments. Where C was told (in certain and unambiguous terms) to return for a follow-up visit or to book another appointment, and failed to do so, then numerous Commonwealth authorities support a finding of CN. Some courts have been sympathetic to the patient who does not keep an appointment, make a follow-up phone call, etc, although the reasons for denying any CN have been carefully articulated (e.g., there was some plausible explanation for C's non-attendance; or that it was more the responsibility of D to ensure that C followed up). In the New South Wales case of *Kalokerinos v Burnett*,[d] C consulted her GP, who advised her to come again if she continued to suffer from having vaginal bleeding; but he failed to arrange an alternative referral to a specialist that was more convenient to C. C's

[a] (Ont SCJ, 16 Apr 2003) [157].
[b] (1990), 108 AR 352 (Alta QB) [148].
[c] [1995] QCA 106.
[d] [1996] NSWCA 324, [40]–[41] (per Clarke JA) (overturning trial judge's finding of no CN).

[65] (QB, 15 Jun 2001).　　[66] [2007] EWCA Civ 397, [8].　　[67] [2007] IEHC 207.

condition worsened, and she suffered daily vaginal bleeding, but for more than four months did not return to the GP or seek any further medical attention. She was eventually diagnosed with cervical cancer. **Held:** 20% CN. In the Western Australian case of *Le Brun v Joseph,*[e] C was making good progress with physiotherapy, but failed to keep two appointments. **Held:** no CN. The reasons for non-attendance were plausible.

Failing to seek medical treatment. Wherever C ignores a condition which, as a matter of common sense, ought to have been checked out; or where C knows of a particular propensity to a medical condition in the family but ignores 'warning signs', CN is possible. Some Commonwealth courts may also be unimpressed with patients who discharge themselves post-operation without permission. In the Alberta case of *Strichen v Stewart,*[f] C knew of a history of cancer in her close family and had been recommended to attend for yearly check-ups. She failed to turn up for mammograms, and was then diagnosed with breast cancer. **Held:** no liability against D. Otherwise, 35% CN would have applied. In the Malaysian case of *Tan Ah Kau v Govt of Malaysia,*[g] C discharged himself from hospital, while in post-operative recuperation. **Held:** 20% CN. He 'felt that the facilities at home were better since his wife and children could take care of him', but that was careless behaviour. In the **British Columbia** case of *Zhang v Kan,*[h] C failed to insist to her GP that she have an amniocentesis test, when C knew that, due to her age, she was at high risk of having a child with Down's Syndrome. A child with that condition was born. **Held:** 50% CN. C was 'a sophisticated and experienced businesswoman' who had researched the topic of amniocentesis, and did not submit to the test, against her gynacologist's advice.

Failing to follow instructions. Patients frequently disregard their doctor's instructions, which has sometimes cost the patient damages. In the Alberta case of *Dumais v Hamilton,*[i] C disregarded D's, her surgeon's, instructions not to smoke in the week following a 'tummy tuck' operation. C did smoke immediately after the operation, which caused necrosis of the tissue, leaving areas of disfigurement. **Held:** 50% CN.

[e] [2006] WADC 200.
[f] [2004] ABQB 612, [90].
[g] [1995] MLJU 183 (HC).
[h] [2003] BCSC 5, [61]–[63].
[i] [1998] ABCA 218, [15]–[17].

On the other hand, some Commonwealth judges have considered contributory negligence by a patient to sit most uneasily with the concept of medical negligence, where vulnerable, sick, worried and unknowledgeable patients put themselves in the hands of competent medical practitioners for advice and treatment. As the Irish High Court said, in *Ryan v Bon Secours Hospital*,[68] '[i]n the doctor/patient relationship there is a total reliance placed by the patient upon the doctor', and that the doctor–patient relationship was distinguishable from the employer–employee scenario, because a patient 'cannot be presumed to have any prior knowledge regarding the nature of his ailment, what possible diagnoses might be open, what tests might be appropriate, the significance of any such tests, or any possible or appropriate treatment', whereas 'a finding of contributory negligence can be made against an employee who has acted

[68] [2004] IEHC 77 (also reported under the name, '*Philp v Ryan*', at the same neutral citation).

in a way which perhaps lacked ordinary common-sense, or was contrary to some training which he had received'. The Fiji High Court called the possibility of contributory negligence against a patient, in *Moli v Bingwor*, as a 'startling proposition'.[69]

Notably, English law suggests that the doctor–patient relationship does *not* represent a fiduciary relationship. In *Sidaway v Governors of Bethlem Royal Hospital*,[70] Lord Scarman said (in his minority opinion, but no other member disagreed with this observation) that the relationship simply could not be compared to that of a solicitor-client or trustee-beneficiary (confirming Dunn LJ's view in the court below,[71] that the fiduciary relationship 'has been confined to cases involving the disposition of property, and has never been applied to the nature of the duty which lies upon a doctor in the performance of his professional treatment of his patient'). Subsequently, in *R v Mid Glamorgan Family Health Services Authy; ex p Martin*,[72] Popplewell J reiterated that, in *Sidaway*, the 'notion of fiduciary relationship was expressly disavowed'. This is in contrast to some other Commonwealth jurisdictions (including Australia and Canada), where the doctor–patient relationship has been expressly held to be fiduciary in nature.[73] It is ironic, then, that contributory negligence seems to be more frequently countenanced where the doctor–patient relationship is seen as a fiduciary relationship involving trust and confidence, than in a jurisdiction where it is not so acknowledged.

A greater acknowledgment of a patient's personal responsibility and self-determination is the most obvious reason to support an extended interplay between contributory and medical negligence – supported by Lord Steyn's statement, in *Chester v Afshar*, that '[i]n modern law, medical paternalism no longer rules'.[74] English judges have been equally willing to acknowledge that times have moved on from when 'doctor knew best',[75] and in extra-curial comment, Lord Woolf observed that '[t]he contemporary approach is a more critical approach'.[76] Whilst those observations have been made within the context of what a patient can expect of a doctor, surely the sentiment has equal ramifications for what a doctor may *expect of a patient*. In other words, if the pendulum is swinging toward a less indulgent attitude toward patients, then they may come to be treated exactly as would road users, employees and invitees – whereby a reasonable standard of care is expected of them all. A greater use of contributory negligence would take into account the *reality* that an effective doctor–patient relationship simply cannot exist in a vacuum of misinformation or non-cooperation – it is a relationship of 'shared responsibility'.[77] Moreover, it is hardly likely that contributory negligence would subvert the principles of trust and reliance upon which the doctor–patient relationship is based. Undoubtedly the trial judge, when assessing the percentage reduction warranted, will give due weight to

---

[69] [2003] FJHC 279 (no CN).   [70] [1985] AC 871 (HL) 884.

[71] [1984] QB 491 (CA) 515.   [72] (1993) 16 BMLR 81 (QB).

[73] e.g., in Canada: *McInerney v MacDonald* (1992), 93 DLR (4th) 415 (SCC) [17], [19] ('The relationship between physician and patient is one in which trust and confidence must be placed in the physician. The physician-patient relationship is a fiduciary relationship': La Forest J). In Aust: *Breen v Williams* [1996] HCA 57, [15], [19] ('the doctor acquires an ascendancy over the patient'; '[w]hilst duties of a fiduciary nature may be imposed upon a doctor, they are confined and do not cover *the entire* doctor-patient relationship'); *Johnson v Biggs* [2000] NSWCA 338 (Giles JA) ('the doctor has a fiduciary relationship with the patient, in which the patient places trust in the doctor to listen to the patient's concerns').

[74] [2004] UKHL 41, [16].

[75] e.g.: *AB v Leeds Teaching Hosp NHS Trust* [2004] EWHC 644 (QB) [115 (re organ harvesting); *B v An NHS Hosp Trust* [2002] EWHC 429 (Fam) [94] (re disabled patients); *R v Bournewood Mental Health Trust, ex p L* [1998] UKHL 24, [1999] AC 458 (HL) 473–74 (re mental health legislation for incapacitated patients).

[76] Lord Woolf, 'Are the Courts Excessively Deferential to the Medical Profession?' (2001) 9 *Med L Rev* 1.

[77] A term used, e.g., in: *Tai v Hatzistavrou* [1999] NSWCA 306, [56].